THE WORK OF THE GODS IN TIKOPIA

Ariki Kafika and Ariki Fangarere at Takerere (1952). The Ariki Kafika, wearing his ritual necklet of coconut fronds, is reaching back for areca nut to chew after the kava rite. His spear, used as a staff, stands behind.

LONDON SCHOOL OF ECONOMICS
MONOGRAPHS ON SOCIAL ANTHROPOLOGY
Nos. 1 and 2

THE WORK
OF THE GODS
IN TIKOPIA

BY

RAYMOND FIRTH

*Second Edition with new Introduction
and Epilogue*

UNIVERSITY OF LONDON
THE ATHLONE PRESS
NEW YORK: HUMANITIES PRESS INC.
1967

First published by
THE ATHLONE PRESS
UNIVERSITY OF LONDON
2 *Gower Street London* WC1

Distributed by Constable & Co Ltd
12 *Orange Street, London* WC2

Canada
Oxford University Press
Toronto

Library of Congress Catalog Card No. 67–10515

Printed in Great Britain by
WESTERN PRINTING SERVICES LTD
BRISTOL

PREFACE

By the passage of time this book has now acquired the character of an historical document in Polynesian ethnography. The Tikopia religious cycle which, adopting a title from the vernacular, I termed 'Work of the Gods' and which I observed in 1928–9 and again (with James Spillius) in 1952, has now been completely abandoned for more than ten years. That small sector of the Tikopia community which in 1952 still carried out the pagan rites converted to Christianity soon after a disastrous epidemic in 1955. This book then describes a vanished past, a set of institutions not known to many of the younger Tikopia themselves.

On the second expedition to Tikopia in 1952 my observations, confirmed and enlarged by those of Spillius, paralleled very closely those made on my first expedition. The degree of similarity and variation noted in 1952 was examined in *Study in Ritual Modification: The Work of the Gods in Tikopia in 1929 and 1952* (Royal Anthropological Institute, Occasional Paper no. 19), 1963, by Firth and Spillius. (This work is referred to as RM in the postscripts to chapters and elsewhere in this book.)

In 1966 I was able to make a third visit to Tikopia, accompanied by Dr Torben Monberg, and together we studied the effects of abandonment of the pagan Tikopia religion.

Material from the original monograph has been cited by various writers and in particular has been used extensively by William J. Goode (*Religion Among the Primitives*, Glencoe, Ill., 1951). In the light of these circumstances the main body of the work has been left almost exactly in its original form, though it has had to be re-paginated. Postscripts to some chapters indicate points of comparative interest which I observed on the 1952 expedition, and an Epilogue describes the aftermath of the Work of the Gods by 1966. A new Introduction indicates the significance of the religious cycle in more general terms than did the original treatment, which was primarily empirical. In order to reduce the volume of the work much Tikopia vernacular text has been eliminated, since this can be of interest only to linguistic specialists. A few small corrections have been made to the spelling but in the absence of a systematic study of Tikopia language, inconsistencies still remain occasionally. For better reproduction the diagrams have been redrawn and some new Plates have been substituted. I have retained the present tense throughout the book although all rites have now been abandoned.

The Work of the Gods can be regarded as Volume I of my studies of Tikopia religion. Volume II consists of a series of collected papers to be published with the title of *Tikopia Ritual and Belief* (Allen & Unwin, 1967); Volume III will be *Rank and Religion in Tikopia*, a general account which was originally intended as a companion work to the present ethnographic study, but which has been long delayed, partly in order that I might complete the analysis after the major change from paganism to Christianity.

In addition to the acknowledgments made in the first edition of this work, I should like to express my recognition of the great help I received from James Spillius on my second expedition to Tikopia. Together we participated in a number of rites of the Work of the Gods, and his comments and further observations after I left reinforced my own findings. I would like to acknowledge here too my recent companionship with Torben Monberg, which helped me greatly in my inquiries in 1966.

I am indebted for finance of my first expedition to the Australian National Research Council, of my second to the Australian National University, and of my third to the University of London, the London School of Economics and Political Science, and the Wenner-Gren Foundation for Anthropological Research; to all these bodies I express my gratitude. I wish to acknowledge particularly the generous help received from the Wenner-Gren Foundation in the pursuit of my Tikopia studies as a whole. For many facilities in the field I am very grateful to members of the Melanesian Mission and to government officials of the British Solomon Islands Protectorate. I also owe thanks to Mrs D. H. Alfandary for help in preparing this work for publication.

Finally, I am much indebted to Anthony Forge, not only for his technical advice in the preparation of this new edition, but also for several helpful suggestions of substance in the Introduction.

London   RAYMOND FIRTH
October 1966

CONTENTS

FIGURES

PLATES

Plates 1–8 between pages 256 and 257

Introduction to First Edition

The Tikopia ritual cycle known as the Work of the Gods was the most spectacular of my discoveries in this isolated community in the British Solomon Islands Protectorate. Although a few of the rites had been briefly mentioned by the Rev. W. J. Durrad, and by Dr W. H. R. Rivers, who used Durrad's valuable material, there was no hint in these accounts that the rites were anything but isolated performances. It was only indeed some months after my arrival in Tikopia that I realized the complexity and highly organized character of the ritual.

A knowledge of the cycle of the Work of the Gods is of basic significance for the understanding of Tikopia culture. It is one of the most elaborate expressions of the system of rank and of the religious beliefs of the people; it has important economic aspects; it is related to their institutions of marriage; it sets the formal seal on their most fundamental form of recreation; and provides sanctions for many of their most basic values. From the point of view of comparison with other Polynesian cultures the Work of the Gods is of great interest since its analogies with such rites as the *makahiki* of Hawaii and *inasi* of Tonga suggest interpretations of them which cannot be inferred from the existing fragmentary and obscure accounts.

In this monograph I have concentrated on giving an ethnographical account of the phenomena, leaving for later publication the major part of the theoretical interpretation. This course has been dictated by the bulk of my material.

In the account I have drawn a distinction between the events which I witnessed, those which took place during my stay but which through other occupation I could not see, and those which were formerly part of the cycle but have now been abandoned. Those rites which I did not see I discussed with a number of informants, particularly with the Ariki Kafika, the Ariki Tafua, and their sons. Since it was only a decade after the abandonment of the

rites of Tafua, the reconstruction of them by the original participants may be regarded as substantially accurate.

It will be seen from the account that I was a participant and not
merely an observer when I attended the Work of the Gods. This
naturally facilitated my investigations, though in a few cases the
rules of *tapu* by which I was bound prevented me from examining
closely the material objects used. In addition to my personal
observation, I had many conversations about the organization and
the meaning of the ritual with the most prominent participants.
My principal informants here were the chiefs and members of
their families, and the elders Pa Rarovi, Pae Sao, and Pa Fetauta.
I also had many discussions with other men not in positions of
rank, who gave me therefore other points of view. But in particular I owed a great deal to the premier chief, the Ariki Kafika,
who after his initial suspicion had been allayed invited me to
participate in all his ritual and imparted to me a great deal of his
unique knowledge. Without his co-operation and that of his eldest
son Pa Fenuatara my work would not have been possible. This is
particularly the case in regard to the texts of the formulae used.
I obtained these from each chief and elder who was responsible for
a rite and checked them from other informants, but since so many
of them were recited by the Ariki Kafika alone it was only with
his help that I could obtain a full account. Most of these formulae
were recited during the ritual in tones too low for the audience to
hear. The correspondence between the different versions I obtained, however, leaves no doubt as to their substantial correct-
ness. But it must be emphasized that all these formulae quoted are
representative since they are recited as *free formulae*, absolute adhe-
sion to a traditional set of words not being required. To save space
I have not given the original Tikopia text in cases where it is
substantially the same in several successive formulae; in such cases
the translation is taken from a native text in my notebooks. All
material in quotation marks throughout the account is a translation of native statements recorded on the spot, in nearly every case
in the vernacular. It may be noted that the first draft of this monograph was written in 1929–30, soon after I returned from Tikopia
when the events were still fresh in my mind.

The account presents a great mass of detail. This has been included because it is most significant to the people themselves, and
to the structure of the ritual cycle as a whole. In particular it shows

the degree to which small items of behaviour have been integrated into a consistent scheme, and also how this integration still allows of the exercise of individual and small-unit privileges within the workings of the major institution. This involves a theoretical problem which I hope to discuss in a later publication.

I am indebted greatly to Mr E. R. Leach for making the drawings from my original sketches. I am grateful also to the Rockfeller Research Fund Committee of the London School of Economics for a grant which has assisted materially in the preparation and publication of the manuscript.

London 1939   R.F.

Introduction to Second Edition

SOME THEORETICAL OBSERVATIONS

I take this opportunity of re-publication of this account of the Tikopia Work of the Gods to expand some of the theoretical aspects referred to only briefly at the beginning and end of the original study. I wrote this monograph originally because, as I explained, so much had been reconstruction and hypothesis in the study of Polynesian religion that it seemed important to describe in a systematic way, from personal observation, just how some Polynesians did carry out their traditional religious rites. Moreover, so much discussion of religion in anthropology had relied on analysis of isolated items of belief or ritual that it seemed also important to give as detailed account as possible of a long-continued and complex *sequence* of rites, in their social setting. Now, while we need much more systematic theory in the anthropological study of religion it is still my conviction that such theory needs to go hand in hand with more meticulous and more refined empirical observation.

There is something of a paradox here. It is often assumed that having more data will make interpretation easier. I think that on the contrary it will often make interpretation more difficult because more variations will have to be fitted in. And no claim for 'abstraction' will help us here; uncomfortable exceptions to our theories cannot be dismissed. All the more should we not burke the facts if we suspect that they may render our task of explanation harder; we should indeed seek them on such account. This lesson in scientific methodology, which we should have known since at least the days of T. H. Huxley, and which Boas, Goldenweiser, Malinowski and their contemporaries held before us, has recently been pressed upon us from another angle by Karl Popper and I. C. Jarvie.

It may be argued that empiricism in the ritual field is fallacious, that we can never get the 'facts' of a religious situation in their completeness, if only because the presence of an observer in itself conditions the situation, and his record of what he observes is distorted by his personal vision. There are no final answers here. But granted that every anthropologist refracts what he sees through his personal prism, the more closely and the more often he records what he thinks he sees, the more chance have others of judging the validity of his interpretations. At the end of this introduction I offer some general propositions about the nature of ritual; it will be for the reader to judge how far they conform to the detailed descriptions in the body of the book.

The first problem is to try to deepen our understanding of the significance of the ritual cycle. During the last half-century, the existence of a growing body of Christian Tikopia has provided a kind of foil against which the sincerity and depth of conviction of the pagan Tikopia could be tested. To the pagan Tikopia the meaning of the Work of the Gods was clear: in major outline the performances were a formal traditionalized means of maintaining contact with powerful spiritual beings and inducing them to look with favour upon the Tikopia by the grant of food and health. The spiritual beings were conceived as being in reciprocal relationship with the leaders of particular lineages and clans, though the benefits to be derived from them were regarded as spread rather indifferently over the whole population. Contact with them was to be maintained partly on the same pattern as contact with powerful human beings, that is, by presentation of gifts and conduct of abasement. But they had to be treated with even more deference and even more formality. In particular, they had to be addressed by special titles not necessarily known to ordinary men and in much more elaborate set phraseology. To render their benefits specific and reinforce the material claims made upon them, these spiritual beings were associated individually with material equipment or resources such as canoes, temples and foodstuffs. This was the significance of the Work of the Gods as presented by the pagan Tikopia. In their own eyes they validated this interpretation by reference to traditional stories of the doings of these spiritual beings in past times, especially in relation to their own experience.

But the acceptance of Christianity by some Tikopia before 1928, and still more by 1952, meant that there were Tikopia who did not accept this interpretation. Many Christian Tikopia still did so. They believed in the reality of the spiritual beings and in the significance of rite and formula in attempting to secure material benefits from them. But such Christian Tikopia believed – on the evidence of their own statements – that the traditional spirits had lost much of their power in the confrontation with the Christian God; consequently the validity of the performances to obtain benefits from them was materially lessened. Judgments were expressed comparing the prosperity accruing to the traditional rites unfavourably with that accruing to Christian church services. Another Christian view which appears to have gained greatly in strength during the last couple of decades or so, as the number of people who once participated in the traditional rites grew very small, was that the very conceptions of these traditional spirits were false. Ritual performances such as those in the Work of the Gods were regarded then as not merely inefficient but entirely misdirected and vain.

An anthropologist, whatever be his own personal attitude to an experience of spiritual reality, presumably adopts neither of these major viewpoints. If he holds that spiritual experience is real, in the sense of being autonomously generated by external influences, he still will hardly argue that the spirit conceptions of the Tikopia can simply be taken at face value. The 'spirits' they recognize do not exist independently under the names and forms assigned to them by the Tikopia. On the other hand, if an anthropologist holds, as I do, that such spirit concepts are ultimately part of human attempts to envisage modes of order and mobilize support in the world around, he will still not argue that the phenomena are purely illusory. His concern is with the relationship of these beliefs to other features of the social life. Whatever be his conception of functional theory in anthropology, he tends to assume that the character of these beliefs and associated rites can be correlated in a broad way with some significant features of the local society. He will also tend to regard these beliefs as ways of representing significant issues in the confrontation of the individual man with his own nature, with the necessities of life and with the demands of an external social world.[1] From this point of view such spirit concepts in their systematic interrelationship serve to provide a

[1] See my 'Religious Belief and Personal Adjustment' (1948) in *Essays on Social Organization and Values*, 1964, pp. 257–93.

framework by reference to which human activities can take a definite, regular and planned form.

These beliefs are expressed in many ways, informally as well as formally. What we term ritual is in part a formal expression of beliefs and translation of them into social action. But ritual, because of its purposive orientation, has a requirement of spatial and temporal sequence. Spirit beliefs may be systematic in the sense that the different items of belief, when formulated and considered, can be envisaged as a logical, ordered arrangement, the various elements being consistent with one another. I think it will be clear from the account in this book that most of the Tikopia belief about gods and spirits is of such systematic type.[1] But in belief there is no necessary progression or development of the same ordered sequential character as must occur in ritual. Tikopia spirit belief is not without its developmental side – a great deal of statement about spirits made by spirit mediums is of this kind and some of it might be classed as almost free fantasy. But the development of this material is not promoted or hampered by space-time requirements and can occur in any order. Ritual on the other hand is bound by these requirements.

My point here is that while belief systems are relatively freer to develop personal variants, ritual systems involve a definite framework of progression, the activities comprised therein being regulated accordingly in the time and energy expended. For any set of ritual operations to be even moderately efficient, a considerable amount of organization of men and materials is needed.

I am not concerned here with Tikopia spirit beliefs 'as such', i.e. as a framework for the organization of experience, by 'making sense' of the Tikopia relation to their own society and the external world.[2] Here I am concerned with the problems of the integration of belief and activity in this particular religious cycle of the Work of the Gods, both internally and in relation to Tikopia society. I am also concerned to demonstrate the significance of variation within it.

First let us consider the programme of the Work of the Gods. The cyclical nature of these performances is a consideration of

[1] Detailed issues of the character of the Tikopia spirit world will be dealt with in *Rank and Religion in Tikopia*.
[2] This will be treated elsewhere – see *Tikopia Ritual and Belief*, 1967, and *Rank and Religion in Tikopia*.

cardinal importance here. It must be reckoned as a very considerable feat for members of a society without a calendar to plan and
maintain such a highly intricate system of performances for six
weeks twice a year. Despite the Tikopia belief that the rites were
instituted by a single culture-hero at a far-off point in time, it is
probable that they were constructed piecemeal, with accretions
over a long period. But in 1928–9 and again in 1952 it was clear
that ordinarily well-informed Tikopia kept the sequence of rites
of the Work of the Gods 'in their heads' so to speak. That is, they
were capable of outlining the programme in a single description
and of relating different parts of it to one another in sequence.
This they could do without calendrical dates but using a combination of natural changes in vegetation, moon and stars with small
numbered sequences of nights. The result was a remarkable degree
of integration at the time-sequence level and also at the level of
human activity. Not only was the programme intellectually conceived, it was also physically carried out. Day by day numbers of
men and women assembled in various places, produced food and
engaged in technical operations, fitting in their activities in a
highly complex manner.

What enabled them to preserve this integration and maintain
the elaborate programme with such effectiveness? In conceptual
terms undoubtedly the traditional beliefs that upon the power of
gods and spirits depended the prosperity and indeed the life of the
people provided a very important sanction for the regular repetition of the rites. But another important factor making for preservation of the traditional scheme was the economic involvement
of the participants. The performance of the rites in due sequence
was regarded as an obligation, a duty laid upon the performers by
their overall religious ideology. But the performance of each
major rite was normally accompanied by the presentation of
offerings of food to the gods and spirits thought to be concerned.
Only a minute fraction of these offerings was thrown away, the
bulk being retained and put back into circulation, as it were, for
ordinary human consumption. Hence the correct performance of
rites necessarily brought with it the achievement of the day's meals.
From this point of view, what was dedicated to the gods and
spirits apart from the miniscule sacrifice of food morsels to them,
was a certain amount of time and energy in assembling and going
through the ritual motions. Most of the technical operations

involved in the ritual programme were also of value from a utilitarian point of view. In a way then the performance of the ritual programme was just another kind of projection of economic activity and as such carried with it the ordinary sanctions of economic motivation.

Another type of sanction tending to promote the maintenance of the ritual programme was that of the status involvement of the participants. Performance of the ritual was a duty, but its accomplishment was normally a matter if not of self-congratulation at least of self-justification. It will be apparent how often in the course of the Work of the Gods leading individuals and their family, lineage or clan took pride in the fact that they alone carried out a specific rite or played a unique, specific part in a rite. The ingenious way whereby obligation was interpreted as privilege and the status of the individuals concerned maintained or enhanced by ritual performance gave very important backing to carrying out the ritual cycle in prescribed form. Each individual might not care too much about what happened to others, but he was very intent that proper recognition should be given to his own 'day', his own 'rite', 'formula' or 'role'. For each to say that he occupied his own prescribed place in the scheme meant that all were concerned to operate the scheme as a whole. Moreover, each main participant kept a jealous eye on the contributions of those who were in a sense his rivals as well as his co-operators, and knowledge of this helped to keep each contributor up to the mark.

One final factor which I think helped to maintain the programme was the attention aroused by its flexibility. The main framework arranged the major groups of rites in a set order, and within each major group the sequence of rites too was normally invariable. But there was room for some variation. There was some discretion for the leading chief as to when the whole sequence should begin and at various points in it how many nights should elapse before a new ritual should be undertaken. There were also possibilities of aggregating or separating rites for different items such as sacred canoes according to the state of the food supply. All this tended to introduce an element of uncertainty and speculation into the conduct of affairs, and so tended to keep interest in these affairs alive, since people might have to revise their plans in accordance with the turn of events. There was also another important source of variation – what may be termed the institutionalized decision of men who controlled certain phases of the ritual. This was usually linked with a change in personnel. When a new ritual elder succeeded in his office he marked his new role by altering the day on which his predecessor had celebrated his sacred canoe or temple.[1] When a chief died, to signalize his passing and to serve as a memorial to him one of his elders might allow a sacred canoe to drop out of the ritual programme for a season or so. Such happenings were part of the very stuff of the ritual cycle and tended to focus the interest of people more strongly upon it.

A striking feature of the conduct of the Work of the Gods was the intricate commingling of esoteric and exoteric features in it. This occurred in several ways. Ritual and economic activity were linked together in the very construction of the whole cycle since one manifest intent of the ritual was the promotion and sanctification of economic process.[2] Work and rite tended therefore to alternate, each as it were supporting and leading to the performance of the other. But within what can be properly regarded as a ritual performance the sacerdotal and mundane elements intermingled. The performance of the ritual made such demands upon the principal officiants that they equated these with ordinary work and used the same term (*fekau*) to describe them. The provision of the ritual materials for offering required a considerable expenditure of time and energy not only in obtaining them from the sea and the cultivations, but also in preparing them for consumption. The conceptualization of offering was such that once the ritual materials had been presented to the gods and ancestors they could be for the most part withdrawn and used as food. Again, the 'atmosphere' of the ritual occasion allowed of quite rapid oscillation between recognition of the sacred by silence and obeisance, and recognition of the profane by allowance for human error or by response to the humorous suggestion of incongruity.

My argument from this is that the sacred and profane elements did not merely exist side by side as aspects of ritual, as Leach has pointed out,[3] but *necessarily* did so in a ritual cycle of this kind.

---

[1] See *Social Change in Tikopia*, 1959, pp. 239–40.
[2] This has been brought out and re-examined very effectively by Goode, *Religion among the Primitives*, 1951, pp. 106–20.
[3] *Political Systems of Highland Burma*, 1954, p. 13.

This was in part a function of time span and degree of commitment to enterprise. If a rite takes place as an isolated item, then it can be a focus of high sacredness to a degree of intensity which may bar almost completely the entry of exoteric elements. But if the rite is one of a series demanding concentration of energy day after day for weeks or even months, then the climax needs to be relieved by some process of alternation. As I see it the relation between the sacred and the profane is one of reinforcement in a kind of pulsation necessary for refreshment and restoration of expended energies. Sociologically this applies not merely to the energies of individuals but to the maintenance of relations of cooperation between individuals in group arrangements. Mechanically, allowance for the exoteric aspect is necessary for the provision of food and other resources. Sociologically it is necessary to retain the interest and co-operation of individual and group participants.

The high level of integration attained in this ritual cycle was based only in part then upon mystical elements; it rested also upon the interlocking of these elements with others in the mundane field.

This interlocking varied in content at different phases of the ritual cycle and assumed various forms. For maximum social effect it was concerned with groups of some scale, either major lineages or clans. An interlocking mechanism of fairly simple form dealing with large-scale groups was of the type where the groups combined, as in the dances of Marae, to provide a *sequence* of days' or nights' performance. The place of each social group in the series was determined by the place of the others, and the contribution of each group thus tended to be defined by comparison with that of the others. This occurred on the material plane, as in comparison of each clan's or lineage's provision of coconuts or areca nut. It also occurred on the social plane, as when the Ariki Kafika objected to a special dance of Taumako (p. 322) on the grounds that his own clan had not been warned and given a similar opportunity. Moreover, the significance of splitting up the festival into days or nights on a clan basis was that of necessity this established a ritual precedence. The people all danced together at various points in each day or night, but the convention that each day and night 'belonged' to one or other clan meant that the *order of physical performance* was correlated also with an *order of ritual grading*. It could have been that the Tikopia graded the days or nights in reverse order, beginning with the clan of lowest rank and ending with that of highest rank. (They did at times use such a process of ritual ascent – 'grading from the rear' – in some kava formulae.) But for the dance festival the convention was one of ritual descent – grading from top to bottom – so that the clan of lowest rank ended the series. Further interlocking was obtained by the process of symmetrical food exchange.

An analogous type of interlocking was where one group provided the materials for the ritual performance by another. Traditionally when the sacred mound in the temple of Kafika was renewed each season, the sand was drawn from the canoe court of either Tafua or Taumako. These three clans were thus maintained in a relationship of interdependence such that each season saw Kafika dependent upon Tafua and Taumako alternately for the proper accomplishment of its rite, and Tafua or Taumako obliged to furnish the material. But this also helped to define the relationship of Tafua and Taumako to each other since the alternation between them helped to establish their ritual equivalence in this respect as against other circumstances in which one or other had ritual precedence.

Another type of interlocking was of a more particularistic kind, since it was regarded as resting upon the recognition of an historical situation created by genealogical ties between two persons. The *Ara o Pu* (p. 131) was an example of a relationship between two clans based upon that between two chiefly lineages alleged to have been created by an ancient marriage. As a result the chiefly lineage of Taumako stood in a relationship of grandson to grandfather *vis-à-vis* that of Kafika. This representative status[1] involved a transaction of food exchange, generation after generation. This was primarily a relation of equality since, while grandparent may be regarded as senior to grandchild, the presumed antiquity of the original relationship was such that the original grandchild in his turn was treated as a revered ancestor by the grandparent's modern descendants. The gift of food from Taumako to Kafika

---

[1] Cf. *We, the Tikopia*, pp. 268–70. Analogous phenomena have been described under the terms 'positional succession' (Audrey I. Richards, 'Some Types of Family Structure among the Central Bantu', *African Systems of Kinship and Marriage*, 1950, p. 224) and 'perpetual kinship' (Ian Cunnison, 'Perpetual Kinship: A Political Institution of the Luapula Peoples', *Rhodes-Livingstone Institute Journal*, no. xx, 1956, pp. 27–48.

was very substantial and recognized as an indication of wealth. But in its turn the reciprocal gift by Kafika was intended to match the original presentation. This ritual exchange, which was carried out in conditions of considerable anxiety and suspense, taboo and mystic contributions, was one of the items which helped to maintain the two clans in relationship.

A linkage of a theoretically more asymmetrical order was that indicated by the items of major value, such as temples or canoes, operated by one clan but regarded as the property of a god of another clan. Several canoes, ordinarily treated as owned by specific lineages with their leading men as responsible administrators of the property, were credited to the control of spiritual beings attached to other groups. The concept of 'ownership' here became a very complex one. At the mundane level the canoe was owned by the people who run it, and no-one else had any voice in the way it should be used. All that happened was that seasonally a bark-cloth vestment and a basket of food were taken to the head of the lineage concerned in the other clan. But this economic act was regarded as symbolic of a relationship at a mystical level, and was an acknowledgment of superiority in this particular respect. In theory at least the spiritual being could dictate what should be done with the canoe in practice. The situation with certain temples, notably that of Resiake of Taumako, was similar. And yet while the relationship was ordinarily treated as one in which the god of one group controlled the property of another group, at a sociological level the situation might be interpreted as one group controlling to some degree the god of another through his putative involvement in their property. Empirically for the purpose of ritual this was almost what seemed to occur. There was ostensibly subordination of men of one group to the *god* of another, but there was no subordination in this respect of the men of one group to the *men* of another. We have here a ritual relationship, not a political relationship.

A relationship which can be truly termed political, which involved the exercise of power to alter people's behaviour, was shown in other aspects of the ritual cycle.[1] There is no single office of centralized authority in Tikopia. The chiefs of the four clans are each autonomous and the constraints to which any of

[1] Cf. Goode, *op. cit.*, pp. 159 *et seq.* In Tikopia the politico-religious connection 'becomes almost an identification'.

them may be subject are imposed by the logic of practical circumstances, not by a theory of government. The chiefs are ranked, but
this is a ranking of ritual and social precedence, not an order of
political authority. The Tikopia system of government is a centralized, *conjoint* authority system (see *Social Change in Tikopia*,
pp. 255–63). But pragmatically the conventions of the traditional
ritual system did imply certain political effects. The religious
primacy of the Ariki Kafika endowed him with the power of
decision in regard to the major events of the programme of the
ritual cycle. This meant that at his word, so long as the religious
sanctions were operative, other chiefs and people had to apply
their time and energy, and much of their material resources, along
the channels which he laid down. Moreover, in so doing they
made acknowledgment of his primacy. The ritual cycle itself
was believed to have been instituted by his ancestor and prime
god. Therefore, periodical acknowledgment of this recognition
was made to the Ariki Kafika in material and symbolic kind.
From this point of view, the major events of the ritual cycle
operated in a kind of pyramid form with the critical acts of the
Ariki Kafika at their apex. The clearest illustration of this was the
system of control of the sacred canoes. Each chief and most of
the ritual elders in each clan had one or more sacred canoes which
were represented by eight or nine of their number, the *taumauri*,
which served as a representative point of application of many of
the most sacred rites. In their turn the *taumauri* were represented
by Vakamanongi, the leading canoe of them all. This belonged to
the Ariki Fangarere, last of the chiefs in ritual precedence. But it
was dedicated to the Atua i Kafika, prime god of the leading chief
in ritual precedence. This ritual inversion gave a status to the Ariki
Fangarere which helped to maintain his 'parity of esteem' with
the other chiefs. But it was the Ariki Kafika who gave the word
as to when and how the leading canoe should be celebrated, and
by implication assumed the role of speaking for all the sacred
canoes throughout the community. In this way the sanctions of
belief which maintained the ritual cycle served as a force of
political integration.

It is clear that this Tikopia ritual cycle was preoccupied with
technological and economic ends. One expressed object was the
attainment of food not merely for the specific occasions but
seasonally and generally. Moreover, the object was not simply to

provide for the wants of the person performing the ritual, but also in many cases to cater for the prosperity and well-being of the whole Tikopia community. From this point of view the element of representation or implied delegation was very strongly marked. On the personal side each chief spoke for his clan, each elder for his lineage. In many rites the Ariki Kafika spoke for the community as a whole. On the material side single objects stood for their species and items of one species could stand for a whole range of types. This was exemplified particularly by the role of the yam in the whole ritual cycle. Appeals were constantly made for food, for the breadfruit to fruit and for other crops to yield abundantly. Foods of various kinds were laid before the gods as offerings, but the only vegetable which was ritualized as part of the cycle of the Work of the Gods was the yam. The prime place given to the Work of the Yam puzzled me at first because the yam, though a useful and prized foodstuff, is not the most important in the Tikopia food provision – taro and breadfruit exceed it by far in volume of production. But from a Tikopia point of view the fact that the yam can symbolize all vegetable foodstuffs is independent of its precise place in the roster of food. It is its representative quality, not its bulk, that is being celebrated. Granted this, utilitarian considerations may be given some significance. From the point of view of ritual performances extending over more than a fortnight, a vegetable which has certain powers of durability is useful. The leaves of taro wilt very soon after it is dug, and the corm begins to decay in a few days. Breadfruit likewise does not last long. But the yam may be kept in good condition for a great length of time and can be thus ritualized with economy and ease.[1] Pragmatically in the formation of the ritual cycle the time schedule must have been adapted in a broad way to the material properties of the objects ritualized.

[1] A question is whether relative difficulty of cultivation and greater variability of yield may not have impressed upon the Tikopia the desirability of ritualizing the yam above all other vegetables. This is an interesting possibility, which I cannot fully check. In Tikopia, however, which lacks the large yams of mainland New Guinea, no great *technical* attention was given to the yam, and it is my impression that its variability of yield was no greater than that of breadfruit. The question of utilitarian factors combining with others as a basis for ritualization is of great interest, especially in the light of the treatment of this issue by Lévi-Strauss, who has used in part Tikopia material. (*Le Totémisme Aujourd'hui*, 1962, pp. 93–5; cf. Firth, *Primitive Polynesian Economy*, 1939, p. 65; Firth, 'Twins, Birds and Vegetables: Problems of Identification in Primitive Religious Thought', *Man* (N.S.), vol. I, pp. 1–17, 1966.)

In some respects the ritual cycle of the Work of the Gods corresponds to the cults described by Frazer and by Durkheim. Frazer's account of the public functionary whose role it is to control the weather and especially to ensure an adequate fall of rain is very reminiscent of the role of the Tikopia chief, especially the Ariki Kafika, in the Work of the Gods. His account of the sacrament of first-fruits as being an act of communion with a deity or powerful spirit, allied to the notion that these fruits are a gift bestowed by the gods upon man, who is bound to express his homage to his divine benefactors by returning to them a portion of their bounty, is illustrated by the rite of the Hot Food.[1]

But although in some respect there are close analogies with the cults of vegetation and other practices which Durkheim categorizes as 'positive rites', the Tikopia Work of the Gods differs in many respects from the stereotype presented by the classical anthropological writers. This is partly because the stereotype is psychologically naïve. One difficulty in accepting Frazer's characterizations of priest and magician (either in opposition or in combination) is the lack of sophistication they show. The priest is characterized by an 'awful sense of the divine majesty' and a 'humble prostration in the presence of it', mingled with 'certain lower motives'; the magician by 'a haughty self-sufficiency and arrogant demeanour towards the higher powers'. And when priest and sorcerer were not yet differentiated, as Frazer saw the situation in some parts of Oceania, the ritual performer uttered 'prayers and incantations almost in the same breath, knowing or recking little of the theoretical inconsistency of his behaviour so long as by hook or crook he contrived to get what he wanted'. In the rites of homoeopathic or imitative magic the practitioner wishing to make rain is presented as simulating rain by sprinkling water or mimicking clouds, and so on. Now, in the conduct of Tikopia chief and ritual elders, elements of all these characteristics described by Frazer can be found. Yet they are not the most marked features and appear in combination with other more plausible attitudes. There was apt to be an intellectual awareness and an emotional sensitivity about the conduct of the Tikopia priest which made it both more intelligible and more sympathetic to me than Frazer's stereotype. The Ariki Kafika, in praying for rain to fertilize the crops, did not pour water on the ground or make motions to imitate clouds. He

[1] J. G. Frazer, *The Golden Bough*, abridged edition, 1925, pp. 62, 479–88.

spoke of rain and clouds by way of appeal, and where he sym-
bolized them did so in verbal imagery and not by crude signs. So
also in other respects the Tikopia pagan priest was much more
complex, much more allusive, much more 'poetic' in his rite and
formula than is the public functionary presented to us by Frazer.
Even Durkheim, though much more subtle, gives an over-simpli-
fied presentation of the 'positive rites' concerned with the increase
of Australian aboriginal food supply. According to him these
positive rites have one common characteristic: 'They are all performed in a state of confidence, joy and even enthusiasm . . . men
celebrate them with confidence, joyfully anticipating the happy
event which they prepare and announce.' They are joyful feasts
'marked with the gravity which a religious solemnity always sup-
poses, but this gravity excludes neither animation nor joy'.
Durkheim distinguishes such rites very sharply from what he calls
piacular ceremonies which suggest not only the idea of expiation
but also of misfortune, and are therefore celebrated in a state of
uneasiness or sadness.[1] As a prime example of this type of ritual he
instances mortuary rites. Now from various phases of the Work
of the Gods it will be clear that the notion of piacular in Durkheim's sense was to be found right at the heart of these 'positive
cults' of fertility and care for prosperity. Durkheim states that
'everything of evil omen' necessitates a piaculum. In the Tikopia
canoe rites the term *Anea Pariki*, the offering of fish to the adze-
gods, itself denotes ill omen – 'evil things' – and the period immediately before the rite was celebrated was one of anxiety and
even fear (p. 103). From time to time during every ritual sequence
anxiety was apt to be displayed lest the offerings to the gods were
insufficient or the gods failed to respond to the appeals made to
them.

There has been a constant trend in anthropological and sociological studies of religion to classify rites as Durkheim suggested
in terms of the ritual attitudes which characterize them. It is clear
from the Tikopia ritual cycle that this contrast between the 'posi-

---

[1] Durkheim's usage differs to some degree from that of Robertson Smith, who
introduced the term piacular to anthropology. Robertson Smith regarded piacular
ritual as in its later form a sacrificial gift in atonement for sin and in its earlier form
a sacrifice of the life of a victim representing in some way an analogy to communion with the life of god and worshippers. *Religion of the Semites*, rev. ed., 1907,
pp. 397–401; 1st ed., 1889, pp. 378–82. Durkheim, *Elementary Forms of Religious
Life*, translated by J. W. Swain, 1926, p. 389.

tive cult' of fertility rites and alimentary communion and the 'piacular rites' of anxiety and atonement is one of elements, not of whole ritual performance. As with the taboos of the 'negative cult', the opposed elements are closely associated together in one integral rite. The evidence of the Tikopia ritual cycle reinforces once again the trend towards the destruction of the classical dichotomies in anthropological religious thinking, except as analytical elements.

The aggregation of different kinds of ritual attitudes as elements in a common performance is brought out very clearly by examination of many of the ritual formulae uttered in the course of the Work of the Gods. Elements of propitiation and request in asking the gods for welfare; of acknowledgment with thanks for benefits and an eye on the future; of compulsion or at least command in that many phrases are in the form of instruction and hortation to the gods – all were present and intermingled. The distinction between private and public rituals also appears as an empirical separation only, not one which can be taken at face value in sociological interpretation. Most of the important rites of the Work of the Gods traditionally involved large numbers of men and women, the latter usually occupied behind the scenes. But many other rites attended by only a handful of men, such as most of those for the yam, were not valid only for the participants. They had representative status for the community as a whole.

In examining the Tikopia ritual cycle, then, we find that the ordinary criteria of interpretation of ritual cannot be applied in any very simple way. We are concerned with the intentions and attitudes of the participants, but in a relatively complex and sophisticated form. We are concerned also with the significance of the ritual for the status of the individuals concerned and for the general structure of the society. Here too no euphoric mood of Durkheimian collectivity will serve. Tikopia ritual relations are highly complex and involve status assertion, competition and even conflict within the general framework of a balanced adjustment of roles in an hierarchical system.

It is clear that the Work of the Gods was performed as much for the sake of society as for that of religion. Social integration was maintained by various devices. These included the recognition of the opposition of sectors of the society – those in the traditional temple area, Uta, and those in the beach villages, Tai; those within the turmeric-making sphere and those without – the 'hot food' and the 'cold food'; those opposed and yet linked together by the formal food exchanges at the dance and other periods. They included also the device of conceiving a religious pyramid of gods which validated a ritual pyramid of precedence of chiefs and so gave a special tone to their political quality. On the other hand, relations of equality and autonomy were emphasized at many points in the rites performed separately by the four chiefs and even by some of the leading ritual elders. Moreover, the device of associating chiefs and leading elders as individual representatives of their groups with specific items of the ritual cycle gave each at certain points in the cycle an outstanding role in the performance. Each of the major personages had then a species of hereditary ritual capital upon which he could pride himself and which marked him out individually from all other participants. Inducement was thus given to him and his associated kin to assist in the perpetuation of the rites, in order to continue to validate his own status and not merely because of loyalty to the system as a whole. It was by this intricate combination of esoteric and exoteric, taboos and inducements, fear and respect, penalties and rewards, loyalty to lineage and to clan leaders and opportunity of self-assertion and status validation that I believe the ritual implementation of the religious beliefs of the Tikopia was maintained.

The traditional Tikopia religious system with its cycle of the Work of the Gods has now been abandoned. Alternative pressures and inducements, and the evidence of prosperity attainable by means other than the traditional pursuit of ritual, stimulated the move to change. But modification of pattern had already resulted from personal suggestibility at one period and the effects of disaster at another. To Tikopia themselves the process of modification was not seen as a challenge which would necessarily destroy the ritual fabric at one blow. They recognized that changes had taken place in the past, that adaptations had been made, often consciously and purposely. They saw that adaptations could continue to be made then while they still preserved the essence of the ritual system. Indeed by some instructed Tikopia themselves far-reaching modifications were suggested to meet the new situation and still keep the major ritual purpose intact.[1] In short, what destroyed the

---

[1] In 1952 Pa Raropuka suggested in a talk with me that because of the famine the work of the canoes, and of Somosomo and certain other rites, should be

Work of the Gods was not the successive modifications which the Tikopia religious attitudes showed every capacity to absorb. It was the series of competing pressures and inducements which led them individually and in groups to abandon the whole traditional ritual system for the alternative system of Christianity. With their steady conversion to the new religion the number of pagan ritual participants dropped so low that continuance of their ritual system became increasingly difficult. In the end it was the superiority of the alternative system in the social and economic sphere which facilitated the change of religious conviction and the abandonment of traditional religious practice. What was evident throughout the history of the Work of the Gods over nearly half a century was the flexibility of this practice and the power of adaptation inherent in this aspect of the 'primitive' religious system.

I now want to raise a few general issues about the nature of primitive ritual. It is useful to take as a starting-point Leach's view that ritual is a form of symbolic statement which 'says' something about the individuals involved in the action – particularly by expressing their social status – and so makes explicit the social structure.[1]

It will be obvious to a reader of this book that Leach's essential propositions are fully borne out by the Tikopia ritual cycle of the Work of the Gods. Chiefs, ritual elders and many other participants, including women, were enabled to demonstrate their social position thereby. But ritual usually involves *critical acts* which are the core of the performance and upon the performers of which public attention is focused; often, as with the Throwing the Firestick, the rite is named by the participants accordingly. Now in the 'language' of ritual the critical act may 'say' something different according to circumstances. In one type of ritual status, emphasis may be upon personal action – he who *does* the critical thing is not only the focus of public attention but also is socially recognized as the legitimate holder of the status achievement. Such was the position of Pa Rarovi, bearer of the sacred Fire to the dances of Marae – he continually revalidated his status by this critical ritual

dropped, and only the work of the yam, the re-carpeting of Kafika temple and the turmeric manufacture be retained – in other words, only those rites immediately under the aegis of the major deity of Kafika. 'Look at the Ariki Tafua,' he said, 'he has abandoned his rites and he has not been struck by famine.'

[1] E. R. Leach, *op. cit.*, 1954, pp. 11–16, 174.

act (p. 349). But a status mark of another kind is when a person is recognized not as the doer of the act but the *controller* of it – to be able to say that it is *his*, and to dictate when, how and by whom it shall be performed, as the Ariki Kafika controlled the Work of the Yam (Chapter 4). Still other status indicators may be given by being allowed to *participate* in ritual, though having neither a controlling voice nor a critical role – as was the case with the cupbearer in a kava rite. Hence it may not necessarily be the ritual performance in itself which makes the symbolic statement about status; it is the fact of performance, the role of performer or controller, which is recognized as a privilege and which is the structural expression. Ritual may 'say' something, but in a sense it may not matter precisely *what* is 'said'; it is the act of 'saying', the *when* and *how* that matter, from the social point of view. I think that perhaps Leach has had this in mind in stating how the *pattern* (my italic) of ritual 'represents' or describes status relations within the community (p. 174). For while ritual 'says' something to the participant individuals, its significance comes in no small degree from the fact that it is not just a simple, single free symbolic utterance; it is a formalized piece of behaviour, repetitive, even routinized. It has 'said' the same thing before and will say the same thing again. It expresses social status by reaffirmation, and by expectation of future performance of the same type.

If ritual 'says' something about individuals, to whom are the things said? Presumably, unless one accepts the reality of postulated spirit powers, the symbolic statements are being made to other members of the society. But as a mode of symbolic communication ritual is not of a very refined order; it is gross and imprecise, as compared with spoken language. This is why the bodily acts of ritual have so often subjoined to them a spoken formula. As a mode of communication in a society, then, ritual may say relatively few things about the social order, and say mostly what people already know. Granted that this is so, the things that it conveys may be of cardinal importance. Rites are of many kinds, and different kinds communicate different symbolic messages. Rites of initiation not only mark the accession of novices to new social position and privilege; they also may convey information of educational value. Mortuary rites assist the survivors to adjust to the final absence of a member of the group;

they may also serve as a means of social control. Installation rites of a chief or king not only emphasize the importance of the office, but also notify to the participants the assumption of a moral commitment by the office-holder.[1]

In such ways ritual not only represents, describes and maintains the social order; it may also help in the formation and development of the social order. It can have an adaptive and even creative function. By giving occasion for the public assumption of roles it also gives occasion for interpreting and modifying them, and so for re-shaping the social order. But as it does these things, by the very messages of status-involvement and exercise of initiative that it conveys it may also be a source of competition and disunity; one man's ritual asset may become another man's social affront.

With this is linked the fact that ritual may serve as a mode of personal expression as well as a mode of social communication. Its expressive function may be re-phrased as being a mode of communication to the self, but such a rendering does not do justice to its values. On the expressive side, ritual may provide a preface or an accompaniment or a stimulus to technical action; it may even be a substitute for action where the technical basis is not firmly assured. This is in line with Malinowski's view. Moreover, as he also has argued, one can assume that every individual has emotional dispositions and tensions arising from his relation to the external world, including members of his own society. This seems to me to be evident from a great deal of Tikopia verbal and non-verbal behaviour, and that what ritual has done is to provide a routinization and canalization for such tensions. These are not left for random expression, but are assigned their time and place for explicit mention and acting-out.

In Tikopia the verbal concomitant of ritual, the formula of address to gods and ancestors, is prescribed in general form, but has a considerable degree of flexibility when it is repeated. Such *free formulae* allow of a combination of conventional patterned statement with individual, idiosyncratic modes of expression. In this sense ritual thus enables something to be 'said' about the

[1] These various aspects have been well brought out in recent works by Audrey I. Richards, *Chisungu: A Girl's Initiation Ceremony among the Bemba of Northern Rhodesia*, 1956; M. Fortes, 'Ritual and Office in Tribal Society', and C. D. Forde, 'Death and Succession: An Analysis of Yakö Mortuary Ceremonial', both in *Essays on the Ritual of Social Relations*, edited by M. Gluckman, 1962.

personal order as well as about the social order. It may be asked – what about the participants who do not take the lead in ritual procedures, or those members of the group concerned who do not even participate in the ritual? (Though anthropological descriptions do not always point this out, such non-participating members of social groups are not at all uncommon.) Here one can postulate that ritual performance operates vicariously, through identification. A theory of assignment of responsibility to lineage head or other status leader means that a junior member of the group can have the expressive function of ritual performed for him on a representative basis. That this does not necessarily completely dispose of his tensions *vis-à-vis* the external world is revealed by the fact that sometimes a ritual leader is criticized by such junior members for performing the rites 'inefficiently' – too late, in wrong order, with insufficient attention to detail, etc.

There is a further point related to the level of scrutiny or of dissection of ritual procedures. Holistically, the communicative and the expressive functions of ritual seem to be well borne out. But at the level of detailed procedures many 'ritual' actions cannot be regarded as in themselves 'saying' anything – or at least anything significant – about the social order. A lot of ritual actions must be regarded as essentially *contributory* to a final symbolic statement – part of the 'build-up' necessary to completion of the pattern. But as separate items each may be 'saying' something about the state of mind of the person who performs it. Here the line between technical and ritual is once again not easy to draw. Even apart from this what may be conceded as a ritual act without technical significance may still have only a minimal symbolic significance, if indeed its symbolism can be discerned at all. When in the Work of the Canoes the sacred canoe adzes were lifted down from their shelf in the temple (p. 69) this was an act without technical implication. It might be regarded as an indication that they were being removed from a quiescent state to one of nascent activity, and therefore the gods associated with them had to be placated. But the action seemed to be regarded as having a quality of danger in itself; it was a 'marker' or 'indicator' action, one which was significant in the general context rather than one which stood for something other than itself.

This leads to a further point. Most ritual involves a commitment of resources, even if only of time and energy. Its significance as a symbolizer of social status tends to lie essentially in this fact. But such a commitment means that whatever be the function of ritual as a symbolic re-statement of some aspects of social structure, a most important focus for the whole ritual scheme is upon the efficient use of resources. Even where no very obvious apparatus or items of wealth are involved there is still the notion that a rite can be well or badly performed. This means that relation of means to ends in terms of concepts of neatness, speed, appropriateness of spoken word or bodily act is regarded as relevant to the ritual situation. This seems to be so apart from aesthetic elements of judgment, and apart from the notion that errors in ritual are deleterious to the results. In short, concepts of efficiency lie at the heart of ritual as at that of technical procedures. It is from this point of view that an apparent antinomy can be once more resolved. 'Ritual' and 'technical' are in many contexts opposed. 'Work' is normally a technical concept, yet we are dealing here with the 'Work' of the Gods. My analysis shows, I hope conclusively, that not only are technical and ritual interwoven as differentiated but linked procedures, but they share some of the same qualities through being expressive of the commitment of the persons who perform them.

But why these two modes of expression – why must some things be said indirectly, in symbolic statement, about social structure? As I see it, anthropologists provide the answer in some such terms as these. In any society, ritual follows a certain idiom, a cultural convention of sequences of behaviour. This idiom provides a code for expression and communication of ideas and emotions in terms which are at some remove from the ordinary speech and other behavioural conventions. Hence 'statements' can be made in a manner less brusque, more protracted, more behaviourally involved, than with ordinary language. The indirect form of 'statement' which the coded expressions of ritual provide also allows of extensive commitment of time and energy with great scope for variation to which values can be attached. Moreover, the endowment of ritual with positive moral values strengthens its acceptability as symbolic statement.

But there is a general point which relates to our understanding of the whole concept of ritual: the sequences pursued in it are in a sense self-validating; the achievement of its ends is in the last resort a matter of faith. It is not just a lack of observation of the processes involved – the chemical and biological changes that take place when a yam put into soil starts to grow are no less 'mysterious' to most of us than are the relations between spoken formula and yam growth to the Tikopia. But whereas the yam ritual is for the most part a non-experimental closed system, the yam technology is capable of a very great degree of modification and experiment. Moreover, an alternative faith-system may be accepted in replacement of the traditional ritual system, as justification of a set of technical procedures. Hence while a people such as the Tikopia may lose confidence in the effectiveness of their traditional ritual they do not conceive of a similar abandonment of their technology; or at least such abandonment tends to be much slower. Some critical evidence in support of this view is given in the Epilogue.

I

General Character
of the Work of the Gods

The aim of this chapter is to give a synoptic view of this Tikopia ritual cycle, with some general observations on its character. It will be realized from the detailed descriptions which follow that this synopsis is not merely an anthropological abstraction, but is a coherent scheme recognized by the Tikopia themselves.

To assist the reader it may be pointed out that the rites fall into several main divisions: a symbolic act to initiate the cycle; a re-sacralization of canoes; a re-consecration of temples; a series of harvest and planting rites for the yam; a sacred dance festival; several memorial rites on the sites of vanished temples; and in the trade-wind season, the ritual manufacture of turmeric.

All this ritual is integrated under the name of the Work of the Gods. This concrete title embodies two concepts, first that of a religious sanction behind the ritual, and secondly that of the ritual as a series of obligations, involving the expenditure of goods and of time. The religious sanction lies in the fact that the ritual cycle is believed to have been instituted primarily by one deity, the principal god of Kafika, who at the same time is worshipped by the chiefs of the other three clans. But into the scheme are drawn also other gods and chiefly ancestors. There is no elaborate system of mythology to explain how the ritual cycle came into being. The Tikopia state simply that the deity of Kafika instituted the rites, and that they themselves are perpetuating his traditional doings. But this attribution, slender as its foundation may seem, imbues them with a strong reverence for the ritual and the sacred objects connected with it. Such attitudes of respect are described in the later chapters. They are linked with definite beliefs that the rites are essential to maintain the fertility of crops and success in fishing, as well as the general welfare of the island as a whole. But apart from the reverence shown to specific objects and at specific moments of the ritual, the Tikopia show a very matter-of-fact attitude. The ritual involves a great deal of preparation of food and other work in plaiting mats, making thatch, repairing canoes, and cleaning the scene of operations, and these tasks are carried out much as ordinary events are, with a great deal of talk, joking and grumbling, with some dilatoriness and evasion of obligations. The Ariki Kafika said to me 'It is truly work, friend.' He himself displayed considerable devotion to his duty, in staying for a long time in Uta, deprived of company, and in rising early to perform his rites. But associated with this 'business' attitude is an element of great interest and some pleasure; the people as a whole look forward to the time when the Work of the Gods will begin, and nowadays Christians as well as pagans inquire eagerly when the firestick will be thrown. From this point of view the most attractive aspect of the ritual is undoubtedly the sacred dance festival. Before I realized the full meaning of the Work of the Gods and had heard this title I was told about the *Taomatangi*, the dance to quell the wind, by people who were obviously looking forward to it, and I thought for a time that this was actually the name for the whole cycle and the centre of it. So strong is the inducement to participate that a few of the more daring young men who have joined the Christian faith sometimes let their hair grow – a sign of unregeneracy – and attend the dance. One such case occurred when I was there. The young man was then barred from church for several months, but was finally readmitted by making a formal apology to the Christian teacher, accompanying it in Tikopia style with a basket of food.

FIXING THE TIME FOR THE RITUAL

A question of some importance is the basis on which the decision to begin these seasonal rites on any given day is taken. The Tikopia have no fixed calendar and no names for the months or for the days or nights of the month. They count moons or nights of the moon for specific purposes, as in estimating pregnancy or periods between events, but they use no tallies to assist them in this (see Postscript). The term *tau*, meaning literally 'a measurement' or 'count', is used for a season and sometimes for a year as a whole, but has no great precision. It is said that some *tau* have six months and others seven, or that after six months have elapsed the *tau* goes on into the seventh. It is in fact a seasonal period rather than a calendar period and refers primarily to the most marked climatic phenomenon in the island, namely the alternation of the trade-wind with the monsoon period.

This seasonal change, which is accompanied by changes in economic pursuits such as fishing, is the main basis for the seasonal ritual, as is shown by the fact that the ritual is called by the names of 'the Work of the Trade-Wind' and 'the Work of the Monsoon', respectively. About April the wind, after veering through several points, settles down to blow steadily with moderate force from the south-east or east-south-east and continues thus with hardly any intermission for about six months. (Since I was in Tikopia only twelve months I cannot say how much variation there is in the advent of the seasonal wind, but I gather that there may be several weeks.) During this period the temperature is often lower than in the other part of the year, clouds drift across the sky, and sometimes obscure it for hours together. During the turmeric manufacture, for instance, a day of bright sunshine was a novelty. About October the trade-wind dies away and is replaced by a variable period of normally light winds alternating with flat calms. The days are often very hot and cloudless. Occasionally the wind, which may have come from any direction from south-west to north, suddenly sets in strongly from the north-west and may rise to gale force for a few days. Rarely, perhaps once a decade, it becomes a hurricane which destroys houses and crops. Such a hurricane occurs only in the *raki* – the monsoon, and never in the *tonga* – the trade-wind season. This is alluded to in a traditional song, and it is said that though in the monsoon the noise of the rising wind makes a man wake and go out in anxiety to strengthen his house, in the trade-wind season he sleeps soundly.

Though the main index for the Work of the Gods is thus given by the seasonal change it is correlated with and corroborated by other factors. The Tikopia have no sidereal calendar but they do use astronomical observation to some extent as an aid in their time reckoning. Thus it is said that when the Pleiades rise then 'the ocean has begun to bite' – that is, the fish rise and are plentiful. At this time also birds and rats raid the food crops, man sets traps for them, and himself feels hunger. It is said that turmeric manufacture is sometimes regulated by the rising of the Pleiades but that it is usually arranged without such reference – 'it is made haphazard simply'. But the position of the stars is used as a general guide. The Ariki Kafika said that when the Pleiades appeared above the sea in the east, in the dawn, then that was a signal for the Work of the Trade-Wind to begin. At this time Taro, another star, still stood high up at dawn, but by the time it had descended in the heavens then the work was in full swing. Again it was said that the rising of Taro gave a signal for the approach of the work.

The Work of the Monsoon is also so guided. When it is seen that Manu, a bright star, has passed the zenith in the evening, then the time to throw the firestick for this season's work has arrived. Saraporu, another prominent star, stands midway in the western heavens in the evening at this time; towards the end of the Work, when the dance festival begins, Saraporu has gone below the horizon in the evening.

The Tikopia thus do not use these stars as definite determinants for the beginning of their rites but as general indicators and controls; their most important function is in giving the signal to prepare for the work rather than actually to begin the work.

Another token of the approach of the Work in the monsoon season is given by the arrival of the migrant turnstone (*turi*). This bird comes from northern latitudes every year about October. The Tikopia are ignorant of the real nature of the migratory phenomenon and hold that the turnstone comes from the sky where it has been staying during the trade-wind season. Its habitation there is called the Heavens of the *Turi*. 'The *turi* come; they come down from the skies; an ancient tale in this land.' The Tikopia have observed that in the trade-wind season there are hardly any of these birds about, save a few who 'dwell constantly', staying all the year round; but that when the monsoon comes they arrive in crowds. I was told 'Now the *turi* is a token of the monsoon. As men sleep, the Ariki Kafika hears the *turi* crying from above. The *turi* have come down and fly wailing above in crowds. Then the Ariki Kafika says "Man of the monsoon has cried. Nights there you are also." Then he does the things in Uta here.' The 'nights' and the 'things' are the rites of the Work of the Gods.

The condition of vegetation is also an important guide. The *Erythrina*, known as *ngatae* or *kalokalo*, changes its appearance with the seasons. It is the tree of the principal deity of Kafika to whom most of the ritual is dedicated, and when its red flowers begin to appear then it is the time for the Work of the Trade-Wind to begin. When the flowers are fully out in a blaze of flame then this is the correct time for turmeric-making. Since the blood-red turmeric is the pigment of the deity the symbolism is clear. A general token of the approach of the ritual season is given also by the maturity of the yam. When the first leaves which the vine has put forth, known as sacred leaves, have fallen, then the yam is ready for digging. Then, it is said, the Ariki Kafika goes and throws the firestick, and the Work proceeds. These factors all help to set the general time for the seasonal rites, but do not decide the actual day of commencement. This lies at the discretion of the Ariki Kafika. He is helped to his decision by the natural phenomena mentioned, but also by certain social phenomena. One of these is the confirmation of his intentions by his principal god, speaking through a human medium, and another is the general opinion of the other chiefs and the people. Thus before the Work of the Trade-Wind in June 1929 his medium Pa Motusio became possessed by the god during a rite held after a thunderstorm. He asked 'Will anything happen nowadays, or is it yet some way off?' The chief replied 'It is some way off, but it has arrived' – meaning that the time was near. The god answered 'Yes indeed, your moon there will stand' – he meant that the ritual should begin in the next month. There was some disagreement at this time between the Ariki Kafika and the Ariki Taumako. The latter had suggested that the Ariki Kafika should hurry up and get on with the Work, and held that the thunderstorm had come because the Ariki Kafika had been staying on in Faea instead of going to Uta to throw the firestick. The Ariki Kafika held that the thunder was simply a mark of the good nature of his deity in clearing up the sky (which is indeed the usual Tikopia interpretation) and pointed to the fine weather which we were then enjoying as proof. Moreover he pointed out to me very strongly that the time for the ritual is quite at the discretion of the Kafika chief. This is the position generally held. In this case he said he would have been willing to let the ritual begin earlier, but he could not do so for fear of the yam, which was not mature until then.

To sum up: there is no fixed date for the seasonal ritual, and the day on which it begins is governed by the decision of the Ariki Kafika who is guided in fixing the time by the various factors mentioned conjointly. It is probable also that the chief takes into account the phases of the moon in fixing the time when the rites should begin, though I did not record any statement on this point.

Since flying fish cannot be caught with the aid of torches when the full moon is up, the date is probably fixed so that the *faunga vaka* rites will coincide with a time of relative darkness. This would seem to explain statements relating to the moon such as that mentioned above.

PROGRAMME OF THE RITES

The order of the rites of the Work of the Gods is traditionally fixed, though the space between them lies to some extent at the discretion of the Ariki Kafika. But any ordinary Tikopia knows the sequence and can visualize it clearly. During the rites of the monsoon season I took down an account of those of the trade wind season from Pa Te Arairaki, a man of the chiefly house of Kafika, who however had no responsibility in the matter. I give this account here since by comparison with the programme as actually followed it shows that the sequence of rites is not simply a matter of dictation by the chiefs but is common knowledge to the people as a whole. The account was given to me in running form with no prompting on my part.

'In the nights of the trade-wind the firestick is thrown; we dwell and then pluck the *repa* (for the yam rites—there is no *faunga vaka*). The next morning make the kava of the yam; the next morning to Takerekere, the kava of Pu Ma. Waking on another day the seed tubers are prepared (*utu*), that is they are made sacred and the Work of the yam is made to them. After three or it may be four nights the yam cultivation is cleared; the morning after the tubers are cut; the morning after is *soani autaru*. The morning after the mat of Vaisakiri is cut, and the morning after the noonday rite of Vaisakiri is performed. The morning after the temples are re-carpeted, and the morning after come Nukuora and Taumako (temples). The yam is buried. It remains there while the chief dwells counting his nights, it may be two or three. Then the yam cultivation is burned. The morning after the *fakaora* is performed, and the morning after the yam is planted. The morning after is *soani to* (a secondary planting rite). Resiake is re-carpeted. On the morning of the next day the sacred digging stick is stood up and the noonday rite of Resiake is performed. On the morning of the next day, Kafika is re-carpeted. On the morning of the next day it is Somosomo; we go and clear. He who has prepared his *roi* carries it to Somosomo – he who marries into Kafika makes then his *roi*.

In the morning of the next day Pa Rarovi makes his noonday rite. The next morning we, sa Kafika, do so. The next morning it is sa Tavi. In the evening the *roi* is prepared. On the morning of another day the kava is made and we disperse, going then to cut new aqueducts, and go and turn over the sacred turmeric, the name of which is the *akoako*. In the morning we go and make a good head of water – we sa Kafika – while the people of Taumako and Tafua go and turn their turmeric. Then letting pass some days, whatever they may be, when the waters have been increased and the digging out of the turmeric from the woods is finished, then filter sheets are sewn.

'On the morning of the next day the turmeric is grated. When grated the next morning it is filtered and its *uruango* is made. The day on which it, the *akoako*, is filtered, is that on which the turmeric of the chiefs of Taumako and Tafua is grated; then on the morning of the next day the turmeric of the Ariki Fangarere and the other chiefs is filtered – they are another company. The next morning the turmeric sleeps in its enclosure. As the night descends it sleeps in the *rotoa*. The next morning the turmeric cylinders are prepared, and in the evening the *akoako* is baked. When the land is dark, it is brought out, and in the morning the chiefs ask if the *akoako* has fallen well or has fallen badly. If it has fallen well it is tied up and hung up above. And the turmeric of the Ariki Fangarere and the other chiefs is baked that night. In the morning, other companies bake theirs and take it out. In the morning it is carried to Kafika and we go and daub. We come then and in the evening set up the *uruango*. In the morning at dawn the spirits fly away, they are invited to go and we beat the canoes and whoop. Then the chiefs go and daub with their turmeric in their houses in Uta. Then we dwell and whatever may be the number of days that pass, Nukuora prepares *roi* – it is the house of the Ariki Fangarere in which the Ariki Kafika makes kava.

'The next morning daubing is also done, and in the evening the people go and prepare the *roi* of Marae. The next morning the Marae is cleared and Matangiaso and Rarofiroki are re-carpeted. Then in the evening the *vetu* is performed; it is the day of sa Kafika. The next morning the *vetu* is again performed – it is the day of sa Tafua and sa Taumako together. The next morning it is finished and we lay hands on the intervals between the temples (a rite known as *popo i a vasia fare*). The Ariki Kafika says to Tafua and

Taumako that Vakamanongi will fall singly, its *ururenga* will be performed alone. But if not it is done collectively. The canoes of the chiefs are done all together. Then we go to Tai to carry on with the canoes. The next morning the *maro* of the canoes are spread. When this is finished we go to Takarito. When its re-carpeting is finished we come and dwell. One man dwells and then makes the *ururenga* of his canoe, another man dwells and makes the *ururenga* of his canoe. Now it is finished.'

This account shows in the first place how a Tikopia man not responsible for the organization of the rites can carry in his memory a sequence of more than thirty separate days. Reference to the actual programme shows that this is a fairly accurate description of what occurs. Moreover it is a good illustration of the verbal symbolism of the Tikopia. The account is practically un-intelligible to the reader—despite the fact that I have translated it to make the technical terms as clear as possible. For almost every ceremony the Tikopia have a cliché, a cryptic reference which cannot be understood without a very full knowledge of the actual procedure and the explanations given by the people themselves. The meaning of these statements will emerge in the following chapters.

To facilitate reference in the following chapters I give here the programmes for the Work of the Gods in the two seasons, on the basis of what I was told and what I observed. The numbers refer to the sequence of events on separate days though since in some cases the intervals between the rites are variable, the total number of days occupied is usually more than indicated here. The names of the clans given in each case show the chief under whose aegis the ritual is performed. It will be seen that the greatest share is taken by the Ariki Kafika.

A. The Work of the Monsoon

I.	Throwing the Firestick	Kafika
II.	Preparing *roi*	All clans
III.	Canoe rites. *Faunga vaka*. Day of the Chief	All clans
IV.	Canoe rites. *Faunga vaka*. Day of Elders	All clans
V.	Canoe rites. *Faunga vaka*. Day of *taurukuruku*	All clans
VI.	Canoe rites. 'Evil things'	All clans
VII.	Canoe rites. *Fainga vaka*. Vakamanongi	Fangarere
VIII.	Canoe rites. *Fainga vaka*. *Taumauri*	All clans
IX.	Canoe rites. *Fainga vaka*. Other sacred canoes	All clans
	Yam rites. Plucking *repa*	Kafika

x.	Yam rites. First-fruits	Kafika
xi.	Yam rites. Takerekere kava	Kafika
xii.	Yam rites. Seed tubers *utu*	Kafika
	(Ariki Kafika stays in Uta)	
xiii.	Yam rites. Yam kava	Kafika
xiv.	Yam rites. Yam kava	Kafika
xv.	Yam rites. Yam kava	Kafika
xvi.	Yam rites. *Autaru*; tubers cut	Kafika
xvii.	Yam rites. *Soani autaru*	Kafika
	Resiake perfumes	Taumako
xviii.	Yam rites.	Kafika
	Resiake re-carpeted	Taumako
xix.	Yam rites.	Kafika
	Resiake noonday rites	Taumako
	Vaisakiri mat	Fangarere
xx.	Yam rites.	Kafika
	Resiake, oil	Taumako
	Thatch of temples	Taumako and Tafua
	Vaisakiri, etc., re-carpeted	All clans
xxi.	Yam rites. Yam buried	Kafika
	1st night; premier temples re-carpeted	All clans
	Kafika thatch 'stolen'	Kafika
xxii.	Yam rites.	Kafika
	2nd night; Thatch of Kafika	Kafika
	Ara from Taumako	Taumako
xxiii.	Yam rites.	Kafika
	3rd night; Kafika re-carpeted	Kafika
xxiv.	Yam rites.	Kafika
	4th night; Noonday rites of Pa Rarovi	Kafika
xxv.	Yam rites.	Kafika
	5th night; Noonday rites of Taumako	Taumako
	Ara reciprocated	Kafika
xxvi.	Yam rites. Cultivation burned	Kafika
	Freeing the Land	All clans
	Temples re-carpeted in Tai	Taumako and Sao
xxvii.	Yam rites. *Fakaora* of yam	Kafika
	Temples re-carpeted in Tai	All clans
xxviii.	Yam rites. Yam planted	Kafika
xxix.	Yam rites. *Soani to.* Ariki Kafika visits Tai	Kafika
xxx.	Mapusanga re-carpeted. Messengers to chiefs	Kafika
xxxi.	Proclamation at Rarokoka. *Roi* made	All clans
xxxii.	Dance festival. *Taomatangi*; day sa Kafika	All clans
xxxiii.	Dance festival. *Taomatangi*; day sa Tafua	All clans
xxxiv.	Dance festival. *Taomatangi*; day sa Taumako	All clans
xxxv.	Dance festival. *Taomatangi*; day sa Fangarere	All clans
xxxvi.	Dance festival. *Uranga afi*; night sa Kafika	All clans
xxxvii.	Dance festival. *Uranga afi*; night sa Tafua	All clans
xxxviii.	Dance festival. *Uranga afi*; night sa Taumako	All clans

XXXIX.	Dance festival. *Uranga afi*; night sa Fangarere	All clans
XL.	*Popo i a vasia fare*	All clans
XLI.	Takarito re-carpeted	Kafika

B. Work of the Trade-Wind

I.	Throwing the Firestick	Kafika
	(Interval of three days)	
II.	Yam rites. Plucking *repa*	Kafika
III.	Yam rites. First-fruits	Kafika
IV.	Yam rites. Takerekere kava	Kafika
V.	Yam rites. Seed tubers *utu*	Kafika
	(Ariki Kafika stays in Uta)	
VI.	Yam rites. Yam kava	Kafika
VII.	Yam rites. Yam kava	Kafika
VIII.	Yam rites. Yam kava	Kafika
IX.	Yam rites. *Autaru*; tubers cut	Kafika
X.	Yam rites. *Soani autaru*	Kafika
	Mats of Vaisakiri and Sao plaited	Fangarere and Sao
XI.	Yam rites. Yam kava	
	Temples re-carpeted	All clans
XII.	Yam rites. Yam buried	Kafika
	1st night, Nukuora re-carpeted and	
	lesser temples	Taumako, etc.
XIII.	Yam rites	Kafika
	2nd night; Mapusanga re-carpeted	Kafika
XIV.	Yam rites	Kafika
	3rd night; Mapusanga re-carpeted	Kafika
XV.	Yam rites	Kafika
	4th night; Mapusanga re-carpeted	Kafika
XVI.	Yam rites. *Fakaora* of yam; cultivation burned	Kafika
XVII.	Yam rites. Yam planted	Kafika
XVIII.	Yam rites *Soani to*	Kafika
	Tafua and Taumako re-carpeted	Tafua and Taumako
XIX.	Fiora; thatch made	Tafua
XX.	Fiora; day of mats	Tafua
XXI.	Fiora; day of sa Tafua	Tafua
XXII.	Fiora; day of sa Fusi	Tafua
XXIII.	Fiora; day of sa Rarupe	Tafua
XXIV.	Fiora; 'rubbish' cleared	Tafua
	Resiake perfumes	Taumako
XXV.	Kafika thatch 'stolen'	Kafika
	Resiake re-carpeted	Taumako
XXVI.	Kafika thatch	Kafika
	Resiake noonday rite	Taumako
XXVII.	Kafika re-carpeted	Kafika
	Resiake oil	Taumako
XXVIII.	Somosomo; day of mats. Marae cleared	Kafika

XXIX.	Somosomo; noonday rite Pa Rarovi	Kafika
XXX.	Somosomo; noonday rite Pa Kafika	Kafika
XXXI.	Somosomo; noonday rite Pa Tavi	Kafika
XXXII.	Turmeric rites. *Akoako* turned; aqueducts repaired	All clans
XXXIII.	Turmeric rites. *Akoako* dug	All clans
XXXIV.	Turmeric rites. Kafika turmeric begun	Kafika
XXXV.	Turmeric rites. Other chiefs' turmeric begun	Other clans
XXXVI.	Turmeric rites. Ariki Kafika daubs turmeric	Kafika
XXXVII.	Turmeric rites. Ariki Tafua daubs turmeric	Tafua
XXXVIII.	Turmeric rites. Ariki Taumako daubs turmeric	Taumako
XXXIX.	Turmeric rites. Ariki Fangarere in Nukuora	Fangarere
XL.	*Ururenga* of Marae. Kafika noonday rite	All clans
XLI.	*Ururenga* of Marae. Tafua and Taumako noonday rite	All clans
XLII.	Muafaitoka kava. *Popo i a vasia fare*	All clans
	Canoe rites. Vakamanongi rite	Fangarere
XLIII.	*Taumauri* rites	All clans
XLIV.	Takarito re-carpeted	Kafika
	Fainga vaka of sacred canoes	All clans

The programme as presented here represents the full cycle of rites in the traditional form, as they were carried out until about 1918,[1] that is about a decade before my arrival. At this time, however, the Ariki Tafua became a Christian and abandoned his participation in them. Moreover all the elders living in Faea followed his example. Thus in the ritual which I saw certain items were missing. These were principally the re-consecration of the canoes of Tafua and Marinoa, the re-carpeting of the temple of Tafua, the formal proclamation at Rarokoka, and the ritual of Fiora. All of these except the Rarokoka proclamation, however, had their analogies in the rites of the other chiefs and elders, so with the help of information from the Ariki Tafua and other people it was easy to see how the full cycle had operated. Moreover, the Ariki Tafua had not abandoned his manufacture of turmeric, and when I participated in it carried it through with the full set of rites in respect of his ancient gods, with the exception of the formal making of the kava. It will be noted that the other chiefs have made certain ingenious adjustments to meet this defection of Tafua, as at the dance festival.

The performance of the Work of the Gods is not purely an

---

[1] I gave this date originally from Tikopia accounts. From Melanesian Mission records, the date of the conversion of the Ariki Tafua was probably later, about 1923.

esoteric activity; it has a definitely exoteric side. The food provided for the ritual serves also the daily wants of the groups concerned, and its preparation is carried out as in ordinary domestic life. For conciseness I have omitted a great deal of this economic and domestic material from my account. Moreover during the ritual cycle family life and kinship relations go on much as usual. When the Ariki Kafika is living in Uta, kept there by his religious ties, his family accompany him. One difference is, however, that because of their comparative isolation these people are very eager for news. When I arrived in the morning I was usually asked at once 'Speech concerning Faea or not?' – meaning, was there any gossip abroad there? And people who came over to attend the rites were asked 'Did our village go out torchlight fishing? How many fish?' and so on.

The fact that the preparation of food is an important adjunct to most rites gives an interesting index for time correlation. As the fire in the oven house begins to burn a white column of smoke ascends from the roof peak and is seen by the people around the margin of the lake. They remark to one another 'The oven of the chief (or whoever it may be) has begun to smoke.' The houses themselves are hidden by the foliage but the Tikopia know well the location of each. When important rites are in progress a number of these smoke pillars are to be seen from afar and their sequence provides quite an efficient means of correlation when, as often happens, cooked food has to be assembled or exchanged by a number of different households. Other indices to the state of food preparation are the grating of coconut for puddings and the pounding of the pudding in a wooden bowl. Passers-by hear these sounds from a distance and so can advise other groups of comparative progress. Indices such as these obviate the need for any fine measurement of time during the day.

Most of the ritual practices in the Work of the Gods include a kava ceremony. A full analysis of this cannot be given here, but in its full form the kava rite consists of four elements:[1] the offering of bark-cloth to the deities and ancestors; the recital of a long formula to them individually with the stem of a kava plant as the medium; libations of cups of kava to them; and the throwing of offerings of food and betel materials to them. The performance of the kava has, however, many variants according to the ritual with

[1] Details will be given in my *Rank and Religion in Tikopia.*

which it is linked, and many of these variants are noted in the following chapters. In brief, they result from the fact that the rite is oriented to different gods and ancestors, or to the different functions which these fulfil in different places and on different occasions.

Certain theoretical problems are raised by the material of this book but their answer can be given here only in empirical terms. One such problem is the type of integration which exists in the relationship of the four clans and their component kinship groups. These clans are politically autonomous, each under its own chief, whose decisions are not governed by any higher authority. In the religious sphere they are ranged in an order of precedence as follows: Kafika, Tafua, Taumako, and Fangarere. But the Ariki Kafika is *primus inter pares* and not the sole controlling authority. The question is then how do the clans and the chiefs maintain effective co-operation when any one of them is theoretically free to break away from the system? The answer, it would seem, lies partly in the religious sanction which attaches to the performance of the Work of the Gods, backed up by the belief that the Atua i Kafika is supreme among the Tikopia deities. But this in itself is not enough. In a great measure integration is achieved by the concatenation of the daily events which, as it were, carry along with them the chief and people of each clan in the stream. To fail in co-operation at one point would have repercussions at many others, and it is clear that the Tikopia do look upon the Work of the Gods as a coherent system of activities. Moreover at specific points the chief of each clan and even the ritual elders of the most important component groups of each clan have specific privileges which for the time being elevate them to a position of pre-eminence and allow them opportunity for self-assertion and the expression of prestige. Apart from the Ariki Kafika the Ariki Tafua has his proclamation at Rarokoka and his utterance over the kava house in Marae. The Ariki Taumako has his Resiake rites which he dedicates to the Atua i Kafika, and his presentation of the large food basket of the *Ara o Pu* for which he receives compliments from Kafika. The Ariki Fangarere has his pride of place before the temple of Muafaitoka. And elders such as Pa Rarovi, Pa Marinoa, and Pa Tavi have each their specific 'days'. These special privileges are highly esteemed by the people of the group concerned.

In the traditional Tikopia system these forces were powerful enough to maintain co-operation. But nowadays it is true that the Ariki Tafua, under the influence of a powerful external thrust, has broken away from his fellow chiefs. But even in his case the factors mentioned still exert a pull. Though a Christian, he grew angry when told that only a few of the elders of the Ariki Kafika were in attendance on him in Uta; his sons told me with evident pride how their father used to recite the formula in Marae in tones that rang round the hills, and how even the Ariki Kafika had to bend his head in respect on that occasion. And at one point it became a serious question whether the old chief would not abandon his Christianity and go back to take up the rites which he had forsworn.

Another problem which emerges from the material is that of variation in Tikopia ritual. Broadly speaking one can distinguish four types of variation. Firstly there is that which is not culturally significant immediately, being a slight modification introduced by an individual performer, as in the amount of food accumulated or the time allowed to elapse between one performance and another. Secondly there is that which is culturally significant at once and is regarded as an error – as when the Ariki Kafika forgot to include the single 'stolen' thatch in the repairing of his temple or to plant the sacred yam tubers. The third type is a variation of cultural significance, but which is classed not as an error but as an improvement – as when the Ariki Tafua suggested the merging of two days of the canoe rites into one and this was agreed to by the other chiefs; or as when Pa Rarovi substituted certain phrases in his kava formula for others. A test here to the Tikopia is given by results. If the crops and the fishing are still successful and no illness or other disaster overtakes the land then the variant is a good one, presumably having received the approval of the gods. The fourth type of variant is that which has presumably occurred in the past and which is now culturally established – as when the house of Mapusanga tie leaves of cordyline on to their sacred canoe when it is being re-consecrated, or as when certain temples have particular sacred objects which must be washed or otherwise treated specially during their ritual. A function of this last type of variant is clearly in giving an individuality to that particular rite and an opportunity for differentiation and special prestige to the group responsible for it. The problem of what constitutes an error and what an acceptable variant in ritual cannot be examined here. But it is plausible to infer that variations tend to be acceptable, first if they do not invalidate or threaten the whole ritual system of which they are a part; secondly if they do not involve a radical readjustment by other groups as well as that immediately concerned; and thirdly when they represent obvious economic and social advantages. There may be occasions on which variation is introduced on a large scale and cannot be effectively resisted, as in the defection of the Ariki Tafua. Here an attempt is made to meet it by adjustment which in itself involves a further variation. In the course of generations such variation may become part of the traditionally accepted practice. If, for instance, the heathen Tikopia can resist Christianity for another century then the anthropologist of A.D. 2028 may find that the simple assembly of the three chiefs at Rarokoka and the splitting of the clan Fangarere for reciprocal presentations at the dance festival may have come to be regarded as the 'original' forms of the ritual. It may be put forward as a proposition for the study of Polynesian cultures that these have been much more flexible in the past than has often been assumed, and that what we have to consider in any single island group is not merely a mixture or fusion of elements from other groups but a very high degree of local variation, arising in part from consciously motivated individual change, and in part from the establishment of errors and defections from traditional practice as recognized cultural forms. To put the point in another way, Polynesian cultures must be regarded not as static arrangements resting upon an original fusion of diverse elements, but as a dynamic arrangement with a tendency to variation perceptible in each generation, and with a selective process by which some at least of these variations are built into the cultural system.

Postscript

A comparative table of the programmes of 1928–9 and 1952 is given in RM, pp. 11–20.

According to Pa Motuata and Pa Panapa in 1952 the nights of the moon were reckoned as follows:

(*a*) 'The moon has disappeared' – about 4 nights when no moon visible; 'it has stood among the spirits'.

(*b*) 'It has stood among men' – about 10 nights, counting first, second, etc. (first quarter).

(*c*) 'Its body has become whole and big' – about 7 nights (full moon). These are the nights for bird-netting.

(*d*) 'It has begun to decline' – about 4 nights, counting first, second, etc. (last quarter).

(*e*) 'It stands on the crest of the dawn'; 'in the middle of dawn'; 'it breaks with the dawn – that is its last night, then it vanishes' – 3 nights.

Note that the phases of the moon recognized by the Tikopia correspond only approximately to those recognized in the West, and overlap them.

2

Throwing the Firestick

The opening rite of the ritual season is the 'Throwing of the Firestick' (*te pe o te potunea*).[1] The direction of this event is one of the special duties and privileges of the Ariki Kafika, the principal chief of the community, and the choice of date rests largely in his hands. When he has finally decided to begin the seasonal ritual he rises early in the morning and proceeds to Uta, the district where the most sacred temples stand. He usually has announced his intention a day or so previously to the other chiefs, his elders and the immediate members of his family. If for any reason his decision has been taken hurriedly without warning, he despatches messengers as soon as possible to advise the Ariki Fangarere, the other chief who is associated with him in this rite, and as many other people as he may think necessary. On such flying missions his sons or grandchildren are usually sent, but any youth who is at hand or whom he meets in the path may be pressed into service. These messages are of an advisory nature, and are not regarded as imperative commands. People who are busy with their own work often absent themselves, a proceeding which is regarded by them as justifiable, though this view the chief did not fully share when I heard him comment on it.

In the *tonga*, the season of the south-east trade-winds, the attendance at the ceremony is small. On the occasion of my visit in June 1929 the party consisted of the Ariki Kafika, his wife and grandchildren, one of his principal elders, Pa Porima, and a kinsman of the latter, a simple good-natured fellow who was willing to work. In the previous *raki*, the monsoon season, a much larger group had attended, comprising the chief, his three principal cousins, his sons, his chief elders, including Pa Rarovi, and his co-chief, the Ariki Fangarere.

The first-comers to Uta arrived soon after the sun had risen

---

[1] A detailed comparative description of Throwing the Firestick in 1952 is given in RM, 1963, pp. 7-10.

above the shoulder of the mountain. Without waiting for instructions they proceeded to rake out with their fingers the oven in the chief's kava house, and build a small fire. A long stick was laid in the middle of the fuel to provide the ceremonial brand over which the rite was to be performed, care being taken to arrange it so that its centre portion might be burned through. By this time the Ariki had come and taken his place on the ordinary coconut leaf mat which was his seat at the rear of the house. The oven was in front of him to the left, his private doorway in the corner behind him on the same side, while his elders and other clansmen sat facing him at the other end of the hut by the common entrance. Such was the usual arrangement at any kava ceremony in the building. The *position* of the participants in any piece of ritual is regarded as being of great importance in Tikopia.

Every ceremony has its domestic side as well as its social and religious aspects, and on the efficient provision of small details of equipment by members of the household depends the smooth functioning of the ritual. Food must be cooked and wrapped in readiness, water bottles filled and at hand, mats and other objects produced at the appropriate moment. The performance of any piece of religious ritual is, in fact, similar to that of a play, an adequate rendering by the actors being conditioned by efficient organization behind the scenes, and by the presence of a number of assistants who do not appear on the stage. This is seen most clearly when someone's lapse of memory about some purely practical detail threatens to throw the ritual mechanism out of gear. For example, on the first occasion of 'throwing the firestick' at which I was present the chief forgot the cincture of bark-cloth which he winds around his waist before beginning the recitation of any sacred formula. When he arrived in Uta he found that it had been left in his house in Tai at the beach village over a mile away, and it had to be fetched.

The women and children of the party were settled in the dwelling hut a few yards inland from the house where the firestick ceremony was held. Normally only men and boys take part in the esoteric side of ceremonial. The domestic side – the preparation of food and provision of water, the plaiting of floor-mats and arrangement of bedding – is the care of the women. This represents not so much a deliberate and conscious exclusion of females as a traditional division of spheres of interest; each sex has its own duties and responsibilities in the general scheme of religious ritual. Greater sacredness is associated with the work of the men, but whenever their immediate rites are over they return to the common resting place, and the women engage them eagerly in everyday chatter and discussion of the latest news.

After a while the fire began to die down in the pit, and inquiry was made by the Ariki whether the firestick had burnt through yet. 'Hey! that thing, has it divided?' he asked. The oven attendant went over to examine it, then laconically replied 'Yes!' 'Lay it down first and come to rub the charcoal', said the chief.

One end of the firestick was pulled out from the glowing mass; it had burnt through in the centre as desired. The assistant laid it down at the edge of the oven and powdered a little charcoal on a stone. Then he pressed his right forefinger in it, and advancing to where the chief was sitting with folded arms, knelt down before him, and while the latter inclined his head, drew the fingertip lightly down his brow. The resulting black vertical stripe was a sign that the chief was about to conduct an important piece of religious ritual.[1] When the man retired he was careful to observe the ordinary rule of Tikopia etiquette and not turn his back upon his superior. The black stripe is known as the *pani*. I was first told that it was a decoration, but later it was described as 'the *pani* of the god', in this case of the supreme deity of Kafika. It was also termed 'a token of the *faunga vaka*'. The *pani* may not be applied by anyone. The proper person is a kinsman 'in good relationship', that is a brother, a maternal uncle or sister's son of the chief. If no such man is present then the chief applies the mark himself.

'Go and lay it down; lay it down outside', said the chief to the assistant with the firestick. It was lifted carefully, being sacred, laid on a freshly cut banana leaf, and set out under the eave of the house, its butt or unburnt end pointing inwards. New leaves were spread there beforehand as a carpet for it – a token of respect paid to objects or persons of distinction. A point of spatial significance here was that though the firestick ceremony was described as a type of kava rite, the stick was laid on the mundane side of the house

[1] The chief, being fond of a laugh, on a later occasion purposely jerked his head as the mark was applied, so that it was crooked. This accident gave amusement to the audience, but discomfited the marker.

by the oven and not on the more sacred side, as a kava stem would
have been.

So far the chief had taken no active part in the proceedings.
Now he donned the ritual garment known as the *riri*, winding it
in coil after coil about his waist, above his ordinary garment. The
riri is the special cincture donned for important sacerdotal occasions, but its use is not confined solely to chiefs. It is the simpler
counterpart of the robe or vestment of the priest in a fully clothed
community, and its object is the same. It serves to mark off the
person officiating in ritual matters, while the assumption of the
garment is a preparation of the person himself for his approaching
communion with an extra-normal sphere of life. The chief then
tied on the *kasoa*, a necklet simply made by tearing off a pair of
adjacent pinnules from a coconut palm frond. This is again the
token of the chief engaged in sacerdotal affairs, since none but he
may use the palm frond thus, and even he will not assume it without occasion. This plain V-shaped green necklet projecting stiffly
over his breast is a striking piece of regalia, far more impressive
in its simplicity than any bizarre arrangement of beads or other
gauds. In Tikopia eyes it is the main symbol of chieftainship (cf.
Firth, 1959, Plate 5). At the conclusion of each day's events the
necklets – there may be several by then – are removed and hung
up by the chief on a bar at the rear of the house above his seating
place, where others rest, brown, shrivelled and thick with mould.
Being sacred they cannot be left to lie carelessly around.

Now came the most vital moment of the rite. The chief moved
from his customary seat to the border of the oven and with legs
crossed and hands resting in front of him faced the firestick, looking along it. In high tones, at first clearly audible, then trailing off
to a low murmur, he recited the formula, inviting ritually his
fellow chief of Fangarere and those of his elders who were present
to countenance or confirm this ceremonial act of 'throwing the
firestick'. He concluded with several phrases of invocation to his
deities.

The actual text of the formula used, with some supplementary
remarks, was given to me by the Ariki Kafika himself. A translation of what he said is:

Arriving in the morning, someone lights the oven and lays the stick
of firewood in the oven; it is there, there till it parts. Then I ask the man
who lit the oven 'Has it parted?'

He calls to me 'It has parted.'
'Go and drag it back.'
Thereupon he drags it back hither, carries and lays it on the oven side of the house.

I wind round my cincture, tear off the necklet, and hang it in position. I call out:

> 'Pa Tafua! Pa Taumako! Pa Fangarere! Pa Rarovi!
> Pa Porima! Pa Tavi!
> Your assembled elders there give countenance to the sacred thing here on its morning will be thrown away for the barring of the land.
> Calm be your land.
> The land shall stand in obedience to us.
> *Marie!*'

The firestick is not thrown, it is sacred; but its talk only is made: Firestick was thrown yesterday.

This statement draws attention to the fact that the firestick is not actually 'thrown' (*pe*) as the name of the rite suggests; as already noted, it is merely laid down on a prepared carpet of leaves. It is too sacred an object to be roughly treated. Sometimes it is not even handled by the chief, though apparently it is the custom for him to touch it with his fingers and thus make contact with it before it is finally set out under the eaves.

The meaning of the formula is briefly: the 'barring of the land' refers to the taboo on noise and public amusement; the 'calm' is desired to facilitate fishing; the names cited are those of chiefs and elders who by implication concur with the act of the chief in performing the rite. Additional phrases may be added as occasion warrants. Thus when I heard the Ariki recite the formula during the actual ceremony he reinforced it with an invocation for the wind to drop, using the honorific form of words: 'Lay down the sacred necklet to sleep down below', since a high wind had prevented the canoes from going out to fish for some days past. He then concluded with the appeal

> Anything weighty for the kava
> Gather together to the setting sun
> *Marie*.

This is one of the characteristic endings of the kava formulae, inviting the gods to remove oppressive influences.

When the recital of the formula was ended the firestick was

left in position under the eave while arrangements were made to prepare the food without which no ceremony of any importance can ever be carried out. It is essential to make these offerings to the gods. The quantity of food prepared at these ceremonies was roughly proportionate to the number of people engaged at the time. Thus the Ariki gave orders on this occasion 'Get some *masi* (paste of taro, etc., mixed with coconut cream) to make a little food bowl for us friends. We are not many, and the portions for offerings are only three.'

Usually one of the party is sent off to the orchards to bring back the coconuts required. When it is desired to hasten proceedings, however, or nuts of the right stage of maturity are difficult to obtain, a small reserve store slung in pairs over a beam of the house inside is utilized. This is termed the *fakana* and is regarded as being sacred, in that the nuts are intended for religious purposes only; they are never used to embellish an ordinary meal. When they are taken, fresh nuts are hung up almost immediately to replace them. This was done on the second occasion on which I was present, though coconuts were scarce at the time.

In this case, as in many others, the preparation of the food occupied a long time, and it was not till several hours after the firestick rite that the oven was finally ready for the second part of the ritual.

The second or confirmatory part follows at once upon the completion of the food arrangements. It consists essentially of the ritual of the kava, which is the fundamental feature of all Tikopia religious life. This practice involves a set of offerings to his ancestors by the chief or elder who is entitled to officiate; the recital of their names with appropriate invocations to them; and the association of this with the kava, in the form of a stem of the plant used as a vehicle of the formulae, or of libations of the liquid prepared from the chewed root. The kava ceremony has many modifications and a great variety of *atua* (supernatural beings) to whom it is addressed. In its most general type, however, the kava follows a definite formal order of events, and is intended not so much as a unique specific rite as a confirmation of some other individual ritual act. It sets the seal upon this, places it before the notice of the appropriate deities and thus relates it to the general universe of religious affairs.

On this occasion the kava invocation was very long, since the chief appealed to all his deities and ancestors. A typical phrase that I caught was 'Let a calm fall for a token of our work that has been performed.'

After the kava rite a meal was eaten from the food prepared, including the offerings, and the party then dispersed.

THE MEANING OF THE FIRESTICK RITE

The reader will ask what is the meaning of this act of 'throwing' the firestick. What is the significance of opening the cycle of the Work of the Gods by burning a piece of wood, and why is it described as 'thrown'? It may be said at once that the Tikopia had no specific reply to my queries on these points. They said that it was the custom from of old, and that there was no legend concerning its origin or meaning. One can see a fairly obvious symbolism in burning the stick in two, a symbolic act of *parting*, of separating the sacred from the profane period. But I could get no definite Tikopia statement of this general interpretation. Moreover, it is the rite as a whole and not the moment of the burning of the stick that sets the seal of sacredness on the land, nor is the pronouncement of the words 'sacred thing' a specific moment at which the interdiction comes into force. The firestick must be regarded as a traditionalized symbol, in which the original meaning has been swallowed up in its present general context.

Nor do the linguistic usages help in further interpretation. The term *potu*[1] *nea* means literally 'bit of a thing'; *potu* being a short piece, as *potu mami*, an end of bark-cloth, and *nea* being the general word for thing. In ordinary speech *potu nea* is used specifically for a bit of firewood. The word *pe* again means ordinarily 'throw', as *pe ki atea*, throw it away. It has a less violent significance, however, in some cases, as in the expression *pe tua*, 'turn one's back', and it can even mean to 'split off' or 'divide up', as applied to the division of a party of men engaged in turmeric manufacture. That the general meaning of 'throw', however, is present to the Tikopia in the firestick rite is seen by the explanation of the Ariki Kafika quoted above, when he felt it necessary to tell me that it was only a manner of speaking to say that the stick was *pe*.

Hence the use of the firestick, its burning and its orientation have their meaning for the Tikopia as traditional usages with definite values attached, values in which the sanctity of the occasion, the

[1] The word *potu* with long *o* is different, and means a village.

ritual position of the Ariki Kafika as the premier chief of the island, and the interdiction that follows the rite all form a part.

The meaning of the rite will be better understood after an examination of its immediate effects. The performance of this symbolic act, brief as it is, has now rendered the land *tapu* and formally instituted the period of the sacred ceremonies. From this moment the way of life of the people changes and receives a fresh orientation. They must now act circumspectly: no one is expected to shout or make other loud noise in the whole island, no parties may sit out on the beach and talk, as is their wont, and dancing, the favourite evening amusement, is suspended. At night people are supposed to sit within their houses, and the Ariki Kafika may even periodically patrol the paths to see that this prohibition is observed. As a rule, however, he remains within doors, and the executive control of the island is left to the chiefs of Tafua and Taumako. The Ariki Tafua said to me – even though he was now a Christian – 'The Ariki Kafika merely sits; I and my brother of Taumako guard the land. Not a man may whoop!'

Rather more latitude is allowed to the people of Kafika clan than to others to walk abroad at this time, the reason being that their principal deity is the originator and basis of all the ritual, and their proprietary rights are therefore stronger.

On the whole, these restrictions are fairly closely observed. To the casual passer-by the absence of folk on the beach and under the trees gives the village the appearance of being almost deserted – the main element of life being provided by children, who are always difficult to restrain completely. In the monsoon season the villagers did not even go to bring in food from the cultivations on the day on which the firestick was ceremonialized. The taboo of the trade-wind season is less rigid. During my last month of residence the sacred time came round again, the firestick was thrown, and the land became *tapu*, but the young people still continued to dance in Potu sa Kafika, a village near the south end of the beach. Those in Namo refrained since they were directly across the lake from the quarters of the chief in Uta. But the former hamlet, being round the shoulder of the mountain ridge, was out of his ken, and the beat of their sounding-board in the dance could not be heard. When the chief later came to hear of it he muttered remarks about hurricanes which might come and open the eyes of the disturbers of the taboo, but nothing more was done. If he had actually happened upon such a dancing party they would have scattered before him, but discreet enjoyment is allowed unchecked in this season.

To *forua* for any reason, to shout or yell the conventional *Iefu!*, a shriek of fear or anger, is banned, and a deliberate breach of this rule is regarded as an offence. An illustration may be given. While the party were waiting in the kava house for the firestick to be burnt a screech of '*Iefu!*' was heard at a little distance. At once the chief sent off a lad to inquire who was the transgressor and why. After being away for a considerable time the boy returned to announce that it was one of his brothers-in-law in an orchard close by and that he had whooped in anger at having found some of his coconuts stolen. He had set up a taboo sign to prevent interference and had returned to find both green and dry nuts taken. 'Why didn't he give you a pair of coconuts to bring back?' interrupted the chief – his idea being that a man who yells at such a time ought to offer some compensation. But none was forthcoming. One of the attendant elders grunted: 'Didn't he see that the oven in the house here had begun to smoke?' In other words he should have noticed by this token that the ceremony was in progress and refrained from giving vent to his annoyance. All were indignant at his breach of the observance, but this soon passed off in the talk about the prevalence of theft in the cultivations, which was very rife at the time, and which indeed excused the offence.

Any loud noise or report is anathema at this time, particularly in the district of Uta, at the inner corner of the lake, which is the scene of the most sacred rites. On one occasion when I was with him the Ariki Kafika showed some forethought. On his way to Uta in the morning he stepped aside to the house of one of the principal elders of the island, a man not of his own clan, who had a cultivation in Uta, and told him to go and cut down a sago palm to provide food for himself and children – the firestick was going to be thrown. The ring of his axe could not be allowed to profane the silence of the sacred place once the rite had been performed, so the man hastily obtained assistance and completed the work before the oven in the house of the chief was ready.

SUBSEQUENT ACTIVITY

The throwing of the firestick is a significant event for all the people of the island though so few of them attend the actual ceremony. It means that they must obey certain rules of taboo, and it marks the opening of a season of excitement and hard work, of submission to a definite and rigid routine. Hence great interest is always taken in the movements of the Ariki Kafika about this time, and gossip soon passes the word round that he has gone to perform the sacred rite. When once it is learnt that the firestick has been thrown the next question is how many days will be allowed to elapse before the actual work of the ceremonial cycle begins. This lies at the discretion of the Ariki Kafika. At the conclusion of the firestick rite the people ask him 'How many days shall we allow to pass over?' He answers formally 'Pass over some days to cut dried mats.' By this is meant that sufficient time will be allowed for coconut leaf to be cut and plaited into floor-mats, which must dry properly for use.

Those people who have to provide mats as part of their duties then set to work to prepare them. The men or boys of the household go out, climb the palms, and cut down the amount of leaf required, then carry it home, four or five of the large leaves being a usual load. The women split each leaf, beginning at the tip, and tear off the two sides with fronds attached, rejecting the thick midrib. The two sets of fronds are then laid side by side, and plaited, at first with a twill pattern, but finishing off with a check when within a few inches of the border. The result is a long trapezoidal mat tapering from head to tail in accordance with the taper of the original leaf.[1]

Meanwhile the chief observes the condition of the sea, since it must be calm enough to allow of fishing at the conclusion of the canoe ceremonies. When he judges that the weather is becoming suitable he sends a messenger round to the other three chiefs with the laconic communication: 'Your sacred things make *roi* tomorrow.' The chiefs assent formally 'Yes.' The reference to 'sacred things' is to the objects of high religious importance associated with the canoe ritual. The *roi* is a special type of food used

[1] Tikopia etiquette takes account of the form of the mat, and the head (*uru*) is superior as a seating position to the tail (*muri*), a fact which enters into the arrangement and disposal of mats in all social and religious life. The diagrams of rites show the way in which the mats are laid; it is a formal feature of the occasion.

at the kava ceremony which prefaces the lifting down of these objects from their place in the house and the carrying of them to the canoe stations in the beach villages.

The peculiar feature of the *roi* is that the food is prepared and put into the oven in the evening, left to cook throughout the night and then removed the next morning for use in the ritual. On the morning after the reception of the message from the Ariki Kafika the chiefs send out members of their households and other clansfolk to collect food. This consists of taro and breadfruit. It is brought to the respective chiefs' houses in Uta, where by custom the *roi* is made. The ground is first carpeted with coconut leaves, a mat is then laid on top – the spot is carpeted since the *roi* is sacred. On this are placed leaves of the swamp taro which are large and thick, and above them leaves of limp, scorched banana. These latter are laid crosswise one over the other. Then leaves of taro, termed *pota*, are carefully placed on top again, reverse side uppermost. All these leaves are the wrappings of the *roi* and the innermost of them, the *pota*, with *vati*, a kind of spinach, are eaten. Those of banana and swamp taro are unfit for food. During this phase of the work the coconuts are grated and converted into cream. A few handfuls of sago flour are mixed with it to thicken it and give body to the food when cooked. Raw taro and breadfruit are sliced into small pieces, which are laid on the leaf pile, and the coconut cream is squeezed over the top, care being taken to hold up the edges of the leaves and prevent the liquid from dripping to the ground. The sticky mass is wrapped up firmly and taken to the oven where it is covered over and left to cook. The making of the *roi* is an event of importance since it is associated with one of the most weighty types of kava ritual. The party detailed for the work is usually small, comprising when I saw it four men and a couple of women. The chief himself does not always appear when the *roi* is being made, but delegates the work to some of his kinsfolk. Sometimes he attends, if his other tasks allow, entering into conversation, and even giving assistance, as by seating himself at one end of the mat and holding up a side of the leaf container as the coconut cream is being poured over the food.

On this occasion the chief and people of Fangarere make their *roi* at their own house, instead of combining with Kafika, as they do for many rites. In former days, when Tafua clan took part, they made two lots of *roi*. One lot was eaten in Uta – they were the only clan to do this – and the other was carried in the usual way to the canoe court, at Namo. This was said to be because they had two major sacred adzes instead of one.

With the setting of the *roi* in the oven the day's work is ended, and all is now in train for the canoe ceremonies, which begin the following morning.

3

Ritual of the Sacred Canoes

The seasonal canoe rites of Tikopia comprise three major series of events – the *Faunga Vaka*, the *Fainga Vaka*, and *Anea Pariki* – each of which will be examined in turn.

The canoes of Tikopia are classed ritually into two types, *vaka tapu*, sacred canoes, and *paopao*, secular craft. In this book we shall be concerned only with the sacred canoes, which, however, for ritual purposes are representative of Tikopia craft as a whole. Each sacred canoe has its own spirit guardians (*atua*) and these vessels, their *atua* and their human owners are integrated into a system which follows that of the general social and religious organization. The essence of the rites described in this chapter lies in the re-consecration of the canoes to their work, renewed appeals to their tutelary spirits to stand by and procure fish for them, coupled with offerings to these spirits of the first-fruits of their harvest from the sea.

Sacred canoes are possessed by the chiefs, their ritual elders, and other heads of the most important kinship groups. The owner-ship of these vessels is complex. Theoretically they are the property of the chief of the clan, despite the fact that the immediate pos-sessor in each case has ordered the building of the craft, paid the craftsmen for it, shelters it in his own canoe shed, has full rights of use over it, and is fully responsible for its upkeep and repair. The expression is, 'The canoe of the chief is resting with So-and-so.' This is in accordance with the general principle of centralization of ownership.[1] All valued property of the people of a clan, includ-ing their houses, canoes, land and bonito hooks, is held in theory at the disposal of the chief. It is theirs, but ultimately it is his too; in the last resort their interest in it will give way to his. Moreover, in case of crisis the theory becomes actual practice; no member of a clan can hold property against his chief. On the other hand the chief uses his privileges for the benefit of his clan and in

[1] See *We, the Tikopia*, 1936, pp. 376–85.

popular speech he is identified with his people when it is a question of collective action. In Tikopia eyes his overlordship and control are not only justified but natural, since it is he who is responsible for the people's welfare. He is their principal link with their ancestors and their only link with the supreme gods. He alone can perform the basic kava ceremonies which form the root of Tikopia religion.

From this point of view it is easy to see how the sacred canoes are held. For when a man of some standing in the community is building a canoe which appears to him to be a worthy vessel, he approaches his chief and with his permission places it under his authority – an act which is described by the term *fakataurongo*. The requisite kava is then performed and the chief assigns to the vessel its guardian deities – the *atua tau vaka* – nominating among them as a rule an ancestor of his own. The kava ceremonies for this craft are then performed periodically by the chief and gifts of food are made to him on these and other occasions by the owner of the canoe.

In this manner the threads of the whole nautical and fishing organization which forms such an important aspect of Tikopia life are drawn together and find their focal point in the chiefs of the four clans. The links are neatly provided by the dual structure of the social and religious system in matters of authority and government, the elders and heads of families deferring to the chief, and in matters of ghostly power the deities of their groups and canoes deferring to his. The structure goes still higher in the institution of the *taumauri*. These represent the acme of sacredness in canoes. They are special craft, held only in the possession of the four chiefs each of whom has two (three in Tafua, perhaps), and have their root, as the natives say, in the fact that they are all under the ultimate control of the one supreme *atua* of the Kafika clan.

Concerning him Pa Motuata, of the chiefly house of Taumako, said 'When he departed from this land, then his canoes were made, and obeyed (were dedicated to) him. They were built by the chiefs, who caused his bark-cloth offerings to ascend on to them. He was made the great god of this land. The chiefs performed rites to him, and, as they continued to dwell, the things that were done in this land were his only. So it is with the rites that are done by the chiefs now.' And Pa Fenuatara of Kafika said 'Things of the chiefs which are done there, are things which were separated from Kafika, from the one chief (the Atua). He made the presentation of their sacred adzes, and their *taumauri*.'

His primacy among the gods is correlated with that of the Ariki Kafika among men. Hence the chiefs of Tafua, Taumako and Fangarere, each supreme in his own clan, owe allegiance through their possession of the *taumauri* canoes to the Ariki Kafika. The importance of this as a bond in the social and ceremonial life is obvious. It means that through the canoe ritual the Ariki Kafika has ultimate control over the sea-going practices of the whole community.

The *taumauri* are not all equal in ritual importance. Of the eight (or possibly nine) of them, four, Tafurufuru of Kafika, Suakava of Tafua, Te Rurua of Taumako and Vakamanongi of Fangarere occupy pride of place, and are the main object of the *faunga vaka* rites. (All the remaining canoes are called the *fua riki*, the 'little fleet'.) Moreover, as mentioned later, Vakamanongi is premier even among these. The result is to produce some interesting complications in the ritual system.

Before describing the canoe rites it is necessary to give an account of the highly sacred objects with which they are concerned. There are two sets of these, both emblematic of the most essential canoe-building tools, and closely associated with the sacred canoes by a common system of tutelary spirits. The first objects are the sacred adzes; the second a group of items known as 'sacred things', the nature of which will be discussed a little later.

THE SACRED ADZES

The sacred adzes are termed *toki tapu*. They are truly sacrosanct. They are kept on a special shelf at the side of the temple and are handled by no-one but the chief, and then only on ceremonial occasions. By women and children they are not even seen, nor is their very existence divulged to casual observers.

Each of these adzes has a large clam-shell blade, nearly a foot long, thick and elliptical in section with a sharp edge and slightly tapering butt. It is almost pure white in colour and finished with a very smooth texture. The blade is lashed to a wooden haft of the conventional Polynesian type but larger than that used for an ordinary working adze, and roughly carved in a series of notches extending part way up the handle. Both this and the sinnet lashing have to be renewed every decade or so. The blades are said to have come down from immemorial antiquity; they represent the type of adze in use before the introduction of European steel tools. But the *toki tapu* are of a different order from the ordinary working blades, being larger and more magnificent, apart from the sanctity attaching to them.

Actually there are two kinds of *toki tapu*, the large type just mentioned being termed the *matua toki*, the 'principal adzes', and the other, a smaller type, being their *pipi*, their 'protectors'. The former only are used in the canoe rites. Nearly all the large adzes are in the possession of the chiefs, though the elder of Marinoa has one, which he employs in his canoe rites, and the elder of Ngatotiu had another, which, however, I think was never used in public ritual.[1] According to most statements the Ariki Kafika has one adze of the large type, the Ariki Tafua has two, the Ariki Taumako two, and the Ariki Fangarere one. The Ariki Kafika on one occasion told me that the Ariki Tafua and the Ariki Taumako had four each, and the Ariki Fangarere two; but I feel sure that he was including some of the smaller adzes in his reckoning. It was not advisable for me to attempt to verify the actual numbers in each case, and it is not of material interest. Moreover, on the adoption of Christianity the Ariki Tafua had his adzes buried in his temple of Tafua, an event that nearly resulted in a fight through the anger of the other chiefs.

The two major adzes of the Ariki Tafua have personal names, one being called Te Otaota and the other Te Ngutusivi. These mean literally 'The Scrapings' and 'The Parrot's Beak' respectively, but the origin of the names is unknown. In a conversation with the Ariki Tafua he denied that any of the adzes had names, but later I was told by his son that those cited above were correct, and that the chief would not reveal them that day because commoners were present in the house. The Ariki Kafika later corroborated these names. It was agreed that no others had names, though the adzes of Tafua and Taumako had descriptive titles, *te matua toki* and *te toki i tai*, the 'principal adze' and 'the adze of the seashore'. (The prime ones are termed also *faingatā*.)

---

[1] I was given this last specimen secretly from his brother Pa Tekaumata (now dead), and it should be in the collection of the Australian National University in Canberra. For further details and illustration see my 'Ritual Adzes in Tikopia', 1959 (reprinted in *Tikopia Ritual and Belief*, 1967, pp. 213–25).

There are several stories concerning the origin of the sacred adzes, disagreeing on certain points. All versions coincide in saying that 'the adze of the shore' of Taumako is associated with the sacred canoe Tukupasia, and like the vessel itself was brought from Tonga by the ancestor of the clan, Te Atafu. The canoe of course is a replacement of the original vessel, but the adze is said to be the original blade. Concerning it a tale was related to me by Pae Avakofe, acknowledged to be the most learned man of Taumako.

According to this Te Atafu had made friends with Singano, chief of the people of Nga Faea, who then occupied the western district. He lived at Vokisa, near the north end of the great dart-throwing ground.[1] On account of their friendship Te Atafu left his sacred adze there, and went to live with Te Foe, chief of Taumako, by whom he was adopted. On returning for the adze he was refused it by Singano, on the ground that his friend was now living in a different district, under the protection of another chief. Te Atafu determined to retrieve his prized possession. His particular deity (embodied in the reef-eel) had accompanied him from Tonga, and Te Atafu ordered him to go and spy out the hiding place of his treasure. The deity went in advance and located the adze, tucked in the thatch of Singano's dwelling. Te Atafu, following, peered in and saw his erstwhile friend asleep. The whereabouts of the adze were made known to him through the body of the deity glowing like fire (hence his name, Pusiuraura). By this light the Tongan entered, seized his property and stole away to his house on the other side of the island. With this adze he continued to re-sacralize his canoe, and on his death it passed to his son, the most famous of the Taumako ancestors, from whom it has been handed down in the chiefly line to the present day.

Opinion differs about the origin of the other major adzes. The Ariki Tafua, on the occasion quoted, told me that the *toki tapu* were fashioned by men. He said that in olden days people who dived for the giant clam (*toki*) were few; if they found a large one they cut it and ground a blade from it. If it was large the chief would see it and add it to his collection. But this probably refers to the *pipi*, since he had just described how a small *toki tapu*, like a gouge, had been handed on to men by the god Rata. 'Rata spoke to men to follow his *toki tapu*; when he should die, men should follow his adze.' The chief said that when men looked at

[1] See my 'Dart Match in Tikopia', 1930, p. 68.

this adze they found it small, and poor, so fashioned newer and larger ones for themselves.[1]

According to the Ariki Kafika the major *toki tapu* (with the exception of that of Te Atafu) originated with Pu ma, otherwise known as Tafaki and Karisi, principal gods of his clan. He said 'The sacred adzes are their own which they made, their own which they ground.' According to Pa Vainunu, there was no detailed story of their origin, but they were said to have been made by Pakora, a female deity, and by her handed over to the Atua i Kafika, supreme culture-hero of Kafika, and principal deity of Tikopia as a whole.

It is admitted generally, however, that in olden times the majority of the large sacred adzes were in the possession of the chiefs of Kafika, and were distributed by them to Tafua, Taumako and Fangarere. About eight generations ago Te Atafu, the Tongan, married Matapona, a daughter of the Ariki Kafika, Veka. She held the position of *Fafine ariki*, chieftainess, a rank peculiar to the eldest female children of the Ariki Kafika and carrying with it certain privileges. On her marriage her father gave her one of his valued *toki tapu*, to be kept by the Taumako clan, which she and her husband were re-founding. Later she returned and carried away another of the precious objects, and still later a third, without asking her father's permission. Considerable licence is allowed by a man to his daughter, but this repeated abstraction of his sacred adzes angered the old chief, as his own clan and his heir were being robbed. 'What is this?' he asked. 'Why don't you leave a *toki* for your brother?' 'His *toki* is there!' said she, indicating the one remaining adze. The Ariki was annoyed and gave vent to his feelings in a *tautuku*, the native term for a speech predicting evil, the utterance of which is supposed to affect the destiny of the person who is its object. He said to her in phrases which have become classic, 'Go with your adze then; you are going then be bitten evilly by its observances. Things oppressive of your adzes there then shall go with you, but the adze of your brother shall be here, its lightness only; not any practices for it.' In other words the *toki tapu* of Taumako which the woman had carried off should bear an evil character and their handling should be accompanied by danger to their possessors from supernatural influences. But the

[1] According to Pa Tekaumata the clam is an embodiment of the Atua i Faea, the Octopus God, who 'enters' it.

sole remaining adze of her brother and his descendants should be free from ill hap. 'The observances' to which he made reference are those performed to propitiate the guardian deities who are in charge of the adzes. When the *toki* of Kafika is taken down from its 'House', a kind of shelf or beam at the side of the building, no special care is necessary beyond the ordinary rites common to the occasion; but when one of Taumako is taken down the whole clan bring food and valuables and set them as gifts before the Ariki lest they die. It is only by this means that the evil influence laid upon the adzes by the chief of old is averted. Such was the story of the Ariki Kafika.

Another adze was given by a Kafika chief to Pu Tafua roa, chief of Tafua clan, since he was a *tama tapu*, 'sacred child', to Kafika, his mother having been of the chief's family. And still another was presented by the Ariki Kafika of the time to Fakaarofatia, also his *tama tapu*, who was the progenitor of the present Fangarere clan. (There is a discrepancy here, if the Ariki Kafika had only one adze left after the raid by Matapona.)

These sacred adzes are regarded as property to be carefully guarded. Pa Vainunu said that one is never handed over to another chief. 'It is not given, because should it be given, the chief and his clan (the donors) will die. Its speech is "the life of the clan".' When I reminded him of the adzes given away by the Ariki Kafika he answered that in this case the evil effect was not produced because they were given by the chief to his daughter or his 'son' – otherwise they would not have been handed over.

The adzes are kept hafted, but the haft decays after a time. When the haft is to be renewed a great ceremony takes place, and in fact it is usually combined with the building of a new sacred canoe of the chief. After the log has been roughly trimmed the chief goes off with the *toki tapu* to 'sharpen' it. Nowadays he does not actually sharpen the blade, but merely cleans it lightly. A stone, which is termed the sacred grinding-stone, lies at a spot called Fakaseketara, near Matangaika, on the path to Maunga. The stone is carpeted with coconut fronds, and a bundle of fresh nuts stands near as the 'vivification' offering. The chief takes the adze from his shoulder and lays it on the fronds. A coconut shell of seawater is brought, together with pumice stone. This is dipped in the water and rubbed on the edge of the adze, while a formula is recited. The blade is then washed with water and laid down, while libations of coconut milk are poured to the deities of the adze. Either then or on the following day (accounts differed) the blade is loosened from the lashing, and the new haft is bound on. It is said that the haft may be fashioned by a commoner who is a craftsman, but that the lashing is done by the chief. The adze is then returned to Uta.

The *toki tapu* of each clan have their supernatural beings, *atua tau toki*, in charge of them, and they are invoked on formal occasions, as in the *faunga vaka* rites. The following are the deities of the adzes of the four clans (those of the adze of Marinoa are given later).

KAFIKA	TAFUA	TAUMAKO	FANGARERE
Tafaki	Tuna toto	Tafaki	Tupuafiti
Karisi	Pusi uri	Karisi	
Pufafine	Pusi toto	Pusiuraura	
....	Te Kau Sukumera		
Faivarongo	Tufaretai		
	....		
	Keretapuna		
	Kauaka of Rata		

A number of these adze deities are primarily associated with the sea, either as sea-gods proper, like Tufaretai, or personifications of forms of eels, like Tuna, Pusi and Tupuafiti. But others, particularly those of Kafika, have no such obvious orientation.

In the many accounts I received of the adze-gods their names did not always coincide. This divergence would seem to be due in the first place to the insufficient knowledge possessed by some of my informants. The chief of the clan is the only person who actually utters the name of the god in the rite, and he does it softly, so that others do not hear. Even such a usually well-informed man as Pae Sao, for instance, told me that the *atua tau toki* of Kafika were called Nga Ariki, whereas the chief assured me that this title was used in Marae, the sacred ground in Uta, and that in the canoe court these gods were called Tafaki and Karisi – 'names among the adzes only' he said. In the first section of the table (above the dotted line) I have accordingly listed the names of the adze-gods as made known to me by the respective chiefs.

The second reason for the divergence seems to be a difference between the type of sacred adze. The large shell blades described are not now used in the more active part of the canoe ritual. They are represented in each case by a small hafted working-adze, termed *toki fakatu*, or *faingata*. Nowadays, since the introduction of a few European tools, the small adze has a blade either of a plane iron or of a broad chisel; in former times it also was of shell. It is said that the chiefs looked at the iron when it came, found that it was not easily broken like the shell blades, and so bound it on instead. Though these working-adzes substitute for the larger and more sacred tools in the canoe rites, they have other uses also; they are used in actual canoe-building and other timber work, and again, in symbolic form, for witchcraft. Thus the Eel-god, Pusiura-ura, of evil propensity, is associated with the working-adze of the Ariki Taumako, which is the immediate representative of the ancient *toki tapu* of the canoe Tukupasia, from Tonga.[1] This ancient adze is kept in Tai, near the beach, and not in the temple in Uta, as the others are. Hence in Uta and in any of the rites connected with the 'sacred things' Tafaki and Karisi are invoked, while in the canoe yard of Tukupasia the kava is made to Pusiura, as adze-god. The gods cited at the bottom of the lists of Kafika and Tafua are in the same category, as gods of other adzes than those kept in the clan temples, or gods used for other functions. I have not space, however, to analyse the evidence here.

To sum up, the essential function of the primary *toki tapu* is in the sacralization of canoe rites, and they appear at the building of a new sacred canoe, and at the six-monthly ritual of the *faunga vaka*.

DIFFERENT TITLES OF THE GODS

A slight digression will be useful here to clarify much of the later description. In the list given above, and still more in the accounts of the various rites given later, some of the gods appear more than once under different names. These are not mere synonyms; the same *atua* bears different names according as his function varies, a feature which complicates the system very much. These various names or titles are known as *rau*. Not only may one chief possess several *rau* for one of his deities, but other chiefs may also have *rau* for this same deity. The deity thus invoked under a diversity of names is regarded as a unity, a single being; he is the 'property' of the one person by traditional association, a supreme claim which is recognized by everyone; the other people have merely an

[1] For an account of the supposed powers of this adze in killing borer in timber see my *Primitive Polynesian Economy*, 1939, ch. IV.

'interest' in him, entitling them to appeal to him in certain specific cases.

Thus for the premier *atua* of the Ariki Kafika the chief has a name (Mapusia) and two additional honorific titles (Toku Ariki Tapu and Toku Ariki Fakamataku, My Sacred Chief and My Terrifying Chief) which he uses selectively according to the nature of the ritual in which he is engaged. Each of the other chiefs has also a *rau*, a name for this *atua* different from that used by the Ariki Kafika, which they employ in the most sacred ceremonies. The Ariki Kafika speaks of this deity as 'my own deity', or 'the deity in this family' – a claim which is openly acknowledged by everyone. The other chiefs simply have 'names' for him, implying a certain limited relationship on their part. If it were ever a question of opposition of interests, which is hardly likely, seeing that the spheres of influence are different, it would be the Ariki Kafika and not any other Ariki to whom the *atua* would listen and to whose wishes he would accede. On the other hand the Ariki Kafika has *rau* for various *atua* of the other chiefs and even for some *atua* of the *pure*, as they also have for each other's deities. Here a similar position holds. Each *atua* is in traditional association with some one chief or elder, 'belongs to him', but is in such relationship with certain others as gives them the special right of appeal to him. As a general principle no chief or elder invokes an *atua* who does not belong to him or of whom no *rau* is included in his ghostly armoury.

As an example of the diversity of titles I give a selection of those of the conjoint Kafika gods, known generically as Pu ma. Their principal names and functions are as follows:

Title	Sphere	Invoked by
Pu ma	in Kafika temple and generally	Ariki Kafika
Nga Ariki	in Marae	Ariki Kafika
Tafaki and Kafisi	in the canoe court	Ariki Kafika
Ruafuti	in the canoe court	Ariki Tafua
Ruaariki	in Taumako temple	Ariki Taumako
Papakitera and Papakiteua	in Vaisakiri temple and Taumako temple	Ariki Fangarere Ariki Taumako
Papakitengaio and Papakitetofu	kava of Raropuka	Elder of Raropuka
Ruaeva	kava of Korokoro	Elder of Korokoro
Ruaeva and Ruatoto	kava of Sao	Elder of Sao

This interlocking system of deities obviously fortifies the unity of the religious organization of the Tikopia community, and through it also the general social structure. On the other hand it also allows for the exercise of special functions and privileges by the heads of the different kinship and religious groups.

SEQUENCE OF 'FAUNGA VAKA' RITES

Each day in the rites of the *faunga vaka* has its own name. The first is the Day of the Adze, so called because the sacred implement is taken down and employed in the rites. An alternative description is the Day of the Chief. This term marks the contrast with the second day, which is known as the Day of the Elders. On the first day the necessary food is provided mainly from the resources of the chief and of his close kinsfolk, and is shared out among the elders and people, the chief and his family keeping practically none of it for themselves. In Kafika clan the largest share goes to Pa Rarovi, the principal elder. 'The coconuts are oriented towards Pa Rarovi' was what I was told of the *fakaora* rite (see later). On the second day, however, the position is reversed. The chief is now the main recipient of food, and the heaviest burden of contributions falls on Pa Rarovi, who is assisted to a less extent by his fellow elders. Hence the name of the second day. But it is significant that the chief, though here the official recipient of the main share of the food, does not omit to send a contribution to help Pa Rarovi, a division of his functions which is common in Tikopia ceremonial and is according to custom.

The third day of the canoe rites is termed *te aso tau rukuruku*, a name for which I could not find any exact interpretation, but which was said to be based upon the fact that the sacred objects are returned to Uta and hung up (*tau*) then.

Of late years this has been combined with the Day of the Elders. This was done on the initiative of the Ariki Tafua, who said that the affair was unnecessarily protracted; and that since no canoes were specially celebrated, this day ought to be omitted. His lead was followed by the other chiefs. This man has since become a Christian and has withdrawn from the sacred ceremonies of the old gods – though he still firmly believes in the existence of these deities – but his modification was introduced before he was influenced by and became a convert to the new faith. This is not the only change in institutions effected from within the community itself. There is in some respects an elasticity in Tikopia ritual which would be surprising to an observer who is expecting a strict adherence to traditional forms. Actually such variation is probably only the normal process of change which goes on in any living culture.

We can now begin the description of the rites themselves, on the morning of the first day.

PRELIMINARIES TO THE RITUAL

The cycle of canoe rites of the monsoon season began after the *roi* had been placed in the oven to cook slowly through the night. On the following morning all the people of the clans woke early, for in theory and also in practice such proceedings begin before sunrise. The chiefs slept in their houses in Tai, that is, the beach villages, and came over the lake by canoe before the land was properly light, each to his own temple.

I was present that day at the rites of the Ariki Kafika. I had preceded him to the temple ground, having been warned by one of my friends in Matautu to get there before dawn if I wished to see what happened. (When I was at the making of the *roi* the day before the chief and his sons had tried to deceive me by a great show of friendliness in inviting me to come to the beach village, where I would have missed the initial temple ritual.) When the chief saw me outside his temple he was very angry, and asked why I had disobeyed him. I answered that he had tried to deceive me, and that I wished him no harm, but merely wanted to see all that occurred. He made no reply on the spot, but sent a messenger to bring me into the house, where I saw all that took place. Since I had thus been present at the preliminary sacred proceedings he then took the line that I was free to attend all his ritual in the future; I had seen the most intimate affairs of the gods and the sacred emblems, so I might as well continue. Later his attitude became extremely friendly, and I owed a great deal to his explanations, and to his sponsoring of me.

When the Ariki Kafika disembarked from his canoe, and our little contretemps was over, he pulled up a kava plant from a clump which grew close to the temple, and then went into the oven house. He wound a new bark girdle round his waist and took his usual seat on the mat. Two of his principal elders entered, one being Pa Rarovi, the highest in status, who carried a small empty basket. It was his task to carry the 'sacred things' (see later) round to the beach village to the canoe yard. First he had to be consecrated to the work. The three men sat silent for a few moments, then Pa Rarovi crawled over the floor till he came to the chief, to whose right knee he pressed his nose in the salute of respect. He drooped his head. The chief took from his own neck a circlet of twisted cordyline leaf, and tied it round the neck of his henchman, murmuring as he did so a short formula.

> The cordyline leaf shall be joined, Ancestors,
>   Tafika and Karisi
> For the shouldering of your sacred things.
> Bar the epidemic disease
> And uncover welfare
> For the carrying of your sacred things.[1]

The ostensible purpose of the necklet was to safeguard the henchman from any ill consequences of his having handled the sacred objects; it was termed the *pipi*, the 'protector' or 'preventer'. At the same time it served to single him out as the person selected for the task and to emphasize the importance of his duty. The atmosphere during the conduct of all these ceremonies was one of reverent care and attention when the transport of any of their religious emblems was involved, and a serious mien characterized the chief and his more responsible assistants. Great attention was also paid to details of procedure; slight variations, introduced in ignorance by partially qualified workers, were immediately corrected by the older well-informed men sitting by. Little or no separate training for novices was thus required. Every piece of ritual was a fresh training ground for them.

After having the necklet tied, Pa Rarovi returned to his place.[2] The *roi* was then taken from the oven and put into a basket. The ritual charcoal stripe was applied to the forehead of the Ariki. 'Mark that it may be good' I heard him murmur to the kneeling

---

[1] In giving me this formula later the chief said 'This speech is "sacred things" – sacred indeed, friend!'

[2] It may be noted that a reef knot and not a 'granny' knot was used; the former is the *tutaki maori*, the 'true join'; the latter is the *tutaki nga atua*, the 'join of the spirits', and is not used in tying. Even small children are expert in making a reef knot.

man. After this he distributed areca nuts to the others. This is a frequent social practice which corresponds to the handing round of cigarettes in our own culture, and is regarded as one of a chief's duties of hospitality.

An adjournment was then made to a temple standing on the seaward side a few yards nearer to the lake shore. This large building, known by the name of Kafika, is extremely sacred and is the ceremonial heart of the clan, erected by their ancestors in the time when men were as gods and gods were as men. Each clan has its temple of this type, a lofty building bearing the clan name, sheltering the sacred adzes and other ritual objects, and serving as the scene for most esoteric rites. They are called by the name of *fare*, in distinction to the more ordinary *paito*, and can be termed 'temples' with more reason than is usually the case with religious buildings of primitive peoples. They are in fact edifices now used solely for religious purposes and presided over by the principal deity of the clan, of whom however no image or figured material symbol is preserved therein. The temples are floored with coconut leaf mats, of the same type as used in dwellings, with the qualification that each mat marks the burial place of an ancestor, or is representative of him. No oven exists in these temples. To serve the need a smaller oven house stands inland, bearing in each case the same name as the temple, or an affiliated name. Thus Resiake, the temple of Taumako clan standing in Ravenga, has its oven house of the same name alongside. The temples of the clans of Kafika, Tafua and Taumako in Uta have Kafika Lasi, Tafua Lasi, and Taumako Lasi as their respective adjuncts. Lasi ordinarily means large or great but is here not literally applicable, as the 'Great Kafika' is about one-fourth the size of its neighbour. But the house containing the oven is also sacred, and the custom of styling it 'great' is apparently an honorific expression.[1]

The party which assembled in the temple was small, comprising myself, the chief, a couple of his elders, and one of the latter's small sons. The kava stem was brought in and the liquid prepared. The *roi* was brought in and laid on the seaward side of the house, where the most important rites were performed.

---

[1] According to Pa Ngatotiu in 1952 the chief temple (*matua paito*) is the oven house, usually inland. 'They the chiefs give weight to their temples inland.'

LIFTING DOWN OF THE SACRED ADZE AND THE
'SACRED THINGS'

After the *roi* was set down a sacred adze (not the shell one but the
plane iron) was laid by the side of the chief. The large sacred adze
was then taken down from its shelf and laid on the mat too. It was
replaced at the conclusion of the ceremony; it is not removed from
the house. When it was lifted down the chief recited:

> Lift down with power sacred things, Ancestors Tafaki
>   and Karisi!
> Lift down for welfare.
> Turn to your starboard
> To bring fish to your sacred things
> To make your evil things.

Here the emphasis is first laid on the beneficial results to accompany the disturbance of the sacred adze from its position; this in
itself is a warning to the spirits that events of moment require
their attention. The general benefit to be granted is sought in the
beginning of the formula, which then proceeds to the specific
requirements – namely that fish be plentiful when the canoes
finally put out to sea. The reference to starboard depends on the
fact that this is the side from which all fishing is done; no one casts
out a line on the port side since it is encumbered by the outrigger.
The expression 'evil things' – *anea pariki* – is a technical one, used
to denote the rites of offering to the deities the first-fruits of the
catch on the return of the canoes from sea. The implication of the
term will be discussed later. *Anea tapu*, the other sacred objects in
their small basket, were then lifted down too. This was accompanied by the recital of a formula of similar tenor, though shorter.

> I eat ten times your excrement Pu ma!
> Things sacred are being lifted down this morning.
> Lift down with power
> Lift down for welfare.

When the objects were in position the kava stem was brought in
and placed on top of the basket containing the *roi*.

The Ariki then raised the adze and laid it by the side of the basket, put on his new bark-cloth girdle and necklet of palm leaf,
turned, and lifting the end of the kava stem, recited an invocation
over it. This was different from the ordinary kava formula, being

a special set of phrases adapted to the immediate purpose of the
ritual.

> I eat your excrement Pu ma!
> Turn to your sacred things
> That are being lifted down this morning.
> Lift down with power
> Lift down for welfare
> And turn to your starboard side
> To your evil things that they may be easily
> performed.
> Ascend a fish to your fleet
> For the making of your evil things.

This formula is in the same strain as those already given. It
involves simply a repetition of the demands for efficacy and well-
being for the act of lifting down the sacred objects, and then en-
larges upon the request for the fishing to be attended with success.
Such is the general tenor of all the invocations of the canoe ceremonies. It may be noted that the request for fish is proffered with
the one ostensible object – to facilitate the performance of the
ceremony of 'evil things' before the spirits. This attitude is not
feigned but real. It is highly desirable that such an event should
come to pass as soon as possible. At the conclusion of the recital
two loud claps were given by the man seated at the kava bowl
and cups of the liquid were carried to the chief in the usual way.
Two of these were poured out to Tafaki and Karisi as adze deities
and they were addressed again as follows:

> Your kava Pu ma Tafaki and Karisi
> I eat ten times your excrement
> Turn to your kava
> To your sacred things which
> Are being lifted down on this morning . . . etc.

This double libation was followed by the parcel of *roi* being
opened and morsels of food thrown out to mark the offering. A
nut of areca was also thrown away to serve as the betel of the gods.
A third cup of kava was then poured out by the Ariki to his
ancestors, with the words:

> Your kava, the Elders.
> I eat ten times your excrement.
> Turn to act as sea experts.
> Stand on your starboard side.

The appeal is to the former chiefs of Kafika, referred to in the kava as the Elders.

After the kava ceremony there was a slight pause; the stem of the plant over which the formula was recited was put outside the inland door, and the *roi* set near another entrance; both were removed from the ritual positions which they occupied. As a rule that part of the house near the doorways is the non-sacred spot where objects are deposited to await the correct moment, while nearer the centre and on *mata paito* is a position of esoteric importance. The small basket containing the sacred objects (*anea tapu*) was then taken out by Pa Rarovi. Standing outside the house he took a new piece of bark-cloth and wound it round his waist. Setting the kava stem in the little basket he thrust a stick through the top of this and lifting it on to his shoulder strode off along the path around the lake. The elder of Porima bore the *roi* with the bunch of areca nut in like fashion and followed. The chief then shouldered his adze, hanging the blade over his back, with the haft hanging free down his breast. This was the ceremonial position. Thus equipped he moved off to head the procession, for the other chiefs in accordance with his message had prepared their *roi* and taken down their sacred objects with similar rites. The chiefs assembled on the path by the lake shore, and without delay moved off in formal order of precedence, the Ariki Kafika leading, a few yards behind him coming the Ariki Taumako, while the Ariki Fangarere brought up the rear. In former days the Ariki Tafua, whose canoes were at Namo, went off alone round the northern side. The path wound around the lake shore, sometimes hidden from view by the intervening thickets, then breaking out again along the margin of the water, and it was an impressive sight to watch the dignified chiefs stride along with their free upright carriage, the rays of the early morning sun lighting up their new cinctures. The Ariki Kafika alone wore an orange waistcloth, the turmeric-dyed cincture which was the emblem of his principal god. (Etiquette on this occasion did not allow me to accompany the procession on land, so I kept abreast of it in a canoe paddled by some of the returning attendants. I was told by Pa Rangifuri that if the leading chief meets a man on the path during the procession he clears his throat as a signal for the man to get out of the way.)

While the rites were in progress in Uta the majority of the people remained in Tai preparing the canoes for the coming of the

chiefs. Each clan assembled at its own canoe court, or canoe yard,
a clear space of ground in front of the sheds of the sacred vessels.
This space is termed *mataforau*, literally *mata aforau*, the face or fore
part of the canoe shed. Each chief and principal elder has his own
mataforau, which is the scene of the major rites connected with
canoes and fishing. While the chiefs were in Uta the canoe court
of each was cleaned up, weeds and dead leaves being removed;
the canoe was taken out of its shed and laid athwart the place;
palm leaves were cut and put by the side of the vessel in ritual
positions, mats were set in place, and any plaiting needed was completed. Youths had been sent off to pluck coconuts, and the women
set to plait baskets to hold food. By this time the sun had risen
well above the horizon.

THE KAVA OF THE ADZE

The chiefs now appeared from Uta, and walking along the beach,
dispersed each to his own canoe yard. They had been preceded
there by the bearers of 'sacred things' and of the *roi*, who had
deposited their burdens in the appointed places near the canoe. At
the canoe yard where I was the Ariki Kafika walked over to the
vessel and stood by it. Then lifting the adze from his shoulder he
struck a sharp blow with it on the interior of the hull. As he did so
he murmured a few sentences:[1]

> Cut with power your canoe, Sea-expert Chief.
> I eat ten times your excrement.
> Turn to your own canoe.
> Stand firmly
> That the 'evil things' may be done.

The object of this ritual act was to attract the attention of the
deities of the canoe, and induce them to provide fish when the
vessel went to sea. They were addressed collectively as the *Ariki
tautai* – Sea-expert Chiefs – and not individually by name.
The exact reason for making a cut with the adze is discussed
later.

The chief then took his seat in the canoe court, sitting on his
mat with his back to the canoe. He laid the adze to his right on
another mat reserved for the sacerdotal objects, while the sacred

---

[1] This formula, with others of the canoe rites, etc., was later given to me by
the chief himself, and corroborated by other men.

things in the basket were set at the end of this same mat, which was close to the stern. (See Fig. 1.)

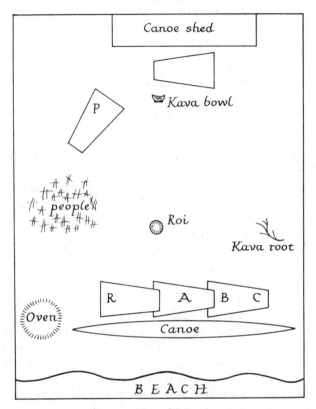

FIG. 1. Kava of the Adze

A, chief; B, adze; C, 'sacred things'; P, Pa Porima; R, Pa Rarovi

The kava of the adze – *te kava te faingata* – was now performed. A fresh necklet of fronds was tied by the chief on top of the one he already wore. He rose, walked to where the kava stem was laid with its root pointing seawards, then sat down and faced the stern of the canoe, lifted the end of the stem and began to recite over it.

The formula was long since the Ariki addressed first his supreme deity, the culture hero, then Pu ma, the two brothers, then Pu Fafine, the Female Deity, and finally his line of chiefly ancestors. The invocation addressed to each of them ran much as follows:

That is your kava Mapusia!
I eat ten times your excrement.
Turn to your kava
And turn to your fleet
To stand on your starboard side
As sea expert.
Be active the sea expert
A *para* or a *marie* or a *varu*
For the making of your kava
Your kava that is not within grasp.
Multiply hither from the ocean
Ascend a fish to your fleet.

Here the commencement of the kava is followed by the usual scatological declaration of abasement,[1] after which comes the appeal to the deity to turn to the proceedings and assist the fishing fleet. As is commonly the case, the request is justified, not by reference to human desires for food, but rather by pointing out diplomatically the need for fish in order to complete the appropriate ceremonies to the deity himself. It is alleged that his kava is not within grasp, that is, an adequate provision of food is not assured, hence his assistance is required. It is immaterial which of the large fish he thinks fit to send, the *para* or the *varu* or the *marie*, the latter being a variety of shark. A general note is sounded in the petition for the fruits of the ocean to be great, and the invocation finishes with a request that fish may be induced to rise for the fleet. The term used, *māroro*, actually signified the flying fish, called *save* in ordinary speech, but is here given a generic meaning to include all fish. The reason is that the flying fish usually comprise the bulk of the catch in any case. Even if the large fish stipulated do not appear the ceremonies can still be performed with the *save*. Another phrase frequently employed as an alternative is 'May the shark when hooked proceed quietly' – to its fate and not rush open-mouthed at the canoe.

One form of expression used in the kava of these canoe rites refers to the belief in the active participation of a tutelary deity in the fishing of the vessel. He is imagined to go out with adze or staff, strike down the fish he desires, and bring it to the canoe, where it is hooked by the crew. The material evidence of this is

---

[1] The Aiiki Kafika said 'One appeals in the eating of excrement; one does not speak naked (that is, in bare phrases); one invokes them to behave well.'

given by gashes seen in the head or sides of the fish. A form of words used to stimulate the deity in this respect is:

> Bite, thy adze
> On the head of the fish,
> To come to thy starboard side.

In comment on these formulae the Ariki Kafika said 'The kava is not made to this or that; it is recited to the *fakamanu* (the efficacy) of the canoe. It is done at the wish of the chief. If he speaks for *ora* (welfare), he speaks. If he is fit, he speaks for all things; but if he is unwell, he speaks only for sea expertise (*fakatautai*).'

The conclusion of the long invocation was marked by the loud '*Marie!*' The Ariki laid down the kava stem and returned to his seat. An attendant then got up from among the crowd, took the *roi* and set it before the chief, spreading leaves as a platter. Portions of the food were laid on these as offerings to the deities.

The *kava raurakau*, 'the kava of the leaf', was then performed, this being a special kind of ritual only adopted on a few of the most important occasions in this series of ceremonies. Another attendant, a young man, broke off a twig from the kava stem and taking a leaf of the large swamp taro knelt before the chief. He passed the twig to the chief, who took it in his right hand, waved it under his lips and returned it again. The attendant tore off a small piece of leaf, which the chief rolled into a little conical cup. The man then bent over with hair unbound, as is the custom at the kava, chewed vigorously the end of the twig and allowed his spittle to drop on to the taro leaf. When a certain amount had accumulated he straightened up, and poured the liquid into the leaf cup held out by the chief. The latter then swung round towards the sacred objects, made obeisance with the cup to his forehead and poured out a libation. Again the formula was repeated to Pu ma, the guardians of the sacred adze.

> Your kava, Pu ma, Tafaki and Karisi
> I eat ten times your excrement
> Turn to your fleet.

The kava-impregnated saliva was a ritual substance of especial potency.

The passing of the twig of kava close to the lips of the chief was done in order to render it and the rite associated with it mild and

equable, attended by no evil consequences. The Ariki Kafika said
to me on this point – 'The twig is plucked and waved before the
mouth of the chief. It is done that it may be mild.' The esoteric
tapu of chiefs in Tikopia is not stringent, but much virtue is
thought to reside in their hands and their lips. With the hand they
throw offerings of food and pour libations, with the lips they
utter the sacred formulae to the gods. Hence their *mana*, their
efficacy and power, is especially potent in these members. The
waving of the piece of kava under the mouth has the effect of impregnating it with the efficacy of the chief and rendering it beneficent.

The kava which had been prepared meanwhile in the bowl was
announced, and cups were borne forward to the chief, who was
still facing the stern of the canoe. The first and second cups he
poured after having made obeisance; these were for Pu ma. While
the bearer waited kneeling with a third cup the chief broke off
areca nut and betel leaf and threw one portion in front of him,
the remainder behind over his left shoulder. During this time the
portions of food were distributed to the elders present, that their
kava might be performed. The first portion was set out before Pa
Rarovi—the principal elder, who was seated also with his back to
the canoe on his own mat to the left of the chief. A cup of kava
was brought to him and he poured it out with the usual brief
address to his main deities. Other cups were taken to the chief,
who invoked such of his gods and ancestors as he desired, throwing small food offerings from the *roi* after each libation. A portion
of food had also been laid at the side of the canoe court. This was
the offering to Pu Fafine, the female deity of Kafika, who was one
of the guardians of the sacred adze, and of the canoe court. A cup
of kava was poured alongside this and the food 'thrown' in the
usual way by one of the attendants, who looked at the chief as he
did so and called '*Ia!*' This was to attract the attention of the
chief, who thereupon murmured a short appropriate formula.
The crowd of people attending the ceremony who were seated
round the fringe of the court had shares of food allotted to them,
and after the last cup of kava had been poured they all began to
eat. In this the chief joined, after he had first rubbed off the black
stripe from his forehead with a piece of coconut fibre and adjusted
his necklet to fit more comfortably. He ate but sparingly, then
drank from his own water bottle. He broke up the bunch of areca

nut, and distributed a share to his principal elders and other important people, who all began to chew betel. A general buzz of conversation now ensued, but the chief remained silent.

The canoe court was at the head of the beach, so that the seaside
path ran right past it in full view; during the ceremony and for
some time after my attention was attracted to parties of people
carrying loads of husked fresh coconuts in baskets along the path.
They were bound for the next village where the Ariki Taumako
was holding his canoe ceremonies. The Ariki Fangarere was also
officiating, in his canoe court adjoining that of the Ariki Kafika,
from which it was separated only by a thicket. In former days the
Ariki Tafua was engaged in like manner in the court of his canoe
'Suakava' in Namo. Custom ordained that the Ariki Kafika, as
premier chief, should begin his ceremony before the others.

The next half-hour or so was a free period. The Ariki and Pa
Rarovi removed their cinctures and walked away, while the crowd
dispersed and adjourned either to the empty canoe shed, which
opened in to the court, or to Taramoa, the house of Pa Fenuatara,
eldest son of the Ariki, which stood close by. This large building
could accommodate several score of people, sitting around and
talking, smoking, chewing betel and preparing fishing tackle.

THE FAKAORA

Meanwhile the green coconuts had been brought in from the
orchards, and bundles of sprouting nuts set outside the *mata paito*
of the house Taramoa. This was the ritual position in which all
such food waited until the proper time came to bear it to the scene
of action. About mid-morning the coconuts were carried to the
canoe court and arranged by three or four men in the shape of a
rough V, leaving a lane down the centre. About twenty-five baskets, each holding five or six coconuts, together with three or four
bundles of sprouting nuts, and an odd basket or two of breadfruit,
made up the heap. When he judged that preparations were complete the Ariki sent a boy to inquire, 'Is the *fakaora* finished in
the canoe court?' When the messenger returned and said 'It is
finished', the chief went out and took his place again with his back
to the canoe, followed by Pa Rarovi. The crowd of clanspeople
again assembled for the ceremony. It may be noted that male
children were not debarred from attendance, but no female was
allowed in the canoe court. Children are often brought on such

occasions simply for convenience in household management, and because the parent likes to have his son with him. There is also the idea that the child thus learns from earliest years the conduct of the ceremonies and can begin to assist therein with confidence. Moreover it is thought that the deities look with favour upon persons who attend their rites regularly, though this aspect of the matter does not receive very serious consideration.

When the chief was seated another necklet was handed to him and he tied it on. Charcoal was also prepared; 'Make it well', said one man to another. The black stripe was then once more applied in silence to the forehead of the chief. He seated himself in the centre of the lane in the heap of coconuts, facing the stern of his canoe. The rite was called 'the kava of the *fakaora*' but no kava plant was employed; the formula recited was quite short. The elders in attendance acquiesced with the usual '*kona! kona!*' after the introductory reference to their names.

The Ariki said:

> Satinamo! Pa Porima, Pe Torokinga.
> You assembled elders there, confirm the vivification
> By me struck hither for the clan.
> Orient there to the sacred adze of Pu ma,
> *Marie.*

The object of this invocation is to announce formally the coconuts which have been gathered for the rites of the sacred adze. Hence the elders are ritually summoned to countenance the act. Certain terms which are used need explanation. 'Satinamo' is the special name or title of Pa Rarovi and is affiliated in sound to that of the Ariki Kafika, which is Tinamo. The expression 'By me struck for the clan' refers to the coconuts plucked or 'struck' by the agents or assistants of the chief – he himself does not take part in gathering them – on behalf of his clan for whose benefit these ceremonies are performed. The word translated as 'orient' signifies 'to point' or 'lay' a thing in the direction of another and is used for any formal alignment of an object. In this case the heap of coconuts with the lane down the middle is set towards the stern of the vessel, where the sacred objects are lying. In the original the word *matauringatā* is used for 'adze'. It is a sacerdotal term. 'Secret speech of the chiefs', said the Ariki Kafika in comment on it, and certainly I have heard the word nowhere else. There are in fact a number of such expressions, synonyms used by the chiefs in their kava formulae for other terms in more common use.

The term *fakaora* interpreted literally means a 'making alive', a 'vivifying'. It has become, however, a technical expression for one of the set of ceremonies which accompanies any important sacred enterprise, such as the reconstruction of an ancestral house, or as in the present case, the seasonal preparation of the chiefly canoes. The *fakaora* usually takes place about mid-morning and may be succeeded by the *fakaoatea*, a kava ceremony of much the same type. The latter means literally the 'making midday', since it often takes place about noon, but both of these terms have come to acquire a purely conventional technical significance. The explanations given by informants are apt to bear this descriptive character. 'Its vivifying that, the vivifying of the sacred objects, were taken down from above, were laid down below.' In other words the rite in this case has the function of consecrating the act of removing the sacred objects from their ordinary position to employ them in the canoe ceremonies. The basis of the term seems to lie in its literal interpretation, in the idea of the ceremony giving welfare to all concerned, including the objects of the rite. One man described it thus: 'The vivifying of the canoe, to make hither welfare for us – and the canoe.'

The ceremonies of this first day were performed in connection with the primary *taumauri*. To the *fakaora* ceremony of each of these canoes, 'Vakamanongi' of Fangarere clan, 'Suakava' of Tafua (formerly) and 'Te Rurua' of Taumako, the Ariki Kafika sent his contribution, a basket of green and a bundle of sprouting coconuts. He thus associated himself with their consecration. The gift was exchanged, or reciprocated by a similar one, so that the net result was the same for each party. The custom was thus of small economic import but provided a link in binding together the social and religious structures.

Slips in organization sometimes occur; in the particular season now described the Ariki Kafika forgot to send in the contribution to 'Vakamanongi' on the initial day. Recollecting this the next morning he ordered it to be taken, and the reciprocal basket was then sent in return.

A libation of coconut milk followed the *fakaora* formula. As the Ariki returned to his seat a couple of men jumped up and placed several baskets in front of him. The nuts were collected into one of these, a few breadfruit set on top, and the other baskets thrown away. Some sprouting coconuts were laid beside the pile.

The chief then hung the adze on his right shoulder and turned to the stern of the canoe. Selecting a coconut from the basket he held it before him in his left hand, and grasped the haft of the adze in his right. With his eyes on the nut he said in low tones:

> Pa Rarovi, Pa Porima, Pe Torokinga,
> You assembled elders, there countenance here to
>   the coconut of Pu ma which will be cut open
> Cut with power.

With three forceful blows he cut round the top of the nut, and shouldering the adze again took off the top of the nut and threw it out in front of him. He transferred the nut to his right hand and raising it to his forehead as he bowed, poured out the liquid. He said:

> Your liquid there Pu ma, Tafaki and Karisi,
> I eat ten times your excrement.
> Turn as sea experts.

The empty nut was smashed in with a blow from the back of the adze and cast, with the words '*Anea tapu e tongi*', behind over his shoulder. He then broke up a section of cooked breadfruit and threw out a small piece in front while the remainder was cast behind. Areca nut and betel leaf were treated in like fashion. The top of the coconut is thrown in front since it is *tapu* to children and may not be eaten by them – 'it is thrown on a spot which is not trodden upon'. The nut itself is thrown behind, and eaten later. So also with the other items. With each of them the Ariki repeated the formula as above, substituting appropriately the terms food and betel for that of liquid. This marked the conclusion of the rite and the chief turned again to the front. 'There it is finished, will be distributed then', said a spectator to me. Immediately three men sprang up, seized each a basket of coconuts and went round among the spectators, handing out to all a share. Someone called out 'Go and distribute singly', that is, give one only to each person to begin with until the extent of the supplies can be gauged. Advice of this kind is frequently given by members of the crowd to people who are serving out food. In a short space of time everyone had received coconuts, each child had one, ordinary adults had three or four, while every elder and person of importance had a basketful allotted as his portion. In one basket there was a melon, a fruit occasionally grown by the Tikopia. This was set before the chief. On this occasion the lion's share was given to Pa Rarovi. Everyone now dug in the eye of his coconut, drank and smashed it with a stone or with a squeeze of his hands, and ate the flesh. The chief did likewise, but before drinking poured a few drops of the milk on to his mat in front of him, without ceremony. This was a libation to his ancestors, rarely omitted under any circumstances.

'Our clan is drinking throughout?' asked one of the servers after completing his task of distribution. This care to see that all present are provided for is a mark of Tikopia food allocation, and is a feature of their hospitality. When all the people had drunk and eaten they took away in the disused baskets any coconuts remaining from their share. People from the Taumako village were to be seen returning along the beach about this time with coconuts, but the ceremonies of Fangarere were not yet complete.

On one side of the canoe court, not far from the bow of the canoe, was a small depression in the ground. This was the oven in which the food for the most important seaside canoe rites was to be cooked. It was said by Seremata 'The *umu tonga* is kindled for the "sacred things" there in the canoe court.' The origin of the name *umu tonga* could not be explained by the Tikopia. *Umu* means oven, and *tonga* normally means the trade-wind, or the south-east, whence that wind comes, but it is not held that there is any connection of this kind. The oven, like most of the ritual appurtenances, was under supernatural control. It was in charge of Pu Fafine, the Female Deity of Kafika. After each season's rites the pit is filled in again, and becomes overgrown with grass. The cleaning away of this, and reshaping of the oven was consequently one of the first day's tasks, and was done soon after the *fakaora*. It too had its appropriate formula, though it was such a small affair. A man drove a stick into the ground and levering up the soil called to the Ariki 'Here! the oven.' The chief then softly recited:

> Pierce with power thy oven
> Thy *umu tonga* Pu Fafine
> Clubbed be a shark
> For the firing of thy oven.

After this the oven was prepared for use, and breadfruit and other food placed therein to cook. The day later became overcast and rain fell, an unpleasant event for the people tending the oven, so a shelter of thatch on poles was quickly raised. The time of waiting for the food to cook was passed there in betel chewing and conversation. Some of the young people of the clan had been out with nets on the reef, and returned with a few fish. These were laid for a time on the canoe court in formal acknowledgment to the deities and were then brought to the oven.

When the food was finally ready the Ariki again donned his cincture, had the black mark put on his forehead, tied a fresh coconut frond round his neck, and took his place on the canoe ground. Lifting up the kava stem he recited a formula over it as in the case of the initial rite of the adze. When finished he returned to his seat and the food portions were set out before him from baskets of breadfruit and taro, together with a bowl of pudding. Again the *kava raurakau*, the pouring of the kava-impregnated saliva from the leaf cup, was performed, followed by libations of the liquid prepared in the usual way, and offerings of food and betel.

The ceremony concluded with a meal, the principal one of the day. It will be remembered that the food eaten so far comprised only a small portion of *roi* in the early morning, followed by a green coconut or two later on. By mid-afternoon everyone had acquired a healthy appetite. After the meal the oven was again got ready, *roi* was prepared and put in to cook for tomorrow morning's events.

Towards sunset the evening kava took place. This was a much simpler rite than the others, the liquid being prepared in the bowl and libations poured, with no kava stem and no elaborate ceremonial. Half a dozen cups sufficed, the Ariki pouring libations to his principal gods, while one was poured by Pa Rarovi to his family deity, and others to the Female Deity and to the kava bowl.

The formula addressed to the Female Deity ran:

> That is your kava Pu Fafine
> I eat ten times your excrement
> Turn to act as sea expert
> Carry a shark to your starboard side.

This deity is one of those who are responsible for bringing the fish to the canoes, hence the appeal in the last lines. As she is a woman she follows the custom of her sex and carries burdens on her back. Hence the term used in the original implies the binding of a load across the shoulders by means of a strap of bark-cloth crossing diagonally under the breasts. After this rite the basket containing the sacred objects was placed in the canoe shed for safety during the night.

The most interesting feature of this evening rite was the provision of special food baskets by the Ariki and his elders. These were ordinary small household food containers with a double handle, which did not usually appear on ceremonial occasions. The common name for them is *longi*, but those of good workmanship used by chiefs and men of rank are called *raurau*. Hence an alternative name for this particular evening kava was *te kava o a raurau*, the 'kava of food baskets'. The chief and his elders had each arranged that a small quantity of food, comprising pudding or other delicacy, as well as taro or breadfruit should be ready and hot in their own houses, just before the time of the evening ceremony. The basket was then filled, put into another, brought along to the canoe court and given to its owner. The technical term for such a specially prepared food basket is *fonokava*. 'Each makes his *fonokava*', is the saying. The important feature of this custom, however, is the exchange of food which normally accompanies it. It is possible for a man to eat from his own basket, but usually the baskets of the elders are all set before the chief, who then redistributes them, keeping one for himself, giving away his own basket to someone else, and allotting the rest among the various men present. Thus no one eats the food which has been brought from his own house. Commoners who have not brought baskets share in the food of others; Tikopia etiquette ensures that a man shall not sit hungry in the presence of others who are eating. Where a man of rank from one clan attends the ceremonies of the chief of another clan it is the custom for him to make his *fonokava*, or have it made for him, and present it to the chief when the evening kava is finished. Advancing with the basket grasped in both hands he squats before the chief, lays it down, then retreating without turning his back, he sits down at a distance. This is an act of homage to the chief, an acknowledgment of his tacit permission to attend the ceremonies. Etiquette prescribes that the chief must eat of the food gift thus provided, while he usually hands the basket from his own household to an attendant with instructions to go and set it before his guest. Formalities of this kind distinguish the intercourse of men of good breeding in Tikopia. Some men are versed in all the niceties of such observances; others through ignorance or carelessness neglect them and thus not infrequently give offence. (On this occasion I was sponsored by Pae Sao, of Tafua clan, who took me in charge and coached me, since I had come to Ravenga from Faea, where I was living in the village of his chief, the Ariki Tafua. He had the *fonokava* made for me in his house, and instructed me to present it to the Ariki Kafika, who gave me a basket of food in return.)

If no food is brought to the evening rite this is performed with green coconuts, which are pierced and libations poured from them. As its name implies the evening kava closes the day's events.

THE DAY OF THE ELDERS

The proceedings of the second day followed closely those of the first, but were begun in the canoe court. As before, I attended the Ariki Kafika.

There was an early morning kava rite, for which the *roi* from the *umu tonga* was used. The chief donned the same cincture as on the day before, and the charcoal stripe was put on his forehead. But this time there was some difficulty in finding someone of proper status to apply it, since most of the men present were either 'sons' or 'sons-in-law' to him. Finally his father's brother's son put it on. When he went up to the chief he did not crouch low, but merely bent his knees. 'Don't stand up!' said the chief to him, laughing. Thereupon he knelt down, and all the crowd laughed. Such joking, which is quite permissible in the early stages of a ceremony, does not detract from the solemnity of the actual rite, which is treated with great seriousness.

The ritual then proceeded precisely as on the preceding day. Afterwards the younger people dispersed to collect food and prepare the oven, while the older men sat in the canoe shed and discussed fishing, most of them re-snooding their shark-hooks or rolling cord for lines the while.

Later the *fakaora* rite took place, with much food; I counted twenty-five baskets of green coconuts and seven bundles of sprouting coconuts assembled. This time, in addition to the *taumauri* Tafurufuru, three other canoes were brought out; all were placed with the outrigger to seawards. In the rite to the guardian deities the chief cut each canoe lightly twice inside the hull, but omitted the vessel for which the rite was performed the day before. After the sequence of operations, the food was distributed. Pa Rarovi received only four coconuts and a single sprouting nut brought from the Fangarere village, whereas a great number of nuts were set before the chief. When all were drinking from their shares Pa Fenuatara said to Pa Rarovi 'The coconuts are many, brother-in-law', a polite acknowledgment of the latter's liberal provision.

It is important to note here a divergence between the original programme as notified to me and the actual programme as I saw it. In the original programme the remainder of the day's rites were carried out as on the previous day, and on the third day the principal performance was the dismissing of the gods and the return of the 'sacred things' to Uta. But owing to the initiative of the Ariki Tafua years before, this now took place in the afternoon of the second day.

DISMISSING THE GODS

After some further talk on fishing the canoes were prepared for sea. The *umu tonga* was got ready for the last time. When the food was being removed after cooking all the canoes were swung round and set in line at the head of the beach, with their bows pointing to sea. Branches of coconut palm were laid down for them to rest on. The food from the oven was laid in the court and the chief prepared himself for his part. He donned his cincture, then stuck in the back of it the tail of a coconut leaf with a few green fronds remaining, which made a very effective splayed ornament. He then tied round his neck the usual frond, and turned to face the stern of his canoe. A green coconut still in its original state, with the husk on, was lying by his side; he took this up, wrapped it in another section of coconut leaf and then with a strong blow from the back of his adze smashed in its side so that the liquid poured out over his hands. Hastily he raised it to his head in obeisance, sprayed it over towards the stern of his canoe, then rose to his feet and with quick dancing steps ran round the edge of the canoe court past the *umu tonga*, waving the nut first to one side and then the other. 'It is waved to and fro that the coconut milk

may pour out.' As he passed the *umu tonga*, he sprinkled it liberally. (I came in for a good share of this, the chief being no respecter
of persons who were in the 'line of fire'.) Without pausing he ran
on to the stern of each canoe, still scattering the liquid in showers,
then holding the nut in one hand, he removed the coconut leaf
with the other and brushed the stern with it twice. He treated the
next vessel likewise, then on completing the round he halted
at the head of the beach a few yards away and drawing back
his arm hurled the coconut as far as he could out to sea. As
this last action was performed the cooks of the *umu tonga* broke
with a loud crash some inverted coconut cups that had been laid
in the bottom of the pit. The whole performance was over in a
very short space of time. The chief returned to the canoe court,
laid down the adze, which he had been wearing on his shoulder
hitherto, took up the kava stem and recited a long invocation over
it. This was of precisely the same type as has already been indicated, its burden being to secure fish for the fleet. Food portions
were then put out, a whole bowl of pudding being set on one
platter and the usual offerings made and libations of kava poured.
The *kava raurakau*, the chewing of the twig and pouring of the
spittle from the leaf cup was also performed. One basket of breadfruit was set aside as a 'basket for Uta', to be taken over for the
ritual of 'sacred things'. After this the chief discussed fishing with
his elders.

The object of sprinkling the canoe was said to be to drive off
the deities of the vessels who had been in attendance at the ceremonies of the last three days, and to induce them to go out to
sea and begin their task of assembling fish ready for the operations
of the fleet that same night. It was said 'The deities of canoes are
bathed; they have been long present at the preparations that have
been made; that is their going. Some deities will go to the sea,
while other deities go to the sky.'

The oven was said to be sprinkled that the food cooked therein
might be rendered mild and pleasant, that in being taken from the
sacred oven of the goddess it might not have ill effects when it
rested in the belly of man. 'The oven is sacred, therefore it is
sprinkled to be mild, because our food has been cooked in the
oven.' The oven is to provide the necessary food for the ceremonies of the *faunga vaka* and it is only used when the sacred
objects are displayed. As it is said 'The oven is lit for the sacred

objects there in the canoe court.' The sprinkling then is really a removal of the *tapu*, a de-sacralizing of the oven now that its function has been fulfilled for the season.

The ritual principle of the act of sprinkling, which appears in other departments of Tikopia religion as well, is comparable to that of the *asperges* in the ceremonial of the Christian Church. The scattering of drops of fluid acts as a medium for the conveyance of the exorcizing or other formula pronounced by the officiating priest.

The breaking of the coconut shells in the oven, which is done simultaneously with the throwing of the green coconut out to sea, is the signal for the deities to depart, and is a fairly obvious piece of symbolism. It is termed the scattering of the gods. The loud crash is a hint to such of them as may be located in the ground in or near the oven to be off. (Cf. the 'Despatch of the Gods' after the turmeric manufacture, pp. 453, 463.) The act of the Ariki in cutting with his adze at the side of the canoe, as described earlier, was explained by one informant as being analogous. He termed it 'the scattering of the sheltering deities'. The idea in this case is that the adze cuts at the sinnet lashings of the vessel and so stirs up its guardian deity, who lashes with his tail at the starboard side and so drives away other supernatural beings who may wish to interfere or work harm.

Short formulae were uttered at various stages of the rite. As the Ariki smashed in the coconut with the back of his adze he said:

> The green coconut will be split on this morning here
> Split with power your green coconut Pu ma
> I eat ten times your excrement
> Unfold welfare from you two.

Then as he passed the oven and sprinkled the liquid over towards it he said:

> Sprinkle with power thy oven Pu Fafine.

As the canoe was brushed with the dripping fronds of coconut leaf he said:

> Sprinkle with power your wood, Sea-expert Chief.
> I eat ten times your excrement.

While finally as the coconut was hurled out to sea he called:

> Carried hither be the green coconut.

The purport of all but the final formula is probably clear enough. In this formula the request to have the coconut carried hither has a metaphorical significance. It is conceived as being borne out to sea by the departing spirit beings, and later brought inshore again in the shape of fish, most desirably in the form of a shark. The formula is another, somewhat obscure symbolic way of appealing to the spirits for a bounteous catch.

On the completion of this kava of the *umu tonga* the assembled people divided up, some to go over to Uta, to carry out the ceremonies there, while the others, by far the greater number, remained to make final preparations that night. During the day the talk had turned consistently on fishing. The men had to be out all night, sleeping, if need be, on the thwarts of their canoes, but it was said that the strong element of competition between the various crews, especially those from the different clans, would keep most of them awake. The hope of everyone was to haul up a shark – some indeed spoke of it already as a certainty, though others expressed cautious doubts. Some related dreams which they had the night before, and for which they and their friends tried to find interpretation. Pa Fenuatara discussed a dream in which he went to sea and his foot was covered with excrement. He asked if it was 'a fish dream or not'. Another man said 'Oh! Yes, a fish dream.' 'I don't know', said Pa Fenuatara. He pondered again, 'Will "evil things" be performed tomorrow or not?'

Satisfaction was expressed that the day had dawned well and promised a smooth sea for the evening; a recent fall of rain too was welcomed as helping to calm the waves and to give life to men and the land. Changes of the weather are nearly always interpreted at once in terms of their reaction upon food supply.

THE RETURN TO UTA

Then came the return of the sacred objects to Uta in formal style.

Before the conclusion of the meal from the *umu tonga* one of the elders, Pa Torokinga, stood up and began to gird himself with a new cincture of bark-cloth. He had not partaken of the food as it was his task to bear the sacred objects back. I was told that it is the custom for a different elder to officiate on this return journey from on the outward one. Moreover, the representatives of certain family groups alone possess the privilege. No-one of the chiefly family, neither the Ariki nor his sons nor even his patrilineal cousins, may do so; it would invoke a breach of *tapu* and, it is thought, would probably result in the death of the carrier or a near relative. Hence of the *paito pure*, families of elders, only those which by origin are not connected with the *paito ariki*, chief's families, are in a position to carry out the task. In Kafika clan these are the houses of Rarovi, Raropuka and Torokinga;[1] in Tafua, Sao, Notau and Korokoro; in Taumako, Ngatotiu, Farekofe and Ratia; in Fangarere, Nukufetau. They are known as *paito ke amo* – 'families who may shoulder' – the specific object concerned being understood. The chiefly and allied families are said to be barred since they are *tau toki*, 'adze-possessors'. The gods of the sacred adzes are also those of *anea tapu* and might injure them.

After girding himself the bearer set off (about 4 p.m.) with the 'sacred things', in a small basket enclosed again in another basket on one end of his shoulder-pole, and the kava root fixed to the other. Various people with baskets of food followed at a distance, while the chief brought up the rear. The people of Taumako, waiting by their canoe court, fell in when those of Kafika had passed along the beach path, and were followed by those of Fangarere. The three chiefs again moved in due order of precedence. On the afternoon under observation, however, the Ariki Fangarere, an old man, and afflicted with an ulcer in his foot which prevented him from walking easily, followed the procession in his canoe round the lake shore, keeping practically abreast of the other chiefs, but slightly behind them, in his proper place. Three other canoes paddled straight across the lake with baskets of food, and the betel materials and water bottles of the chiefs, who carried nothing but their adzes. I was in one of these canoes. Everyone stepped out briskly along the path so that in twenty minutes or so they arrived, just as the sun was sinking behind the high ridge which towered at the back of the Uta shore. The canoes paddled gently in order to allow the chiefs to reach their destination first. Arrived at Uta they separated without words, and each went to his own house, put away his adze, and prepared for the kava. I went with the Ariki Kafika as before.

This time the rite was performed in the open. Mats were laid down, one for the Ariki and another for the kava bowl. A large basket of food from the canoe court was placed in front of the

[1] In this generation the son of the Torokinga house was not eligible; he was a sister's child of the Ariki Kafika. Said the chief 'he has sprung from me'.

chief, and green coconuts were prepared for drinking. The chief poured libations of kava to the guardian deities of his adze, and to his ancestors. He was assisted by six men, three preparing the kava, and three the food. When this was finished the Ariki removed his waist cincture and his necklet, also the coconut fronds from his girdle. These were all hung up in the adjacent house since they were sacred objects. The people then drank and ate the coconuts, after which they chewed betel. In the midst of the ensuing conversation the Ariki Kafika remembered to ask 'The kava of Pa Taumako, is it finished?' 'It is finished', he was told.

THE 'SACRED THINGS'

Now that the part played by *anea tapu* in the canoe ceremonies has been described their nature may be explained. Like the sacred adze, they are (or rather were) objects of value in canoe-building. In olden times, I was told, they were *muriroa*, long volute shells (*Terebra dimidiata*) of a creamy colour splashed with vermilion, which were used according to tradition as augers for boring holes for lashings. In former days, before the introduction of European steel tools, the woods used in canoe-making were of a softer type than those employed today. *Puka* and *poumuri* were the favourites instead of the modern *fetau* (*Calophyllum* sp.), a hardwood.

A point of great interest in connection with these 'sacred things' is that many generations ago the shell *muriroa* were replaced by *fao*, iron spike nails, which seem to have come to Tikopia long before the first actual visit was made by white men. The local myth is that they were the gift of an *atua*, one of the deities of the Ariki Tafua, by name Tufare, or Tufaretai. This spirit desired to secure valuable objects for himself, and so went out on the ocean face to search. After seeking for a long time he returned with the *fao*, which were embedded in a slab of wood. This slab was brought by him inshore on the tide '*mori saere, mori saere*', says the tale, this phrase indicating the bobbing motion of the plank on the waves, which is dramatized as representing the motions of the deity in proffering his gifts. When the slab finally came ashore with the *fao* sticking up from it – tradition says four at each end – the chiefs took counsel and decided that it was a gift from the gods, and divided up the prize among them, two for each. The spikes were then utilized to replace the shells as canoe tools and sacred objects for the ritual. Though tradition makes no mention of the fact, a chief then living, who was the official human medium of the god concerned, was probably instrumental in identifying the plank as the result of his god's efforts, and giving instructions accordingly. Pa Saukirima, whose tutelary deity is Tufaretai, said that the nails came to Tikopia before the time of his father and his grandfather – and he was an old man in 1928. He described the bringing of them as an act of pity on the part of the deity. 'His canoes were hewn, hewn, in this land, and there was not a thing to bore them with. Thereupon he sent to search, and brought back the things to bore the canoes. He looked and looked, and there was nothing for the making of canoes; there was no iron to bore the canoes; thereupon he went to seek it.' Since the Tikopia stress the antiquity of this event, and the spikes have apparently rusted away to a fraction of their original size, it seems probable that the plank came from one of the very early European vessels in the Western Pacific, before the Tikopia became acquainted with any white people. If the spikes were of comparatively recent origin they would be regarded as ordinary material objects and no more; of interest from their European source, and valued from their association with ancestors, as in the case of certain relics of La Pérouse, brought over from Vanikoro more than a century ago. But for them to have become embedded in the very centre of Tikopia canoe ritual and supplied with a supernatural origin suggests that they were probably the first pieces of iron to come to the island. No Tikopia admits that the plank drifted to shore of its own volition; it came as the direct result of the searching by the deity. The idea of Pa Saukirima, a heathen, was that Tufare went to the Atua o te Fekau – the Christian God – to obtain the iron from him. 'Who else has it?' he asked me, logically. And in Tikopia style he added that Tufare presented a *maro* of bark-cloth to God in exchange for the nails.

It is difficult to convey the atmosphere of sanctity which surrounds these objects which practically no-one but the chief of each clan sees. Even when taken out of the temple for the canoe rites they remain enclosed in their little basket, and are handled with the utmost care and reverence. I did not see them myself, and made no attempt to do so. It would have been an act of desecration that would have wrecked my chances of further work on Tikopia religion. But in addition to being told what they were by the Ariki Kafika, the Ariki Tafua and Pa Saukirima, I was given an account of how John Maresere, a native of Uvea who was taken as a 'son' by the Ariki Tafua, was entrusted on one occasion with the bearing of the 'sacred things' of Tafua. He took the opportunity of peeping into the basket, and long afterwards said to another member of the family 'They are only nails', in disgust. (It may be noted that Maresere did not reveal to Rivers any of his knowledge of this aspect of the Work of the Gods.)

It will be remembered that a somewhat similar replacement of shell by iron has taken place in the case of the small sacred adzes carried by the chiefs. The use of the sacred adzes and the 'sacred things' in the canoe ritual is clearly to be correlated with their function as the most important tools in canoe-building. The sanctity attaching to them is a sacralization of implements essential in the work, a recognition of their symbolic vital importance.

SPRINKLING THE CANOES

As the sun went down the fleet got ready for sea. Each village had its own canoes and as the tide was falling they were carried down the beach early and set in the water on the reef. They were then paddled or pulled by men walking alongside out into the vicinity of the 'channel', in reality no more than a narrow fissure or indentation in the solid fringing reef. This night 'the assembled darkness was long' – i.e. the moon set early. Lines had been prepared during the day, hooks seen to, new traces bent on, nets repaired, and torches made. These consist of a couple of dry coconut leaves, taken from the roof of the house, set together and the fronds grasped in handfuls and roughly plaited. The maker begins at the base of the leaf and swiftly works upwards, tying strings of strips from the midrib of a green coconut leaf with a single bow knot at intervals of about a foot. As the torch burns down in use the holder reaches up and pulls clear a string, thus releasing a fresh section to flare up. Three to eight torches are made per canoe, depending on the length of the span of darkness, and both men and women prepare them.

When the moon was low the crew assembled and got into the canoes, torches were lit, and the craft moved down the channel. I was not with them, but was told that each vessel performed a brief rite termed *te fekau o te ava* (the work of the channel). The word was given to 'untie the fire'. A torch was raised, a string was pulled away, and a shake caused it to burst into flame. By custom the torch was held up towards the east or north, not on the west or south. One of the crew held his long-handled net ready. When the light flared up he called aloud to the chief of his clan, who was on shore, 'Behold! recite a formula hither, Pa Kafika, for the work of your vessel.'

The chief of course was too far away to hear this. But he told me that he was aware by the sudden flaring of the torches that the ritual moment had arrived, and sitting in his house, looking out from the eaves, he recited an appeal to the guardian deities of his fleet.

> Prosper well thy timber, Sea-expert Chief.
> Rattled as a coconut leaf be thy starboard side.
> The jumping fish, broken be its neck
> To slide down into the sea below.

This formula needs some commentary. The use of the generic term timber for its specific product the vessel is common in Tikopia invocations. 'Prosper' refers to the flying fish, that they may be plentiful. The abbreviated diction of the formula applies the word directly to the canoe which it is hoped will benefit by the plenitude of fish. The next phrase indicates a desire that the fish in their flight shall be so abundant as to knock with a continuous rattle against the side of the canoe. 'Jumping fish' is another name for garfish, which skims above the surface of the water at great speed when disturbed and is capable of inflicting a dangerous wound. The sharp long snout, thin and set with rows of tiny teeth, embeds itself in the flesh like a spear point to a depth of several inches, and breaks off in the wound, the fish escaping in the confusion. People are frequently thus pierced in the leg or hand, and weeks of serious illness and disability, with even permanent lameness, may follow. There is a natural desire that the 'jumping fish' may be warded off by the guardian deities.

I was given several variants of this formula, all of the same type. Pa Nukurenga of Taumako said 'This speech is made throughout the land. We the clan of Taumako announce to the Ariki Taumako, but when the canoes of Kafika go fishing, they announce to the Ariki Kafika. The one speech is lifted.' As a general point it may be noted that no Tikopia formula is regarded as invariable.

This rite is known as *fifinga vaka*, 'sprinkling the canoes'. No actual sprinkling is done, but the idea is conveyed partly by the dipping of a fishing net of each vessel in the sea, and partly by the formula, which is of the nature of a benediction to equip the canoes with a 'shower' of fish.

As each vessel performed its rite and addressed the chief it moved off in line through the channel, and, once beyond the reef, took up position in the rough crescent of the fleet, which was to sweep up and down the coast. The handling of the fleet demands organization and team work. The torches are raised at a signal from the leading canoe and caused to flare up, when the flying fish, attracted by the lights, rise from the surface and, if the wind is strong, skim along for many yards high above the water. A man in the bow and one in the stern stand with long-handled bag-nets and with a quick flash of the net intercept the fish in the air as they come within reach. A turn of the wrist and the net is spun round, enmeshing the prize, which is then dropped with a backward jerk into the hold of the vessel. Quickness of eye and speed of hand are essential. An expert will net his hundred fish on a good night; a clumsy fisherman will get no more than a score.

On this night of the *fifinga vaka*, I was told, when the first flying fish was caught, the man took it out of the net, killed it, and then banged it against the side of the canoe, while he uttered a formula to bring other fish. This was done only for the first; the others were merely dropped into the bottom of the vessel. (Each canoe has its own custom on this occasion but the general proce-dure is as described.) In the morning when the fleet returned the question was asked – 'Who got the first flying fish in the fleet?' and some prestige was gained by the man and the canoe that secured the prize.

After the inshore waters had been swept a number of times and a sufficient quantity of flying fish had been secured, the canoes settled down individually for line work. In this they mainly tried for fish of medium proportion. But the size of tackle used and the fish sought after always depend on the season of the year, the wind, the set of the tide, the state of the moon, the position of the fishing bank and other factors, all of which the experts calculate. Heavy lines and large steel hooks – in former times of wood – were lowered in the hope of catching a shark, the ambition of every member of the crew. The night passed thus, interspersed with spells of dozing, until the approach of dawn indicated that the time had come to return. (Most of the Tikopia sea-fishing is done at night; this is an ordinary event to the crew.)

THE THIRD DAY

As the fleet came inshore and approached the channel in the morning people began to gather on the beach after their toilet and eagerly watched the vessels. They commented on the way in which each was handled in the channel, identifying the craft, the steersman and crew, and speculated on the catch. The word went round 'A canoe is dashing up spray', though to me the vessel was barely distinguishable. This was a sign for a large fish, given by the paddlers. The type of signal caused it to be identified first as a *para* and then as a shark that had been caught. 'Where does it come from?' was asked. 'From the east' was the reply. This was an attempt to identify to which clan the canoe of the successful fishermen belonged, since there is rivalry between the clans. One by one the vessels shot the line of breakers and emerged into the comparative quiet of the shallow reef waters. They separated and each canoe made for its own village. As they drew up to the beach children rushed down, the catch was lifted out and taken up to be examined while the craft was carried up on to the level ground and left in the shade. Lines and nets were taken out, washed in fresh water and hung out to dry. The fish were carried to the canoe court, where they were set down to await the arrival of the chief, who had been engaged in Uta.

RITE OF HANGING UP THE 'SACRED THINGS'

Soon after dawn, while the chief still slept, I went with a party of three men in a small canoe across the lake to Uta, in order to get a fire going and make preparations for cooking fish. A couple of lake fish were carried over; these had been netted during the night by men who did not go out with the fleet. Theoretically, every vessel, fully manned, took part in the *fifinga vaka*; but in practice a few vessels were left without a crew, since some men were indisposed and others preferred to spend the night in attending to nets on the lake. There was method in this division of forces since it reinforced the chance of obtaining fish for the ceremony should the canoes be unsuccessful at sea. The canoe halted along the shore to collect firewood, then proceeded on its way while the paddlers speculated on the night's work. A dispute occurred as to which clan had secured the shark signalled from the fleet just before our party left. One man said it must be Taumako, another that it must be Kafika; the arguments of the second were more conclusive since he had a fish dream in the night, in which he went out and pulled up a shark. As it turned out, the shark belonged to Taumako after all, which was galling to the chief and people of Kafika.

When preparations were well in hand the chief arrived and took his seat in the large house. The fish and other food when cooked were carried out to the spot where he was waiting, the charcoal stripe was put on his forehead and the coconut frond necklet assumed. A stick of kava was laid across the central food basket. The chief then performed a rite similar to that of the day before. He stuck the branching fronds of the 'tail' of a palm leaf in his girdle at the back, then laid a green coconut in a further bunch of palm fronds. He held the nut for a few seconds, murmured a brief formula, then lifted his adze and smashed it. Rising to his feet he ran round the side of the temple waving the streaming nut to and fro and sprinkling the milk on all sides. Reaching the far end of the building he stopped and threw the nut under the eaves outside. He then poised the piece of coconut leaf and threw it too, to slide along the mats to the eave. The method of its fall was said to be an index of whether the fishing was successful or not. The chief then returned with stately steps to his usual seat. Facing the basket of food he picked up the end of the kava stem and invoked his deities in the usual manner. I noted that Pa Te Arairaki, who was new to this rite, had to ask Pa Porima whether he should prepare for the kava of the saliva or not. The kava of the saliva was made, followed by the libations of the ordinary liquid and the throwing of food offerings, at the conclusion of which the Ariki removed his coconut frond decoration and wiped off the charcoal mark from his forehead. This rite of sprinkling, which was the counterpart in Uta of that performed in the canoe court over the vessels and the sacred oven, marked the conclusion of the rites of the *faunga vaka*. The sacred objects were then hung up once more, and the sacred adze replaced on its shelf.

Portions of food were allotted and all ate, while a discussion was started on the fishing, of which the full news had been brought by the later canoe in which the Ariki came. The catch secured by the vessels of Kafika was not satisfactory, and a critical analysis of the reasons was begun. Laughing abusive remarks were passed on a clumsy man, who, standing in the bow, got only ten flying fish, whereas his companion in the stern secured fifty. The fact that one crew was composed entirely of lads with not a *tautai* (sea expert) among them was also stressed. Much of the talk also turned on what the achievements would have been if only certain factors had been different, as if more canoes or different people had gone out. 'If our fleet had fished completely nothing could have come near us!' was a sentiment which all seemed to share, while one or two people boasted of their own hypothetical prowess. 'If I had fished,' said one stay-at-home seriously, 'the canoe would have secured a good catch.'

DIFFERENTIATION BETWEEN CANOE RITES

The rites which followed were those of the *fainga vaka* and *anea pariki*. The latter clearly is a first-fruits rite, an acknowledgment to the deities of the fish secured through their good graces. I found it difficult at first, however, as an observer, to perceive the functional distinction between the *faunga vaka* and the *fainga vaka*; to understand why a canoe should require two separate sets of ceremonies of more or less the same type to attain the one object. Differences in detail of observance were clear, but threw no light on the underlying motive of what appeared at first to be practically a repetition of previous rites. Analysis of the meaning of the names did not afford much help. *Faunga vaka* is literally the 'lashing of the canoes'; i.e. the overhaul preparatory to their going to sea; while *fainga vaka* signified 'doing' or 'preparing the canoes', which seems to convey much the same idea. Both in fact are purely conventional terms. The Tikopia were quite clear that there were two sets of ceremonies, and that there was an essential difference between them, but it was not easy to get from them an explanation of just where this essential difference lay. The type of answer commonly given was that the *faunga vaka* signified the overhaul of the vessel, scrutiny of the outrigger, replacement of it if it had begun to decay, and renewal of sinnet lashings. '*Ma fau o a vaka*' was the phrase, 'For the overhauling of the canoe.' The phrase *fainga vaka* on the other hand was said to represent the making of food for the canoe: 'If a man is seen on the road with breadfruit or taro he will be asked "Where are you going?" "I am going to the *fainga vaka* of the so-and-so family" he replies.' My questions as to the meaning of the *fainga vaka* elicited also such a reply as

'Make the food for the canoe; its kava is made for the fish to come to it' – a statement which seemed to apply equally well to the preceding *faunga vaka*! Such literal explanations told me little; they were significant only as indications of those features most prominent in a Tikopia definition of the phenomena. A more relevant point of procedure was that whereas in the *faunga vaka* no bark-cloths were actually hung on the canoe, in the *fainga vaka* they were so displayed.

The real distinction, as I found after considerable inquiry, was in the personnel of the supernatural beings addressed in each case. In the *faunga vaka*, as has been shown, the *atua tau toki*, the guardian deities of the adze, and 'sacred things' were invoked, together with the ordinary deities of the kava. In the *fainga vaka* the deities of the kava were also summoned, but the rites were primarily addressed to the *atua tau vaka*, the guardian deities of the canoe itself. Hence there is one point of difference: in the *faunga vaka* each rite was of a *collective* kind, that is, it was valid for all the canoes of the clan at once whereas the *fainga vaka* had to be performed *separately* for each canoe in order that its own tutelary deities might take part. The second set of rites was then not a repetition of the first, but a particularization of it. For the Tikopia it is especially significant as it involves a much more definite participation of individual families as canoe owners and food providers, and more personal responsibility.

To illustrate this particularization in the *fainga vaka* the tutelary deities of two canoes may be specified. In each case there is a myth which accounts for their special attachment to the vessel, stating how the craft was given to men from the gods.

The sacred canoe of Porima house is called Kau Rotuma, and is believed to be the direct descendant of the vessel which brought the ancestors of Kafika to Tikopia. Hence the *atua tau vaka* of Pa Porima for this craft are:

> Tafaki and Karisi (i.e. Pu ma) – Kafika ancestors
> Te Atua i te Uruao – principal deity of Porima
> Pu Fafine – female deity of Kafika
> Pufine i Taufiti – female deity of Porima

The sacred canoe of the house of Maneve, called Te Aroimata, is believed to have been acquired in the spirit world by Rakaitonga, the ancestor of Taumako, from the Atua i te Uruao, the deity of

Porima. Its gods then include this deity and his crew. When the canoe was brought into the Taumako clan the chief took it over as a sacred vessel, and allotted to it some of his own gods in addition. One was Rakaitonga himself, as was natural, since he had secured it; the others were the eel-god of Taumako, and a female deity. Hence there are seven *atua tau vaka* whose bark-cloths have to be spread at the *fainga vaka*, as shown below.

Poungaru – Atua i te Uruao	2 orange cloths
Tiaremuna – crew of Poungaru	
Matavaka – crew of Poungaru	3 white bark-cloths together
Vakamaofa – crew of Poungaru	
Pu Lasi – Rakaitonga	2 orange cloths
Pu Tautonga – eel-god	1 white cloth
Pakora – female deity	1 white cloth square

This last example shows the intimate relationship that often exists in myth between the gods of the various kinship groups, a relationship that frequently emerges in ritual and economic terms, as illustrated by the rites of Te Akaumoana and other canoes later.

It must be emphasized that while well-informed men know approximately who are the gods of the various sacred canoes, particularly the principal ones, they do not know all the details. Pa Nukurenga said to me of his vessel Te Aroimata 'We, the men, each hides the god of his canoe. Great is their weight. Of the canoes laid up there, some have three, others four, others two *maro* (i.e. bark-cloth offerings to their deities). We who make the rites of the sacred canoes, each has a deity of the canoe for himself. One person does not know the deity of another; the chief only knows.' Hence the *fainga vaka* rites have an individuality for each vessel, with the chief of the clan as the common factor of linkage.

We may now return to the observed sequence of ritual. The *fainga vaka* as performed in the monsoon season allows of alternative procedure, owing to the differential rank of the *taumauri*. The premier canoe is Vakamanongi, of Fangarere. It is 'the canoe in front'; 'Vakamanongi is a loftier canoe; the fleet is below' it was said. Hence when the early morning kava was over on the third day the Ariki Kafika despatched messengers to the other chiefs to inform them of the arrangements. This was a matter of great interest for the folk in the beach villages, since they had to get ready the food. The first canoe which returns from Uta is always

eagerly asked 'How are the canoes?' or more simply 'How?' If
the answer is 'the canoes will be gathered together' then it is
known that all four main *taumauri* will perform their *fainga vaka*
rites on this same day. If, however, the messenger says 'Vakamanongi will fall singly', then it is understood that only this craft
will be celebrated. In this case the other clans will perform the
first-fruits rite (*anea pariki*) alone this day, and postpone their *fainga
vaka* till the next. It may be noted that the Ariki Kafika speaks of
the Fangarere canoe as his, in apprising the other chiefs of the day's
plans. 'My canoe Vakamanongi will fall singly', he says, if he
wishes it to be celebrated alone. If he wishes the other *taumauri* to
perform their rites at the same time he sends word to the chiefs of
Tafua and Taumako 'Your canoe will shift to the outrigger of
Vakamanongi.' This is described as 'honorific speech' to that
vessel, since the outrigger side is the inferior one. It is a figurative
expression, as each canoe remains in its own court all the time, and
the orientation does not carry out the words. As far as I could see
the decision of the Ariki Kafika in this matter depends upon the
quantity of food, especially fish, available, and upon how energetic he feels.

In the season described, Vakamanongi was allowed to 'fall
singly', that is the clan of Fangarere performed its ritual alone on
the first day of the *fainga vaka*. On this day the people of Kafika
celebrated *anea pariki*, the first-fruit rites, and the following day
also. The next day they carried out the *fainga vaka* for their *taumauri* Tafurufuru in the morning, and similar rites for their other
sacred canoes in the afternoon. The people of Taumako did likewise, as would have those of Tafua had they still been participants.
The events of Kafika, which I attended, will be described in their
order here.

'EVIL THINGS'

The first rite of 'evil things' of Kafika was performed in the canoe
yard of the *taumauri* Tafurufuru. Fig. 2 indicates the arrangements.
Various items of fishing paraphernalia were assembled. Besides
two canoes, two flying-fish nets used the night before were sticking out of some bushes, a roll of the sinnet cord used in deep-sea
fishing was hung alongside, and some of the flying fish caught,
still raw, were also strung up. Coconut leaves were laid outside the
canoe shed. An important point of ritual was that the green mat

on which the sacred canoe tools had been laid was still open in
its original position. It was not to be folded up until the rites of
'evil things' had been completed, and lay there as a reminder, so to
speak, that the account between gods and men was still unsettled.

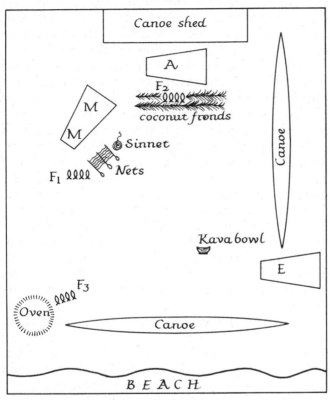

FIG. 2. 'Evil Things'

A, chief; E, mat of 'evil things'; F 1, 2, 3, fish in successive positions; M, elders

The Ariki arrived from Uta some three hours or so after sunrise
– where it will be remembered he had been 'hanging up' the sacred
objects. He took his seat on a mat spread for him at the end of the
canoe shed. On his coming the fish previously hung up were laid
on the coconut leaves in front of him. They lay there for a few
minutes, and were then set by the side of the canoe court, close to
the *umu tonga*. This was by way of formal announcement of the
catch.

The kava bowl was set at the seaward end of the court and the liquid was prepared while two baskets, one of breadfruit and another of flying fish cooked on leaves over a fire, were set before the chief. The attendant untied them and set out portions for the chief, the kava bowl, and the deity of the canoe. A note of colour was then given to the ceremony by the application to the chief of turmeric, a vermilion pigment mixed with coconut oil. A young man stood behind the chief, and dipping his fingers in a little of the pigment in a leaf, smeared a broad red band round the chief's belly, sides and back, just above the waistcloth. Turmeric was the decoration in honour of the principal god, his 'perfume' (cf. p. 416). The kava was then clapped and the first cup was poured by the chief on the mat by his side. This was to various deities of his kava. Following on this a *marotafi*, a piece of bark-cloth, orange-dyed with turmeric, was brought to the chief, unfolded by him, and laid towards the stern of the near canoe. A cup of kava was handed to him and he poured it on the mat beside the cloth. The bark-cloth was the vestment of his supreme deity, and the kava his libation. Food offerings were then thrown, after which another cup of kava was poured to other deities by the chief and then one by Pa Porima, which concluded the ceremony. The fish and breadfruit set in front of the chief were removed and dealt out to the crowd, who had as yet eaten nothing, since they had awaited the arrival of the party from Uta.

A certain continuity was observed in the composition of the various groups. Thus the people who went to Uta the previous evening went this morning also; they were known as 'Sa Uta' as against 'Sa Tai', the people who remained on the coast and performed the work in connection with the canoe court.

The ceremony of *anea pariki*, when performed by itself in the canoe court above the beach, is not of very great sacredness; it becomes so however when it is performed in Uta or if it is combined with the rites of the *fainga vaka*. In the first case it is said to be *mama*, light, as compared with the second, which is *mafa*, heavy. The term *palasu*, which has an even more literal meaning, is also used to signify a ceremony of importance or 'weight'.

In the interval, while waiting for the next event, the chief and his elders sat either in the canoe shed or in his adjacent house, talking, chewing betel, and smoking, while the ordinary rank and file of the clan went off to the woods to collect food. On their return the oven was prepared and late in the afternoon preparations were again made for the kava. The same arrangement was followed as in the morning, but this time the fish formed a much larger portion of the meal. The kava ritual was of the simple type, libations only being poured. Care was taken to make special food offerings to the deity of the canoe, a piece of breadfruit being thrown towards the bow with the announcement ' *Ia!* ' and portions of fish to the stern. A meal concluded the day's activities. As these had been in effect the offering of the night's catch to the gods, fish naturally formed the greater portion of the food supply. I was told 'It is made only to the fish; rites of evil things are made considerable with the fish, while the food is little' – the 'food' meaning, of course, vegetable supplies such as taro and breadfruit. A command frequently given at such a time emphasizes that it is primarily a fishing ceremony. 'The remaining bait to be cooked for the cold kava of fish.' The 'cold kava' is one of the lesser grades of ritual. The 'bait' refers to the fact that the flying fish are used to bait the hooks for a larger fish, hence some of the catch are consumed in this way at sea.

The curious term *anea pariki* may now be examined to see why it is that a rite of celebrating the first-fruits of fishing should be called 'evil things'. The Tikopia explanation was that it represents an acknowledgment to the gods of the adze for their efforts on behalf of men. If this is done then relations between gods and men remain on a pleasant footing. But if men are slack, and either do not catch fish, or neglect to perform the appropriate rites with them, then the gods become angry. Said the Ariki Kafika to me: 'Evil things truly, friend. If there is no fish, it is made with a man, and the man dies. The man has been struck by the guardian deities of the adze that he may die for the making of their "evil things".' If the *anea pariki* are not made for some days after the canoes have gone to sea, it is believed that some person will sicken and die; it is known then that the gods have taken their victim. According to Pa Raropuka, in Taumako the decision lies primarily with the chief. The deity Pusi enters his human medium before *anea pariki* is performed, and asks:

Where shall Tumoana cut?
Shall he cut among the news of the ocean,
Or shall he cut among the news of the land?

This means, where shall the god's adze strike – among fish, or among men? With which sacrifice shall 'evil things' be made? If the chief calls in reply 'Strike at sea', then the deity will kill a fish to be brought to shore by one of the clan canoes. But if the chief sits without a word, then the deity will kill a man. Pa Raropuka said that the Taumako clan were bad; their god killed if no fish were caught.

Hence there is always some haste to get the ceremony over, and if bad weather prevents the fleet from going out or if the catch is poor, uneasiness is felt in all the villages. It is during this time that the mats lie open in the canoe court and everyone is relieved when they are folded up; it is the sign that the due rites have been completed. The custom is for Kafika clan to perform *anea pariki* three times at least, including once in Uta. If no large fish is obtained, but only flying fish, then it will probably be made twice in Uta for safety. Taumako perform their rites four times, once in the canoe court, once in Uta, once in Ravenga at the sacred house Resiake and then finally in the canoe court again. The day chosen depends largely on the catch of the preceding night. The chief looks at it and if it is substantial says to his people 'Here! We shall go and make "evil things".' The rite is spoken of either as 'evil things of the canoes', or 'evil things of the canoe court'.

On this occasion the Ariki Kafika again performed 'evil things' on the following day, the fourth of the canoe rites. On this day also a subsidiary rite took place, the re-consecration of the canoe shed of the chief's vessel Tafurufuru.

About sunrise the chief was seated in his canoe court with a score or so of flying fish, the first product of the night's work, on a mat in front of him. The place was empty of canoes, for Tafurufuru and the other vessels of Kafika were out at sea with the fleet, and had not yet returned. As the sun got up, however, they began to come inshore and were a subject of comment to the crowd of people on the beach. Naturally everyone was more particularly interested in the vessels of his own family and clan, and the chief himself was no exception to this. A swell was breaking on the reef, and the channel was none too smooth. A canoe which approached it from the side instead of facing straight in, aroused his ire, while the sight of Tafurufuru riding in on the crest of a wave in daring style caused him to curse vigorously. Exasperation passed, however, in interest in the catch. The numbers obtained by each canoe, and the comparison of the fishing of Ravenga with that of Faea, with which district there was constant rivalry, occupied attention for some time.

The arrival of the *monotanga* from Fangarere (see later) diverted the conversation; it was a large household basket filled to bursting with a mass of taro tubers and pudding, and topped by orange bark-cloth. At the same time the gift for Taumako was borne past, a similar great package of food covered with a white bark-cloth. On the receipt of this the usual morning ritual took place, the *monotanga* – 'the kava of Vakamanongi', as it was termed – being the chief object. The basket was opened in front of the chief, the orange bark-cloth was laid towards the stern of the canoe, portions of food were set out and libations of kava poured. That the rite was a celebration of the fishing was indicated by the presence in the canoe court of a flying-fish net, several rolls of sinnet and a smouldering torch, all articles brought from the canoes.

Preparations were then made to go out fishing again, for at this time work was fairly continuous. The economic organization demanded some care. Arrangements were made for some people to get food from the cultivations, and for others to procure fish. Messengers were sent to men likely to form canoe crews, and young men who were unwilling were persuaded to go. As it was, one canoe was unable to get a full crew of men, and made up its complement with three boys.

While the fishermen were away an oven was prepared in a hut adjacent to Taramoa, the house of Pa Fenuatara, eldest son of the Ariki Kafika.

RE-FURNISHING THE CANOE SHED

The next event was the re-furnishing of the canoe shed which housed Tafurufuru. Every craft has a shed of its own, a long structure with a lean-to roof almost touching the ground on the low side. The sheds of some sacred canoes are *tapu*, being under the aegis of one or more deities of the group owning the vessel. The presence of a deity is manifested by a material object, a mat, a stone slab, or a conch-shell. There is a distinction here between *vaka fai tapakau*, canoes having mats, and *vaka se ke tapakau*, canoes without mats, known as *vaka fakaangiangi*. In Kafika, for instance, Sapiniakau has no mat in its shed, and hence no ritual as here described, whereas Tafurufuru has such. 'Canoes with mats' are primarily the *taumauri*.

The seasonal rite of re-consecration involves replacing of coconut mats and other perishable material, followed by the usual kava ritual.

It is a Tikopia custom to utilize the structural members of a building as foci of religious interest or embodiments of deities. In this case the principal post at the far end of the shed was the embodiment or token of the gods Tafaki and Karisi, otherwise Pu ma. At the foot of the post lay a mat, while the post itself was decorated with leaves of cycas tied in place with a narrow strip of bark-cloth, of which one end hung down in a long streamer. These ornaments of the post were a token of respect and honour to the deities. (A more detailed discussion of the function of such things is given in Chapter 5.)

On this occasion the food from the oven was brought into the shed and set in the middle of the floor, which was covered with a debris of old thatch and coconut leaves. Mats were set out, one for the chief and another for his elders, that of the former being nearer the sacred post. The kava bowl was likewise set in position. When all was ready the Ariki said – 'Wait till I go and re-furnish.' He rose, walked to the far end of the house, removed the old mat and laid in its place a new green one fresh plaited, untied the streamer and took away the dead cycas leaves, replacing them with a fresh set and binding them with a new white length of bark-cloth. He then returned to his seat and performed the kava. He faced the mat and cycas leaves as he did so.

Since the principal post of the shed was the pillar of the two deities, Pu ma, an orange bark-cloth offered with obeisance by the chief was theirs also. As it was said 'The bark-cloth spread out there is spread out to Pu ma – Pu ma are two, Tafaki and Karisi.' Theirs also was the display of cycas leaves bound to the post. This was described by Pae Sao as a decoration conferred on them by Tafito and Pufine Taufiti. (Tafito is the premier god of Fangarere; Pufine Taufiti is one of the Rua Nea.) The strip of bark-cloth which bound the leaves to the post was called *te noa*, a general term for a tie, but which was used as a technical term for all such pendent streamers in temples. The other supernatural being who shared the canoe shed was the Atua Fafine, the female guardian of the canoe. The mat at the foot of the post, though known generally as the mat of the gods, was in reality her resting place alone. It is from this that the kava ceremony received its name – 'the kava of the mat'. In the Kafika canoe shed this female deity and Pu ma were the supernatural beings principally invoked. The canoe shed of each chief had its own female deity, in Kafika known as Pu Fafine, in Fangarere as Pufine Ravenga, while Tafua and Taumako had each 'A Rua Nea', 'Two Persons', the euphemistic conjoined title of a pair of evilly disposed goddesses. It was said that these deities sometimes take material shape, and are to be found in the embodiment of a stone at the foot of the principal post of the canoe shed. 'When the canoe shed is built they embody themselves in a stone, a stone slab of light rock. When we dig the post, there it is in the soil, found there in the bottom of the hole of the post.'

As far as the floor itself is concerned the female deity is in charge, and it is because of her that certain prohibitions are in force when men sit in the shed of one of the chief canoes. 'The canoe shed is *tapu*.' People may not sit above the floor on stools or upturned bowls or blocks of wood as they do elsewhere, but only on mats. Moreover, no man may sleep face downwards there, a position which is quite allowable in a house. The reason for these observances is to be found in the belief that female deities sometimes desire to have connection with mortal men, and in this event the man sickens and may die. Positions such as the above are suggestive, and might be construed as invitations to the goddess; hence they are to be avoided. The general principle obtains in Tikopia religion that male *atua* are peculiarly dangerous to mortal women, and female *atua* to mortal men on account of this sexual bias. As natives said to me, 'Friend! the female deity is bad; she is concupiscent towards us, the males.'

An interesting instance of probable Melanesian contact is afforded by the cycas. Its common name is the *rongorongo*, but it is also known as the *melemele*, apparently a reduplication of the name *mwele* by which it is known in Mota and adjacent islands, where also the leaves are used as taboo badges and the like.

During the performance of the kava which had re-consecrated the canoe shed the fishermen had been away in their craft. They returned in the early afternoon. Most of the people on shore had been busy in attending to the large oven. This was to provide the food for a further rite of *anea pariki*, and a considerable amount of work had been devoted to it. Finally all was ready and chief and elders took their respective seats. An attendant applied the band of turmeric round the waist of the chief. The usual kava ceremony was then performed, omitting the recitation of the formula over the stem of the plant, but with a large number of libations to the various deities. Portions of taro pudding, three in number, were laid by the side of the canoe which flanked the group; these were for the deities of the vessel. A single cup of kava was carried from one to the other and a little of the liquid poured out beside each food portion. This was the 'kava of the canoe'. A special point was made of taking a cooked fish from the basket, removing its wrappings and pinching off a piece of the flesh to throw towards the stern of the canoe. This was an essential gesture of the rite, since it offered to the canoe deity there the produce of his beneficence.

The food, including the portions which had been laid beside the canoe, was then distributed among the crowd and all ate heartily. The fishing of the morning was keenly discussed – it had not been good. Much speculation was indulged in as to what were the various fish which had bitten but were not hooked, the manner of biting and pulling being described in detail in each case for public judgment. Humorous anecdotes enlivened the theme, and were well received.

After the oven was emptied for this last ceremony the *roi* was placed in it for the morrow. From this was to be served the *kava fakaafuru* in the morning, a rite of particular weight and importance to mark the *fainga vaka* ceremonies of the chief's *taumauri* Tafurufuru.

'FAINGA VAKA' OF A 'TAUMAURI'

As mentioned earlier the *fainga vaka* is a rite performed individually for each sacred canoe. Its principal ritual elements are the anointing of the vessel with oil and the offering of bark-cloth to its tutelary deities. But one feature of especial economic interest arises from the integration of the tutelary deities of the vessel in a wider scheme.

Whenever the kava is made for a sacred canoe it is the custom for the owner or possessor of the vessel to make a special large basket of food and carry it to his clan chief, as a gift. This is termed the *monotanga*, and being in the nature of an acknowledgment of his suzerainty the chief does not reciprocate it. Here is one of the few occasions on which the rule of reciprocity is abrogated. But what happens when a chief celebrates his own canoe? The custom of the *monotanga* holds also in the case of the *fainga vaka* of the *taumauri*, with the difference that the chief concerned sends a basket of food to each of his fellow chiefs when his own canoe is celebrated. The net result is that each chief has to send out three separate gifts in connection with his own canoe, but receives as equivalent three baskets from the canoes of the others. In each case the *monotanga* is topped with a single piece of bark-cloth, and here certain distinctions are observed. Tafua, Taumako and Fangarere clans all send orange-dyed cloth with their gifts to the Ariki Kafika, and plain bark-cloth to each other. The Ariki Kafika, on his part, sends an orange cloth to the Ariki Fangarere and plain cloth to the Ariki Tafua and the Ariki Taumako. The orange cloth means that the gift is offered to the Atua i Kafika; the plain cloth that it is to the other canoe deities in each case.

The food for the *monotanga* of these principal canoes is cooked in the evening of the *fainga vaka* ceremony, removed from the oven the next morning, and sent off to the other chiefs. The sacerdotal name for the *monotanga* of the *taumauri* vessels is 'te ara o nga atua – the path of the gods.' It is said too that in olden days when the rites were celebrated for Vakamanongi, each chief shouldered a contribution of green food in person and went to the ceremony. This is significant of its importance, for normally a chief does not shoulder things, or bear any burdens. Nowadays, however, this duty is delegated to his wife or son.

The fifth day was one of great interest and activity to the Kafika folk. The oven with the *roi* was uncovered soon after sunrise. Special attention was paid to the *fakapoke*, a large mass of pudding which was to form the centre piece of the *monotanga* of the canoe, including the various gift baskets. I heard Pa Fenuatara ask Pa Siamano, his father's cousin, 'Is the *fakapoke* large?' 'What?' the elder replied sharply. 'Was it made by children? We two, I and the chief, made it.' The younger answered smoothly 'It is well.' A busy party of men and women had gathered round the oven, and by degrees the various packages of food were ready and set in line. One was designated 'the basket of the canoe', for use in the rites of the canoe court. Another, crammed into a household basket (*longi*), was destined for the Ariki Fangarere, while another for the

Ariki Taumako (and formerly one for the Ariki Tafua) was put into a large openwork basket of the type called *popora*, which held it more easily. It will be remembered that the gift from Fangarere to Kafika was contained in a *longi* while *popora* were used for those to the other chiefs. These differences of detail are extremely important to the Tikopia; they are points of traditional procedure for which usually no reason except tradition can be assigned, but with which good manners demand compliance. Such social obligations connected with a rite are in their way just as weighty as the religious duties. A number of baskets of the elders (*popora nga pure*) were also made up, one for each. These represented their share of the food. The remainder was put into baskets to be distributed later among the crowd assembled at the ceremony.

Considerable care was exercised in the food apportioning, which was so organized that the various baskets were not confused. This was essential, since the type, quality and quantity had to vary considerably according to the destination of the basket. In the bustle of uncovering the oven, preparing the food, and packing the baskets, with a score or more people actively engaged, it was surprising that no mistakes occurred. At last the food was carried across from the cookhouse to the canoe court, the bearers being carefully instructed about each basket.

The chief and his elders took their appointed seats, and the people of the clan assembled in numbers, for this was one of the great rites of the season. (See Fig. 3.)

The charcoal stripe was put on the forehead of the chief, and the vermilion turmeric band smeared thickly round his waist, with a ring on his upper arms in addition. Then came one of the special rites of the *fainga vaka*. The Ariki, still seated on his mat, selected a few sprigs of an aromatic shrub laid in front of him, took up a bottle of coconut oil, and carefully poured a few drops on to the leaves in his hand. (Formerly gourds were used as containers, but nowadays glass bottles have superseded them.) Setting down the bottle he leaned forward and rubbed vigorously at a spot on the side of the canoe, near the stern, where a dark stain showed the effect of former applications. This was the rite of 'oiling the canoe'. The chief accompanied his act with the recital of a formula, which he gave me later, as follows:

> Anoint with power your timber Sea-expert Chief
> Anoint for welfare.

I eat ten times your excrement
Turn to your timber
Rise with your fish,
A shark, a *varu*, a *para*;
And be properly abundant your timber.
Fall sleeping into the sea below.

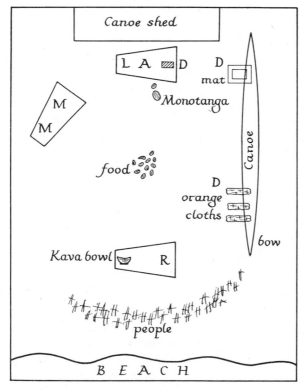

FIG. 3. Celebration of Tafurufuru Canoe

A, chief; D, *maro* offerings; L, aromatic leaves and oil; M, elders; R, Pa Rarovi

This formula was said to be a general one, used by the chief on all occasions when he had to perform a *fainga vaka* rite. It is of the 'telescopic' variety, so that a fairly literal translation such as the above still leaves its meaning rather cryptic. The first four lines are fairly clear, though it should be noted that the term 'anoint' is active in form and passive in sense, and that it and its adverb *manu* though grammatically linked are dependent for their significance on different subjects. To put it more concretely, it is the chief who performs the action of anointing, while it is the sea-expert chief, the guardian deity of the vessel, who supplies the power. The term 'rise' is explained as 'the sea to rise', that is for fish to come nearer the surface and so be available. In the last line but one the real subject is omitted; it is the flying fish that are required to be abundant for the advantage of the canoe ('wood' or 'timber' is always used as a synonym for 'canoe' in such formulae). The request to 'fall sleeping into the sea below' refers to the undesirable garfish in the hope that it may remain below and not disturb the fishermen by its dangerous flight. For the conventional self-deprecatory statement of the eating of the excrement of the deity the reason is given thus: 'Eating excrement only to the guardian deity of the canoe that his mind may be well disposed, that he be not angry hither towards us.'

A similar formula for his *fainga vaka*, though somewhat shorter, was given me by the Ariki Taumako.

> I eat your excrement Tafaiata!
> Turn to your timber is anointed there
> Anoint with power
> Anoint for welfare
> To ascend a flying fish on to your canoe.

Tafaiata is the special name used by this chief in his canoe court when addressing the Atua i Kafika, to whom he also has limited rights of appeal. In such case it is Te Rurua, the *taumauri*, that is celebrated, since it is dedicated to this principal Kafika deity.

After the anointing with the aromatic leaves and oil came the important rite of spreading the sacred vestments. These are similar in nature and function to those used in the ordinary kava cere- mony. They are normally pieces of bark-cloth which are spread out as offerings to the tutelary deities of the canoes. They are kept solely for the use of the vessel, each deity has his or her own type, and there is a special position in which the cloth must be laid.

The actual form of the ceremony for the canoe Tafurufuru was as follows: The chief took first the *maro kie*, a small mat, finely plaited from a soft variety of pandanus leaf, and decorated with a deep red border of dyed fibre in a zigzag pattern. This he laid on the stern of the vessel, over the spot on which he rubbed the oiled leaves. He next took a pile of orange bark-cloths and raising them to his head in obeisance, laid them on the mat before him. An attendant – in this case his eldest son – picked up several of them and laid them across the starboard gunwale, with the broad end hanging down to the ground outside. Three were so placed amidships towards the bow. A *mami* or large white square of cloth was laid on the ground near the bow. This was for the Female Deity – '*te maro a Pu Fafine*', the white square being a woman's garment, whereas the longer strips of cloth were appropriate only to male deities. The *maro kie* was the property of the deities of the adze, i.e. Pu ma, here celebrated as deities of the canoe itself. The other cloths were assigned to the Atua i Kafika and other deities of lesser status. When all the *maro* were set out the vessel presented a picturesque appearance, the light straw colour of the pandanus leaf contrasting with the bright orange or vermilion of the turmeric-dyed cloths, while the bright turmeric bands on the body and arms of the Ariki added a further note of colour to the scene.

The Ariki now put on his necklet of coconut frond, and the kava stem – a large one for this occasion – was laid with its root towards the stern of the canoe. The chief again took up a handful of the aromatic leaves, and rubbed them over his chest and upper arms, bruising them in the process so that they would be still more pungent. The scent of the leaves is believed to be pleasant to the nostrils of the deities, and this act represents an attempt of the chief to attract their attention still more favourably towards him, the performer of their ceremonies. He then turned to the stem of the kava, and after the usual appeal to and confirmation from the assembled elders began the recital of a long formula, the customary kava of the canoe court, which has been described earlier. The first two libations were poured by the chief towards the stern, that is Pu ma; the next two on the mat in front of him, to his other gods and his ancestors; the fifth cup was poured by Pa Porima to his own principal deity; the sixth and seventh by the kava bearer to the other deities of the canoe; the eighth by Pa Porima to his other gods, and the ninth by Pa Rarovi to his gods. The *monotanga* were then topped with bark-cloth; that for the canoe court of Te Keo, of Fangarere, with an orange cloth from the mat of the chief, and that for Te Rurua, of Taumako, with a plain cloth from the bow of the canoe. They were borne off with a stick of kava in each case. (A slip in the organization occurred here; the four portions to be used by the elders Pa Rarovi and Pa Porima as offerings to their gods were forgotten, until a protest caused them to be set out.)

I had been told by Pae Sao that if a visitor of rank attended this kava rite etiquette allowed him, in fact compelled him, to present several *maro* to the canoe. Coached by Pae Sao, I did this. After the ordinary bark-cloths had been spread out I rose from my seat and laid two pieces of red calico at the feet of the chief, one for the *maro* of the canoe, and the other as its honorific support. I then laid a white piece on the bow of the vessel, for the Female Deity; and another red piece at the chief's feet with the words 'The *maro* of your father and your ancestors.' The chief and his people were at first taken aback by my act, since I had been coached in secret, but a murmur of appreciation then went round, and my gesture of acknowledgment of hospitality and recognition of the gods helped me greatly in my future work. Some time later, however, the Ariki told me with a laugh that I had made one mistake – the white calico should have been laid on the ground, and not on the canoe itself! The calico was afterwards parcelled up and kept as part of the ritual offerings to the gods, for future use.

'FAINGA VAKA' OF OTHER KAFIKA CANOES

The ceremony just completed marked the end of the *fainga vaka* for the principal *taumauri*, but the rest of the *vaka tapu* of the chief still remained to be celebrated. The main vessel was described as a *vaka fai tao*, i.e. a canoe, the rites for which are performed with food cooked in the oven overnight and taken out early in the morning. The others were termed *vaka fai mata* – 'canoes cele- brated green', since the food used to make the requisite offerings was brought in from the gardens and cooked the same day. Hence the rites for these vessels are always performed in the late after- noon; their offerings rank somewhat lower on the ritual scale.

On this day three canoes of Kafika were celebrated, namely Karoata, belonging to the Ariki and kept in his village of Potu sa Kafika; Sapiniakau, also his property and kept adjacent to his residence in Sukumarae; and Kaveitau, the canoe of Pa Torokinga, one of his elders, which was hauled up in its shed in Te Roro, on the far lake shore. It is the duty of the family possessing the canoe to prepare the necessary baskets of food for the ceremony, including the *monotanga*, which is given by them to their chief. The preparation of the food entails a considerable amount of work, and the family concerned obtain assistance from brothers-in-law, nephews or neighbours, who come along with contributions of raw food and join in the work. When cooked the food is carried to the canoe court, where the vessel is drawn up, and is termed the oven of the canoe or the kava of the canoe. The principal basket is topped with a piece of plain bark-cloth. The rite as I saw it was practically the same as that performed in the morning for Tafuru-furu, the essential elements being the anointing of each vessel, the spreading out of bark-cloths for their respective deities, and then in conclusion, to give efficacy to the performance and stamp it with the seal of esoteric authority, the full kava ritual. Only two canoes were present; Kaveitau, having been out of repair for some years, remained in its own shed and 'its kava only was brought hither', i.e. only the obligatory basket of food. Accordingly no actual rites were performed over it, but it was included by implication in the kava formulae. The canoe gods of Karoata were said by Pa Fenuatara to be Tumoana and Pu-i-te-Moana. The former, he said, was Pusiuraura under another name; he was an *atua* of Pu ma, having come with them to Tikopia by swimming under their canoe. His arrival from Tonga with the canoe Tukupasia was later. Pu-i-te-Moana was formerly a man, by name Tifenua, a son of the Ariki Kafika Maranga. The canoe gods of the craft Sapinia-kau have been described elsewhere.[1]

An interval of a few minutes occurred when the kava was over, and the Ariki then went across to the canoe court, a few yards away, where his vessel Tafurufuru lay. Here four large baskets of food were resting, three being the respective *monotanga* of the canoes, and the other, placed slightly in advance, 'the basket of the elders', i.e. of the ancestors of the chief. Portions of food were set out in front of the chief, orange cloths were unfolded and kava was prepared in the bowl; of this the chief poured five cups – three towards the stem of the vessel for Pu ma and Te Atua i Kafika, and two for his ancestors. This ceremony did not relate to the other craft just celebrated, though it arose from their presence. The chief had duly performed the rites for the deities of these canoes and had received the *monotanga* from the respective owners in acknowledgment. He in his turn then made recognition to his own particular deities, notably the Atua i Kafika, by this

[1] See my *Primitive Polynesian Economy*, 1939, ch. IV.

subsidiary rite. It was the 'announcing' of the food to his god, in accordance with the usual custom that a chief or elder, on receiving a large gift of food from any source, places it on the ritual side of his house, opens it and throws small morsels in offering. The present case gives another instance of how the threads of the social organization are drawn together, in that the gods of the ordinary *vaka tapu* are once more linked with those of the *taumauri*. It may be objected here that two of the three vessels celebrated were under the immediate ownership of the Ariki himself, and that a repetition of the offerings was superfluous. This, however, was not the case, since the gods of each canoe were different, and the supreme deities must have their due every time.

When all was over the food was divided among the crowd who attended, the ritual elders receiving the largest share. As the work of sorting out and wrapping up the food was ended the sun was just going down. Sometimes at this juncture the Ariki leaves for Uta in order to perform a ceremony known as '*Te Ara o Pu*'. Description of this, however, will be most appropriate after the account of the remaining canoe rites is completed.

Two or three canoes as a rule are celebrated at the one time, and this performance goes on at intervals of a day or so until all the vessels have been re-consecrated. In Kafika clan on the following day – the sixth – Kau Rotuma, the craft owned by Pa Porima; Peru-i-te-vai, that of the Mapusanga family, who were close relatives of the chief, and Ariki-taufenua, that of Pa Rarovi, were celebrated. In former times a pair of other canoes, Maratau, belonging to Pa Raropuka, and Te Arai-moana, owned by the family of Totiare, both residing in the district of Faea, were also celebrated by the Ariki Kafika. But since Christianity has claimed these people their *fainga vaka* have fallen into desuetude.

By tradition, variations of procedure were observed at the ceremonies of certain specified vessels. One of these was Peru-i-te-vai, which was decorated for the occasion with streamers of the young creamy light-green fronds of the coconut, cut before they had properly opened out. These were tied on at the junction of thwart and gunwale, and leaves of a ruddy variety of Cordyline were also used. This was termed the 'significant mark' of the canoe and was a decoration confined to this vessel and two others only – Kakeafanga and Tereata, both of Taumako clan. A point of importance is that a special *monotanga* topped with an orange cloth was carried to the Ariki Taumako when the rites of the Kafika canoe were performed. This gift was termed 'the betel of Peru-i-te-vai', and originated in the fact that this vessel came from Taumako in past time. It was in fact regarded as the ultimate property of the chief of this clan. 'It is held by us, but obeys the Ariki Taumako' the people of Kafika said to me. Peru-i-te-vai is the name of an ancestor of the Mapusanga family who first built the vessel, and it was called after him. The connection with the group of Taumako, however, lies in the realm of religious belief, and only becomes apparent when the significance of the name is examined. *Peru* means in ordinary speech 'curved' or 'crooked', and '*Peru-i-te-vai*' means therefore 'curved in the water'. I was told in fact that it is a euphemism, a descriptive honorific term for the sinuous twinings of the eel, the material representation of Pusi-uraura, one of the most important deities of Taumako. The reason why the *monotanga* from the canoe was sent to the chief of that clan was that the Kafika ancestor when he first built the craft dedicated it to the Taumako deity, whose name he bore and under whose control it consequently came. The ancestor Pu Mapusanga was a 'sacred child' of Taumako, i.e. his mother came from that clan. The reason why the vessel Peru-i-te-vai is ornamented in this special manner is that the young coconut frond and the ruddy cordyline leaf are the aromatic emblems of Vai Atafu, the Heaven which is the dwelling-place of the god Pusiuraura. It is held that this Heaven is situated in Tonga, whence the god came. The fact that Kakeafanga and Tereata canoes also had this special form of decoration meant that they too had the eel-god as their tutelary deity. The position of Peru-i-te-vai between Kafika and Taumako is an illustration of the type of dual property rights and economic obligations which help to bind together the various clans in a social network.

CANOE RITES OF THE ARIKI TAFUA

Till this point the sequence of events has been described as it occurred in the canoe rites of the Ariki Kafika. This has been done for two reasons – in the first place the intricacy of detail is so great that confusion is lessened by adhering to the programme of one particular chief and clan; and in the second since the Ariki Kafika is the chief of highest rank on the island, the rites which he per-forms are often fuller than those of the other chiefs, and he has many special duties which they do not share. Generally speaking the ceremonies of the other chiefs follow the same course as those which appear above; certain differences of procedure exist, however, arising from those unique privileges of individual office which make the study of Tikopia social and religious life so interesting and yet in a way so exasperating to the observer who is seeking to reduce it to a set of general principles.

Only the most outstanding variations in custom can be mentioned here. It will be realized that each chief, since the bulk of his spirit guardians are different in name and in attributes from those of the other chiefs, has to employ a slightly different mode of procedure and address towards them.

I saw some of the canoe rites of the Ariki Taumako, particularly the *fainga vaka* of his vessel Tukupasia, but there is no marked difference in his procedure and that of the Ariki Fangarere from that of the Ariki Kafika. Rites of the Ariki Tafua, however, followed a somewhat different plan in the days when he still practised them. Unlike the other chiefs he held most of his canoe rites in Namo, the strip of coast to the north of the huge bluff Fongatekoro. Here in 'the eye of the land' was situated the canoe court of Suakava, his most sacred craft.

I received from the chief himself an account of his canoe ritual, the substance of which is given here, in the historic present tense, as the information was taken down.

The Tafua clan carry out the same initial rites of the *faunga vaka* as do the other clans, save that as mentioned earlier, they prepare two lots of *roi*. They also bear an actual sacred adze to Namo in addition to the *faingata* carried by the chief. When the Ariki lifts down the adze from its resting place he recites a formula of an unusual kind. He says:

> Blood-red Tuna!
> I eat ten times your excrement.
> Turn to your adze which will be lifted down.
> Turn to your implement which will be laid down.
> You, cause a flying fish to climb on to your
>   starboard side
> For the making of your evil things.
> And let your tail be lashed to starboard of the
>   fleet of the chiefs
> That the guardian canoe deity may go, go, astray;

That his eyes may be fogged
Lest you and I be splashed hither.
Let your sinnet be firm in your hair
To perform your deeds on your starboard side.
Distribute among your fleet;
Give fish only to the large canoes,
Suakava and Rama-i-katea and Fiti-mua.

This is an appeal to the principal *atua tau toki* of Tafua, Tuna the eel-god, to send fish to the canoes of his own chief, and blind the eyes of the deities of the other chiefs so that their vessels may be unable to haul up any large catch. The formula is an interesting expression of the desire for prestige and success in advance of his rivals that animated the old Ariki, and was still manifest in 1929.

The first part of the recital is of the usual invocatory type, requesting the deity to turn to the sacred adze. The deity is conceived as sitting in his abode, unwitting of what is desired of him until the disturbance of his sacred implement, coupled with the calling of his name, attracts his attention. His interest and assistance are believed to be demonstrated in a physical and quite human way; that is, if he wishes to be helpful he turns to face the supplicator; his neglect or anger, however, is indicated by the presentation of his back.[1] The reference in the second part of the formula to the lashing of the tail is understood when it is remembered that Tuna is the personification of the eel. The tutelary deity of a canoe accompanies it on the starboard side, that which is free from the outrigger and on which the fish are caught, so that in consequence the swishing of the tail of the intruding god is imagined to confuse the rightful guardians, to befog their eyes with the swirl and foam, and to cause them to wander astray in their attempts to bring in a shark or other large fish to their particular vessel. The capture of such a prize gives great pleasure to a chief. 'His whoop of delight rings out, *Iefu!* he rejoices', said the Ariki Tafua. He added, 'The chiefs burn in the rivalry of their performance', meaning that there is great competition among them. The failure of any of his vessels to get such a fish, conversely, is a blow to a chief. It means that he lacks influence with

---

[1] This correlation of favour and disfavour with the view of the countenance or the reverse is also held in Oriental culture, and emerges very clearly in our own literature when under the influence of Hebrew thought. 'Turn not thy face from us, O Lord', 'Avert not the light of thy countenance' are sentiments the expression of which is perfectly intelligible to a Tikopia.

the gods. He is not *manu*, he has no success. From this one can understand the appeal of the Ariki Tafua that he be not put out of countenance by his rivals. It is interesting to note, too, how he cleverly draws his deity into the same predicament by the use of the dual 'thou and I', suggesting that if the *atua* does not hamper the canoes of the other chiefs they will be both 'splashed hither', that is be put to shame by the splashings which signal the large fish hauled in by the others.[1] The custom among male Tikopia is to wear the hair long; when work is to be done it is bound up out of the way in a knot on the top of the head, in order that it may not impede the sight. Such is the purpose of the sinnet mentioned in the formula – it must be light and firm lest it slip at the critical moment. Following this beguilement of his rivals the *atua* is asked to see to the needs of his own canoes and to apportion the catch among them so that each of the principal craft receives a large fish. The smaller vessels may be neglected, but it is essential that the *taumauri*, the three canoes of which the names are given, shall be supplied.

It will be noted that this major canoe deity of Tafua is credited with a limited understanding on the one hand, and with super-human power on the other. He is regarded as having some of the physical characteristics of the eel, the mental endowment of man, and the capability of a spirit.

This action of the Ariki Tafua would not have been viewed with a good grace by his fellow chiefs if they knew of it. In past years before I came he had had great success with his canoes in compari-son with theirs, and in his belief this was due very largely to his instructions and to the power (*manu*) of his deity. That he made appeals of this nature was kept a secret in his family. As a matter of fact in giving me the formula set down above he implored me not to reveal to the other chiefs that he had used such tactics, lest they be offended with him. They had, however, some suspicion of his methods, for his character was well known. He was des-cribed as having been very prone to utilize all forms of *tautuku*,

---

[1] I owe an interesting Chinese analogy to Dr Michael Sullivan. When Po Chü-i was Governor of Hangchow in A.D. 823 it was his duty to compose addresses to the spirits that controlled the rain. To one spirit he promised 'singing and dancing, drums and bells' if it rained within five days. But if the spirit 'just sits calmly watching while the crops go dry it will not only be a disaster for the people, it will also be a disgrace for you. It is for you to decide!' (Arthur Waley, *The Life and Times of Po Chü-i*, 1949, p. 148.)

black magic, so it was surmised by the leaders of the other fleets, though in the absence of real proof, that the continued success of his vessels had been accompanied by some such spiritual sabotage against those of his rivals. His real accomplishments at sea appeared to be due to a combination of his own undoubted efficiency and driving power, coupled with skill in fishing on the part of his crews, a knowledge of some good banks, and a rather unusually long run of luck.

After the sacred adzes and the other sacred things of Tafua have been lifted down the kava is performed, and the deities of the adze are invoked. For this clan they are 'Blood-red Tuna', 'Black Pusi', 'Blood-red Pusi', 'The Group of the Rosy Tail', all gods associated with the eel, in this order, and lastly Tufaretai, the personal deity of the chief on his mother's side (see list earlier). Some of the attributes of these *atua* will be discussed later in connection with the manufacture of turmeric. No other deities, nor any of the *kau firifiri*, the chiefly ancestors, are summoned to this kava.

When the Ariki Tafua goes round to Namo he takes his seat in the canoe court, not close to the canoe shed or to the craft itself, as do the other chiefs, but thirty or forty yards away; such is the custom in his clan.

For the kava of the *faingata* in the canoe court, the same set of tutelary deities of the adze is invoked, and a somewhat similar appeal is launched as before to bewilder the gods of the other chiefs. Thus the Ariki recites as part of his formula:

> You should divide in two
> To bring hither the young coconut.
> To my fleet give fish this night
> Lest we be splashed hither then.
> And be lashed to be misty
> The fleet of the chiefs;
> Do not cause any fish to ascend to it.

The significance of the latter part of the formula will be clear in the light of the explanation already given. The injunction—

> Be lashed to be misty
> The fleet of the chiefs

– forms one of the 'telescopic' expressions beloved of kava reciters in which certain phrases of an idea are slid into others. The expression here quoted refers to the tail of the eel-god disturbing the water before the eyes of the guardian deities of the other canoes.

Some comment is necessary on the first two lines of the formula. It is suggested by the Ariki to the group of deities that they divide into two parties in order to accomplish their task the better. The reference to the bringing of the green coconut, which the Ariki smashes and finally flings out to sea, means that the next morning the deity is expected to bring in a shark, i.e. one caught by the crew, as a token that he has heard and complied with the request. This is alluded to figuratively as the coconut returned again to shore. Hence the chief has a special reason to look out to sea in the morning to see if his canoe is scattering spray in the appropriate signal.

The ceremony of the green coconut is performed with more elaboration by the Ariki Tafua than by the other chiefs, since this fruit is the emblem of his principal clan deity, Raki-te-ua by name. It is in fact regarded as being his head.[1] Hence before being smashed the nut is held up against the forehead of the Ariki as a mark of respect to the nut and the deity. 'It is conveyed to the face of the chief to touch it, because he is going to split the countenance of Raki-te-ua, that is the coconut.' As he performs this act of ceremonial obeisance the Ariki mutters;

> Raki-te-ua and Blood-red Tuna!
> Turn to your young coconut.
> To be split on your starboard side
> Split with power.

The nut is then smashed with a blow from the adze. 'Thereupon the Ariki rises up, waves the nut around, sprinkles it on his canoe, runs then and sprinkles it on the sacred objects, runs also to the beach, and waving the coconut as he goes down, calls out

> Be carried away the young coconut
> Where are you two to carry the coconut?

Then he comes to the beach, calls out

> Be carried away the young coconut

and hurls it out to sea.' Such is the account of this rite, which was practically the same as that performed by the Ariki Kafika.

During the fishing itself the gods are not forgotten and appeals

---

[1] See my 'Totemism in Polynesia', 1930, p. 298.

are addressed to them by people of rank. One invocation of considerable interest is peculiar to Tafua. The custom of *fai soko* is common, whereby at the ceremonies of a family or clan the men who have married women of this group go along with a bundle of firewood to help in the preparation of the oven and the cooking. The gods, too, *fai soko* in the approved style. One of them named Feke, the personification of the octopus, is held to be married to Nau Fiora, who is a female deity of Tafua. Consequently he rests under this obligation, and whenever the sacred ovens of this clan are fired Feke is supposed to come along and lend his supernatural assistance. A Tikopia is never chary of reminding his gods of their duties, so that this matter of oven-tending is brought to the notice of the Octopus Deity in cases where the fishing of Tafua is not proving too successful. The following formula is addressed to him by one of the leading fishermen while waiting in his canoe:

> Feke! May a fish bite
> Stick your bundle of firewood on to a shark.
> What is your oven to be made with?
> You will keep on, keep on (loafing), then arrive on shore
> To find the *taori* performed that Pufine may dance.

In this formula Feke is adjured to make haste and send along a fish, not to come empty-handed, but to fasten his contribution of firewood on to a shark and bring that too – in passing, as it were, without giving himself too much trouble. Otherwise what will be the use of lighting the oven?; there will be no fish to cook in it. Then he is twitted with the fact that if he delays much longer he will land to find that his wife, spoken of as 'Pufine', 'Ancestress' has given him up as dead, and the *taori*, a ceremony to liberate her from her mourning of widowhood, is being performed so that she can dance once more. 'Unless he brings a fish let him not marry', said Pa Rangifuri to me in comment on this.

This address has an ironical note, rare though not unknown in the dealings of men with their gods. The style is more free and colloquial than is usual in such formulae, but it must be admitted that there is every excuse for an impatient fisherman!

In the various kava rites of a chief the deities invoked are not always the same. For the celebrations connected with the sacred adzes the gods of these implements only are called upon. For the 'great kava' of the *umu tonga* on the canoe ground, however, more deities are summoned. As it is said 'the gods are brought hither'. The order of invocation for this consecration of the oven of Tafua is as follows:

Raki-te-ua	principal god of clan, and coconut
Tuna	eel-god of the lake
Pusi	eel-god of the reef (and Taumako)
Tufaretai	god of Fusi lineage
Toki-tai-te-kere	god of lineage of Sao, Korokoro, etc.
Tarikotu	god of Fusi lineage

Feke and Pufine i Fiora, who are among the deities in charge of this oven, are also usually included in the list, but their position is lower than that of these mentioned above. For the kava performed at the re-furnishing of the canoe shed a somewhat different set of deities is invoked:

Raki-te-ua	
Tuna-toto	
Pusi	
Matapula	Tafua name of Atua i Kafika
Tangata-katoa	mythical ancestor
Rua-futi	Tafaki and Karisi

The chiefly ancestors are also appealed to on this occasion, but selectively; and choice of the few who are actually named in the formula rests with the Ariki.

The rest of the canoe rites of Tafua are performed as described for Kafika.

CANOE RITES OF THE ELDER OF MARINOA

The account of the procedure of Tafua has served to elaborate our first description of the canoe ceremonies of the chiefs. In order to appreciate properly the complexity and importance of these rites in the life of the whole community it is essential to refer also to the special privileges of one of the principal elders of the Ariki Kafika, the Pure i Marinoa. Though not a chief he has nevertheless chiefly status in this respect, in that he possesses a sacred adze and by immemorial custom he performs his own canoe celebrations. These comprise both *faunga vaka* and *fainga vaka*, and in general arrangement are similar to what has already been described. In common with those of the Ariki Tafua these rites have now been discontinued owing to Christianity, but the account of them which I received from the holder of the *pure* office, Pa Fetauta, who used to perform them, presents some points of interest.

The lineage of Marinoa, which includes several other house names, as Fetauta, and is also known as Nga Fiti, constitutes an important element in the Kafika clan. Their seat is in the district of Faea, on the opposite side of the island from Ravenga, where the Ariki Kafika and the other chiefs celebrate their fleets. On the morning of the first day of the ceremonies, 'the day of the chief', the elder of Marinoa sits in his house, and orders his relatives to go out to their orchards and to his own, and pluck coconuts. These are for the rite of revivification of his principal canoe, or as he expressed it 'That is my canoe, the canoe of the chief; is carried its *fakaora*.' The phraseology used indicates the concept of dual ownership which operates in regard to the sacred canoes of the elders.

According to Pa Fenuatara this canoe, Te Akauifo, 'is held to be the *paopao* of the Ariki Kafika'. It was given by the Kafika chief to the original ancestor of the Marinoa group. This man said to the chief at the *faunga vaka* rites of Kafika, 'I am going, and when I wake in the morning I shall not come.' The Ariki assented 'Yes indeed! Go and sleep, and when you wake, stop then for the re-lashing of my *paopao*.' Such is the story on which the present semi-independent procedure relies.

The *fakaora* of the vessel is carried to Ravenga, where the elder duly attends the rites of his chief. But towards evening he says to the chief, using his formal title, 'Tinamo! I am going.' The chief replies 'Yes! Proceed to go. Go to cook the food portion for the making of the sign of our canoe.' On this conventional phraseology the elder departs to Faea, taking with him his share of food from the day's distribution. This is placed in the oven in his temple, Marinoa, together with the usual *roi*. In the morning the oven is uncovered, the sacred adze is taken down and the kava made. Calling on the various deities of the adze in turn the elder says:

> You, Te Araifo!
> Turn to your adze which has been lifted
> And has been laid down.
> Turn with welfare.

Similar phrases are recited to Meteua, Rata, Fakasautimu, Pungatere and Pakora. The first two, with Te Araifo, are said to have come in times past from Fiti, that is from Vanikoro and the adjacent islands of the north-west. Fakasautimu is a spirit, the result of a miscarriage in the Marinoa house some generations ago. Pakora is the conjoint name of the two female *atua* known as A Rua nea, of whom one is termed Nau Taufiti and is held to be the wife of Pu Taufiti, another name for Rata. The progenitor of the house of Marinoa himself originated from Taumako, the Duff group, according to the Tikopia legend – hence the alternative family name of Nga Fiti, the People of Fiti – and these deities are associated with his canoe.

The elder of Marinoa resembles a chief in that he has at his kava a person to support him and utter the '*kona! kona!*' of confirmation. This man is the head of the family of Tarafanga, whose special ritual duty is to wait on the elder in this fashion. He is not himself an elder in rank, but acts as such to the elder of Marinoa when the latter officiates at a kava ceremony. This is the only instance in Tikopia where a man not a chief has a formal assistant at his kava and it is spoken of by the natives as a privilege of great weight, indicative of the importance of the head of this particular lineage.

When the canoe rites are being performed it is the preliminary duty of Pa Tarafanga to carry the 'sacred things' of Marinoa down to the canoe ground (I am uncertain if these are *Terebra* shells or nails). To equip him for this service the elder of Marinoa knots the circlet of Cordyline leaf round his neck and commends him to the care and attention of the gods.

> You all the gods!
> Look hither on the man who is carrying the sacred
>   objects that he may be well.
> His cordyline leaf will be cast
> Cast for welfare.

The celebration of the vessels is carried out in the manner already described, the charcoal stripe being put on the forehead of the elder as if he were a chief. The necklet of coconut frond is also assumed, though normally when the kava is performed in the house of Marinoa the ordinary ritual necklet of an elder, the cordyline leaf only, is donned. The features most worthy of note as differing from the rites of the chiefs are the specific gods invoked, and the individual turns of expression in the formulae addressed to them.

When the elder goes with his adze to strike the blow on the inside of the hull of each canoe he says:

> I eat your excrement, Guardian of the Adze!
> Turn to your canoe.
> Resound inland, resound for welfare;
> Resound in the sea waters, turn as sea expert.

Here an onomatopoeic term (*paku*) refers to the hollow sound as the blade of the implement strikes the hull. The idea of this appeal is that when the canoes go out the deity will stand and bring fish to them. It may be noted that in this ritual act the Ariki Kafika addressed the Ariki Tautai, the Sea-expert Chief who is the deity of the canoe, whereas the elder of Marinoa calls on the deity of the sacred adze. The function of each is the same in this connection – namely, to secure fish for the vessel.

On his return, when he sits down in the lane of coconuts to perform the kava of the *fakaora*, the elder recites:

> I eat your excrement, Guardian of the Adze!
> Turn to your kava in your adze;
> Turn with welfare.
> And you all the Elders,
> Turn you hither with welfare;
> Turn to your kava in your adze.
> I eat your excrement.
> And you all the *Fuanga*
> Turn hither;
> Lift up the orphaned one
> Cast away on that spot there;
> Lift you hither.
> And anything unpleasant for the kava
> Lay aside to the setting sun there.
> *Marie!*

The ending to this formula is that usually employed in the ordinary kava. The *Fuanga* are the deities of the mother's family, to whom it is the privilege of every man to appeal.

For the pouring of libations from the green coconut the words used are:

Your liquid there Possessors of the Adze
Revolve precisely with welfare to your kava in your adze.

As the *umu tonga* is later cleared out the workman drives a stick into the ground and calls 'E! the oven!', glancing as he does so towards the elder. 'Go you and dig' the latter replies. Then while the pit is being dug he murmurs:

The oven of the adze will be dug out
Dig with power
Dig for welfare.

For the rite of sprinkling on the concluding day the elder, after smashing the coconut, runs first to his principal canoe, the *tau-mauri*, and calls:

Here! Sprinkle away with power
Sprinkle one thing, a flying fish to climb on to the
canoe
For the making of 'evil things'.

Then he runs on to the sacred objects, then past the *umu tonga*, on to the other canoes and finally to the beach, whence he casts the nut into the sea. So doing he recites the words:

The coconut, which has been thrown away, throw
with power;
Directed hither be the coconut;
Directed hither as sea expert,
Directed to welfare,
Directed to a shark,
Carried hither be the coconut.
You Saunipariki! be directed hither the coconut.

Saunipariki is the name of a former elder of Marinoa who is regarded as having great power among the gods, hence he is especially invoked in the formula.

The sacred objects are then carried back by Pa Tarafanga, and the elder follows with the adze. This is laid on a mat in the house and the people go and fire the oven. When the food is cooked they eat, but the elder does not partake; he sits alone on his mat, and does not eat until after the kava is performed. Such temporary fasting before a ceremony is fairly common among persons of rank. All night the sacred objects lie on the mat. The next morning the elder comes and performs the rite known as the sprinkling of the sacred things. No formula is recited during this act, but 'they are sprinkled for the deities to turn hither with welfare'. The elder then returns and hangs up the adze with the words:

> I eat your excrement Possessor of the Adze!
> Revolve precisely with welfare
> Your adze will be hung up,
> Hung with welfare.

After the kava is made the elder goes down to the beach to see the canoes come in and learn the result of the night's fishing. The ceremony of *anea pariki* is then performed in acknowledgment to the guardian deities of the sacred adze. Deities of the canoe are included in this in recognition of their services. Thus in the case of Te Akauifo canoe, the principal vessel of Marinoa, in addition to the gods of the adze already mentioned, Saunipariki, ancestor of the elder, is also addressed by name in the kava ceremony, he being a tutelary spirit of that canoe. The kava bowl only is prepared, and each of the major deities has his libation. The ancestral spirits, generally termed Nga Matua, the Elders, are here addressed collectively as Nga Tautai, the Sea Experts, in honour of their nautical powers. In the evening the same procedure is repeated.

The *fainga vaka* of Marinoa also displays certain features which are different from the corresponding rites of the chief of Kafika. For Te Akauifo the canoe shed is re-furnished as in the case of the other *taumauri*. The food from the oven of the mat, as it is called, is prepared and carried to the shed. Here is no special post to be decorated as with the canoes of the chiefs, but a small platform or shelf is covered with a leaf of the umbrella palm. The crux of the ritual consists in the renewing of this. The elder of Marinoa goes up, replaces the old dry leaf with a fresh one, and strews on it leaves of the *kava pi*, an aromatic plant somewhat resembling the Canna. This last is termed the 'perfume' of the shelf. The aromatic leaves, the shelf and the canoe shed are all under the control of the guardian deities of the adze. To them a formula is recited as the shelf is covered.

> Your shelf the gods
> Will be covered
> Covered for welfare
> And turn to be sea experts to your canoe.

The remaining rites are conducted in the usual way. The bark-cloths are spread out in the following manner:

> on the ground by the bow, to Fakanatai, a deity of the canoe
> over the stern (white cloths, topped by an orange one) to the deities of the adze collectively
> along the gunwale, to Rata, Meteua, Fakasautimu, Foatai and Te Ama (the latter pair also gods of Fiti), individually.

In all seven *maro* are spread.

The next day the two other sacred canoes of the Marinoa group are re-consecrated. Of these one, Saunipariki, is named after the ancestor already mentioned who held the office of elder some generations ago, and is under his spiritual control; the other, Pungatere, is named after the son of Rata, and he is consequently the tutelary deity of the vessel. A *monotanga* from all these craft is carried to the Ariki Kafika as overlord, and is the usual large basket of food, topped in this case by an orange bark-cloth, denoting that the offering is made to the Atua i Kafika. When the gift is brought to the Ariki he takes it to his canoe court and 'announces' it to his principal deity in the manner already described.

When the *fainga vaka* of another Marinoa canoe, Te Akau-moana, is made, the *monotanga* is sent to the elder of the house of Sao, of Tafua clan. The reason is that in ancient days two elders of Marinoa, Rangaro and Maone, were 'sacred children' of Sao. On their death they went to the abode of the female deity of Sao, Makupu, in Ruamotu. There they saw the canoe and said 'We desire that canoe.' It was given to them, and transmitted to their descendants, being built by their successor Vaiangafuru. 'Great is the *manu* of the canoe', I was told.

Two other craft, Te Akauroro and Te Akautu, have similar cross-clan relationship, through their tutelary deities. The former is the titular property of the Ariki Taumako, but 'it has its basis in Korokoro' (of Tafua). When the kava of the canoe is made, in addition to a basket of food for the Ariki Taumako, one is sent to Pa Korokoro. This latter is reciprocated, but that to the chief is not, 'because the canoe is his'. This vessel is dedicated to Pu ma, in their Korokoro title. Te Akautu is the canoe of Niumano, of Taumako. But it is a 'canoe from the gods', in this case from Te Akauponopono, the residence of Semoana, a sea deity, who is the joint deity of several houses of Tafua, and acknowledgment is made to them in the rites performed over it.

Thus within the general system of canoe rites described, there are subsidiary links between kinship groups, which still further make for an interlocking scheme of privileges and practices.

'THE PATH OF OUR ANCESTOR'

Some days after the canoe ceremonies of Kafika have begun a spectacular presentation of food is made to the chief of this clan by the chief of Taumako. The gift is termed *Te Ara o Pu*, '*Pu*' being the honorific title applied to the progenitor of the Taumako clan. The origin of the gift will be explained later.

The ceremony of *Te Ara o Pu* may occur as an interlude in the rites of the *fainga vaka*, or may be postponed for a few days. During the season of my attendance it was held twice, the first time on the principal day of the *fainga vaka* and again about a fortnight afterwards, during the proceedings connected with Kafika temple. It is not planned to take place on a fixed date but depends on the catch of the fishing fleet, as the main item of the gift is a cooked shark. Made with this as its basis it is termed also '*anea pariki o Pu*' by analogy with the ceremonies noted earlier. If no shark is available the presentation is deferred for some time, and if the fleet remains unsuccessful it is then made with smaller fish alone. The securing of two sharks by the vessels of the Ariki Taumako in the season under review accounted for the duplication of the gift.

When the shark was caught by a canoe of Taumako the chief was notified. The following morning the fish was taken to Uta and sanctified by the performance over it of the 'cold kava', after which it was cooked in the oven of Taumako temple, together with a large mass of vegetable food. When ready the food was laid first before the mat of the Ariki Taumako, who performed a brief kava ceremony over it. It was then carried at once to Kafika Lasi about fifty yards away.

Meanwhile preparations had been made for its reception. A coconut mat was laid under the eave of the house, the head projecting outside, and the Ariki Kafika took his accustomed seat, with his kava equipment and assistants in attendance. A number of the clan had assembled including besides the chief several of his sons, brothers and nephews, a couple of his elders, the Ariki Fangarere and four or five commoners. As the time drew near for the uncovering of the oven in Taumako all listened keenly for the first sound of the pounders thudding in the wooden bowl as the pudding was prepared. This was the signal for the people of Kafika to get ready. I was told:

That is its observance; the oven is uncovered, and pounded to reverberate that the Ariki Kafika may hear. Thereupon the Ariki calls out to a man 'Go and grope for stones; the oven there has been pounded hither.' Thereon he goes then and gropes.

This statement needs some explanation. While it is the obligation of Taumako clan to make the magnificent present of food it is the duty of Kafika people to facilitate its carriage. By custom one man alone must bear the gift, and as it consists of a huge basket of pudding topped by three smaller baskets of fish and mixed edibles, the weight is considerable. As a matter of fact it is just as much as a well-built man can stagger under. The communication way between the two houses is a narrow path between the bushes, often blocked by branches of sago palm to prevent depredations on the areca nut of either of the chiefs. These barriers must be removed. Also there are a number of rocks in the path, half-buried in the soil. These have been there from olden times, and no attempt is made to remove them. They are in the nature of customary obstacles. It is the task, however, of someone from Kafika to go out and locate them under the debris of leaf mould, twigs and grass and clear them so that the man bearing the load of the *Ara* may see where he is going and not trip and fall. This is not mere politeness, for if he stumbles and the food drops, or as much as touches the ground, it may not be carried further at the moment, but must be returned to Taumako and an additional gift prepared. In such circumstances failure to clear the path properly might involve Kafika in a shameful suspicion of negligence because of greed, so that they are very scrupulous on this matter.

When this task was finished the man returned and soon the double clap of the hibiscus fibre was heard from Taumako as the preliminary kava was performed. 'There it is clapped, now it will be brought hither', commented the Ariki Kafika, and all sat tense and silent, watching under the eave of the house. Quietly the kava liquid was prepared in the bowl. The sound of a heavy footstep was heard and a whisper, 'He has come', passed round. Slowly the bearer approached, his arms straining to hold the four baskets. As his legs appeared by the eave the Ariki called out loudly, breaking the silence in formal request.

Come you Ancestor and lay it down!

On the word the bearer set down his burden as gently as possible on the mat provided, and mutely backed away and disappeared to his own house. No attempt at communication with him was made by the Kafika people beyond the formal speech of the Ariki. This was in consequence of the *tapu* which surrounded the whole proceeding.

The baskets were seized by the folk inside and set before the mat of their chief, the cords were loosened and offerings of the food to the gods were arranged, one placed by the chief's feet, another by the kava bowl. Libations were then poured in the usual way. This was termed '*te kava o te ara*' or '*te kava o anea pariki*'. Portions of the food were then distributed among those present and they ate. As the gift was so large the greater amount of it was still unconsumed. This was apportioned out among the various 'houses' of the clan. Even if no representative of a 'house' was in attendance a food share was nevertheless set aside to be carried to them, for this was an event of a major importance to the clan, a gift made not to their chief alone, but to them as a whole. A point was made of praising with great emphasis the quality of the food. '*Great* is the fineness of anything sa Taumako make' was a typical remark passed by an elder. As was the local habit, encouraging comments were made inciting others to eat; such comments also could serve as a polite acknowledgment of the food, though the donors would hear of them only indirectly through the usual channels of gossip. 'The *ara* of our ancestor brought hither for us' said the eldest son of the chief sententiously, with the implication that the consumption of such a gift was a duty as well as a pleasure.

Mention of this attitude of obligation to partake of the gift raises the question of its origin. By Tikopia tradition it is attributed to the act of Pu Lasi, 'Great Ancestor', the progenitor of Taumako, son of Te Atafu the Tongan. The latter married a daughter of the Ariki Kafika of the time, the 'chiefly woman'. Their son, accompanied by his mother, brought one day a present of food to his grandfather, a token of affection not at all uncommon in Tikopia life. The old man said to his grandchild 'Come you and lay it down.' The gift then was continued annually and after the death of the two persons concerned was perpetuated by their descendants, thus becoming symbolic of the tie of relationship between their clans. Irrespective of the individual kinship between the chiefs of Kafika and Taumako, for ceremonial purposes the Ariki Taumako behaves to the Ariki Kafika as a man does to his mother's kinsman, in virtue of this tie of many generations ago. The *ara* is the most formal occasion on which this relationship is expressed. It receives its name, according to the Tikopia story, from the fact that the means of communication between grandson and grandfather was this track running between the temples of Taumako and Kafika. Hence the burden carried along it in later days was called '*te ara*', 'the path'. Moreover the words used originally by the Ariki Kafika have become a set mode of address. Chiefs of later generations, however, have incorporated the title '*Pu*', 'Ancestor', in the speech out of respect to this revered forebear, since the convention is that he comes in person each time as the bearer of the food. This is a figurative concept; it is understood that the actual person concerned is a human being in the flesh. The insertion of this appellation is explained thus by the Tikopia:

His grandfather goes on, goes on till he dies, and then his sons and his grandsons dwell later, and so they use the term *Pu* for him. And so it goes on in this way, another Ariki lives, '*Pu*' then, another Ariki lives, '*Pu*' then. It is held that it is he who comes. No Ariki who lives may have a different name for him, he says '*Pu*' only. But his grandfather of old said merely 'Come you and lay it down', and did not say '*Pu*'.

Respect for the original chief does not allow him to be spoken to merely as 'you', but his name is too sacred to be uttered, so he is addressed as 'Ancestor'. A similar usage obtains in the case of a sea-going canoe belonging to the Taumako clan and named after the same renowned ancestor. Its real name, that of the original man himself, is Rakaitonga; this is far too *tapu* to be bandied about in the mouths of the common folk. The vessel is accordingly called always '*Te Ingoa o Pu*', 'The Name of Ancestor'.[1]

---

[1] The original craft of the name, now replaced by the Tikopia, is in the Auckland War Memorial Museum, as a result of the interest taken by Captain H. Burgess, former master of S.Y. *Southern Cross*, in acquiring specimens of ethnographical importance for public collections. This is the only vessel of its type, the Tikopia *vaka tapu*, to be obtained by a white man, though there are smaller non-

The derivative term '*Pu tangata*', commonly used in addressing grandfathers, men of similar seniority, and ordinary male ancestral spirits, is not used towards this important forebear of the people. To my inquiry as to whether this term was permissible a negative reply was given:

The name '*Pu tangata*' is not uttered because he is of olden time, therefore he is '*Pu*'. Not a woman, not a child may speak at length (i.e. the long form of the expression) concerning him; they speak shortly, they '*Pu*' only. It is prohibited, because he is the chief who originated from among us.

Since this word '*Pu*' is also used to describe other deities of note this progenitor of Taumako is known for distinction as '*Pu Lasi*' ('Great Ancestor'), an honorific title that is specially his own.

After this digression regarding the terms of address which it is proper to use towards this sacred ancestor, and which are in themselves of great importance in Tikopia eyes, attention may be directed to one phase of the gift which throws considerable light on the correlation between the display of food-wealth and prestige in the Tikopia social economy.

Reference has been made to the prohibition against lowering the food to the ground during the time in which it is borne from the one house to the other. This interdiction springs from the sacerdotal importance of the gift and the desire to prevent it from any contamination. It has, however, further implications of an economic nature. If the bearer should stumble or let his burden slip so that any of the baskets touch the earth they are all returned to Taumako, and the members of the clan assemble 'to wait for their ancestor' – that is, to await his appearance in a spiritualistic medium, who will offer comment or give instructions regarding the situation. Then they go out again to the orchards and collect supplies for a second batch of food which is prepared and carried in as before. When the fresh baskets have been brought to the kava house of Kafika and the ritual performed over them the former gift is brought also, but to the dwelling-house, not to the sacred house, and left there to be consumed. This food is rejected by Taumako 'because their ancestor is angry in that his *ara* from Kafika was caused to fall by them'. Kafika thus receive a twofold

sacred canoes in the collections of the Australian National University in Canberra, and the Museum of Ethnology in Cambridge. ('Te Ingoa o Pu' was re-rigged by a party of Tikopia who accompanied Spillius to Auckland in 1953.)

present. It is rare that such an event occurs, but it is not altogether unknown, and the occasions are handed down by tradition. In olden days Pu Oliki of the house of Morava let fall his burden by the way, as also did Pu Resiake of noted memory. In each case a double gift was then carried to Kafika. My inquiry revealed, however, that both times the mishap was premeditated, not accidental; the bearer did not stumble, but purposely let his legs sink down beneath him. And the reason was to be found in the desire for self-advertisement. The Tikopia themselves have a perfectly clear understanding of the matter. When I expressed surprise at the carelessness of the bearer in letting such a *tapu* burden drop the answer was given, 'It did not fall; it was simply made to fall by him. Such is a custom of a wealthy man, because his food is abundant.'

This incident also throws an interesting sidelight on the relation of rank to law in this primitive society. It is not by keeping the law but by breaking it that the man is in a position to demonstrate his superiority, and this is then made manifest by the value of his atonement. It is in fact the payment of the penalty which heightens his prestige. The situation seems somewhat of a paradox, but this is more apparent than real. For the wilful contravention of the social rule is followed by a proud compliance with it, and it is this latter which earns him his reward in the judgment of society. There is the further point, that this is but another illustration of the principle that status begets status. For only men of assured position could thus dare to infringe such a regulation deliberately, with the object of calling attention to themselves. In the cases cited above both men were offshoots of the Taumako chiefly house, one of them, Pu Resiake, being a noted *toa* – a person of strong passions and great fighting power – who consequently could brave the possible exasperation of gods and men. In a mere commoner such conduct would be described as 'desire of boasting', and would be promptly condemned. In addition to the resentment of the ancestor at seeing his rule broken the aspirant to fame might have to reckon with that excited in the recipients of the gift, who are placed in a certain position of inferiority when they come to make their present in return.

The matter of the counter-gift must now be considered. (In order to preserve the unity of the account of the *ara o Pu* the time sequence will be disregarded slightly and the description of the return gift incorporated here, whereas it actually occurred later during the re-furnishing of the sacred houses.) Like nearly all food-donations in Tikopia the *ara* has its *tongoi*, its counter-gift. In this case it was a huge basket of food, prepared a few days afterwards in Kafika and carried over to Taumako under the same conditions as obtained for the *ara* itself. As a point of terminology, when the *ara* is spoken of in connection with the *tongoi* it is often called *fonākava*, a word of generic application to certain ceremonial gifts of cooked food to a chief. As with the initial gift, a great deal of attention is paid to the food. Custom demands on this occasion that it be packed in a large *longi*, a household basket, which is strengthened by strips of fibre torn from the mid-rib of a coconut leaf threaded through the fabric. This forms a network extension in which the enormous package of pudding, breadfruit and taro reposes. The Ariki himself supervises the preparation of the gift very intently, and when it is complete orders it to be carried out under the eave of the house – not through the door, as it is a *tapu* burden – and set down at the entrance of the path to Taumako. Here he performs a simple kava ceremony over it, '*te kava o fafo*', 'the kava of outdoors'.

The bearing of the basket when I witnessed the event provided some moments of interest. It speedily emerged that no-one wanted the task, the reason being that the weight of the load, which is carried in front of the body, places a great strain on belly and arms. One and another of the men present were named, but each had some plausible excuse for refusing. With a view to encouragement an old man pointed out that while the *ara* itself might not be raised aloft on the shoulder, no such prohibition really applied to the return gift, which could be thus more easily handled. This, however, met with no response. At last a bearer was found, his stipulation being that the others should help him to lift the load from the ground and settle it in his arms. This was done, and he started slowly on his way. After a few yards, however, he found that he was unable to cope with the weight, and called for assistance. It was apparent that he was genuinely distressed, and that the precious burden was beginning to slip. A swift consultation took place among the anxious watchers at the end of the path, as a result of which Pa Taramoa, a son of the Ariki, sprang to his side and carefully took the basket from him, including with it the customary stick of green kava, which in default of other means of holding, he carried between his teeth! Thus equipped he completed the rest of the journey in safety. The people of Taumako, of course, as etiquette demands, were quietly sitting in their house during these proceedings; in no circumstances could they lend assistance. When the first bearer returned, somewhat shamefaced, he made an apology for his weakness, but was approved by the Ariki for his action. Better that he should call for help and transfer his load than remain silent and suffer it to touch the ground, which would indeed be the act of a fool! The Ariki added that he would have carried the basket himself if it had not been that he had strained his back a few days previously in lifting a canoe. To my question of surprise – for a chief does not normally bear a burden – he replied that it was quite proper for him to undertake this task. Its associations placed it in a different category from ordinary loads.

The gifts connected with the 'Path of Pu' are not an integral part of the canoe ceremonies, but an adjunct to the *fainga vaka*, by reason of the fish caught during this period. The probability of obtaining a shark, and the general atmosphere of ritual interest which obtains at this time, make it the most appropriate for the *ara* exchange. Its primary importance is in providing a means of reinforcing the traditional link between Kafika and Taumako clans, and that this is effective is seen by the manner in which the personality of their great ancestor forms a real background to the event. I felt that the commemorative aspect of the gift was very strong in the minds of the people of both clans, the interest of Kafika being hardly less than that of Taumako. While to Taumako this ancestor was the founder of their clan, to Kafika he was their greatest 'sacred child', and moreover, through subsequent intermarriages most of the latter could claim kinship with him.

SUMMARY

The sequence of canoe rites in the Work of the Gods has now been described. Their detailed theoretical implications cannot be discussed here, but a brief review of the complex set of performances will indicate important Tikopia religious conceptions.

The most obvious aim of the ritual, it is clear, is to secure fish. But the fish are not wanted simply for human consumption, but to provide the gods with suitable offerings. Thus the ritual has the aims in the first place of bringing the deities once more formally into contact with the canoes made by the tools which they ultimately furnished; in the second place of stimulating the deities to provide the wherewithal for their own worship; and in the third place of strengthening the bonds between deities and the kinship groups associated with them. The seasonal aspect of the ritual indicates too that it is in the nature of a re-dedication of material fishing equipment to its tasks, a re-charging of it with efficacy. And in so doing, the ritual secures that these items of equipment, particularly the canoes, are in fact overhauled and made technically more effective. Moreover, the ritual provides a socially unifying occasion for the Tikopia community as a whole – elders are brought together under their clan chief, and the chiefs under the Ariki Kafika. Occasion is given by specific rites for the exercise of individual privilege, but the total result is an integration in technical, ritual and social terms.

Postscript

In July 1952 I witnessed the canoe rites of the *Ururenga Nga Vaka* (cf. Chapter 13, p. 465) for Tafurufuru of Kafika and Te Rurua and Tukupasia of Taumako (see RM, plates 1*a* and 1*b*). Owing to the food shortage there was considerable telescoping of rites. In particular, the prime sacred canoe Vakamanongi did not have a day devoted to its rites alone. 'Vakamanongi will not fall singly, friend, because the famine is great; the major sacred canoes (*taumauri*) will be celebrated together', said Pa Fenuatara to me. He added 'The (other) canoes will be celebrated or not; it rests with the men, the famine is great. The rites will be definitely performed only for the *taumauri*. As regards the "little fleet", they'll be celebrated or not, famine has fallen upon us, it depends on the canoe owners.' In the event, of the *taumauri*, Tafurufuru was not drawn out of its shed, since the Ariki Kafika was ill and not present to celebrate it, and neither was Te Ingoa o Pu, of Taumako, since Pa Nukutapu who operated it had fever, and was up to no more than lending a hand to his chief. Karoata, of Kafika, was not celebrated at all, though a *taumauri*, because the lineage of Torofakatonga, who operated it, said they had no food for the ceremonial presentation (*monotanga*).

For the four main *taumauri* the special *roi* was prepared. Owing to the food shortage only Kafika lineage itself contributed the food for Tafurufuru. The Ariki Taumako was helped by contributions from kinsmen and one of his elders, but one of the baskets of *roi* left overnight in the oven was stolen, to the horror-struck surprise of most people since this was a flagrant breach of taboo.

Monotanga were sent as follows:

(1) From Tafurufuru to the Ariki Fangarere, and to Vainunu lineage.

(2) From Te Rurua to the members of the chiefly lineage of Kafika in Taramoa – where Pa Fenuatara was living. This basket was divided by Pa Farikitonga (son of Pa Fenuatara), Pa Karua and Pa Nukuva (as representatives of other branches).

(3) From Tukupasia to Pa Fatumaru – said to be an ancient custom.

(4) From Vakamanongi to the Ariki Kafika, living in Teve, and consumed by about eighteen members of the household.

Thus, though also the inter-clan and inter-chief presentations were curtailed, even during the famine some recognition of ritual obligations was made. The Ariki Taumako observed that the coconut problem was not so grave in the trade-wind ritual cycle as in the monsoon cycle as the 'coconut kava' was not then performed over canoes.

4

The Work of the Yam

The principal vegetable foodstuffs of Tikopia are held severally under the control of the chiefs of the island by a traditional division, authorized by a myth,[1] by which these foods were partitioned among the principal gods. By this title the Ariki Kafika has jurisdiction over the yam, the Ariki Tafua over the coconut, the Ariki Taumako over the taro, and the Ariki Fangarere over the breadfruit. Each chief has his own set of rites to secure the prosperity of his food, and much of the Tikopia religion is of the type of a fertility or nature cult.

The yam (*ufi*) is a constant element in the food supply of the Tikopia. It is not so important from the economic point of view as the taro, the breadfruit or the *pulaka* (*Alocasia* sp.), but it is of value because of its durability, since it remains sound for a long time in storage. There are several varieties, one being the *ufi vaea*, with a short tuber rather bigger than a large potato. It is this which provides the special ritual type known as the *ufi tapu*, the sacred yam, which is not a distinct variety, but a certain sanctified set of tubers and their product. The other types can be planted and harvested at will.

The yam is the premier food product in ritual, and its rites alone belong to the seasonal cycle of the Work of the Gods. Those of the taro, coconut and breadfruit are performed separately. The ritual of the yam, indeed, is considered as the heart of the Work. The yam is conceived as the property of the Atua i Kafika, and represents his 'body'; the rites performed by the Ariki Kafika in connection with it are held to be a perpetuation of the deeds of their principal god. Hence an atmosphere of reverence, and even of awe, surrounds the ritual.

The yam rites comprise two major divisions – those of harvesting and those of planting. The whole round of activities takes about twenty days to complete. In the monsoon season it follows

[1] See my 'Totemism in Polynesia', 1930, p. 296.

the work of the canoes. The initial rite of the yam takes place on the same day as the more important events of the *fainga vaka* conclude, and for a short period the affairs of the yam and those of *anea pariki* proceed side by side. In the trade-wind season the yam rites follow the 'throwing of the firestick', after a few days' interval. In both seasons the rites are the same. In the monsoon season, however, the amount of yams harvested is greater, and conversely, that of yams planted is greater in the trade-wind season.

The following account combines my observations of two seasons' ritual.

THE PLUCKING OF THE REPA

The yam being a vegetable, it is natural that cooking should occupy an important place in the preparation of it as an offering to the gods. The oven used is that in Kafika Lasi. To assist in retaining the heat during cooking, leaf covers are used for all ovens, and those employed here are of special esoteric importance. By the end of each season the covers become very tattered, for they are used for every kava rite, whatever be its object. The opening rite of the work of the sacred yam consists in the renewal of them, and thus religion and practical aim are fused together. The oven-covers are here termed *repa*, from the principal type of leaf used, and the initial rite is *te koto o te repa*, *koto* meaning 'to pluck'.

The making of the covers is traditionally a female task. On the appointed day in the monsoon season ten women, mainly the wives and daughters of men of Kafika family, and of the elders of the clan, assembled in Uta at the house of their chief. From there they moved off through the woods, keeping in touch with one another. The leaves used had to be large and of heavy texture, and they collected not only those of the *repa* itself, but also those of breadfruit and giant taro. Their task was definitely a ritual one. They were invested with a strong *tapu*, expressed particularly in a rule of silence. They were not allowed to hold any conversation with people met in the orchards. Indeed, when it was known that the *repa* was to be plucked that day most people avoided the area. The Ariki Kafika said to me 'Great is the sacredness of the *repa*; not a person may go and call out to the crowd who are plucking the *repa*, no, absolutely not!' Some latitude, however, is allowed so long as due reverence is observed. On this occasion Seremata of Taumako (incidentally, a Christian) was working in his orchard with his niece when the group of women were seen approaching. The girl hid, but the man plucked green coconuts and silently presented them to the women. This received commendation from the Ariki Kafika when he heard of it. 'A good fellow', he said.

When the women had filled their baskets they returned to the oven house and prepared thick pads, by pinning together a number of leaves with short lengths of the mid-rib of the sago pinnule. The completed pads were piled on top of one another, so that a heap three feet or so in height rose from the middle of the floor. 'How many *repa* pads?' asked the chief. A woman answered 'Fifty-seven.'

While engaged in this process, too, the women had to observe certain restrictions. They had to sit quiet in the house while working, and if a man passed by they did not call out to him for news or for betel ingredients or for tobacco, their usual habit. The sanction behind this rule was the same as in the case of the isolation during the plucking of the leaves. It is believed by the Tikopia that these women, while engaged in the sacred task, are under the protection of Te Atua Fafine, the Female Deity, who is the tutelary genius of women. In fact, they are actually identified with her. 'They who are doing the work there, it is she.' I could not obtain a more precise definition of the relation conceived to exist between the women and the goddess. The logical discrepancy between single spirit and multiple representation, for instance, was not acknowledged by the Tikopia, who regarded this splitting of the personality of the goddess as quite simple. Other instances of the temporary identification of human beings with spirits will be given later. In this case since the women represented the Female Deity it was especially prohibited to men to have speech with them.

When the pile of *repa* pads was finished it was covered with a huge taro leaf, and the workers sat round to await the arrival of the Ariki Kafika. He had been occupied with the anointing of his canoes in the beach village, hurrying this on as much as possible. Food was distributed at the end of these canoe rites, but the chief did not wait for more than a snack. 'You eat still; we are going to Uta', he said to the crowd, and hastily bespeaking a couple of assistants, got his canoe brought round to the landing place and paddled over the lake. With him he took the *monotanga* of each canoe celebrated that day. The food gifts were spoken of as if they were the actual vessels. 'How many canoes will be carried to Uta?' was asked. The carriage of these baskets was an illustration of the manner in which prearranged surplus supplies from one rite were utilized to form an integral part of another. For these *monotanga* from Tai provided the food offerings for the yam kava in Uta, and their bark-cloths were used as *maro* for the deities in this new rite. Conversely, advantage was taken of the proceedings in Uta and the presence of the chief at the yam rites to 'announce' the canoe baskets in due form.

On the arrival of the Ariki the kava took place without delay. The baskets were opened out, one being set before his mat for Te Atua i Kafika and another laid by the rear post for Te Atua Fafine. The orange bark-cloths from them were arranged by the chief and spread out as offerings to his main deity with the words:

> That is your vestment my Sacred Chief.
> I eat ten times your excrement.
> Your body, our yam, will be celebrated here tomorrow.

Poroporo, the term translated as 'celebrate', denotes a first-fruits rite performed for any principal crop.

During this and the succeeding ritual most of the women were seated on the *tuaumu* side of the house in the place appropriate to them near the oven. The very fact of their presence in the building at all during a kava ceremony showed that it was a ritual of unusual type, connected with their patroness the Atua Fafine. Normally, as in the canoe rites, though they may take part in the work of the oven, they retreat to the dwelling-house close by when the sacred rites begin, and leave the field to the men and boys. But on this occasion it was their privilege to be present. Still more remarkable several of them actively busied themselves in the various services of the kava. One woman opened the baskets and distributed the food, another, the chief's daughter, acted as cup-bearer. If no male attendant had been present the post of kava maker would also have been filled by a woman. Kafika is the only clan where females can thus officiate at the kava ceremony.

Libations were poured; the first two were for Pu ma, the third for the Atua i Kafika, and the fourth, at the side of the house, for Pu Taufiti, an *atua* of Marinoa mentioned in connection with the canoe ceremonies. In the kava house of Kafika the last-named was the guardian of a small shelf overhead and was not directly concerned with the *repa*, but an acknowledgment was made to him just the same. The first two cups for Pu ma were also a courtesy libation, as these gods were not immediately connected with the yam ceremonies. 'Their own kava is poured simply; they come hither to the yam? No! The yam has only one deity, the god in this family', said the Ariki, meaning by his last statement the Atua i Kafika. These courtesy offerings to the highest gods of a clan were usual, and illustrate an important point in Tikopia ritual – that the kava ceremony in any particular case has a general as well as a specific function. Thus in the present instance while it was a consecration of the *repa* oven-covers to their sacred office, it also contributed towards the wider aim of keeping the high gods in contact with their worshippers.

Though an air of solemnity is usual on these occasions, I observed at one *repa* rite the cup-bearer, a novice, being instructed *sotto voce* by the kava-maker. The latter, a 'son' of the chief, was a wag, and slyly told the cup-bearer to pour a libation on top of the pile of pads. It would have been an act devoid of meaning, and out of keeping with the ritual, but the cup-bearer, in all innocence, happened to mention it to the chief. The old man started in surprise, then seeing it was only a joke, laughed heartily. He told the company, who laughed too, though one woman made a scornful comment.

After the rite the food was shared out among the women, who ate with much chatter and laughter; it was their first proper meal of the day. The chief eats or not as he feels inclined. On this occasion he abstained and chewed betel. The other two men present drank coconut milk, but neither ate. The pile of *repa* was left in position for the rites of the morrow. By the time that the last parcels of food had been wrapped in leaves and the house floor made neat, the end of the day was approaching.

The scene on this summer evening was very peaceful. The quiet was emphasized rather than disturbed by the murmur of the surf on the distant beach. Out in the lake a fish jumped, and a few birds were whistling softly in the woods up the mountain slope at the back. Occasionally the faint tones of a voice came across as one man called to another by the lakeside, his words indistinguishable, while a regular flurry and splash told of a bather out of sight. The women set out with their backloads of food along the narrow path running round the shore of the lake, while the chief embarked in his canoe. Once out from the bank he too seemed to be influenced by the quietness, and squatting in the bow with his back to it, hands clasped round drawn-up knees, sang gently to himself as the paddles softly dipped and gurgled.

FIRST-FRUITS AND THE 'HOT FOOD'

The next day brought one of the most spectacular events in the series of yam ceremonies, not only for the observer, but also for the Tikopia themselves. This was the competitive rite of the *kai vera*, the 'hot food'. It was preceded by a celebration of the first-fruits of the crop, termed the *poroporo mata* since it was first performed over the yam in a raw state (*mata*).

Preparations started early as usual. In the monsoon season by the time the sun was above the horizon, that is before 6 a.m. in our reckoning, about twenty men had gone off to the cultivation on a mountain slope some distance away to bring back the yams. Most of these people were of Kafika clan, but a few from Fangarere and other clans were present also, either because they had wife or mother from Kafika, or from curiosity to see the noted rites. Among them was the heir of the Taumako chief. The eldest son of each chief generally makes a point of attending at least once the most important ceremonies of the other chiefs soon after he has reached manhood in order to obtain an insight into the main religious practices of the whole community. The work of digging did not take very long, each mound being loosened with a stick while the tubers were groped for and removed with the hand. About fifty or sixty yams were obtained. Some of the party dug while others climbed coconut palms to pluck fresh nuts, and one or two collected loads of firewood. The yams of the sacred hillock alone were not touched. On the return journey a certain order of precedence was observed owing to the *tapu* of the crop. The men walked in single file along the narrow path, the bearers of the sacred yams going first, followed by the bearers of the coconuts and then by the remainder of the party. The way had to be left open for them by all other traffic, and the ordinary folk of the villages took care to keep out of sight during their passage. But their task is accomplished so early as a rule that no-one else is abroad, and the paths are in consequence uncontaminated. I myself saw that the regulation was regarded seriously. For after watching the digging of the sacred yams in the trade-wind season I came down the hillside to talk to a man who was up a palm gathering coconuts. When our conversation was finished I started off down the path, but was softly hailed by him and asked politely to step aside and allow the yam carriers to go first to the house. This I did, and a little later they appeared, passing without a word, and not even looking at us as we stood close at hand. This was a great contrast to the usual freedom of Tikopia manners, for passers-by are always expected to exchange salutations; failure to do so implies that a person is either angry or, as in the present instance, engaged on a sacred mission. In the trade-wind season three men only formed the digging party. One of them, son of the chief, complained that 'the yams had been planted down to the realm of the spirits', that is, they had been set in too deeply, and that therefore the crop was poor.

At this particular period the Ariki was still living in his house in the beach village. On the morning of the yam digging the members of his household ate an early meal of cold food from the oven of the day before, but the Ariki did not eat, practising a ritual abstinence. Soon he took his canoe and went over to Uta, there to await the arrival of the working party. These set down their burdens outside the entrance to the temple. They squatted around, talking and chewing betel. The women were inside the oven house. Each had doffed her ordinary skirt and wrapped herself in a brand-new one. No garment that was soiled or dirty was permitted for the work which they were about to perform, the everyday long narrow strip of bark-cloth used as a belt alone being retained. Here again the women were held to impersonate the Female Deity, and this, in conjunction with the sacredness of the yam rites, required from them a ceremonial cleanness.

Firewood was broken up and the oven started, a work which had to be performed by the men alone, while the women sat around and chewed betel. On this important occasion the direction of affairs was assumed by the eldest son of the chief. The order was given for a couple of men only to remain to prepare the oven while the remainder were invited to go and sit in the temple in order to make a good show for the kava. The reason for this was that the gods should be satisfied with the attention paid to their institutions.

The first rite of the morning was ' *te kava a niu* ', 'the coconut kava', so called because for it were used the nuts brought with the yams. The Ariki had bathed, had donned a fresh bark-cloth, had the charcoal stripe applied to his forehead and tied the *kasoa* round his neck. The charcoal stripe in this case was essentially a mark to distinguish the rites of the yam from those of the ordinary kava. The Ariki said of the yam ceremonies

They are divided off as different from the kava, they are not made naked to be just the same as the kava, therefore they are separated apart. When I go and plant, I shall also put on the *pani*.

By not being 'made naked' he meant that they had this extra touch of decoration applied to them.

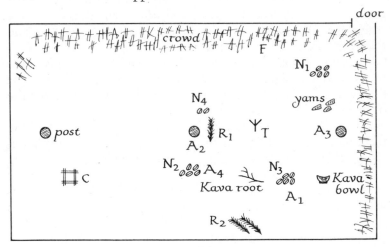

FIG. 4. Kava of the Coconut

A 1, chief in usual seat; A 2, chief at centre post; A 3, chief sits facing yams, with back to post; A 4, chief sits before pile of coconuts; C, bamboo crate; N 1, coconuts in first position; N 2, coconuts as offering; N 3, coconuts from which libations poured; N 4, coconuts offered near centre post; R 1, new coconut frond; R 2, old coconut frond; T, wooden stage

Thus arrayed the Ariki went over to the temple to perform the rite (Fig. 4). The usual seat of the chief was on the side of the building nearest the lake shore. There he took up a bundle of aromatic leaves placed by his side, arranged it in his left hand, and grasped a bottle of coconut oil in his right. Picking up also several fronds of cycas he went over to the huge centre post of the house. Sinking to his knees he laid the cycas down and poured a few drops of oil on the leaves. Then standing up to his full height he

raised the bunch above his head and with swift energetic movements rubbed it up and down the surface of the post, bruising the
leaves and impregnating the house with their pungent scent. As
he did so he recited the formula of the *kaukau pou*, directed to promote the welfare of the land and to avert sickness. The invocation
was addressed to the Atua i Kafika, to whom the central post
belonged.

> I eat ten times your excrement, Mapusia!
> Your post will be anointed on this morning
> Anoint with power
> Anoint for welfare
> Swept away be epidemic disease from your crown
>   of the land.

The cycas fronds were then laid on the coconut leaf mat which
extended up to the base of the post on the north side; this was the
memorial mat of Te Atua i Kafika. The old fronds from the previous season were removed and laid on the 'adze house' supporting the sacred adzes used in the canoe rites. These fronds were
sacred from their associations, hence, as it was said, 'they are not
carried and thrown away at random; that is their depository from
of old'. The Ariki went then to the end of the house near the
entrance doorway and sat with his back to the pillar there, facing
the pile of yams. He recited another formula, very short, appealing
for formal confirmation from other chiefs and his elders for the
'body' of his deity dug that morning, that is, the tubers. He concluded with an appeal for their fecundity. This invocation was
termed '*te fakasao o te ufi*', 'the sanctioning of the yam'. The
Ariki murmured:

> Pa Fangarere, Satinamo (Pa Rarovi), Pa Porima, Pe Tavi,
> Sanction me you (all)
> To your body, Mapusia
> Of which this is the morning of its consecration here.
> Fertilize the share of the sacred yam
> Fertilize the share of the yams of Fangarere
> Fertilize the share of the yams of Porima
> Fertilize the share of the yams of the whole assembly of elders
> *Marie!*

The term translated as 'fertilize' (*fi*) has the concrete meaning of
'sprinkle' or 'shower', but in the above formula bears the more

abstract connotation. On the second occasion on which I witnessed the yam ceremonies the recital of this formula over the pile of tubers was forgotten for a time. Suddenly its omission was recalled by someone and the Ariki was advised. He was annoyed both at his own slip and at not having been reminded sooner. 'Why did you not call to me before?' he asked sharply of the crowd, who remained sheepishly silent. The piece of ritual had then perforce to be undertaken out of its turn.

At the conclusion of the celebration of the newly dug crop the Ariki returned to his seat. Immediately afterwards the bundles of yams were taken out to the oven house, save only for a pair of tubers which were hung up on a bar at the far end of the building as an offering to the deity. 'The seed tubers of the Atua i Kafika' they were called. More aromatic leaves were brought to the Ariki, together with oil, and with them he smeared his chest and upper arms, after which the Ariki Fangarere did likewise.

The scent of the bruised leaves is pleasing to the nostrils and for this reason the practice is much favoured by the Tikopia at their dances. The esoteric use of the leaves is parallel to that in everyday life: since its savour when applied to one's body makes one agreeable to other human beings, so also it is to be expected that it will render one agreeable to the gods. And the chief as the foremost medium of communication with the gods was the most appropriate object for its application. A statement on this point is 'the anointing of the god that he may have desire towards the Ariki, his floor mat. But if the perfume and the oil are not applied, then he will act disgustingly towards the Ariki.' The mention of the Ariki as the floor mat of his deity seems curious, but it is comprehensible when it is realized that it is an expression of his formal abasement, similar in thought to the statements of 'eating excrement' in formulae. More precisely, it refers to the belief that the Ariki serves in his own body as a resting place for the god when he comes to attend the ceremonies in which he is invoked. If this body is not made sweet for his arrival, then he will be angry and wreak evil upon the chief and his family, spoiling their crops or visiting them with sickness.

The next portion of the rite was the recital of the formula over the kava stem which was brought in through the small door at the end of the house specially reserved for it, and aligned with its root towards the centre post. Crouching over it the Ariki held up the end and recited a long invocation which began on this occasion with an appeal to the father of the chief, then proceeded back through his ancestors to the principal gods. The kava stem when removed was not left near the house, but was carried down to Takerekere and laid on a stone slab there at the side of the path. Gifts of areca nut and betel leaf were thrown towards the central post for the Atua i Kafika. Then came the cry of 'carry the offering'. A bundle of coconuts was deposited near the post on the lake side of the house, and the Ariki seated himself before it with reverent mien, his arms folded and head bowed. Libations of kava were brought to him and he poured them with a special procedure, the same as that adopted with the *raurau kumete* (see *infra*). The libations were to: Pu ma; the Atua i Kafika; the premier god of the Ariki Fangarere; and the ancestors of the Ariki Kafika, in this order. An essential feature of the ritual on this occasion was the piercing of the eyes of green coconuts and the shaking out of their contents on the appropriate floor-mats as further libations to gods and ancestors. This was termed 'the pouring of liquid of the gods', while its object was 'the despatching of the yam', apparently a ritual mark of its transition from the soil to the oven. The distribution of the coconuts for food and drink among the twenty-eight men assembled and the apportionment of the areca nut indicated the end of the ceremony, and the subdued atmosphere gave way to talk and laughter.

Such was the *poroporo mata*, the sacralization of the raw first-fruits. Its object was to announce formally the crop to the gods, and so open the way to a free use of it by the community in general. The explanation from the Tikopia point of view was: 'The yams of the *poroporo mata* are brought hither first that the kava of the chiefs may be made first, that people may go and dig their yams for food, the kava of the chiefs having been completed beforehand.'

The other chiefs and certain of the elders of high rank in the other clans had a ritual interest in the yam to the extent that they also performed a 'yam kava'. This was merely a repetition of their ordinary kava procedure, and had none of the intricacy of ceremonial which took place in Kafika. As was the custom the Ariki Kafika waited until the other chiefs assembled in Uta on this morning, and then began his rites. The Ariki Taumako delayed till he heard the reverberation of the kava clapping in Kafika, and then proceeded with his ceremony, while the Ariki Tafua (in former days) and the elders who were in most distant houses out of earshot allowed a short time to elapse after their arrival to ensure the priority of the Ariki Kafika before they began. The precedence of the real controller and main officiant of the yam rites was thus maintained. This brief rite concluded the share of the elders in the yam operations for many days. The Ariki Fangarere attended the proceedings in Kafika, and behaved like a member of that clan. 'He goes with the crowd; he eats the hot food.' His own separate yam kava was not performed till later.

A PRIMITIVE COMMUNION FEAST

Preparations were then made in the oven house for the spectacular ritual of the 'Hot Food', in which use was made of the yams ceremonialized in the temple. All the tubers were scraped by women, who, clad in their new skirts, sat in a line on the *mata paito* side of the house. This was contrary to ordinary etiquette, and so emphasized the ritual nature of their task. So situated, they were in a definite order of precedence. First was 'the woman of the sacred yam', that is, the wife of the Ariki Kafika, next came the woman of Fangarere, then those of Porima, Tavi, Fenumera and lastly of Rarovi. The yams were served out to them in this order. Leaves were laid on the floor and each woman scraped the refuse from her tubers on to them. The work was done in haste, not in the usual leisured style of the preparation of food: as each yam was finished it was thrown down and another grabbed up. The work was *tapu* and there should be no loitering. Then the women retired to their own side of the hut again. While on the *mata paito*, engaged in their scraping, they had been invested with supernormal attributes. That was the reason why each wore her new skirt, 'because it is the Female Deity who has decorated herself and is going to prepare things'.

A count was made of the number of men who would be present at the rite, and a yam was set aside for each, with a couple of small ones in addition as offerings to be placed in the *raurau kumete*. There were thirty men in all at the monsoon season's rite, but fewer at the trade-wind rite. The great anxiety of the Ariki and other men on the latter occasion was that the yam crop should be sufficient to meet the needs of the kava and other rites on this day. I heard the question asked repeatedly 'Will the kava be attained or not?' They feared the god, who otherwise would punish them for what he deemed to be their neglect or meanness. Said the Ariki:

His kava is made to be sufficient; therewith he is lauded. But if it is not made weighty towards him he is angry with us, he is bad; he holds that we have gone to bring the crop here, but instead have left it and hidden it from him in the bushes.

If the true yam crop should suffer disaster, as occasionally happens, then *taumako*, a species of yam with a prickly vine, regarded by the Tikopia as a different food type, is called into service. In the last resort *pulaka* or even taro would be used, but this would only be done in extreme circumstances and might not be acceptable to the deity.

When the tubers of the 'hot food' had been picked out, the remainder were cut up in ritual style. Pads of the *repa* made the previous day were taken one by one from the heap by a male worker and held while another, sitting on *mata paito*, sliced the yam on to them, a few pieces to each. The *repa* were piled on the floor. After the fire in the oven had burned down the stones were spread out, and the entire tubers put in. The *repa* pads were lifted one by one and their contents shot into the oven, the pieces of vegetable not being touched by the hand. According to one opinion this was merely because they were slimy, but according to the Ariki, it was in deference to their *tapu*. Still, as they were handled freely both before and after, this observance, which was real enough, was probably just an element of the rite as a whole, without special significance in itself except as it gave the affair greater solemnity. The new *repa* pads were used to cover the oven, this being the first occasion on which they were called into service. (The rite of the sliced yam was termed *kava sofe*.)

The rigid division of labour by which the women scraped the yams and the men cut them up and set them in the oven was one of the ritual features of the day. Both sexes usually take part somewhat indiscriminately in the work of cooking, but on this occasion the oven was *tapu* to women. The actual origin of this differentiation is unknown. It is a traditional feature of the ceremony correlated with the fact that the food prepared therein is peculiarly the property of the great Atua. 'We do not know why it is sacred; it has been the custom from of old.'

Shortly before noon the oven was uncovered and the food removed. The *raurau kumete*, a shallow wooden dish of unique shape (sketch given in Chapter 5), which was the special sacred property of Kafika, was washed in the lake. By custom it was lined with two leaves of *rau tea*, a plant with large oval light-green foliage. When the tubers intended for it had been placed inside, the dish was carried to the main building and set in its ritual position on the seaward side close to the centre post. This represented the portion of food offered to the gods Pu ma, and its position so far in advance of the other offerings near the most sacred part of the house was held to be the reason for using the special receptacle instead of the ordinary leaf platters.

Leaves are prohibited; they are not carried forward. The portion in front is done with bowl alone.

Preparations were made for the 'hot food' by providing each person in the house except the Ariki Kafika with a large leaf of *rau tea*, which he held cupped in his hands. An air of tense expectancy now gripped the crowd and speech was only in whispers, for not only was this one of the most sacred rites of Kafika, but it was one carried through in great haste and demanding alertness from every participant.

A basket had been filled with the yam tubers, smoking hot from the oven, in the other house. Suddenly as the men sat quiet, each holding his leaf between his knees, the bearer of the yams burst in through the doorway, and at once began to distribute his load. The tubers were not dealt out in the ordinary polite style at the feet of the assembly, but hurled out to them as the bearer strode along the line. The first yam was thrown to the man seated at the kava bowl, and the distribution then proceeded as fast as possible without a break till the far end of the house was reached, when the participants were all served. Each man on receiving his yam caught it deftly in his leaf-covered hands, bent over and at once with a great show of haste began to bite, or rather mumble, at it – for it was still piping hot! This was in the nature of a race. The first person to be successful in swallowing a mouthful of the scalding food made a sucking noise or chirrup with his lips (*e miti*), and on hearing this all looked up and laid down their yams. Then there was a general inquiry, led off by the Ariki, 'Who chirruped?' A modest acknowledgment was made, and the identity of the person was confirmed by people on either side of him. Immediately after this another man entered with a basket containing the pieces of cut yam, and began to distribute them among the gathering, while the Ariki seated himself behind the *raurau kumete*.

The kava libations in connection with this were a variant on the usual procedure. The Ariki was seated with arms folded and head bowed, in reverent humility. The bearer of the kava came to him, crouched at his back and held out the cup. Without turning his head the chief reached round with his left hand, took the cup under his right armpit, transferred it to his right hand, and then making obeisance by raising it to his forehead, poured it out in front. These movements were made so that not for one moment did he avert his face from the sacred presence of the deities, believed to be seated, invisible, in front of him. Four cups in all were poured in this fashion. The first two, emptied near the dish, were libations to Pu ma, Tafaki and Karisi; the third, emptied to the side towards the centre post, was for Nga Matua, the ancestors of the chief, including the most important deity of all, the Atua i Kafika; while the fourth, poured to the front again, was offered to Te Atua i te Uruao, 'The God in the Woods', who was the principal deity of Porima but was invoked in this building by the Ariki Kafika. Morsels were pinched from the yams in the dish and thrown to these gods, after which the Ariki returned to his former seat. An assistant emptied the *raurau kumete* in a ceremonial manner by a quick jerk of the leaf lining, which laid the contents on the matting. The dish itself was brought back and put in place on the *toko tu*, a wooden staging which served as the repository for sacred objects. A second journey was made to collect the yams, one of which was given away as an ordinary food portion, while the other, wrapped in its leaf covering, was laid in a small food basket belonging to the chief and hung up on the *toko tu*. The people then ate their shares of food.

Immediately the rites of the *kava sofe* were over the tension relaxed. 'The kava of the gods is finished', someone said. People began to talk over their experiences. They told how their lips were burnt, how tears came to their eyes, how they made puffing noises in the endeavour to cool off their burning morsels. One man described another who, unable to bear the heat of his mouthful, spat it out again. The bearer of the basket complained that his fingers had been 'cooked' with handling the tubers, and wondered plaintively if they would blister. Laughter arose from a group of youths who had watched Pa Sukumarae. This clumsy man, instead of catching his yam, had let it roll away from him under the eave of the house, whither he crawled to redeem it. The sight of his large bare posterior thus elevated from under the wall at this moment was too much for the restraint of the young. 'We are laughing at Pa Sukumarae, just like a dog going outside', said one of them, while another described his actions as being like those of a cat pursuing its rat!

The clue to this curious ceremony lies in its relation to the principal deity of the Kafika clan. Besides being called the *kai vera*, the hot food, this rite is also termed the *kai tapu*, the sacred food. (Some idea of the importance and significance of the 'hot food' ritual to the Tikopia may be gleaned from the fact that the same name *te kai tapu*, the sacred food, is applied by them to the Christian service of Communion, which they themselves regard as being of somewhat the same nature.) The rite is sometimes also called the *kava tapu*, the sacred kava, though actually the kava proper does not appear in it. In being classed by the Tikopia as a form of kava ceremony, the essential point is that it is an act of communion with the god and commemoration of his institutions. By tradition the *kai vera* was set up as a rite by the Atua i Kafika while he still lived upon earth; he wanted, it is said, a kava which would be different from those normally celebrated. According to the Ariki Kafika, the Atua ate only hot food; nothing cold ever touched his lips, hence the ceremonial *kai vera* follows his personal habits. And to this day he himself attends the rite to observe that it is duly carried out. The Ariki Kafika does not have a yam given out to him, though there is one remaining in the basket. He refrains because as he sits there watching the scene, he is believed to be the god in person come down to witness his kava. The Ariki himself made a statement to me which is worth quoting in full from the light it throws on the concept.

Tera ku nofo kuou; ko ia; sise kai; ku tuku ke fai tana kava e Te
There have sat I; him; not eats; has left to (be) made his kava by the
Fanau. Kuou tera te atua ku au o nofo i a kuou. Ku au ki a kuou,
Brethren. I there the god has come to sit in me. Has come to me,
e faia te ariki palasu; mai mua rei, te Ariki Kafika te

because the chief weighty; from formerly then, the chief Kafika the
ariki palasu. E mafa i a ko ia.
chief weighty. Is heavy from him.

In freer translation 'I who have sat there am him; he does not eat
since he has left his kava to be made by the Brethren (the family
of principal clan gods). I there am the god; he has come to sit in
me, because I am the chief of importance. From olden times the
Ariki Kafika has been the chief of prime importance since he has
been rendered so by the god.' This statement is somewhat confusing in its sudden transition from first to third person. The meaning
is that for the moment of this sacred rite, while the body and flesh
are still those of the chief, they are acting as a vessel for the god
within, who is thus seeing out of the eyes of the Ariki and reposing
within his limbs. 'The body is that of the Ariki but the eyes glaring
out of it are those of the god' is the explanation which Tikopia
give. The reality of this psycho-physical dualism is firmly credited
by them. It finds further expression in the organized institution
of spirit mediumship, of which the present case is hardly to be
reckoned as an example because of the transient nature of the manifestation. The Ariki in his statement gives the reason for the selection of himself as a vehicle for the deity – he and his ancestral line
are the premier chiefs in the island, because they are the direct
descendants of the great god.

The chirrup is taken as a sign by the god that his kava has been
properly performed, and on hearing it he at once leaves his human
resting-place. 'The chirrup is given, the god then goes, his kava
has been good.' It is held that the person who first makes the token
sound that he has consumed his portion of hot yam is in special
favour with the god from this time forth. '*Ku tu i te Atua*', which
may be translated as 'He stands in with the god.' When the idea
is grasped, that the Atua is present in person to watch the perpetuation of the rites he set up, then the gravity of the occasion, the
tension of the participants and the eagerness of their competition
can be understood.

To have chirruped at the 'hot food' is a mark of social distinction, though the winner receives no material prize, and does not
appear to take great personal pride in his achievement. When the
first-comers arrive back from Uta in the afternoon the question
is put to them 'With whom did the honours stand?' In the monsoon season it was Pa Porima, but it was said that usually Pa

Fenumera, of Fangarere, was the victor. This man was said to have cheeks and throat 'like iron'. I myself participated in this as in the other rites of the Work, and in the trade-wind season, by accident more than by design, I managed to chirrup first, and was awarded the honours. Pa Fenumera was then absent, but meeting me some time afterwards he said with a smile 'I hear that you won in the "hot food". You would not have done so if I had been there.' I saw no reason to challenge this claim.

An evasion of obligation may occur in even this most sacred ceremony. It is said that some men, shrinking from the possible pain involved in biting into the steaming hot yam, only make pretence thereto, bending over and moving their empty jaws until they hear the chirrup which relieves them from further action. It does not appear, however, that such a shammer would ever dare to utter the sound himself.

When a novice attends the 'hot food' he is always instructed by his elders how to act – to spread his *rau tea* leaf in both hands; not to hold it up, but to keep it down in the lap; to open his legs out so that the end of the yam may not burn his calves as he bends over it – apparently a real danger – yet not to draw up his knees, a position which is always forbidden in sacred buildings. Contrary to the usual custom of the kava, small boys are not encouraged to attend and the Ariki sent away his grandson, saying that the sacred kava was coming on. The food itself must be finished completely by the men who take part. It is *tapu* and may not be eaten by women and children. The yams of the *kava sofe* do not matter, so that when the remains are being handed over to be parcelled up and taken away for later consumption it is always stated which are from the tubers of the sacred yam.

After the meal was over the Ariki Fangarere and the elders present were sent off by the Ariki Kafika to perform the kava in their own houses. In this, a simple ceremony, each man invoked his own personal deities for the general prosperity of the people. Meanwhile the younger men left to pursue their own affairs, and some of the seniors remained for a time in the house with the Ariki Kafika, smoking, chewing betel and talking leisurely. 'The kava of the gods is finished' was the sententious observation which closed the proceedings.

The fundamental importance of the ritual of the Hot Food lies in its function as a kind of elementary communion feast. Not only does the god of the yam, the Atua i Kafika, attend the ceremony in person, watching through the eyes of his chief, but the yam itself which is consumed is the actual body of the god, partaken of in common worship.

The succeeding rite, the *kava sofe*, is so called since the yams have been sliced (*sofe*) in pieces.

A sample formula used at the *raurau kumete* rite – the actual words recited vary according to the wish of the chief – was given me by the Ariki Kafika.

A. As the cups of kava are poured he says:

> (First cup):
> Your kava, Tafaki!
> I eat ten times your excrement.
> Turn to your kava
> Stand firmly in your Kafika.
> Your kava has not been attained
> Make it great from yourself from the sky
> Cover over firmly the sacred necklet (the wind)
> Let calm fall
> For a good word for us from the crowd
> Lest we be laughed at.
> Pour out your calm on the crest of the land
> And press down the sacred necklet.
> Be it dragged by you two to the north,
> To go drifting calmly there.

> (Second cup):
> Your kava, Karisi!
> I eat ten times your excrement,
> Turn to your Kafika.
> Stand firmly, you.
> Scatter out the head of the land (the breadfruit)
> For the making of your rites.

> (Third cup):
> Your kava, my Sacred Chief
> I eat ten times your excrement.
> Turn to your standing place,
> Stand firmly in your land.
> Uncover welfare from your soiled foot below.

B. (As food offerings are thrown):

> Your food, Pu ma, Karisi and Tafaki!
> I eat ten times your excrement
> Let the earth fruit.
> Turn to your kava,
> Let the yam root
> For the filling of the *raurau kumete*,
> For your food portions,
> And the throwing of your food.

> Your food, my Sacred Chief.
> I eat ten times your excrement.
> Let a bit of a shoulder-burden spring up here for you;
> Scatter out the head of the land for the making of your rites.
> Stand firmly, you.

The general purpose of the formulae is to induce the gods to give fine weather at sea, and plenty of food on land, for their own sakes as well as for that of men. It will be noted that breadfruit as well as yam is requested.

The precise injunctions in these formulae may vary considerably, and only the chief knows exactly what he has said on any occasion. According to Pae Sao a tradition was that in olden times the yams harvested were of great size, and when the people ate them they became ill. Nowadays, he said, if a man finds such a huge yam and eats it, after a time sickness seizes him. His skin becomes bright and shiny, and his limbs swell. This affliction comes to commoners only, not to members of the chiefly families. Hence the formulae recited by the Ariki Kafika are intended in part to ensure that the yams will be good for the belly of man, said Pae Sao. But there is no specific mention of this in the examples given above.

THE RITUAL OF THE UNSCRAPED YAMS

The next day there was another characteristic yam ceremony, performed not indoors but out in the open air, on the main path that ran along the lake shore. A few feet nearer the water was the site of a small house named Takerekere, long since subsided into the lake, and in former days the rites took place within its walls. According to the old men another name for this house was Tauapepe. Vestiges of its posts were last to be seen about twenty years before. Two mats were laid across the path, one for the Ariki Kafika and another, some yards away, for his kava bowl.

To begin the proceedings the early morning kava was performed; it was called also the cold kava, because the yam hung up the day before in the small basket on the stage in Kafika house was taken for the food offering. After the libations of kava were poured the yam was returned uneaten to its place in the building. Meanwhile assistants had collected raw food from adjacent orchards and this was placed inland at the door of the house Rarovi,[1] till the kava was finished. Food was cooked; ordinary yams and the variety called *taumako* are generally used, but if these are scarce then taro, *pulaka* or even breadfruit are pressed into service. A bunch of green coconuts was also brought. Shortly before the oven was ready the men plaited from coconut leaf small open baskets like flat dishes. These were termed *lingilingi*, and were simply made with the ends tied in knots. They were six in number to serve as platters for the food offerings to the gods which were set out on the open path. The first two offerings towards the lake side were for Pu ma, one being for Tafaki, the other for Karisi. These were known as *taumafa i mua*, 'portions in front'. The next, in line with them but further down the path, was for Te Atua i Tafua, and opposite this on the inland side of the path was that for Sa te Kamali. This last are deities whose habitation is the adjoining shrubbery, which grows where once stood the building known as Te Kamali, a temple of the Rarovi family. In its generic reference the word *kamali* means 'a sacred place'. The offerings just mentioned are *taumafa i muri*, 'portions behind', being of lesser importance. The final two platters were set before the Ariki Kafika and the Ariki Fangarere, who were sharing the same seating mat, and were offerings for their chief deities in each case, i.e. for Te Atua i Kafika and Te Atua i Fangarere. When the kava had been prepared in the bowl a libation was first poured by the cup-bearer to the initial offerings. He looked at the Ariki Kafika who murmured:

> Your kava there Tafaki
> Turn to your kava in Takerekere.

Another cup was poured beside the second offering and a similar formula was addressed to Karisi. The cup for the Atua i Kafika

[1] See plan of Uta in *We, the Tikopia*, 1936, p. 386.

was handed to the Ariki who poured it himself beside the food at his feet and said:

> Your kava there Mapusia
> I eat ten times your excrement
> Turn hither to your kava in Takerekere.

The Ariki Fangarere did the same in his turn. A fifth libation, to the Atua i Tafua, was accompanied by the words:

> Your kava there Raki-te-ua
> Cause the coconuts to sprout
> For the preparation of your food offering.

To the last cup, poured beside the inland platter, the Ariki said:

> Your kava Sa te Kamali
> Turn your backs
> And face the direction of the gods.

In comment on the last two formulae it may be noted that the Atua i Tafua is tutelary deity of the coconut, so that it is appropriate for him to be asked to increase its fertility. Other phrases of the kava may be added to supplement those given, according to the wish of the Ariki and his conception of the needs of the land at the moment. On one of the occasions when I was present the weather had been unsettled for some time previously and the appeal was completed by the request for a calm to fall. The desire expressed for the *atua* of the Kamali to turn their backs, which is against the usual principle of kava invocations, is due to the fact that they are regarded as beings of malignant power, whose interest in human affairs is to be discouraged. Hence they are given food and kava and respectfully asked to face the other way and let their attention be occupied with the things that the other deities are doing! As a conclusion to the ceremony a coconut was pierced and the liquid shaken out by the Ariki at the head of his seating mat as a further libation to Pu ma.

A hearty meal was eaten after this rite, for it was *tapu* to eat cold food in the morning before attending, and this was the first oven of the day. This rule also applied in the case of the 'hot food' of the day before, and it was said that anyone infringing it would have become ill.

The characteristic feature of this ceremony, and one which was extremely unusual at Tikopia meals, was that the tubers of yam and *taumako* which constituted the food had been cooked with the rough dirty skin still on, and had to be peeled with the fingers into the platters. Each man had to do this for himself before beginning to eat, even the Ariki, whose food was normally dressed with care by other hands. Such was the custom of Takerekere, which might not be altered. There was according to the Tikopia a verbal association between the name of the glade 'Ta-kerekere' and this peeling of the food which had been 'cooked dirty' (*tao kerekere*), though they did not know if there was any etymological connection. The peelings and other debris from the meal were left in the platters, and these were not thrown away at hazard but carefully set in line at the side of the path. There they remained till they decayed, no passer-by daring to touch them, since they partook of the sacredness of the place. As each season comes round a new set is deposited, and by that time the former has practically disappeared.

The kava of Takerekere is very sacred. Only the Ariki Kafika, the Ariki Fangarere and two or three necessary assistants attend, and other people take care not to intrude. Though the spot where the rite takes place is actually a portion of the main route round the lake, and is daily in constant use, all travellers avoid the neighbourhood till such time as the ceremony is over, and utilize the less convenient subsidiary tracks which run through the bush at the back. The path is spoken of as being blocked, but there is no material obstruction set in the way; it is merely the respect of the people for the ritual. 'They know that we have begun to sit here; the path has become sacred', said the Ariki Kafika. Passers-by later in the afternoon look to the side of the path and see the platters there; thereupon they tell anyone they meet on the road 'The kava is finished', and all know that the road is once more open to traffic.

SANCTIFYING THE SEED TUBERS

On the first day, when the yam crop was dug, all the tubers of Kafika were removed and used as food with the exception of a few at one end of the *puke tapu*, the sacred hillock which was the principal object of ceremonial during the planting. These few remained till the day after the Takerekere rite, when they were taken out and the little hut known as the *fare ufi* (see later) was razed to the ground. These residual tubers were the sacred *pupura*, the basic seed for the planting six months hence.

The cultivation of the sacred yam involves a considerable amount of care and foresight. There are two crops in the year and the planting of one season is not done with the tubers from the crop just dug, which would not grow, but with those from the crop of the preceding season. Each family which has a proprietary interest in the yam has always to keep a set of tubers in storage to provide for its maintenance. The yam which comes to fruition in the trade-wind season is not of great quantity, but the yam harvested in the monsoon demands a large party of workers to perform the principal tasks.

To fetch the seed tubers, only one or two men were necessary. They made a special journey up to the cultivation early in the morning, and on their return to Uta put the yams into a new coconut leaf basket, well plaited, and laid over them bunches of aromatic leaves from the fragrant *akoako* and other shrubs. The basket was then stood on the *mata paito* side of the house in token of its sacerdotal importance. This rite was termed *te utunga pupura*, literally 'the filling (of the) seed'. The exact application of these words is obscure. *Utu* in this phrase is an archaic expression. When questioned on the matter Tikopia said 'It is ancient speech, from former times.' Normally *utu* means 'to fill' as of a water bottle or other vessel, so that in this case the term supposedly refers to the filling of the basket with its seed tubers.

The ceremonies connected with the sacred yam are almost inseparable in some aspects from those relating to the renovation and re-furnishing of the temple of Kafika, in that theoretically the same god controls both, and practically their rites take place in the same place and overlap or even merge on certain days. The *utunga pupura* for instance with its attendant kava is also made the occasion for the 'carpeting' of Kafika Lasi, the oven house which is the common scene of operations.

After the seed tubers had been brought in food was prepared. The Ariki went alone to Kafika Lasi where three freshly plaited mats were lying folded, still green. He donned his cincture and taking up one mat laid it on the shelf at the back of the house, the repository of the sacred adze, the *maro* of the gods and other sacred objects. Sprigs of aromatic leaf were then scattered on the new mat, after which the seed tubers, old and new, were taken from their baskets and laid on it, and more leaves were put over them so that they lay in an aromatic bed. This rite, 'the putting to sleep of seed tubers', was accompanied by the recitation of a formula to the Atua i Kafika.

> I eat your excrement my Sacred Chief
> Your body will be put to sleep
> Gods and men have become habituated to your body
> Which will be put to sleep
> Poured be your calms on your crown of the land.

The object of the ritual is the preservation of the seed from contamination, the sanctifying of it to its vital purpose of propagation. In Tikopia terms 'Such is the custom from former times; it is made sacred, it is not left below to become soiled, it is deposited up above.' The yam, being so closely connected with this premier god of the land, is conceived as his body, a piece of symbolism which is largely verbal and does not appear to any extent in the actual performance of the rites. It is implicit to some extent, however, in the 'putting to sleep' (*fakame*) of the tubers on the shelf. *Fakame* is a ceremonial term used also for certain aspects of birth and incision ritual. The word *mē* (substantive and verb) with its causative *fakame*, and their reduplicatives *meme* and *fakameme*, undoubtedly bears the basic idea of 'sleep'. It carries with it, however, also a derived meaning of 'to lie down'. If a person is sitting in a house talking and seems tired his host will say '*Me ki raro*', 'Lie down', not necessarily to sleep, but merely to continue the conversation from the more convenient reclining posture. It is possible that there is something of this secondary meaning in the *fakameme* of the seed tubers.

This ritual act is of considerable sacredness, so that noisy conversation, which is deprecated at any time during the yam ceremonies, now becomes especially undesirable. Elderly people sometimes remark to young folk 'Don't go about making a noise! The body of the deity is put to sleep.' The importance of the yam as the 'body' or material symbol of this powerful being is emphasized in another way. When a quarrel occurs about land boundaries the disputants are very prone to express their own feelings and annoy their adversary by slashing down growing foodstuffs such as banana trees in the debatable area. From this destruction, however, yam plants are immune, '*e tapu*', it is forbidden, since they represent in a sense the Atua himself, and wantonly to hack them about would be to incur his anger.

It is a feature of Tikopia ritual that the specific is made also to serve the general purpose. The formulae recited usually include in their phraseology appeals which transcend the immediate object of the occasion. Among other matters that of weather is one which calls for most frequent entreaty by the Ariki for intervention on the part of his gods, and phrases to this effect are interpolated freely into all ritual addresses. The request for a calm is perhaps the commonest of these. After setting the seed tubers in position the Ariki took up another of the new mats and laid it in position on his ordinary seating place. Here again he made another appeal for fine weather.

> Let the calm fall, Ancestor!
> Listen to the fact that your body has been put to sleep
> That the sun may shine that it may be clear for your mat.

The amount of emphasis laid on the desire for clear calm weather depends of course on the conditions prevailing at the time. During the yam ceremonies of the monsoon my account of one day's events includes reference to the variety of ways in which the Ariki repeated appeals of this nature. Phrases desiring calm weather were recited with great frequency, not only in conjunction with the various libations of kava, but rather noticeably, between them when no actual rite was in progress. Each time the introductory word *to* (fall) was uttered with great vehemence, in such a way as to leave no doubt as to the reality of his sentiments, and in my diary I find recorded at this time 'Seas heavy; no fishing on Ravenga coast', which provides the explanation.

After the 'carpeting' ceremony ended the Ariki remained alone in the house, in contemplation, till the time for the kava arrived. This was a joint celebration for the yams and the re-laying of the mats. Inland in the dwelling-house a special basket of food was being prepared. This was termed *te longi o te ufi* – the household food basket of the yam – though actually it was not a *longi* but a *popora*, a large basket, that was used. Each lineage of the yam group, i.e. the chief divisions of Kafika and Fangarere clans, made one of these and brought it to Kafika Lasi house where it was set in the middle of the floor for the kava to be performed over it. Each family prepared its food contribution in its own house, independent of its fellows. The kinsfolk of the Ariki Kafika made their oven in the dwelling-house adjacent to the sacred buildings, the people of the Ariki Fangarere were busy in the house Fangarere a few yards away, while the people of Porima and Tavi made their *longi* in their respective houses in Uta, and those of Rarovi and Fenumera in their dwellings in Tai. It was optional to do the work either in the lake houses or the beach villages; in the latter event the food baskets were brought over by canoe in time for the ceremony. Where so many households were concerned, tardiness in some quarters was inevitable, and much energy was spent by the Ariki and his family in obtaining news of the progress of the various ovens, and finally in sending out messengers to hurry up the laggards. At last all were assembled and the ritual began. The food basket of Kafika stood foremost and alone, while those of the rest were in a pile in rear, as befitted their inferior status. As this rite was an important link in the chain of yam celebrations the kava invocation was recited over the stem of the plant, and the orange vestment, significant of the appeal to the Atua i Kafika, was spread. The meal when the rite ended was the first of the day for the Ariki, though it was almost evening. By fasting before the sacred ceremony he maintained its taboo unimpaired.

When the offerings to the gods were set out from the baskets care was taken to open every package so that all contributed. This ensured also that any particularly good parcel of food was announced before the deities, a matter of some importance. For if the best food was not formally set out they might imagine that it was being purposely withheld, become offended and retaliate by storms, droughts or other afflictions. One day, when a minor yam kava ceremony took place, cups of sago pudding were prepared in the oven as a delicacy for the Ariki and myself, but through some oversight on the part of his son were not laid first before the deities. They were served direct from the oven to be eaten after the ritual. On discovering the cup in his food basket, the Ariki became annoyed. 'What will the *atua* do when they look at it, look at it, and see that it has not been put with the offerings?' he remarked severely.

One of the features of the 'food basket of the yam' ritual was the exchange of contributions. Each basket brought was re-allotted under the direction of the Ariki as in the case of the canoe rites. Another custom of the day, an extension of the food exchange, is that any person may, if he so desires, prepare a special basket termed *fonokava*, in addition to the basket of the yam, and present it to the man of his choice. In such case the gift will be reciprocated (*tongoi*) either the next day or, if the recipient has already heard of the intention, on the same afternoon. Such a *fonokava* is made from motives of respect for the person to whom it is given, or in order to gain his favour for some project.

LIFE IN UTA

From this day onwards till near the conclusion of the season's rites the Ariki Kafika does not return to sleep in the beach village but remains in the dwelling-house in Uta, whither the women of his family carry his roll of bedding. He may walk abroad to visit his orchards, or go over to Tai to take part in torchlight fishing, but he must always return immediately afterwards to his house in Uta. '*E tapu*', 'it is prohibited', for him to reside again in Tai till the Work of the Gods is completed. It is customary for some of his elders to follow his example, but they are not always willing to do so, since Uta is a quiet spot, far from the bustle and excitement of the coast, and the mosquito problem is unusually acute. When the question of joining him was raised by an old man in the monsoon season the Ariki politely said that he left the decision to the elders concerned – 'it is done according to their own thought'. But none seemed eager. Pa Rarovi, the principal man of rank, whose place it was to give the others a lead, sat pulling a banana leaf to strips and looking at the floor, while the others stayed silent and gazed uneasily about them. At last one of the relatives present interjected 'Shall the Ariki come and stay here alone?' This also drew no response. Desultory conversation was renewed, and the upshot was that none of them came. This shirking of obligations irritated the Ariki exceedingly, though he voiced his annoyance only within the circle of his own family. In the trade-wind season the same thing occurred. On my way home from Uta one evening I happened to meet the Ariki Tafua and told him this. Though a Christian the old chief at once became very indignant. 'It is their place to do so! Shall the Ariki be left to carry on the Work of the Gods alone, with only his family to help him?' he grumbled, and more to the same effect.

Though the Ariki Kafika has great influence and controls the religious affairs of the island his word is not always strictly obeyed.

It was pointed out in Chapter 2 that the 'Throwing of the Fire-stick' imposed a taboo on the land so that people could no longer sit in groups on the beach in the evenings. This prohibition, how-ever, is not always upheld as the days go by and the Ariki goes away to reside in Uta, especially if the weather becomes oppres-sive. Then the people, who at this time of the year like to go and sit under the trees above the sand to get the cool breeze, are apt to begin to get careless about the observance and congregate again, especially the younger and more thoughtless of them. Their action is not necessarily approved by others with a greater sense of responsibility. 'Their mind is like that of children' it is said. If the Ariki happens to notice them then they scatter at once and dis-appear into their dwellings. If he catches sight of them unob-served he goes to his house, seizes a club and returns, brandishing it and shouting 'May your fathers eat filth! You go back to your houses!' upon which they vanish, terrified. Such incidents are not common, but I was told that they have occurred. 'That is the cus-tom from olden times' it was said.

The Ariki obeys no special food restrictions at this time, save that he refrains from eating in the morning before certain of the most sacred rites lest he pollute them. But the present Ariki Kafika, being of a highly strung nervous temperament, sometimes fasts for a couple of days and nights before such an event – not from religious asceticism, but because in his own words 'I think of the Work that is to be done, and all food is bitter in my stomach: it has no flavour.' Often too, he told me, he does not sleep during the night prior to an important ceremony. Such abstinence is purely a matter of personal constitution.

Life is very quiet in Uta during these days. The Ariki has his mat spread in the house, and with his winged head-rest within reach, spends much time talking and chewing betel. When he tires he lies down and pillowing his head continues the conversa-tion. His wife busies herself with plaiting or other household work while other members of the family come and go in the course of their usual duties or sleep in the middle of the floor.

In these long hours in the quiet of the forest glade, undisturbed by the busy village life, confidence was established and talk flowed easily. Sitting cross-legged with my back against a house-post, or reclining on a pandanus mat, I was able to glean many things from the chief regarding the gods and religious secrets of his forebears.

OWNERSHIP AND CLEARING OF THE YAM PLOTS

The day of the *utunga pupura*, the digging of the seed tubers, marked a stage in the yam ceremonial from which the next important rite was calculated. This was the *autarunga māra*, the clearing of the cultivation in preparation for planting. It took place on the fourth day after the bringing down of the seed tubers. It may be more or less according to the decision of the Ariki. The intervening period is counted by nights, the usual Polynesian method of reckoning time. I was told 'Will be three nights, three nights; will be four nights, four nights.' The people concerned in the yam operations simply awaited the command of the Ariki. They said 'We sit, we listen only to the chief, to be definite.'

During this time there was a daily rite, termed *te kava a ufi*, yam kava, of minor importance. It resolved itself into a family affair of the immediate Kafika household, the main feature being the cooking of the food. The Ariki himself, of course, took no part in the oven-work, so every day one or other of his sons came over to Uta and assisted by a younger relative or two and by any women staying in the house made ready the food. When the oven was uncovered the Ariki was summoned to the oven house, the offerings were set out, the kava bowl was prepared and the usual libations were poured. These were offered as follows on one typical occasion:

Cup 1 to Pu ma
    2 to Pu ma
    3 to Te Ariki Tapu (Atua i Kafika)
    4 to Pufafine (Female Deity, by post)
    5 to Raki-te-ua and Sakura (Atua of Tafua and Taumako)
    6 to Nga Matua (the chiefly ancestors)
    7 to Pinimata (female deity of Porima)
    8 to the *fuanga* (*atua* of chief's mother's family)

Food offerings were thrown out to Futi-o-te-kere (principal deity of Fangarere, etc.); Tuisifo (an ancestor of special power), and the other gods mentioned.

The chief addressed various appeals to the different gods, asking Pu ma for *manu* that the breadfruit might yield a crop, and Pinimata to calm the waves then breaking on the coast. To his ancestors he appealed:

> Excrete you on the vegetation
> Your kava is not secure.

This last could have been mere formalism, but food was actually getting scarce then. A form of words recited by the Ariki on another occasion to his principal deity ran as follows:

> That is your kava my Sacred Chief
> I eat ten times your excrement
> Your body will be planted away to twine, to root
> That your kava may be assured.

The terms twine and root apply to processes of growth, the first describing the curling round of the tendrils as the vines creep up, the second the formation and enlarging of the tubers below ground. The term 'assured' was thus explained 'that the kava may be heavy', i.e. that it may be important with the weight of offerings.

As a rule there were only about five people present for the ceremony and it was not unusual for a girl to act as cup-bearer to the Ariki. After the kava they joined the others in the adjacent dwelling-house and ate. Only those who constituted the essential minimum for the rite made the effort to attend.

The end of the fourth night saw the initial preparations made for planting the next season's crop. Early in the morning, long before sunrise, parties of men from the Kafika villages on the coast made their way to the *māra*, the cultivation up in the hills, and began the work of clearing the ground as soon as the first light appeared. This consisted mainly in cutting the scrub and undergrowth, clearing it away and pulling up the grass and weeds, work described under the general term of *autaru*. A special term, *tata*, however, is used in connection with the yam activities and is not applied to operations relating to taro or other crops. 'Cultivation of yams is cleared this morning', is the way of describing this stage of the work. Theoretically, every lineage of the yam group should have sent representatives to assist in the clearing, but some people failed to attend. 'It is bad that they should stay behind. It is taboo' was the judgment passed by the Ariki, but no form of compulsion was used, nor was their absence regarded as a grave dereliction of duty. One absentee honestly gave as his excuse that he understood that there was going to be an interval not of four nights but of five.

A short account may be given here of the various sites utilized for growing the sacred yam. The ordinary yam may be grown in any suitable spot, but the sacred yam by tradition is restricted to five gardens (*vao*), all of which are under the control of the Ariki Kafika and virtually owned by him. Of these three are in Maunga, the high plateau sloping down to seawards on the north side of the island, one is in Nuku, in the fertile land behind the rock pyramid of Fongo-i-Nuku which stands between the Ravenga beach and the lake, and the last is in Uta, high up the mountain slope at the back of the Kafika orchard, under the foot of the cliffs which ring the ancient crater. In these *vao* a certain rotation of crops is observed, the yam never being planted again immediately in the ground from which it has just been removed, and only rarely in the ground of the season before. 'Is dug hither in one season, plant in another season in another place', it is said. Or in another statement 'Has been dug in this season, bring to another cultivation in another season.' The reason for this rotation is quite clear to the Tikopia: it is done to allow the undergrowth on the recent cultivation to grow tall and mature, whereas if it is prepared again too soon the undergrowth will not have attained its full size and the crop will be poor.

Vao is the name given to any considerable expanse of open cultivated ground. It is only when reserved for religious purposes in producing the sacred crop of either yam or taro that it is called *māra*. Of the five *māra uﬁ* one only is planted each season. Four are used freely in ordinary rotation as conditions allow, but the fifth, known as 'Penusisi' and situated at the edge of Maunga at the head of a distant cliff above the sea, is rarely cultivated. Only twice, perhaps, during his period of chieftainship does each Ariki Kafika give instructions to prepare it. The reason, according to native belief, is that this is the sacred *māra* which was first instituted by the Atua i Kafika and planted by him when he originally set in motion the system of yam rites. It is the prototype of yam cultivations, so to speak, and to crop it frequently would be a cheapening of the ground which he made sacred.

Each *māra* is acknowledged to be under the control of the Ariki Kafika, who maintains it in fief, as it were, from his god. 'That which is done is his' the people say in reference to the Ariki and the cultivation of the yam, meaning that he is ultimately responsible for any activities in connection with it. At the same time, though the chief controls the cultivation as a whole there are a number of individual plots therein, which are held immediately by other lineages of his clan. The ground is cleared as a whole by the working party, but in planting each lineage with an interest there prepares its own section. Thus in a description of the *māra* it is said: 'The single cultivation is cleared; they go and plant, one man there, another there. The yams of the Ariki Kafika there, Pa Fangarere there, Pa Porima there; Rarovi, Fenumera there. Each stands in his standing place. The same allotment is made season after season; no plot is abandoned. When a man dies, and his sons remain, they go then and stand in the place his yams used to stand. His relatives go and plant in the one yam spot.' For the management of each family plot the head of that group stands in the same relation to the members of it as does the Ariki Kafika to the participants in the entire activity – they plant their portions under his control. Participation of people as individuals in the yam group is quite voluntary, but it is obligatory on the major lineages to keep up their traditional interest. The people of Kafika clan alone – including here Fangarere which is ceremonially considered as part of it – have plots in the sacred yam ground. A man of another clan, however, if he is sister's son to the Ariki Kafika may come and plant yams in the plot of the Ariki by virtue of their kinship. On the day of the *poroporo mata* this man goes and digs the larger portion of his yams, brings them to the ceremony and places them with the rest. The remainder he takes out on the day of the *utunga pupura* and carries them to his house for food or to be stored for seed.

The specific ownership of the yam plots will be further considered in connection with planting.

THE SLICING OF THE SEED

Not long after dawn on the same day as the cultivation was cleared, while the working party was still returning, the rite of cutting open the yams was performed by the Ariki. A special mat was laid down on the *mata paito* of Kafika Lasi and on it were set a couple of tubers and the small basket containing the rest of the seed yams from the season before. The Ariki, after bathing in the lake, donned a new cincture and seated himself on the mat facing towards the eave of the house. With a small knife,[1] in former days

---

[1] The Ariki Kafika and other men denied a statement made by John Maresere

a shell of a bivalve species termed *kasi*, he cut the tubers into pieces suitable for planting. Some were severed across but the majority were sliced lengthwise (*fāi*), an operation from which the name of the ceremony is derived. As he wielded the knife the chief murmured softly

> My Sacred Chief!
> Your body will be sliced away on this morning
> Slice with power
> I eat ten times your excrement
> Settle on my head.

Here in addition to the appeal for success in the undertaking he invites the deity to descend on to his head – a request which implies abasement on his part, since the head of a chief is the most sacred portion of his body, and also a desire for the favour which such an act would show. It has already been pointed out how the Ariki is regarded, almost literally, as the seating mat for his deities; they utilize his body as a medium through which they may revisit the world of men.

Meanwhile a younger relative kindled the oven. He then brought a pile of *rau tea* leaves and carefully scraped out the flesh from each piece of yam on to a leaf, leaving a thickness of half an inch or so next the rind. Each rind was laid at the side of the Ariki, who took it up, scrutinized it carefully, then put it down at the head of the new mat in the place of respect. These were the seed to be planted shortly. The Ariki was careful that each piece of tuber had its 'eye' (*mata*). The mature dry yam which was beginning to shrivel slightly was the type desired for the seed, he said, and showed me, as the best, one in which the sprout had 'broken', i.e. had appeared. Some other tubers which were immature or damp were unwelcome to him, since they would not grow so well.

The pulp from the tubers was wrapped up to make three or four small leaf packages, which were then placed on the hot stones of the oven and covered over. Aromatic leaves were strewn over the seed, the mat of which was pulled under the eaves to be out of the way. The Ariki then returned to his sleeping mat to await the

(W. H. R. Rivers, *History of Melanesian Society*, 1914, vol. i, p. 317) that it was taboo to cut yams with a knife. They said such a prohibition had never existed. I certainly saw the knife used freely by them.

progress of the oven. After an hour or so the attendant went to
uncover it, and the Ariki, still lying down in his hut, called to him
'Son! Is it cooked?' 'It is cooked' answered the young man. A rite
of importance then took place in the temple. The leaf packages
were brought from the oven and laid in the *raurau kumete*, and the
kava was performed. Afterwards the leaf packages were shared
out among the few people present, but the Ariki Kafika and the
Ariki Fangarere did not eat. The food, which was simply the
cooked pulp from the interior of the seed yams, tasted very much
like a saltless oatmeal porridge, and the portion was hardly large
enough to be a meal. The eating was primarily a ritual affair. The
rite was termed *te kava tapu*, being more than usually sacred. 'The
food which is scraped is not given to the children and the women,
hence it is called the sacred kava; it is eaten only by big persons
(i.e. by adult men).' It will be remembered that the same prohibition applied to the yams of the 'hot food' which was also a
kava tapu.

   Shortly afterwards each Ariki went to his own house. Their
families, as well as those of their elders, were busy during the day
in preparing another 'yam basket' of food similar to those made
four days before. Towards the end of the afternoon these were
brought along to Kafika Lasi for the kava to be performed over
them. The Ariki entered, inquired if the elders were all assembled,
and when this was so began the ritual. Turmeric was smeared in
broad bands round his arms and waist, a sign that the kava was of
special importance. This was due to its association with the slicing
of the tubers for seed, an operation which, besides being the
figurative cutting of the body of the Atua, was critical for the fate
of the future yam crop. When the kava was over the baskets of
food were exchanged, and a meal concluded the activities of the
day. In all there were only ten people present at the trade-wind
season's rite.

   A humorous touch occurred at one of these functions. A small
boy carrying a big basket came along, and was questioned by the
men at the doorway as to its origin. Satisfied they told him to
enter and set it down, 'on the mat at the back of the house' added
the wag Pa Te Arairaki. The boy started forward innocently, but
pulled up at the sight of a broad grin on the faces of those around.
The mat indicated was the seating place of the Ariki, and the
thought of what he would say on entering to find a fat basket of

food occupying his position fairly convulsed the crowd with laughter. Pa Te Arairaki then tackled the youngster again. 'Does the basket contain a fish?' 'No!' answered the boy, 'none were caught by us last night.' He was then berated with mock seriousness. 'Why haven't you put a fish in the basket? When the food is distributed no fish will be given to you people.' At this threat the boy grinned, since he knew that this at least was all pretence.

RITUAL PREPARATIONS FOR PLANTING

Early in the morning after the clearing of the yam plots the rite of *soani autaru* was performed. I did not see this rite, but was given the following description of it. In the clearing of the *māra* a single shrub has been left untouched in the middle of the field. The saying among the working party is:

The crowd! Clear the ground but leave a single tree for the *soani* of the yam.

And before leaving the field people ask to make sure

Where is the tree which will be left for the *soani* of the yam?
There it has been left standing.

Before sunrise a man arrives at the cultivation, and with a single stroke, if possible, cuts down the shrub and leaves it lying on the ground. A good swinging blow is used that the shrub may fall with a crash so that the deity may hear from the heavens, it is said. Then the man gathers a load of coconuts, together with breadfruit or other food, and returns to Kafika where a simple rite takes place. I attended this with six other people, offerings being made of the coconuts, from which libations were poured when the kava was finished. Later the oven was prepared and when ready in the afternoon the ordinary minor kava was performed again. Appeals were made to the gods primarily for coconuts, then scarce, but since the sea was calm no reference was made to it.

The actual object of this rite is ill-defined. Not even the most well-informed men, including the Ariki Kafika, could throw much light on its origin. The Ariki described it as 'the assisting of the clearing process'. He added 'It is done only to be correct; it must not be done wrongly.' The word *soani* may be a derivative of *soa*, to assist, but is best translated in descriptive terms of the act accomplished. It is 'speech of the yam alone', i.e. it is not used in any other context. In practice it conveys the idea of a secondary or supplementary action, finalizing that which has been done. An analogous rite on the day following the planting of the yam is called *soani to* (*to*, planting) and consists of a similar visit paid before dawn to the cultivation by one man to bring away the sacred digging stick.

Great emphasis is laid in the *soani autaru* on the arrival of the performer before the rising of the sun. This is one of the commands laid down by the Atua i Kafika. Point is given to this injunction by a tale, which forms part of the background of the yam ceremonies. An account of it will help our understanding of the significance of the *soani* to the Tikopia.

Many years ago a man named Pa Ravoro of the house of Vaerama was delegated by his chief to the task of the *soani autaru* at a certain season. In the morning he overslept and while he was still running hastily along the path to the cultivation saw that he would be caught by the sunrise before he could reach it. He was some little distance away when he heard the crash of a falling tree and recognized with alarm that someone – clearly not human – had preceded him to perform his neglected work. Turning to flee in fear, he was struck on the head by a flying stone which gashed his forehead and felled him senseless to the ground. Some time later he recovered, to tell the story in the village. His escape was said to be due only to Te Atua i te Uruao, The God of the Woods, his own family deity, who had taken it upon himself to perform the belated task, and so save his descendant from paying the penalty with his life. Had he not done so in time the man would have fallen a victim to the vengeance of the Atua i Kafika, who, as it was, merely signified his anger by casting the stone at the hapless laggard.

The actor in this little drama came from the lineage of Porima – to which Vaerama belongs – and ever since that time, when for any reason there is danger that daylight will surprise the messenger of the *soani autaru* still on the road, a man from that lineage is sent. It is believed that as the original culprit was protected from a tragic fate by his own deity so once again the god will step into the breach and hew down the tree in time. If a man from Kafika family should go late, since he has no immediate deity to interpose between himself and the outraged god of his clan it is held that he will have to pay the full penalty. It is said, however. that nowadays there is little danger of the messenger being late; people know the story and so they 'sleep wakefully only'.

The shrub left standing must be a fine large specimen; one of the *asonga* or *repa* species is usually chosen. According to Pa Teva there is some idea of a connection between the excellence of the shrub and the vigour of the succeeding crop, but this was denied by the Kafika folk. When pressed for further explanation they merely admitted the curious nature of the rite and appealed to tradition as their guide. The function of the rite is simply a further emphasis upon the sanctity of the clearing of the ground, one of the series of acts which marks the importance of the yam.

The remaining ceremonies in connection with the sacred yam are interspersed by others which celebrate the re-carpeting and re-furnishing of the sacred houses. Thus in the monsoon season the day of the *soani autaru* of the yam by Kafika marks the introductory rite of 'sunning' the aromatic leaves for Resiake, the temple of Taumako. For two more days the ceremonies of Resiake continue, and on the last of these the Ariki Fangarere makes kava for the mats of his temple Vaisakiri. The next day is a very busy one throughout all the community, for most of the ancestral houses of the prominent families are re-carpeted then, and food gifts from each have to be carried to their respective chiefs. Moreover the thatch is pinned together for the repair of the temple of Taumako. The following day sees the re-carpeting of Taumako by its own clan, and of Nukuora by Kafika and Fangarere, while preparations are made for the re-carpeting of the Kafika temple. These various events will be dealt with in detail later in their appropriate chapter; in order to avoid confusion the rites of the yam are here followed to a close. This brief reference, however, and examination of the Programme (Chapter 1) will enable the reader to appreciate the complexity of the ceremonial cycle of worship, and the amount of organization and labour needed to carry out each item of the Work correctly and in proper order.

The yam ritual moves in stages approximately four nights apart. Thus four nights usually elapse from the time of the *utunga pupura* to that of the clearing of the cultivation; four nights pass from this to the time of burying the seed rinds; and four nights more are counted till the cultivation is burned for the morrow's planting. Sometimes for special reasons the interval is lengthened or shortened by a day, but *po fa* (four nights) is the basis of calcula-

tion. For this regularity and symmetry in the yam ritual, tradition
is the only reason assigned.

During the days succeeding the *soani autaru* the kava of the yam
was made regularly each afternoon, while the seed rinds covered
with their aromatic leaves lay on the mat at the side of the house.
This yam kava was of the minor type, as already described.

The next event in the procedure was the 'burying' of the seed,
which took place on the afternoon of the day on which Nukuora
was celebrated. This operation of burying – a literal translation of
the native term *te tanu o te ufi* – was more of ritual than practical
importance. As soon as the kava ceremony in Nukuora was
finished the Ariki Kafika slipped out alone, put the seed rinds into
a basket and went down to Takerekere. A yard or two behind the
seat which he occupied during the rite of the unscraped yams,
shielded from the path by a few bushes, was a round patch of
earth, covered with stones. After lifting these off the Ariki cut
himself a small digging stick and loosened the earth, then refined
it between his fingers, taking out all rootlets and mounding it up.
Removing the seed rinds from the little basket he placed them
firmly in the soft soil, then laid over them leaves of sweet-scented
shrubs, earthed them in and set the stones carefully on top, collecting every fragment and wedging them together for protection.
This operation was done to promote growth in the seed, though
according to the Ariki no formula was recited for the occasion.
That it had an esoteric significance was shown by the use of the
aromatic leaves spread over the seed rinds, thus rendering them
agreeable to the deities. The burying was *tapu* to the extent that
ordinary people did not come to witness it, though I followed the
chief. Two passers-by, I noticed, seeing the Ariki thus engaged,
stood still with their burdens some twenty yards away until he had
finished. After washing his hands in the lake the chief returned to
Kafika Lasi and confirmed his action with libations to the gods.

The next morning, as an adjournment from the ceremonies of
Nukuora, the kava was made in Kafika temple, when the *raurau
kumete*, the sacred wooden dish, was employed with its characteristic rites. This was a very sacred occasion, the deities invoked being
Pu ma, who controlled Takerekere. The rite was by way of epilogue to the interment of the seed in that taboo spot.

Again the days passed while the yam seed remained in the
earth, each day being marked by its small kava ceremony, and

each night being counted to preserve the proper sequence of events. During the fourth night a working party of women, with a youth or two, visited the cultivation. The fallen shrubs and other debris from the clearing were collected and burnt, and the surface of the ground was picked free from rubbish. Moonlight assisted these operations. This was termed *te sunusununga mara* – the burning off of the cultivation. The workers made their way home before dawn broke and other people could emerge from their houses. The 'vivifying' of the yam, *te fakaora*, a kind of preliminary celebration to ensure success in planting, took place the following day. Food supplies were collected during the morning, a procedure termed *ta fakaora*, and the oven was prepared. Each family group with an interest in the yam cooked the food in its own house, and where an elder was in charge he made his kava there. During the morning the Ariki went down to Takerekere and took out the yam rinds, putting them back into their basket and returning them to the mat in Kafika Lasi. The kava was performed and the seed was then examined finally, some further tubers being added.

THE SACRED RITES OF PLANTING

The next morning everyone of the yam group had to be awake long before dawn, for this was the day of planting. I was told 'the yam is planted in the night' – a statement too near truth for my comfort. The reason given was that 'the yam should be hidden in the woods' before people stirred in the villages, so that the paths might not be contaminated by ordinary affairs. It was said that this was the command and practice of the Atua i Kafika, though no express utterance to this effect was known.

One member of the household was told off to wake the others, but the Ariki Kafika, his responsibility in mind, slept little, he told me, and every now and again observed the position of the heavenly bodies to gauge the flight of time. The moon is one index, and the *fetu ao* (morning stars), Putae in the trade-wind season and Aokapu in the monsoon season, are others.

On each occasion I came over from my house in Faea soon after 4 a.m. When the people of the household had been roused from sleep one man was sent off first with the *koso tapu*, the sacred digging stick, a piece of wood some seven feet long, pointed at both ends, one of which was ornamented by some roughly cut notches.

This implement is one of the most intensely sacred articles in the island. Through its association with the yam, the vegetable food-stuff of primary significance, this digging stick has become as it were the prototype of all instruments of cultivation, the material symbol of agriculture. Like all other objects in this particular context it is regarded as the property, even the embodiment, of the Atua i Kafika, and therefore must be handled with extreme care, and only by persons authorized by the Ariki and at the appropriate time. No women, for instance, would dare to touch it, nor is it probably ever seen by them. It is kept normally at the far end of the Kafika temple, and the custom is to hang a few kava leaves over it in token of its unique value and importance. As the implement decays it is replaced by a fresh one, but as its use is ritual, not practical, it lasts for many years without attention. (When the sacred digging stick has to be renewed, a rite is performed: the chiefs assemble at a large stone in Te Roro, on which the Atua i Kafika is said to have sat after descending with it down the hill, and the new digging stick is stood against the stone.) The stick employed in 1928–9 was very frail, so much so that the Ariki, in handing it over to the man who was appointed to carry it, gave the caution 'That one has become aged; go carefully lest you stumble in the path.' The bearer, out of deference to his sacred burden, had a clean white strip of bark-cloth wound as an extra cincture round his waist and a bundle of scented leaves stuck in the back of his girdle. The significance of these in ritual matters has already been explained. The sanctity of the *koso* required also that its bearer should precede the rest of the working party and go alone. Soon after he had disappeared in the darkness another man was despatched with the *fakaora*, a basket containing food from the oven of the day before to provide the offerings in the cultivation, and following him went a youth with the little basket of seed yams. All these articles were *tapu*, hence their bearers had to proceed apart from the crowd so that they were not contaminated. The rest of the party waited for the equivalent of a quarter of an hour or so to enable them to preserve their lead on the road. Then they followed, the Ariki girt with his ritual bark-cloth, but the others in ordinary costume.

Torches, of coconut frond, are forbidden by ancient rule. (As a special concession when I accompanied the party I was allowed the use of my electric torch, of the beam of which the Ariki was glad to avail himself at times.) If the night is dark the unlucky folk have to stumble along the narrow rock-strewn trail as best they can. When the moon is up progress is easier, though there are still black stretches where the path runs beneath thick trees. A further element of unpleasantness to the Tikopia is added by the belief that ghosts may be abroad.

On the way to Maunga the track lies round the lake shore from Uta, turns the corner at Mori, goes on through Te Roro, opens out for a short space at the glade of Somosomo, then goes through the woods again till it debouches on the beach of Namo under the cliffs of Nuaraki. For a little way all sign of a path is then lost in a scramble over rocks till the foot of the ravine Matangaika is reached, where the track now plain once more takes a steep ascent up to the shoulder of Maunga, climbing over the face of massive boulders. The progress of the party should be such that the first lightening of the sky finds them here, ready for the ascent to the plateau on which the cultivation stands. In the trade-wind season the Ariki noticed as we were approaching Namo that a paleness had begun to creep into the eastern sky above the cliff ahead. At once he hastened his step, and exclaimed to the others 'Hurry! the land has become light!' The statement was an exaggeration, but all quickened their pace so that at the last they were almost running over the shingle and rocks along the shore. The steep pull up Matangaika was done with heaving chest, and the race with the light continued along the narrow muddy path through the cultivations. There were several traditional resting places on the trail to Maunga which were used continually by the people on their way to and from their daily work, and at one of these, beneath a spreading *kafika* tree, the Ariki found the bulk of his people, who had come along the Ravenga coast, and awaited his coming. Relieved to see them all assembled, and having won his race with the oncoming day, the Ariki led them more leisurely on to the scene of their work.

As the sky was brightening before the dawn the party reached the *mara*, to which they had been preceded by the bearer of the *koso tapu* and his comrades. Immediately the work began. They all sharpened the ordinary digging sticks which they brought with them, or hastily cut fresh ones from shrubs on the border of the clearing. The bearer of the sacred implement stood alone and silent at the far end of the field; he had held communication with no-one since leaving the house in Uta. The Ariki put on his ritual necklet of coconut frond, and the black charcoal stripe was drawn down his forehead. The crowd gathered round him at the spot selected, the site for the *puke tapu*, the sacred hillock. This was to contain the special seed of which the treatment has already been described. This little mound served as a focus for the performance of all the yam ritual in the cultivation. The making of it was the first procedure of the planting ritual. The Ariki squatted down with his digging stick held before him, and the others formed a ring and followed suit, their sticks all pointing inwards. The bearer of the *koso* came up and, silently standing at the side of the Ariki, directed his sacred implement towards the same spot. Then the Ariki, squatting thus, recited a short formula termed 'the countenancing of the hillock', to place it in proper association with the Atua i Kafika. First calling on his fellow chiefs and his principal elders by name he invited them to confirm or countenance the planting.

> Your assemblage of elders there give countenance to the
>   body of my Sacred Chief
> Which will be planted on this morning
> Plant with power
> Plant for welfare.

As he concluded the formula he drove his stick into the ground and as he did so, uttered a ringing cry of '*Iefu!*' As one man the crowd too drove in their sticks and yelled on the high shrieking note characteristic of the Tikopia. The bearer of the *koso tapu* laid the tip of it gently on the soil. This potent implement is the direct lineal descendant of that used by the Atua i Kafika when he first instituted the cultivation of the yam, hence arises the need to sanctify by its touch the hillock which is to contain the premier seed. It is sometimes said that the sacred hillock is dug by means of this implement, but this statement must be taken figuratively. The staff is held in too much reverence to be used for actual digging, especially when it is old, since the misfortune of breaking it would be far too serious for any risks to be run. To touch the soil with it is sufficient to establish the contact.

After the preliminary plunging-in of the sticks the hillock was dug properly, while the *koso tapu* was carried away to the side of the field and leaned up against a stout tree. The bearer discarded his ritual girdle and returned to assist in the work. Finally the hillock was made satisfactorily. 'It is good, it is good, is it not?' the workers asked. The Ariki inspected it, then took a piece of yam from the seed basket and holding it in his hands uttered a short formula over it.

> Plant with power your body my Sacred Chief
> May a shoot burst out for you
> That your men may be properly prepared by you
> May your body strike root
> May a hinder-end creep for you
> That your sacred kava may be assured.

The seed was then set in the hillock.

It is very difficult to give an intelligible translation of this formula without departing greatly from the literal version obtained from the men participating. The central thought expressed is that the yam so planted may grow well, and that the Atua may be well disposed towards his human dependants. The yam is referred to as the 'body' of the deity, a concept which has already been explained. 'Breaking' or 'bursting' of a shoot is the term used to describe its springing from the parent seed – the object of this being alluded to in the next line, that it may grow and come to fruition to provide food for men, who will thus be properly looked after by the god whose subjects they are. This control of the Atua over his worshippers is implicit in the expression 'your men'. The next phrases convey the request that the yam may root well. The 'creeping of the hinder-end' alludes to the new tubers, that they may grow rearwards, slowly pushing their way further and further outwards into the soil as they increase in size. The purpose of the concluding line is to clinch the invocation. It asks the Atua to cause the yam crop to flourish, not for the sake of men alone, but in order that sufficient food may be obtained at harvest to fulfil all the requirements of his kava.

The first pieces of seed only were planted by the Ariki; he left the others to be attended to by his helpers at the sacred hillock. The remainder of the party then spread out over the near-by strip of ground, which was that of the Kafika lineage, and prepared the other hillocks which were planted in turn. When the yams of Kafika were finished, the planting of which is by custom the first and common task, attention was turned to those of the other lineages. The party split up and a little group of men began work in each plot. The making of a hillock was a simple matter. A stake was driven in, the soil was burst up, a hole a foot or so in diameter was soon excavated, and the soil loosened. Each family had brought its own seed tubers in a small basket. These were quickly planted and the hillocks mounded up and covered with stones. The people worked with speed so that the clouds in the east were no more than red when the task was well on its way to completion.

Meanwhile certain ritual matters were attended to, under the direction of the Ariki. A couple of leaves of coconut had been cut and laid across the sacred hillock as a screen. A long pole was also cut, and to its upper end was attached the *noa*, a trailing strip of brand-new white bark-cloth. The pole was set in the ground, and in the morning breeze the cloth streamed out like a pennant. The object of the *noa* was said to be to stimulate the growth of the yams 'that the things planted may sprout up above'. Its more direct object, it would seem, is to serve as a trespass notice to people, an announcement of the presence of the sacred yam, which can be seen from a distance. For once the *māra* is planted it is *tapu*, and intrusion except by authorized persons who have business there is forbidden, upon pain of punishment by supernatural agencies. The stringency of this rule of *tapu* I myself observed when travelling with Tikopia in the vicinity. Even a peep into the cultivation had to be made with caution, and there was objection to my photographing the growing yams. The bark-cloth *noa* was compared by the natives to the *matini fakapapalangi* (the flag of the white man) which they had seen on occasional vessels.

The yells emitted at the beginning of the digging need explanation. They signalize the momentous occasion of the passing of the period of most intense *tapu*, now that the sacred yam is once more being safely set in the soil. When the yam is planted on Maunga it is the custom for the crowd to give a series of yells, and from time to time during the work the cry of some light-hearted lad goes ringing across the valley. But in Uta only one yell is given, since the place around is sacred in itself, quite apart from its association with the yam. When I attended the planting of the monsoon season, however, the night was dark and stormy, and rain fell heavily near morning. Most of the party were late, to the indignation of the Ariki, who arrived early and began the work, helped only by a very old man and two youths. (The Ariki Fangarere had turned out, but the Ariki said to him 'Come and sit in the house; I am going to plant the yam.' He thought the old chief had better remain behind.) At the planting the chief cursed freely. 'May their fathers eat filth! Lying things!' he said, referring to the promise of the laggards the night before. When the sacred hillock was dug, he was so annoyed that he let out a second whoop in addition to the customary one. When the party arrived he berated them, and they made no answer, knowing they were in the wrong. Later he said 'We shall sit; not a man will come; the time of the yam is over.' On their return the Ariki was mildly chaffed for his second whoop, and he admitted smilingly that 'it was annoyance only'.

The view from the cultivation in the early morning is one of great beauty. In Maunga the clearing is in an upland field which gives an extensive view over a valley. On the one hand is the peak of Reani, and on the other is a gentle undulating slope leading down to the edge of cliffs which rise three hundred feet above the sea. The land is clothed in smooth patches of taro and clumps of chestnut, *kafika*, *vere* and other trees, with the feathery tops of palms and the fingered leaves of the breadfruit. All is suffused with the soft rosy tints of the early morning light on the clouds. But the Tikopia regards the light only as a taskmaster, and hastens on with his work.

When the planting was completed the various plots of the field were marked off by lines of small stakes. The same order is always preserved. First comes the *ufi tapu* proper, i.e. the sacred yams of the immediate Kafika family, then come the yams of the family of the Ariki Fangarere, next follows that of Porima and the others. The arrangement is shown in the accompanying sketch (Fig. 5). No other lineages have a separate interest in the yam. Those such as Marinoa or Torokinga (as above) which desire to be connected with the ritual, attach themselves to whichever of the *kau ufi* group they are most nearly related and cultivate a portion of that plot. There is always plenty of ground available so that such accessions are welcomed as helping to magnify the importance of the occasion. As already mentioned, single individuals from other clans may also take part under certain conditions.

'The count of the sacred yam' was made, by a simple but ingenious method. To ascertain accurately how many hillocks had been planted, a man took a piece of coconut leaf and going round the plot tore off pinnules one after the other and threw one on each hillock. When each had its pinnule he collected these and counted them. This obviated the risk of missing any hillocks, as might have easily occurred if they were counted by eye alone. In the planting of the yam in the *tonga* (done for the crop of the *raki* season) there are usually from thirty to forty hillocks of the sacred yam, or even up to sixty in some years (there were thirty-nine in 1929) and about the same number in each of the other plots, though these are not reckoned up, being of less esoteric importance. The

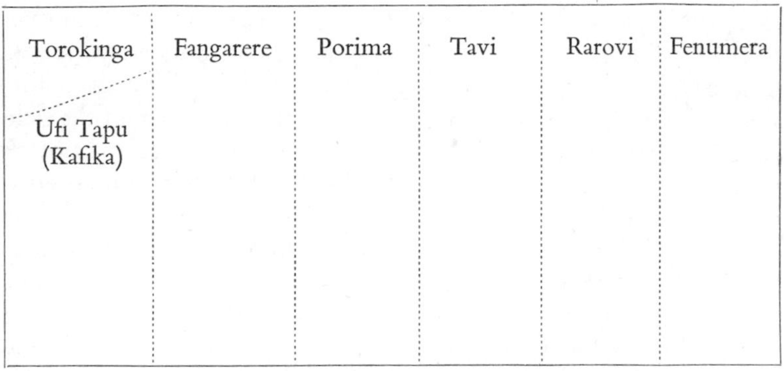

Torokinga	Fangarere	Porima	Tavi	Rarovi	Fenumera
Ufi Tapu (Kafika)					

FIG. 5. Ownership of plots in the sacred yam cultivation
(about 50 by 30 yards at the widest)

field measured about fifty yards by thirty yards. In the planting of the *raki* the cultivation is much smaller, and the *ufi tapu* will be contained in ten to twenty hillocks while some of the other families may not plant at all. The *māra* in 1928 was about ten yards by fifteen, with about twenty hillocks. The reason is that the crop from this season's planting is always poor, being harvested in what corresponds to the winter season (i.e. in June or July) so its main function is that of perpetuating the ritual.

By the time that the last hillocks were finished the sun's rays were beginning to strike across the plantation. Then came the sanctification of the work. Some of the party had been sent to pluck green coconuts from all the orchards near by, a raid of this kind, without distinction of ownership, being licensed by tradition. Several of the nuts were laid on the palm leaves sheltering the sacred hillock; the rest were distributed among the crowd. The baskets of the food brought from the various households were also

set on the hillock. In doing this in the trade-wind season a package
was discovered: opened, it was found to contain the seed of the
sacred yams on which so much care had been lavished, and which
had been forgotten at the last moment! The finding of it caused
little concern; three extra hillocks were hastily made at the bottom
of the plot and the sacred seed planted there. The calm displayed
during this incident threw an interesting sidelight on the Tikopia
attitude towards mistakes in ritual.

The workers drew near and squatted down in respect while a
brief rite was performed. An offering of food was laid out on the
sacred hillock while another with a few coconuts was taken over
to the far side of the field. From one of the coconuts on the sacred
hillock a libation was shaken out by the Ariki, with a short formula to the Atua i Kafika. An assistant at the other side of the field
called 'Here!' pouring at the same moment liquid from another
nut. This was a libation for Pu Fafine, the female deity who resided
on top of the basket containing the sacred yam seed. The phrases
recited invoked success for the planting. The morning's events
were concluded by a meal. After this the party dispersed. The
Ariki with one or two assistants returned to Uta, where the kava
was performed, including the rites of the *raurau kumete*. This was
described as 'the last kava of the yam which has been planted'.

The next morning the rite of *soani to* was carried out, analogous
to that of *soani autaru*, as a supplement to the planting. The sacred
digging stick had been left standing for the night in the field.
About daybreak a man of Kafika family retrieved it – staying the
night if the planting was in Maunga, or otherwise going up for the
purpose. The stick was carried with the same precautions as before,
but by daylight. In the trade-wind season, in former days, the folk
of Tafua, engaged in preparing thatch for their temple, used to
watch anxiously for the bearer, and conceal themselves when he
approached. When returned to its place in Kafika temple the stick
was again hung with fresh kava leaves, and a kava rite, with libations of coconut milk, was performed. The object of leaving the
stick overnight is not clear, but it is regarded as contributing to
the growth of the yam. Tradition is the reason given. 'Plant, plant
the yam, finished, leave the digging stick there; the idea was conceived of old, is taught running down the generations' was the
statement made to me.

The *soani to* completes the cycle of the yam rites, and marks a

definite point in the Work of the Gods. It frees the Ariki Kafika
in the trade-wind season to have a rest for a few days, and in the
monsoon season to officiate at the re-carpeting of his clan temple
Mapusanga. Other chiefs and elders may now begin their temple
rites also. Until the yam is planted no temple or ordinary dwelling
may be re-carpeted.[1] It is *tapu*. If this rule is broken, it is said that a
storm strikes, and houses are unroofed and shaken down. I was
told that this had actually happened; it was due to the anger of the
Atua i Kafika. A hurricane can be explained in terms of a secret
breach of this rule, even though no culprit is known.

CARE OF THE GROWING YAM

The yam rites described are all that fall within the Work of the
Gods. Other operations connected with the growing crop have
ritual also, but this takes place between the seasonal cycles, and
not as a part of them. For completeness, however, they may be
briefly considered here.

There is no precise time at which any of these rites are performed; they depend upon the state of growth of the yam. This
is described by various expressions. The term *kăva* refers to its
growth in general; when the yam is 'dwelling' (*uarangoi*) it has
not yet climbed to the top of the stakes provided for it; when it
has 'fallen down' its leaves have dropped, and the root has grown
down into the earth; when the leaves have dried and fallen off
then it is near the time for it to be dug.

Staking is done after the shoots have sprouted a couple of feet
high, and are showing signs of beginning to curl. It is not done
before since the shoots are 'stiff' and might break off. The staking
is accompanied by the recital of a formula, of which there are
several variants.

One (given me by the Ariki Kafika) which may be used on this
occasion is:

> Your stake will be driven in
> Sever your crown of the land.
> And break out a seed for yourself to climb above,
> For the attainment of your sacred kava.
> Let a calm fall,
> As a sign of your body
> Which will be staked on this day.

[1] But see the correction in RM, 1963, p. 21.

This is an address to the Atua i Kafika to give fine weather and make the yams grow well.

Sometimes the chief does not visit the cultivation, but sends a commoner. This man then recites a formula:

> Recite hither a formula, Pa Kafika, for the stakes
> to be driven in today.
> Smear off the sky,
> Let the eye of the wind be kicked down
> To tumble down below.
> Sever the skies.

This is an appeal for fine weather, through the agency of the chief, who is expected to be exercising his influence with his deity. The chief told me that if the sky is threatening and any yam rites are performed, it will clear up. In another version the chief instructs the yams to climb and hold on to their supports in order that they may be viewed to advantage from the lake, and people may be moved to exclaim in admiration at the sight of them. He says

> Climb up above
> To cling to your bonds
> That you may be seen hither
> From the water of chiefs.

The 'water of chiefs' is the lake, which is regarded as the joint property of the four Ariki of the island, people of all clans being free to set nets there. When people are canoeing over the lake and observe that the yam has grown up well they give utterance to such words as 'Lo! the fine growth of the yam.' After the staking a minor kava ceremony is performed in Kafika Lasi house.

THE STORY OF THE LITTLE HUT

Some time later, when it is observed by the Ariki or some of his family that leaves are beginning to shoot at the base of the yam stems, the yam house is built. This is a small hut, measuring only a few feet in either direction, and roughly constructed of branches and some lengths of sago thatch. It is set in a corner of the field over against the sacred hillock. When it is being built each main structural member is formally announced by name as the work-man puts it in position, so that the *atua* may be aware of what is taking place. This is all the form of words used, the motive being largely to avoid any suspicion on the part of the deity in charge of the yam that someone is surreptitiously tampering with his plantation.

When the tiny house is complete the builders, of whom there are generally three or four, descend to Uta, and prepare the oven in Kafika Lasi. When the food is ready offerings are set out, including one for the Ariki, who is usually absent in Tai. The kava is made in the bowl and the cup-bearer pours out a cup on the mat of the chief, saying as he does so

> Recite hither Pa Kafika for the kava of Pu ma which will
> be poured out.

A second cup is poured, also to Pu ma, followed by cups to the Atua i Kafika and to Nga Matua with repetition of a similar appeal. The idea is that the Ariki in his beach village, aware of what is taking place, will utter the requisite formulae at the appropriate time, without having to come over to Uta for the purpose, since the occasion is of minor importance. Thus the demands of ritual are satisfied by this labour-saving expedient. When this is finished the offerings are wrapped up and carried to the Ariki in his house in Tai. On the arrival of the party he asks 'You prepared your kava bowl?' 'We prepared it', they answer. Thereupon the Ariki throws his own personal offerings from the food brought. If, however, for any reason the members of the working party have omitted to pour the libations then he orders them to go and chew the kava and the ceremony is performed on the spot. In either case *maro* (bark-cloth vestments) are spread for the gods with the brief form of words

> Your maro Pu ma and Mapusia
> Your yam house is built today.

In Tikopia theory Pu ma do not actually attend the yam rituals, but deference is shown them, their *maro* are spread and their kava poured since they are principal gods of Kafika. The Ariki Kafika said that the hut was set up to the Atua i Kafika; it was his, as are all the yam rites. But its origin was given in a legend told me by Pa Fenuatara. A woman and her female grandchild lived in olden times in Maunga and looked after the yam plantations to see that no one stole the crop, dwelling for the purpose in a tiny house in the field. The two of them went down one night to catch fish by torchlight on the reef and while thus occupied the girl smelt the odour of Tongans, their body smell, supposed to be recognizable at a fantastic distance, which is a feature of a number of Tikopia tales. 'Grandmother, Tonga smell rushes hither' she said, but the old lady took no heed. A little later she called out again 'Grandmother! Tonga smell rushes hither.' After several repetitions of this kind the girl was ordered to hold her tongue. The two of them then returned to the cultivation, to Penusisi, and entered the hut to sleep. While they slept the Tongans followed them, and arrived at the spot. They threw a large seine net over the house, completely covering it, and went to steal the yams. Then came a kingfisher, in reality the God of the Woods in bird form, roused the two women and allowed them to escape by lifting up the net. Then he dashed about inside the hut, striking the thatch with his wings to give the impression that the captives were vainly seeking an exit. In due course the Tongans came back, after stealing all the yams. But the kingfisher had managed to conceal the crop of one hillock. On their return they threw darts through the thatch into the interior of the house, meaning to kill and then eat the occupants. The kingfisher, however, called out from inside 'Your prey has gone.' Angrily they burst open the hut, but it was empty, and the bird flew away. Then they went off down to the shore again with their booty.

All that remained of the yam harvest was a single hillock, which became the nucleus for re-propagation, and is perpetuated in the sacred hillock of the present ritual. The little hut of the two women was the prototype of the modern yam house, which is built in the vicinity of the sacred hillock in commemoration of the saving of the yam. The little structure is sacred since it belongs to the grandmother and her grandchild and in reality, according to the Tikopia, they are *atua*, supernatural beings. 'Their shelter-house; it is sacred; no one shall go and enter into it; if he shall enter, he shall be overcome by them', it is said. If a man is rash enough to disregard the prohibition and go inside the hut, then they avenge themselves by having sexual connection with him in his sleep. As a result he falls ill, and may even die. The hut is known as the house of Pufine ma. These two female *atua* are spoken of as grandparent and grandchild, but are also identified with Rua Nea, the well-known pair of malignant sisters who appear in many guises in religious affairs. It is they who inhabit the sacred place of Rarovi, adjacent to Takerekere, and as such are called Sa te

Kamali and are invoked in the kava at that spot. When the kava
of the yam planting is finished the stem of the sacred shrub over
which the invocation is recited is carried down to Takerekere and
put in the *kamali*. The Ariki then briefly addresses these two
women, saying

> Go to the yam which is planted in Matatoa,

mentioning the name of a cultivation in Maunga, or

> Go to the yam which is planted inland,

if it happens to be in Uta for that season. The object of this appeal
is that they may go and watch over the crop, wherever it may be,
and prevent thieving there. It seems curious that the deities thus
summoned to act as guardians are those who in the legend proved
distinctly inefficient at their task, but this is an inconsistency which
is blandly ignored by the Tikopia who believe in their power.

The construction of the little yam house, whatever may be its
historical background, appears then in one sense as an insurance
against theft, by providing a material habitation in the field itself
for the deities associated by tradition with wardship. It is only fair
to note, however, that this is an inference from the situation and
the legend as preserved, and is not based on any direct statement
to this effect, since theft of the sacred yams is a possibility not
greatly to be feared, and the Tikopia is concerned chiefly in building the hut out of compliance with custom.

Apart from staking the vines and putting up the yam house the
only remaining operation in connection with the cultivation of
the yam is the clearing away of weeds. This is done without any
ceremony. Each person who has an interest in the field visits his
plot whenever he thinks fit and grubs out the rank growth which
soon appears there. If he sees the yams of another person choked
with weeds he tells him on his return, 'Your yams have become
overgrown; go and weed!' Then, it is said, the man so notified
will sleep that night and go out the next day and clear his plot.

The yam ceremonial, with its many days of labour, constitutes,
as the people themselves say, the base of the cycle of the Work of
the Gods. Like the ritual of canoes it serves to enlist the omni-
potent gods on the side of an important sphere of economic
activity, it subordinates agriculture to religion and sacralizes it for
the benefit of the community.

Since, however, the yam is not the staple foodstuff in Tikopia, it is difficult to see why it should have premier place in the agricultural ritual. I made inquiry on this point from Tikopia, but got no convincing answer. The Ariki Fangarere gave four reasons for it. The first was because of the appropriation of the yam by the Atua i Kafika. Since he had assumed control of it, and he was the principal god of the land, then its rites took pride of place. This is the usual Tikopia explanation. The second reason was that the yield of the yam is less certain than in the case of the other foodstuffs. Often a man gets only small tubers for his work – hence many men do not bother to plant yams – otherwise it would be a much more important food. Thirdly, theft of yams is common, so again, fewer yams are planted than otherwise would be the case. And fourthly, some chiefs of Kafika superintend the planting of great quantities of yams, while others are content with the 'sacred yam' alone. 'It comes in the energy of the chief; one energetic chief is *manu*; another chief is not.'

The Tikopia argument thus falls into two parts – first that the ritual of the yam is not so disproportionate, if the potential planting is taken into consideration; and secondly, that the traditional character of the rites determines their supremacy. It does seem clear that there is an unexplained historical factor which has determined the situation. The supremacy of the yam ritual at the present day is summed up in the words of the Ariki Kafika: 'No work was to be a close second to it', once it had been initiated by the Atua i Kafika. He added that if another chief than himself attempted to perform rites on the same scale then a hurricane would strike the land. Granted the present position, the yam ritual has two obvious social functions. The first lies in acting as a symbol for all vegetable foodstuffs, providing the major referent for ritual in connection with them. The second lies in its aggregative role, linking the chiefs together by their respective participation, and emphasizing the prime place occupied by the Ariki Kafika. In this way it assists in the maintenance of the political and religious hierarchy.

Postscript

Two themes dominated the discussion of the yam rites in the trade-wind season of 1952 – shortage of food and shortage of personnel.

On the morning when the yam crop was dug one man alone, Pa Timoio of Tavi, did the work; he objected that no young man came to help him, and that in consequence the yams were dug when the sun was already up. With a companion I got to the cultivation in Nuku just as he was coming away. He stopped, without speaking, and no one said anything for a few moments; he gestured silently that he was carrying the yams. Then we began to talk, in low tones, which gradually grew to normal. I took his photograph. He was carrying the yams – about half a dozen – on a small forked stick. He asked my companion, of Kafika, if it would be proper for him to carry the yams across the lake by wading through the shallow portion and so save a long walk – it was taboo to take them by canoe. This was agreed to, and we then went to the Ariki Fangarere, who was impatient to begin the ritual. In the Kafika temple the absence of women from the coastal village was deplored – they had apparently met and decided that the yam crop was not worth while coming over for, and they also resented the fact that the Ariki Kafika had yielded to persuasion and slept in Uta. The shortage of yams for the kava rites was also discussed, and it was agreed that the deficit would have to be made up by coarse taro (*pulaka*).

The rites of 1952 followed the general form of those of 1929, with modifications owing to shortages (RM, p. 12), the most obvious being complete absence of coconuts. Though the group of participants was much smaller than in 1929 their attitude was of the same order: emphasis on the sacredness of the temple and the rites, and on the speed necessary to accomplish the procedures of the 'hot food'. A grandson of the Ariki Kafika was reproved for coming in laughing with a tiny portion of yam in a small leaf bundle for the *kava sofe* rite – p. 153. As I listened to the kava recital of the Ariki Kafika I heard phrases similar to those of 1929: 'your land obeys you', 'let all trees flower', 'let coconuts fruit properly', etc. The flat wooden *raurau kumete* dish (p. 251) was used as before, though this time it contained coarse taro instead of yams. The communion rite of the 'Hot Food' was carried out as before, though this time it was Spillius who was first in the competition (p. 154).

The rite of the 'unscraped yams' (p. 161) took place with minor change in the material accessories owing to shortage of coconut leaf. I specifically checked the food offerings and kava libations and found them to be exactly as in 1929. But in conversation the Ariki Kafika added a few details about the temple that formerly stood at Takerekere. He said the house was controlled by the elder of Rarovi, near whose territory it stood, but it was the Ariki Tafua, as Worker of the Ariki Kafika, who was invited to come and perform the kava there. He added that the temple was abandoned by chiefs of old. Why? 'I don't know; perhaps they objected because it fell in the lake.' His idea was that once the house had subsided into the lake the Ariki Tafua refused to perform there, and the Ariki Kafika took over the ritual obligation. As before, during the sacred rite the path was regarded as 'blocked', though no material obstruction was put in the way. Those having business in the vicinity made a detour. 'They look on us sitting here, and they go away, they do not approach us' said the Ariki Kafika, in similar style to his observation a generation earlier.

For the removal of the seed yam (*utunga pupura*) a grandson of the Ariki Kafika officiated, reciting a brief formula as he pulled out the yams. He handed them in a small basket to a lad of Fenumera, instructing him to carry it to Uta, not to hold any talk with people on the way, and to hurry. The lad in charge explained to me that the yams should be removed at first light, but that we were a little late – as we returned indeed the risen sun was striking the crest of the hills round the lake. On this occasion I noted that the little hut (p. 190) had been constructed close to the set of yam hillocks – the symbolic protective dwelling of the yam guardians, a memorial to watching care.

The remaining yam rites proceeded normally, save for an oversight in not burning off the felled brushwood from the planting area (RM, 1963, p. 23), which embarrassed the Kafika family. But Pa Fenuatara held that the Atua Pouri (of Porima) would do the work after the fashion of spirits, since in any work of the yam he is first on the job. The Atua i Kafika would not be angry since he would know it was a human weakness, not a planned rejection.

(This permissive attitude was probably a modern development.) For the planting of the yams the Ariki Kafika was too frail to attend, so the Ariki Fangarere took his place. It was stated that such was the custom from of old – if the Ariki Kafika was absent on a voyage, or in Anuta, or old as now, the Ariki Fangarere acted as his substitute. This is an illustration of the Tikopia pragmatic attitude towards such ritual gaps.

5

Re-carpeting the Ancestral Temples

Following directly upon the yam ritual come the rites of re-consecration of temples. Here the main features are repair of the buildings by replacement of sheets of thatch, re-carpeting of them with coconut frond mats, and standardization of these practical activities by the performance of the kava. The replacement of mats and thatch represents in a broad way an offering of the products of the land by specific kinship groups to their particular ancestors and deities, and is thus an acknowledgment of inheritance. Variations of procedure occur in accordance with differences in the equipment of the temples, their tutelary deities and the rank of the men who control them. The net purport of the ritual is to bring the gods and ancestors into relation with houses and lands in a manner parallel to that in which they are linked with canoes and fishing.

It is first necessary to explain the nature of the Tikopia temples. They are of the type of the ordinary dwelling-houses and cooking-huts, but usually are somewhat larger,[1] and their importance lies in their specific association with gods and ancestors. They are of three kinds. First, there are a few actual dwellings, in occupation, but having the grave-mats of noted ancestors therein, with one or more of the house posts dedicated to gods of the kinship group. Such is Motuapi, the residence of the Ariki Tafua. His major rites are performed therein, since, now being a nominal Christian, he has abandoned his temples in Uta. Secondly, there are the houses which apparently once served as dwellings, but which have

[1] A plan and description of a Tikopia dwelling has been given in *We, the Tikopia*, 1936, pp. 75–82.

been abandoned as such, and are now visited only for the performance of religious rites. With the burial of increasing numbers of ancestors there they presumably became too sacred for ordinary use. They are known as *fare tapu*, sacred houses. Pae Sao said ' *Fare tapu* are houses which were dwelt in of old. Things went on thus, went on, but coming down to later times, they were not dwelt in. They stand uninhabited, and people go merely to make the kava in them and then disperse.' Thirdly, there are the oven houses attached to the more important of these *fare*, where the food for the rites is cooked. No ancestors have been buried in them, but they are sacred because of the gods associated with the oven, and in some cases with a shelf or other piece of furniture.

The most important temples are controlled directly by the chiefs of the four clans. Their names are: Kafika, Tafua, Taumako (of these clans respectively); Nukuora (Kafika and Fangarere), Resiake (Taumako) and Vaisakiri (Fangarere). They are the primary *fare tapu* analogous among temples to the *taumauri* among sacred canoes. Of the other temples, some are controlled by the major elders, of Rarovi, Sao, Korokoro, etc., and are usually known by the names of these groups; some are controlled by men of lesser status. Whereas in the former the elder performs his own kava as well as less formal rites, in the latter the performance of the kava is the prerogative and function of the clan chief. Hence these houses are known as *paito fai kava o te ariki*. Five of the principal temples, and many of the others also, stand in Uta.

The temples Kafika, Taumako, Resiake, and (in olden days) Tafua, are of outstanding size. Not only are they constructed with a supporting post at each end to carry the weight of the enormous ridge pole (as is the case in an ordinary large house), but they have in addition a post in the centre of the building. This post is one of the principal objects of ritual interest therein. It is under the control of the main deity of the temple – 'it obeys him'; it is spoken of as his post, and it is even ritually treated as his 'body'. Other posts and structural members of the building symbolize other gods, while items of furniture such as a spear, a conch-shell, or a small shelf also may be their emblems or embodiments. These material objects are thus all held as sacred, and their presence intensifies the veneration with which the buildings are regarded. It must be emphasized that the social affiliations of these temples are exclusive to lineages, definite kinship groups whose ancestors and gods are sheltered therein, and whose living members meet at appropriate times to perform the customary rites.

The rites specifically associated with the temples in the Work of the Gods are called *fariki nga fare*. The term *fariki* is most simply translated as 'carpeting'. It applies to any act of laying mats on the floor of a house, or coconut fronds on the ground, whereby persons or things are kept from direct contact with the soil. It has thus an honorific significance. But when applied to these temple rites it has the meaning of a general re-furbishing, and includes not only replacement of floor-mats, but also repair of thatch, cleansing of sacred implements, and all the ritual processes associated therewith. Since the general intent is to maintain the temples in being as foci of religious interest, the rites may be spoken of as a process of re-consecration.

For several days the rites for temples and the yam proceed side by side. And before this, while the Ariki Kafika and his immediate circle of helpers have been busy with yam ritual, other people, in his own and the other clans, have been preparing for the temple rites. During the last week of November 1928, men and boys of each kinship group associated with a temple brought in loads of coconut fronds, which were dressed and plaited into floor-mats by their womenfolk. Before the rites began, each group had three or four such new mats in stock, and others in the making.

MYTHIC ORIGIN OF RESIAKE TEMPLE

One of the most important features of the temple ritual is the re-consecration of Resiake, the temple of Taumako. This building is specifically associated with the Atua i Kafika, thus providing one of the many links between the different clans. Unlike that of other temples, its origin is not assumed *ab initio*, but is explained by a definite story. I give this tale, as narrated to me by the Ariki Taumako.

Resiake was first built ten generations ago, by Tangitari (son of Matakai I), chief of Taumako, who himself lived there for many years. The building stands in Ravenga[1] in a small clearing a few yards off the main path, surrounded by areca palms, bananas and a red-leaved variety of *Cordyline terminalis*. Its name was taken by Tangitari as his house-name, and his descendants are still known as the house of Resiake.

[1] See *We, the Tikopia*, Map (b).

The story is that on the day when the building was finished Tangitari took up his residence therein. In the night he was awakened, and heard a voice call down to him from the sky. It said 'Friend! I desire your house.' He recognized the voice as that of the Atua i Kafika, and accordingly complied with the request. The building was given to the deity as a spiritual residence, that is, he became the chief god worshipped there, and the centre post was taken as the material token of his presence. The Atua i Taumako, who might be expected to be supreme there, is of secondary importance. The Ariki Taumako said to me 'The Atua i Taumako simply stands in my house, but the house obeys the Atua i Kafika, because he called down hither from the sky that he desired it.' Resiake is thus an exception to the rule that a temple of a clan is held under the control of the principal god of that clan; the myth has the function of providing an explanation of this anomaly. Its dedication to the supreme god of Kafika gives the Ariki Kafika no over-right over the temple, but it does give him a special position there should he attend the ritual. His seat is on the *tuaumu* side of the building (the landward side) opposite the centre post.

The rites of Resiake begin the temple ritual in the monsoon season, on the day of the *soani autaru* of the yam. They occupy four days when fully performed. The first day sees the 'Sunning of the Perfumes'; the second is that of the actual repair and re-carpeting; the third is the fixation of this by the *Fakaoatea*, the 'Noonday Rite'; and the fourth is the 'Smearing of Oil'. The first and last are rites peculiar to Resiake, among the major temples.

'SUNNING THE PERFUMES'

The Sunning of the Perfumes is termed *fakarā manongi*. Most sacred houses have their *manongi*, that is a type of plant or shrub with aromatic or brightly coloured leaves or flowers, which are used to decorate the interior at specific places. These 'perfumes' are not simply regarded as decorations, but each is associated with a specific deity. Many of them are used for the cure of sickness, in rites in which the particular deity is invoked. The peculiarity of the *manongi* of Resiake is that it comprises 'things common, things prickly only' – such as the nettle, wild ginger and *silato* (a tree with stinging leaves). To the Tikopia themselves the use of such unpleasant materials for decorating the building is anomalous, but they have an explanation in supernatural terms. This is given later.

Resiake, again, is almost alone in the treatment of its 'perfumes'. Whereas other temples use their greenery freshly cut, that of Resiake is exposed in the open air for a couple of days before being brought inside. The process is termed 'sunning', though actually the exposure to the sun is minimal.

The explanation of the exposure of the leaves and flowers outside is that it is a recognition of the deities of the temple. It is a traditionalized form of offering to them. This is exemplified by the fact that the 'sunning of the perfumes' is not an invariable feature of the Resiake ritual, but is performed at the discretion of the Ariki Taumako. In the monsoon season of 1928 it was not done. The reason given to me then was that no oil for later use with the perfumes had been prepared. But at the time of the trade-wind rites, when the performance did take place, the Ariki Kafika told me that it had been omitted before because the Ariki Taumako had been annoyed with his gods. No shark or other large fish had been hauled in by his canoe after the *faunga vaka* rites, so he had refused to expose the perfumes to them.

The rite of 'sunning the perfumes' is a very simple one. On the opening day of the Work of Resiake a party composed mainly of youths is sent out from the village in the morning to collect foliage of the types mentioned. They do not welcome the task, for obvious reasons. They bring their bundles back to the temple, and the foliage is then laid on a mat under a large chestnut tree near the path. It is then covered with stones kept there for that purpose, and known as 'stones for sunning the perfumes'. The process is really exposure in the open, but not actually to the sun. The next day the foliage is bundled up in a leaf of the umbrella palm, carried into the temple, and hung up, after which a kava rite is performed to sanctify it. It is then available for decoration, as described later.

But I will give here the account of the rites of the monsoon season, as I witnessed them.

On the first day, work began about 8 a.m. There were no 'perfumes' to be collected this day, but preparations had to be made for the repair of the temple on the morrow. The greater part of the day was spent by the chief and his helpers in making sheets of thatch.[1] Food was prepared at the same time, and was ready

---

[1] The organization of this work is described in my *Primitive Polynesian Economy*, 1939, p. 195.

about mid-afternoon. A kava rite was then performed, which would ordinarily have been to sanctify the 'sunning of the perfumes', but on this occasion had merely a general function.

RE-CARPETING AS RELIGIOUS RECOMPENSE

The next day was that of the actual carpeting (*fariki*). Soon after sunrise, a crowd of people assembled and in a short time there was a scene of great activity. Careful examination of the building was made by competent men and any lengths of thatch through which a spot of light showed were marked. Rotten sheets were replaced, others were strengthened by a piece of sago frond beneath. Some men repaired the entrances and the roof where they could reach it from the ground, others brought a rough ladder made from a heavy forked bough with twisted vines as rungs, which they erected inside the building. While one man held the ladder another climbed it and tied on the pieces of thatch, which were pushed up the roof from outside on the end of a long pole. A couple of hours concluded the repairing, after which the men sat around in the temple for talk or sleep. Conversation turned as usual on the fishing of the previous night and visitors from the other side of the island were eagerly listened to while they gave details of the catch and narrated the more striking incidents.

Meanwhile the women under the chestnut tree prepared food for the oven, its basis being taro or breadfruit according to season. On such occasions every family brought a *fiuri*, a donation of raw produce as a contribution to the common stock.

When the oven had been covered for some time the re-carpeting began. Each lineage of the Taumako clan had brought a newly plaited mat, 'the mat of its ancestor'. In the interior of the house the old mats lay side by side in a definite order, each associated with a specific kinship group and either marking the actual burial place of a prominent ancestor or serving as an emblem of his grave, which lay elsewhere. When the word to begin the re-carpeting was given the people swarmed into the house and laid their mats in position, usually above those of previous seasons, but in some cases removing the topmost of these. Each family laid its own mats, but did not interfere with those of another family, or endeavour to make up any deficiencies, even where a neglected mat lay rotting in its place. Some adjustment was needed in places, as space was limited and a certain amount of overlapping was inevitable. For certain positions, indeed, mats had been plaited of specific dimensions. Only a few minutes sufficed for the task and the house had then taken on a fresh and clean garb for the new season. It is this periodic custom of re-carpeting that saves the temples and many other buildings of Tikopia from that unsavoury interior appearance which characterizes so many of the native houses of the Western Pacific.

But the replacement or renewal of the floor-mats is not primarily a practical measure. It is the central feature of the ritual connected with any of the sacred houses, though in point of time and display it does not bulk very largely therein. The mats thus contributed seasonally by each family group are termed *inaki*, a word which has affinities in other Polynesian languages.[1] In Tikopia the *inaki* represents the acknowledgment or return made by the members of a family group to their ancestors or to relatives of former generations, for the use of the gardens and orchards from which they draw their food supply. The conception is that the lands of a family have come down to it from its forebears who have worked therein, tilling the soil and planting trees, and have then departed to the realm of the gods, handing the fruits of their industry on to their descendants. In their spiritual state they still exert an influence on the food resources, being responsible either directly or as intermediaries with the higher gods for their prosperity. The real significance of the *inaki* lies not in its value as floor-covering but as a mark of attention to an ancestor by virtue of which he is induced to continue his favourable interest in the family lands. Should the renewal of a mat be omitted and it rot in the house then the ghostly owner may become annoyed and blight the crops. A Tikopia describes the *inaki* in fact by quite a concrete term which he uses for ordinary commercial transactions; he speaks of it as the *tauvi* for the family land, that is the equivalent in exchange, or payment for it. 'The food from the orchards, that is its payment', 'Na tauvi tena', said Pa Vainunu, laying his hand on the mat of his ancestor Mourongo on which we were both sitting, after the ceremony of re-carpeting in Nukuora. Again the Ariki Kafika described a floor-mat laid by his family as 'the payment for the orchard'. Broadly speaking the richer a man is in land the more

---

[1] Cf. Tonga *inati* (*inasi*), a festival of offering of first-fruits. See James Cook, *A Voyage to the Pacific Ocean*, 1784, vol. I, pp. 336–52 ('Natchee'); William Mariner, *Tonga Islands*, 3rd ed., 1827, vol. II, pp. 168–73 ('*Inachi*').

new mats he has to provide when the day of re-carpeting arises. The *inaki* represent as it were a periodical interest charge payable to one's ancestors in virtue of the mortgage of productivity which they hold over the family gardens and orchards.

These associations of the new floor-mats explain why no one is interested in re-laying any mats but those which belong to him by kinship. To do otherwise would mean that he was paying for something that he had not received. Moreover, unless he was directly descended from the ancestor concerned he would be entirely without standing in the matter. Conduct of this kind is permissible only when a family dies out completely as a social group, that is when no males are left to carry on the name. In this case, if the lands have passed to a man of a collateral branch then he will furnish the new mat every season by virtue of his own distant affiliations. If, however, the lands have gone with women of the group who have married into other families then their husbands may provide the *inaki* as though coming from their wives. Later, their sons may take on the obligation through the inheritance of their mothers' interests. In such cases, however, the provision of the *inaki* is likely to be soon omitted. 'The man eats from the orchard, but he does not bring the mat; he grows tired.' When the original family group has died out it is held that the gift to the ancestor is then no longer obligatory. This omission is not strictly consistent with the Tikopia theory of the *inaki*, but is in accord with the tacit principle that as the degree of relationship decreases so also does the stringency of social obligation.

The real meaning of the re-carpeting of the temples as set out above was first made clear to me by Pa Vainunu, an elderly man of Kafika, whose father had been Ariki of the clan some twenty years before. His explanation was subsequently confirmed from other informants. After indicating the importance of the floor-mats this man went on to point out that the thatch replaced in the portion of roof directly above them was also included in the *inaki*. A characteristic statement made by him is worth reproducing: 'The mat of my ancestor is spread below, while tied down is the thatch from above to shelter my ancestor; because I eat from his places, from his orchards.' It is a common thing for a person to say 'I am going to pin a sheet of thatch to hang up my *inaki*.' It must be noted, however, that the thatch is really a subsidiary element in the *inaki*, since as already described, it is quite often prepared and replaced by communal labour. Moreover if the existing sheets are in good condition at the new season, then they are left in place and the mat alone is renewed, this latter being an invariable part of the procedure.

The custom of re-carpeting has been considered so far in its simpler forms. It is complicated, however, by the fact that lineages divide and families branch off in the course of generations, giving rise to several groups sharing a number of ancestors. The practice is then for each group to provide the *inaki* for its own immediate forebears, according to the division of the family lands among them, whereas the more remote ancestors are attended to either by the senior branch of the family, or shared by mutual arrangement among several members. Thus if a family splits up and agrees to divide its lands the head of the elder branch may say to his junior 'But come you then and renew the mat of our ancestor, and I will have a breathing space.' This intimates that he wishes to discontinue providing the *inaki* for some particular forebear and to hand the responsibility over to his relatives who have now formed a separate social entity, with exclusive rights over certain of the original family lands. Such transferences of obligation are not infrequent, though normally the major responsibilities rest on the shoulders of the representatives of the elder branch of the group. The *inaki* is not provided for every ancestor in the genealogical line. Only those of special note as warriors or leaders, or of critical importance as the starting-point of family offshoots, have their grave-mats singled out for renewal. Again if a man draws food supplies from an orchard in Uta he will renew the mat of his ancestor in the sacred house in Uta, but if his orchards lie elsewhere then he will provide the *inaki* in his house in Tai alone. It also should be noted that though Tikopia always speak of the mats as being provided by the men of the family in point of fact they are always plaited by the women.

Such old mats as are removed from the temples in the process of re-carpeting are termed *punefu*, a name used also to designate one type of funeral gift. Though many of these mats are still in good condition, they are not used again as floor-covering as this would be derogatory to the dignity of the ancestors from whose graves they were removed. They are carried away, each by its own family, and burned.

EMBLEMS OF THE GODS

After the re-carpeting a more spectacular procedure of decoration was begun. This was included under the term *fariki* though not literally implied therein. Resiake, like many other temples, was a veritable arsenal of weapons, which were of interest partly from their historical associations, but mainly because they were regarded as *fakatino o nga atua*, embodiments or emblems of the various deities who were affiliated with the building. It is not held that the object reveals the actual shape of the god; he is spoken of and treated as if he were anthropomorphic. Sometimes it serves as a vehicle of expression for him if he should wish to appear to human eyes in concrete form, but more often it is held that the god does not dwell in it or actually appear in it in person. Thus of one such weapon, the club of Rakiteua, it was observed 'It is termed the embodiment (*fakatino*) of the god, but he does not enter into it.' (*Tino* means body.) A clear distinction is always drawn between the material and the spiritual entity: these objects are not called *atua* themselves; they are known to be only representatives of *atua*. In every case by reason of their supernatural associations they are *tapu*, and must be handled with considerable caution and only at the appropriate times.

In the house Resiake the movable emblems of the gods consisted of four long spears, an arrow and two clubs which occupied prominent positions round the walls. The ceremonial re-decoration of these weapons, which was in effect a mode of paying honour to the gods they served, was one of the cardinal features of the day's events. They were taken down, carried to the lakeside, which was about fifty yards away through the trees, and there stripped of their embellishments of the former season and thoroughly washed. They were then brought back to the house where a mass of greenery of several species of plants had been gathered. In addition to the nettle, wild ginger, and *silato* already mentioned as forming the 'perfumes' of Resiake, bunches of a filmy fern, pink-leaved *Cordyline terminalis*, and the young creamy centre frond of the coconut had been brought. Several people busied themselves with splitting the white coconut frond into a long fringe, lengths of which were bound on the spears about a foot behind the barbed head, and made an effective decoration. A number of strips of bark-cloth had also been prepared. The

actual work of adornment was the ritual task of the Ariki Taumako. Sitting down near the band of assistants he prepared himself by tying on his sacred necklet and girding himself with the
sacred bark-cloth. A definite order was followed in the proceedings. The Ariki took one of the pair of clubs in his lap and with
a bunch of aromatic leaves soaked in coconut oil rubbed the weapon quickly, muttering as he did so a short formula invoking
prosperity from the *atua* whose embodiment it was. This was a
rite equivalent to that of anointing a canoe or other sacred object.
Some fronds of the mature green coconut leaf were then laid on
the club and bound with a strip of bark-cloth. This first weapon
was that of Rakiteua, Te Atua i Tafua, and the mature coconut
frond was his special decoration or symbol, which was appropriate
since he is the tutelary deity of the coconut in the land. The fronds
were termed his *surusuru*, the ornament stuck in the girdle at the
back when a person is going to a dance. The Ariki next took up
three of the spears, which his assistants had encircled each with a
fringe of white coconut frond, and to them he tied a bunch of
reddish cordyline. These were the emblems of Pu ma, Tafaki and
Karisi, who have already been mentioned as prominent deities of
the canoe ceremonies of Kafika. In Resiake they were not thought
to play any very important part, but they had as it were a seat on
the board of spiritual directors of the building, through being
gods of the Atua i Kafika. Their names here, according to Pa
Motuata, were Papakitera and Papakiteua respectively – a literal
translation being 'Knock against the sun' and 'Knock against the
rain', possibly referring to their function as rulers of the weather.
The other club was then adorned, in this instance with a frond of
cycas, and without any rite of anointing. This weapon was the
emblem of Tangiteala, as the arrow was of Te Araifo. These two
are deities from Fitimairaro, i.e. from Vanikoro or the neighbour-
ing island groups.[1] According to tradition these *atua* – in other
words their worship – were brought back by Matakai II, a former
Ariki Taumako who lived about the beginning of the nineteenth
century and made many voyages to and from those islands. The
comparatively recent introduction of these foreign gods has had
no deep effect on the Tikopia religion. There is no special cult
of Tangiteala in Resiake, and he exercises no functions of any

[1] Rivers (*History of Melanesian Society*, 1914, vol. I, p. 231) mentions Tangiteala
by the name of 'Tangteala' as one of the gods of the Reef islands.

importance in the scheme of religious belief of the Taumako clan. He with the other deities from Vanikoro and the West are honoured as stranger gods in the house, and have offerings of food set before them at the *fariki* ceremony. But they remain apart from the older Tikopia gods. Their emblems are grouped together in one corner of the house on a decorated shelf known as 'Te Fare Fiti', 'The Fiti House', the name of which perpetuates their origin. This is described in more detail later. The worship of these gods by the lineage of Marinoa or Nga Fiti, where they are regarded as paramount, is in a different category from that in Resiake. The people of Marinoa hold that they are themselves descended from immigrants from the Duff group, and brought their gods with them thence, at a time much anterior to the introduction of them to Resiake by the Taumako chief.

The fourth spear, a short one, was decorated with a frond of cycas and represented Taufokikimuri, a god of Fangarere clan. To the arrow was attached a piece of fern, the dancing decoration of Te Araifo. This concluded the decoration or 'binding' (*noa*) of the weapons. During the task, which was performed mainly by the Ariki, assisted by a couple of senior men of the clan, there was silence in the house. Only about a dozen persons were present, all males.

The next phase of the ritual was the washing of the centre post of the temple – the emblem of the Atua i Kafika – which had been wrapped in a mat during the *fariki* proceedings. All the main parts of the house are sacred but this especially so. No commoner or woman may touch it; the Ariki alone may do so.

After a short interval a couple of sprigs of aromatic leaves were thrown in from outside through the central doorway of the house. Suddenly there was the sound of hurrying footsteps outside, someone murmured 'He has arrived', and a man entered quickly by the centre door, bearing in his arms a large leaf full of water like a bowl. He had been sent down to the lake to get the water for washing the sacred post, and by tradition the task had to be performed with speed. Delay would have been dangerous as it might be construed by the deity as a want of respect for his power. On his knees the messenger went over to the centre post, while the Ariki, taking the two bunches of aromatic leaves, slipped down the mat from the post. Dipping his bunch of leaves in the water held up to him in the leaf basin he stood up to his full height and rubbed the timber vigorously at about the level of his head. This was repeated several times, then leaf basin and leaves were flung down on another part of the floor. This was the rite of *Kaukau pou*, washing the post, similar to that of anointing the post of Kafika temple during the yam rites. It is also known as the *Furu*, the cleansing. Here also the Ariki Taumako recited a formula during the washing, in invocation to the principal god of the temple to give health and prosperity to the people and the land.

I received two versions of this formula. One was from Pa Vangatau, one of the best-informed of the Tikopia old men, who said that he had been told it by his brother the late Ariki Taumako, with instructions to hand it on at death to the latter's son. But he found this to be unnecessary, he said, since the son, now the present chief, had later been fully instructed by the father himself. This formula is as follows:

> Thy post Mapusia, will be anointed
> Anoint for welfare
> Thy district which stands here obeys thee
> And be kicked away the storm clouds
> To tumble into the sea
> Thy land which stands obeys thee
> Spirit and man art thou.

Respect for the god is here the leading theme. The invocation opens with an announcement of the rite which is being performed, since this is a means of apprising the deity that the handling of his post is not simply unauthorized interference. The statement 'Spirit and man art thou' means that the god exercises jurisdiction in both realms, that of the Heavens and that of Earth, watching over the interests of his people among the gods above and descending also to watch over them among men.

Another version of the formula, different in wording, but similar in tenor, was given me by Pa Motuata, son of Pa Vangatau. Since the phrases used by the chief vary on different occasions, this text is probably as authentic as the one first given. The central theme is the same.

> I eat thy excrement Mapusia
> Turn hither with welfare
> To thy people
> Thy eyes in front to the sky

> Thy eyes in rear to the Uaroto
> Thy district which stands here obeys thee
> Spirit and man art thou.

The phrases

> Thy eyes in front to the sky
> Thy eyes in rear to the Uaroto

embody the same idea as is represented in the conclusion. The Uaroto is the esoteric name for the central post of the temple. The desire is that the Atua keep in touch with the realm of deities while at the same time casting backward glances at his building on earth, so safeguarding the interests of his people in both spheres.

The general object of such rites as the anointing of house posts and the recitation of the associated formulae was expressed by this informant as follows:

The Ariki calls to the deity to have sympathy for him; that the calm may fall, that vegetation may come to the land, and the rain may come, the wind not to blow.

The rite of rubbing at the post, though described as 'washing' or 'cleansing', in reality does not have much effect in this respect. Its validity lies in the fact that it provides a bridge, by contact with the sacred post, between the chief and his god, so increasing the force of the recitation of the formula.

When the washing or anointing of the post was completed, the coconut leaf mat bound to it was partially severed in the middle by the chief and his assistant, and then slipped round the base of the post, where the chief, kneeling, tied it securely. This was the mat of the Atua himself. In this case the old mat was not removed, so that the height of the pile grows every year.

The next feature of the ceremony was the decoration of various other structural members of the house, including the posts and rafters. Streamers of bark-cloth, or bunches of leaves, were tied to them in honour of the several deities they represented. They were termed *a noa o nga atua*, 'Ties of the gods', the basic meaning of *noa* being to tie or bind. The term *maro* is also used of these decorations, since they are in a sense offerings to the gods. The first of these was a bunch of cycas fronds which was tied on a rafter on the seaward side of the house, opposite the centre post.

The club with the coconut fronds was hung up beneath this decoration. The latter, as already mentioned, was the emblem of Rakiteua, the Atua i Tafua; the rafter decoration was for Te Atua i Fangarere, known in Taumako clan by the name of Te Urupaku.

A similar bunch of cycas was next bound by the chief to the centre post, very large leaves being selected since this was the dancing decoration of Te Atua i Kafika. In attaching this ornament the leaves were laid tip to tip, carried to the post and set upright, butts downwards, while the strip of bark-cloth was bound round and made fast. The bunch was then deftly parted and spread with a quick movement thus splaying out the leaves in attractive style.

The next decoration was that of the post at the far end of the temple, the 'seaward post', which represented the interest of the Atua i Taumako there. Here were used the 'perfumes of Resiake' – the nettle, wild ginger, etc., which had been sunned previously. (When the sunning is omitted they are gathered and used fresh.)

The reason for this strange procedure of introducing such unorthodox plants into the scheme of decoration did not seem to be known to most people, by whom it was accepted as simply the custom of that particular temple. Pa Motuata and other well-informed men, however, explained the plants as being the decoration (*rakei*) of Sakura, the Atua i Taumako, who wore them stuck at the back of his girdle. 'His decorations like a man who is going to a dance.' The prickly character of some of the leaves was said to protect him from molestation by other gods.

The gods who go to Sakura are stung; the leaves are called 'his guard' to ward off any other deity from coming to him, so that he may sit alone by himself.

I was further told by Pa Motuata that the special name of Sakura in Resiake was Satai, and this was unknown to the people of the clan in general. But since the same name is commonly used for a group of shore-dwelling *atua* I am doubtful if this is correct.

Leaning against the post of Sakura was a digging stick of ordinary type. This was stated to be the cultivating stick of Taromata, known also as Te Atua i te Marama, who was a son of Sakura, sprung from his body in the realm of the gods. People said of the post and the stick 'It is held that they are father and son standing there.' Both these gods are tutelary deities of the taro, of which the major ceremonies are controlled by the Ariki Taumako.

After the far post was decorated, three *noa* of bark-cloth were then tied by the chief at various places. One was on a rafter over the centre doorway on the landward side, one on the rear post supporting the ridge pole, and another to a rafter at the back. The rear post, known as the inland post, was associated with the kava bowl. The latter had no special spirit guardian, but the post had its own deity, Te Atua i Sao, for whom the *noa* was tied. According to the Ariki Taumako his name for this *atua* in Resiake temple was Tamasia. The *noa* of the rafters were presumably those of Pu ma and Te Atua i te Vai, respectively, but this I did not verify. While the chief was binding these streamers on to the appropriate timbers a couple of assistants tied several to other rafters round the building. These were not for gods, but were marks of remembrance in honour of the late Ariki Taumako, father of the (1929) chief, who lay buried in the central doorway of the house. It was said 'the streamers are simply tied' and did not represent offerings to gods.

The temple of Resiake was distinguished among other buildings of this type by its central doorways, jointly termed *mata tokarua* (two faces); each was under the control of the deity whose weapons hung above. The doorway on the side of the house towards the lake was the property of the Atua i Tafua, while that on the inland side belonged to the Atua i Kafika. Both entrances were *tapu*, the latter exceedingly so. I was told that no-one who was not engaged on a sacred mission, such as that of the bearer of the water from the lake, would dare to enter this doorway; dire trouble would befall him and probably the clan too if he did so. (When I attended the *fariki* rite great agitation was caused beforehand by the rumour that I had been urged by some deceiving ill-wisher to enter the house by this middle doorway. The rumour was quite without foundation, but it took much argument to convince the Ariki that his fears were groundless. His fears were for the sanctity of the house, not for my welfare!) When the late Ariki Taumako was about to die he said to his brother Pa Vangatau, 'I am about to die, speak you to the chief and all the land that I may be laid in the *tokarua* of the Atua i Kafika.' This was promised. After his death people asked which was the spot in which he had expressed a desire to be buried. On being told they objected to carrying out his wish, saying that the place was very *tapu* and they would come to harm thereby. But Pa Vangatau argued that while his brother was alive he made kava to the Atua and with success; calm fell on the sea, rain came at his word. 'The Atua descended to him.' Hence he could fittingly be buried in the doorway of the god he had served. He carried his point, and the grave was dug just inside the entrance. The presence of his grave-mat was the reason that so many streamers were hung for the chief in the interior of the temple.[1]

It was noteworthy that of all the greenery used for the decorations the cycas fronds alone were put into the house through the *mata tokarua*. This was permitted since the cycas was the dance decoration of the Atua i Kafika, who 'owned' the doorway. In conclusion the spears bound with tufts of reddish cordyline leaf were slung over this central doorway, while the Fare Fiti was arranged in the far corner of the building. This Fare (literally 'house') was a simple shelf laid from one wall-plate to another across the corner, and was dedicated to the gods of Fiti. The shelf was decorated with a long fringe of young creamy coconut leaf, split finely, and draped over it. This was termed *a titi o te Fare Fiti*. The emblems of the gods – the club of Tangiteala, the arrow of Te Araifo, and the spear of Taufokikimuri – were then stood upright on the shelf. (Fig. 6 shows the arrangement of streamers, etc.; see also Postscript to this chapter.)

A kava rite was then performed, to sanctify these acts. Afterwards a meal was rapidly eaten, about twenty-five men being present in the temple, while the women ate in the adjacent oven house.

The oven was again prepared, and when ready, libations of the 'evening kava' were poured. After this a man ran from mat to mat with a pierced coconut shaking out a few drops of the liquid at the head of each. The remainder of the nuts with the food were carried outside and a brief meal was eaten. The chief drank from a single coconut, but did not eat, in spite of pressing from various people. He evaded their insistence by declaring that he would eat later. This abstention from food was a matter of personal preference. Afterwards a parcel of *roi* was placed in the oven, to provide hot food for the ceremonies of the following morning.

That night, as also on the following night, the chief, accom-

[1] But see RM, 1963, p. 21, and Postscript to this chapter.

panied by a small party of men, slept in the temple as was the custom. A few women, including the wife of the chief, slept in the oven house, as the temple was *tapu* to them. According to custom also, it was *tapu* for the men who spent the night in the temple to

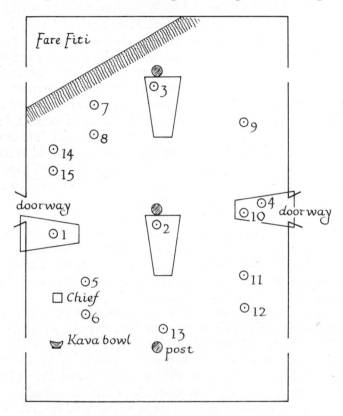

FIG. 6. Decorations and Offerings in Resiake Temple (1952)

1, Atua Lasi and Atua i Tafua; 2, Atua i Kafika; 3, Atua i Taumako; 4, Grandfather of chief; 5, Pu Faisina; 6, Nga Matua (past chiefs); 7, Tangiteala; 8, Te Araifo; 9, Pu Tauratua; 10, Pu ma; 11, Pu Resiake; 12, Pu Nukurenga; 13, Atua i Sao; 14, Pakisiva (Pu Tiu); 15, Te Orofana (Pu Faioa), Tau Fanau i Faioa

sleep face downwards. 'The folk who will sleep in Ravenga, not a person shall sleep face covered downwards; they turn their bellies upwards.' This prohibition was connected with the possible visits of malevolent female spirits.

THE 'FAKAOATEA' OF RESIAKE

The people awoke next morning before sunrise. During the night some men of the clan had gone out fishing; as a result a salmon-trout (a lake-fish) from the net of the chief had been laid at the door of the temple while he slept. Flying fish also were brought over from the coast at an early hour and roasted for the morning kava. Before sunrise the *roi* was taken from the oven and carried in a large basket to the temple. Then began the rite of *foraforanga maro* – spreading the vestments. This was one of the most solemn acts of the whole four days' ceremony, as was evidenced by the early hour at which it was performed, the use of the sacred *roi* for the kava and the serious air of the persons engaged. 'No one may raise his voice while the *maro* are being spread; it is held to be *tapu*', I was told. It was said that if a person in forgetfulness happens to speak loudly at this time or during the subsequent period someone will say to him 'You go and cry out, don't you see the *maro* are spread? Do not speak out loud!' Such a person will accept the reproof and lower his voice lest he be said to 'make sport' of the procedure. The object is the same as that of laying *maro* in the ordinary kava ritual – to present offerings to the deities and to provide them with seating places on to which they may alight to attend the events. Greater importance is given to the *maro* on this occasion, however, since they are the sacred properties of the house itself and remain in position for a day and a night.

The principal items of the ritual were two *maro kie*, finely plaited mats made from a soft-leaved variety of pandanus, and decorated with zigzag patterns in henna-coloured fibre. (The best *kie* are made in Anuta, whence the technique is said to have originated.) The *maro kie* were taken by the Ariki from their bark-cloth wrappings, in which they had been carefully stored from season to season, and laid down on some leaves of *rau tea* in the centre of the house. The first *maro*, a narrow one, was unfolded. Raising it in both hands before his head the chief made obeisance, then laid it near the seaward doorway under the club of Te Atua i Tafua, and covered it with fronds of cycas. This was dedicated to the Atua i Fangarere. Another large *kie* was then unfolded and set at the base of the centre post of the house. This served as base for a smaller *maro kie* with which the Ariki made obeisance as before, laying it on top, and covering it with cycas leaves likewise. This was the *maro* of Te Atua i Kafika. The chief then laid a piece of white bark-cloth by the far post of the house – this was the *maro* of Te Atua i Taumako, his own special deity. An orange *maro* was spread by an assistant on the grave of the late chief, and the ordinary *maro* of the kava were arranged. The usual formulae were recited, libations poured, and offerings of food set out from the *roi*. The pouring of the initial cups of kava was distinguished by the fact that the same procedure was adopted as with the *raurau kumete* in Kafika – the Ariki sat facing the *maro*, and did not turn round to receive the cup, but held his hand behind his back and received it thus from the cup-bearer, who was crouching in the rear. The reason for this is the exceeding sacredness of the Atua i Kafika, who was believed to be present. Less formality surrounded the other libations. The ceremony concluded with a hasty meal, by which time the sun had risen, its level rays stretching across the lake and striking the roof of the house.

The second oven of the day was now prepared and was cooked when the sun was high in the sky, at a time corresponding to about 10 a.m. The food for this occasion was by ancient rule a pudding made from fermented taro paste. As it was removed from the oven a cry of '*Te fakaoatea!*' was given to announce to the people sitting in the temple the progress of affairs. When its preparation was complete in the oven house one bowl was covered and carried as usual into the temple. With the other a curious custom was performed. One man armed with a pounder and another with a small dish of coconut cream went out and waited for the bowl, which was dragged along the ground from the oven house to the temple. As it proceeded the man with the pounder ran alongside and mashed vigorously at the pudding while his partner squeezed the cream over it. The three or four attendants in charge of the bowl did not pause for an instant, but dashed as quickly as possible over the few yards which separated them from their goal. It was said, 'it is pounded on the run'. This procedure aroused amusement among the younger members of the party. The Tikopia could assign no reason for the custom, except that the idea was to present an appearance of haste to the gods in the temple so that they might think every endeavour was being made to serve their portions with all possible speed. These offerings of food were quickly set out and libations of kava were poured beside each, this time with less formality than before.

Such is the *fakaoatea*, the 'midday' food preparation, which is an integral part of the rites of each of the major temples. It does not enter into the re-carpeting of the less important houses. Its function is general, not specific; that is, it is merely one element in the complex series of food offerings of which the purpose is to propitiate the deities of the house and clan and to secure their co-operation and assistance in obtaining prosperity. This procedure in the case of Resiake is sometimes termed 'the midday celebration of the oil'.

A third oven was prepared in the early afternoon to provide food for the evening kava; when this had been removed a package of *roi* was put in, as on the preceding day. For the evening ceremony a large pile of fresh coconuts were brought to the temple. They were termed the *Inu*, the 'Drink', which was here a technical term. The procedure followed was as before. After a hearty meal of coconut most of the people left for their homes in the beach village, a few only remaining with their chief.

ANOINTING THE PARTICIPANTS

The final event in the 'Work' of Resiake was the anointing of the participants with oil. A description of the proceedings was given me as follows:

The Ariki Taumako will stay two nights in Ravenga; in the morning he will make the *fakaoatea*; when night descends on the land carry hither the coconuts; when night descends on the land, near the time when the land will be light (i.e. dawn), grate the coconuts in the night, express the cream, heat then the oil in the night, and take two oil vessels. Hasten up in the morning, then the Ariki enters singly, he and the elder – Pa Ngatotiu, or whoever will apply the oil of the men, enter singly the Ariki or Pa Ngatotiu. Is different the oil of the men, is different the oil of the women. We go and bathe in the morning, and come then to the Ariki. The *roi* has been uncovered; bring it in and stand it in the centre of the house. Leave it there; the kava is not made. We bathe in the oil which has been poured into the palm of the hand, and smeared then on the breast of each man. Finished is our bathing in the oil, the Ariki comes then to sit down and perform the kava. Perform the kava, finished, fold up the *maro*. Finished is the folding of the *maro*, go then to Uta, to Taumako, to pin thatch. Thereupon are completed the things of Resiake.

I was not present at the preparation of the oil, which was not made in the monsoon season of 1928, but witnessed all the other rites. The following is the traditional proceeding in the preparation.

The night of the *fakaoatea* is the time selected. Mature coconuts have been gathered from the orchards of the Ariki and his people; they are grated and the cream expressed. Round about midnight or in the early morning the sleeping men in the temple awake, the oven is prepared and red-hot stones from it are slid into the bowl of cream, which is thus converted into oil by the usual technique. Leaves of various kinds are bruised and dropped into the liquid during this operation to give the oil a pleasant perfume. When it is judged that the process of conversion is complete the stones are withdrawn and the oil put into containers. In olden times small gourds like those now used for holding lime were used; nowadays glass bottles have been substituted. (This is one of the very few ways in which Tikopia religious culture has drawn upon European materials.) A distinction is made between 'the oil of the men' and 'the oil of the women'. The essence of this lies in the fact that the former is the property of the gods Pu ma, whereas the latter belongs to Pufine ma, sister-goddesses. The oil container of the men is filled first, then that of the women, small cups of coconut shell being used to dip the liquid from the bowl. The work is done by torchlight. The preparation of the oil is not an invariable feature of the seasonal rites. If the containers are fairly full already then this part of the 'Work' is often omitted. The rest of the procedure I witnessed myself.

The anointing took place early in the morning. After going down as usual to bathe in the lake the people of the clan assembled, many coming from Tai to be present, though some had not attended the earlier part of the 'Work'. The Ariki took down the oil vessel and sat waiting till they appeared. Then he got impatient. 'Haven't they seen that the sun has risen?' he said in irritation. Whereupon stragglers were hurried up by the earlier arrivals. 'Call out! The Ariki is waiting for them.' At last all the men and boys assembled, and sat along the sides of the house. A man of rank, an elder, was the first to be anointed. He walked up the house and seated himself before the chief, who was at the far end of the building. The chief withdrew the stopper of the bottle, poured a few drops of oil into his right hand and smeared it on the man's chest and upper part of his arms, with a gentle sweeping motion. The man then went back to his seat, while his place was taken by others in turn. Children took part, and were instructed loudly by their elders how to act. A few men remained in their places and refused to be anointed. Little was said to them, since participation is optional. The anointing was treated solemnly by those who were being treated at the moment, though a few jokes passed among the crowd. The people were said to 'bathe' in the oil, though actually it was applied to but a limited area of the body. After the male members of the clan were finished it was the turn of the women and girls. There the Ariki was assisted by an elder to whom he handed the second oil bottle, and who carried out the task. The wife of the chief, as befitted her position, was the first to enter, and was anointed on the upper part of the breast, the upper arms and the back of the neck. Each woman, after treatment, returned to the oven house, the women's abode. (Cf. Plate III in *Tikopia Ritual and Belief*, 1967.)

The general object of the ceremony is to assist in preserving the health and prosperity of the person anointed – 'it is made for welfare', is the explanation. Anointing with oil is a common mode of treatment for physical ills, the efficacy of the act lying not in the ordinary properties of the liquid but in the combined virtue of its association with the deities who control it, and with the hand and person of the chief who applies it or who presides at its application.

Take the *manongi*, rub, take the oil, pour into the hand, rub on his body, that is the cleansing from epidemic disease, from sickness.

If special potency is required a formula is recited to secure the attention of the deities more specifically concerned.

The rites of the *Fakasinu Vaka* (Oiling Canoe) and *Kaukau Pou* (Anointing Post) belong to the same genus as the anointing ceremony of Resiake. This last is called the *Takai Sinu* (Smearing Oil – to be distinguished from the term *taki sinu* sometimes used in this connection, and meaning 'to withdraw the plug of the oil vessel'). This rite is peculiar to the 'Work' of this one temple. It marks the completion of the rites of the building, and forms a kind of clan bond, by giving evidence of common association in serving the clan gods. The anointing is associated too with the investiture of necklets of cordyline leaf, a rite performed also for individual welfare. The 'throwing' of the necklet is not confined to Resiake alone, but is done by the chief of each clan before or after his important 'Work'. An example has already been given in regard to 'Sacred Things' (p. 67). The procedure in all cases is the same, though the formulae recited vary according to the occasion, and if the chief should be in a hurry, or a large crowd of people are to be invested, he repeats only the introductory phrases.

After the anointing, the kava was performed, with food offerings from the *roi*. The chief then carefully folded up the barkcloths of the gods, and stowed them away on the *tokotu*, the staging near the centre of the building. Each major temple has such a staging, with a heavily notched base post. I was told by the Ariki Kafika and other men that the *tokotu* served to protect food and other property from rats in the days when these buildings were actually inhabited by their ancestors.

The 'Work' of Resiake was now finished. I have described it in detail as much of the procedure is common to the re-carpeting of other temples.

Reference to the Programme of Rites given in Chapter 1 will show the main order of events at this time; without it the following description may be confusing owing to the overlapping of the 'Work' of the various temples.

RITES OF VAISAKIRI

The third day of the ritual of Resiake gave the signal to the Ariki Fangarere to begin the 'Work' of his most important temple. The keynote of this was also the re-laying of the mats of ancestors. The conventional expression to describe the first day's operations was 'The floor-mat of Vaisakiri is cut' meaning that the palm fronds for the plaiting of the most sacred mat were gathered then. Another formal expression used was 'The floor-mat of Vaisakiri is plaited' – in preparation for the re-carpeting.

This is an instance of how processes of a primarily technical order, which are merely preliminary to the ritual processes, tend to be elevated into the ritual scheme, and to receive a validity of their own. Thus the preparation of the mat, which has no sacerdotal value in itself, has a day devoted to it, on a par with the actual laying of the mat, which is the only real offering to the god. This elevation of technical processes into ritual processes is a prominent feature of the Tikopia religious system.

Vaisakiri was the principal temple of the Ariki Fangarere, having come down to him, with the orchard in which it stands, from

Fakaarofatia, the ancestor of his clan, by gift from Pu Resiake of Taumako, mother's brother of this ancestor. The temple stood somewhat inland from the main path along the lake shore; beside it was a smaller house, corresponding to the oven houses of other temples, but with no oven therein. It was in this smaller building that the initial rites of the sacred mat took place. The mat itself was destined as an offering to the Atua i Fangarere. A sacred mat for the temple of Sao was also prepared on the same day, to be used as an offering to the Atua i Sao.

The mat of Vaisakiri was plaited on the day that Resiake had its *fakaoatea* rite. The same day the 'midday celebration of the mat' was performed. Food was cooked in an adjacent oven house, and shortly before it was ready the old mat was removed from the *mata paito* side of the house, a basket of clean white sand was spread there, and the new mat was laid on top of it. A kava rite then took place. This was of great sacredness, since the principal clan deity, the Atua i Fangarere, was believed to enter a medium and talk to the people. The explanation of this was 'That is the confirmation of his kava, that he comes among men.'[1] In this case the medium was the eldest son of the chief. From time to time people present murmured 'He (the god) comes to the kava of the chief', and similar comments, showing their firm belief in the reality of the manifestation.

On the following day the re-carpeting of the temple itself took place. The usual oven was prepared, the thatch of the roof was renewed where necessary, and the various floor-mats were replaced by appropriate family groups according to the conventions of the *inaki*. While the temple was being renovated a sacred conch-shell which was kept there was taken down to the lake and washed. Several temples had such shells, called *pu*, a name given to all trumpet-like instruments. In this connection they were known as *pu tapu*, sacred trumpets. After being washed the conch of Vaisakiri was blown vigorously several times. It was old, and its sound not melodious – hence a lad on hearing it remarked 'It does not cry, it merely snores.' The mournful sound rang along the lake shore, and apprised the people of other temples, who were busy with their own tasks, that the re-carpeting of Vaisakiri was well under way.

[1] Some description of mediumistic phenomena has been given in my *Essays on Social Organization and Values*, 1964, pp. 247–54.

Bark-cloth streamers were bound to posts and rafters in honour of the deities of the temple. The principal post, at the far end, was decorated with two separate bunches of cycas fronds. The upper one was the decoration of the Atua i Fangarere, known in this temple by the name of Te Urupaku. The lower decoration was that of Pu Tafatai, a deity of sea-voyaging. His personal name, according to Pae Sao, is Takatosi. The corresponding post at the other end of the temple was that of the kava bowl, and was presided over as in Resiake by Te Atua i Sao, Tokitaitekere. A simple streamer of bark-cloth marked his post. On the left side of the house as one entered was the *toki tapu*, the sacred shell adze with its carved wooden handle hanging over its shelf. This has as its deity Te Atua i te Ava, Tupua fiti, who is called a son of Te Urupaku. The spot was not adorned, however, in any way. Opposite, on the other wall were slung two spears with bunches of cycas tied to them. These, as in Resiake, were embodiments of Pu ma, known here by the same name as in that building. Of the streamers of bark-cloth hung from the rafters, the principal one on the *mato paito* side of the house was for Te Atua i Ravenga, Taufokikimuri, who is also regarded as a son of Te Urupaku. The joint occurrence of this and other names in Vaisakiri and in Resiake was due to the fact that these were the gods of the old Nga Ravenga people. Resiake was built on Ravenga soil and incorporated some of the local deities, and Vaisakiri, though it stands in Uta, is the temple of sa Fangarere, the present-day descendants of the Ravenga folk.[1]

The re-carpeting ritual was concluded by a kava performance, with offering of bark-cloth to the Atua i Fangarere, and invocation of the gods over the kava stem.

RE-CARPETING THE KAVA HOUSES

This day of the re-carpeting of Vaisakiri temple was one of great activity throughout the island. It was the occasion for the re-consecration of all the lesser temples in Uta and Ravenga, and some of those in Tai also. These were the *paito fai kava*, the houses in which chiefs or elders performed their kava on the various ritual occasions through the year. The programme for the day varied for the people of the different houses and clans. Early in the morning the Ariki Taumako performed the 'anointing' in

[1] See my *History and Traditions of Tikopia*, 1961, ch. 7.

Resiake, after which he went to Taumako temple in Uta to superintend the preparation of the thatch there, and was then occupied with the ritual in connection with his lesser clan temples. The Ariki Kafika spent the day at Kafika temple, mainly in receiving the food gifts from his lesser temples, but performed a small 'yam kava' in the afternoon. The Ariki Fangarere was primarily occupied with Vaisakiri, and in former days the Ariki Tafua would have been superintending the thatch-making of Tafua temple, and receiving food gifts from the lesser temples of his clan.

The work of the various kava houses fell into two sections – on the one hand the re-carpeting of the building (including renovation of thatch); and on the other the preparation of a large basket of food known as *fonakava*. (This is to be distinguished from the *fonokava*, a contribution of cooked food on many ritual occasions or at a dance festival.) The *fonakava* was a present to the clan chief, and the importance attached to it was the main reason for the bustle which had seized upon every lineage group. The essence of the *fonakava* is that in native theory it is an acknowledgment to the chief of his suzerainty over the temple of each particular lineage in his clan. His overlordship is purely formal; he enters the temple only rarely, to perform the kava, or may never even enter it at all. But the presentation of the *fonakava* to him twice yearly is a basic link between him and the constituent kinship groups of his clan, and also in native eyes, between his gods and theirs. The *fonakava* is not reciprocated directly, but an indirect reciprocation is given to some extent by a re-distribution of the baskets among the representatives of the various lineages.

Preparation of the *fonakava* demands the mobilization of the resources of each major kinship group, and assistance of affinal kin to some extent. Bananas, breadfruit and taro are required in large quantity, as also mature coconuts for the creamed pudding which is an essential part of the gift. Most of the baskets are brought about mid-afternoon. Where the owner of the temple is an elder with kava privileges he performs his kava over the *fonakava* before it goes to the chief. In any case, the chief himself pours the libations of kava to his gods when it arrives, as a dedication of the food to them. Usually the baskets are *kavaki* (have the kava performed over them) all together. If there are a great number, however, then as soon as three or four accumulate, it is done and repeated for others later. This was the case with the *fonakava* received by the Ariki Taumako in the monsoon season. The following table gives the temples from which the *fonakava* are brought to the chief on this day. Each chief of course acts independently.

KAFIKA	TAFUA	TAUMAKO	FANGARERE
Rarovi	Fusi	Kavasa	Vaisakiri
Porima	Rotuma	Fatumaru	Fenumera
Tavi	Sao	Niumano	
Raropuka	Rarupe*	Kamota	
Torokinga	Motuapi*	Rarokofe	
Somosomo		Maniva	
Te Afua	Korokoro*	Mataioa	
Tongarutu	Notau*	Farekofe	
Fenumera	Samoa	Ngatotiu	
Rakau*	Akitunu	Ratia*	
Fakamaina*			
Vaisakiri		Niukapu*	
Marinoa*	Te Akaukena*	Rangirikoi*	

* *Fonakava* abandoned by 1928.

In recent years the adoption of Christianity by the Ariki Tafua and the people of Faea has caused some modification of the scheme. Those kinship groups in Faea, as Marinoa, Niukapu and Rangirikoi, which formerly sent *fonakava* to their clan chiefs in Ravenga, have discontinued it, while the Ariki Tafua has ceased to receive *fonakava*, either from his Christian kinship groups in Faea or his heathen ones on the other side of the island. These latter still perform the rites of re-carpeting. But like Akitunu, Samoa and Fusi in Namo they retain the *fonakava*; or they present it to the chief in whose village they live, as does the elder of Sao in the case of his house Notoa (see p. 259) in Potu sa Taumako. In all non-Christian houses the rites of *fariki* are, however, unaltered, while in those of Christians the persistence of the belief in and respect for their ancestors and gods lead to a seasonal re-laying of mats in the houses used as dwellings, usually accompanied by food offerings. Some of the sacred houses, as Korokoro, still stand; others as Marinoa, Te Akaukena and Tafua have been allowed to fall into decay. In the case of Rakau, which is the house of the origin of Marinoa lineage, an attempt has been made to cope with the defection of its own people by combining its *fonakava* – nominally – with that of Torokinga, a house of another lineage of the same clan. That of Raropuka is still made every season, since a few faithful members of the family come over every time on the appointed day.

Sometimes of course the re-carpeting of a temple, and the making of the *fonakava* are abandoned for purely internal reasons. Thus the Ariki Kafika no longer receives the customary basket from Fakamaina, a related house of Tavi, since that branch of the family immediately concerned has become extinct. By Pa Tavi then, 'it has been abandoned, because his brothers died completely'.

It will be observed that *fonakava* are presented from Fenumera to both the Ariki Kafika and the Ariki Fangarere – a basket to each. The building is that of the Ariki Fangarere, hence one *fonakava* is given to him; the extra one is an acknowledgment of the overlordship of the Ariki Kafika over the Fangarere clan. The *fonakava* from Tafua and Taumako also on their re-carpeting a few days later are carried to the Ariki Kafika in virtue of his position as the supreme chief of the island.

Though the general form of the *fariki* ceremony is the same for all houses, variations in detail occur. Each has its own peculiarities of custom, '*ona ke faifainga*'. The procedure in the case of some of the most important houses will be described briefly in order to give an idea of this variation, the complexity of the day's proceedings, and the consequent organization needed.

Marinoa (informant, Pa Fetauta):
Principal rite, anointing of main post at end of house, dedicated to Te Araifo. Three streamers tied, for Te Araifo, Tukere (Atua i Ratia) and Rata. Kava performed by elder.

Raropuka (informant, Pa Raropuka):
Kava performed, but no post anointed. But present elder, as sister's son of Porima, made kava in house Sukumarae, belonging to Porima. Main post anointed, dedicated to Pueseia (Atua i te Uruao).

Akitunu (informant, Pa Sukuporu):
No kava performed, but bark-cloth spread: to Tangaroa, a white cloth and an orange one; to 'The Followers of Tangaroa', a white cloth; to Te Kasomera (Eel-god), an orange cloth and a white one; to Vaikirimera, a female deity, child of Eel-god, a white cloth.

Fatumaru (informant, Pa Vangatau):
Principal rite, cleansing of Atua i Fatumaru, a long black stone, paired with stone of Takarito. Stone removed from bed of cycas leaves, washed, smeared with turmeric, and laid back on fresh bed. Kava performed, frequently by Ariki Taumako, since god is important for fishing. Temple is in control of Atua i Kafika, under title of Tauaroaro. Cycas is 'perfume' of Atua i Kafika, and temple has set of stones for 'sunning the perfume' as in Resiake, though of less importance.

Niukapu (informant, Pa Niukapu):
Temple founded on ground formerly occupied by Nga Faea, who were driven off to sea, hence their gods incorporated into list of tutelary deities. Done by founder and family lest 'they would be devoured by the deities, angry at their people who had been killed'.

Kava performed by Ariki Taumako, deities of Nga Faea invoked first, and those of Taumako secondarily.

Invocation of: Feke (Octopus God)

> Taukaveivaru ('Eight Rays'), i.e. tentacles
> Atua i Taumako
> Nga Matua (former Taumako chiefs)
> Pu Niukapu (noted sea-voyaging ancestor)

Temple contained formerly large wooden implement said to be of type used for cutting banana stems before iron introduced; original lost; copy shown to me a wooden imitation of a trade-knife, carved by Pa Rangifuri.

Korokoro (informant, Pa Korokoro):
Principal esoteric objects:
Post at south end, 'body' of Semoana ariki, primary god of Korokoro. Serves as back-rest for Ariki Tafua when he attends kava of temple.
Shelf adjacent to post, that of Semoana ariki and Semoana tu. Centre post, embodiment of Pu ma, under title of Ruaeva. Serves as back-rest for Ariki Taumako at kava; his title for Pu ma the allied name of Ruaariki.
Shelf opposite, and spear above, also of Ruaeva.
Ariki Kafika occasionally attends kava, by virtue of presence of Pu ma in temple. Seating places of three chiefs a token of 'weight' of Korokoro rites.

Principal elements of *fariki* rite were re-decoration of shelves, and anointing of post of Semoana, with performance of kava by elder of Korokoro.

Shelf of Ruaeva laid with fresh branchlets of pale and of red *kava pi*; that of Semoana re-carpeted with a little mat of coconut fronds, plaited to correct dimensions. Formula for re-decoration of shelves:

> I eat your excrement.
> Turn to your shelf which is being carpeted
> Your shelf which is carpeted for welfare.
> Unfold goodness for the man preparing your kava
> And stand your foot firm on your Korokoro.

The last expression conveys the desire that contact between deity and temple should remain unbroken, so that he should be at hand to protect and favour his people.

Formula for anointing the post of Semoana:

> Semoana ariki
> I eat your excrement
> Your post will be cleansed,
> Turn to your chiefly name,
> Your post will be anointed for welfare,
> Haul on the man to be properly hale above
> For preparation of your kava,
> For tying of your sheet of thatch,
> For covering the palm leaf covers.
> Be severed away the illness
> And give good health only.

This formula varies somewhat from the usual type. The allusion to the 'chiefly name' of the deity implies respect. Incentive is given to the deity to grant the request for health by referring to the various activities in connection with his sacred house which can only then be performed by the suppliant. The 'palm leaf covers' are the branches of coconut leaf which are laid, butt downwards, over the rows of sago leaf thatch in order to hold them down. The last line was difficult to translate concisely. It was explained as characterizing 'the man in whom is lacking ills of any sort', i.e. it represents the idea of continued good health.

The above are the principal variants in the rites of re-consecration of the sacred kava houses. It will be realized that the differences in procedure are due largely to the different deities believed to control each house, and the various material objects therein which act as their embodiment or representation. As in the case of the sacred canoes, the ritual system is extremely intricate, but in various ways links kinship groups with their clan chiefs, and at a number of points brings out the acknowledged supremacy of the Ariki Kafika.

A return may now be made to the description of the temple rites in chronological sequence.

RE-CARPETING OF NUKUORA, TAUMAKO AND TAFUA

After the ordinary sacred houses had been renovated on the one day there still remained a few of such importance that they had a special place assigned to their ceremonies in the programme of the season. Such were: Tafua, Taumako and Kafika, the temples of the chiefs; Mapusanga, the house of an affiliated lineage of Kafika; and Nukuora, connected with the Fangarere clan. The rites of the latter were performed on the day that the yam seed was buried, and in the monsoon season Tafua and Taumako were re-carpeted on the same day. Kafika came later, while Mapusanga was re-carpeted after the Freeing of the Land which is one of the salient events in the seasonal cycle. The description of the rites of this last house will then be held over till the next chapter.

Nukuora temple rests under dual control. As the Tikopia say, it is the house of the Ariki Fangarere, in which the Ariki Kafika makes the kava. 'They merely get it ready; when the kava is to be made, they invite me to go and make the kava', the Ariki Kafika himself explained. Thus though in point of ownership it may be said to belong to the Fangarere chief, yet at the same time he acknowledges the suzerainty of the chief of Kafika. The reason is to be sought in tradition. Nukuora is the house built by Fakaaro-fatia, the sole survivor from the slaughter of Nga Ravenga. His mother, a daughter of the Ariki Kafika of the time, ran with her son, then a babe, to her father's home in the night, and was saved by him. Nukuora was erected on Kafika soil, on a site given to Fakaarofatia by the Ariki, and this, combined with the tie created by the act of preservation, accounts for the present overlordship. The continued interest of the Fangarere people in the house is due to the fact that their ancestor lies buried there; hence they maintain the link with their 'origin'. 'To re-carpet the mat of (our) Ancestor' was the reason they gave me for the ritual.

The ritual itself was of the usual type. When the food had been placed in the oven the work of replacing the mats began. Fig. 7 shows how the principal mats were laid, and to whom.

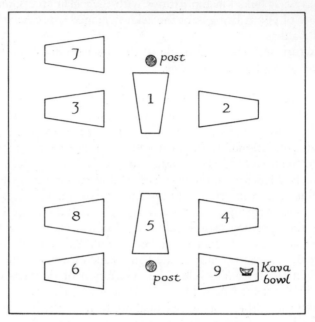

FIG. 7. Inaki Mats in Nukuora Temple

1, Fakaarofatia – double mat provided by Pa Nopu and Pa Fenumera; 2, Father of Ariki Fangarere, provided by chief's own family; 3, Mourongo, ancestor of Vainunu branch of Kafika, provided by Pa Vainunu; 4, Pa Mapusanga (Tariariki), eldest son of former Ariki Kafika, lost at sea (provided by Pa Te Arairaki, of Mapusanga); 5, Atua i Sao, represented by rear post, specifically that of the guardian of the kava bowl; 6, Atua Fafine, Female Deity of Kafika; 7, Pufine ma, female deities of Porima; 8, Atua Pouri, principal deity of Porima; 9, mat of kava bowl

It may be noted that the head of each mat, i.e. the broad end, lay towards the centre of the house – except those laid to the posts. The reason was that in the *fare* as distinct from the *paito fai kava* the usual distinction between *mata paito* and *tuaumu* was abandoned. 'The temples in Uta here, not a *mata paito* for a distinguishing mark.' In Kafika the side nearest the lake was especially *tapu* because, it was said, of the dead chiefs who lay there. This how-ever did not apply in the same measure to Nukuora. There '*mata paito* was made in the middle of the house'. For this reason women if they entered sat round the wall on either side, and men, when they slept in the house, lay with their heads towards the centre, no matter in what part of the building they might be. The importance of the centre posts as representative of the chief gods accounts largely for this attitude since in Tikopia, as elsewhere, respect is implied by orientation of head or face towards the object, whereas feet or back turned in that direction indicates lack of consideration. Great attention is paid to details of this kind. Thus when the kava of Nukuora was about to begin the man seated at the bowl raised the question of the correct position for him to sit in. 'The kava-wringer turns his back to seaward' was the pronouncement made by an experienced listener, and the man sat accordingly. The food was brought into the house – six ordinary baskets, a bowl of pudding and a huge mass in a basket specially woven. This last was the *fonakava*, which was to be presented to the Ariki Kafika. Some of his own family who had attended the ceremony had contributed their share to the *fonakava*, the food thus given having completed a circuit.

The Ariki Kafika tied on the various bark-cloth streamers of the temple. The first was bound round the principal post, for Fakaarofatia, the 'chief' of the house; the second, tied to the rear post, was for Tokitaitekere, Te Atua i Sao. The others, eight in all, decorating opposite rafters in pairs, were for the various deities and ancestors whose mats lay on the floor beneath. These latter streamers were smaller than those attached to the main posts. A pair of long beams ran at the back of the principal post of the house from side to side, about three feet from the ground. These acted as a shelf, and were termed the *fetāraro*. This was the repository for a mass of cycas leaves which were relaid by the chief when he had tied the streamers. For this reason it was known also as the *fare rongorongo* (cycas house). Such shelves exist in most of the more important sacred houses, as Raniniu, Motuapi and Mapusanga, and hold venerated objects; on this account they are all *fetāraro tapu*. That in Nukuora was the property of Pufine ma, and the house itself was under the control of these two female deities and their brother Te Atua Pouri. The cycas leaves laid on the shelf belonged to this last deity. One of the common features of the Tikopia religious system is the parallelism which is held to exist between the realm of men and that of the gods. In this case the 'cycas house' in Nukuora was believed to have as its prototype that which stands in Rangipouri, the particular Heaven which is under the domination of Te Atua Pouri.

These preliminaries over, the kava began. The Ariki Fangarere presented an orange bark-cloth to the Ariki Kafika, who laid it before him with an obeisance. This was for the Atua i Kafika, who, though he had no direct jurisdiction over the temple, being without post or rafter therein, was nevertheless invoked as the supreme deity of the clan. The gods invoked in the kava were in the following order:

Pu ma
Futiotekere (Atua i Fangarere)
Tokitaitekere (Atua i Sao)
Mapusia (Atua i Kafika)
Tuapou (Atua i Porima)
Pufine ma
Fakaarofatia (first chief of Fangarere, and 'sacred child' of
    Kafika)
Nga Matua (chiefly ancestors of Ariki Kafika)

The libations of kava were many 'because it is the principal house of another chief'. The joint interest of the chiefs of Kafika and Fangarere required that the deities of both should be recognized. The order of libations was:

Cups: 1 and 2. by cup-bearer, to Pu ma
          3. by Ariki Kafika, to Fakaarofatia
          4. by Ariki Kafika, to Atua i Kafika
          5. by Ariki Kafika, to Nga Matua
          6. by Ariki Fangarere, to Atua i Fangarere
          7. by Ariki Kafika, to Pu Mapusanga
          8. by Ariki Kafika, to Atua i Sao
          9. by Ariki Fangarere, to his father
      10, etc. by cup-bearer, to remaining gods and ancestors

The invocation of Pu ma, and libations to them, was a significant part of the procedure; Nukuora was the only temple in Uta where they were so invoked with no specific function. Their role, like that of the Atua i Kafika, was merely as primary gods of Kafika, coming, so to say, with the Ariki Kafika.

In the evening the 'coconut kava' was performed, in the open air, on a small grass plot between Kafika temple and Kafika Lasi, but close to Nukuora. *Roi* was also prepared in Kafika Lasi. The following morning the *roi* was used for the 'morning kava' in Nukuora. Besides myself, only four men were present, the two chiefs and two helpers. The rite was an important one, as shown by the *roi*, and also by the decoration of the Ariki Kafika with bright bands of turmeric on belly and arms. Before the kava the chief tied two thick fringes of cordyline leaf to the beams mentioned earlier. These fringes were termed *te kara o Pufine ma*. They were described as being 'perfume of the gods, fringes of the gods'. The *kara* is an esoteric name for a *titi* or fringe, an ornamental dress worn around the waist, generally by women, but sometimes worn by men, above the ordinary costume at dances or on other festive occasions. The *kara* or *titi* in this case were an offering to Pufine ma.

After the recital of the kava formula the offerings of *roi* were set out, thirteen in all, each god and ancestor having his portion placed on his mat. First of all, however, the *raurau kumete* which had been brought in from Kafika was filled and set aside. After the principal libations of kava had been poured the Ariki Kafika, his kava-wringer and cup-bearer adjourned to Kafika temple taking with them the sacred dish, and poured the customary libations of kava to Pu ma and the other deities there. This, which was a highly sacred piece of ritual, was done on behalf of the yam, and the change of place was made since as yam deities Pu ma have no part in Nukuora. 'They have no mat or post there' as the natives said. Immediately this was over the party returned again to Nukuora and the subsidiary libations were poured to the various ancestors and secondary deities there. This completed the ceremonies of Nukuora.

On the same day as Nukuora was re-carpeted Taumako temple – and in former days Tafua – was re-consecrated also. The thatch had been prepared the day before. The ritual was of the type already described for other temples. But a special feature was the laying of two mats under the shelf which held the sacred adzes of the canoes. These mats were plaited the day before by a woman of the family of the Ariki Taumako, after the chief had tied on her a leaf necklet, for welfare. When the mats were laid the chief sat before the shelf, lifted each new mat on to his lap, made obeisance with it, and spread it out. The mats were for Tafaki and Karisi,

guardian deities of the adze. In the following kava rite these two
deities were invoked first; then came the Atua i Taumako, who
was represented by the centre post and the mat adjoining it; and
later Pusi, the reef-eel.

The rites of Tafua temple were described to me by the Ariki
Tafua. The temple itself, abandoned for a decade, was in ruins
in a tangled mass of undergrowth. One massive end post still
stood, but apart from this only the stone pillar which was the
embodiment of the Atua i Tafua remained in position. The canoe
adzes had been buried by the chief beneath the floor when he for-
sook their rites.

The re-carpeting was in all essentials the same as that described
for other temples, save that the lower part of one of the rafters and
not the centre post was anointed. From this peculiarity the clan
of Tafua were sometimes called 'sa Raro-oka', 'The People of the
Lower Rafter', a term that could be applied also to 'sacred children' from the clan. This timber was the dwelling of the Atua i
Tafua during the ritual, while the Atua i Fangarere abode in the
fesisi, the supporting post at its base. These deities were said to
'climb into' their respective timbers. The timbers were rubbed
with oiled leaves by the chief, who recited the following formula:

> I eat ten times your excrement, Rakiteua and Tafito
> Turn to your sacred Lower Rafter
> Which I anoint on this morning.
> Anoint with power,
> Anoint for welfare,
> Your perfumed body.
> Unfold the welfare,
> While unfold properly
> Your sacred coconut there on your crest of the land
> For the perpetuation of the kava.
> And suppress the ills of the coconut.
> Raise the sea's resources
> For the vivifying of the land.
> Rain down your skies.

The term 'perfumed body' refers to the anointed timbers. It is
held that the deities are pleased by the performance, and their
nostrils are delighted with the aroma of oil and bruised leaves.

The subsidiary oven house, Tafua Lasi, was remarkable for the number of mats of deities spread therein (see Fig. 8). Not only the principal gods of the chief himself, but also those of his two principal elders, of Fusi and Sao, were also represented. Then there was a group of deities known as Sa Runga, who had a mat laid for them at the oven-border, and are conceived as fairy-like folk, living on the mountain crest, descending at night to fish, and fleeing back on the approach of dawn. When the oven house was re-carpeted the mats were laid in the order given in the plan. It may be noted that the oven of this house is situated on the opposite side from that which is customary in Kafika Lasi and the other sacred cooking houses.

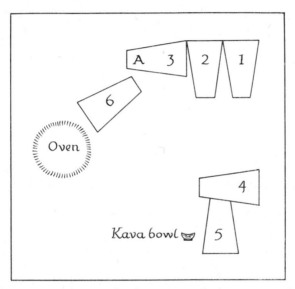

FIG. 8. Re-carpeting of Tafua Lasi Temple (reconstruction)

1, Atua i Tafua; 2, Tuna; 3, Kaufirifiri (past chiefs); 4, Tarikotu; 5, Tokitaitekere; 6, Sa Runga; A, chief

Inland of Tafua stood a third house of moderate dimensions, known as Te Toka. This was re-carpeted by the Ariki at his discretion any time during the ceremonial season. His people in Namo were sent to get fish from the lake, while those in Faea, on the other coast, went out torchlight fishing by night. As soon as a plentiful catch had been obtained word was sent to the Ariki and the ceremony was performed. It was in this house that the late Ariki Tafua, by name Pukenga, was buried at his death some twenty years before (i.e. about 1910). The building was also known as Te Fare Fiti since one of the Atua Fiti, by name Meteua, whose home was said to be in Maunganefu in Vanikoro, was one of the deities there.

RE-CARPETING OF KAFIKA TEMPLE

One of the most important series of rites in connection with the temples was that for the re-carpeting of Kafika.

It is appropriate now to describe the building and its furniture in some detail. The Kafika temple, being the ancestral house of the ranking chief of the island, and under the control of the supreme gods, is, as can be well understood, the principal religious centre of the whole community. It is a large building measuring about twelve yards by six and rising to a height of about fifteen feet at the ridge. Formerly it was both wider and more lofty, but in the repairs consequent upon a severe hurricane which occurred some fifteen years before I arrived its dimensions were lessened for future safety. Kafika, according to tradition, has stood there since the days when men went as gods and gods as men, in that immemorial antiquity before the birth of the great Atua himself, the culture-hero. As generation succeeded generation the temple was rebuilt as it showed signs of decay but preserving continuity through occupation of the one site and incorporation of parts of the former structure. The existing house was erected by Tarotu, a former Ariki (father of Pa Vainunu), about 1900.

The rebuilding of this house is an event of the greatest interest to the whole island. I give here a brief hearsay account. People from all the clans assemble in large numbers, and those of sa Kafika and sa Fangarere collect food and prepare the ovens, while sa Tafua and sa Taumako do the actual work. The former clan has charge of the north end of the house, the latter of the south end, and their division lies at the centre post. The *fare* is of the usual shape, the ridge pole being supported on three huge posts. Every timber of any structural importance in the house has its own special sanctity. The ridge pole – in the present building a trunk of *poumuri* given from the land of Pa Tavi – is usually termed *taufufu*. For Kafika, however, it bears an additional title, Te Fakasiva. When this is hauled into position and settled on the tops of the supporting posts the assembled crowd gives a loud shout, expressive of the safe completion of an onerous task. The tops of the posts are slightly hollowed to receive it, but the real means of security is the *sumu*, the elaborate crossed sinnet-lashing which is the pride of the craftsman. Only a real expert is competent to achieve such work. The central post is that of the Atua i Kafika, and the lashing is termed *Te Sumu Nga Matua* – the Lashing of the Elders. It is *tapu* for any man of Kafika family to make these lashings; the work may be done only by the family group of Rarovi or by those who are immediately descended from Rarovi. Thus for the present house, the central *sumu* was done by Pae Avakofe and Pa Vangatau, brothers of Taumako clan, whose mother was from Rarovi family. The lashing of the post at the south end of the building is termed *Te Sumu Nga Ravenga* and it is the function of sa Taumako to see to it. Pa Vangatau and his brother's son Pa Veterei were responsible for that in the present building. The lashing of the post at the north end – the post of the kava bowl – was the duty of sa Tafua, and was called *Te Sumu Matavaru* – 'The Eight-eyed Lashing'. That standing in 1928 was the work of Pa Akitunu, an expert, dead by the time of my visit. The builders are fed by the people of Kafika while the work is in progress, and on its conclusion are given presents of food and valuables, including bark-cloth and pandanus mats.

A curious feature of Kafika which is not found in other temples is a short stout post standing beside the supporting pillar at the south end of the house. A piece of vine is lashed to them both, and holds the *koso tapu*, the sacred digging stick used in the yam rites. This post commemorates the end of the friendship and rivalry of the Atua i Kafika and his companion Te Samoa. After various feats of emulation, the Atua began to build or rebuild his temple. He went and cut down a *poumuri* tree for a post, then brought it and left it in charge of Te Samoa while he dug the hole. Standing at the bottom he told his friend to lower down the tree on top of him and when he did so, sprang up through the roots and escaped, thus proudly demonstrating his agility and bravery. Then he told Te Samoa to go and dig the hole. The latter did so then in his turn called out in emulation to the Atua to let down the tree. Te Samoa was hoping to follow his rival's example, and shoot up through the gaps in the interlacing roots. The latter, however, foreseeing his intention, twirled the trunk round as he lowered it. Te Samoa was trapped, and the tree descended on his head. To his cry for relief the Atua called 'Sleep then friend! Thy post shall obey thee.' Then he filled in the hole and erected the house. Hence the post is called *Te pou te Samoa*. It was said that the timber now standing was the original *poumuri*; if true it was set in position over 250 years ago. According to one informant the bones of Te Samoa are disinterred when the temple is rebuilt and laid at the base of the post again; it was acknowledged that such was not done for the present structure but that the elders maintain such to have been the practice.

When in the course of setting up the timbers the first rafter is put in position this event also is signalized by a shout from the assembled people. The rafter is situated above the *Tinai Ariki* (see below) and is called *Te Oka o Nga Ariki* – 'The Rafter of the Chiefs'. Its name is said to refer to the ancestors who lie buried beneath the floor. Other rafters have names from various gods of the house. These are *Te Oka o Pu ma*, 'The Rafter of Pu ma'; *Te Oka o Fanau*, 'The Rafter of the Brethren'; *Te Oka o te Atua lasi*, 'The Rafter of the Great Deity', i.e. Te Atua i Fangarere. 'All the gods are complete all together in the house' I was told.

The *Tinai Ariki*, mentioned above, is a large mound of sand occupying the greater part of the south-eastern quarter of the house, and covered with special long mats. Its proportions are impressive in the dim light of the house, and the importance due to its size is accentuated by the fact that it is the place towards which the most sacred ritual, as that of the *raurau kumete*, is oriented. It is held to be the seating place of Pu ma, or Nga Ariki, 'the Chiefs', as they are called in this house when they descend to be present at the kava. In ordinary times they are considered to be absent; they are present only for the 'Work' or for other ceremonies. The mound is theirs and as such is sacred. When it is re-sanded it is believed that if a stone were to fall on the heap it would fall 'to the realm of the gods' and if a person were to stand on it he likewise would sink from sight. 'It is termed the ocean.' This accounts for the precautions presently to be described (cf. Epilogue).

On one side of the *Tinai Ariki* near the centre of the house stands the *Kaufata*, a kind of open crate of bamboo about four feet long. As a material object in the temple it is held to be the property of Pu ma – though constructed by the Atua i Kafika, according to one informant. It has its counterpart, however, in the realm of the gods and this is used in times of epidemic by malevolent *atua*. It is believed that they travel with it along the beach paths and snatch the spirits of any mortals they encounter therein, putting them into the *Kaufata* as container, wherein these people must die. The passing of this ghostly receptacle is a time of dread for all in the villages, and they cower close in their houses lest their souls be reft from them. The wooden structure in the house, according to Pa Vainunu, is correctly known as *Te Vaka a Kofe* (the vessel of bamboo); its spiritual counterpart above is the *Kaufata*. This latter term, however, is commonly used for both the material and the immaterial object. The vessel itself is a flimsy structure. I was told that when it needs repair the Ariki Kafika alone performs the task. No one else may remain in the building with him; all the people stay outside while he relashes it. To accommodate it during the repair and re-carpeting of the temple two pegs are lashed to rafters on the side of the house, and on these it is suspended. The Ariki alone lifts the *Kaufata* to and from these supports, owing to its sacredness.

On the same side of the house as the *Tinai Ariki* and the *Kaufata* – i.e. towards the lake – stands the *fare toki*, the adze house, constituted by a pair of beams under the eave, on which rest the adzes and the 'sacred things'.

In the centre line of the house but near the rear, or north end, stands the *tokotu*, a staging of a type mentioned already. That of Kafika is said to be of great age. Originally it was undercut in notches as that of Resiake (which is a recent replacement), but this section of the timber has now sunk deeply into the ground. Elderly men told me that Pu te Roma, who lived many generations ago, was famed as an expert in the manufacture of *tokotu*, and constructed most of these now existing in the various temples.

The presence of these objects, some affiliated with gods, others with ancestors, most of them sacred, all of great age or reproductions of ancient things, is one of the factors accounting for the reverence displayed by the Tikopia when they enter this building.

As in the case of the other sacred houses there is no indiscriminate renovation of the building. Different sections 'belong' to different lineages or family groups, who lay down their mats on the floor and replace rotten thatch above. Unlike most of the houses, however, these divisions are marked off by rafters, making for more rigid compartments than usual. Fig. 9 indicates these spheres of influence as I noted them in 1929. The kinship groups concerned were those of the chief himself (sa Kafika proper), sa Fangarere, sa Rarovi, sa Porima and sa Tavi. Sa Kafika had the south end of the temple, where the chief's father and other ancestors were buried. This end is known as *te inaki tapu* for this reason.

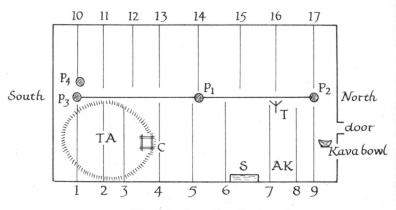

FIG. 9. Ritual Sections of Kafika Temple

AK, Ariki Kafika; C, bamboo crate; P 1, centre post; P 2, north post; P 3, south post; P 4, post of Te Samoa; S, sacred adze shelf; T, wooden stage; TA, Tinai Ariki; 1–3, 10–12, rafter sections of sa Kafika chiefly family; 4–6, Sa Tavi; 7–9, Sa Porima; 13–16, Sa Fangarere; 17 and north end of house, Sa Rarovi

The first day of the ceremonies of Nukuora marked the virtual beginning of those of Kafika, in that the initial piece of thatch for repairing the house was then formally pinned together. The expression used was 'the leaf is stolen'. A man of the clan went out early in the morning before the land was properly light, cut a single branch of the sago palm and returned with it. This was made up by the Ariki Kafika during the day into a sheet or two of thatch. The term 'stolen' is only a figure of speech; the branch was actually taken from the orchard of the Ariki himself, and Tikopia were emphatic that there was no idea of theft from either the Ariki or the deity in charge of the orchard. Pae Sao said, 'Not stolen from orchards (in general), stolen from our own orchard; a custom it is from formerly.' Later the sheet of thatch was sacralized by a small kava rite made formerly with the *fonakava* of Nukuora as basis, or nowadays with that from Taumako. About midday occurred the investiture of a woman from the family of the chief, her duty being to plait the mat for the sacred adze and 'sacred things' of Kafika. This piece of ritual was not elaborate, taking place in the dwelling-house.

On the following morning, that is, the concluding day of the Nukuora rites, the bulk of the thatch for the temple of Kafika was prepared. This work was termed 'the great leaf pinning of Kafika', and was treated primarily as an economic task. Neither the Ariki Fangarere or the Ariki Kafika scrupled about assisting the workers.

In the evening occurred one of those picturesque features of the ritual on which the Tikopia themselves love to dwell in narration – *Te Asunga One*, 'The Scooping of the Sand'. It is a frequent practice of the Tikopia in re-furbishing the graves of their ancestors to bring a basket or two of white coral sand from the beach and spread it on top to give the place of burial a neat and cleanly appearance. In the case of the Kafika temple this has been elevated into a ritual procedure, surrounded with severe *tapu*. In the monsoon season a dozen women, of Kafika or married out of that clan, assembled at the time when the sun was low over the western hill crest and proceeded to Potu sa Kafika, where they each plaited a small basket from fresh coconut leaf. They then set out when the sun had disappeared behind the hills, going in single file along the beach path round the bluff of Fonga te Koro till they reached the level expanse of Namo. Arrived at Suakava, the canoe yard of the sacred vessel of the Ariki Tafua, they halted and spread out in line along the edge of the beach, where the low bank of coral boulders met the sand. Facing up towards the canoe shed they sat down in groups of three or four and scooped out several large holes with their hands. It is from this that the rite takes its name. The sand taken out was used to fill the baskets. While this was in progress no one approached them or called out to them nor did they chatter among themselves, save to pass the few necessary comments on their work. For a man, in particular, to have interfered with them would have been the gravest breach of religious etiquette; he would be certain, according to the Tikopia, to have brought on himself death, or at the least severe illness. (I received permission to observe the proceedings only on condition that I did not set foot on the canoe ground and made no attempt to talk with the women – conditions which of course I kept.) When the baskets were full the women rose all together and walked in single file up to the canoe shed, where they stood for a moment. A man of Kafika clan approached the leading girl in the line and silently handed her a large mat, then retired without a word. She advanced to the canoe shed, laid down the mat, and set her basket upon it, after which the other baskets were passed to her along the line and stacked in one by one. This was done deliberately without haste. Another mat was laid on top covering the heap, and the women then withdrew, as they came, in single file, and walked off the canoe ground. Then they sat down in a group and discussed where they would spend the night. They could elect to sleep together in a single house, or go each to her own dwelling. The decision was specifically stated by the men to be taken upon their personal preference. A reasonable interpretation seems to be that the traditional privilege of spending the night together undisturbed emphasizes their exclusiveness, increases the amount of public attention given to them, and to some extent allows them an assertion of their female group independence.

In the monsoon season the women went as described to scoop the sand in Namo, and set it in the canoe shed of Suakava; in the season of trade-winds, the sand was scooped out in Ravenga at Maraniniu, the canoe court of the Ariki Taumako where the shed of his sacred vessel Te Rurua stood. Alternation is thus made between Tafua and Taumako clans for the provision of material for the Kafika ritual. This is yet another instance of the close interrelation maintained between the autonomous clans in the religious system.

The sand thus obtained was no ordinary material. It was that of the gods Pu ma, and was used on the following day to spread on the *Tinai (Nga) Ariki*, their sacred mound in Kafika house. The removal of it was the duty of women alone, since the task was under the jurisdiction of the Atua Fafine, the Female Deity of the clan. She in fact is held to enact the spiritual counterpart of the work of the women.

It is grasped by the Female Deity. The Female Deity comes to scoop up the sand; that is, goes with the women. The women come among the men, while she comes among the gods to scoop up the sand. The deity of the women goes together with them.

More clearly it is meant that the goddess of the women, the Female Deity, accompanies them on the task and that she duplicates in the realm of gods on the spiritual plane, what they perform

in the realm of men, on the earthly plane. As in the case of 'Plucking the Repa', the deity 'assists in the work' though of course
remaining invisible all the while. This antithesis, and yet parallelism, between the realm of men (*i a tangata*) and that of the gods (*i a
nga atua*) is a constantly recurring feature of Tikopia discussion on
religious matters.

Out of respect to their patroness and the sanctity of their task
the women are supposed to wear clean new bark-cloth skirts for
the occasion. When I saw the procedure this rule was followed by
only one or two of the party, the reason being given, 'because the
land is under restriction; therefore they gird cobwebby; they are
girded with anything poor'. Mourning for the recent death of
relatives was the reason; new clothing might savour of a festive
spirit alien to that of their grief. Hence they girt themselves with
their usual garments dirty, frayed and ragged like a spider's web
from use.

The association of the scooping of the sand with the Female
Deity is the explanation also of the *tapu* imposed on the presence
or interference of men.

The next morning, at dawn, the women rose, assembled at the
canoe ground and, taking their baskets of sand, carried them round
the lake to Uta and set them outside the temple of Kafika, where
they waited till the re-carpeting.

While some people prepared food for the oven others repaired
the thatch of the temple. When this was done they left the building, and the Ariki Kafika came alone to perform the preliminary
ritual. (I was allowed to stay with him and watch.) First he
'bound the post'. For this a mat threaded with a length of young
palm frond was passed in to him through the sacred doorway at the
northern end of the building. He wrapped the mat round the
centre post, with a short formula appealing for efficacy and welfare. Then he lifted the *Kaufata* on to pegs on the wall, and sat
down in his usual place.

Meanwhile the crowd outside had been getting ready. Mats had
been collected for the *inaki*, and each of the women concerned
with the sand-digging the previous night had donned a kind of
collar or ruff by slipping over her head a torn leaf of *rau tea*. A few
of them had also a fillet of green leaf round the brow. These were
their insignia and protection for the sacred task to come. New
skirts were also donned for the occasion. The women crawled into

the house by the door at the south end, led by Nau Kafika, the wife of the chief, and squatted under the eaves. With the assistance of one or two men on the other side of the house they removed the long mats which covered the *Tinai Ariki* and passed them out under the eaves. A pliant rib of a coconut leaf stripped of its fronds was now passed in and with it the wife of the chief smoothed over the top of the mound. The baskets of sand were then brought and the material was scattered on the mound with a sprinkling action. As this was done the crowd sat silent in the house; the Ariki alone murmured:

> Scatter your Tinai Ariki
> With the sand from Suakava.

This was an invocation to the gods Pu ma; an appeal for their approval. (In the trade-wind season the name of Maraniniu was substituted for that of Suakava.) The whole operation occupied several minutes; it was very *tapu* and was watched with great interest by all. It was held that in the sprinkling of the sand the wife of the chief represented the Atua Fafine, who was actually embodied in the mortal woman. 'The Female Deity stands after the manner of the gods; is not discovered' (i.e. is invisible). She was regarded as preparing the place for the mats of Pu ma.

When the sand was spread new mats of great length, formed by tying ordinary ones together in pairs, were laid over the mound, the object being to avoid setting foot upon the sacred place during the process of re-carpeting it. The remainder of the mats for the rest of the house were brought in by degrees and the floor was completely re-covered on the principles described earlier. One mat termed *matua tapakau*, the principal mat, was laid at the foot of the shelf of the sacred adze. All the women now retired from the building, followed by the men, and the Ariki again remained alone to complete the work. (The men tried to induce me to go too, but the chief let me stay.) He removed the binding of the central post and laid it at the foot, on the south side. This was the mat of Te Atua i Kafika. Another mat was brought and laid at the north side of the post; this was for Te Atua Lasi. The sacred digging stick of the yam was set in position at the end of the house, the *Kaufata* crate was lifted down to its place on the mound of the gods, and the vestments of the temple were deposited on the *tokotu* staging. In conclusion the *epa*, a small pandanus leaf mat, was laid on the large coconut leaf mat of the Atua Lasi and covered with some cycas leaves. This mat lies there always as an offering to this deity that he may avert disease from the land, in particular epidemics, over which he has special control. The sacredness of all these objects is the reason why the presence of the common people was not desired at this time.

The practical side of the seasonal 'spring-cleaning' and repair of the temple was now over, but the consecration of this work remained. The chief said to me 'It is finished', and went to bathe. Then he rubbed his chest and arms with aromatic leaves, and sat in his house till the oven was ready. After a while he was reminded that he had forgotten to re-carpet the shelf of the oven house, Kafika Lasi, so did it. He laid on the shelf a leaf of the umbrella palm, and strewed aromatic leaves on it. This was for Te Atua Fiti, to whom the shelf was dedicated. A bunch of a small variety of areca nut was also added, for the betel-chewing of the god.

The oven was now uncovered and the food taken to the temple where the chief and the men of the clan, a score in all, assembled for the kava. First the chief went with oil and aromatic leaves to anoint the central post.

'I eat your excrement, my sacred Chief' he began and continued the invocation in the usual manner. He then renewed the cycas leaves on the *epa* mat, and laid the old ones on the adze shelf. On returning to his seat he rubbed his body and arms with the oiled leaves as a prophylactic measure, as did the Ariki Fangarere also. The kava was then begun, the usual rites, including those of the *raurau kumete*, being performed. Since this was the occasion of the re-carpeting of the temple, however, the *fonakava* had been prepared for the Ariki from his own food supplies. This was carried up and stood beside the *raurau kumete* in formal offering to the gods. Such ceremonial items were not omitted, even when, as in the present case, they practically involved the presentation of food by a man to himself. It was held that the gods were looking on, ever watchful for their offerings. As the kava was of special importance on this day a large bunch of areca nut was brought, and set up opposite the centre post. While the food portions were being allotted the Ariki rose and with hands clasped in front of him in humility went to the bunch, plucked off a nut and laid it at the foot of the post, saying

Prepare a betel wad for yourself.

He was addressing the Atua i Kafika.

After the requisite libations had been poured a hearty meal was eaten by the crowd. It was now about 4 p.m.

The single piece of thatch may be remembered, the 'sacred leaf' which was 'stolen' and prepared two days before. Normally this would be inserted in the roof above the *inaki tapu*. In the monsoon season of 1928 however, on my inquiring for it at the end of the day, the Ariki suddenly recollected that it had been forgotten and was lying out among the trees at the back of the house. This was regarded with amusement and not as a serious mishap; the Ariki announced his intention of using it for the repair of his own dwelling-house. This is an instance of how the ceremonial machine does not always work smoothly and with automatic precision. Since the functioning of the ritual system depends upon *men* such minor adjustments have frequently to be made. (Compare a similar lapse in the yam-planting noted on p. 188.)

In the trade-wind season the 'Work' of Kafika finished on the day of the re-carpeting. In the monsoon period, however, it continued for two more full days, being characterized mainly by extensive food preparation. For the first of these the responsibility was assumed according to tradition by the lineage of Rarovi; for the second the onus lay on the clan of Taumako. The rites in each case were termed the *fakaoatea* and were analogous to that already described in the case of Resiake. The *fakaoatea*, so called because the food is ready about midday, is a kind of finalization or clinching of the ceremony already performed, and the more important the ceremony the more numerous the *fakaoatea* are likely to be, though there is no direct correlation along these lines.

A characteristic feature of the Kafika 'Work' was the obligation of the group whose *fakaoatea* it was on the morrow to send along a bunch of mature green bananas, fit for cooking, together with a load of firewood, on the preceding evening. These were brought by two men and stood up by the wall of the house. The expression is 'the banana is stood up'. On the first evening it is *Te futi Nga Matafare*, on the second *Te futi Pa Taumako*; Nga Matafare being the honorific title for the family of Rarovi. If the head of either of these groups has no bananas ready for the appointed day then he obtains them from the orchard of one of his relatives; if that fruit should be lacking entirely then breadfruit, or even taro, may be substituted. The Ariki and his people are ignorant of the type of the food that will be sent each evening. 'We do not know whether the banana or whether the breadfruit will be brought.' The term *futi* (banana) is still retained however for the food, no matter what may be its nature; it is the form and not the substance of the gift that is important. But on this occasion it was a bunch of bananas. Early the next morning while it was still dark, the oven was prepared in Kafika Lasi by a couple of young men, relatives of the chief, and the banana was set therein. This operation was timed as nearly as possible that the food might be cooked about dawn, for the performance of the early morning kava.

The kava was performed about 5 a.m. (by my reckoning). Only the Ariki Kafika, the Ariki Fangarere and four of their young relatives were present. The special feature of this rite was the 'Washing' (*fakaranu*) of the temple. The Ariki Kafika laid on the palm of his hand a cordyline leaf, set thereon a water bottle, withdrew the stopper and knelt down. Then he recited a formula calling upon the Ariki Fangarere to confirm the rite he was about to perform, that it might bring welfare. Rising, he went with prancing steps along the temple, jerking the bottle freely from side to side, and sprinkling the water in all directions. At the end of the building he turned, replaced the stopper, walked back to the centre post, knelt in obeisance to the Atua i Kafika and hung the bottle at the base of the post. This performance was analogous to that which took place during the canoe rites; its object was to secure general prosperity. The chief described it to me succinctly, 'Sprinkling of the land to live; that man may live; that food may live.' He concluded by saying 'What I have done, friend, very great is its weight.'

The chief then anointed the centre post again, laid a dilapidated *kie* mat as an offering before the Atua i Kafika, by the centre post, and performed the kava, with the elaborate rites of the *raurau kumete*.

This was the day of the *fakaoatea* of Pa Rarovi, and his 'house' prepared a large quantity of food. In accordance with Tikopia custom the Ariki Kafika ordered a contribution of raw breadfruit to be sent over to this man from the Kafika orchards, though he, the chief, was to be the recipient of the food when cooked. It is significant that the contribution was made at a time when the chief and Pa Rarovi were privately by no means on the best of terms. When I asked the chief if he was obliged to do this he replied 'It is made at our own wish'; that is, omission of it would have been a breach of etiquette, but not of definite obligation.

After the early morning ceremony described above, the Ariki remained in the house and was joined shortly after sunrise by those of his elders who desired to participate in the 'Work'. Meanwhile preparations were made in Rarovi, a couple of hundred yards inland, for the *fakaoatea*. When the food was cooking and it was desired to express the necessary coconut cream the hibiscus stick from which the bark was to be stripped was brought to Kafika that the Ariki might touch it. If he had been absent at the time it would have been laid on his seating mat for an instant, then withdrawn. This was said to be a traditional practice of unknown origin; and its basic idea to be to secure contact with the *manu*, the efficacy of the chief.

When the food was finally ready – it consisted of two bowls of fermented vegetable paste with two baskets of breadfruit and taro – it first had the kava performed over it by Pa Rarovi, with preliminary libations to his own deities. It was then carried to Kafika, to be ceremonialized by the Ariki. This was done by the ordinary kava of the temple including the formula over the stem, and the rites of the *raurau kumete*, after which the food was shared out among the party. The quantity was sufficient for each to have a parcel to carry home with him.

Late in the day, when the sun was sinking, a double rite was performed – 'the evening kava inside the house' and 'the evening kava of outside'. The first theoretically was made with libations of fresh coconuts, provided by the donor of the *fakaoatea*. The Ariki Taumako followed the custom, but Pa Rarovi in recent years had ceased to provide this gift of coconuts, which was a cause of offence against him in the mind of the Ariki. He had become 'tired'. Lapses of this kind sometimes occur, more especially in minor details of ceremonial, since individual sense of obligation of the successive office-holders may vary greatly. On the other hand, a practice which has long fallen into desuetude may be revived by an unusually energetic man, either from devotional interest or from the desire to attract public attention. Such differences cumulatively help to account for the slow change in ritual which must take place through the generations.

For the second rite, which took place in the open grass plot between the houses, the kava bowl was prepared. In each case the food portions were provided from household food baskets the contents of which then served as the evening repast for the group. Each of the chiefs and assembled elders had his own separate food basket in front of him for the ceremony; such was the custom. (The following day, in addition to the coconuts, a couple of baskets of food were sent in by the Ariki Taumako. These were termed *te vai* (the water), or *te inu* (the drink), and were greatly appreciated.) In the evening the banana bunch for the next day was brought and stood up against the wall of the house.

The following morning saw a repetition of the ceremonies of the preceding dawn. This was the *fakaoatea* of Pa Taumako, which meant that this clan under their chief were busily engaged in preparing the food. This was a busy time for Kafika also. According to the modern sequence of events Taumako is re-carpeted on the same day as Nukuora, and its *fonakava*, which is presented to the Ariki Kafika, is a huge mass of food of the type already described in Chapter 3 as Te Ara o Pu. It is in fact the second of the presentations to be made. Ordinary *fonakava* and *fakaoatea* are not reciprocated, but custom requires that the *ara* be repaid in kind. On the day of the *fakaoatea* of Taumako, therefore, the people of Kafika took the opportunity to make their return gift. As both the *ara* and its reciprocal have already been dealt with in full in Chapter 3 this reference will suffice here. The remainder of the day's rites followed the form of those of the preceding day. In the evening the 'banana' of sa Kafika was set up against the wall of the temple. The next morning the oven was again prepared in darkness and the kava made at dawn, but this time it marked the end of the 'Work' of Kafika. Then came the Freeing of the Land, to be described in the next chapter.

One feature of the Kafika rites was that the chief and a few of his men followers spent the greater part of each day in the building, going out only for a short time to bathe. Hour after hour they sat, talking, smoking and chewing betel. During the 'Work' of Resiake the men were accustomed to sleep in the house at night, and to recline during the day-time if they chose. This was not the practice in Kafika, where the men left at night in order to go and sleep in their houses. During the day, moreover, it was most strictly *tapu* to lie down at full length in the temple. Everyone sat upright either with legs crossed or feet stretched out in front. The prohibition on reclining is a greater hardship than one might imagine, since it does not allow of short periods of relaxation which relieve the strain of the unsupported upright position. Even a small post at one's back is no permanent relief. By the end of the second day several of the family heads, who were elderly men, began to complain of the ache of their 'broken backs'. If over-come by the desire for rest or sleep one might leave the temple at any time and go and lie down in Nukuora or another of the adjacent houses, but such a shirking of obligations would be hardly consistent with the dignity of an elder, so most of them adopted a stoic attitude. A touch of humour was given on the morning of the concluding day by one of the younger men who was not of the party in residence. The kava ceremony being over at an early hour, he suggested with a grin that the assembly of elders go back and finish the day in the temple. The answer was a very decided negative from the Ariki!

The *tapu* against lying down in Kafika house was said by the Ariki to be of comparatively recent origin, and to have been instituted by a chief of the clan. In former times it was not un-common for the principal men of the island to harbour murderous thoughts towards one another. On a certain occasion, he said, the elder of Rarovi, while lying on his mat in the building, kept watching the Ariki Kafika to see whether he was awake or asleep, that he might catch him off his guard and kill him, thus securing the chieftainship for himself. This unsettled the nerves of the Ariki who gave orders, in consequence, that when the 'Work' was per-formed in the temple all the people should keep sitting up, and this custom has been continued by his successors to the present day. This explanation has the air of a rationalization, but is now believed to be the cause of the *tapu*. Another custom of the 'Work' of Kafika temple is to keep a fire going all the time that the party is in residence there. It was lit each morning as soon as anyone arrived, and was kept alight throughout the day. A peculiarity of the fire was that it was fed not with wood, but with the husks and shells of the coconuts used many days ago for the *poroporo* rite of the yam. When the flesh had been extracted from the nuts the remnants were stored in a corner of the temple, by the inland door, for this occasion. The fire was described as 'the fire of the yam', but the exact nature of its connection with the yam rites (apart from the origin of the fuel) was vague, and nothing definite was known of its ritual value. It was kindled 'for the smoking of the house', but no reason could be given for this.

This account has not covered all the temple rituals, but since some of them take place after the Freeing of the Land it seems more convenient to preserve the chronological order, and describe them in the next chapter.

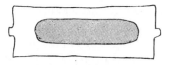

FIG. 10. Sketch of *Raurau Kumete*
(about 2 feet long)

Postscript

The rite of 'Sunning the Perfumes' of Resiake was not performed in 1952 (cf. p. 202). The Ariki Taumako said then, as had his father in 1928, that the performance of the rite was associated with the preparation of coconut oil (cf. pp. 218–19). But whereas in the former case the 'perfumes' were omitted because there was no need to prepare oil, in the latter they were omitted since there were no coconuts available because of the hurricane and drought. So the kava alone was performed. 'It is termed sunning perfumes, but the kava only is made; but if there are coconuts, the perfumes are prepared.'

In re-drawing the plan of Resiake temple for this edition some fresh information has been included about symbolic memorials to ancestors. Again I was told (by Pa Motuata) that the centre post of this temple was dedicated to the Atua i Kafika, and the rafter to which cycas fronds were tied, to the Atua Lasi, the principal god of Fangarere. (The Ravenga side of the temple was controlled by him.) But I was also newly shown by the Ariki Taumako in circumstances of great ritual respect an antique wooden representation of Tuna, the Eel God, said to have been brought to Tikopia by invading Tongans when they killed and ate the daughter of Pu Resiake. (Cf. *History and Traditions of Tikopia*, 1961, pp. 118–19.) In the ritual distribution of offerings, none was set out for this image; it was a passive rather than an active symbol. Among the offerings noted in 1952, not specifically recorded in 1928 though doubtless then made, was one to Pu Tauratua (or Pu Kamota) the spirit medium (*tauratua*) of the founding ancestor Pu Lasi; he was buried on Fongatekoro, but his *noa* of bark-cloth was tied to the rafter above where the food offering was placed. Other offerings were to Pu Nukurenga, ancestor of Maneve lineage, and to Tau Fanau i Faioa, a pair of brothers who took part in the expulsion of Nga Faea; their mat was re-carpeted by their modern representatives, of the lineages of Aneve and Turau.

The re-carpeting of Vaisakiri (p. 221) was performed in a small subsidiary temple in 1952. The Ariki Fangarere said that when his father became a Christian the old temple inland was allowed to fall into decay. The sacred spears had been allowed to rot in the temple, and the conch-shell had disappeared, he knew not where. The sacred shell adze had been given away to one of the Melanesian evangelists, and had therefore been replaced by a sacred implement given him by the Ariki Kafika and Pa Fenuatara. The chief complained of the small number of participants in the rite – apart from me, there were only himself and his two small sons, one of whom prepared the kava and the other served as cup-bearer. The chief said it was not like the days when I was there before. If on other occasions other men attended it would be only one or two. 'They don't go to church and they don't come to the kava. They go and steal in the woods instead!'

For the re-carpeting of Kafika temple my original record of symbolic memorials and offerings was confirmed in detail. But an additional minor piece of information was given to me by Pa Motuata, to the effect that a mat at the far side of the *Tinai Ariki* was for Pu Tanakiforau, chief of Kafika about six generations ago (see *We, the Tikopia*, 1936, p. 347). The Scooping of Sand for Kafika (p. 241) took place by 1952 only from the canoe yard at Maraniniu, of Taumako. The canoe shed of the Tafua sacred canoe at Suakava in Namo, long abandoned, had decayed and there was consequently no ritual place on which to set the baskets of sand for the night.

By 1952 when a number of lineage houses were re-carpeted, because their owners were Christian, food presentations (*fonakava*) alone were given to the chief, and no kava was performed. Such houses cannot be described as temples, the link with the chief being political, not religious (cf. RM, p. 30). This was true of only very few houses in 1928–9.

The houses re-carpeted at this stage (not all on the same day) in the trade-wind season of 1952 were:

KAFIKA	TAFUA	TAUMAKO	FANGARERE
Siamano	Sao?	a Kavasa	Vaisakiri
Tongarutu	Notoa	a Kamota	Fenumera?
Paoari		a Rarokofe	
Timoio		a Maniva	
Motusio		a Aorere	
Nukutauo		a Raniniu	
		b Fatumaru	
		b Niumano	
		b Farekofe	
a kava made by chief		b Ngatotiu	
b kava made by ritual		c Mataioa	
elder		c Ratia	
c no kava made		c Tafora	

Details regarding the Kafika houses will be found in *Social Change in Tikopia*, 1959, pp. 240–3.

The only Tafua houses concerned were the temple of Sao in Uta and the dwelling Notoa in Tai. It was very doubtful if Sao was celebrated; if so its *fonakava* would have been carried to the Ariki Tafua. When Notoa was re-carpeted, a little later, its *fonakava* would be carried to the Ariki Taumako, under whose protection the Sao lineage members in Ravenga lived. (See *Social Change in Tikopia*, 1959, pp. 221–2.) Kava details are given of the Taumako houses. Ratia, the re-carpeting of which had been abandoned before 1928, had come back into the sphere of celebration. But no elder of Ratia had been appointed when the last one died; his eldest son, Pa Nukurotoi, had become a Christian. So he made his food presentation to the chief, but no kava was performed. The same had occurred with Mataioa, and probably with the new house Tafora. Rarokofe, re-carpeted by Pa Nukufuti, was celebrated later than the others, and irregularly. This was done in accordance with the custom that after a chief died some of his adherents would alter their procedures as a mark of respect to him – abandon a sacred canoe, or alter the time of re-carpeting a temple. The forceful character of the Ariki Taumako, and the loyalty of his clan to him, is shown in the comparatively large number of houses re-carpeted at this period, with formal presentation of food to him.

A few details may be added here about Raniniu, temple of the Ariki Taumako in Tai, near his canoe yard (cf. pp. 242, 260). According to the Ariki Taumako in 1952, the fringe at the seaward end was dedicated to Pu Veterei (Pu Taumako Lasi) and the other on *mata paito* was for Pu Raniniu, 'my ancestor', whose name was linked with that of the house. He had been a 'seedling chief' who died at the age of about ten years (Pa Motuata said stillborn) and had become a powerful spirit. The temple also held various important relics, including a broken spear used by Pu Resiake to kill Kaitu of Tafua (*History and Traditions of Tikopia*, 1961, pp. 148–9). The Ariki Taumako took me over to see this weapon. He said 'Let's crawl over quickly, the place is taboo.' We stayed about a minute while he showed me how the deed had been done. Then he said 'Let's withdraw, the place is taboo.' In the house also was a wrist ornament of Matakai II, the Ariki Taumako who voyaged frequently to Vanikoro. A couple of little cylindrical boxes contained bonito hooks. The chief had not looked into them – 'sacred things'; he discussed showing the hooks to me but decided better not. Also there was an *useru*, a bundle of sage pinnule ribs bound together and used by chiefs to beat time to the ritual dirges known as *seru*; this was a replacement of an earlier implement. Raniniu was re-carpeted four days after the bulk of temples. An orange bark-cloth was offered to Pu Lasi, the originating ancestor of Taumako, and a white bark-cloth to the eel-god of the sacred adze, under the name of Tumoana (a name which the chief uttered in a whisper, hardly moving his lips).

6

Freeing the Land

It will be remembered that the initial ceremony of the seasonal Work, the 'Throwing of the Firestick', plunged the whole of the island into a state of *tapu* which prevented the people from dancing, from shouting loudly, and even from sitting in groups on the beach in the evening for general conversation. This *tapu* was most intense during the period of the yam ritual, and in fact was said to have its foundation in this. The removal of the *tapu* constitutes a restoration of freedom, and is marked by the performance of all those things which have been interdicted. Loud shouting, conch-blowing and other penetrating noises are indulged in, people emerge once more from their seclusion, and dancing begins among the young folk that very evening.

The ceremony of 'freeing the land' is called '*fakatanga o fenua*', *tanga* being the term of opposite significance to *tapu*. The expression '*Te kere e masofa, e tanga fakalaui*' applies to the freeing of the soil from restrictions likewise. The 'freeing of the land' takes place a couple of days before the yam is planted, and after dark that same night the burning-off of the yam cultivation is done by the women.

The morning of the appointed day was one of great excitement. From earliest dawn the children were awake, and told by their parents that today the land was free, they ran about through the village between the houses, shrieking at the topmost pitch of their voices. When the sun got up the din increased as adults, too, showed off their lung power. '*Iefu! Iefu! Iefu!*' rang along the shore, and was answered by similar whoops from the hill slopes round the lake, whither people were by this time dispersing to their work in the cultivations. Mingled with the high-pitched notes of the voices was a dull hollow boom, caused by beating the buttresses of the Tahitian chestnut tree. This was the *pakū* of timber, in contrast to the human *forua*, both being conventional means of expression. The noise continued spasmodically for an hour or so, after which only an occasional yell was given according to some person's fancy.

During this time the Ariki and his attendant elders were gathered in Kafika temple where they performed the final kava of the building just after sunrise. After this was over they sat and talked, discussing chiefly the fishing of the previous night, since fish were a necessary part of the *fakatanga* offerings. If the sea had been too rough for the canoes to go out, then nets would have been set in the lake. Actually, however, in this case a breakdown in the organization occurred. It was the duty of the family of the Ariki, who were living in Tai, to go out the evening before and procure a catch. They were feeling slack, however, and failed to do this. When a youth arrived as messenger from the head village he was at once asked for details of the fishing. He replied that two canoes from the village of Taumako had gone out, but none from the Kafika village. The Ariki was very annoyed. 'May their fathers eat filth! Excrete in their gullets! No fish for the *fakatanga*?' The Ariki Fangarere, sitting with him, also chimed in: 'Shall the *fakatanga* be abandoned?' Then the Ariki asked how many fish had been secured by the Taumako canoes and on being told – seven and ten respectively – began to be appeased. For etiquette ensured that the best portion of the catch would be sent along for the rite.

The Ariki then gave instructions to several youths to begin the preparations for the more formal celebration of the *fakatanga*. They must return to Tai, collect a crowd of boys, then break down a number of coconut fronds and return, whooping as they came, by the path round the lake to Uta. On this mission they departed.

The breaking or cutting of coconut leaves was a further sign that the *tapu* had been removed – it was a subsidiary element of the ritual directly related to the ceremonies of Kafika temple. 'When the land is *tapu* not a man shall go and cut coconut leaf. Now it is freed for coconut leaf, and we carry coconut leaf hither', the chief explained to me. Once coconut leaves had been cut and laid on the roof of the temple the leaf became *tapu* for all the people, a state of affairs which lasted for four days. No-one might cut the leaf either wantonly or for utilitarian purposes, even so much as to cover the thatch of his house or to make baskets. For the various meals of the ceremony dry baskets only were used; no fresh ones were made. This observance was correlated with a

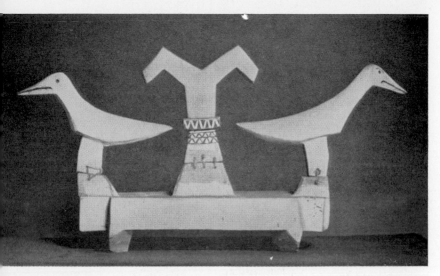

1*a*. *Turi* and *Manutapu* as canoe ornaments (1929). The naturalistic *turi* (turnstone) flank the conventionalised symbolic form of the bird. (This sculpture, the work of Pa Fenuatara, was lost in London during the war.)

1*b*. Preparing food for the rites of Resiake (1929). The Ariki Taumako (far left) with bushy hair directs and participates in the Work.

2a. Kava rite (1929). The Ariki Taumako is about to throw offerings of areca nut in a rite outside the temple of Resiake.

2b. Kava rite (1952). The Ariki Taumako, son of the chief in 2a, recites a kava formula for his sacred canoes.

3a.Filling the basket with sacred yams (1952). The little yam house stands to the right.

3b. The kava-maker at Takerere (1952). Pa Timoio of Tavi fills a pipe after the rite is over. His fan is stuck at the back of his belt.

4a. Offerings in Marae (1929). Flying fish and raw breadfruit laid before a stone of Pu ma in the Freeing of the Land.

4b. Offerings in Marae (1929). Pa Porima lays cooked food before the stones of Pu ma in the kava of Marae.

5*a*. Kava of Marae (1929). Water is poured into the kava bowl.

5*b*. Kava of Marae (1929). The Ariki Fangarere withdraws backwards, crouching in respect, from Muafaitoka.

6*a*. Kava of Somosomo (1929). 'Clapping' the kava. The Ariki Kafika is sitting with back to the camera, Pa Tavi to his left and Pa Rarovi to his right.

6*b*. Kava of Somosomo (1929). Pa Rarovi plucks an areca nut as offering.

7a. Kava of Somosomo (1952). The Ariki Kafika recites a formula over the kava stem. The Ariki Fangarere and Pa Timoio attend.

7b. Kava of Somosomo (1952). The Ariki Kafika throws a foot offering. Note the stone of the turmeric enclosure at his back.

8a. Kava of Somosomo (1952). The Ariki Kafika recites the formula of the evening kava near the lakeside.

8b. Kava of turmeric manufacture (1952). The Ariki Kafika pours a libation ango in front of the eaves of his house after the turmeric has been filtered. His grandson assists as cup bearer. His spear, a ritual token, is stuck in the ground nearby.

belief that to cut coconut leaf at this time was to invite one of the dreaded storms which sometimes arise in this season and cause considerable damage. The completion of the ceremonies of Kafika removed this ban. Hence on the evening before, the Ariki said to his family as they were leaving Uta for the beach village, 'You go and sleep, then wake to go out in the sea to make free the land. We here will sit and wait. If you shall sit, and not go out to sea, then let someone come and break hither the coconut leaf and bring it with him to Uta here, that we may know.' In other words, he gave instructions that the freedom of the land was to be marked by the cutting of coconut fronds, if by nothing else.

This was the task of the youths already mentioned. After an interval of an hour or so they could be heard returning, with yells and shrieks and the blowing of rough trumpets made from rolls of pandanus leaf. At last they emerged on to the Marae. They were walking in single file, the foremost carrying coconut leaves cut in Tai, the others a fish tied to a stick, or a breadfruit plucked as they came along, and all were shouting vociferously. All were clad in ordinary costume. They ceased their yells, then laid down their burdens close to the path which ran across the centre of the Marae, and went to squat down at a distance at the side of the temple of Taumako. The Ariki, girt with his cincture, came down from Kafika and went over to where the food had been laid. Squatting down he uttered a formula, the 'announcing' of the fish and breadfruit to the other chiefs.

> Pa Tafua, Pa Taumako, Pa Fangarere your assemblage of
>   elders there
> Countenance me in the land which is freed this morning.

After thus figuratively appealing to the other chiefs for con-firmation of his act in removing the *tapu* he turned to the food and divided it into portions. These were allotted to the principal clan deities, each of whom had a stone slab in the Marae at which his special offering was deposited on this and similar occasions. There were five portions, of which the first, with the coconut leaves, was carried by an assistant and placed at Muafaitoka, in front of the sacred house Rarofiroki. (A description of Marae and its ritual features is given in Chapter 9.) This first portion was for the Atua Lasi of Fangarere. 'There is your share, Futiotekere', murmured the Ariki as he handed it to the attendant, calling upon his own

name for the deity. The next was set for Pu ma, and the others for
Rakiteua, Sakura and Nga Anuta (gods of the island of Anuta,
seventy miles away), each with a similar utterance. All the clans
were thus embraced in the rite. Sometimes the Female Deity is
also included in the division of offerings under the name of
Ruanofine.

'Conveyed that they may look at it', was the expression used
for these offerings. They were made that the various deities, each
seeing his portion placed by his stone, might be satisfied that they
were not forgotten when the land once more reverted to its
mundane state.

When this was finished the Ariki rose, collected the sticks with
which the fish and breadfruit had been carried and walked down
the path towards the group of youths. These stood up and as the
Ariki looked meaningly at them they gave a single united shout.
They then dispersed and went to their own houses. This marked
the carrying of the *fakatanga* from the shore inland to Uta, the
sacred district, the heart of the island. The land was now completely free from its special *tapu*.

The food offerings were carried to the houses of the respective
Ariki who were in residence in Uta. If they had not been there the
food would have been taken to the house of the Ariki Kafika
alone, for consumption. Food had been cooking in the oven
meanwhile, and was now taken out for the performance of the
kava. This was a minor ceremony with libation of the usual type.
'The Work is finished', said the Ariki, at its completion.

This de-sacralizing ritual was performed in the monsoon season
only; in the trade-wind it was omitted by custom, and the actual
planting of the yam marked the freeing of the land. The reason, it
was alleged, was that in the monsoon alone was there danger of
high winds and storms. But there was some inconsistency in the
statements about the duration of this *tapu*. The basis of the whole
period of restriction from the Throwing of the Firestick to the
Freeing of the Land lies in the deference paid to the sacred yam.
This is made clear by a body of explicit statements as well as by
the behaviour of the people. Thus:

The origin of things that are done, the yam only. Works of the
tonga, originate in the yam, works of the *raki*, originate in the yam.
Originate in him, because he is the chief who is superior.

In other words, the ceremonial cycles of both seasons (including their *tapu*) have their foundation in the yam, that is in Te Atua i Kafika, its controller, who is the supreme chief and deity of the island.

In enlarging upon this point it was said that while the yam is above ground the land is *tapu*; it is only when it has been planted and buried out of sight that restrictions are abolished. Thus the chiefs will then say 'Go and dance; the yam has been planted; has become lost down below.' People are then at liberty to dance, sing and play as they please. In this the ceremonies of the *raki* and of the *tonga* do not quite agree. In the latter the disappearance of the yam beneath the soil coincides, as in Tikopia theory it should, with the removal of restrictions. In the *raki*, however, it follows the 'freeing of the land' with an interval of a full day between, so that actually the licence of noise is regained before the yam is planted. This lack of coincidence between theory and practice was not satisfactorily explained by the Tikopia, who were apparently content to follow traditional modes of thought and action without analysing carefully the relations between them.

The day of the 'Freeing of the Land' saw the continuance of the ceremonies of the sacred houses, a number in Tai being renovated and re-carpeted on this occasion, including Raniniu, an important house of the Ariki Taumako, and Notoa, the dwelling of Pae Sao. The next day others in the beach villages were celebrated, including Vangatau and Veterei, both under the control of the Ariki Taumako, who went upon invitation and performed the kava therein. Meanwhile the Ariki Kafika had gone back to the work of the yam, this day being its *fakaora*. The following morning the yams were planted, and no houses were re-carpeted on this day, because of the *tapu*. It was believed that if the prohibition were disregarded a storm would burst, unroof the offending house, and others also. Such a consequence, it was said, had actually happened in former times. The next day was the *soani to* which completed the activities in connection with the yam and freed the Ariki Kafika from restriction. Now he could go abroad freely once again and dwell once more in his house by the shore.

RE-CARPETING OF MAPUSANGA

The day following the chief attended the re-carpeting of Mapusanga, the last of the temples to be celebrated in the monsoon season. The ceremonies occupied but the single day. A feature of note in Mapusanga – as also in Raniniu – was the *kara*, a fringe made from cordyline leaf split and joined, similar to that described for Nukuora, but much larger, the *kara* of Mapusanga being six feet long with a fringe eighteen inches deep. Its preparation was a formal matter. Two women, young and unmarried, went in the morning to Rakisu, the plain at the south end of the island, and brought back a load of yellowed leaves. They then sat down on the *tuaumu* side of the house and split them, finally plaiting them together in the requisite form. This work lasted several hours, and during it no one might speak to them. The men, who were engaged in preparing food, sat in the house and talked among themselves, but ignored the women, who went quietly on with their work. Children who intruded were chased out again with the remark that the *kara* was being made; 'It is *tapu*.'

The *kara* of Mapusanga was said by Pa Te Arairaki, immediate owner of the temple, to be that of Pu ma. That of Raniniu, where the same procedure obtains, was said, by the Ariki Kafika, to belong to Pu Veterei, a former Ariki Taumako. After his death, it was said, he went to reside in Ngarumea, a land beneath the sea, and from there returned with a bevy of *atua* to be represented in Raniniu. Hence the cordyline fringe in that house is termed ' *Te kara sa Ngarumea*.' But according to Pa Motuata, of Taumako, there are two fringes in Raniniu. One belongs to Pa Raniniu, a stillborn brother of Pu Veterei, who is buried under a raised mat in the temple (see p. 254); the other, of sa Ngarumea, is that of Pu Veterei.

As part of the ornamental furniture of Mapusanga a spear was hung up along one of the side beams. It was an ancient weapon of different shape from those of Tikopia, with spikes close-set behind the head and a much lighter and thinner shaft. It was said that formerly long spines of bone were set at the end of its wooden barbs, in which case it would be very similar to a typical weapon of the Western Solomons. However, tradition relates that this spear was one of a group of seven which came ashore in company with a woman from Nanumanga, a land to the north. Her canoe was lost at sea, and she drifted to land. One of the spears was in Vaisakiri, one in Resiake, one in Rangateatua, the dwelling of the Ariki Fangarere, and one in Mapusanga, while the others, formerly hung in Tafua and affiliated houses, had perished. (It is interesting to note the manner in which these weapons have been absorbed into the Tikopia religious system, being taken over by the various chiefs and made to serve as embodiments of their respective gods.)

When the oven with its mass of food had been covered, the replacement of the mats of the house took place. At the same time the spear was taken down and, with a sacred shell trumpet, was washed in the sea. The shell was then blown a number of times on the way up from the beach and also outside the eaves of the house, thus giving the signal that the food was cooking. Both these sacred objects were then deposited on a mat in the house. Later, when the oven was uncovered, a messenger went over to Uta to summon the Ariki Kafika. All preparations were made for him, the *fonakava* and other food baskets were placed before his seat, and a man sat behind the kava bowl. The chief entered, seated himself for a moment, then went and hung up the spear and the shell trumpet. He then lifted down the *kara*, which had been folded in a mat, and rolling it up tightly, poured a few drops of oil in it. Rubbing the fringe round in his hands to impregnate it thoroughly he tossed it on a mat, then, after putting on a necklet of Cordyline leaf, he tied up the new *kara* in place of the old ones hanging from the roof. A couple of smaller fringes were spread out on a mat near the rear end of the house by Pa Rarovi, after which both men rubbed their bodies and arms with oiled aromatic leaves. These subsidiary fringes were one for a former Ariki Kafika who was lost at sea, and the other for Pu Veterei, the Ariki Taumako mentioned above.

This completed the decoration of the house, and the kava ritual followed. This was the same as performed for the Kafika temples in Uta, save that a final libation was poured to Te Atua i te ava, Tupuafiti, the adze deity of Fangarere, who was invoked only in the kava of Tai. A meal concluded the events of the day, after which the *fonakava* was carried to Uta by canoe and left at the house of the Ariki Kafika. It may be noted that the closeness of the kinship between the people of Mapusanga 'house' and the chief – they are all 'the one family' – did not release them from the obligation of making the ritual basket of food and presenting it to the chief. Since he was the suzerain of the temple and they were its immediate owners, they complied with the general custom of the *fonakava*.

In the evening, a formal announcement was sent by the Ariki Kafika to each of his fellow chiefs, summoning them to attend the following morning at Rarokoka, a small open glade in Uta. There in former times an annual proclamation was delivered by the Ariki Tafua.

7

The Proclamation at Rarokoka

Of the many ritual formulae in use in Tikopia none can have been more striking than that formerly recited as a public address or proclamation at Rarokoka. Not only was it picturesque in setting – the glade in the forest, the rising sun, the expectant silent crowd, and the towering figure of the chief of Tafua rolling out the phrases – but the speech itself was remarkable for its dignity and rhythm and for the moral code which it promulgated. The ideas contained therein can no doubt be paralleled from those held by other peoples in various parts of the world, but rarely in a primitive society has expression been given to them in such a formal explicit statement of the duties and obligations incumbent on its members.

The *fono* as an address to the people by a man of rank is known to other Polynesian cultures.[1] In Tonga harangues were made to the commonalty by the chiefs on matters of agriculture, political duty, and behaviour at public ceremonies, and also on minor questions of the repair of a noted canoe, the freedom of a plantation from tribute or the improvement of the conduct of young chiefs towards women they met on the road. In Samoa the *fono* is the actual group or assembling of *matai*, of titled men of a village district or island, and public announcements or addresses are made there. In Tikopia, however, the *fono* differed from this. It was not of frequent, irregular occurrence as occasion required, but a specific unique event, occurring once only in the year on the day fixed by the sequence of ceremonies in the seasonal cycle.[2] Again,

[1] e.g., William Mariner, *Tonga Islands*, 3rd ed., 1827, pp. 229–31; Basil Thomson, *The Diversions of a Prime Minister*, 1894, pp. 85–94; Margaret Mead, *Social Organization of Manu'a*, 1930, pp. 10–18.

[2] As I came to realize later, other *fono* of a secular character also took place in Tikopia from time to time as need dictated. (See my *Social Change in Tikopia*, 1959, pp. 100–5.) The Rarokoka assembly was the only regular *fono*.

it had not the character of a personal extempore speech on some affair of the moment; both matter and phraseology were prescribed by tradition. Moreover, it had strong religious associations, and the chief who spoke was deemed to be the mouthpiece of the gods. In other words the sanction of the *fono* in Rarokoka was not simply social and political, exercised through the authority of the presiding chiefs, but was intensely religious as well, receiving its validity from its superhuman origin. It is essential to understand this in order to realize the force of the impression produced on the audience by this recital.

I have spoken of the *fono* in the past because owing to the defection of the Ariki Tafua the actual address is no longer given, and this is one of the few events of the ritual cycle which I did not observe. But I obtained full accounts of it from several informants, and in particular was given the text of the formula recited, by the Ariki Kafika and by the Ariki Tafua. It was the latter who had the privilege and duty of reciting the *fono*. Nowadays, in the absence of this chief, no move has been made to secure a substitute. The three other chiefs merely meet at Rarokoka in the early morning, sit for a while in their appointed positions and talk, and then return home. No crowd of people assembles, as formerly. But both the continued meeting of chiefs, denuded as it is of dramatic accompaniment, and the lack of attempt to replace the Ariki Tafua, are indices to the specific religious meaning of the *fono*, as will be seen later. For convenience, I give the rest of the material in this chapter in the historic present, as it was made known to me.

THE PROCLAMATION IN FORMER DAYS

The first act in connection with the *fono* takes place on the evening of the re-carpeting of Mapusanga. When the rites of this temple are over the Ariki Kafika sends a formal announcement to each of his fellow chiefs:

> You group of elders there,
> Wake for your Masauma tomorrow.

Masauma is the sacramental name for the Marae of Rarokoka. On receiving the message – for which of course they are prepared – the chiefs assent formally 'Yes!' This notification is termed 'speeding the messengers of the chiefs'.

Rarokoka, or Masauma, is a small glade in the forest to the

north of the large Marae of Uta, and in it are standing several large stones, representing the principal clan gods.

On the following morning the Ariki rise early, get into their canoes and paddle across the lake in order to arrive at the place before the rising of the sun. There the chiefs of Kafika, Taumako and Fangarere take their seats by the stones of their deities, while the male members of each clan, who have assembled earlier, sit down in the rear of their respective leaders. The people of Tafua take their appointed place also, but their Ariki remains in his sacred house till the assembly is complete. When all is ready, clad in a new white cincture, he walks down the path from the building to the Marae. A careful watch is kept by the crowd, and as he appears someone whispers 'He has come', and all heads are immediately bowed. Not a man, not even the chief of Kafika, may look up as the Ariki enters to deliver the *fono*. 'He will enter and make his speech, not a person shall look at him, alone he will speak.'

When the Ariki has halted and surveyed the crowd he calls out to the Ariki Kafika

Deliver the address you Tinamo.

But that chief with bowed head replies

Deliver the address you Worker (Faifekau).

As Tinamo is the personal title of the Ariki Kafika, so Faifekau is that of the Ariki Tafua, since he is the executive officer of the supreme chief. Hence he assents 'Yes!', and proceeds to carry out his task.

I give below two versions of the formula he used to recite. Text I was that supplied by the Ariki Kafika, Text II that supplied by the Ariki Tafua himself. The latter is fuller, not only because the reciter may be expected to provide a more complete text, but also because it includes some injunctions which were said to have been deleted from the recital in the last generation. For ease of comparison I have divided the recital into sections.

TEXT I

(1)   *Te oro o Ravenga*
       Na niu, na kaula
       Ke tuke maru.
       Ke maru i nia?
       Ke maru ki a rongo o fenua.

(2)   *Te oro o Namo*
       Na niu, na kaula
       Ke tu ke maru.
       Ke maru i nia?
       Ke maru ki rongo o te fenua.

(3)   *Tangata ne fenatu ku faia ko ana nea*
       Puni ki roto ko ona ngutu.
       A ke forua ke ea?
       Ka fenatu te tangata o paito nga ariki
       Nai fainiaria?
       Te atua o te fenua e sokotasi.

(4)   *Tangata ne tu atu ki tona tofi*
       Kai ki tana foi niu
       Kae tao ki raro tana foi puru.
       Te fakaarofa ne fenatu
       Ono ki anea o paito nga ariki ku fakapini mai
       Au fakapini atu ko ni nea mona
       Kae peri ke ea?
       Ka poi o kaia?

(5)   *A tangata ne taufirifiri*
       Fekite i roto te ara
       Fai taranga fai taranga
       Mavae ki tua
       Tasi poi i a ko ia.

(6)   *Tangata tau tofi, ana nea e tu i tona tofi*
       Te tapa o tona manava
       Kae te vae ara te tofi o nga ariki.

TEXT II

(1)   *Te oro o Namo*
       Na niu na kaula
       Ke tu ke mau.
       Tuku Ravenga,
       Na niu na kaula
       Ke tu ke mau.

(2)   *Nia o ta tangata ne riro i nga uta*
       Ne mataki i tona fiakai.
       Te vae ara te tofi o nga ariki.

(3)   *Fenatu te fakaarofa o ono atu ki anea o te maru ku fakangiti*
          mai
       Au fakapini atu ko ona nea
       Kae peri ko ana nea
       Ka poi kaia?

(4)   *Te tangata ne tu atu ki tona ngangea*
       Ka kai tana foi niu, tao ki raro ke maopopo
       Kae peri ko ana nea
       Ka poi kaia?

(5)   *Te tangata ne kau ki tona nofine ke poi*
       Uru atu ku pa i te tuakoi ke foki
       Ka ku uru atu kua uru ki mua, kua uru kese fuere, kua
          uru ki take ngangea.

(6)   *Te tangata ne poi fakaangavare*
       E fakarongo ake ka fati ke ena i tona manava
       Kae titi fakaoti
       Nia ka fakamau ko tona manava?
       Ke tuku ko tenea ke ena i tona manava ma fakamau o tona
          manava.
       Kae titi fakaoti
       Ka poi kaia?

(7)   *Te tangata ne me atu ki tona fafine*
       E fakarongo ake ke masike
       E sokotasi te tangata sokotasi te fafine
       Tena te faki o te foi niu kae te kae o te vai.
       Ka meaki te tangata ka fakauruuru,
       Tefea tona tafito i rakau ka fakauruuru ki ei?
       Ka fakauruuru fuere o poi o kaia.

TRANSLATION I

(1)   The path of Ravenga
       Its coconut, its areca nut
       To stand to ripen.
       To ripen for what?
       To ripen for news of the land.

(2)   The path of Namo
       Its coconut, its areca nut
       To stand to ripen.

To ripen for what?
To ripen for news of the land.

(3)   Man who went his things have been stolen,
Press together his lips.
And he would shout to what end?
When the man of chiefly family goes
He will make something for him?
The deity of the land is one.

(4)   Man who stood over in his garden
Let him eat of his coconut
And stack below its husks.
The commoner who went,
Saw something of the chiefly families which has been prepared
Let him come and tie up something for himself.
But he will destroy to what end?
Will he go and steal?

(5)   Men, with murderous thoughts towards each other,
Meeting in the middle of the path,
Let them have speech, have speech,
Separate back,
Each go on his way.

(6)   Man owning an orchard, his things which stand in his
     orchard.
The fortifying of his belly.
But the border of the path, the orchard of the chiefs.

TRANSLATION II

(1)   The path of Namo
Its coconut, its areca nut
To stand firm.
Allow Ravenga
Its coconut, its areca nut
To stand firm.

(2)   Anything of a man's hidden inland
Observed in his hunger.
The border of the path, the orchard of the chiefs.

(3)   Comes the commoner to look at things of the *maru* which
              have been pressed together.
         Return, bind up his things.
         But if he destroys his things,
         Shall he go and steal?

(4)   The man who stood over in his place
         To eat his coconut, stack it down to be complete.
         But if he destroys his things.
         Will he go and steal?

(5)   The man who ordered his wife to go
         Goes out, has struck the barrier, to return
         But has gone out, has gone in front, has gone apart only,
              has gone to another place.

(6)   The man who went to face around
         Feels that it will break and stay in his belly
         But voids completely
         What shall bind his belly?
         Leave the thing to stay in his belly for the binding of his
              belly.
         But void completely
         Shall he go and steal?

(7)   The man who slept with his wife
         And feels thus let him rise
         One male and one female
         That is the plucking of the coconut and the carrying of
              the water bottle
         The man who will persist in creating himself a family
         Where is his basis of trees he will create his family for?
         He will make a family merely to go and steal.

It is regrettable that the sonorous rhythm of the original cannot
be reproduced in translation. As the texts are critical documents
the rendering has been made as literal as is possible consistent with
clarity, and a more detailed linguistic analysis than usual is
desired.

INTERPRETATION OF THE FORMULA

In Text I the *fono* opens with the command that the coconuts and
areca nut in the lowlands of Namo should be allowed to remain

until they are mature. The coconut is mentioned since it is the keynote to the food supplies of Tikopia. The indispensable element in all the better foods is coconut cream, obtained from the flesh of the brown mature nut. If the nut is plucked while it is still young and green it is much better for drinking purposes, and the flesh being soft is pleasant for immediate consumption. Forming only a thin layer in the interior of the nut, however, it is of much less food value than at the later stage. What is probably the most discussed point of the Tikopia agricultural economy is the establishment of an equation between the consumption of young and of properly matured nuts. The green coconut is provided extensively for ceremonial purposes, and is also utilized largely as refreshment by people working in their orchards. Too reckless a consumption of the green coconuts, however, means that there will soon be a dearth of the older nuts for creamed puddings. Hence in any but times of great plenty, there is a perpetual conflict of opinion between the young people and their elders, and between the commoners and the men of rank. In domestic life the married men and the elders accuse all the bachelors and youths of eating green coconuts too freely; the young men deny it and accuse their elders of slander, or speak of theft by persons unknown. In the wider social sphere the chiefs in the privacy of their families discuss the gluttony of the commoners and the wealth of coconuts that would be theirs if they would exercise more restraint, while these latter in their turn bemoan the poverty of their orchards. From the point of view of mere living, a dearth of mature coconuts is of no importance, since the coarser kinds of food provide all the requirements of nutrition. But Tikopia custom requires that every gift of food shall contain a package of creamed pudding. This applies to social as well as to religious presentations. Hence a time of scarcity of dry coconuts is a time of social embarrassment, for most people have difficulty in procuring the requisite nuts from their own orchards or in borrowing them, and unless they do, they will be shamed by the non-fulfilment of their duties. A Tikopia will go on short commons himself and eat rough food, but he will not neglect the appropriate periodical gifts to his chief unless the time is one of great stress. A central idea of the Tikopia social economy is that the interests of the commoner should always be subservient to those of the chief; the food supplies of the commoner should be held in readiness for public occasions of which his chief is the sponsor. Stealing of coconuts in seasons of scarcity is not infrequent, and the chief unwittingly may be a participator in the spoils. But such theft is regarded as evil, because of the disturbance which it causes, and the premature loss of food which is sustained.

This preliminary explanation allows the general tenor of the opening part of the *fono* to be perceived. It is an injunction in favour of economy, and against theft, to preserve both coconut and areca nut. The reason is asked in a rhetorical question, and the answer is given – that they may mature for 'news of the land', that is for the important public events initiated by the chief. The use of such a metaphorical phrase is dictated, as will be fairly clear, by the fact that such festive occasions set the whole land talking. The proclamation is first repeated (Section 1) for the benefit of the lowlands of Ravenga, on the eastern and southern shores of the lake, and then (Section 2) applied to those of Namo, on the north shore. The district of Faea is not mentioned, possibly because by tradition the text of the *fono* received definite formulation in the period prior to the occupation of Faea by the present inhabitants. The term *oro* might be regarded as a poetical form of *ara*, path, and is so translated by some informants. More correctly, however, according to the Ariki Kafika, it is an abbreviation of an archaic term *orooro*, equivalent to the modern *rauraro* meaning lowland. Another form of this word is seen in the name of Te Roro, the flat expanse at the foot of the cliffs on the northern side of the lake, which is in reality Te Orooro (o Namo).

Section 3 is a caution not against theft, but against giving way to unbridled passion when one's food has been stolen. The common practice of a Tikopia on being robbed is to stand up and shriek at the top of his voice, varying this by curses of the excretory type which serve as a vent for his feelings and apprise other people of his loss. Such conduct is pardonable, but may be unwise. For if a chief or a man of chiefly family is in the vicinity he will come to inquire the cause and soundly rate the noisy one. Such disturbance of the peace is a breach of etiquette and will have to be atoned for by a gift of food. Hence the aggrieved owner is advised to 'compress together his lips'. What is the use of shrieking? Does he wish to pay a fine to the next man of rank who comes along? The statement that 'the god of the land is one' is highly figurative. It means briefly that the chief is the sole source of authority in the land. This being the case, it is implied, what does a commoner mean by making such a noise and, as it were, arrogating to himself the privilege of a chief? It must be said, however, that the command to refrain from advertising a theft and to suppress one's feelings is disregarded and with impunity by many Tikopia. And on such occasions public sympathy is with the sufferer. No one, however, would dare to yell in such fashion close to a chief's house.

Section 4 opens with an appeal for orderliness in the orchards. The man who goes to his property is requested to eat the coconut which he desires and then to stack the husk properly beneath the tree, i.e. with the outside surface uppermost. This is in conformity with religious usage, and is normally observed since the coconut is regarded as being under the control of the Atuai Tafua, and the symbol of his head. Hence out of respect to him the husk and shell are carefully packed together in an inconspicuous fashion, and not left to lie about the ground. 'It is prohibited.' Of husk which has been thrown about it is said, 'It has been scattered stupidly – the man has made sport with the gods and the chiefs.' A chief seeing the husk thus lying around will whoop in anger. The reference to this in the *fono* has also a further implication; it is a warning against theft. For a man who is interfering with the coconut trees of another without authorization is in haste lest he be seen, so that he rarely takes the trouble to stack the residue properly.

The next sentences are a variation on the theme of the duty of commoners to consult the interests of their chief. For if a commoner, going to his lands, observes that on those of a chiefly family a taboo has been placed to restrict consumption and conserve the choicer items, then let him go and do likewise for himself. It is an indication that a chief is preparing for some public function to which he himself will be expected to contribute when the time comes. Let him therefore take heed and practise economy that he may be able to play his part. But if he continues to consume his food supplies indiscriminately without reserving any portion, what will he do when the occasion arrives? Will he go and steal in order to fulfil his obligations? – such is the thought expressed.

The term *peri* also involves further shades of meaning. In disputes over boundaries, or the ownership of gardens, one or other of the contestants may in anger destroy (*peri*) the crops at the debated spot, by slashing them with a knife or pulling them out. But in the above statement it is rather a warning against wanton consumption of food supplies.

Section 5 is designed more expressly for the preservation of public order. Private feuds are not uncommon in Tikopia, generated as a rule by either of the two universal causes of strife – land and women. Such men are said to *ramarama*, or *firifiri* towards each other, harbour in secret murderous thoughts which turn over and over in their minds. Usually such men seek to avoid each other, taking separate paths to their work. If they should meet a wordy argument is the result, ending often in blows. By the *fono* they are enjoined to dispute in speech only and that this being concluded they should turn their backs and each pursue his own way.

The final section (6) gives a formal definition of one aspect of the rights of ownership of the chiefs over the orchards of their people. For while the food supplies which remain hidden from sight in the interior of the orchard are those of the owner himself for his own consumption – 'for the strengthening of his belly' as it is vividly expressed – such of his trees as stand on the outskirts are regarded as bearing fruit for the benefit of his chief. Hence it is said that 'the border of the path is the orchard of the chief'. This is a real prerogative which chiefs have, though the exercise of it is left largely to the initiative of the actual owner. He himself observes the food – it may be a bunch of bananas – marks when it has reached maturity, and then cuts it and carries it along to the chief's house.[1]

Text II of the *fono*, which may be regarded as supplementing Text I, opens in the same manner, enjoining that the coconuts and areca nut be not plucked before their time. The term *mau* here employed signifies 'firm', 'undisturbed', and ultimately conveys the same idea in this context as does *maru*, meaning ripening till they fall on the ground.

The second section of Text II coincides in intention, though not quite in form of expression, with Section 6 of Text I. The third and fourth sections of Text II are similar to Section 4 of Text I, with slight variations in phraseology. The *maru* referred to in the former is an executive official, of whom there are several in each

[1] See my *Primitive Polynesian Economy*, 1939, p. 215.

clan, brothers and cousins of the chief, their function being essentially the preservation of public order. The expression *fakangiti*, meaning literally to 'squeeze together', here carries the same significance as *fakapini*, meaning to 'plait together'. It is the custom when it is desired to keep a bunch of bananas to encase it in a plaited cover of coconut leaf – which is implied here.

The remainder of Text II embodies a number of ideas not suggested in the first version. The fifth section is involved in its phraseology, but the central theme is clear enough. It is in the nature of advice to married couples against pursuing their quarrelling to the bitter end. The husband is warned that if he drives his wife away – 'orders her to go' as the stock phrase is – he may find it difficult to get her to return, if once he allows her to get beyond the immediate confines of the home.

The proposition contained in Section 6 is very interesting. Put bluntly, as the native understands it, it states that endeavour should not be exerted to make evacuation as complete as possible, but rather to allow the secondary faeces to remain *in situ*. Thus stability is afforded to the belly. The basis of this idea is the physiological concept of the *tanga kai*, the food bag in the stomach, into which all food from the throat goes, in which the transformation into excrement takes place, and from which the ordure is voided. This idea of the stomach as a simple single chamber for food with throat and rectum respective doors of entry and exit explains why a merely moderate evacuation is thought to lessen the strength of the craving for food, whereas the accomplishment of the act with finality leaves the stomach completely empty and so brings on the desire for food immediately. (The psycho-analytical equation of faeces with wealth may be compared with this.) In discussing this question it must be remembered that defecation is to the native a perfectly natural human process as much so as eating, of which indeed he realizes it is the logical result. Hence there is not the same atmosphere of embarrassment surrounding it as exists in our own society. But this does not mean blunt reference to the act. The Tikopia has his niceties of speech as we have, though they are concerned with different situations. Thus in the presence of affinal relatives, as mother-in-law or father-in-law, less definite terms are substituted, the use of which marks refinement and good breeding, and so also in the presence of chiefs and elders.

In the present instance the language of the *fono* is clear and direct enough, but the precise terms of the act are avoided. Thus the expression *fakaanga-vare*, meaning 'to face in a direction indefinitely', is the conventional substitute for the actual descriptive terms for defecation, *tiko*. *Fakaanga-vare*, though metaphorical in origin, has now however come to acquire a specific, concrete significance. This change from metaphorical to concrete meaning is an illustration of a familiar linguistic phenomenon. The English term 'to relieve oneself' is an analogous usage. It will be noted that the other terms used in this part of the *fono* also follow the same lead; they allude to the act of defecation without employing the common direct words.

The concluding section (7) of Text II contains a still more remarkable injunction – one which is hardly to be expected in the moral code of a primitive people. The problem of population seems to have exercised the minds of the Tikopia ever since the earliest times of which tradition gives record. The small size of the island, and its absolute isolation, which formerly has barred the possibility of migration as a means of overflow, has led on the one hand to a very clear appreciation of the dangers of over-population and on the other to very definite types of social mechanism for its prevention. The majority of these do not fall within the compass of our present study; to one only, and that the most unexpected, is reference made in the *fono*. The Tikopia, like most Polynesians, has quite a clear understanding of the primary facts of the procreation of children, and appreciates the part played by the male organ and the male seminal fluid. By the practice of withdrawal before ejaculation, then, the procreation of children can be avoided and population may be kept within reasonable limits.[1] Human impulses in this field, however, are notoriously difficult of control, and this preventive measure, though known to the body of Tikopia people, is practised only to a moderate degree. The tendency is always for an increase in population towards the subsistence limit. In the *fono* of former days, then, advantage was taken of the public occasion, and solemn effect of the address on the minds of the people, to proclaim the advisability of married men exercising restraint of this kind. The language used, like that

[1] For a more detailed discussion of this see *We, the Tikopia*, 1936, pp. 408–17; *Primitive Polynesian Economy*, 1939, pp. 42–5. Since about 1952 a great deal of migration has taken place from Tikopia, mainly for employment in the central islands of the Solomons – see *Social Change in Tikopia*, 1959, pp. 66–9. This migration, and epidemic disease, have restricted the population on the island.

of the preceding section, is indirect but clear. The specific terms for copulation and ejaculation are avoided, and polite substitutes are employed. Thus the term *me*, 'sleep', is used, its specific connotation being indicated by the particle *atu* indicating motion away from the subject and the preposition *ki* meaning 'towards'. By the words 'The man who sleeps over towards his wife' the idea of marital sexual connection is thus conveyed. The term *fakarongo ake* is subtly used. It means 'to feel' and in conjunction with the adverb *ake* which indicates 'in an upward direction' applies to the critical moment in tumescence when ejaculation is about to take place. The sentence is in fact elliptical; in ordinary conversation a Tikopia would add '*ka pusa ko na nea*' ('will ejaculate his organ'). It signifies then that the husband is adjured 'to rise' that the consequence of complete intercourse be averted. The reason for this restraint is hammered home in the next phrases which are familiar in many another context to all Tikopia. 'One male and one female. That is the plucking of the coconut and the filling of the water bottles.' The complete household is in Tikopia theory composed of four persons, the husband and wife, with a son and a daughter. This makes for a correct economic adjustment, while it does not impose too heavy a strain upon the food resources of the family. The boy assists his father and does the more energetic 'odd jobs' such as climbing the trees to pluck fresh coconuts, cutting leaf for thatch, and preparing the hibiscus fibre for expressing coconut cream. The work of the girl, *par excellence*, is that of keeping the family water bottles full, a task which is not so light as it may seem. In addition she helps with the work of the oven and in other household tasks. This is the ideal social unit. If the family is much larger there is an increase in food consumption without a corresponding increase in the value of the labour power. The man is reminded by the *fono* then that if he persists in creating a large number of offspring – the metaphor *fakauruuru*, 'making many heads', is primarily applied to the branching out of a bushy tree-top – he may not be able to increase his food resources proportionately. The *tafito i rakau*, the 'basis of trees', refers to the standing vegetation which provides so much in the way of supplies – coconut, breadfruit, *natu*, *voia*, banana, *vere*, *fukau*, *kafika* and others, and which cannot be increased *ad lib.* in a limited area of ground. The alternative to restriction of population is presented in a query which forms almost a refrain at the end of each set of phrases – will the person go and steal? In other words, the probable consequence of his improvidence is that he will incur social obloquy.

It was stated by the Ariki Tafua that in more recent years this section of the *fono* was usually omitted from the recital. The delicacy of the subject may account for this, since to Tikopia this matter is normally one only for extremely private conversation.

To sum up the general character of this remarkable proclamation it will have been observed that it is primarily a part of the mechanism for the preservation of social order. It cautions against theft, against disturbance and brawling, it advises economic forethought in the provision for events of public importance and enjoins restraint in the matter of procreation in the interests of communal welfare. It is thus seen that the concepts involved are of a developed moral order – if one agrees that the standards of morality need not be coincident with those of our own society. The Tikopia themselves emphasize this moral element in the *fono*, that it inculcates good as against evil conduct. 'The *fono* is made with speech; is made only for the good; evil doings to be abandoned', said the Ariki Kafika.

It will be noted also that the *fono* emphasizes strongly the status and privileges of the chief, and thus tends to maintain the social and political stability of the community. It is possible that in times past the chiefs may have used the *fono* as a means of advancing their interests as against those of the commoners. This is implied in a statement of the late Ariki Taumako, a man of exceptional benevolence, and held in great veneration by all Tikopia. He spoke privately to the present Ariki Tafua, shortly after his accession twenty years ago, and I give the latter's account of it. The old man said:

'Hey! Son! I am going to speak to you. The sacred *fono* abides with you?'
'Yes! It abides with me.'
'The affair is complete in you, but we two father and son alone hold speech. I am going to bar you. Anything causing men to go to sea, abandon it.'

This means that after being satisfied that the knowledge of the *fono* had been transmitted fully to the new Ariki Tafua, he assured him that the matter then lay entirely at the latter's discretion, but that he, occupying the privileged status of 'father' in the classificatory sense, wished to give a word of advice. He wanted dropped out of the *fono* any pronouncements which might cause dissension among the people and lead to a possible 'suicide voyage'. The Ariki Tafua told me that he promised to do this.

But this concept of the proclamation as an assertion of chiefly privileges is certainly not the main aspect of it in the eyes of commoners. All with whom I spoke treated it as a pronouncement in the interests of law and order. Thus Pa Rangifakaino, a commoner of Kafika, said to me 'It is a proclamation to the land to go about properly, to stand well; for the things of men which stand on the border of the path not to be seized; for men who find that their food has been stolen not to whoop; and not to throw on to the path their banana stalks and skins to spread them out on the path of the chiefs' (i.e., not to litter up the main highways, which are under the control of the chiefs).

SANCTION AND BREACH OF THE 'FONO'

We have now to consider the sanction for the *fono*. There is no doubt but that the proclamation was listened to with great reverence by all the people. It is difficult to say to what degree they observed the precepts therein laid down, but it cannot be doubted that such a public promulgation of some of the main points of the moral code exerted an influence in tending to preserve the social order. The sanction of the *fono* as of so many other Tikopia matters was the backing which it received from the principal gods of the land. They were supposed to come and address the people through the mouth of their representative the chief of Tafua. This is the reason for the respect shown by the bowed heads of the assembly. While I was writing down the words of the *fono* (Text I) the Ariki Kafika said to me, 'Great is the weight of your writing that is being done. Because the *fono* of the gods is being made – is based on the *fono* of the gods. That is the Brethren who have come to *fono* – the Great God, Rakiteua, Sakura, Oatuatafu have assembled to go and *fono*. That is their own *marae*, Rarokoka.' The Brethren are four of the chief deities of the island, the first three names mentioned being those of Te Atua i Fangarere, Te Atua i Tafua and Te Atua i Taumako, in that order. Their association with the glade of Rarokoka is told in a myth of origins.

This religious ascription stands behind the inclusion of the *fono* in the ceremonial cycle of the season. It provides one more example of the manner in which social, economic and religious interests are intertwined and buttress one another in the maintenance of the communal life.

There is one interesting breach of the sanctions of the *fono*, however, which illustrates the complex motivations of Tikopia conduct.

Every head should be bowed when the Ariki Tafua appears. But occasionally the rule is broken. If the chief catches sight of an upturned face as he strides on to the *marae* he calls out to the offender 'Who is the person who looks on the *fono* of the gods?' The culprit, it is said, is overcome at the disgrace of discovery. 'Very great is the shame of the man.' Immediately he rises from his seat and hurries away to the beach. There he hauls down his canoe, and paddles out to sea to commit suicide, in conformity with Tikopia custom in cases of intense disgrace. But on further inquiry it appeared that there was a less dramatic alternative. The first, in fact, was the theoretical rather than the actual outcome. Going to his gardens and orchards the offender strips them of large quantities of taro, breadfruit, bananas, and coconuts, and prepares several great baskets of food. Assisted by his relatives he bears these at the end of the day to the Ariki Tafua. Then, wailing his humility, he crawls to the chief over the floor-mats, presses his nose to the chief's foot and knee and follows this by the chanting of a dirge. Thus he abases himself and by the presentation of the food is absolved from any further consequences of his fault. (This is the customary method of reinstating oneself in Tikopia society after committing any offence against a chief.)

This breach of the regulation of the *fono*, however, displays one peculiar feature. In times past, I was told, there were a few cases in which a man deliberately refrained from bowing his head on the entry of the Ariki and made the propitiating gift of food in consequence. This apparently strange conduct is explained by the Tikopia as being due to the fact that the person concerned was a man of great wealth in land and food and committed this breach of custom designedly in order to display his riches by heavy compensation, and gain a reputation. No man of low birth would dare, however, to expose himself in this manner; only a person of chiefly family could afford to ignore possible criticism and draw attention to himself so boldly by what was after all an outrage upon tradition. (Compare the *Ara o Pu* for an analogous situation.)

The thread of the events may now be taken up again. After the delivery of the proclamation there is a pause. Then the Ariki Tafua inquires formally of the other chiefs as to the manner in which they shall make the sacred *roi* for the morrow. 'We shall make *roi* in the mouths of the ovens, or we shall make it in the green?' This refers to the preparations for the sacred dance festival which begins the next day. By the conventional expression 'the mouths of the ovens' is meant the joining of the people of each clan together to their respective chiefs to make a communal food portion in the sacred house in Uta, each person bringing his contribution. By 'in the green' (*mata*) is meant the cooking of separate packages in the various houses of the principal families. Some people thus make the *roi* in Tai, others in Uta. The chiefs decide which policy will be best on this occasion, and give their reply. When their decision is made public the people rise and go off to their cultivations in order to carry out the plan. Whatever the procedure adopted, the families of Sao and Fusi; Niumano and Fatumaru; Rarovi and Porima, make the *roi* in their respective houses. They do not combine with the other people of their clans, this aloofness being their privilege. Since these families are those of the most important elders their food is called the *matua roi*, the principal *roi* of the clan.

The sacredness of the *roi* depends upon its being used to provide offerings in the most important religious ceremonies. It is said then to be made by the chiefs' elders for their respective deities. 'Each makes it for his god.' When this food has been consumed the leaves in which it has been wrapped and the basket in which it has been carried are not used again for ordinary food, as is the normal custom, but discarded. In clearing up the debris of the meal instructions will be given by one person to another. 'Roll up the leaves and the little basket and throw it away, it is something sacred.' Other wrappings are obtained in order to carry away the food scraps.

8

The Dance to Quell the Wind

After the freeing of the land from *tapu* an air of excitement began
to pervade the villages. The forthcoming rites, with their religious dancing of an unusual kind, were by far the most spectacular
of the seasonal cycle, and claimed the interest of the people to a
high degree. Over and over I was told enthusiastically 'Beautiful
dances', and young folk, in particular, looked forward to them
with eager anticipation.

The dance period was divided into two sections, referred to as
the *Taomatangi* and the *Urangafi*. The former, which came first
on the programme, consisted of four days' rites, with dances performed for a short space of time in the late afternoon, while in
the second period a different set of dances began at dusk and continued throughout the night till dawn. These took place around a
sacred fire which was not allowed to die down, hence the name of
Te Uranga afi, the flaming fire, by which this period was known.

Taomatangi may best be translated as quell the wind, *tao* meaning to press down, and *matangi* being the wind. This term was
used more generally to cover the *Uranga afi* nights as well and
was associated with the belief that these sacred dances have the
effect of keeping trampled down, as it were, the violent gales
which sometimes spring up at this season.

Pa Vainunu said of the *Taomatangi*, 'Its idea is the suppression of
the wind, the wind not to storm in nights of the summer; the
custom of the land of old. It is done for the work which is performed, things of the chiefs which are done; kava is made in Uta,
while the chiefs call to the wind not to blow.' The association is
vague, but it explains the archaic and esoteric expression often
quoted, '*Te raranga nga atua e mori ke siki*', interpreted in more
usual speech as '*Te fekau nga atua e fai ke oti*' – meaning 'The Work
of the Gods is performed that it may be finished.' The idea is that

it is a good thing to complete the various ceremonies as speedily as is consistent with the programme in order that no untoward events may arise. It can be easily seen how the existence of such a belief tends to promote the efficiency of the performance of the seasonal ritual, and maintain it.

According to the Ariki Taumako, in former days the *Taomatangi* took place rather later, after our New Year, in fact as near as possible to the actual hurricane season. It was determined, he said, by the time of appearance of the stars Manu and Saraporu – 'adjusted to the stars not to blow hither'. When they appear in the morning in the south-eastern sky low down over the horizon, they are regarded particularly as harbingers of storms. He said that the fixing of the dance period was simply a matter of traditional lore (*tara tupua*) and that there was no actual myth (*kai*) in connection with it. But in recent years the Christmas festivals on the other side of the island led the heathen to seek to maintain their precedence, so that the ancient rites were put forward into an earlier month.

There is, however, a further belief in the function of the *Taomatangi* dances. As with most of the principal religious rites, there is the idea that their performance tends to bring prosperity on the land, to induce the gods to grant that efficacy which is subsumed under the term *manu*. I was told 'The singing which is performed by the lake, we men do it only to the gods; it is made to the *manu* of the gods; all the chiefs sing to the gods to make hither the *manu* for the land to be well.' In all this the premier god is the Atua i Kafika – 'his is the *Taomatangi* which is made' – though he does not figure to any great extent in it.

MARAE

The scene of these activities is a glade in the forest in Uta opening on the eastern side on to the lake; bordered inland on the north side by the sacred houses of Nukuora and Rarofiroki, and to the south by those of Kafika and Taumako with the wall of aromatic shrubbery which surrounds them. The main path from Ravenga to Namo round the lake shore traverses the spot, and joins it up with Takerekere and Matavi, a combined smaller glade, a hundred yards to the north.

The dancing place in Uta is known as Marae. The term is applied descriptively to other open spaces used for religious rites, but is reserved as a proper name for this one alone which is the chief of them all. Marae is one of the most sacred spots in Tikopia, both from its general association with religious rites, and also, more particularly, because in it stand a number of rough stone slabs, each of which is representative of one of the chief gods of the island. According to native ideas the slab serves as his 'seat', or more strictly, back-rest, during any kava ceremonies performed there. These stones are not regarded as *atua* in themselves but are spoken of as the embodiment (*fakatino*), or confirmation (*faka-patonu*), of the *atua*. Each male *atua* is said to sit cross-legged with his back against his stone; the female *atua* to sit with legs straight out before her. The custom of gods thus agrees with that of men. (Towards the end of the *Taomatangi*, when I ventured to take photographs, Tikopia asked if I had not seen the *atua* in the mirror of the camera, and seemed surprised that they were not visible.) Because of this association with the deities it is *tapu* to walk indiscriminately over the ground. Except to carry out a definite piece of ritual no one in ordinary times may step aside from the path. Though the track through the glade was used as a main highway by many people daily during the year at no time did I see anyone ever set foot off it and tread the *tapu* soil. As a result of disuse after each season's festivities the ground becomes rapidly overgrown with grass and weeds to a height of several feet, and before it can be utilized again it must be thoroughly cleared. This task then forms the initial rite of the *Taomatangi* and is of the greatest sacerdotal importance. It is termed the *Tanga i Marae*. (*Ta*, the generic meaning of which is strike or build, is also used for operations of cutting palm fronds, etc. Its use for the grubbing out of grass and weeds may be in token of respect to the Marae.)

This ceremony, like so many others already described, took place soon after daylight. On the occasion on which I saw it I had arrived early in my canoe in order to precede the crowd. The Marae itself was quiet, and wet with dew, and no-one else was there. The people soon arrived by canoe or on foot, and went to join their respective chiefs. Some gathered in the houses to chew betel and smoke; others waited near the lakeside.

While the crowds assembled round the Marae the Ariki Kafika remained in his house. When all was ready he was notified and came down to the border of the sacred ground. There he wound round his waist a new piece of bark-cloth, and tied the coconut leaf round his neck. When he appeared the men – there were no women or girls present, any such being inside the houses inland – gathered in from all sides and arranged themselves around the edge of the Marae in a ring, crouching down, with hands stretched out ready to clutch and tear up the grass when the word was given. A chief who is elderly need not participate. The Ariki Taumako, who was young and energetic, crouched with the rest. The Ariki Kafika alone stood erect. Drawing in a preliminary breath he called out the formula for the clearing of the Marae. It was quite short, and of a type already described.

> Pa Tafua, Pa Taumako, Pa Fangarere, Satinamo (i.e. Pa Rarovi).
> Your assemblage of Elders there give countenance to the Marae of Pu ma which will be cleared away on this morning.
> Clear for welfare.
> Be swept away epidemic disease from the crown of the land. *Marie!*

The formula finished on the word *Marie*, on hearing which everyone began in haste to root up all the vegetation immediately in front of him. The Ariki Kafika on the completion of his recital dropped down and worked away with the rest. No definite plan of organization was followed, but each member of the party gradually worked inwards, clearing all within reach as he went, until in a surprisingly short space of time, a matter of a couple of minutes, the lush herbage had been reduced to piles of rubbish, which people hastily seized in armfuls and ran to throw into the bushes by the side of the lake. Speed is an essential feature of the affair since it is held that one should not delay in setting about the work of the gods. After the initial clearing, which was but superficial, a more thorough survey of the ground was made, and a second load of vegetation removed, leaving only very short grass and weeds. A protruding bush or so was chopped out at the side of the Marae, a work which was superintended by the Ariki Kafika. After this the people returned to their various clan-stations. 'Marae has been cleared', they said.

Now that it was bare and open to inspection the chief features of interest in it could be clearly seen. Fig. 11 indicates their relation to one another. The surface was fairly smooth but hardly

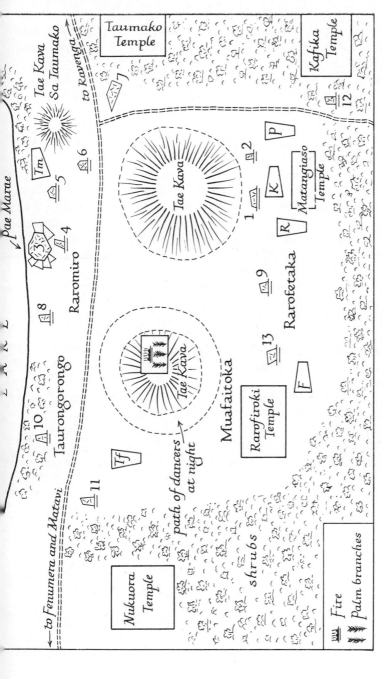

FIG. 11. Marae in Uta

Stones: 1, 2, Pu ma; 3, Atua i Kafika; 4, rest for sounding-board; 5, Atua i Anuta; 6, Atua i Sao; 7, Atua i Taumako; 8, Atua i Tafua; 9, Atua Fafine; 10, Rua Nofine; 11, Atua i Niumano; 12, stone for *roi*; 13, rest for sounding-board. *Mats:* K, Kafika; Tf, Tafua; Tm, Taumako; F, Fangarere; R, Pa Rarovi; P, Pa Porima level, since two large low mounds occupied much of the centre space. These were known as *tae kava* (literally 'kava refuse'), and on them the kava bowls of the chiefs were prepared. The fibrous residue from the sacred liquid was shaken out there; hence by hyperbole that name was given to the mounds, as if they had been built up of the refuse of generations. A third much smaller mound, bearing the same name, lay towards the south end of Marae. Mention has already been made of the stones representative of the principal deities of the island. Immediately in front of the small hut Matangiaso, on the upper side of the ground, were two such pillars, each a couple of feet high, side by side. These were the stones of Pu ma, Tafika and Karisi, or Nga Ariki, as they were known in Marae. A yard or so behind them was spread the seating mat of the Ariki Kafika, whose gods they were, and whose offerings were made primarily to them. Near by, close to the path from Kafika, stood another stone, under a *fetaka* tree. This, however, was not representative of any deity, but merely existed to indicate the spot where the *roi* was to stand.

I was told 'It is the distinguishing mark of the placing of the *roi*; there is no *atua* who may be embodied therein, no, the stone simply was set up there.' According to Pa Motuata, however, it was the stone of an *atau* of Nga Fiti, whose name is lost to memory.

At the lower side of the ground, adjoining the lake, in the open space between the trees, lay a tumbled heap of rocks, with the water lapping their edges. This was known as *Pae Marae* – the Slabs of Marae. The most important of them was a broad flat stone which was perhaps the most sacred object in Tikopia. It was described as *te fatu tapu o te paenga* – the sacred stone of the heap of slabs. This was the stone of Te Atua i Kafika. An inclined pillar in front of this served as support for the sounding-board during certain afternoon dances (*fatu fakamau o te nafa*), and another stone at the south end of Rarofiroki served a similar function during the night. Such a stone was also termed *te fakarave o te nafa*, meaning that under it the sounding-board was fitted or engaged. To the left of Pae Marae, looking towards the lake, was another pillar, which was the seat of the Atua i Tafua, while near to it, further back in the shrubbery, was the stone of Rua nofine, two female deities of the Tafua chief. To the right of Pae Marae stood the stone of the Atua i Anuta who in Tikopia, through ancient association, was under the control of the Ariki Taumako. Near to it was the pillar of the Atua i Sao. A few yards away, almost flush with the ground, lay the stone of the Atua i Taumako. A myth concerning this stone and that of the Atua i Kafika is given briefly in Chapter 9. On the upper side of Marae, between Rarofiroki and the seats of Nga Ariki, leaned the stone of the Atua Fafine, the female deity. In rear of this was the space called Rarofetaka which was the seat of the women at such times as they attended the ceremonies. As the men had their stations near their respective clan deities, so the women were posted near to their goddess.

On the north side of the Marae, among the gnarled roots of the huge *puka* tree which bordered the path, stood the low stone of Te Atua i Niumano, son of the Atua i Taumako. A little further along the edge of the ground towards Pae Marae was the Taurongorongo, the space in which dancers waited to join the ring during the night festivities, swaying their bodies and shuffling their feet in time to the rhythm. Further still towards the centre lay Raromiro, another space where the men sat to chant their sacred songs in response to the women at Rarofetaka. All these spots, though distinguished by separate names, were quite close together, since the Marae was in all not more than fifty yards long. This minuteness of distinction of locale, with profusion of names, was an essential feature in the complex yet precise organization of events.

During the rites of Marae, each clan had its basic station; this was in rear of its own chief, his seating mat being near the seat of his principal god. Thus Kafika squatted outside the north end of their temple, between it and the hut Matangiaso; Tafua used to be at the north side of the ground, near the main path and the stone of their god; Taumako were at the south end of the ground, also near the main path, while Fangarere took post at the end of the temple Rarofiroki (see later). Thus the chiefs and their clansmen were roughly at the four corners of a rectangle, each group facing towards the centre of Marae.

RAROFIROKI TEMPLE

It may have been noted that the Atua i Fangarere alone of the principal deities had no stone in Marae. In place of this he had a small temple which was representative of him, and served as his seat when he wished to descend to the kava. 'The god of the

Work, there is no stone for him. That is his stone, the house which stands there, Rarofiroki; therefore the Ariki Fangarere goes and makes obeisance to it.' The name Rarofiroki may be derived from the fact that a tall umbrella palm, the fruit of which is known as *firoki*, waved its crest overhead. Thus the hut was indeed 'Under the palm fruit'. By the Tikopia, however, it was said to have been named from the dwelling of the god himself in Rangi, the Tikopia Heaven. The tale of its origin is bound up with the history of the island. After the slaying of Nga Ravenga, a fearful epidemic of the type known as *te kemo* came upon the land, and the people died by scores. This was the result of the anger of the Atua Lasi at having had his clan wellnigh exterminated, and as he is the controller of disease, he could easily make his displeasure felt. At last to appease his anger Pu ma, *atua* of the chiefs of Uta, announced through their mediums that a *fare* should be built in Marae. This was accordingly done, the house was named Rarofiroki after its counterpart the house of the Atua Lasi among the gods, and the plague was stayed. At this time the sole survivor of Nga Ravenga was the child Fakaarofatia, who afterwards became the progenitor of the Fangarere clan. To pacify the god still further Fangarere was appointed by mutual consent to be the premier group in Marae. The Ariki Tafua, as executive for the Ariki Kafika, performed the kava to the Atua Lasi before this house. Later when Fakaarofatia grew up he joined the Ariki in the ritual and spread the *epa* mat to his deity (see *infra*). Thus Rarofiroki came to be one of the most sacred houses in Tikopia.

It was distinguished by having on top of the ridge a carved slab of wood running along it from end to end. This was termed *te papa purou*, the covering plank, or *te papa tapu*, the sacred plank, since the figures which were cut out of it were religious emblems of great importance. 'Great is the weight of the slab', said the Tikopia, referring to its sacerdotal, not its physical quality.

One of these carvings, the most sacred, was known as *te iofa*; the other was *te manu tapu*. I could not discover what creature, if any, the *iofa* represented (but see Postscript to Chapter 9). The *manu tapu* ('sacred animal') was said to be a type of *turi*, a general name for several species of wading birds, in particular the turnstone (*Arenaria interpres*). The living *turi* is not regarded as sacred, but its conventionalization, the *manu tapu*, is highly so. After some objection by the Ariki Kafika had been overcome Pa Fenuatara sketched for me the two carvings on the plank of Rarofiroki, and my sketch, based on his, is seen in Fig. 12. Later he carved the

FIG. 12. *Iofa* and *Manu Tapu*

manu tapu in wood and mounted it as a parting gift to me. He flanked it with two *turi* modelled in naturalistic style, and for decoration whitened them with *rimu*, a living growth gathered from the reef. The *manu tapu*, however, he left in self-colour, explaining that it was too sacred for him to smear over thus. The carving did not meet with the entire approval of his father, who thought his son was meddling with sacred things. It was brought to me covered by a cloth, and handed over with the stipulation that women and children and persons of no consequence generally should not be allowed ever to see it. (This carving was unfortunately lost about 1940, during the War – see Plate 1*a*.)

These emblems of course belonged primarily to the Ariki Fangarere, and his principal canoe bore the carved bird on its bow or stern cover. I was told by Pa Fenuatara that when this vessel is taken out for fishing, should one of the crew by accident strike the wooden figure, the trip is immediately abandoned, and the canoe brought to shore. The crew arrive wailing and when the news is spread abroad the whole clans of Kafika and Fangarere assemble and cry, gash their foreheads with knives, tear the skin on their cheeks and give vent to other manifestations of grief. Then they go over to Uta, pull a plant of kava, collect quantities of taro from the cultivation, and *masi* from the store pits, and go and stand it by the starboard side of the canoe. Then the kava ceremony is performed to appease the anger of the deity whose symbol has been thus outraged, and people come from all parts of the island to take part in the mourning ceremony.

Other chiefs do not infringe on the privileges of the Ariki Fangarere in the use of these emblems. On the subject of the carved *turi* Pa Fenuatara remarked:

The name in this land is 'the sacred creature'. It is prohibited to the chiefs and the populace; the Ariki Fangarere adorns his vessel and his house – the assembly of chiefs, no! The chief who desires to stand the *turi* on his canoe, does so and goes to sea, but when he returns he is overwhelmed by the waves in the channel; he is swamped; split is the canoe, broken. As done by me, no, it is good, because I am the sacred child.

In other words, Pa Fenuatara might mount the *turi* on his canoe with impunity since his mother came from Fangarere clan. Because of this he was able to carve these emblems as a gift to me. Apparent exceptions to the rule that no other chief may utilize them as canoe decorations were also explicable on this basis. Thus in 1928 two canoes of the Ariki Taumako, Kakeafanga and Te Ingoa a Pu, both had the *turi* on the covers. These were carved and set there by Pa Veterei, now dead, who was also a 'sacred child' to the Ariki Fangarere, though not of close kin. The *iofa*, however, was more sacred. No one, not even Pa Fenuatara, would have ventured to set this on his vessel. It was *tapu* to the Ariki Fangarere alone.

The beliefs and rites described above illustrate the reality of the religious veneration in which these objects were held by the people. The *manu tapu*, i.e. the *turi* (not the *iofa*, as the text states), may be seen in a photograph taken by the Rev. W. Durrad in 1910.[1] The slab has since fallen down and decayed, and in 1928 had not yet been renewed. I was told that when it is to be carved again all four Ariki take part in the rites, in token of their joint interest in the house and its deity. The wood selected is that of the bread-fruit for its lightness. When a suitable tree has been chosen the chiefs assemble, each with his sacred adze on his shoulder, and march up to it in line. The Ariki Kafika leads the procession. As he reaches the spot he takes the adze from his shoulder and makes a cut at the tree, reciting as he does so the formula:

> Cut with power be thy slab Te Varotea.
> Cut with power be thy slab Futiotekere.
> Face towards the head of the land thy slab,
> And be parted the epidemic disease from the
>   crown of the land

[1] Reproduced in Rivers, *History of Melanesian Society*, vol. 1, p. 339, Fig. 1. More modern illustrations of *iofa* and *manu tapu* are referred to in the Postscript to this chapter.

He then steps aside, and is followed by the Ariki Tafua, who repeats action and form of words likewise. His place is then taken by the Ariki Taumako, who is succeeded by the Ariki Fangarere. When each has performed his share of the rite the experts come to fell the tree and dress and carve the timber, the latter part of the work being done beside the house Nukuora at the edge of Marae. For this people assemble from all other villages and a large quantity of food is brought together, to form the feast which marks the importance of the occasion. The formula given above is an invocation to the Atua Lasi, under his name in Marae and his name in Kafika, to give food and health to the people. The 'head of the land' is an esoteric term for the breadfruit. The bulbous fruit of this tree is said to be the head of the Atua Lasi. There is thus to the Tikopia a close social connection between the Ariki Fangarere, the breadfruit, the Atua Lasi, and Rarofiroki house – a connection which could be pursued further as regards disease, death and spirit homes. The control of the Atua Lasi over epidemics gives particular point in the above formula to the customary appeal for health and protection.

Though the house of Rarofiroki is primarily under the jurisdiction of the Ariki Fangarere, as being the property of his god, he comes last of the four chiefs to deliver his formula. This is due to his inferior rank. The opposition between precedence and proprietorship which might otherwise occur is obviated by the use of the *rau*, the separate titles of the god. Thus in the present instance the Atua i Fangarere is known variously as Te Atua Lasi and Tafito to all the people, Te Urupaku in the kava of Fangarere and Taumako. Futiotekere in that of Kafika, and Te Varotea in that of Marae, that is in the kava of the Arika Tafua.

PREPARATION OF TEMPLES

This digression has been necessary in order that the true importance of Rarofiroki in Marae should be understood. The first task after the clearing of Marae was to repair this house. A few lengths of thatch were replaced where desirable, while the Ariki Kafika stood by to watch the process, and repeated a very brief formula of the usual type, notifying the god of what was being done and requesting that it might have auspicious results.

Attention was next turned to Matangiaso. This was a tiny hut, no more than breast high above the ground, and a few feet long.

It was said by the Ariki Kafika to have been a small house of Pu ma from older times, though they have no ritual place therein. When it is rebuilt, as is needful occasionally, kava of the usual type is made in Kafika Lasi. Like Rarofiroki, Matangiaso was never inhabited, but served merely as the shelter for certain sacred objects. Chief of them was the *nafa*, or short trough, of carved wood which was beaten as a sounding-board to mark the rhythm of the dances. The one I observed was old and broken so that in actual practice a non-sacred timber was employed. When it gets too rotten to be handled easily the *nafa* will be replaced by another specially hewn for the purpose. In this case the *nafa* was removed, and a few repairs were done such as the replacing of the plaited ridge cover.

The technological aspect completed, the sacerdotal now came to the fore. One of the most sacred spots in Marae was the *mua fare* of Rarofiroki, the space immediately before the house on the side toward the lake. Here was the spot where to Tikopia eyes the Atua himself made his appearance to men for the ceremonies, and where his kava was poured several times daily. It was known by the esoteric name of Muafaitoka and in recognition of its importance in the rites it was carpeted with coconut leaves, over which a pair of coconut mats were laid. One mat was for the Atua i Tafua, the other for the Atua Lasi. These corresponded to the two main doorways of the house, the one to the east being that of the Atua Lasi while the other, to the south, was that of his brother deity. At the same time fronds of areca palm were laid down before the *aro fatu*, the two stones of Nga Ariki, and over them a fresh coconut leaf mat was set. A spot on the mound immediately in front was carpeted with areca palm and banana leaves – this was the place where the kava of the Ariki Kafika was to be prepared.

The Ariki himself now entered Matangiaso hut with a small green mat, and laying it on the floor, proceeded to tie a number of streamers of new bark-cloth to the rafters. These were for the various gods within. Accounts varied as to who they actually were. One version stated that there was a deity named Te Ama-fakaro, and that he was an *atua* of the drifting foam on the sea. It may be noted that this name was that of Te Atua i Raropuka as invoked in the game of dart throwing, and that the 'foremost dart' of sa Kafika was known as Matangiaso.[1]

[1] See my 'Dart Match in Tikopia', 1930, p. 75.

Pa Te Arairaki gave the names of the *atua* as Pu Ase and Angi-angi (being two names of Pu ma), Nuku-i-tafa-tai (or Pu-i-tafa-tai) and Te Atua i Matangiaso, known as Te Ama fakaro. The two streamers he said were those of Angiangi and this last god. The Ariki Kafika himself said that he had not heard of these separate deities. He knew of three *atua*, who were gods of the sea foam, and had no individual names, being termed collectively Nuki-i-te-tafa-tai. He received this information from his predecessor, and from the late Ariki Taumako. The difference of opinion on this point is not material, since the hut Matangiaso played no important part in ritual – which is probably the reason for the variation of evidence. The sole rite of interest in connection with it was the washing of large helmet shells, which took place a little later. A large leaf was brought from the lake, full of water. Pa Rarovi, whose function it was to officiate, entered the house with the water and washed the shells. As he did so he called 'Ia!' to announce his work to gods and men, and the Ariki then recited a formula:

> Wash with power your bodies
> Nuku-i-te-tafa-tai.
> Pour out your bodies to go in the wastes
>   to seawards.

This is an invocation addressed to the deities of the sea foam, whose material embodiments are the shells, to give efficacy to the rite, and also to proceed to the open ocean, far from land. The point is that sea foam is the result of breaking waves, which make trouble for canoes and fishermen. Hence in directing these gods to remove their body, i.e. the foam, to the ocean wastes, the Ariki is in reality making an appeal for fine weather at sea. But he invokes the effect, not the cause, the foam gods, not the sea gods. According to Pa Te Arairaki, who was a collateral kinsman of the Ariki, actually in the elder line, and received his information from a different source, the formula for the washing should have been addressed to Pu Ase, Pu Ase-kau and Nuku-i-tafa-tai, requesting the parting of the line of foam (*tafe*) on the reef. Another allied meaning of *tafe* is the *miro*, the wake of a canoe, which is the 'body' of Nuku-i-tafa-tai. From the common elements in these variations, however, it is clear that the deities of Matangiaso are foam gods and the object of the rite and formula is to cause them to retreat and leave the sea calm.

After the Ariki Kafika had completed his task, the Ariki Fangarere entered Rarofiroki and tied the various streamers to the rafters and post. The formulae for these were of the same type as those given in the case of Nukuora, Vaisakiri, etc.

THE KAVA OF MARAE

The more important part of the ceremony now began. Each Ariki took his seat at the traditional position (see Fig. 11) and his kava was brought – a root and stem of the plant bared of leaves – and laid on top of a large basket of food, the *roi* prepared the night before. The basket of food of each chief was set near his seat. That of the Ariki Kafika was laid against a stone to the right of the pillars of Nga Ariki. Next to it was put the basket of Pa Porima, whose seating mat, dedicated to his chief deity, Te Atua i te Uruao, rested at the side of Matangiaso. On the other side was the mat of Pa Rarovi, by which his *roi* was laid. These two men had their special seating mats in Marae on account of their position as principal elders of the Ariki Kafika.

After the washing of the shells in Matangiaso and the return of Pa Rarovi to his seat, the Ariki Fangarere rose from his mat and went with a small finely plaited pandanus mat under his arm down to the front of Rarofiroki. There he sat on the coconut leaves, facing the house. The mat was termed *te epa* and was the seat of his Atua (cf. *fakaepa*, 'to do honour to', 'to praise', in a general sense). He unfolded it, held it up in both hands breast high, uttered a short formula, and then, making an obeisance with it, laid it down by the side of the house. Then he returned to his place.

The *roi* was now carried from its respective positions out to the centre of the ground. This, like all other rites of this place, was done in a definite order. The bearer first brought the basket of Tafua, then that of Fangarere, then that of Kafika, and finally that of Taumako, the food of the elders in each case following that of their Ariki. The primacy of Tafua was due to the special functions of that chief in Marae, and Fangarere was next since it was the Atua Lasi, the god of that clan, who was the chief object of the present ceremonies. When the baskets of food had been heaped together the 'kava house' was constructed on them. The sticks of kava were lifted and stood with their tops together so that they formed a pyramid.

The next rite was that of the recital of the kava. This was essentially of the same type as the repeated invocation of deities by each chief in his own private ceremonies, but was invested on this occasion with much greater solemnity and grandeur, and had a number of special features associated with it. It was not performed in full when I was present, owing to the absence of the Ariki Tafua. I insert here, however, the account of it I received from several sources. The recitation of the formula was the privilege of the Ariki Tafua – a privilege which was highly valued and was the subject of great pride on his part, inasmuch as he stood erect to execute his office, while the rest of the people, including his superior chief, the Ariki Kafika, sat in silence with bowed heads. This was in his capacity as Worker to the Kafika chief, and was on the same plane as his position as reciter of the *fono* in Rarokoka. Unlike the normal kava formula, this one was recited aloud, in fact shouted, and men who were present before the defection of the Ariki Tafua said that the resounding tones of his voice rolled round the hills in Uta, and could be heard like the rumblings of thunder from over the lake.

The Ariki stood up, girt with a new waistcloth and with two fronds from the tip of the coconut leaf, the symbol of his deity, stuck at his back. He laid one hand on top of the 'kava house', the erection of stems, and turned towards the north. Then he began his recital.

> Tinamo! (the Ariki Kafika) for your own making of the *roi*, for your own digging of the kava prepared for the assembly ground of the gods.
>
> For your elders and their own making of the *roi*, for their own digging of the kava prepared for the assembly ground of the gods.
>
> Pa Taumako! (i.e. the Ariki Taumako) for your own making oɩ the *roi*, for your digging of the kava prepared for the assembly ground of the gods.
>
> For the making of the *roi* by your elders, for their own digging of the kava performed for the assembly ground of the gods.
>
> Pa Fangarere! (i.e. the Ariki Fangarere) your digging of the kava, your own making of the *roi*, prepared for the assembly ground of the gods.

For your elders and their own making of the *roi*, their own digging
    of the kava prepared for the assembly ground of the gods.
(Then he calls to himself – the Worker:)
    My own making of the *roi*, for my own digging of the kava pre-
    pared for the assembly ground of the gods.
    For the making of the *roi* by my elders, for their own digging of
    the kava prepared for the assembly ground of the gods.

The confirmation of the kava is finished!
Your kava there, the Chiefs!
You two excrete hither food for me;
Excrete on to the head of the land.
Your water, your soil
Has become parched.
And urinate down below
Your sides of the heaven
And prepare excrement
For the head of your land
Which has stood orphaned.
And raise your waters
On your reef
For giving life to your land.
And brush away epidemic illness
From the crown of the land.

Thy kava there, Te Varotea!
Excrete thou hither food for me,
Excrete on to the head of the land.
Your water, your soil
Has become parched;
And urinate down below
Your sides of the heaven
And prepare excrement
For the head of your land
Which has stood orphaned.
And be brushed away epidemic illness
From the crown of the land.
And raise your waters and your reef
For giving life to your land.

Thy kava there, Sakura.
Thy kava there, Rakiteua.
Thy kava there, Oatuatafu.

Thy kava there, Ruanofine
Open thy basket
And prepare nourishment for thyself
For the crown of the land,
And the edge of the reef.
Things burdensome for the kava
Put away, to the sun which is sinking there;
Marie!

The formula opens by calling on each chief in turn, in virtue of
his having made the *roi* and pulled up the plant of kava for the
ritual of Marae, to confirm or countenance the invocation to the
gods. This is the implication, though the actual invitation is not
delivered but merely announced as completed. The introduction
differs considerably in this respect from that which opens the
ordinary kava. Mentioned in each case after the chief are his principal elders. In the previous chapter reference was made to the
making of *matua roi* separately by a certain number of elders, and
here is the formal recognition of that act. The invocation proper
opens with an appeal to Nga Ariki, i.e. to Tafaki and Karisi. They
are asked in symbolic language to excrete upon the land and its
inhabitants, i.e. to give profusion of foodstuffs. A plentiful
appearance of breadfruit (the head of the land) is likened to the
excrement of the gods voided upon the trees. An appeal is also
made to their sympathies by the pathetic – and not necessarily
correct – statement that the springs have dried up and the land is
parched. They are asked then to pour down the skies in rain by
the symbolism of urination. The formula then proceeds along
normal lines, invoking in order Te Varotea, i.e. the Atua Lasi;
Sakura, the Atua i Taumako; Rakiteua, Atua i Tafua; and
Oatuatafu, another of the Brethren, also a deity of Tafua. It concludes with an appeal to Ruanofine, two female deities of Tafua,
who are believed to possess a typical woman's basket, which they
are asked to open in order to disburse food to the land. The actual
form of the recital of the kava of Marae thus differs considerably,
notably in its freer use of scatological symbolism, from the normal
invocations, though the underlying ideas are of precisely the same
kind. This is regarded as the premier kava of Tikopia. In addition
to this the Ariki Tafua also 'possesses' another form of recital
which he uses for all ordinary ceremonies. The kava of Marae
should be recited only in Marae.

I obtained this formula in several texts, the principal ones being from the Ariki Tafua himself, and from his eldest son Pa Rangi-furi. The latter was an excellent informant and wished always to illustrate his data. On this occasion he was standing up in his house, girt with a new waistcloth, and with considerable excitement began reciting the invocation in proper form. Suddenly I noticed gooseflesh begin to appear on his arms and body. He began to tremble, then stopped and sat down quickly, saying shakily, 'You have seen? The god jumped on to me. He has heard his formula recited, and has come to his kava.' He was much disturbed at the thought that by imitating the procedure of Marae he had summoned the deity of his clan who had entered him as a medium. When he sat down, however, the symptoms disappeared; later, after my reassurance, he continued the formula, but in a moderated tone, and without performing the appropriate actions.

When I saw the rites in 1928 the Ariki Tafua had ceased to attend the *Taomatangi*, so that though the other procedure was still carried out, his invocation was replaced by a short formula of confirmation recited by the Ariki Kafika. He remained seated on his mat, while Pa Fenumera, a man of Fangarere chosen for this duty, went and stood by the 'kava house'. The substitute version, which was formerly recited on occasions of unavoidable absence of the Ariki Tafua, was practically a repetition of the invocation recited for the clearing of Marae earlier in the day.

When the recital of the formula was finished the *fare kava* was dismantled, and the kava stems were apportioned (literally 'thrown') to the stones of the various deities of Marae. The kava of the Atua Lasi was first laid at Muafaitoka, then that of the Atua i Tafua was set by his stone, and that of Te Atua i Taumako, Rua nofine and Te Atua i Anuta followed in this order. 'It is distributed among the gods.' Packages of *roi* were then carried in the same order and set by the stones.

The pouring of libations was the next item of the ritual and this too was done with much greater solemnity than usual. Indeed I could not help but be impressed by the quietness and reverence of all the proceedings there, the haste to perform duties and the absence of slipshod methods, all of which was in contrast to the normal habits of the Tikopia. The kava bowl was brought in from the wings as it were, i.e. from the non-sacred area, by Fenumera.

For these rites the kava-maker is girded with leaves of *rau tea* over his ordinary bark-cloth held in place by a belt of sinnet rope. If he be an elder he dons a new bark-cloth for the occasion. This is the traditional dress of the persons who have special duties to perform in Marae. For the opening day of the *Taomatangi* of 1928 Pa Fenuatara was kava-maker. Though he was the eldest son and heir of the principal chief of the island yet he wore the *rau tea* leaves; he was still 'a common man'.

The kava-maker seated himself behind the bowl on the mound facing Rarofiroki and was followed by the cup-bearer with a water bottle and piece of kava, which he proceeded to chew (Plate 5a). The usual method of preparation was followed, but a new bundle of hibiscus fibre was used as a strainer, and special care was taken to see that all residue was removed from the liquid, which should be clear. 'He looks to see that it shall be clear absolutely.' The reason I was told is that if any of the fragments remain in the liquid when the libations are poured, the deity who is thought to drink thereof will choke, and thereupon disappear from the cere-mony. This is known by the fact that the man who has been pre-paring the kava, or the medium, when as deity he drinks from the cup offered him by the Ariki Tafua, topples over and falls insensible. The people at large, if they witness such an accident, say at once 'The kava was not clear, the god choked; the leavings are still there.' Then they rush up and drag the kava-maker or the medium away to revive him. 'Great is the weight of the kava of Muafaitoka', it was said.

The knowledge of this makes the kava-maker very careful, and no event of this kind had been known to happen within recent memory. While the kava was being made the cup-bearer sat with bowed head, the cup in his hands.

ENTRY OF 'THE GREAT GOD'

The cardinal feature of the ceremony was the entry of the god upon the scene – a display of spirit mediumship similar to that described in the rites of Vaisakiri house. The medium, who was at that time the eldest son of the Ariki Fangarere, appeared sud-denly from the house inland, girt with a new cloth, with bands of turmeric on arms and belly, the black charcoal stripe on his forehead, and the splayed cycas leaves at his back. Trembling slightly, he seated himself on the mat of the Ariki Fangarere, his head moving slightly from side to side. When the kava was nearly ready he rose quickly and took his seat in Muafare, that is at Mua-faitoka, facing the north end of the Marae. His trembling became more violent, and his locked hands rattled on the coconut matting. Suddenly he emitted a shriek, then with head swinging rapidly from side to side he began to speak in loud, metallic, curiously prolonged tones. This was regarded by the Tikopia as the voice of the deity speaking to his brothers among the gods. There appeared to be no doubt in the minds of the people as to the genuineness of the phenomena witnessed; I heard someone whisper as the medium appeared, 'Our ancestor has come.' In former days, as the medium sat there the Ariki Tafua was handed a cup of kava by the attendant, and poured it out, exclaiming as he did so:

> Thy kava there Te Varotea.
> Drink thy kava,
> And drip down on thy house of the Brethren.

This interpretation of the last phrase is uncertain but it probably refers to breadfruit and other crops to be 'rained down', as it were, by the deity upon the people. As he emptied the cup the Ariki passed it behind him, then stretching out his hand palm up, he called:

> *Kau kaina, kaina, tae Te Varotea*
> *Io-oo rei!*
>
> By me eaten, eaten, excrement Te Varotea
> Aye!

The final words of assent, '*Io rei*', were taken up by the assembled people, who dwelt on them in a prolonged shout which echoed round the hills. Thus the clans as a whole joined in the affirmation of humility. 'The whole land assents entirely, not a person remains', it was said with pardonable hyperbole. A variant of the formula substitutes 'We' for 'I' in the announcement of eating excrement. The god, i.e. the medium, may sometimes drink kava at Muafaitoka, though this did not happen when I was there. According to Pa Fenumera it is a point of etiquette in presenting the cup not to hold it straight to his lips, as is usual, but to proffer it with the front of the wrist held towards him. He will then take it himself and drink.

This rite was termed 'the Conveying of the God to the Skies', since it was regarded as an act of formal and reverent dismissal. It was in fact the parting homage of one god to another. For the native conception was that in the person of the Ariki Tafua it was actually the Atua i Tafua who sat there and who in spiritual guise raised up his brother in his arms and so sped him on his path to the heavens. This rite is not performed nowadays.

A slight digression is necessary to explain this ritual whereby the principal god of Fangarere is believed to appear to men. For a long period after the building of the house Rarofiroki, I was told, the Atua Lasi sought no human contacts. About four generations ago, however, a chief of Fangarere, Te Atua Vao by name, married a woman from the chief's family of Tafua. They had a son, Rakeimaitafua (also known as Sumutangata, or Pu Fenumera), who became a medium for the spirits in the ceremonies of his father. Seeing this, the chief deity of the clan took possession of him and used him as his vehicle, or 'god-anchor', *tauratua*, for his appearances in Marae. 'When he became a medium, the Atua Lasi flew on to him, he was decorated by sa Tafua, by his mother's kinsfolk, to convey him and bring him hither. They lifted him up, bore him in their arms and set him on the mat at Muafaitoka that the deity might possess him. Therefore he was called by the name Rakeimaitafua (Adorned by Tafua).'

The action taken by the clan of his mother in thus decorating him was to gratify the evident desires of the great deity and also to honour both their nephew and themselves in the eyes of the community. Because of his maternal affiliations Rakeimaitafua became the object of favour on the part of the Atua i Tafua. He was the latter's 'sacred child' and received much *mana* from the god in consequence. While he acted as the vehicle of the Atua Lasi the prosperity of the land was great. Both the breadfruit and the coconut fructified, while chestnut, taro and yam also flourished. His end, however, was tragic. On one occasion when the ritual season came round he refused to listen to the entreaties of his relations and instead of remaining to take his place as medium of the Atua Lasi he lowered his canoe and set off on a voyage to Anuta. He never reached his destination, being lost at sea, 'trodden down' as the natives say, by the vengeful deity. If the god had been allowed to 'run to men', to have made his appearance on earth as usual, all would have been well, but thus deprived of his customary vehicle of materialization, he followed and slew him. Ever since then one of the chief's family of Fangarere has acted as medium for the god.

It has been mentioned that the pandanus mat spread at Muafaitoka was a token of respect to the Atua Lasi from the Fangarere chief. But when the medium came down in a state of possession by the god he was not allowed to sit on it. He was a god, but he was a man also, and being a man, to use the pandanus mat would mean death for him. As he was about to sink down on it the mat was deftly jerked from beneath him by the watching Ariki and he rested on the coconut matting alone. It will be remembered that it was believed to be the Atua i Tafua, not merely the Ariki, sitting in front. The medium then was usually chosen from the *afu* of Tafua (i.e. those born of women of that clan), so that on his arrival the god would have consideration for his relative and not let him sit to his death.

To return now to the actual progress of events in Marae. After the recital of the formula of abasement the kava was 'clapped' at Muafare, and a cup was brought and poured by the cup-bearer to the foremost stone of Nga Ariki in front of the Ariki Kafika. The reason for this was the primacy of these two gods in the Marae, since they were the deities of the Atua i Kafika when as a man on earth he initiated these ceremonies. Hence in all rites acknowledgment was made to them. The next cup of kava was poured to the Atua Lasi at Muafaitoka. This was done formerly by the Ariki Tafua (now by the Ariki Fangarere), after which he retired to his seating mat a few yards away (Plate 5*b*). There used to be a division of function between the Ariki Tafua and the Ariki Fangarere based, according to the natives, on ancient usage since the days of Fakaarofatia, whereby the chief of Tafua performed the kava and offered it to the medium to drink, while the Fangarere chief had control of the *epa* mat and threw food offerings from the *roi*.

The kava of Muafare served also to provide the libations of the Fangarere chief. As soon as it was begun the bowls of the other three Ariki were brought in and set near their seating mats while their kava was prepared. Each chief then poured the libations to his own clan gods in the usual manner, and threw offerings from the basket of *roi* allotted. The procedure of the Ariki Kafika was marked by the preliminary attentions he paid to his gods, Nga Ariki. He rose from his mat, and with bowed head seated himself on the mat laid before the two stones. Two cups of kava were brought and with each he made obeisance. This in Marae corresponded to the ritual of *raurau kumete* in the temple of Kafika. Like other deities these two were imagined to drink of the libations, sitting cross-legged each before his stone. 'They drink of the kava which is pouring down; when it has poured out they two have drunk.' The Ariki returned to his seat, and poured the ordinary kava, cups being also given to his elder, Pa Rarovi. The first meal of the morning then took place.

The custom on this occasion was for the *roi* to be exchanged: no chief might eat of the food which he had brought to Marae. Consequently on the conclusion of the kava the *roi* of sa Kafika was carried to sa Taumako, and that of sa Taumako to Kafika, while a similar exchange used to be made between Tafua and Fangarere. The reason for this was given simply as 'the custom from of old'. It was however in agreement with normal Tikopia usage, which promotes the exchange of food at large assemblies. An exception to the rule of reciprocal presentation was in the case of the families of Fusi, Sao, Niumano and Fatumaru. Each elder of these presented a portion to his chief and then, with his immediate kinsmen, fell to upon the remainder of the package. As each chief received his basket from another it was opened and the contents were apportioned among the crowd in rear. All ate heartily, with animated conversation, but each clan group kept to itself in the neighbourhood of its chief; people did not wander from one to the other.

Like other important rites, those of Marae had their *fakaoatea*, performed not at noon, but about mid-morning. On the first day, that of the clearing of Marae, this was provided by the Kafika clan. A basket of *roi* with a stem of kava across the top was carried from the house inland and set at the bottom of the ground. The Ariki Kafika then recited a short formula. The kava was then removed and laid with the previous stem at Muafaitoka, while the *roi* was laid between the two mounds in the centre of the Marae. Portions of the food were distributed to each chief – these were for ceremonial purposes only, since the meal had just concluded. The kava-maker and cup-bearer, who had meanwhile been in retirement at Fenumera after the previous rite, came in again and the liquid was prepared with the same ceremony as before. The Ariki Fangarere went down to Muafaitoka and the first cup of kava was handed to him there to pour to the Atua Lasi. The second was taken to the mat before the stones of Nga Ariki, the third and fourth to the other two chiefs. Other cups were then filled and carried as quietly as possible to the chiefs, in order of precedence, an assistant cup-bearer being called in for the purpose. For the *faka-oatea* the kava was prepared in a single bowl, not separately as in the previous rite. The various offerings were then 'thrown', the Ariki Kafika rising to officiate for that of Nga Ariki, then return-ing to perform the same service for his other gods at his seating mat. The Ariki Fangarere then lifted the *epa* and replaced it on his own seat, while the cycas leaves which covered it were stuck in the top of the roof of Rarofiroki.

This concluded the rites for the time being, and the members of the various clans now mingled and chatted. The Ariki visited one another informally to talk and chew betel. A common sub-ject of conversation was the size of the crowd that had assembled, the significant absentees, their reasons and the like. On the occa-sion of my visit about seventy men and youths were present. A small private kava ceremony was performed in Kafika Lasi by the Ariki Kafika but this was of no great importance, libations alone being poured to some of his clan deities. Of the rest of the people most went to Tai to continue their ordinary work, or pay visits to the houses of friends and relatives.

At this point the description of events may be interrupted to give a few general observations on the structure of the cycle of activities. The *Taomatangi* proper lasted for four days, each of which was associated more particularly with one of the clans. Thus the first day, that on which the Marae was cleared, was termed the 'day of sa Kafika', and for this the basket of *roi* which constituted the *fakaoatea* was provided by this clan. Likewise they were responsible for the accumulation of a large quantity of areca nut, which was distributed among the men and women present at the dance. This areca was also termed '*te aso*', 'the day', from a linguistic transference. The order of precedence of the clans was strictly observed. The second day was thus 'the day of sa Tafua' who (until conversion of their chief) were responsible for *fakaoatea* and areca nut; the following was 'the day of sa Taumako' while 'the day of sa Fangarere' concluded the period. The *Urangafi*, which immediately followed, was divided in similar style, the first night being that of sa Kafika, the second being associated with sa Tafua, and so on. Here the stress was laid not so much on economic contribution, but on the type of song chanted, certain kinds being restricted to certain nights, with very close clan associations. This will be considered in the next chapter.

When I saw the dance festival, however, adjustments had been made to meet the defection of the Ariki Tafua and his clan. The 'day' and 'night' of sa Tafua still remained in name, but the people responsible for the areca nut, etc., were different. The solution found was to split one clan, that of Fangarere, into two sections, one of which, the immediate kinsfolk of the chief, remained as 'sa Fangarere', and the other acted as 'sa Tafua'. This was very ingenious, since Fangarere was the smallest in numbers by far. If either Kafika or Taumako, which were each about the same size, had been split, the traditional balance of exchanges between them would have been disturbed, but by dividing Fangarere into two approximately equal sections equilibrium was kept. Another reason for selecting Fangarere people to fill the place of Tafua was possibly that their premier god was of outstanding importance in Marae.

In the following account the description of the part formerly played by sa Tafua is given in terms of the traditional scheme, as the Tikopia themselves described it. It must be remembered, however, that the actual persons taking part were people of sa Fangarere.

By ancient rule, the ordinary offices of Marae, especially the apportionment of betel nut, the setting up and redistribution of the 'kava house', were done by men of sa Tafua, in particular by those of the family of Sao. The reason was that since the Ariki Tafua was the 'Faifekau', the 'Worker', in esoteric affairs, of the Ariki Kafika, it was proper for his clansmen to carry out the ordinary duties therein. Sa Sao and sa Fusi have a peculiar right in this respect since their principal deities, Te Atua i Sao and Te Atua i Fusi, were believed to be the *atua faifekau*, the 'working gods' of Marae. This position was regarded as an honour and a privilege, not as in any way degrading. On account of its sanctity very strict rules had to be observed as to conduct of affairs in Marae.

Men who performed such offices as cup-bearer or distributor of food had to appear in correct costume, with hair loosened, not tied up on top of the head. Except when actually engaged in carrying objects, they had to adopt a conventional posture – the body respectfully inclined forward, the hands clasped in front. The method of walking was stiff and stilted, due to the weight being thrown mainly on the toes and ball of the foot, and movement was hurried and jerky. The object was to convey the impression to the gods that the person was moving rapidly about their business, yet with due regard for the sacredness of the ground on which he treads. According to Pae Sao, the cardinal rules which he himself observed in performing the tasks of Marae were, first, to go lightly, and not let his feet thud on the ground; and secondly, to go quickly – only ignorant people move slowly – while he adopted the correct position of hand and head as already mentioned. Pa Fenumera of Fangarere, who in 1928 performed many of the offices in Marae and was acknowledged as being well versed in such matters, said, 'Distributions of Marae are clutched quickly. One runs, runs in going.' By this he meant that quick action was imperative; in apportioning areca nut one should grasp the bunch, wrench it apart and fling down the pieces, moving almost at a trot the while. There must be no pause, no slow consideration. But on account of its taboo no-one walked idly across the Marae and the cup-bearers kept to the track between the mounds and did not take the shorter route across the centre.

In order to accomplish his task in Marae in the minimum of time, a man of the Sao family muttered a special formula to himself prior to rising to proceed on his duties:

> You, Tokitaitekere
> Turn up your foot sole that I may hasten
> I am going to distribute the things of the chiefs.

He called on his god by name to speed him on his way by assisting the soles of his feet to turn up more rapidly. Moreover the formula served as an announcement to the god of the intentions of his messenger so that he knew the man was not merely trespassing on his domain. The people of Fusi substituted the name of Tarikotu for that of Tokitaitekere in the recitation. This was made known to me by my friend Pae Sao for the occasion when in conformity with the usage of visitors of rank I rose after the *aso* to make customary presents to the deities of the Marae. He coached me carefully, and insisted that I recite the formula to enlist the co-operation of his god. (This man did not attend the *Taomatangi* of 1928, since his son was absent from the island on a vessel, and festive conduct would be therefore unbecoming in him.)

Towards the middle of the afternoon the contributions of areca nut began to accumulate. Since this was the day of sa Kafika it was their responsibility, and in theory at all events every man of the clan contributed his share. A bunch of *kaula* (a variety of areca nut) or in lieu several of the less valued *fuariki* was the rule, but if a man had many trees in his orchards he might give more. Each bunch had a few leaves of betel tied to the top and was stood on a mat outside the house of the Ariki. The *aso* was in two sections: one for apportionment among the men, the other, not so large, among the women. On this day the *aso* of sa Kafika was distributed mainly among the people of sa Taumako, with smaller quantities to those of Tafua and Fangarere, while those of Kafika each received only a single nut or a couple as their share. On the second day Tafua provided the betel, of which the largest portion went to sa Fangarere, while the third and fourth days reversed the position of the first and second respectively. By such means equivalence was maintained in the presentation and reception of gifts.

PREPARATIONS FOR THE DANCING

As the sun went down towards the western cliffs preparations were made for the dance. To avert evil influences and secure welfare some of the women came to the Ariki and got circlets of twisted cordyline leaf tied round their necks, with the recitation of the usual formula.

The antithesis between dancing and taboo has already been discussed with regard to the ban imposed after the throwing of the Firestick. In ordinary life, after a death has occurred, all the members of the immediate family group, and others of close kin, as the mother's family, are subject to a form of taboo which restricts them from eating certain of the choicer kinds of food and from indulging in any of the outdoor amusements, or even appearing abroad by day. This becomes less severe as time goes on, until at last the initiative is taken by a more distant relative, who without announcing his intention brings food and turmeric to the bereaved household. Despite protests he anoints the mourners with the red pigment, thus by decorating them in festive manner breaking the prohibition under which they lie. While the turmeric is being applied, and for some time after, the bereaved family break out into extravagant wailing, and chant dirges in memory of their lost one. After a time the expression of their grief subsides and they are constrained to eat. This ceremony is termed the *furufurunga kere* – the 'Washing of the Soil' – and frees the mourners from their voluntary seclusion.

On the evening before the clearing of the Marae for the *Taomatangi* dirges could be heard chanted from many of the houses of the village. It was a recognized time for release of restrictions, and the relatives of those people who had been in mourning for some months made a point of anointing them then in order that they might be able to take part in the festive season. Mourners for a recent death, however, were not so treated, nor if it were proposed would they consent; the demands of their affection had not yet been assuaged.

For the dances of Marae elaborate decorations are worn. New bark-cloths are donned, and over them men of rank wear a mat kilt, and commoners green banana leaves. Leaf fringes are worn on the head, tassels of flowers or leaf in the ears, rings in the septum of the nose, and necklets of leaf or the sweet-smelling white frangipani blossom. Unmarried people often also stick such a blossom in the hair above the brow. Trochus-shell rings are worn on the arms, coconut-shell rings on the fingers, and beads of shell or coconut shell on wrists and ankles. A spray of leaves, or a bouquet of flowers and fruit, is set at the back of the belt. Much time is spent in the choice and preparation of these ornaments, and both colour and scent are taken into consideration. So much, in fact, is smell important that the preparation of ornaments in general is known as *fai manongi*, 'preparing scents'.

SONGS AND DANCES OF THE 'TAOMATANGI'

The dances held in Marae, like other features of the Work of the Gods, follow a definite traditional arrangement. This systematic organization refers primarily to the songs which are basic to the dances. The characteristic elements of the system are: firstly, the division of the songs into a number of named types, which are performed in a recognized sequence; secondly, the association of some types of song, and of some individual songs, with a particular clan, to which they 'belong', with the chief of that clan as the primary 'owner'; and thirdly, the maintenance to some extent of an order of songs within the particular type, the first few at least following a definite sequence.

The division of the songs into types rests partly upon the rhythmic patterns upon which they are based, and partly upon their content – as for instance whether they are of the 'dance type' or 'dirge type'. Some traditional compositions, the origin of which is unknown, form the archetypes; others, composed by 'historical' persons, have been framed to fit a particular type. The association of a particular song with a particular clan rests primarily on the fact that the song is dedicated to a god of that clan, or secondarily, on the attribution of the song to a member or ancestor of the clan as composer. The sequence of songs within a type depends also to some extent on the gods to whom they are dedicated, the songs relating to the most important gods tending to come first on the programme. But here adventitious factors of selection in the past seem to have complicated the arrangement.

This systematic arrangement holds both for the 'days' of the *Taomatangi* and for the 'nights' of the *Urangafi*. The fundamental feature in it is the provision of definite occasions for the chanting by each clan of its 'own' songs, which from the religious point of view honour its own gods in particular, and from the social point of view allow it to give expression to its special individuality and privileges. It will be noted, however, that the co-operative aspect of the ritual is still maintained; all four clans participate on each occasion, no matter what songs are being sung, or whose 'day' or 'night' it is. Thus the gods of each are honoured in turn, and are treated as the gods of all, due attention being paid to the recognized hierarchy.

I recorded in all more than sixty songs chanted during this festival of Marae, and it is not possible here to give the text of each. But in this and the next chapter I give what may be termed the special 'feature songs', the key-points of the ritual, in their context of performance. In addition I give as an appendix to this chapter a few samples of other songs, choosing those which occupy the more important positions in the recital.

As an example of the proprietary attitude to these songs the *vetu masanga* may be mentioned. These are sung at Fenumera, on the 'days' of sa Kafika and sa Tafua only. They are regarded as belonging to the Ariki Tafua. I obtained some texts of them first from some men of Ravenga, partly because we had all been present at the dance together, and partly because I wished to get check material. When later I applied to the Ariki Tafua for them he was very annoyed on finding that I had received them already. He said these songs were his: to impart them to me was 'stealing'. This is the same principle which applies to kava lists and basic myths of social origins. One factor in the situation is that the man who 'owns' them is believed to hold the authentic version in his memory. In practice I usually found that he could give me a complete version, but that other men were often equally well versed. In the case of the songs of Marae this tends to be particularly the case, since they all chant the songs together.

We may now return to the descriptive account of events on the first day.

The people began to assemble for the initial dance when the shadows began to creep out over Marae. Like other important ceremonies it had to be done in the shades of evening, or late afternoon, not under the full glare of the sun.

First, however, came the rite of 'the Drinking', which was essentially a series of kava libations connected with the offering of fresh coconuts to the gods. A large pile of coconuts was brought into Marae and set down on the lower side of the path, while baskets of food were laid before each of the chiefs. The pile of nuts was then divided up, and the man officiating seated himself by the stones near the water; then the Ariki Kafika called out the confirmation formula. The coconuts were then apportioned: the first lot to Fangarere, the next to Taumako, the next to Tafua. The stones at the bottom of the Marae had each their share, as also the mat of Nga Ariki. The kava was made at Muafaitoka, cups being carried to the various Ariki in turn as already described. After this brief ceremony the chiefs went to join the crowd, which, after gathering at Fenumera, had gone to Matavi to await their arrival.

The first dance was the *Vetu*. A hollow square was roughly formed, the people facing inwards with the side nearest Marae constituted by the chiefs alone. After a moment's silence all looked at the chiefs, and a wild yell broke out, '*Iefu!*' The song was now started, the time being kept by clapping of the hands with a rising motion. Hence the expression 'Is crashed (clapped) the *vetu*.' At first the demeanour was restrained and the arms alone were swung. Gradually, however, the rhythm was felt more and more deeply, and, though with no change of tempo, the excitement began to grow. Bodies turned in unison first to one side, then to the other, while the knees bent and rose in co-operation with the swinging of the arms. The song was chanted in high tones in quick time. The correct method of beating time was not to clap the hands lethargically together, but to lift them high up – in completion of the movement. The more vigorous of the dancers thus exhorted the others 'Lift them up!' in an endeavour to animate the proceedings still more. Towards the end of the stanza, when a kind of refrain was introduced with the words '*Riele, riele*', the hands were not merely allowed to swing up and down, but urged up in a sweeping gesture, and the volume of sound waxed accordingly. As the dancers became more fired, stamping with the foot was also introduced to synchronize with the simultaneous clap of the hands. The spectacle was a dramatic one.

Each song ended with a whoop that made all the cliffs of Uta echo and re-echo. A short pause ensued before the next song was raised, during which the participants remained silent, mostly with eyes cast down to the ground. It was noticeable also during the dance that the men avoided each other's eyes but looked up to the hills, or out over the lake. This persistent gazing at the mountain crest was a symptom of the self-consciousness which the dancers felt at facing one another thus – 'they are shy', I was told. Moreover it was taboo to laugh or joke during the proceedings, since the dance was that of the gods. By fixing their eyes on a distant point of the landscape any tendency to laughter was thus minimized. The *vetu* varied considerably in melody and also in rhythm, while a variant of the clapping, with one hand raised on high and the other meeting it from below alternately, was characteristic of certain dances. The signal to commence was given by the Ariki Kafika, who called out '*Osepo!*', a conventional cry which had no special meaning. At the conclusion he was supposed also to call '*Forua!*' ('shout'), when all the men obey. But complaint was made by the older members that the crowd acted stupidly, and began without the preliminary signal, and shouted at the end of the songs without waiting for the order which it was the privilege of the chief to give.

After four songs had been given in Matavi, the group moved off, singing, led by the chiefs in due order of rank, to the near-by place of Fenumera. Here they re-formed and after a short silence the whoop was given again and other *vetu* were sung. These were of a different type and were known as *vetu masanga*. After four songs or so the dancers again moved off in single file, led by the Ariki Kafika, out on to Marae. Arrived at Raromiro, that is the position towards the lower edge of the ground, between the path and the lake, they all sat down, facing inland.

The women meanwhile had been busy, and before the men entered, they seated themselves at the side of Nukuora, facing towards the lake behind a number of new coconut mats. The women had all donned clean skirts for the occasion and had circlets of twisted cordyline leaf round their necks. The mats which were unfolded were dedicated to the Atua Fafine, behind whose stone they were ranged. They were known as 'principal mats', and might not be used by the women as seating places. 'It is taboo, they do not go and sit on the mats spread out.' Male deities had no part in this rite; the dichotomy of the sexes operated on the spiritual as well as on the earthly plane. 'It is taboo; male deities do not go to the women.' It was believed in fact that each party not only represented but actually embodied the deities of its own sex who had come to attend the singing.

It is held we the men who chant, that is the gods, the Brethren.

The women likewise were held to be the material embodiment of the Female Deity. For this reason no conversation was exchanged between the men and women; the taboo of Marae required the strictest decorum. On the entry of the men the sounding-board was brought from Matangiaso hut and set in position before the Ariki Taumako. This sacred board – looking like a trough – was under his control. 'It is his', the Tikopia said, meaning that he alone had the privilege of beating it for the dance. A low seat of wood on four legs was slipped under him and a song was started by the group of men. All clapped gently with one hand on another, or with hand on knee, while the Ariki Taumako beat with his hand on the sounding-board. The women were silent.

The songs now given were of quite a different type from the *vetu*. They were known as *sore* and were classed under the generic name of *fuatanga* (dirges), whereas the *vetu* were *mako* (dances). The special feature of the *sore* is that they are drawn from a much larger range of songs, many composed in quite recent times; they have been chanted in the first place as an integral part of a particular type of festival of a chief, known as the *seru*. The songs of the *seru* itself are divided into three sections: the '*seru* in front', those 'in the middle', and those 'behind'. The first two sections comprise 'dirges of the deities'; the third section consists of songs to the chief composed by his clansfolk. It is from the first two sections that the songs of the *sore* are chosen. Each section is marked off by a song of a different tempo, and the same principle is used to sub-divide each section. And in each of the first two sections one song, the *matai* of the *seru*, takes prime place from its dedication to all the major deities of the land. It is composed by the chief giving the festival. The songs of the *sore* in particular represent homage by each clan separately to the common deities. As 'dirges of the gods' they are intensely sacred; they embody names which under ordinary circumstances are never repeated by the common people, and are invoked only by the chiefs in their kava.

As with the *vetu*, the chanting of *sore* was regarded as a serious matter, and the behaviour of the participants was very restrained. There was no joking or laughter; each sat quietly in his place. The Ariki were in the centre of the front rank, with men of importance immediately flanking them; the rest of the crowd were ranged behind, indiscriminately in several rows, no order of clans being observed.

After four or five songs had been chanted the *aso*, or *anea kamu*, of betel was brought in. This was done by two men detailed beforehand, who carried the heavy loads from the inland house. They came down the path, along the front of Marae, passing the people till they came to the Ariki who was the principal recipient of the gift. On this, the first day, it was the Ariki Taumako. Setting the bunches down in front of him, slightly to his right side, they did not turn round, but marched off the Marae by the opposite exit, with hands clasped and heads bowed in orthodox style. Thence they walked round again to the house, making a circuit, and entered with the second load, and after that a third, mainly of betel leaf. A special song was chanted for the bringing of the betel, but after this the singing of the men ceased.

The women now began their *sore*, beating time with fans held in their hands while their betel was also brought in in similar fashion. The bearers of the betel did not move down Marae to join the crowd of men when their task was finished, but sat apart near the station of their clan.

The distribution of the betel was done with care, by two men of the clan which provided it. A large bunch of each variety of areca nut, garnished with betel leaf, was carried first for the Ariki Fangarere and laid on his mat. A single bunch of *kaula* followed for the Ariki Kafika, a gift for the Ariki Tafua equivalent to that for the chief of Fangarere, and a specially large mass for the Ariki Taumako. The bunches were then taken by the servers and broken up for distribution among the crowd. The people of Tafua and Fangarere got moderate shares, the people of Taumako received large portions, those of Kafika only a single nut each, in accordance with the principles already discussed. The special bunch carried to the mat of the Ariki Kafika was for his principal deity; it was not torn up and distributed by the chief afterwards but kept by him for his own private consumption. After the distribution the men began a further set of songs, while the women paused and arranged the apportionment of their betel in turn.

By now the dancing and singing had been pursued for nearly two hours. Hence the clapping was not nearly so vigorous as at the commencement, and some people made hardly more than a pretence at beating time. At last the songs ended, and the crowd dispersed.

The 'evening kava' was then performed, by each chief separately, his own bowl being set near his own seating mat. The procedure in this followed the normal course. No one partook of food from the baskets of the chiefs, and after sitting for a short time in general conversation everyone went home. This concluded the rites of the first day, the day of sa Kafika.

FOOD EXCHANGE ON THE DAY OF SA TAFUA

The next day was that of sa Tafua. Since the Marae was clear the first ceremony of the day was that of the kava of the *fakaoatea*. This, a single basket, formerly prepared by the family of the Ariki Tafua, was brought into Marae, and the chiefs were summoned to sit upon their mats. Nowadays, as mentioned earlier, this *fakaoatea* is prepared by Pa Fenumera of Fangarere clan, whose family has taken on the responsibilities of the second day, including the provision of betel and areca nut. The rite was quite simple, being in fact a replica of that performed the previous day. The party was small, comprising only half a dozen men in addition to the chiefs. The rest of the time passed as before. This was the 'day of decoration of the land'. On the previous day it was taboo for people to indulge in too much ornamentation, the opening dances of the season being a matter of the greatest solemnity. On the succeeding days, however, the tension had relaxed somewhat, and ornaments were much more liberally used, as also was turmeric pigment, Moreover this freedom extended to the actual dance itself, in which considerably more laxity of style was permitted. The reason given for the constraint of the first day was that it is 'the day of the Atua i Kafika' and the people must show respect to him. On this initial occasion, according to Tikopia distinctions, movement should be almost solely of the vertical type, as the swinging up and down of hands, or the stamping of feet. Later, however, lateral movement of body, arms and legs is allowed; one can *dance* instead of merely sing and clap. The principal difference in the procedure lay in the performance of individual dancers in the square. After the song had been chanted for some little time, and the rhythm was properly adjusted, one of the recognized experts emerged from the ranks with little sidelong jumps, his fists clenched and alternating, one close to the body, the other extended to the side, rather after the fashion of a boxer. With bent knees he progressed by short movements of the feet up the centre of the square, body swinging, turning first to one side and then to the other in perfect time to the song. His head was thrown back, and his face bore a fierce expression. Each rhythmic change of position was accompanied by a grunting '*Uh! Uh! Uh!*' or '*Ih! Ih! Ih!*', a sound which was taken up by some of the dancers in the square in token of encouragement. This was known as the *fakai* of the dance, and had no special significance apart from its rhythmic value. The movements of the performer were varied from time to time by opening the hands and throwing wide the arms as if in a gesture of appeal, while the steady advance of the feet and the swaying of the body proceeded. This was the *sava*, the display of individual skill which was much admired as the crowning point of the dance. Anyone might *sava* provided that he was sufficiently expert, and young men were often urged to go and do so by their elders.

The ceremonial dancing season, like so many other Tikopia

institutions, has as one of its important features the making of
reciprocal presents of food. In the *Taomatangi* these exchanges
take place between the women. The grouping here again is on the
basis of clans, the people of Kafika exchanging with those of
Taumako and those of Tafua with those of Fangarere. The packages of food concerned are termed household food baskets though
in reality they are baskets of the largest size. In name the transaction is one which concerns the women alone – *a longi nga fafine*
is the term used – but actually all the resources and manpower of
the household are mobilized to assist in the preparation of the
gifts. The time of selecting partners for the occasion is in the
evening of the 'day of sa Tafua', after the *sore* have been sung in
Marae. When the men have dispersed the women wait in their
places at Rarofetaka, to make the arrangements. The method is
for the women of Taumako and Fangarere to sit silent while those
of Kafika and Tafua announce their choice respectively. A woman
says 'I desire so and so.' Someone who hears this will pass on the
information to the person concerned, 'You have been chosen by
such and such a family', and the procedure is complete. No objection is ever made by the person selected: this would be a grave
breach of etiquette. One woman may be chosen by several of the
opposite group: this is quite in order, though it means of course
that a corresponding number of packages of food will have to be
made by her family for the return gift.

The choosing of food baskets, or agreeing of food baskets, as it is
termed, is done on the evening before the actual presentations are
made in order to allow due time for the collection and cooking of
the requisite amount of food. Though in theory the women of the
primarily recipient clans are supposed to sit silent while the choice
is being made, actually they appear to enter into the conversation
and give their opinions freely.

Though many of the partnerships are traditional ('Its food
basket from of old'), there is always a certain number of free
decisions to be made. Moreover some rearrangement is often
necessary, since people try to spread out the obligations as far as
possible so that no family is omitted, and others are not over-
loaded. The result is a babel of talk for many minutes. The women
are left to settle the affair themselves, and no man goes to take part
in their conversation. As a rule, however, the chiefs of the two
clans concerned meet informally afterwards and discuss the

arrangements to ensure that no serious omissions have been made.

On the next morning, which was the 'day of sa Taumako', the *fakaoatea* rite was performed at an early hour – somewhere about 8.30 a.m. – in order that the people might be free to prepare the food for the exchanges. When the kava was over the men went off to their orchards accompanied by some of the women of their household, and plucked coconuts and breadfruit or dug up taro. Everyone was very busy, for each family group was preparing its oven. The social emphasis of the reciprocal presentation had now entirely passed from the women to their respective households and it was now these which were spoken of as conducting the exchanges. Much discussion went on about the baskets and about the various households which had been linked together. Representatives of one or two families which had been overlooked in spite of the arranging of the night before wandered about from house to house, trying to find partners, and in order to accommodate them some 're-shuffling' took place. The fact of cardinal interest to a family was that their food basket had to be made for presentation; the precise group which was to be the recipient of it was important, but to a less degree. But to be entirely left out of the scheme of exchanges would be a reflection on their name and social prestige. The number of food baskets which a single family has to reciprocate is a rough index of its importance in the society; the household of a chief or man of rank is usually 'bound' to several other families of the opposite clan, that of a commoner to one alone. Thus in the actual season under review the family of the Ariki Kafika were linked to three other families – that of the Ariki Taumako; that of Kamota, also of Taumako clan; and that of Notau, a family group of Tafua resident in Namo. The first of these exchanges, that between the households of the chiefs of Kafika and Taumako, is a standing arrangement of traditional origin (as also was one between the Ariki Tafua and the Ariki Fangarere). That with the Kamota group was concluded on the previous evening at the 'choosing of the food kits', while that with Notau was the result of a visit from a woman of that family earlier in the day. Exchanges are often thus settled by friendly agreement before the evening discussion. The departure in this case from the rule that Kafika clan is linked only with Taumako and Tafua only with Fangarere is due to the fact that the abandonment of these ceremonies by the Ariki Tafua has disorganized the arrangements of those of his clan who live in Ravenga or Namo and still attend Marae.

The social unit concerned in the exchange is not, except in rare cases, the individual household of parent and children, but the extended family, the members of which gather to assist their head.

An interesting mechanism enables people not directly involved in an exchange, and not wishing to go some distance to join their own family group, to affiliate with that of a neighbour or friend. A person who thus desires to take part in the system of exchanges may 'seek the food basket' of another. He goes with a contribution of taro, etc., to the place where the food basket of the person of his choice is being prepared. He gives in his supply to be absorbed, and in due time when the return basket is received from Marae he will be allotted a share of the food. This institution of 'seeking baskets' is very useful, since it enables orphaned youths, single men, old widowers, and other people without near relatives to join in the system of exchange and share in the product without taking upon themselves the full burden of the whole basket.[1] Moreover it gives opportunity for a mark of friendly attention from one person to another. Though a man may be busy in his own family group with its food basket he can assist that of his friend or neighbour by sending over a lad with a bundle of taro or breadfruit. All such contributions are welcome since the amount of food required to equip a basket is great.

As the sun sank the 'baskets' began to arrive. Canoes came over the lake loaded up with the large green baskets, filled to bursting with food, and with the feathery tufts of the sprouting coconuts hanging over the gunwale. They put in at the landing place among the trees at the bottom of Marae and unloaded, then moved off along the shore, while the packages were carried up and set down at Rarofetaka, at the side of the house Nukuora. Other baskets were carried in on the backs of women, who were assisted to remove their burdens by husband or male relatives. The men came in shouldering a bunch of bananas, or some taro or coconuts at the end of a pole. Most of the baskets were set indiscriminately on the ground, but certain ones had a definite position assigned to them. These were *a longi o a tapakau* – 'food baskets of the mats' – so called because they were placed on coconut mats which had been spread out for their reception at the edge of Marae. The laying of

[1] Cf. my *Primitive Polynesian Economy*, 1939, pp. 326, 328–9.

such mats was a privilege which belonged to only a few of the principal families in each clan – in Kafika, that of the Ariki and his elders of Rarovi, Porima and Tavi alone. One basket in each clan was termed *te longi o mua* – 'the food basket to the fore' – so called since it stood in front of all the others. It was the gift of the Ariki which was destined for the other Ariki; a preliminary kava rite was performed over it in the house as soon as it was prepared, and it was lifted out from under the eaves on *mata paito*, not through the ordinary doorway, in token of its sacerdotal importance. It was in fact directly associated with the gods of each clan, and after it reached its destination the kava was performed over it likewise before it was apportioned for food. The 'baskets of the mats' were exchanged only against each other, and as each family of rank had one only it followed that gifts of this type took place only between the principal family groups of the clans. Thus in the case of the Ariki Kafika mentioned above, the basket which went to the Ariki Taumako was the 'basket of the mat', whereas that which went to the group of Notau was not. (The 'basket to the fore' of the chief was of necessity his 'basket of the mat'.) There were thus three grades of food gift in the exchange.

The Basket to the Fore	the principal basket of the chief, to be presented to his corresponding chief.
Baskets of the Mats	the main food baskets of the principal elders, presented to other elders of similar status.
Baskets	the general baskets exchanged between commoners, or men of rank and commoners.

When the baskets had been set in position and a kava rite performed, the *vetu* and the *sore* were sung as on previous days. The distribution of the betel was effected as before, but this time a large share was given to the Ariki Kafika, another to Pa Rarovi, and four moderate bunches to the chiefs of Tafua and Fangarere, while the Ariki Taumako received only a small bunch. This was his 'day', so that he reciprocated the allotment of the 'day of sa Kafika'.

The dancers dispersed, and the evening kava took place, after which came the exchange of the baskets. Before being handed over each basket was cut through at the top band. The only reason which could be given for this was that it was an old custom, but it presumably had the effect of preventing the basket from being used again.

In addition to the ordinary routine of the *Taomatangi*, according to which certain songs and dances are prescribed, there are items which are sometimes performed as 'extras'. One of these is the *tau*. This is a dance which takes place when a boy of rank comes to the ceremonies of Marae for the first time as a novice. As a rule this happens at the first *Taomatangi* festival after he has undergone the operation of incision.

When the dancing season arrives an oven is made in the clan temple of the lad and the *tau* is sung. It is repeated over and over as if it were a new song being learned for the first time. After the food has been eaten the people assemble outside and again go through a preliminary practice. The men who are about to take part on Marae decorate themselves in a peculiar fashion by bands of turmeric smeared across the temples from the corners of the eyes, and down the cheeks from the sides of the nose. This is the distinguishing mark of the group of *tau* dancers in contradistinction for example to the performers of the *uru* (see later). Valuables are also donned for the occasion, including new bark-cloth, beads, etc.; while the boy is decked with a new waistcloth, has many ornaments hung upon him and is smeared with turmeric on breast, neck and cheeks in token of his social importance.

During the time that the oven is being made and the song chanted some of the relatives wail. The ostensible reason is that they are ashamed for their kinsfolk who are going to perform the *tau*, and desire also to show affection for their child. The wailing, however, is of the same nature as that which takes place at incision, marriage and other ceremonies. It is a formal method of signalling the entrance of the boy on a further stage of his career, and expresses the interest of the relatives in him and their sympathy with him in the social crisis through which he is passing. More generally it is a reaffirmation of the bond of kinship.

In a pause in the *sore* the people of his clan rise up, with the lad in their midst, while the people of the other clans remain seated, and sing and dance the *tau*. The boy also is encouraged to take part and is supported by his mother's brothers (real and classificatory) who stand behind him and at the sides, even in front of him, grasp his wrists and hands in theirs, and perform with them the motions of the dance. The object of this is to give the lad moral support in the face of the spectators – he is shy, the Tikopia say, in the sight of all the people. How true this attribution of shyness may be is uncertain; the real function of the *tau* and its procedure is undoubtedly the formal recognition of the rank and social prestige of the boy and honouring of his family. Moreover it serves as a public demonstration of the amplitude of his maternal kinship affiliations. The action of the mother's brothers in supporting him is termed 'the honours of the definite child', and the more men surrounding him the greater is the distinction accorded him. By the 'definite child' is meant that the presence of so many maternal kin to assist is a proof that he is accorded full social recognition by his mother's family group. As Tikopia continually seek concrete forms of expression for social relations they say 'Such a boy is not allowed to fall down in the *tau*.' When this sight is seen in Marae it gives rise to approving comment: 'The land will make speech. That one there is a definite child; he does not fall down.'

The *tau* may also be performed for guests of rank, and then their arms also are supported by their maternal kin.

The movements of the *tau* differ somewhat from those of the *vetu* and other *mako*. The dancers rise to their feet with fists clenched and bent knees, and begin to sway the body from side to side, with one arm advanced, the other held close to the breast. The body is thus turned slowly to the left, and bent over, the right arm extended and the head bent down. A prolonged swing downwards is followed by a quicker upward movement and a toss of the head, after which the function of the arms is reversed and the body sways to the right in a corresponding movement. This is repeated many times, the rhythm of the song being followed. The feet are kept firmly planted on the ground, and no one moves from his position in the ranks. Songs of the *tau* which are performed in Marae are sacred.

The type of dance just described, for which an oven is prepared, is termed the *tau nunga*. Sometimes, however, a clan will decide to perform a *tau* even though they have no boy of rank to introduce to the *Taomatangi*. For this no food is made and no special term is used. As is always the case they hold the *tau* on their own day; it would not be etiquette to select the day of another clan for the purpose.

During my attendance at Marae a *tau* was performed by sa

Taumako, and aroused considerable discussion afterwards. The chief and his cousins had determined on such a dance, but had not announced their intention beforehand. When the time came they stood up, and wished the men of the other clans to follow suit. Some complied, others remained seated at first but were brought to their feet by exhortation from the men of Taumako, and the dance was performed. The Ariki Kafika remarked laughingly afterwards: 'I remained sitting down, but Pa Tarikitonga looked at me furiously and said "Those who do not stand and dance will have to go out to Tai" so I stood up. His eyes looked as if they were about to drop out, and he appeared as if to fight me!' (The idea that the Ariki Kafika could be compelled to dance on pain of being banished to the beach village was humorous.) The Ariki gave as his reason for sitting down: 'I refused because we had no *tau* yesterday for our day.' His grievance was shared by the men of Kafika as a whole. They felt that in introducing this special dance without warning the people of Taumako were arrogating to themselves prestige in the affairs of Marae which was not rightly theirs; that mention should have been made beforehand, that they too might have had a *tau* of their own. Such an attitude on the part of one group against another for a real or fancied slight is not an uncommon feature of these ceremonial proceedings.

The concluding day of the *Taomatangi* was 'the day of sa Fangarere', but was also termed *te aso tauvare*. The explanation of this latter term presented difficulties to the Tikopia, who merely said 'It is the same as the speech, "the stupid person".' This, however, shed little light on the point. The reference may be to the somewhat confused order of events on this day, or to its lesser importance, but no-one could speak with certainty on this. The procedure, however, differed from that on the previous occasions. The *fakaoatea* was made in Fangarere temple, and during its preparation the three other Ariki attended. The kindling of the oven was the signal for the chiefs to assemble, and while the smoke was billowing through the house they sat and talked and chewed betel. The Ariki Kafika, as befitted his position, occupied the mat at the head of the house, while the other Ariki sat at the foot. Pa Rarovi had the duty of tending the fire, in which he was assisted by other elders. It may be noted that each Ariki brought with him, or sent with some member of his household, his contribution of raw food to the oven of his host. When the food had been prepared the company began to sing dirges. These were of various types, including *vetu*, and their performance lasted for some time. Like the ceremonies of Rarofiroki its primary object was to pay honour to the Atua Lasi, the chief god of Fangarere, and other senior deities of the Marae.

When the songs were finished a man of Fangarere brought in bunches of areca nut and bundles of coconuts, from which offerings were made to the deities of Marae. The chiefs then went to Marae, and performed the kava of the *fakaoatea*.

The *aso tauvare* was characterized by a fishing expedition conducted towards midday by a large number of people, more especially young men. Armed with pole net or hand net, they swept the reef and bagged all that came their way. The catch was cooked and eaten in the beach villages in Tai; but if the fish had been very plentiful some would have been brought to Uta and given to the chiefs.

Later in the day the areca nut was collected. I noticed that on this occasion the Ariki Kafika observed to the Ariki Fangarere, 'Great is the quantity of betel.' This praise was by way of tactful comment, for everyone knew that the people of Fangarere clan, including their chief, were not wealthy and their stock of areca was not large. Pa Fenumera, who had now assumed the responsibility of the Ariki Tafua, was of this clan also, and was comparatively poor. On this account Pae Sao, his friend, sent over five bunches of areca nut for his 'day' remarking to me in comment, 'He is a bat; he has no betel.' 'Bat' is a term of commiseration or contempt applied to a person who has little wealth; the reason for the metaphor is, as natives say, that the bat is a creature possessing no property of its own.

During the course of the afternoon several bunches of taro, leaves and tubers complete, were brought into Marae and set by the stone which marked the depositing of the *roi* on the first morning. They were termed the *putu*, and were to provide the *fakaoatea* of Kafika on the morrow. After the usual *vetu* and evening kava the people dispersed; thus ended the day of Fangarere, which was the last of the *Taomatangi*.

SONGS OF THE *TAOMATANGI:* A SELECTION

'VETU'

(1) A foremost *vetu* of sa Kafika

> *Tafito:* Te ata ne tafa i te tonga E!
> Kau ono mai – o
> Ko Reani ra E
> Turi oke i te toi.
> A uru o a maungo
> Ka nokotanumia
> E te tai roroto.

> *Kupu:* Ai-e! A uru o a maungo
> Ka tanumia
> E te tai roroto.
> Riele, riele!
> Kakea ke oko ai
> Ko Reani ku rere tu i runga.

> Translation: The dawn broke in the east, O!
> To me appeared
> Reani then, O!
> Risen in the sea.
> The crests of the mountains
> Which were formerly buried
> By the swollen tide (empty ocean).

> *Ai-e!* Crests of the mountains
> Buried
> By the swollen tide.
> *Riele, riele!*
> Mounting, and now to be reached.
> Reani has flown and stands on high.

This song was said to have been composed by an early chief of Kafika and 'to have been left in progression to his grandchildren of later days'. Its theme is the returning voyager sighting at last the peak of his island home, amid the ocean wastes. In a version given by Pa Fenuatara the last line but one runs '*Kake ake i oku vae*' – 'climbing up from my feet'. His explanation was 'Joy has mounted up from his feet to go into his body above, because he has looked upon Reani arisen. Thereupon the man says that he has been saved, that he will arrive at the land on shore.'

The sacredness of this song lies not in its content, but in its antiquity.

(2) *Vetu* of sa Kafika

Tafito: *Ku moe a kolo*
I oso
Ku moe a kolo
O pisa.

Kupu: *Te folau loa*
Taua ku moe
A kolo o pisa
Ko niu na ku moe
Loloki ie!

Safe: *Ku moe*
A kolo o pisa.

Translation: Penis has slept
In vagina
Penis has slept
In sheath.

The long voyage
We two have slept
Penis and sheath
Coconut there has slept
Female fluid *Ie!*

Has slept
Penis in sheath.

I obtained the text of this from Pa Fenuatara, who said 'Great is its weight, brother!' He further commented upon its sexual character. 'It is the giving of a mind to the land; that the men shall not go foolishly to the women, that the women shall not go foolishly to the men.' His argument was that sex references in such a sacred context impressed upon people the need for control. This point of view (which he gave me quite unsolicited) was later opposed by Pa Rangifuri strongly when I put it to him, on the grounds that such words inevitably tended to arouse desire. 'How then do they give people minds?' But as I observed, in the actual chanting of the song a serious demeanour is maintained.

(3) An initial *vetu* of the day of sa Taumako

Translation: Stood then the wind O!
Deities of the monsoon.
Manu will descend,
Will blow a hurricane hither.

Riele, riele!
The trade-wind stands.
I sleep
My sleep is sound
The wind will blow hither a hurricane.

This song is said to have been composed by Faisina, a former Ariki Taumako, who taught it to his son, from whom it was passed down. The song is a well-known one. The version above was given by Pa Fenuatara. An expanded version was given by the Ariki Kafika, mentioning also Saraporu, allied with Manu in the production of hurricanes. The theme is the danger of hurricanes in the monsoon season, contrasted with the safety of the trade-wind season, when a person hearing the rising wind may nevertheless sleep soundly. The song is by way of propitiation, tending 'to quell the wind'.

'VETU MASANGA'

(4)

Translation: I was made to grow
That I might fly away
To the crown of the *vetu* O!
Dancing among you.

Dancing among you
With back-decorations, O!
Dancing among you
Standing up from the bearded one
Dancing among you.

This *vetu* was said to have been composed by Tisasafa, the ancestor of the chiefs of Tafua, who is alleged to have sprung from the beard of a dead Tafua chief. The song refers to this. 'He thought of it, and left it to the chiefly group of Tafua. This is a weighty *vetu*; it is performed only on the day of sa Kafika and the day of sa Tafua', said Pa Fenuatara. The translation of the song is approximate only, because of the licence of grammatical forms.

(5)

First stanza: *Euo, iai o*
                 Euo, iai o
                 Rongo!
                 Ka Aniaio
                 Anivetu.

Second stanza: *Aniaio*
                 Kanisava
                 Teretere
                 Euo, iai o
                 Euo, iai o
                 Rongo!
                 Aniaio
                 Anivetu.

Third stanza: *Aniaio*
                 Anipanipa
                 Ne loa
                 Euo, iai o, etc.

Fourth stanza: *Aniaio*
                 Kanisava, Moitekava
                 Euo, iai o, etc.

This *vetu* was sung with a lilting, undulating rhythm. The characteristic of the *vetu masanga* is that they each have a refrain, to which each stanza returns. '*Vetu* which goes in the one place, that is the *vetu masanga*. It sticks to the one base, therefore it is termed twin *vetu*.'

These 'twin *vetu*' are primarily the property of sa Tafua. According to the Ariki Tafua, who gave me the text of some of them, they were all composed by Tisasafa. According to Pa Torokinga, who also gave me texts, two only of the ancient ones, '*Euo, iai o*' and one beginning '*Mako sivo*', were composed by him, and the others by the Atua i Kafika. Pa Torokinga said that the role of Tisasafa as composer was due to his having been the 'Worker' of the Atua i Kafika. He added that *vetu masanga* are *tapu*. Ordinary *vetu* can be composed by any chief, he said, but 'twin *vetu*' only the Ariki Tafua may compose. His new songs are inserted in between the songs of the Atua. This privilege he has as 'Worker' of the Ariki Kafika.

This song is untranslatable. 'There is no speech in it we recognize', said the Ariki Tafua, in giving me another of the same type. Aniaio, Anipanipa, Teretere, etc., were said to be the names of a canoe-crew. Pa Torokinga said it was not known of what canoe, whether a vessel of the gods or of men. The Ariki Tafua said that they were the names of the crew of the canoe which went to Varuka to invite Tisasafa, his ancestor, to assume the chieftainship of Tafua, according to the myth.[1] But though portions of some of the names can be interpreted as Tikopia words (*sava*, for instance, meaning the movements of the arms in the dance), the names themselves are not current, and no gods are worshipped under them.

Pa Torokinga said that *vetu masanga* 'are composed simply to names'. Then he added that the speech in most cases is 'evil speech' referring to genitalia, at the same time that it represents personal names. He also put forward the same view as Pa Fenuatara on this point, that the intent of these sexual songs was the instruction of the people. Brought to a consideration of the importance of the sexual act by the setting of the songs they do not merely 'go foolishly' in such matters.

'SORE'

(6) The initial *sore* of the days of sa Kafika and sa Tafua, an ancient song, of only one stanza

> *Turi kou sore*
> *Turi kou sore, turi kou sore*
> *Turi vonusio.*
> *Turi farakura i matau ra*
> *Eketia e ai a*
> *Eka te atua ne to ifo mai Rangi*
> *Saungatia i Maunga Rafa.*
> *Kaia kove*
> *Sina kaea kaea.*

[1] See *History and Traditions of Tikopia*, 1961, pp. 71–4.

This song, known as a *sore matangi*, was said to have been composed and sung by the Atua i Kafika while he lived among men. Its theme is the *turi* (turnstone), the sacred bird of Fangarere, 'the deity fallen down from Heaven'. But most of the song is untranslatable in detail. 'Great is its importance', said the Ariki Kafika.

(7) The second *sore* of the days of sa Kafika and sa Tafua

> *Tafito:*   *Kau pipiki ki Rangi-mata E!* (bis)
>
> *Kupu:*   *Tu ki Rurupeo o mata rei.* (bis)
>
> I clasp Rangi-mata O!
> Standing on Rurupeo to gaze.

This also was composed by the Atua i Kafika, and refers to the speeding of the gods through the heavens from one point to another. Rangi-mata and Rurupeo are names of different sections of the heavens.

(8) A third *sore* of sa Kafika

> *Tafito:*   *E Asoaso i aso*
> *E Asoaso i aso*
> *Mai ra*
> *Si ki oko mai ra.*
>
> *Kupu:*   *Kau tuku kau sava*
> *Moi-o, moi-o*
> *Kau sava ki Retonga*
> *Moi-o, moi-o*
> *E au se fai ia*
> *Te totoro a te unga*
> *Nai se ukuakina*
> *Moi-o, moi-o.*

I received this text from Pa Motuata, who said that it was composed by the Atua i Kafika to Asoaso, his grandfather (actually, by the genealogies usually accepted, his father). It was described as 'a dirge of parting from his grandfather'. The meaning of some of the phrases is doubtful, but the theme is that Asoaso has become old, 'crawling like a hermit-crab and the Atua is dancing in his grief'. At the present time it is a Tikopia custom to perform a 'parting dance' over the corpse of a young person, and this *sore* seems to be analogous. Retonga was said by my informant to be a sacred name for the east (*tonga*).

(9) A *sore* of the day of sa Tafua

Translation: Tuisifo has sped from the west
The wind enters for a storm.
Be it pressed down firmly
That the sky be clear.

Your lightning has kept on flashing, Sakura.
It draws near to the west, O!
The Tafito is turning to the east, O!
Black storm clouds will arise.

Now it is the Matapupula.
Pounded are the sides of heaven;
The mother and son
Descend from the north
With their red clouds.

This song is typical of the *sore* which come from the *seru* of recent chiefs. It was composed by Pukenga, chief of Tafua, who died about 1910, and is sung only on the day of sa Tafua, as their 'foremost *seru*'. Its theme is one of praise to the principal gods, whose names are mentioned.

I received this song in several versions, with minor verbal differences, that given here being from Pa Vainunu. The song pays reverence to the storm-powers of the deities. Tuisifo is a former Ariki Kafika, credited with great power, and appealed to here to go from the west to the south to stop the coming storm. In the second stanza the Atua i Taumako and the Atua i Fangarere are invoked; in the third, the Atua i Kafika under his Tafua title of Matapula (reduplicated), and the Atua i Tafua and his mother, the Atua Fafine. The association of the gods with various wind-points may be noted. (According to Pa Vainunu the 'son' in the last stanza is Oatuatafu, but the Ariki Tafua said that it was Rakiteua.)

(10) A *sore* of the day of sa Fangarere

Translation: Rakiteua,
                Stand in the Marae.
                You are a god,
                Hearing the kava.

                Climb up, Sakura;
                The Surumanga, O!
                Let your chiefly deity stand
                That I may do reverence to him.

This song was composed by the present Ariki Fangarere, in honour of the Atua i Tafua and the Atua i Taumako.

In reviewing this selection of representative songs of the *Taomatangi* two general points may be briefly made. One is the difference between the modern songs and those believed by the natives to be ancient. The former are clear in meaning, granted the 'poetic licence' of the composer; the latter are often cryptic, and even untranslatable. The other point is that despite the clear-cut privileges which organize the songs on a clan basis, the compositions belonging to each clan are not at all restricted in theme to its own gods, but range over the hierarchy of gods of the whole community. I should also like to stress again that whatever the theme of the song – and some of them show no particular religious feature in the text – they are all chanted with great reverence, and are held as equally sacred. Their value to the Tikopia lies in their context, not in their words as such.

9

The Dance of the Flaming Fire

The Dance of the Flaming Fire, the *Urangafi*, followed immediately upon the *Taomatangi*, and in ordinary conversation the latter term was often used to cover both. The essential difference between them in point of procedure was that the one was held in daylight, the other from dusk till dawn. The *Urangafi* was even more popular as a festival than the *Taomatangi*, since whereas all the daylight dances were sacred to a high degree, those which were performed during the latter part of the night were practically free from taboo. The women joined in and in the early hours of the morning the sexual interest of the songs became very marked. For this reason much larger crowds attended the second period of the festival. To Christians participation was prohibited, since it implied the worship of the old gods, but so attractive was the spectacle, and so appealing the rhythm and the choruses, that more than one of the young men, unable to resist its spell, had abandoned discretion and mingled with the dancers. For this they were publicly reprobated and put out of Church for a year. Reinstatement was gained by preparing a present of food, and going to express contrition to the Melanesian Christian teacher. The very aged and infirm, persons who were ill and their attendants, and more numerous, those who were under restraint because of mourning, did not take part in the festival. They were spoken of as '*sa Tua*' ('Those at the Back'), whereas in contradistinction the people who did attend were known as '*sa Roto*' ('Those Within'). No esoteric value attached to these terms.

The Dance of the Flaming Fire, like that to Quell the Wind, was divided into four sections. Thus the night of sa Kafika opened the festival, and this was followed by the nights of Tafua, Taumako and Fangarere in this order. The term *night* includes the period of daylight as well. It is in fact the normal Tikopia habit to count the passage of time by *po* (nights). (Cf. p. 41 and Chapter 4 on the intervals between yam rites.)

The night of sa Kafika was begun in the early morning by the kava of the *putu*. This was performed by the Ariki Kafika in Marae before sunrise in connection with the bundle of taro left the day before against the stone. The rite was simple and comprised no more than libations to Pu ma and the other chief gods. The *putu* was then prepared for cooking, the peculiarity on this occasion being that the tubers were not scraped, but the stalk base alone was broken away from the tuber with the thumb-nail – no knife might be used. 'Its manner is to be stripped only; it is not scraped, it is cooked dirty only.' By the time the oven had been covered the crowd had begun to arrive. Theoretically it was still *fenua po*, the time of darkness, but actually it was quite light and the sun was rising. The last act to be performed was the clearing of Marae for the second time. The men, numbering between forty and fifty, assembled round the edge of the ground and squatted down with hands outstretched as on the previous occasion. Once more the Ariki Kafika repeated the formula, and the ground was speedily cleared of all weeds and rubbish. This time much more attention was paid to it, and all the surface vegetation was removed, leaving the ground bare but for the roots of fern. As an accompaniment to this rite, the *pae Marae*, the stones at the border of the lake, were carefully washed, water being brought in a large leaf of giant taro for the purpose. It is the custom not to use a bowl or ordinary water bottle. The care of this task was left to the Ariki Taumako, or in former times the Ariki Tafua, the Ariki Kafika being busy superintending the work in Marae.

The large flat stone previously mentioned as that of the Atua i Kafika was the principal object of attention; it was exceedingly taboo, and could not be used as a seat by anyone; nor could any person set foot upon it. Unwittingly I broke this rule of *tapu* and stepped upon this stone during the ceremonial washing. Though previously warned I had mistaken its position. The deep moaning grunt from all the men around and the absolute silence maintained afterwards by everyone indicated the sacrilege which I had committed. No one ever referred to it again. During the nights of the dance it was said to be permitted for chiefs, and for commoners as well, to lay their heads on the stone as a pillow, but I did not witness any use of it in this way.

A man climbed the umbrella palm which stood over Raro-firoki temple and broke off a few of the leaves and some of the fruit. The latter, the *firoki*, were planted at the south end of the Marae, but without ceremony, and I understood that there was no particular significance in the act.

When the Marae had been cleared the Ariki Kafika cried:

We who have fallen hither to the place of crowds, a night then shall be for us.

This was a formal announcement that the ensuing night would be devoted to dancing, that is that the *Urangafi* would take place and not the substitute performance of the *Purunga kava* (see end of chapter).

THE 'URU'

The next performance of the day was the *uru*. This ranks with the *vetu masanga*, the *fu tapu* and the *tuaro* as one of the primary recitals of Marae, *a mua o te Marae*, being extremely sacred and more in the nature of a formula than a song. The pronouncing of the *uru* is properly the privilege of the Ariki Tafua, to whom it is commonly said to belong. The characteristic features of this recital are the use of wands by the attendant crowd, and the markings of charcoal displayed.

Previous to assembling in formal ranks the men gathered in a group at Fenumera, where charcoal was powdered, and each person was given two horizontal stripes on the upper right arm. This was the *pani marara* which was held to be the mark of the Atua i Kafika for whom the ceremony was performed. The chiefs bore the mark as well as commoners. It was essentially a ritual sign, not a mere decoration.

For the actual performance the men stood in a circle at the entrance to Marae with heads bent, eyes directed to the ground and wands lowered. The Ariki Kafika, deputizing for the Ariki Tafua, then recited the formula at the top of his voice. It was divided into a number of sections (*taunga*), the end of each being marked by a lowering of the voice and a slight pause. After a moment the voice was pitched in a higher key, and the recital of the next section began. The fifth section concluded with the words:

Neti neti ne pisa ia.
Osi o!
Forua!

which were repeated over and over again, and after each imperative '*Forua!*' the crowd of men gave vent to wild yells of '*Iefu!*' The formula itself was recited in loud tones, with clear enunciation and a commanding manner. The final section, the *taunga pese*, was chanted by the group as a whole. For this they raised their wands and walked singing on to Marae, headed by the Ariki Kafika. When Pae Marae was reached, they stopped and arranged themselves into ranks for the succeeding dance, the *vetu*.

The formula of the *uru* was as follows:

Taunga mua:	*Osiosi O!*
	Pe ea?
	Oio io manu
	Ara paia a!
Taunga muri:	*Osiosi O!*
	Pe ea?
	Oio io tu
	Ara paia A!
Taunga:	*Tenei penapena vaka nei*
	Ufiufi vaka nei
	Fausia vaka nei
	Osi moi
	Osi moi!
Taunga:	*Tutu afa ka ni afa*
	Tutu afa ka ni afa
	Osi moi
	Osi moi!
	Te fou kupenga
	Ke mouo moi se iko
	Te fuo romongo
	Te fou kupenga
	Ke moua moi se iko
	Te fuo romongo
	Osi moi
	Osi moi!

Taunga:	*Tenei te kata nei*
	A mate a te pure nei
	Mo te fia kai touo,
	Tou fia kai touo.
	Neti neti ne pisa ia
	Osi o!
	Forua
	Neti neti ne pisa ia
	Osi o!
	Forua.
Taunga pese:	*Tapetape ki na nuku e tu*
	Tapetape ki na nuku e tu
	Fetukuokino ea
	O io
	Fetukuokino ea
	O io.

Like certain of the songs in Chapter 8 the *uru* is not capable of adequate translation, being apparently framed in archaic language, and referring to incidents in myth not fully preserved in the memory of present generations. Some of the words and phrases are not understood by the Tikopia themselves. The *uru* is not, however, a dead relic in the midst of the performances of Marae, but is a ritual item of the utmost importance. The significant thing to the Tikopia is not the original meaning of the words of the recital, but the fact of the recital itself as an element in the ceremonial cycle, and what they take to be the allusive suggestiveness of the language. A textual analysis of the formula with the help of Tikopia comments is illuminating from this point of view. For the terms '*osiosi*',[1] '*osi moi*', '*ara paia*', no translation could be given by informants. Of them it was said 'Speech of old, we do not know it, speech of the growth' – i.e. of the time when Tikopia culture is supposed to have been formed by the gods. Of the word *manu* in the first section it is known only that it represents an appeal for efficacy. The idea is that the *uru* mentions certain of the most prominent of human activities in order that success may be granted them. 'The dirge (i.e. the *uru*) is

[1] In Samoan, *osi* means to pledge or offer, and *osiosi*, dance; and *pisa*, to make a noise (cf. *tapisa*, sound of revelry). So these terms may originally have been merely encouragement to enjoyment. (See G. B. Milner, *Samoan Dictionary*, London, 1966.)

made to the god to listen to the speech to grant efficacy to canoes for the vivifying of man.' Hence in the third section the statements are made

> This is the preparation of the canoes here
> Covering of the canoes here
> Lashing of the canoes here

embodying instructions to repair the vessels, shelter them from the sun and attend to their sinnet lashings.

The fourth and fifth sections are thought to refer to the antagonism between the Atua i Kafika and the Fanau, the Brethren, the band of deities (Atua i Tafua, etc.) who are held to have arrived in Tikopia from abroad and striven for mastery of the land. The *afa* is the storm, and it was suggested that the phrases are a derisive song directed by the Atua against his opponents, inviting them to raise a storm against him, which he beats down by lifting his hand.

The translation then is:

'The storm threatens, but what a storm!' The verb *tu*, meaning 'to stand', is used of the black clouds standing in a quarter of the sky, and threatening to burst over the land. In the following part of the section considerable mutation of vowels has occurred, a common phenomenon in Tikopia songs, the *a* becoming *o* for greater euphony in singing or reciting. In ordinary speech the words are:

> *Te fua kupenga*
> *Ke maua mai se ika*
> *Te fua ramanga.*

That is

> The catch of the net
> To secure a fish;
> The torchlight fleet.

This is an appeal for a good catch when the fleet goes out at night for flying fish.

The next section, in which the Atua is represented as speaking, states how the Fanau laughed at him, but that they came only through their desire for the food made from the turmeric, the *tauo*. They 'laughed to death' at him – the metaphor is actually a Tikopia one, '*e kata ki te mate*' – but they came in reality to obtain the things which he had made. According to Tikopia belief the Atua i Kafika is responsible for the conversion of the turmeric to human use, but the incident to which reference is here made is obscure.

Of *neti* the meaning is unknown but *pisa* is a term for female genitals found in other old songs. The significance here, as also in the last section, which is sung, is evidently erotic, involving a veiled reference to the sexual act. '*Tapetape ki na nuku e tu*' is stated to be indecent speech. It may be rendered as 'Knocking on her hamlet standing there', where *nuku*, ordinarily a local prefix, is used as a synonym for the place of particular sex interest.

In former times it was the custom after the *uru* for the wands to be poised and hurled into the lake after the fashion of darts, but nowadays this is not always done.

The *uru* was followed by a couple of *vetu*, after which the per-formers washed off their charcoal marks and sat about in the shade under the trees. The *fakaoatea* from the taro of the *putu* was now brought into Marae. The Ariki Fangarere then entered Raro-firoki and brought out the *epa* mat which he laid at Muafaitoka with the customary formula and obeisance. After covering it with leaves of cycas he returned to his seat. When the kava was made he again went to Muafaitoka and the first cup was handed to him there. He recited the brief formula to Te Varotea in high appeal-ing tones, ending again with the *Io* which was taken up by all those present with a loud cry. As the Ariki uttered the concluding words he raised his hand palm up to the level of his shoulder in a gesture of offering, after which he poured the kava. Other liba-tions and food offerings were made as usual, after which the mat was put away.

The remainder of the day till late afternoon was spent in work, conversation or sleep according to individual fancy or responsi-bilities. Some people went to collect food, others to fish; the Ariki Kafika occupied himself with pinning together the thatch for the shed which was to shelter the evening fire. Children were sent off to get flowers, cordyline leaves and fruits to provide ornaments. 'Go and get perfumes for us', they were told by their elders. This was the greatest occasion for decoration, and people brought out all their stores of beads to string them round neck and wrists. Conversation turned almost wholly on the coming dance and discussion of the fine sight that would be presented.

THE 'TAUME'

A rite of some importance towards midday was that connected with the *taume*. This was the name applied to the dry spathe of the coconut which was the most important ceremonial element of the occasion. Like most other sacred objects it was 'announced' to the gods beforehand. The *taume* and the *afi*, the coconut spathe and the fire, were regarded as the property of Pa Rarovi and were managed by him. Food was prepared at his house in Uta, and when it was ready a *taume* was laid ceremonially by him on his seating mat at the head of the building. As he performed this action he recited the formula to ask the chiefs to countenance the rite.

> You Tinamo, you Pu Tafua, you Pu Taumako,
>   Pu Fangarere!
> Countenance me you the assemblage of Elders
>   for the *taume* this (being) its day on which
>   it will be announced.

The chiefs were not in attendance, and his request was a purely formal one. Then the kava was made and formulae were recited to dedicate the *taume* to the service of the gods and to invoke their assistance in the coming dance. This was an important rite, 'a weighty kava'. I attended the rite and Pa Rarovi later gave me the formulae.

The appeal uttered over the kava stem was as follows:

> You Taringamoea!
>   Turn down with your household of brethren
> And your group of workers there
>   To the *taume* of your day which has been
>   decorated for the Marae of Pu ma
> That the sky may be fine and the sky be clear that
>   your fire may blaze.

This invocation is to the Atua i Sao, whom Pa Rarovi addressed by the special title of Taringamoea. He is asked to incline towards the speaker in order that he may be able to secure good weather for the dance. As an inducement to the deity it is pointed out that these conditions are necessary to the activity of his fire. The 'house of brethren' means the children of the deity.

As a substitute the expression 'Turn together with your children' may be employed, said Pa Rarovi. The term 'decorated' or 'splendid' refers to the enhancement of the occasion by the attendance of the people and their performance. It is a term of praise, but conveys the suggestion that while the day is the god's its effectiveness is due in no small measure to the interest taken in it by his worshippers. Towards evening the 'drink' of coconuts was sent into Marae and the kava was made there.

The rite of the *taume* then took place. The men, all decorated for the dance and each with a coconut sheath in his hand, assembled at Takerekere and awaited the coming of the chiefs. When the kava was finished they entered, whereon the crowd rose. All seated themselves on the row of flat stones on the upper side of the path which once flanked the former sacred house of Rarovi. The chiefs were in order of precedence, the Ariki Kafika being nearest to Fenumera. Each person held his *taume* on his lap, supporting it across the palms of his hands, the point of it being to his right. As the row of men was facing towards the lake, the *taume* thus pointed to Marae. Here as elsewhere the precise orientation of the sacred objects was a matter of concern. When all were in position Pa Rarovi entered and seated himself at the head of the chiefs. Of his premier position on this occasion he was intensely proud, and indeed it was regarded by the community as a whole as a signal mark of his importance.

After sitting for a moment Pa Rarovi raised a cry:

Taringamoea!

upon which all made obeisance with the *taume*, raising it to their foreheads. They took up the call on the antepenultimate vowel and ended it with 'Oooo-uri?' Pa Rarovi then began to sing, in low tones, so that the words could not be properly heard. The chiefs alone joined with him; the crowd as a whole remained silent, save that at intervals in the song, following the example of the soloist, they repeated the cry and the act of obeisance. This, the song of the *taume*, was the especial property of Pa Rarovi. He said it was not made known by him to other people, but would be handed down to his son. He spoke of it to me as 'The forefront of my kava, this, the *taume*!' With its solo and the interspersed cry in which the crowd of men joined it ran:

Shout: *Taringamoea!*

Song: *Ko nga tama moe mo*
Moe mo mo e mako
O ara ra.

Taringamoea!

Fua te marama
Fua te marama.

Taringamoea!

Fuasa asaka
Tutu ki Retou
Ko matou e si ki vae atu.

Taringamoea!

Oue nunu E!
O te ra mai u-o.

Taringamoea!

A matou rara
Suru ki Retua
Ma rau tataka
Suru ki Retua
Se umata ke fare kou ura toto.

Taringamoea!

Ke raumisi raumisi
Te rau tao

Taringamoea!

A fafine kere i o ma ki tongo.

The song is composed of seven stanzas or groups of phrases (*kupu*) which are divided off by the chorused cry of 'Taringamoea', the name of Te Atua i Sao. The rites of the *taume* are under the jurisdiction of this god, who, it will be remembered, is one of the two 'working deities' of Marae.

As in the *uru* and other pivotal chants of the festival, the language of the *taume* is of a different character from that used in everyday conversation, and contains a number of words which are said by the Tikopia to be of archaic form. Thus of some phrases it is said 'speech of former times: it has disappeared'. The absence of any very precise meaning for individual words and phrases, however, is not detrimental to them in Tikopia eyes. Their value is essentially symbolic and lies in the correct recital and conjunction of them, not in their individual significance to the people who sing them. An essential in all these songs is to preserve the authentic version as believed to have been handed down through the line of ancestors from the gods themselves. Thus Pa Rarovi said to me, 'We who sing the speech, sing it to be correct, that the deities may see that it is correct.' Moreover because of its sacred character the song must be rendered with due reverence. Despite the strange, even humorous, sound of some of its words to modern ears, any tendency to laugh must be suppressed, and no jokes or careless ways of behaviour are permissible.

The central theme of the *taume* song is a series of brief allusions to activities of the coming dance. Thus the first stanza speaks of 'the children', in this case the people, sleeping, then waking to dance. Then comes the wish that the moon may shine and be full for the occasion. *Fua te marama*, an archaic form, was explained as 'the moon to be good for the dance'. *Fua* here is probably connected with its basic meaning of 'to fruit'. So also it is desired that the sun shall be favourable; i.e. that bad weather shall not interfere with the festival. The fifth stanza deals with the aromatic leaves used in the dance and refers to those 'hung up in former times'. The concluding line of this stanza contains an obscure reference to the rainbow, *umata*, and links it with the blood-red flames, presumably of the fire, *ura toto*, which is to be made. The rainbow serves as an omen to the Tikopia, but why it is mentioned here is not known. In the final stanzas the language is of the erotic type common to several of these sacred songs.

When the song was finished the men rose and, headed by Pa Rarovi, walked slowly in single file to Fenumera, and thence on to Marae. Each person carried his *taume* at breast height on his palms. At the invitation of Pa Rarovi I walked with them, bearing my *taume* with the rest. When the first mound was reached the leader knelt down, again performed obeisance with the *taume*, and laid it on the ground. Then he passed on. Each member of the group followed suit, so that a pile of these coconut spathes was formed. This was the fuel for the fire for the night's dancing.

After depositing their burdens the men formed in lines at the lower side of the Marae, the Ariki Kafika and Pa Rarovi being in front. The sounding-board – often a small old canoe – was carried in, and supported against the stones at the Pae Marae. Sometimes a shout of 'Osepo!' introduces a *matavaka*, and a song is chanted, ending with a yell of 'Iefu!' before the sounding-board is carried down. When the board was in place a man took his place behind it, commenced to beat, and the dance began. This was the *matavaka*, the dance of the canoe prow, so called from its most characteristic feature, the tossing heads and masses of flowing hair which were held to resemble the movement of the bow of a canoe on the waves, and the flying spray thrown out on either side. The dance is very striking and rhythmic. The *matavaka*, however, was only a preliminary to the ritual events; it was the same dance which at ordinary times was beaten almost nightly on the beaches.

DANCE OF THE BAMBOO

After a short time an interlude was provided by a dance of a highly sacred character. A long pole, a dry bamboo stem, which was kept stored against a tree on the north side of Rarofiroki, was brought to the entrance to Marae at Fenumera. About a dozen men, six on either side, arranged themselves along it, holding it with one hand, and grasping a light wand in the other. Then they struck up a song and with curious jerking movements and gestures began to advance on to Marae. Holding the pole horizontally, they crouched low, moving with stiff-legged short jumps, bending their heads from side to side, and singing the while. In this manner the dancers brought the pole to the south end of Marae, where they laid it down, in front of the seat of the Ariki Taumako. (Before the dance each chief had seated himself on his mat, while those of his clansmen who were not participating squatted behind him.) When the pole was set down the dancers stood looking down upon it and resting their wands on it, while they continued their song. Concluding the stanza with a few phrases, spoken in ordinary tones, they turned abruptly away, each side facing outwards, and pointed their sticks to the ground. Again they sang, then finished again with the spoken phrases and walked off. The bamboo was then removed.

The significance of this dance lay in its mythical associations. It was termed the sacred dance, and was indeed one of the most sacred of Marae. Its descriptive name was the Dance of the Bamboo, but it was also known, more familiarly, as the Dance of the God. It was believed to have originated with the Atua i Tafua in the days when the gods lived as men upon the earth, and conducted the ceremonies of Marae. Each Atua was seated in his place, the Atua i Fangarere at Muafaitoka, the Atua i Taumako at the south end of the ground, Pu ma at their stone pillars and the Atua Fafine on the inland side, when the Atua i Tafua entered with his bamboo, singing his song. 'His idea, he was exhilarated, he rejoiced.' It was a jesting song, made in derision against his brethren, with the object of causing them to laugh. He was successful in all but one instance. As he went from one seat to the other, making his gestures and singing, one god after another broke down and chuckled. The Atua i Taumako alone succeeded in retaining his gravity, and refused to laugh. It is for this reason at the present time that the dancers at the conclusion of their song set down the bamboo before the Ariki Taumako, who is the representative of the god. For this reason also, the Ariki, however much he may feel amusement at the dance, must not show it, but keep an unmoved countenance in conformity with the behaviour of his deity.

The introduction of the *mako tapu* at each successive ceremonial season is thus the perpetuation of an ancient jest and its rebuff, solemnized and sacralized by being enshrined in mythic lore.

The point of the whole affair lies in the character of the dance. Baldly stated, it is nothing more or less than a pantomimic representation of the movements of man in copulation, with the gestures reinforced by the allusions in the song. The bamboo, swung in jerking thrusts as the dancers hop slowly along, represents the action of the male organ.

Further point is given by the explanation of one informant that the song and the dance were primarily directed against the Atua Fafine. She was the mother of the Family of Gods, but several of them, in particular the Atua i Fangarere, had entered into sex relations with her. The Atua i Tafua, who presumably had refrained, then composed the song, deriding and at the same time amusing his relatives by allusion to the crude facts of the case. I received versions of the song from several informants, with little variation. I give here that which appeared most coherent. (It was not possible to catch the complete wording when the song was actually chanted in Marae.)

> *Tafito:*   *Ea ea simotoro*
>   *Ea ea simotoro*
>   *Ie koli! Ie kola!*
>   *Ie koli! Ie kola!*

> *Kupu:*   *Mo vero kou raverave*
>   *Nonue nonue*
>   *E piro revoi*
>   *Ka mapapa te masoa*
>   *Nonue nonue*
>   *E piro revoi.*

> *Kupu:*   *Malaki tau E!*
>   *Malaki lulu E!*
>   *E vau*
>   *E tangi i te varo.*

> *Safe:*   *Io! Semu*
>   *Ia koki!*
>   *Ia koka!*

The words of the song are foreign to ordinary conversation: like those of the *uru* previously mentioned they are held to be archaic, and their meaning can be explained only by elderly, well-informed men. The stanzas do not embody any continuous statement or set of ideas, but merely present a number of words of erotic significance in conjunction. A coherent translation then is not feasible; it is necessary only to know the significance of the various key-words in order to apprehend the purport of the song. *Simotoro* means the genital organs, of which *simotoru* and *semotou*, given in other versions, are variants. According to one informant it was the *membrum virile* that is thus indicated. Another held that the word is the equivalent of *mimi*, the female genitalia, and regarded it as derived from *motomoto*, a virgin. The cry of *Ea ea simotoru* thus would express the desires of the singer: 'He wishes for a virgin.' *Koli* and *kola* both refer to the sexual act, being euphemisms derived from the ordinary word *koni*, which is, however, not used in polite speech. Of these words it was said 'they are made to curve', i.e. they are a roundabout means of alluding to the ordinary term. *Mo vero kou raverave* describes the act of entry (*vero* meaning to 'lower down') and the motions of thrust and withdrawal ('the thing of the man is connected with the thing of the woman'). *Raverave* means to connect or lock. *Nonue* is a figurative term for the female genitalia, while *revoi* applies to the *rugae* or to the interior of the vagina as a whole. *Piro* is the normal adjective used to describe anything of unpleasant odour; this is a kind of stock gibe flung by the men at the women in lewd conversation and song, and alluding to their organs. *Te masoa*, or in another version *te maloa*, is a figurative term for the testicles, these being compared to the fruit of the masoa plant. *Mapapa*, onomatopoeic in etymology, signifies 'clapping', and the allusion here is to the striking of the testes against the body of the woman during congress.

The first two stanzas were sung as the bamboo advanced across the Marae. After it was laid down the third stanza was sung.

In this *malaki* is another allusive term for the act of connection, the syllable *ki* denoting a squeak or more broadly any small sound. The explanation was 'When persons copulate the penis "squeaks" into the genitals of the woman.' *Lulu* describes the entrance of the male organ into that of the female. Another version gives this word as *ulu*, a form of *uru*, a verb in ordinary speech meaning 'to enter'. The same rendering concludes this stanza thus:

> *E tangi te valo*
> *Ulu E!*
> *E tangi te valo.*

Both here and in the text given the meaning is obscure. Informants tentatively suggested that *valo* or *varo* represented the female genitalia, but were uncertain as to how these could be said to 'mourn' (*tangi*). On this one point they were all agreed, however, that it was the act of copulation which was described. It is possible that the 'mourning' or 'wailing' of the female parts is a symbolic mode of stating that the act of penetration has been accomplished – such a form of speech is sometimes met in other songs.

The final stanza was sung before the bamboo was left on the ground.

The word *semu* is used, though sparingly, in ordinary speech in the sense of *kaisi*, i.e. to ask or beg. Here, however, it is probably a variant of *simotoro*, the male organ. The phrase '*semusemu to ifo*' occurring in one version was translated as 'penis drop down', meaning that it is inserted and rests in the vagina. *Koki* and *koka* are again variants on the theme of *koni*, the sexual act. *Ia*, like *ea*, *ie*, *tau E* (*Ue* in one version), is a euphonic particle introduced to allow the rhythm to be maintained.

The song as a whole is thus an agglomeration of terms, more or less archaic and disguised, descriptive of male and female genitalia and the act of sexual intercourse. As such, it was clear from discussion, it has certainly the tendency to provoke amusement in a Tikopia audience, particularly as it consists largely of a play upon words, wherein the direct terms of normal usage are avoided. But it is a point of etiquette in Marae to regard the song with all gravity and suppress any amusement. The fact that it is of high antiquity and sacred, a legacy from the gods, does not render this difficult. Since at the same time the speech is recognized as being lewd, women are prohibited from hearing it, and when the time for the performance arrives, they retire to the houses inland.

The solemn performance of song and dance in which the language and gestures are of what is commonly called a 'lewd' type is an interesting phenomenon, which has its parallel in ritual in other parts of the world. It receives its sanction from its religious and mythic basis. Its precise function or place in the social life of the community is somewhat difficult to comprehend, since this emphasis on a sexual theme appears to be irrelevant to the religious and economic interests of the Work of the Gods. The significance of this dance in the immediate context has been explained, but its social functions are probably to be sought in more indirect fashion. Its importance in the ceremonial cycle may lie, in addition to its value as an integral part of traditional ritual, in the element of sensation which it provides, acting as a fillip to the imagination of the people, a point on which their interest can be focused and maintained, and an attractive feature of the ritual. On the other hand it is perhaps part of an attempt at sacralization of the sexual side of life, by associating these impulses with religion and myth, and thus assisting in their regulation. But it may also be fairly argued that this and the other sex songs provide a sanction for the use of 'bad speech', that is bawdy references, in ordinary life, by projecting their origins into mythic antiquity. The second point, that of teaching sense to people, which seems to be a rationalization, is the only one mentioned to me by Tikopia.

THE SACRED FIRE

After the Dance of the Bamboo preparations were made to construct the shed of the Fire for the ritual of the night. The thatch of the shed had been pinned together by the households of the chiefs during the day, each chief himself as a rule taking part in its manufacture. While the dance of the *matavaka* was being performed in the late afternoon poles were cut and quickly set up in position on one side of the mound where the kava of Muafaitoka was made. The shed was a simple shelter of thatch, a roof without sides. It was the custom to carry the materials on and off Marae at the run. The shed was completed just as it was getting dusk, and the evening kava was prepared immediately. No chief ate from the food basket set before him in Marae, but each waited to have a meal with his family outside his own house.

The next rite was the bringing of the Fire. This was the special duty and privilege of Pa Rarovi, and was allied with his control of the *taume*. But it will be remembered that all items of ritual are under the jurisdiction of gods of the men who respectively own them. The Fire was partly under the control of Taringamoea (also the god of the *taume*) and more especially of Pufine i Ravenga, a female deity, known in this particular function as Ruataka.

The crowd of men sat around in the vicinity of the houses waiting for the fire to be brought. Pa Rarovi, who had gone off alone, was meanwhile in his house preparing the torch; he waited until he considered that the correct time had arrived to perform his task. This was one of the crucial moments of the ritual, and his attitude was indicative of his importance; he knew that he could delay all the proceedings and keep the four chiefs waiting with impunity. A couple of his male relatives kindled a small fire on the *mata paito* side of the house close under the eave. Pa Rarovi took some fronds of the areca palm (*kaula*) and broke them into smaller sections, each with a piece of rib that would stick into the ground. Laying them down he took up a torch which had been plaited of dry coconut leaf, and seated himself on a mat outside the house near the eave. He held the torch so that its end rested on the ground by the fire and the butt was inclined over his head. He then began to chant softly to himself and rubbed the end of the torch along the ground, approaching it slowly to the blaze, until it caught alight. This was the *tutunga afi*, the Kindling of the Fire. The chant was a formula of the confirmatory type to invite the chiefs to countenance the rite which he was performing:

> You Tinamo, you Pa Tafua, you Pa Taumako, Pa
> Fangarere
> Countenance me your assembly of elders there in the
> Fire of Pu ma and the Brethren
> Which will flame away on this night.

When the torch was blazing thoroughly he rose, laid it down for a moment and then picking up the pieces of areca frond set them on his right arm and the torch above. As it was about four feet long the flaming top stood up diagonally above his head, and his shock of bushy hair was lit to a warm brown by the glow, while his face, as he stood with bent head, rested in shadow. He moved off with stately step along the special track leading from his house to the main path, a way which was sacred, and was trodden only by the bearers of the Fire of the Gods. As another special privilege, Pa Rarovi allowed me to follow him, on condition I uttered no word to him or the spectators. His progress was extremely sacred, and though people gathered at the entrance to Marae to await his approach, none might speak to him. Children in particular were warned to keep out of the way, but some, in spite of restraint, insisted on dashing along the path to catch a glimpse of the torch-bearer and were roundly cursed by the adults in consequence. When the glow of the fire was seen approaching all retreated, and the people near the path drew aside, squatting down out of respect. As Pa Rarovi walked slowly along he crooned softly to himself the Song of the Fire, which was practically identical with the refrain or conclusion of the song of the *taume* given earlier.

Nearing the open space of Fenumera, Pa Rarovi raised torch and leaf, made obeisance to them, and then went on into Marae. There he sat down beneath the shelter, and kindled the Sacred Fire, using for the purpose some of the *taume* and the residue of his torch. The areca fronds were then stuck in the ground to act as a kind of shield from the blaze, and he remained there to attend to the Fire.

The entrance of the Fire was accompanied by complete silence on the part of the crowd.

The Sacred Fire was maintained thus all through the night, fresh *taume* being added whenever it died low. A man was always seated behind the leaf screen to tend it; in olden days, it was said, two men shared this task. When the watcher tired, after an hour or so, he made a sign to one of the dancers, and this man dropped out of the ranks and relieved him. The man who had just been released backed away from the fire in a respectful crouching attitude and joined the throng. It was primarily the task of the men to tend the fire, but towards morning it was permissible for a woman to act as relief. Under no circumstances must the fire be allowed to die out, or to remain untended. After his preliminary vigil Pa Rarovi took no further part in this, until just before dawn, when he slipped into his place again.

As soon as the Fire was brought, the men began to arrange themselves for the further rites. The people of Taumako gathered at the southern end of the Marae, those of Kafika and Fangarere at the northern end, beside Rarofiroki. The dance of the *matavaka* was begun again, and followed by a dirge which was sung as a preliminary to the bringing up of the sounding-board or 'trough' from its position by the stones by the water's edge. The actual accomplishment of this was signalized by a vigorous clapping of hands. This was the signal of 'the conveying of the trough'. The Ariki Kafika had previously been seated in his house inland, for the 'trough' and the handling of it was the affair of the Taumako clan. When he heard the clapping he knew that it was in position for the performance of his office. This was the beating of the *fu tapu*, the sacred *fu*, which was at once the most picturesque and the most revered of all the dances of Uta.

THE 'FU TAPU'

The substitute sounding-board, the *ta*, had also been brought, and was held firm against the stone which stood at the south end of Rarofiroki. The trough (*nafa*) itself was not beaten, since in the first place it was too infirm to be roughly handled, and still more it was the property of the Ariki Taumako, and was used by him for patting during the *sore*.

The Ariki Kafika took his seat behind the sounding-board, gripped the two wooden beating sticks, and waited till complete silence reigned over Marae. When all was quiet he began to beat, a single stroke, with a long pause between each. Then he began in low measured tones the song of the *Fu tapu*. Every word was clearly articulated, and there were no drawling cadences, as is common in Tikopia songs. The melody itself was of an unusual type, and was associated with this one song only. It was sung nowhere else but in Marae as a prelude to the nights of sa Kafika and sa Tafua alone.

The text of the song, recorded in Marae, and checked by the Ariki Kafika, is as follows:

> *Turou, e turou*
> *Ariki o Namo*
> *Mamaru mamaru*
> *Ariki o Namo*
> *Fu io io*
> *Fu io io.*
>
> *Somotio tu*
> *Kouro tu*
> *Fu io io*
> *Fu io io.*
>
> *Tukutuku ifo i te ava E!*
> *Kae au ko te ika E!*
> *Rere mai te tokape*
> *O asu ki oi*
> *Fu io io*
> *Fu io io.*
>
> *Ko Tafaki tefea?*
> *Ko Tafaki tenei*
> *E tu ifea?*
> *E fu io io!*
>
> *Ko Karisi tefea?*
> *Ko Karisi tenei*
> *E tu ifea?*
> *E fu io io.*

The song is believed to have been composed by the Atua i Kafika when he lived upon earth, in honour of his own deities, Pu ma, here addressed by their personal names, Tafaki and Karisi.

Translation: Respected, are respected
    Chieftains of Namo
    Reverenced, reverenced
    Chieftains of Namo
    Fu io io
    Fu io io.

    Samutia standing
    Kaura standing
    Fu io io
    Fu io io.

    Lay it down in the channel O!
    And then comes the fish O!
    The *tokape* rushes hither
    To scoop it up.
    Fu io io
    Fu io io.

    Where is Tafaki?
    This is Tafaki
    Where is he standing?
    Is hidden indeed!

    Where is Karisi?
    This is Karisi
    Where is he standing?
    Is hidden indeed!

As usual, some of the words were obscure, even to the best-informed men of the community, among whom were the Ariki Kafika, the owner of the song. But from him I obtained the following comments.

The opening words *turou, e turou*, sung very slowly and distinctly, are what the Tikopia class as *taranga fakaepa*, honorific speech. They are used principally in reference to chiefs. When, for instance, a man is striking blows with an axe, or producing any loud booming noise in the vicinity of where a chief is staying, someone of influence and authority will say:

'*Turou ra! te ariki e tapu.*' 'Have respect there! the chief is sacred.' (There is a causative verb *fakaturou* formed from this.) The term *mamaru* is of similar type. It is derived from *maru*, meaning 'soft', and is used in similar situations. Thus it will be said to a man in rebuke, '*E! sise e maruia e a ke te ariki e tapu e nofo?*' 'O! is not reverenced by you the chief who is sacred sitting there?'

Ariki o Namo refers to Pu ma, Tafaki and Karisi. They are mentioned as chieftains of Namo, since they are held to have been the original rulers of Kafika, and the ancient honorific title of the Ariki of Kafika, still borne by each successive chief, is Tinamo, Ruler of Namo (cf. Tui Tonga, termed in Tikopia Ti Tonga). *Somotio* is a form of *Samutia*, the vowels having undergone mutation in the song. By one informant (of Taumako) this was said to be an alternative name for Karisi and to be very sacred. He begged me in fact not to mention that he had made it known to me lest he be bewitched for his effrontery. The Ariki Kafika, however, said that the meaning of this word was unknown to him. *Kouro*, a form of *kaura*, was said to be the areca palm (*kaula*, of which two varieties, the *kaula tu*, standing palm, and *kaula raro*, low palm, are distinguished). The third stanza was held to be an appeal to the gods for fish, of which the *tokape* is a variety. The description applies to the use of the bag net, the *kuani*, which is let down at the end of a sinnet line. The *tokape* flock into it to devour the bait and are then hauled up. The concluding stanzas ask of the whereabouts of Tafaki and Karisi, question and answer following in dialogue form. Concerning the words *fu io io*, which form a kind of refrain to each stanza, considerable difference of opinion existed. The Ariki Kafika gave the meaning of the phrase as 'sharp-edged' and contrasted it with *fu tokotoko laui*, meaning an even plane surface. In this sense *ioio* is connected with *te io*, the edge, as of a box, and *te ioioanga*, the corner, as of a field; while *fu* may be translated as surface or aspect. The Ariki said in explanation of the refrain, '*A kaokao a atua e ioio*', 'Ribs of gods are edged', and placed his hands to his sides in illustration of the sharpness of outline. The word *fu*, however, in ordinary speech means 'hidden' and *io* is the word of emphatic assent. The refrain may be then translated as 'hidden indeed'. It is in this sense that other informants understood it. Their idea was that the gods, angry with men, hide from them, and go off to the sky. The object of the song is to induce the gods to return again to earth. It is from this, these informants said, that the name of the dance, 'The sacred hiding', is derived. It is evident from this disagreement in interpretation by the best informants that a great deal of individual guesswork has been brought to bear on the song.

Before the song began half a dozen men, including the Ariki Taumako and some of his near relatives, detached themselves from the group at the bottom of Marae and in the dim light crouched in a curved line round the periphery of the *tae kava* mound. They held fronds of the areca palm in each hand or leaves of a species of cordyline, the *ti mea*. They crouched motionless while the tempo of the song quickened and the rhythm changed from a single slow alternative beat to two single beats followed by two double beats. As the beat quickened still more, and the song swelled out, there was a sudden movement from the crouching figures. With a simultaneous leap they sprang high into the air, throwing their arms above their heads, and waving across each other the palm fronds held in their hands. With an agility surprising in men of such heavy build they sprang again and again, almost without a sound, for they landed on their toes each time. It was *tapu* to thud to the ground in the dance. Even the waving of the palm fronds was done silently. They leaped and crouched, swung their leaf fans, and turned to one side and to the other with set gestures, in conformity with the rhythm. Then they stiffened again into immobility as each chanted stanza ended.

It was a weirdly impressive spectacle, especially to one who saw it as I did, in the moonlight, which was yet not bright enough to give an air of reality to the scene. As background there was the still lake, with the rock pyramid of Fongo te koro rising on the further shore and its black reflection reaching across the silvered waters to the foot of the Marae. In the glade there were the dark mass of people clustered by the open lakeside, the figures of the dancers, the firelight flickering on them and on the thatched roof of the shelter and the sitting figure of the attendant dark and motionless, shielded by the screen of palm fronds. The rhythmic beat of the sounding-board, regulated by the high-flung arms of the chief as he wielded the polished striking sticks and intoned the ancient chant, contrasted strongly with the noiseless movements of the dancers as they leapt and postured with waving limbs and flowing hair.

It seems a legitimate assumption, though it cannot of course be verified, that these highly sacred dances, dedicated to some of the most important gods of the people, represent one type of ancient

Polynesian religious cult, of which only the vestiges have been preserved by tradition in Hawaii and elsewhere.

The *fu tapu* and the dances immediately following it are regarded as the property of sa Taumako, to be performed only by men of this clan and sons of women of their clan. The songs which serve as their accompaniment, on the other hand, are held to belong to the Ariki Kafika and his 'house', and the privilege of beating the measure and leading the singing is accordingly theirs.

THE 'TUARO'

As soon as the *fu tapu* was finished the beat of the sounding-board changed, without a break, to that of the *tuaro*. Each type of dance had its own special rhythm. The beat of the *tuaro* may vary, depending on the character of the song which it accompanies: 'some *tuaro* are beaten progressively; other *tuaro* are beaten in a rising manner'. In the first style the hands are kept fairly low and the beat is a steady throb; in the second the hands are flung high after each stroke, giving a lighter nervous feel to the rhythm. 'I alone am expert', said the Ariki Kafika to me. His assumption of sole knowledge was really an expression of his privilege and no more, since in strict accuracy there were quite a number of men capable of officiating at the post. The technique, he said, would be transmitted by him to his eldest son when he himself reached old age, and I noted that Pa Fenuatara sat near him on the second night and watched his style.

The dance of the *tuaro* comprised practically the same series of movements of arms and legs as in the *fu tapu*, save that they were in quite regular time, and the dancers did not spring into the air. The songs were traditional, and followed a fairly definite order.

The initial song, of which the position never varies and which is most sacred, is given below.

> *Tou ra, Sakora*
> *Tou ra, Sakora*
> *Matakina tou ra, Sakura*
> *Oie! turou Sokuro*
> *Oie! turou Sokuro.*

According to tradition the origin of this song is to be found in the acts of the Atua i Kafika when he instituted the ceremonies of Marae. He desired to be supreme there, so set up his stone at what is now the Pae Marae. It was a lofty pillar, but he was offended by the competition of that of the Atua i Taumako, which was as tall, and trod this down flat. This is the stone as it now rests in Marae. Not unnaturally the Atua i Taumako was annoyed at this slight put upon him and through his agent, the sun, planned revenge. The sun shone strongly without ceasing, day after day, and concentrated its rays upon the stone of the Atua i Kafika. At first it had no effect, but gradually the rock cracked with the heat and pieces began to fall away. The Atua i Kafika observed the crumbling of his pillar with dismay, and tried to restrain it by pouring water upon it, but without avail; it split to pieces. In the end the once massive pillar was reduced to a number of slabs, which form the present Pae Marae. In acknowledgment of the victory of the Atua i Taumako, the Atua i Kafika composed this song, mentioning his adversary by name and doing reverence to him.

> Thy sun, Sakura
> Thy sun, Sakura
> Observed thy sun, Sakura.
> Oie! respected, Sakura
> Oie! respected, Sakura.

I recorded fourteen *tuaro* altogether. Most were very short and some were untranslatable, even by the Ariki Kafika, who was most entitled to pronounce on them. I may add that the chief's ignorance seemed absolutely genuine, and was corroborated by the inability of all other informants to supply any more cogent explanations.

These 'unintelligible' *tuaro* are the first to be sung, and after them come several which are comparatively clear in meaning. Nothing is known about the composition of the former, save that they are regarded as very ancient, and the latter include three which are held to have been composed by former chiefs of Tafua, a few generations ago, and one by the great-grandfather of the Ariki Kafika. It therefore is a reasonable inference that the former are older, their original wording altered and their meaning lost in the course of oral transmission. But I would argue that this is not necessarily evidence of any high degree of antiquity, and does not allow us to conclude that here are the relics of an archaic speech of Tikopia of an essentially different culture from that of

today. The range of variation I have recorded when different informants have given me the text of the same song, in the chanting
of which they themselves have taken part only a few days before,
shows the flexibility and liability to change inherent in the
Tikopia system of performance and transmission. The more
recent *tuaro* have as theme the acts of invading Tongans, or sea
voyages.

SOCIAL ASPECTS OF THE DANCING

After the set of *tuaro* had been performed a change took place. The
most sacred dances of the night had now been completed, and the
tension noticeably relaxed. Joking and laughter began. The Ariki
yielded his post to a younger man and the beat of the dance was
changed to that of the *matavaka*. This was the real beginning of
the night's enjoyment. The band of dancers round the circle was
now augmented by practically all the non-Christian men of the
island and the dance became a social rather than a religious function. The ritual element, however, was not wholly discarded. The
dancing circle was formed round the periphery of the mound on
which the fire was situated, and one part of the circle passed close
to Muafaitoka. Even at the height of the dance due reverence was
paid to this sacred spot. As each performer approached it he
quietened the swing of his head and limbs, straightened up his
body and walked with bent head and hands clasped in front of
him round this portion of the circle, facing outwards towards the
taboo place. Though his feet moved in time with the beat and the
music of the dance he did not swing his body – 'he does not
dance'. This was the conventional mark of respect to the Atua
Lasi and his house Rarofiroki. On moving away the performer
broke into the swing of the dance once again.

The rhythmic motion of the *matavaka* was intoxicating, as I
found when I took part in the dance each evening. The insistent
throb of the sounding-board went on and on, and blended with
the chorus of voices, now swelling, now dying down, but never
quite ceasing. The dancers moved round and round in the ring
with short steps, knees bent, feet wide apart, arms swinging simultaneously with the movement of the feet and heads swinging
regularly with hair tossing like the waves of the sea. The people
kept close one behind the other, and their exact and regular movement gave the circle an air of corporate life, independent of the

coming and going of the individuals who broke into or fell out of it from time to time.

Everyone was ornamented with head fringes, beads and scented leaves, and many people, especially women, carried fans in their hands. The women joined in the dance late in the evening. Their attitude was different from that of the men; they did not sway from side to side, spread their feet apart or toss their heads, but bent their backs, and dropping their hands down low, moved up and down with a curious shuffling step. They had their own dancing line near the centre of Marae, which undulated up and down in the vicinity of the stone of the Female Deity, but they also joined the ring of the men and circled around the fire. When the dance was in full train and excitement was high this ring formed a tightly packed mass. People who were awaiting their turn to slip in, 'marked time' as it were, at the Taurongorongo at the bottom of Marae, swaying to and fro and shuffling their feet in time to the music. Those who dropped out for a rest sat down on the tree roots or stones near by in little groups and discussed the dance, chewed betel and smoked or went to sleep. Some, more luxuriously inclined, went to a near-by house and lay down on a floor-mat with a wooden head-rest. Food was occasionally brought along and eaten but no organized meal took place.

The dance went on without a pause through the night, and the majority of the crowd did not sleep. From time to time a change of attendants took place by the fire, or one man relieved another at the sounding-board, but the function proceeded with scarcely a perceptible check.

The early hours of the morning was for the young folk, perhaps, the most colourful time. For by then all were thoroughly soaked in the rhythm of the performance. At this point ancient custom permitted the introduction of erotic songs. Of these there were two kinds, the *tauangutu* and the *feuku*. The distinction between them lies in this, that in the former there is grossness of speech, but figurative expressions, and veiled phrases alone – some of them quite poetic in their imagery – convey the intended suggestion. In the *feuku* as a rule, all indirect allusion is cast aside, and the plain crude physiological vocabulary is employed. The Song of the Bamboo in particular is an example of a sacred *tauangutu*. These songs, though usually erotic to a high degree, are not love-ditties. They are essentially of derisive kind, a challenge to the opposite sex, imputing bodily imperfections and absence of virtue, linked with unbridled desire. They are sung alternately in challenge and answer and the object of the one sex is to reciprocate and if possible surpass the song of the other. The atmosphere is one of humour, and some of the songs have certainly wit in them. Because they embody *taranga pariki*, impolite speech, they are relegated to a late period of the dance. It would be highly improper to perform them in the presence of *tautau pariki* (persons in a relationship of constraint), as for instance a man and his father-in-law.[1] When the night has worn on most of the elder folk who comprise one term of these relationships have danced their fill and withdrawn, leaving the field open to the young people. 'When we see that the *tautau pariki* have gone, then we perform *feuku* and *tauangutu*.' The presence of both fathers and sons, who are under constraint of relationship in certain other respects, is not considered to constitute *tautau pariki* for the purposes of Marae. During the dance period, it was said, the women are under the protection of the Female Deity. The male deities, at times, desire the mortal women whom they see on their dancing ground, but the Female Deity interposes and will not allow them to obtain their desire.

The dance continued without interruption till the flush of dawn reddened the sky. When light began to creep over the land everyone mustered at the dance ground, and all the sleepers were summoned to swell the number of performers. The dance became rapid and vigorous. As the first rays of the sun began to appear Pa Rarovi, who had again taken his place beside the fire, suddenly stretched out his hands to the screen of palm fronds and toppled them over on to the flames. These went out almost immediately and the dance stopped at the same moment. This was the ceremonial 'Touching of the Fire' and marked the end of the night's festivities.

The shed of the Fire was then dismantled, the roof being lifted off in one piece and laid at the side of Marae for use the following night. After this the men adjourned to the bottom of the Marae where the *vetu* was clapped once. The morning kava was performed by the Ariki Kafika and the Ariki Fangarere, the chiefs of Tafua (formerly) and Taumako attending on their

[1] See *We, the Tikopia*, 1936, pp. 509–27, for a discussion of dancing, sex and kinship.

respective days. Many of the crowd then went off to their homes to sleep.

The ceremonies of the *Urangafi* were of the same symmetrical form as those of the *Taomatangi*, in that each clan had its own night, and in connection with this prepared its *fakaoatea* of food on the appropriate day. Pa Rarovi, whose ritual of the *taume* and the *afi* was an integral part of each evening's performance, had a constant duty of making the kava in his own house each afternoon. This was termed *Aumumu taume* and was a minor rite, a reinforcement of the major one which took place on the initial day. Every night of the Fire Dance was not of the same esoteric value. Those of Kafika and Tafua, which led off, were of more weight than Taumako and Fangarere, a position which was to be correlated with the respective status of the chiefs. Associated with this differential importance, the *fu tapu* and *tuaro*, the most sacred dances, were performed on the first two nights only; this was analogous to the performance of the *vetu masanga*. The majority of the *matavaka* which constituted the bulk of the choruses for the night were common property and sung indifferently on any occasion, but those which were introductory were always the specific property of the clan whose night it was. Examples cannot be given here for lack of space, but they are of the same type as the songs already published (in *We, the Tikopia*).

Since the Dance of the Flaming Fire is essentially an open-air festival, it depends for much of its success upon the state of the weather. 'The *Urangafi*, its spoiling one thing – the rain', said the Ariki Kafika. If the sky is overcast during the day, as evening draws on it is watched very anxiously. On one occasion when it had started to rain the Ariki after grumbling a little called out loudly 'Clear up the sky, Pu ma!', an appeal to his deities to mend matters. Even when it rained, however, the dance was not abandoned. I was told that as a rule it is not even shortened. People came from the villages carrying leaves of the umbrella palm over their heads, and girt, not with *kie* and other fine clothes, but with leaves of *rau tea*. This was the 'bad weather vesture'. The fire was lit, the sounding-board beaten, and all night long they danced in the wind and the rain. This is an index of the importance of the ritual, for the Tikopia dislikes rain and will not get his skin wet unless for some very good reason. Occasionally a concession is made. Thus after a thoroughly wet day Pa Rarovi came to the door of

the house of the Ariki Kafika, and told him to remain seated on his
dry mat in Marae with the other Ariki and not to take part in the
taume rite since the stone slabs in Takerekere were soaking wet.
This night was exceedingly stormy, with very heavy rain, and this
time the dance was stopped by Pa Rarovi in the early hours of the
morning. Most of the crowd had abandoned the scene and were
sleeping in the various houses round about, while eight or nine
young people were left to carry on the dance. Round and round
they went, untiring, but drenched with rain and lashed by the
squalls which came sweeping over the lake. Pa Rarovi said afterwards 'I had compassion on our young men and maidens; I put
out the fire.' This action was approved by public opinion.

FOOD EXCHANGES

Apart from its religious performances the *Urangafi* has its set of
transactions of social and economic importance – an exchange of
food baskets similar to that of the *Taomatangi*. The reciprocal gifts
already described, centring primarily on the women, are regarded
as being of the greater ceremonial importance: 'Its making
weighty that which was made inland', it was said, since the baskets
of the women, which are deposited at Rarofetaka, are made of
much greater size. For those of the women, moreover, it is taboo
to use breadfruit or banana as the basis of the food. Taro must be
used, or if a woman has no taro at command, she will draw upon
her reserve stores of *masi*, or in the last resort will go and dig her
yams and grate them up. This taboo rests on the differential value
of these foods for consumption. Pudding made of breadfruit or
banana is deemed to be inferior to that prepared from taro or yam,
hence for the baskets of the women it is etiquette to employ the
latter alone. For the baskets of the men, however, which are of
less ceremonial importance, it is permissible to use the foods of a
lower grade.

The arranging of the baskets of the men took place on the
second day of the festival – *te po sa Tafua*. The initial presentation
was made on the third day, *te po sa Taumako*, and the exchange
was concluded by a reciprocal gift on the fourth day – *te po sa
Fangarere*. In this respect the affair differed from that of the women
where the reciprocal presentation took place on the same day. The
arrangements were made carefully and methodically. The procedure was simplified by the custom that all the *longi nga fafine*,

exchanged by the women, were made and exchanged again in the *longi nga tangata* by the men. Thus in the case of a married couple the wife, during the *Taomatangi*, exchanged a basket with a woman of the opposite clan. As a result, in the *Urangafi* the two husbands exchanged likewise. An unmarried man and his sister followed a similar rule. Hence there is never much difficulty in allotting partners, since if two family groups have been linked by their womenfolk, a pair of men – it does not matter greatly who – is easily found for the second exchange. For other unmarried men (of whom a great number always attend the festival) one procedure is to go methodically through the list of family groups of one clan, naming them in turn, and settling partners for the the principal young men in each. In arranging this any baskets previously fixed for each 'house' are kept in mind, and when the total for any group reaches three or four, then a halt is called. But I heard this termed excessive. 'A household is plentiful, two, three their baskets, then cease', was laid down as a guiding rule by some people. When the number reached the desired point the Ariki or someone else in authority called 'Stop', and the discussion passed on. 'Anyone who is left (in that kin group) stick him on to another man', was the instruction of the elders.

A bachelor may arrange his own basket beforehand instead. He goes to the dance on the first night with a *surusuru*, a branch from a scented shrub, worn as a back ornament, and sticks it in the waist belt of the friend whom he selects as the object of his food presentation. When the allotting of baskets is being decided he informs the meeting of his choice, or someone else does so in his absence. Mutual discussion is thus the basis of the organization of this important set of transactions.

The next day the work of preparing the food for the baskets began – on the part of sa Kafika and sa Fangarere alone, since sa Tafua and sa Taumako reciprocated the following day. The same distinction was made as before between the ordinary baskets and the 'foremost baskets', which one chiefly family presented to another. For this a minor kava ceremony was performed before it left the house of the donor.

A novice who has come to the ceremonies of Marae for the first time, makes a presentation of a much larger amount of food than the normal. Besides the huge basket which forms the main portion of the gift there is a secondary basket and usually a bundle of sprouting coconuts or a bunch of bananas in addition. The large basket is termed the *matua longi*, the smaller one *na taotao* ('its support'), or the *taotao longi*. In former times every man made both of these – though less imposing than those of a novice – but of recent years the minor one has been discarded by common consent of the chiefs. In the season described in our account the Ariki Kafika and the Ariki Taumako had a conversation and agreed to conduct the exchange on a single-basket basis (except in the case of novices, who were to be allowed to present both baskets).

The religious ceremonies of each day did not vary: after the morning kava came that of *fakaoatea*; the 'drink' took place late in the afternoon while in the evening after the *taume* rites the evening kava was a prelude to the dance.

The technique of presentation of the men's baskets differed in some respects from that of the women's baskets. The *longi o mua*, or the *longi o Marae* as it was sometimes termed, destined for the Ariki Taumako, was carried out to the ground and placed on the mat of the Ariki Kafika, the donor. Those of the rest of Kafika were set at the clan-station in rear of that of their chief. When the evening kava was to be made, after the *taume* had been brought, the *longi o mua* was carried from the mat of the Ariki Kafika and placed on that of the Ariki Taumako. Simultaneously a kinsman of this chief brought across a small food basket and a bunch of coconuts and set it before the chief of Kafika. The real reciprocating gift for the basket was made the following day, but this was by way of preliminary acknowledgment. The idea was that – theoretically – the Ariki Kafika, having been busy all day with the preparation of the gift to his co-chief, would be without food, hence the Ariki Taumako sent him a kind of 'sustaining present'. The next day, when the return gift was made from Taumako, the Ariki Kafika sent over a corresponding basket. Between the chiefs of Tafua and Fangarere a similar series of secondary presentations used to take place. Exchanges of this nature indicate the complexity of the system of reciprocal gifts, and also the endeavour which is made to preserve its symmetry.

During this satisfaction of the obligations of the chiefs the baskets of the commoners had remained in position. After the kava was over and the dancing of the *matavaka* began the presentation was made; the baskets of Kafika and of Tafua being carried to the stations of Taumako and Fangarere respectively, and placed near the seat of the chief. As each consignment arrived it was announced to him. The people of the recipient clans were dancing the while. Later they assembled and their chief made known to each man the position of his basket in the mass.

Certain baskets were not formally presented in this manner. If the oven was ready very quickly in a household, by the early hours of the afternoon, the basket might be filled and sent along to its destination immediately. The saying was 'Send along the basket that it may arrive for their hunger at the midday.' In this case of course it was not stood in Marae – the practical object of the food gift has here taken precedence over the ceremonial aspect. Of such a basket it was said 'it was sent in by the back way'.

On the next day, which was the fourth of the *Urangafi*, the reciprocal baskets were prepared and presented with a similar procedure to that already described.

FINAL RITES OF THE DANCE

This was the night of sa Fangarere, the final occasion of the Dance of the Flaming Fire, and its importance was stressed by all. It was *te te po*, the remaining night, *te po fakamavae*, the night of parting, and efforts were made to render the dance as vigorous as possible. 'The dance will be packed closely this night: the crowd are separating', was stated by men of rank and echoed on all sides, and the emphasis given to the word *ngingiti* (pack tight) indicated the strength of their wish. On this evening the *vetu* was introduced before the *matavaka* began. I heard the Ariki Taumako, turning to one of his young relatives, say, calling him by name, 'Koroa-manongi! Go and *sava*; this is the last night, go and *sava* in the dance.' The young man was bashful and objected, but was prevailed upon to obey. *Sava*, it will be remembered, is the term for the admired solo movements performed in the square while the rest of the dancers clap the *vetu*.

The evening and the night followed as before, though the scene was if anything more animated, and the dancing towards morning more furious. At last dawn broke, the fire was extinguished and in the grey light the dancers dispersed.

The concluding rite of the *Urangafi* was one of great sacredness. It was a kava rite of the ordinary type, but its specific object was to render the Marae *tapu* so that once again no one might set foot beyond the border of the path. The 'Work of the Gods' was finished there, and therefore the place of the gods should not be profaned.

For this kava the Ariki should not sit on separate mats; they assembled and occupied the one seating mat, at the side of Rarofiroki. The Ariki Kafika took the head, next him (formerly) was the Ariki Tafua, then the Ariki Taumako, while the Ariki Fangarere occupied the tail. The *epa* mat and some leaves of cycas lay there also. When all were seated the Ariki Fangarere rose and laid the *epa* with appropriate obeisance before his Atua at Muafaitoka, and covered it with the cycas leaves. Then he returned to his seat, while the kava was prepared. This occasion was noticeable for its solemnity: the men who entered the Marae did so on tiptoe, and spoke only in whispers.

When the kava was ready the maker glanced at the Ariki Fangarere, who rose, went down to Muafaitoka, and poured a libation to his deity. As he did so he recited the formula of abasement, ending with the *Iorei!* which was taken up by all the crowd. I was told that as a general rule the spirit medium of the Atua Lasi entered Marae for this ceremony, and seated himself at Muafaitoka. At the recitation of this formula the Atua was believed to leave the medium; this was the signal for his final departure from Marae now that the rites had finished there. The medium did not come, however, on this occasion. The next cup of kava used to be brought to the Ariki Tafua, who handed it to the Ariki Kafika, who poured it out. This was a mark of respect to the premier chief. Nowadays it is handed direct. Other cups were then handed to the chiefs of Tafua (formerly) and Taumako, who poured their customary libations. The *epa* was then folded up, the cycas leaves stuck in the roof of Rarofiroki, and the various seating mats of Ariki and elders were folded and carried off to their houses. This was the conclusion of the ceremonies in Marae.

Each Ariki then went to his temple where he performed the kava to his own immediate gods. This was done with full libations, omitting none of the deities. In Kafika, for instance, the Ariki poured the kava to Pu ma before the mound of the Tinai Ariki.

These rites have as their essential object the re-establishment of the state of *tapu* which has been disturbed by the constant traffic, the presence of women and children, the noise and the dancing.

The first kava of the morning was termed *te kava po te Marae* – 'the kava for extinguishing the Marae', whilst the other was known as *te kava po te vasia fare*, 'the kava for extinguishing between the houses'. Both might be described as ceremonies of 'clearing up' after the confusion of the last few days; the restoration of the peace characteristic of the sacred district of Uta.

THE 'PURUNGA KAVA'

In the normal way the festival of the *Urangafi* follows that of the *Taomatangi*. Sometimes, however, in former times, by a decision of the chiefs this was not held, but the rites of the *Purunga kava* were substituted instead. The following account is hearsay only.

The Ariki slept in Uta on the night after the dance was finished, then rose early the next morning and went to Matorotoro where there are a number of stone pillars and slabs which served them as seats and back-rests. Matorotoro is a small point of land jutting out into the lake in Te Roro, about half a mile from Uta, and is a spot of traditional associations. While the chiefs sat and talked their followers went through the orchards in Uta and brought a small quantity of coconuts and other food. This was known as the *aru*.

A minor kava rite was performed over it, and the Ariki then proceeded by canoe back to Uta, to Masauma, or Rarokoka as it is more generally called, the small Marae where the *fono* was delivered (see Chapter 7). There they seated themselves at their appointed posts, and a much larger *aru* was then collected, even the heights of Maunga Lasi being laid under contribution. When the food was brought the kava house was set up as in the *Taomatangi*, and the kava of Marae was recited by the Ariki Tafua. The Ariki then went and sat in their respective houses, and each partook of food. They waited until the sound of a shell trumpet was borne to them across the lake from Tai, then boarded their canoes and met in the beach village at the house of whoever of them had made preparations for their reception. The house selected was one of the lesser sacred buildings of the chief, and the choice lay between Raniniu, Rangieva, Mapusanga, or Rangateatua. The clan of the chief who was acting as host had meanwhile been extremely busy; since early morning the ovens had been going, and as a rule they collected food the day before in order to have an abundance.

The large *aru*, which had been brought over from Uta, was divided into three portions. One portion was cooked in the oven to supplement the feast, another was set in its green state on the *mata paito* of the chief who was the host, and the third was carried back to Rarokoka to provide food for the next day.

When the oven was ready, the *aru* was 'announced' by the Ariki Tafua, that is a formal acknowledgment was made to the gods, offerings of it were thrown, and the Ariki ate together in the house.

The next day the oven was made in Rarokoka, and each Ariki recited his own kava. An interval of a day or two then occurred until the signal was given by the Ariki Kafika to recommence the ceremonies. Such intervals serve a very useful purpose – they allow people to recover their normal equilibrium, to accomplish tasks which have been neglected in the performance of their ritual obligations, to inspect their orchards and cultivations, to plant *taro* bases which have accumulated and to manufacture or repair tools and implements for which the need is pressing.

When the Ariki Kafika gave the word a round of ceremonial dancing began. The people assembled on each successive day at the Marae of a different chief, who, assisted by his clan, prepared large quantities of food for their reception. In this the Ariki Fangarere joined himself with the Ariki Kafika, partly on account of the intimate relation of the two clans, and partly on account of the comparative poverty of Fangarere. The first day's performance took place at Te Akauroa, a sandy flat on the beach below Potu sa Kafika, since swept away in a great storm about 1918. *Roi* was made the previous evening, the chief and the principal families of his clan each making their *fonakava* for themselves and their guests. On the day of the festival the chiefs decided whether or no 'the whole land should be divided apart', that is whether the people should dance as a single group, or should divide into two dancing groups, those who attended the *Taomatangi* forming one (*sa Taomatangi*) and those who for various reasons had stayed in Tai forming another (*sa Tua*). In this latter case a form of competitive dancing was the order of the day.

That same evening the *roi* was made again, and the following day the people assembled and danced at Faretapu, the Marae of the Ariki Taumako. Again the *roi* was made, and on the final day the dance took place at Matautu, on the other side of the island, in the Marae of the Ariki Tafua. Here a *feasinga* of competitive dancing usually took place between the two districts, the people of Faea forming one group and those of Ravenga another. Each day the formula of the kava was recited by the Ariki Tafua, but the *fare kava* was not set up – it being a ritual structure confined to Uta alone. For the ceremonies of the Marae in Tai a fresh stem of kava was plucked each day, the Ariki Tafua sat down, held it in his hand and recited his formula. Each Marae has its principal gods, to whom chief place was given on these occasions. In the Akauroa Nga Ariki (Pu ma) have control; in Faretapu it is Sakura, the Atua i Taumako; in Matautu it is Oatuatafu, a deity of the Ariki Tafua, who presides over the channel in the reef. In the Marae of Tai, as distinct from those of Uta, only one kava bowl was used for the ceremonies of the conjoined Ariki; this was the bowl of Tafua, and from it the other chiefs were served with cups of kava with which to make their libations.

This distinction on the part of the Ariki Tafua, together with the fact that he alone recited the kava formulae there, is in keeping with his other privileges as the Faifekau, the 'Worker' who performs the ritual offices for the Ariki Kafika. Here as elsewhere, however, special function has given rise to privilege and social prestige, and the Ariki Tafua was wont to plume himself on the fact that he, and not the Ariki Kafika, carried out these rites.

The dancing in Tai was of a less formal character than that in Uta. The *vetu*, and other highly sacred dances, because of their *tapu*, were absent from the programme. Women and children, moreover, attended without hindrance. The *Purunga kava* was not wholly free from ritual restraint, however, and the dances ordinarily performed for amusement were not introduced. The *matavaka tapu*, the 'canoe bow', fairly sacred, with songs referring to the deities, was the prescribed type. The performers, however, did not circle round and round as in the *Urangafi*, but marched up and down as in the ordinary dance.

The *Purunga kava* was performed on occasions when it was desired to push on more rapidly to the end of the ceremonial season. In former times, after the conclusion of the *Urangafi* in Uta the dance was 'conveyed' to Tai and performed in the Marae of the main villages in a manner similar to that of the *Purunga kava*. In both cases this procedure was known as 'the causing to tramp of Marae', since figuratively speaking its rites were borne through the island by the feet of the crowds as they assembled at the various dancing grounds. Like the *Purunga kava*, this conclusion to the *Urangafi* is no longer in vogue, since the Ariki Tafua is no longer available for the performance of the kava. Nowadays then, an interval of two or three days generally elapses before the final piece of ritual of the ceremonial season, that is the 'carpeting' of Takarito.

Postscript

In July 1952 Pa Fenuatara explained to us that the Work of Marae was being omitted that season since the Ariki Kafika was at that time too unwell to travel to Uta, and no one else, neither common man nor chief, could perform his critical ritual tasks there. (The rites were carried out in November 1952, and attended by Spillius.)

I obtained some additional information concerning the *manu tapu* and *iofa* symbols on the top of the temple Rarofiroki. The Ariki Fangarere gave me a canoe ornament representing *manu tapu*, which he said had been carved by Pa Fenuatara. The chief said that before Pa Fenuatara, Pae Avakofe had been the carver of these ornaments, but it was open to anyone to make an example. Only the Ariki Fangarere, however, could set it up on his canoes – on both bow and stern if desired. I asked if it were taboo or not. 'Oh no! It's all right,' the chief replied, 'it's a custom of the clan', and he handed it to a child without any formality, to go and wash it clean of soot and dirt before presenting it to me. He added that the ornament was carved of breadfruit wood. His attribution of lack of sacredness to the object was possibly a reflection of the change in view as Christianity advanced. In 1952 Pa Fenuatara carved two samples of *iofa* for us. After some pressing he also identified the *iofa* with Manu, the spirit of a constellation in the sky, who was believed to be largely responsible for hurricanes. It is plausible that this symbol should be associated with the Ariki Fangarere. (For illustrations and discussion of *iofa* and *manu tapu*, see my article on Tikopia woodworking ornament, *Man*, 1960, No. 27.)

As regards the Dance of the Flaming Fire, by 1952 Pa Rarovi had become a Christian and abandoned the rites of the *taume* and the *afi*, his special privilege. But despite his claim that he 'owned' them, these rites were carried on by the Ariki Kafika, in order that the dancing could proceed as before. In 1952 Pa Rarovi asserted once again the importance of his former special position in the Urungafi, and recited to me again his formulae. The text followed very closely the version he gave to me a generation before, with merely a slight change in the order of words at the end. One identification, however, he made slightly differently. In 1928 he had told me that Taringamoea, the deity invoked in the Taume rite, was one of the names of the Atua i Sao, his name in Rarovi. In 1952 he said that this was the title of the Atua i Raropuka, in Marae, parallel to the titles of Tupua-uri for Pa Raropuka and Te Ariki-uri for himself in the kava; the origin of the deity was in Raropuka. Now in 1928 he had been much under the influence of Pae Sao, and it is possible that he then accepted the latter's contention that the Atua i Sao and the Atua i Raropuka were really one. In the meantime, he and Pa Raropuka had shared the Work of Marae after the Ariki Tafua had reverted to paganism for a period, so this aspect of the identification may have been more fresh in his mind. Once again he repeated that the basis of the Fire was in the female deity Matangi-mai-muri (Pufine i Ravenga) (see p. 348), though he did not mention the title Ruataka as he had done previously. He added that it was she who (in spirit form) kindled the Fire, which was her glowing body. The shield of branches round the fire was to shelter the ordinary people from her, lest they be overcome by her and made ill.

In 1952 I also had an account from Pa Raropuka of how after the reversion of the Ariki Tafua he was summoned with Pa Rarovi to the Ariki Kafika. The chief said 'Now you two brother elders there, which of you is going with the Fire?' 'Then he pointed to me,' said Pa Raropuka, 'and I assented. So when the Work of Marae was carried out, we didn't go haphazardly according to our wishes, we went to the chief and we all agreed.' (This confirmed that Pa Rarovi was claiming more than he was entitled to, in asserting that he had sole rights to the Fire.)

Deserted Gods in Takarito

The carpeting of Takarito is a piece of ritual of a different type from that which has gone before.

In order to understand its significance it is necessary to go back into Tikopia traditions. Nga Ravenga, said to have been the former inhabitants of the greater part of the eastern district of the island, have already been mentioned. At the time of their extermination, and for the space of about two generations afterwards, it is said, the western side of the island was occupied by a people known as Nga Faea,[1] a name associated with the present name for this district. Nga Faea in their turn became the object of the same land-hunger on the part of the chiefs which had destroyed Nga Ravenga. The Ariki Tafua of the time, seeing the success of his confrère of Taumako with the latter, determined that he also would acquire territory for himself, and to that end attacked Nga Faea. In this, according to tradition, he was aided by 'houses' from the other clans. Indeed one version of the tale has it that the initial impulse came from the elder of Marinoa who persuaded the Ariki Kafika to make kava and by magic unsettle the hearts of Nga Faea and induce them to abandon their lands. Be this as it may, the result was that Nga Faea, apparently threatened by attack, and not liking to meet the fate of Nga Ravenga, chose the more dignified though no less fatal course. Led by their Ariki, Tiako, they prepared their canoes, gathered their women and children together, and, figuratively speaking, with banners flying, pushed off into the ocean wastes – to perish. They left but a few children as survivors, and the fertile lands thus vacated were soon occupied by the eager retainers of the chiefs.

The importance of Takarito lies in the fact that it is the site of

[1] For details about Nga Faea, see my *History and Traditions of Tikopia*, 1961, pp. 136–43.

the old Marae of Nga Faea corresponding to the sacred dancing ground of the chiefs in Uta. In times long ago, I was told, each of the districts of the island had its own Kafika, the temple; its own Marae, the sacred square; and its own *Taomatangi* festival; the Ariki Kafika was, as now, *primus inter pares*, and the Ariki Tafua, as his Faifekau, his executant, went from one set of ceremonies to the other, to recite the Kava of Marae.

At Takarito stood the dwelling-house of the chief of Nga Faea, close beside the dancing ground, and when the last chief abandoned the lands of his fathers, he sent a message to the Ariki Kafika to come and occupy the site, use the food of the adjoining orchard, and perform the ceremonies to the gods. For in addition to its importance as a 'historical' relic, Takarito has yet another claim upon the interest of the people. There, on the site of the ancient house, lies the Atua i Takarito, a deity of the most sacred character. He is the abandoned god of the vanished chiefs of Nga Faea, and it is on his behalf that the Ariki Kafika concludes the ceremonial season with the 'carpeting' of Takarito. The *atua* is embodied in a stone, round and heavy, which is kept covered by cycas leaves and a coconut mat.[1] It is *tapu* to disturb this stone or even to look upon it at unauthorized times, and tales are related of how even in recent years inquisitive people have suffered for their temerity. A decade or so ago, so I was told, two girls who were out in the woods were led by curiosity to tamper with its coverings, and one of them even dared to touch the stone with her foot. The girls went home, and soon after they became ill. The one who had been most forward in meddling with the stone died, the other recovered, but with a diseased leg from which she still suffers. More recently, since the establishment of Christianity in Faea, one man in his zeal for the new faith, and contempt for the old, ventured to tamper with the deity. He took it out of its wrappings and rolled it away, some little distance. Then he went away, but told no-one. Later Pa Fangatoto, a man of the 'house' of Siku, the members of which are descended from the former chiefs of Nga Faea, and who consequently have a proprietary interest in their *atua*, found what had happened and hastened to

[1] The account given of this rite by Rivers, *History of Melanesian Society*, vol. I, pp. 338-9, is the first record of it, but contains many inaccuracies. It was based on the description by a Motlav mission teacher, Ernest Wirit, who had not seen the rite but had been told about it by a Tikopia.

report the sacrilege to the Ariki Kafika, not daring himself to touch the stone. The Ariki came, in great anger at the disturbance of the sacred relic, and replaced it. He complained to the missionary teacher, a Motlav man, of the lack of toleration which the new converts displayed and prophesied evil would come upon them. The offender had been accused of the deed but denied having taken any part in it. Not long afterwards, however, he became afflicted with frightful yaws in the arm, rendering it useless. In the eyes of the Ariki Kafika, who told me the story, and of many other people, Christian as well as pagan, this was his punishment.

The Atua i Takarito is related to that of Fatumaru, mentioned in Chapter 5. The former is named 'Sefu', the latter 'Sefuia', associated names which are known only to a few people. Both are said to be used for purposes of black magic by the respective chiefs who have charge of them, that of Takarito by the Ariki Kafika, and that of Fatumaru by the Ariki Taumako. Both are known by the natives as *fuateka*, a term which is applied to the 'spider-shell', but which also denotes a foetal monstrum of which limbs are lacking or which is otherwise imperfectly formed. When used of *atua* it signifies that they are not equipped with powers of locomotion and a full complement of organic parts – though potent in supernormal affairs. Another name for the Atua i Takarito is 'Te Kerepuna' and it is by this title that he is addressed by the Ariki Kafika on formal occasions. It is not only, however, in perpetuation of a traditional obligation that this deity is recognized in the seasonal rites. As the deity of Nga Faea, he was held responsible for the fecundity of the fruits of the earth in their district, for the breadfruit, the coconut and the taro, and also for the continuity of the fish supply on the reef and off-shore. Of these benefits he is believed to be still master, so that there is a direct incentive for the Ariki Kafika to appeal to him in order to conserve them for the people. On investigation indeed, I found that Te Kerepuna was identified with the premier god of Nga Faea, Feke, whose normal embodiment is the octopus.

The ceremonies of Takarito began after sunrise, on Christmas Day, 1928. The Ariki Kafika advised his elders and others whom he desired to attend, and the cortège moved off along the track to Faea. I accompanied it. On the way parties broke off and went to their cultivations to collect food for the day. Some taro and breadfruit were wanted, but the main requisite was coconut. 'The coconut only shall be considerable', said the chief, addressing the people at large, who echoed his words with emphasis. The custom is for the proportion of cooked food on this occasion to be small.

On this day, all the orchards of Faea, without privilege of family or clan, were laid under contribution, and from each a few coconuts, or a bunch of bananas, or a couple of breadfruit were taken. This was in the nature of a levy on the produce of the district; it was termed *te aru* and was sanctified by tradition.[1] The toll on each person's plantation was not heavy, and no owner interfered with the collecting party. Such conduct indeed would have been definitely sacrilegious; they were *tapu*. I was told that the correct procedure is for the gatherers of the food not to speak to any person whom they may encounter in the woods. They are regarded as representing for the time being the material embodiment of the Atua, Pu ma.

While the majority of the men were away collecting provisions the Ariki and a few followers proceeded to Takarito. The first rite performed there was the Clearing of the Marae, which was done in the same manner as that of the ground in Uta. There were about fifteen men present. The formula, which I obtained from the chief on the spot, was as follows:

> Pa Porima and your assembly of Elders there
> Countenance me in the Marae of Pu ma and Te Kerepuna
> Which will be cleared away on this morning.
>   Clear for welfare,
> For the reef edge and the head of the land.
> And let the sky be rent apart.
>   *Marie.*

In this invocation the Ariki appeals first to his elders to confirm the performance of the sacred rite in the usual way. His request to the deities, Pu ma and Te Kerepuna, to look favourably on the reef edge, i.e. the sea, is an appeal for a plentiful supply of fish, while the mention of the 'head of the land' is for fecundity of the breadfruit. The 'parting of the sky' is a synonym for fine weather; it refers to the breaking up of heavy clouds.

This influence on the elements is a characteristic feature of Tikopia religious rites and formulae. The greater the importance

---

[1] Discussion of the *aru* is given in my *Primitive Polynesian Economy*, 1939, pp. 260–1, *Social Change in Tikopia*, 1959, p. 159.

of any piece of ritual, the greater its effect upon the weather. The carpeting of Takarito is a very important rite. 'Completion of the Work of the Gods – tremendous, friend! My house here, a house of weight!' said the Ariki to me, indicating the glade in which we sat, and the former dwelling of chiefs. In proof of this power the chief was able to point to the weather of that very day. In the morning heavy black clouds covered the sky, thunder was heard close overhead – and to all appearances a violent storm was about to ensue. However by midday the clouds had rolled aside, the sun was shining, and a beautiful day was the result. Hence a manifestation of the power of the old gods! If the weather has been bad for a long time, too much sun, or too much rain, then the kava is made in Uta to obtain a change. If this is unsuccessful then the Ariki Kafika comes to Takarito and performs the ceremonies there. This is said to act without fail.

The next rite was the washing of the god. The centre of the clearing was spread with palm fronds on which the Ariki seated himself; this was his ritual position. Two men who had been previously appointed for the task had plaited a pair of small baskets from coconut leaves, one to fit inside the other. They went to the spot where the god was lying, removed the cycas leaves and put the stone into the baskets. One man held these, while the other manipulated the stone, a task which taxed his strength, for it was very heavy.

My presence as a guest prevented me from examining the *atua* closely, on account of its *tapu*. From what I saw of it, however, it appeared to be a sphere of light-coloured, greyish-brown stone, about a foot in diameter, and of irregular surface. According to the natives it had a face, equipped with eyes, nose and mouth, but this I was unable to verify. It is probable that, as in the case of other such sacred stones in other parts of the world, peculiarities of natural formation have been taken as anthropomorphic characters.

One man who had performed the offices in connection with the stone described it to me thus: 'Great is its weight; heavy just like iron; it is small, it is round.' He continued, 'Baskets are plaited, circular like this' (curving his arms in illustration). 'Two baskets are made and it is enclosed in them. A large stick is cut; if a small stick is used, it breaks, the large stick is good alone.' The narrator indicated a stick of about six inches diameter as being necessary to sustain the weight of the stone when carried. It is said to be very

hard, so that a knife or an axe would be broken on it – though no-
one would ever put this to the proof on account of its *tapu*.

The bearers of the stone are most properly men who are *tama
tapu* of sa Kafika, i.e. whose mothers are from that clan. The
informant mentioned above, Pa Nukutau, said: 'Because I sprung
from sa Kafika, because my origin came from there, therefore I
went to shoulder it.' It is not always the same person who under-
takes this task in successive seasons. 'Wishes a man to go and carry
it, he goes; wishes another man to go and carry it, he goes.' The
Ariki Kafika himself does not handle the stone at this time. 'The
chief does not go and touch it; the common people only.' In
substantiation of this and other statements regarding the *atua* Pa
Nukutau said 'My truth; I it is who looked at it; I who lifted it.'

As the stone was lifted out of its bed one of the men thus occupied called out to the Ariki '*Ia!*' in formal announcement of the
act. 'The deity is lifted' was the expression used by the people
commenting on this.

The men enclosed it in the baskets, thrust a stick through the
top and, shouldering it, carried it down the path which led to
the beach at Matafanga. This was called the sacred path, since it
led direct from Takarito, and was the road of the god. On ordinary days the path was used freely for all purposes, but on this
occasion everyone kept clear of it – they hid, it was said, on the
approach of the bearers; in other words, they remained within
their houses if in the vicinity.

A few years ago a dramatic incident occurred which illustrates
both the sacredness of the rite and the dread which is entertained
of the *atua* by the people at large. The bearers were carrying the
stone down to the beach for its customary cleansing when they
noticed that someone – probably a child – had deposited excrement in the path. Since this would have been defiling to the *atua*
they turned aside from the sacred track, and went along by the
house of Niukapu which stood near. In due course they returned,
and the kava was prepared. As the ritual was being performed the
chief and the people were astounded to hear a succession of
whoops from the direction of the shore. '*Iefu! Iefu! Iefu!*' Several
men at once seized their axes and ran down in anger to find
out who it was who had dared to violate the sanctity of the
occasion in this challenging fashion. They discovered the culprit,
Pa Niukapu, outside his house. Raising their axes to strike, they

lashed him with their tongues. To their abuse and reproaches the offender answered not a word but sat with bowed head, and wailed. At last he said 'Launch my canoe; I am going to sea' – a notification that he would commit suicide in expiation of his offence. Then the Ariki Kafika had sympathy for him since in times long past the ancestor of Pa Niukapu, a famous navigator, had perished at sea in the same canoe as his nephew, the ancestor of the Ariki Kafika. The traditional saying is '*Te kerekere o te Ariki, ne poi ma ko ia*', 'The earth of the chief, who went with him', meaning that he supported the chief by his presence in his last moments, and accompanied him to his ocean grave. This ancestral link still counts for much, and was responsible for the lenient attitude of the Ariki on this occasion. Instead of confirming the intention of suicide he said, 'No! We are angry because you have whooped like this; but there is no need to go out to sea.' Finally after more talk the party returned and finished their rites. Later, after the group dispersed, the Ariki and Pa Porima sat on at Takarito. Then came Pa Koroatu, the brother of Pa Niukapu, and Vaitere, his son, with gifts of bananas and breadfruit to the chief. Crawling to him along the ground, they pressed their noses to his knee, as the custom is, in token of their humility. 'The one fool in Tikopia', said Pa Koroatu of his brother. The apology and the present were accepted by the Ariki, and the incident was tacitly buried.

But the most interesting point remains. It was the Ariki himself who told me the tale, as we sat together on the palm fronds in Takarito, and he added, in comment, 'Pa Niukapu was right!' In elucidation of this curious statement he explained that the diversion of the bearers from the sacred path brought the stone right past the side of the house. It was an *atua pariki*, an evil deity, in that it was fraught with the potentialities of causing sickness, and Pa Niukapu feared therefore the possible hurt to his children. It was as an objection to this disregard of the welfare of his family that he had made his protest. Of course from the Tikopia point of view this justification of his reason for action in no way removed Pa Niukapu from having to suffer the consequences.

To return now to the bearers of the stone. After carrying it down to the water's edge they removed it from its baskets, and carefully washed it in the sea. When it was thoroughly cleansed they enclosed it again and carried it back to Takarito.

At the moment when he judged that the *atua* was being washed the Ariki recited a formula to it.

> Thou hast arrived at thy flat of the sea, Ancestor!
> Excrete on to thy flat of the sea,
> To climb hither a sea creature
> For the fish offering of thy kava.
> The land has come in conclusion to thy chiefly house
> Which has been carpeted singly on this day.
> Cause to lie down, thou, Ancestor,
> The eye of the wind
> To tumble below
> As a witness to your house
> A sign of thy own kava on this day.

This is primarily an appeal for the *atua* to grant bounty from the sea wherein he is now being washed. The 'flat of the sea' is a figurative expression for the reef waters. The appeal to the *atua* to excrete at the sea-edge is a metaphorical way of expressing a desire for the creatures of the sea to multiply; the scatological figure of speech represents the humility of the speaker and exalts the deity.

The theme of the formula then changes to praise of the *atua*. It is pointed out that the people have assembled in the concluding rite of the season at his chiefly house, that is the glade of Takarito where the house once stood; and that this house is re-carpeted alone on this day. The inference is that it is accorded primacy of place. The deity is then further requested to push down the clouds which come from the wind quarter, i.e. to mend the weather, and this service is pictured as being a token of the importance of the occasion and of Takarito.

As usual the choice of phrases in the invocation lies with the Ariki; he can make his appeal short or long as he wishes. If the preceding period has been one of drought, and rain is desired, then he substitutes an alternative form of words:

> Turn then, Ancestor, to the sky
> To rain for a witness of thy sacred house
> Which will be carpeted singly on this day.

When the time came for the return of the stone all the party were alert for the first sounds of its approach. When the bearers finally emerged from the leafy mass of shrubs which embowered the path, the people drew back and remained quiet while the stone was replaced in its bed, and covered with fresh cycas leaves. Again the formal announcement was made to the Ariki. When the *atua* was once more safely deposited the Ariki addressed it again. This time he invoked it for the products of the soil, as formerly he appealed for those of the sea.

> Thou hast arrived hither in thy earth, Ancestor,
> Excrete on thy soil that it may fruit
> To be secure thy kava and thy food portion;
> And send down hither the coconut
> For the preparation of thy liquid
> For the pouring of thy liquid.

The 'pouring of the liquid' meant the libations of the coconut kava which followed.

After the *atua* had been brought back from the beach and was once more set in its bed the kava was performed with a few coconuts obtained from the adjacent orchard. The libations were for his deities, including the Atua i Takarito. The Ariki then went to sit under the shade of a tree, to await the arrival of the *aru* party.

Towards midday the food gatherers assembled, each man carrying a large load on his shoulder. Breadfruit, bananas, coconuts and areca nut were the chief items collected. These were set in the middle of the Marae and after a time the Ariki notified the crowd of his intention to go and 'announce' the *aru*. He squatted before the heap and recited a formula similar to that already given as a preliminary to the clearing of the Marae, and appealing in the same way for fertility of the breadfruit and other crops. The crowd of men present was then counted – there were of course no women or children – and the *aru* was apportioned among them. Green coconuts formed the midday meal; the bananas and breadfruit were set aside to be taken home. Some of the breadfruit had previously been taken to Teve, the house of the Ariki Kafika in Sukumarae where the oven was prepared, four men, one from each of the clans, acting as cooks. In order that the proceedings might be accelerated as far as possible no pudding was prepared; the breadfruit was simply cooked whole. The cooks were not forgotten in the distribution of the *aru*; piles of coconuts were set aside for them.

Mention has been made of the coconut mat the head of which

covered the sacred stone. This mat marked the site of the ancient house of Takarito – in which the stone formerly lay, in the same manner as the Atua of Fatumaru rests nowadays in Fatumaru – and lay on the grave of Pu Forau, the father of Tiako, the chief of Nga Faea who led his people out to sea. Pu Forau, who was buried by his mother's brother, Pu Tafuaroa, was said to pillow his head on the stone of the Atua. Two groups of his descendants, the houses of Siku and Torokinga, exist at the present day, and the elder of Siku (or Ratia), being the senior, should be responsible for the renewal of the mat of his ancestor. (Another mat of Tiako should also be spread in his own house.)

But nowadays he has ceased to do these things. Formerly, while the oven was being made in Teve he brought a newly plaited mat, laid it on the grave, and weighted it with stones on the edges, accompanying this act with the recital of a formula (given me by Pa Ratia).

> Thy mat, Grandsire,
> Will be re-carpeted
> Carpet with welfare.
> And a marine creature
> To be laid hither on the reef edge
> For the vivifying of the land.

The meaning is again that all fish and sea products should multiply and become available for the benefit of the people. Formerly associated with this laying of the mat but now a separate item is the ritual of the kava, performed when the cooked food has been brought from the house Teve. The Ariki Kafika took the principal part in the ceremonial. He recited a long invocation over the kava stem, calling upon all his principal gods in turn to grant fine weather, send fish and cause food to be plentiful. The usual procedure of the kava then followed. Special attention used to be paid to Pa Ratia, to whom cups of the liquid were handed that he might make his own libations to his ancestors and their gods. The first cup he poured to the Atua i Takarito under his general name:

> Thy kava there Feke!
> Excrete on to thy flat of the sea
> That there may be a marine creature
> For the vivifying of the land.

The second cup was poured to Pu Forau:

> Thy kava there Ancestor!
> Push down the skies
> To stand calm
> And the reef edge to climb a marine
> creature.

His last cup was given as a libation to the chiefs of Nga Faea of olden times, many of whose names are said to be lost. A formula was addressed to them collectively that they might all attend the kava and by so doing exert a beneficent influence on it still.

> Your kava there the line of chiefs
> Meet together simultaneously at the kava
> Not a one may remain from among you
> Turn hither with welfare.

At the conclusion of the kava the cooked food was distributed among the crowd, but the meal was a very perfunctory one, and a number of people did not eat at all. The object of the breadfruit was not to satisfy the hunger of the people, but to enable offerings to be made to the deities, after which the people quickly packed up their share of the provender and went off to their homes for a family meal.

The principal ritual formulae for this day's events have been given above, but one addition may be made here. According to Pa Ratia, the carrier of the stone also may recite his own set of phrases to invoke formally the co-operation of the chief. As he takes the stone to be washed he may murmur to himself:

> Recite hither Pa Kafika to the deity who will be washed
> on this morning.
> Wash for welfare
> And push down the skies
> To stand calm;
> And excrete on to the reef edge
> That a marine creature may climb here
> For the land.

But I do not know if this formula was in general use.

The carpeting of Takarito marked the end of the long series of rites which had engaged the interest of the whole island for weeks on end, and demanded assiduous attention and constant labour, especially on the part of the men of rank. Now at last the Ariki Kafika had a breathing space, and the land could revert to its ordinary state, untrammelled by taboos and the daily performance of sacred ceremonies. One significant feature, in fact, was that almost immediately afterwards a period of intensive dancing began, with competitive festivals, held during the day, instead of at night, as ordinary dancing was. This was a kind of exoteric prolongation of the recreational aspect of the Work of the Gods.

Postscript

The rites of Takarito had been abandoned by the time of my return to Tikopia in 1952, after alleged interference by mission teachers, and Christian protests against the *aru*. A comment was offered by the Ariki Taumako in 1952 on the effects of this abandonment. He said 'It's not good, their going and laying hands on it (the sacred stone symbol of the god). Now after they have thrown it away the fruits of Rotoaia and the fish are no longer good. Formerly shoals of fish rose regularly in Faea; after they threw it away the fish come sparsely.'

Even among some Christians there was still a firm belief in the power of the Atua i Takarito. For further details of the ideological struggle between Christian and pagan on this point see my 'Plasticity of Myth in Tikopia', and other comments in *Tikopia Ritual and Belief*.

.   .   .   .   .

I have now completed the account of the Work of the Monsoon season, which represents one-half of the Work of the Gods. The chapters which follow deal with the Work of the Trade-Wind season, which, however, can be covered much more briefly, though the time the rites occupy is much the same.

The interval between the Work of the Monsoon and that of the Trade-Wind, a period of roughly five months, is not without seasonal rites. Apart from the operations in connection with the yam, described in Chapter 4, ritual is performed by the Ariki Taumako for taro planting and harvest, and by the Ariki Fangarere in connection with a breadfruit crop. The extraction of sago, again, in September and February, has its own system of rites.[1] But none of these belong to the cycle of the Work of the Gods and the Ariki Kafika takes no part in the taro or breadfruit ritual.

The beginning of the Work of the Trade-Wind is determined in the same way as that of the Monsoon, by a consideration of the position of stars and the wind, the condition of the yam and other vegetation, and a clinching pronouncement by a spirit medium. In 1929 the programme began in the middle of June. The first rite was the Throwing of the Firestick, but the rest of the programme, especially for temples and canoes, followed a somewhat different order than in the monsoon season. The precise order of events is given in Chapter 1. It is not necessary to give here an account of the complete series of rites I witnessed in the Trade-Wind season, since they followed so closely those of the Monsoon, and differences in detail have already been noted in earlier chapters. But two important series of rites which are not performed in the monsoon season, the 'work' of Somosomo and Fiora, and the ritual extraction of turmeric, remain to be described.

[1] Some details of sago production have been given in my *Primitive Polynesian Economy*, 1939, pp. 135, 288–9; 'Economics and Ritual in Sago Extraction in Tikopia', Mankind 1950, pp. 131–42 (reprinted in *Tikopia Ritual and Belief*).

The Work of
Somosomo and Fiora

The rites of Somosomo and Fiora are composed of a series of incidents which, though in no way spectacular to a casual witness, are yet of the deepest religious interest to the Tikopia. In each case the ritual centres around a house site in an open glade, near the lake, the central feature being the re-carpeting of the site with fresh coconut matting. One cardinal distinction exists, however, between the work of Somosomo and Fiora and that of the temples in Uta – the latter are celebrated twice a year, in both the monsoon and the trade-wind seasons, the former in the trade-wind alone.

In this chapter the work of Somosomo will be described first; that of Fiora really comes prior to it in the chronological order of events, but in the absence of the Ariki Tafua from the sacred cycle its rites have fallen into abeyance in the last decade. The ritual of Somosomo is therefore recorded in full detail, as the result of my personal observations, while that of Fiora, which is very similar, is given as a supplement from description by my informants.

A. THE WORK OF SOMOSOMO

The glade of Somosomo is a picturesque spot on the north shore of the lake, beneath the lofty cliffs leading up to Reani. It is a grass-grown space, less than fifty yards square, traversed by the main path along the Te Roro shore, bounded on three sides by a wall of vegetation and by the lake waters on the other. Inland stands a *puka* tree, its broad leaves giving shade to the participants in the ritual in the noonday heat.

Like many of the other important religious rites in Tikopia

Somosomo[1] is primarily associated with the Atua i Kafika. The orchard inland, which bears the same name, was originally his, near by are the pools at which he instituted the first turmeric-making in the land, and the glade itself is his Marae, where in ancient times rites were performed by him. This is the traditional basis for the present fact that the rites of Somosomo are peculiarly those of the Ariki Kafika and no other chief except the Ariki Fangarere attends them or has any share therein. During the time of the work of Somosomo, indeed, the greater part of the people, including the chiefs of Tafua and Taumako, carry on their ordinary tasks; the Ariki Kafika is left to carry out his rites, and incidentally to seek *manu* for the land.

Originally in the glade there stood a small house, the prototype of which was said to have been built by the Atua himself, and which was annually repaired. This was swept away in the great storm with its accompanying tidal wave which struck the island about 1918, and now the space stands bare. It is the re-carpeting of this site, irrespective of whether there is a roof over it or not, that forms the crux of the ritual.

Here again is another example of special privilege in religious affairs; for of the people of rank who represent the clan of Kafika it is only the Ariki himself, and the elders of Tavi, Rarovi and Porima who are entitled to take part in the work, with the Ariki Fangarere, who as already explained is considered as bound to the Ariki Kafika by peculiarly intimate ties. The Kafika elders of Raropuka and Marinoa are not represented on this occasion. 'They have no mats', it is said. Such privileges are highly regarded. The elder of Tavi, for instance, is very proud of the fact that his mat is one of primary importance, taking precedence over that of Pa Rarovi, who is ordinarily his superior in rank. And the latter plumes himself on the kava formula which he is entitled to recite, which is in addition to that of the Ariki Kafika. In public, each participant is punctilious in recognition of the others, but in private discussion every man tends to exalt his own privileges and depreciate those of his fellow office-holders. Thus I was assured by Pa Rangimaseke, heir of the elder of Tavi, that his 'father' held pride of place among the elders at Somosomo, and that the kava

---

[1] The name Somosomo is given by leading men in Kafika as that of one of the traditional island homes of their people. It is found today as a place name in eastern Fiji. See also *History and Traditions of Tikopia*, 1961, pp. 61, 66, etc.

of Pa Rarovi was very short and unimportant in comparison. He described it as merely introductory to that of the Ariki Kafika. 'Pa Rarovi goes, goes only to announce, announce the kava to the gods. His kava is not long. He goes simply to confirm it to the assembled elders.' Actually, as the formula given me by Pa Rarovi and my own observation on the spot showed, it was a long and weighty invocation. This also was the comment on it of the Ariki Kafika who, in his pre-eminence, is careful to hold the scales even in regard to the relative importance of his elders. It must be noted that the attitude of these men towards each other is not one of struggle for position. This is already fixed for them by their traditional obligations; it is the maintenance of their personal prestige in office and the dignity of their 'house' in their own eyes and in those of the observer that is involved.

INITIAL WORK

The work of Somosomo began on the last day of the re-carpeting of Kafika temple in the trade-wind season. After the final kava was made and the people dispersed some of them went and cut coconut fronds. By a prolepsis in expression it was said that they 'have gone to cut mats in the crest of the coconut' or they 'have gone to slice mats', since the fronds were to be used for this purpose. Members of four kinship groups only took part – Kafika, Tavi, Rarovi and Fangarere. They did not take the material all from one spot, but went through the orchards, selecting a few fronds here and there, some in Uta, some in Te Roro. 'They go slicing walking', it was said. The fronds were not carried to Somosomo on this first day but were set down at a spot on the lake shore in Te Roro known as Matorotoro. Here was *te paenga*, a heap of stone slabs with one standing upright in their midst, resembling the Pae Marae in Uta, and with kindred name and associations. Matorotoro was in myth the residence of the *atua*, Tangatakatoa, 'All men', who appropriated a girl from Tafua to be his wife and thus began a line of deities. Later it was under the control of the ill-fated Nga Ravenga folk, the standing stone marking the place where some of their men were killed. The stone slabs are important apart from the work of Somosomo; they are used as seats by the chiefs who paddle over there from Uta on those occasions when the *Purunga kava* ritual follows the *Tao-matangi* (see Chapter 9).

The coconut fronds were left at Matorotoro all night, while the people engaged in the ceremony went back to Uta to sleep.

The next morning the work began. The first procedure was to clear the Marae of grass and weeds, as at Uta and Takarito. The men assembled at the spot in the early morning, theoretically before sunrise, but actually later, the main point being that the sun had not appeared over the shoulder of the mountain, or his rays struck the glade, before the ceremony began. The working group was small, comprising the Ariki Kafika, Pa Tavi, Pa Rarovi, Pa Torokinga (whose house stood just inland and was used as a basis of food preparations) and a few other assistants. Women might also help on this occasion, though this was not strictly their sphere. The Ariki prepared himself with new necklets and cincture, and called out 'The assembly of elders there! Stand up!' They rose, spread out round the edges of the Marae, and crouched down. The Ariki, standing alone, repeated a formula – which I recorded at the time.

> Satinamo, Pa Tavi, Pa Torokinga,
> Your group of elders there,
> Confirm me in the clearing of the Marae of Pu ma
> Which will be cleared on this morning.
> Clear for welfare
> And be brushed away epidemic disease from the crown
>   of the land.
> *Marie!*

All then began tearing up the grass and weeds with their hands, the chief working with the rest. The invocation was made in the name of Pu ma, since though the Marae is under the control of the Atua i Kafika, they are his deities and are therefore interested in it.

In the midst of the clearing a party of women and children arrived from Uta bearing the sleeping mats and household gear of the chief, who stayed here during the four days in which the ritual was in progress. In former times he used to sleep in Somosomo itself, the house which stood in the Marae, but since its loss in the hurricane he sleeps with his family in Maraetoto, the dwelling of Pa Torokinga inland.

After the glade had been cleared – the centre portion only was laid bare – the men sat down and chewed betel in and around the canoe shed which stood at its eastern end, while some of the young people set the oven going at the dwelling-house. Meanwhile the women of the group went off to Matorotoro to fetch the coconut fronds laid there the afternoon before. Returning, they began to plait the mats which were the principal ritual objects of the day. Here the regulation of the *tapu* came into force.

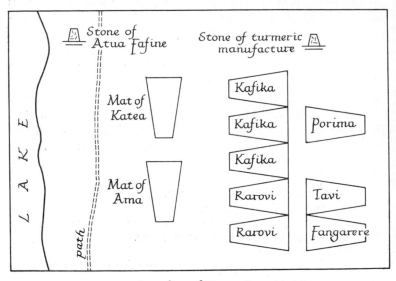

FIG. 13. Spreading of Mats at Somosomo

A brief reference to the arrangement of the Marae may be given here, as shown in Fig. 13. Two stones were standing in the glade, a small one beside the path, and a broad slab set at an angle in the ground, further inland. The former was the representative of the Atua Fafine, the Female Deity, the latter was the mark of an ancient turmeric-making enclosure, said to be that of the Atua i Kafika. Both of these were sacred to some extent. The space at the lake side of the temple site, near the path, was known as Muafare – the Fore-house – and was of the greatest ritual importance. Another spatial distinction was made between that portion of the Marae which lay towards Uta and the stone of the Female Deity, and that which lay towards Tai, the coast, and more immediately, the canoe shed at the eastern end. The one was known as Katea, the other Ama. The use of these words is curious, since they are taken from canoe terminology. Katea is starboard, the side free from the outrigger, Ama is port, the side to which the outrigger is attached. No reason for the application of these terms to the Marae was given, save that they were first introduced by the Atua i Kafika who attached them also to his turmeric-making. As one stands in Somosomo and faces towards Uta, Katea and Ama correspond with right and left, and it is possible that the idea expressed is of this kind. Whatever be the origin of the figurative sense of these terms here, however, it is certain that their use gives a much greater esoteric significance to the spatial division than the mere 'right' and 'left' would do, for which the Tikopia have ordinary words.

The plaiting of the sacred mats was a rite of importance. The women who sat down to plait were supposed to do so in Ama, though they sometimes placed themselves further forward. Moreover they had to turn their backs to the sea coast, not to the lake. The reason for this was that by following the latter course they would be showing disrespect to the sacred district of Uta which lay on the further shore. This is a point on which the elders in charge were insistent. In my presence Pa Rarovi called out to the women as they were standing up to prepare their leaf, 'Your backs, do not turn them to Uta', as a warning. When the actual plaiting began the taboo of silence was imposed: the women might not speak to each other, nor the men to them. This rule was not absolute – one woman asked another about a technical detail of the plaiting, for instance, and when a light shower of rain came on the elders called out to the women to go on working. But this latter was due again to the sacredness of the task: it could not be laid down because of mere weather conditions. All ordinary conversation, however, was barred. Nor might the workers be approached by anyone else. A boy, grandson of the chief, when about to cross the Marae, was told to go inland, by the hedge, and not to go near the women. The Marae as a whole was in fact taboo during the progress of the 'Work' there. During the clearing operations a lad came along the path carrying a food bowl and taro-grater. He was at once stopped and rebuked for not proceeding by an alternative route which ran some hundred yards or more inland and avoided the glade altogether. On his protestations of ignorance, however, and after a good talking to by the older men, he was at last allowed to go past. The taboo extended

also to all details of the sacred work. Thus the women on their
return with the coconut fronds from Matorotoro expressed
their indignation at another, not a participant, who had bathed
that morning near the spot where the fronds lay. 'No one should
go near when the Work is in progress', was the comment passed.

As is customary in Tikopia ritual of this type, where several
different groups are concerned, a definite precedence was observed. For the plaiting of the mats each woman had her place, the
seating order being as follows: at the head of the row, nearest to
the stone of the Atua Fafine, sat the woman of the 'house' of
Kafika; next her was the woman of Rarovi, then the women of
Tavi, of Fangarere, and lastly, in former days, of Porima. No
representative from this last group attended this ceremony in 1929,
however, their sacred mat having been abandoned some years
before. Occasionally more than one woman takes part from
Kafika, as several mats have to be made. These other women sit
always in rear of the principal plaiters. The wife of the head of
the group, from her status as the senior married woman, is usually
selected to fill the office. Sometimes the wife of the eldest son is
given the task, which is looked upon as a duty to be efficiently
performed rather than an honour. When I was present the wife of
the heir of the Ariki Kafika was summoned from her work in the
cookhouse to come and assist in the plaiting but refused. Her unmarried sister-in-law then sent for her to come, with the message
that she herself would attend to the oven. This was obeyed, with
not too good a grace. Each woman plaited two mats, and the
work was competitive in the matter of speed.

While the women worked the chief and elders sat in the canoe
shed – formerly in the temple itself – chewing betel and talking,
on this occasion about fishing. As each mat was finished it was
laid face downwards near the path in Muafare. The mats were
spoken of collectively as 'mats of the forefront' (tapakau o mua), or
'mats of the offering of the forefront' (tapakau a inaki o mua). The
term mua is used here not so much spatially as signifying ritual importance of position. The word inaki was explained to me as
'mats spread out to the deities', the idea being the same as in the
're-carpeting' of Kafika, Nukuora and other temples.

Meanwhile food was cooking in the house inland. It was spoken
of as 'the oven of mats', since its object was to provide food for
the kava rite associated with the laying of the mats in their final

position. The uncovering of the oven thus gave the signal for the rite to begin.

The mats were spread out one by one on the temple site, in a reverent manner, the bearer squatting down in respect while he arranged them in position. The order and orientation of the mats was a point of definite ritual significance, the broad end, the 'head', being turned towards the centre of the temple. The arrangement was as shown in Fig. 13.

The leading position was occupied by the mats of the Ariki Kafika, which were in Katea. The mats of Porima formerly also shared with him in this division, though they were of less importance, as shown by being on the inland side. In Ama were the mats of Rarovi on the lake side, and of Tavi and Fangarere on the other. In addition to all these which occupied the temple site were two mats of even greater sacredness, known as the *Tapakau o Katea* and *Tapakau o Ama*, each being laid in the respective division in Muafare, as shown in the plan. The first was the mat of the Ariki Kafika, the second that of Pa Tavi, and it was the privilege of having this special mat outside the ordinary *inaki* which gave this latter elder his importance in the Somosomo 'Work'. These two mats were distinguished from the others of the ritual by the fact that they, instead of being left open continually throughout the day, were kept folded except during the kava ceremonies. In importance they may be compared with the mats of 'sacred things' in the canoe ritual, the folding of which indicated the conclusion of events. Each group might spread several mats – according to one account Kafika four, Porima, Rarovi and Fangarere two each, and Tavi three. However, I did not see as many as this. The principal mat of Pa Rarovi was known as *te Tapakau o Pouroto*, 'The Mat of Centre Post' – this being the name of his deity.

While the mats were being thus arranged the oven was uncovered and the food when prepared was brought to the Marae for the ceremonies, the 'kava of the mats'.

The kava was made with great formality on this occasion, although so few men were present to take part. Especial attention was paid to the seating of the principal participants, each being on the mat of his own deity. When I was at Somosomo the Ariki Fangarere was absent, while Pa Porima, as already mentioned, had abandoned his mat some years before. With the exception of the

Ariki Kafika, Pa Rarovi was the most important figure there. The ritual of Somosomo was one of the spheres in which his rank was demonstrated; like a chief he had the privilege of repeating a major invocation at the kava. In token of this, like a chief he had a bark-cloth cincture brought him, and girded it round him. The usual procedure of the kava ritual was followed, and the Ariki Kafika repeated a very long formula to the deities for protection and assistance. The libations of the kava then followed. The cup was handed first of all to the Ariki Kafika who poured it after an obeisance, and then to Pa Rarovi and Pa Tavi, returning to the Ariki again when their libations had been offered. As on other occasions, the Ariki Kafika was disturbed at the idea of my photographing his sacred rites. He consented to my camera at Somosomo only on condition that I sat at his back – and not in the Marae proper. Without my camera I was always given a seat among the participants in the rite (cf. Plates 6, 7).

In former days, when the actual house of Somosomo was still standing, the centre post of the building was anointed in a ritual manner as in the case of Kafika or Resiake. This was the task of Pa Rarovi, and preceded the kava offering. Pa Rarovi took his oil and scented leaves and rubbing the post briskly repeated the *kaukau pou* formula (which he made known to me):

> Thou, Ancestor!
> I eat ten times thy excrement
> Turn thou Mapusia to thy post which is being
>   anointed
> Anointed for welfare
> Unfold welfare for thy crown of the land.

The oil bottle used in this rite was kept hung in the house of Pa Rarovi.

More importance than usual attached to the kava of Pa Tavi on this occasion. Not only did he receive several cups, but the first one was given him before Pa Rarovi. In pouring his libations Pa Tavi called first on Tauaroaro, this being a name of the Atua Lasi used at Somosomo – his title to 'Port'.

He said:

> That is your kava Tauaroaro
> I eat ten times your excrement
> Turn to your name in Ama

You are standing in your kava among the chiefs
So turn to your kava in Ama.

The appeal here was to the deity to combine earthly with heavenly
ritual – he attended the kava of the gods; let him do the same for
that of men. This formula and other information about Somosomo was given me by Pa Rangimaseke, heir to Pa Tavi.

The next *atua* to be invoked was Tuna, the eel-god, under the
name of Feseketaki, his title in Tavi. Appeals to Akiti, progenitor
of the family, and to Fakasautanga and Tuarofi, later holders of
the title of elder, followed.

After the kava came the withdrawal to the shade of the *puka*
tree for conversation and chewing betel. Here again was a rule of
taboo. The Ariki Kafika told me that at Somosomo, as during
turmeric-making or at the celebrations of Kafika house, each man
should come equipped with all his betel apparatus – mortar and
pestle, leaf and lime. It is prohibited to take or ask for the gear
of another person owing to the sanctity of these occasions. I saw,
however, that like many other such rules, this was broken un-
ostentatiously, and with impunity.

MARRIAGE GIFTS AND RELIGION

An important feature of the rites of Somosomo (and of Fiora
also) is the presentation of food to the chief of the clan from men
who have married women of the clan during the past year. This
gift is known as the *roi*. The term is 'the name only', since the
food does not consist of the creamed slices of vegetable properly
so designated but of ordinary pudding cooked in the oven overnight, and reinforced by a further supply in the morning. This
subsequent oven is known as 'the second filling of baskets'. At the
first Somosomo celebration following the marriage the gift is of
considerable proportions, and is termed the 'new *roi*'. For the
second and possibly subsequent years the gift is much smaller, and
is called the *peni roi* or 'little *roi*'. Another name for it is the *umu
matasanga*. Thus the question is asked 'Whose is the little *roi* which
has been stood in the fore-house there?' The answer is 'The
matasanga oven of So-and-so.' The amount of food required for
the initial presentation is great – twenty, thirty or forty baskets
may be taken to Somosomo as the gift of one man. Preparations
are begun months in advance, and on the actual day the oven may

be split into two or three, that is several houses may each cook a portion of the food in order that the family may cope with the quantity. In any case, kinsfolk and neighbours come in to assist.

From the oven of the *roi* when opened one basket of food is taken and carried to the house of the wife's parents of the *roi*-maker. No special name is assigned to this gift, which represents their prior share of the *roi* to be carried to their chief. The food is assembled for the Marae in two main sections. The most important is the four large baskets for the principal men at Somosomo – the Ariki Kafika, Pa Rarovi, Pa Tavi and the Ariki Fangarere. The food for these is known as 'the pudding of the baskets'. The other section of the gift consists of a number of smaller baskets each containing two packages. The food in these is much of the same type and is termed simply *te kofu*, the package.

When the gift arrives on the Marae the four huge baskets are arranged in the order of importance indicated above, and the small parcels together in a separate heap. These latter are for the use of the participants in the 'Work' in general.

Some time prior to the Somosomo ritual which I attended a man of the family Nukufetau of Fangarere clan, living in Namo, had married a daughter of Pa Taraoro, also of Fangarere clan, but from a different village, Potu sa Fangarere. As Fangarere and Kafika are for many ritual purposes considered one clan the new husband, Pa Korofatu, and his kin prepared the *roi* and brought it to the Ariki Kafika. The gift consisted of four large baskets of cooked provisions, five bunches of sprouting coconuts and a bunch of bananas, a considerable mass of food. A set of these items was taken also to the Ariki Fangarere in his own house, since he was not present at Somosomo. The food was brought about mid-afternoon, and was carried by women in addition to men. As the bearers advanced into the open space they were preceded by a man holding a bunch of areca nut which he deposited ceremonially on the seating mat of the Ariki Kafika. On his return to his fellows the baskets of food were carried in. The four baskets with such coconut bundles as were stood behind them were, as already explained, for the four principal men present; this is known as *te mori o te anga* – 'the gift from the feast'; the remainder of the food was for division among the other men present.

When families of Tafua or Taumako clan make the gift of the
· *roi* to the Ariki Kafika it is reciprocated by food – of less quantity

– from the midday oven at Somosomo.[1] For this reason the oven-makers keep in mind the possible bringers of *roi* when deciding how much food they will prepare – that is they recall the marriages of Kafika women since the last season's 'Work'. Nowadays the presentation of the *roi* is tending to fall into abeyance among Christians, particularly after the first year of marriage.

When the second trade-wind season comes round again only two large baskets of food are prepared, one for the Ariki Kafika and the other for Pa Rarovi, and these are reciprocated by a single basket as before. The affair may then cease.

But the intricacy of economic arrangements between families connected by marriage, and derivately by the ties of the woman's family to her child, provides for an extension of the gift of the *roi* to a lifelong obligation. It is the custom of a chief on the death of a prominent member of his family to decree, if circumstances allow, that the funeral shall be a *pariki sausau koroa*, wherein gifts of property are made on a much larger scale than usual. Should the child of the woman from the Kafika clan be once included in such a scheme of presentations, then its father would continue year after year to make the gift of the *peni roi* to the Ariki Kafika at Somosomo. 'He does it constantly.' The reverse is also true, since the continual making of the *peni roi* obliges the family of the chief to make the periodic gifts to their 'sacred child'. As the Ariki Tafua pointed out in regard to his own clan 'The foundation of the *tama tapu* lies in the Muafare of Fiora; when the valuables are presented to the sacred child the basis is from Fiora' – that is, from the *roi*.

Again if the husband should go to a mourning ceremony of Kafika, and there be given a mat or bark-cloth sheet in reciprocation for his attendance, then this lays on him a similar obligation. He should present the *roi* season after season at Somosomo. These obligations are not so one-sided as they seem, since on every future occasion of importance a present will be made to the man or to his child in acknowledgment of this seasonal food gift.

One custom which I did not observe may be noted here. I was told by Pa Rangimaseke that from the *peni roi* baskets of food are sent out to the chiefs of Tafua, Taumako and Fangarere. This present is termed 'the companionate path of the gods' (*Te ara fanonga o nga atua*). He explained that the deities known as the

[1] Cf. *Primitive Polynesian Economy*, 1939, p. 321.

Brethren have been collected at the cleansing of the Marae, hence food is sent to their representative the chiefs, 'their presentations to their houses'. The food is not carried to the ordinary dwelling-houses of the chiefs, but to their sacred houses – to Motuapi of Tafua, Raniniu of Taumako, and Rangateatua of Fangarere. There offerings are cast to the respective deities. The food gift is not reciprocated by the chiefs concerned. But I am not sure if this custom should not refer to Fiora rather than to Somosomo, since it appears to be essentially the same as the *fakaariki*, which is performed only from the Marae of Tafua.

A presentation of the *peni roi* of particular interest is that made on behalf of the Ariki Taumako. Between chiefly families, if ancestors of note have been involved in the preliminary obliga-tion, their descendants in subsequent generations take pride in continuing the bond. Taumako remember that the great founder of their clan was the offspring of Te Atafu the Tongan and Mata-pono the daughter of the Ariki Kafika of the day, hence as the fruit of that marriage, each chief of Taumako sends his contribu-tion of food every year to Somosomo. The gift is known as *Te peni roi o Pu*, 'the little *roi* of Pu'. The *Ara o Pu* gift (see Chapter 3) is another item in the set of reciprocal obligations on this same basis.

The *peni roi* of the Ariki Taumako was sent to Somosomo early in the morning, unlike those of ordinary people which arrived in the afternoon. While the sun was still low a canoe came over the water, paddled by two lads, who quietly landed their burden on a mat specially spread out on the *mata paito* side to receive it, and departed as quickly and silently, out of respect to the sacredness of the glade. The gift comprised two small baskets of food, with a stick of kava atop, and formed part of the offering at the first kava rite.

Like so many of the gifts made at the ceremonial season, the *roi* has a religious basis. Its root lies in the deference paid to the Female Deity, the Atua Fafine, of Kafika, under whose watch and ward are the women of the clan. No very clear formulation of the meaning of the gift is made, but it is understood that the per-formance of the kava at Somosomo over the food supplied is a kind of solemnization of the marriage; the union is brought to the notice of the Female Deity, and her sanction assured. As she is responsible to some extent for the creation of children there is perhaps a further point in gaining her favour. A similar institution used to characterize the ceremonies of Fiora, the food gift here being made to the Ariki Tafua by men who had married women of his clan. In this case three large baskets only were prepared – one for the Ariki, one for Pa Saukirima, his chief councillor, and the third for Nau Lasi, by which title his eldest daughter is known. In this case the religious basis of the offering lay in the presentation of it to Pufine i Fiora, the female deity of Tafua. This ritual of Fiora has now been discontinued.

No gifts of *roi* are made in connection with any Taumako temple rites. The Ariki Taumako explained this by saying that according to tradition originally the food present was made for a woman of Taumako and sent to Resiake in Ravenga at the appropriate season. A short time afterwards, however, the woman died. Then the clan, seeing that she was dead, knew that the goddess had claimed her, and resolved to discontinue the custom lest other women die also. Ravenga, in which the Resiake Marae lies, was thought to be bad for the *ora* (life) of women. Hence the *roi* takes place only in Namo – that is, for Somosomo and Fiora.

THE SACRED BASKETS

The next ritual operation on the first day of the Somosomo events was the plaiting of the sacred baskets to be used at a later stage. The work of plaiting had to be done by women of high rank in the clan, one of Kafika representing Katea and one of Tavi representing Ama. Nau Kafika, the wife of the chief, and Nau Vangatau, the sister of Pa Tavi, both elderly, officiated when I was there. Each from deference to her task was clad in a brand-new skirt of bark-cloth. As the sun declined to the crest of the hills overlooking the lake they came on to the Marae, took down the coconut fronds, set up on the inland side of the glade, and began their work, sitting on the *tuaumu* side of the temple. The fronds had previously been stood up in the sun to dry a little. 'Look out a place where it beats down that they may be sunned, stand them up singly', had been the command given. The women proceeded carefully with their work, each intent on producing a creditable basket. As I watched – sitting with the men at a distance – these latter called out to them 'What are you splitting?' The women were observed to be splitting the fronds as they plaited in order to make the work finer. The men wished them to make more speed by using a coarser plait, but they ignored the interruption and went steadily on with their work. This was an instance of disregard of male authority. The men were in charge of the organization of the ceremony as a whole, but the women maintained their independence in their own sphere. Their reputation as plaiters of taste and skill brooked no rough work through haste. The two baskets, oblong in shape and of medium size, were known as *kete roro*, and were named individually and in the same fashion as the principal mats, *Te Kete o Katea* and *Te Kete o Ama*. When completed they were hung up on the bushes on the inland side of the Marae.

As soon as they were finished preparations began for the evening kava, which took place outside the house site, by the lakeside. The two principal mats were now unfolded on the lake side of the house and seating mats for the main participants were spread. In front of each one was set his basket from the *roi* (see Fig. 14).

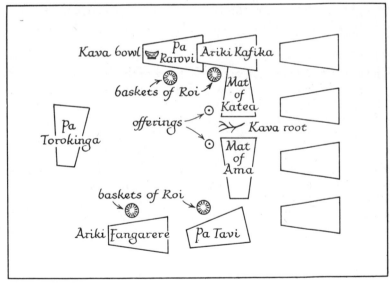

FIG. 14. Evening Kava at Somosomo

The chief and his assistant elders took their seats, the food of the *roi* was distributed, and the portions set out as offerings, one of the baskets of the *peni roi* of Taumako being set before each of the principal mats. The first two cups of kava were poured on to the

Tapakau o Katea and the *Tapakau o Ama* respectively, the one
being announced by the cup-bearer to the Ariki Kafika, the other
to Pa Tavi. Each then recited a short formula to Pu ma, the tutelary deities of Muafare. The phraseology was simple. That of Pa
Tavi, for example, was:

> That is the kava of you two Pu ma E!
> And you Tauaroaro, that is your kava also.

The third cup was handed to the Ariki Kafika, and the fourth to
Pa Tavi, who poured it with the remark

> That is your kava Feseketai
> That is your kava The Fear-creating Chief (i.e. the
> Atua i Kafika).

Pa Tavi, owing to his status as representative of Ama, received his
cup before Pa Rarovi on these occasions, contrary to the normal
usage of the kava. Two more cups were then presented to the
Ariki and to Pa Tavi. The seventh cup was presented to Pa Rarovi,
the eighth to the Ariki Fangarere, the ninth to Pa Porima, and
others followed to the Ariki Kafika and Pa Torokinga for their
usual libations which, with food offerings, concluded the kava for
the day.

A little piece of ritual which took place in the evening was the
setting up of a bunch of raw bananas at a stone at one end of the
Somosomo house site. The stone was a sacred one, but its importance was traditional only – 'It is not known if it be the stone
of a deity of long ago, or simply a stone which has been made
tapu – it is Tikopia!' The custom of the island was to have such
things – such was the attitude. The purpose of the bunch of
bananas was to furnish the food for the early morning kava of the
next day, and the placing of it against the stone, to remain there
through the night, was a rite of sacralization. It was similar to
that performed for Marae in Uta.

This custom was observed on three successive nights, the bunch
being known in each case by the name of the principal provider
of the next day's food – as 'the bananas of sa Kafika', etc.

THE FISHING OF SA RUNGA

That same night saw a curious event. One of the features of the
Somosomo ritual was the provision of fish for the ovens, by net-
ting by torchlight on the reef. I give the following description

from accounts of informants only, as I did not attend the fishing itself. The symmetry of the ritual was preserved even here – two nets were used, the Net of Starboard and the Net of Port – *te Kupenga o Katea* and *te Kupenga o Ama* – the former belonging to the Ariki Kafika and the latter to Pa Tavi. The fish were netted in the usual way.

Then came the symbolism so characteristic of the Tikopia religion, the fiction that certain persons were for the time being deities in the flesh. The two baskets made during the afternoon were held to be baskets of Pufine ma, those two dread sisters who under various names find place in the kava list of nearly every family of note. When darkness fell the baskets were taken by two women, who went down to the beach and there personified the goddesses, receiving the tribute that was their due from the fisher-folk.

They have become Pufine ma there who have gone with their baskets.

The fishing parties started from the bluff of Nuaraki at the northern end of the Namo beach, worked down round Tua Te Koro to Te Rano and thence down the reef to Sukumarae, the village of the Ariki Kafika, a distance of more than a mile. Both men and women took part in the drive, which was known as Sa Runga, a name applied also to spirit folk of the mountain, of fairy type. The two women with the baskets walked in front, and it was a most strict taboo that no-one should hold any conversation with them. As a fish was caught in the net it was taken out and put without a word in the basket on the back of one of the women. Fish from the Net of Katea were put in the Basket of Katea, and similarly with Ama. A fish was put into the Basket of Katea first. As the fishing party came up from the reef on to the beach at Sukumarae a man ran ahead inshore, got a thatch door, and laid it at the tide mark. After the baskets had been put down on this the taboo was laid aside, and people spoke to the two women, whose identity with the female deities was momentarily lost. The baskets were emptied on to the thatch door, and the fish gutted. The catch numbered 40 on the first night in 1929. They were put back again into the receptacles and shouldered again by the women, when the taboo once more came into force, and silence fell upon them. After the gutting of the fish the people dispersed, scattering to either side to give the women free passage. These went ahead again, but returned along the beach. The fisherfolk, falling in behind them in a body, raised a song in honour of the Atua i Kafika, under whose charge the Marae of Somosomo and its ceremonies lay. The first song chanted was a dirge beginning

Mapusia! Mapusia!
Fly on your path . . .

This was the same dirge as rendered in Marae on the day of sa Kafika during the *Taomatangi*. Other dirges of the same character followed.

When the party arrived opposite Raniniu, the sacred house of the Ariki Taumako, on the return journey, the singing was dropped. But as they came abreast of Faretapu another dirge was raised. The reason for the cessation of the song was that the canoe yard of Maraniniu was under control of the Taumako god Pusi, who would resent encroachment of this type by strangers in praise of another god. When the party arrived at Asanga a dirge to Pu, the Taumako ancestor, the fruit of the Kafika woman, was raised. This was a *sore* composed by Tarotu, late Ariki Kafika, in praise of the generosity of the great chief, continued through his descendants, in making ritual food gifts to Kafika. I did not record the first stanza of this song; the second runs

His thought also
Thy path my food
Separated from Taumako.

This refers to *Te Ara o Pu*, sent as described in Chapter 3. Singing as they walked, the people went along the beach, past the cliff face of Te Koro, past the hamlets of Namo, striking up one dirge after another until they arrived back at Te Roro. The two women went on and hung up the baskets in their original position at Somosomo, while the remainder of the party stayed at Maorere, the canoe-landing of the Ariki Taumako nearer the sea. There they sang for some time until they felt sleepy, when they retired to their homes. While all this fishing and singing was taking place, in the dead of night, the people of other clans who had no immediate connection with Kafika remained inside in their houses.

THE DAY OF PA RAROVI

The next morning was the day of Pa Rarovi, the time when he took charge of the ceremonies and in particular had the responsibility of providing the food supplies. This, however, came later. The first item before the morning kava was the offering of the fish caught in the Sa Runga of the previous night. When the people woke in the morning the baskets of fish were taken down and stood side by side on the principal mats, which were now opened after lying folded through the night. The Ariki Kafika then came and 'announced' the fish to the gods. The baskets were then separated and one put at the head of each of the two chief mats. Pa Tavi then went and 'announced' his own basket – the Basket of Port, which had been laid on the Mat of Port. He grasped the end of the basket and said:

> There are fish, Pu ma E!
> Consider fish of Sa Runga brought hither
> For the making of your kava.

The fish were then cooked. This operation was performed very early, as the kava itself took place at sunrise.

The oven in which the banana bunch and a little other food was cooked was prepared while the land was still dark. Hence it was known as 'the night oven'. Owing to the sacred nature of this early kava, and the danger incurred from the wrath of the gods in allowing it to be tardy, great care was taken to see that the oven was begun in time. The working party slept in Maraetoto near by – formerly in the Somosomo temple itself – and one man was deputed to wake the others. The sign by which he went was the Pleiades. When this constellation appears over the crest of Tapukuru, a cliff which stands above the lake shore, then the oven should be lit. By the time that the land is properly light, but before the sun has risen, the oven should be uncovered. Sometimes it happens that the watcher sleeps on, and on waking is scolded by the others. I was told how in the time of Tarotu, the former Ariki Kafika, the man assigned slept late, and Nau Kafika, the chief's wife, went and prepared the oven alone. When the rest of the party awoke and berated the laggard, the oven was already covered and the food cooking.

The banana bunch should be cooked stem and all, an unusual proceeding, and one undoubtedly followed in order to emphasize the ritual character of the food. But in 1929 no 'night oven', strictly so called, was made, since there were no bananas fit for cooking. The early preparation of an oven, however, was still necessary, to heat food for the later offerings.

The morning kava now took place. In preparation for this the fish when cooked had been divided into two portions, and one was set on each of the principal mats again. A detail of interest at this kava rite was the position of the kava stem itself, which after the ceremony of the evening before was 'stood up' – a ritual phrase – by being inclined against a forked stick. Now it was taken down and laid at the head of the chief mat, pointing to Pouroto, the middle of the house. On this occasion Pa Rarovi took pride of place. His function it was to recite the formula of invocation to the gods. A necklet of creamy young coconut fronds indicated his sacerdotal task. His recital was very long, and brought in a great number of his own family gods in addition to the names of deities shared by the Ariki Kafika and other elders. The formula he used is given below in translation.

(Like practically every kava formula quoted, this was obtained by me from the actual user, corroborated in substance from other informants, and checked over again from the original giver.)

> Thou Tinamo, thou Pa Fangarere, thou Pae Tavi,
> You group of elders there, countenance me in the kava.
> The presentation of the kava is complete.
> The kava of the ancestors which I pulled up,
> Let it be pulled for welfare.
>
> That is thy kava Mapusia!
> I eat ten times thy excrement
> Turn to the kava
> Stand firmly on thy crown of the land
> Ward off epidemic disease from thy crown of the land.
> Unfold welfare.
>
> The kava of you two, the Chiefs,
> Stand firm you two in your Kafika
> With the Atua i Kafika on your crown of the land
> Turn to your work.
> Be you firm in your work
> That a calm may fall.

That is thy kava Tauaroaro
I eat ten times thy excrement
Blow gently thy eye of the wind
Turn hither to the works of thy cleansed son.

That is thy kava Rakiteua
Turn to the kava
Agree equally you Brethren to the works of your cleansed
    son.

That is thy kava Sakurafiti
I eat ten times thy excrement
Turn thou to the works of thy cleansed son
Agree equally you Brethren
That a calm may fall.
The presentation of the kava is complete.

That is thy kava Sekeitevai
This is thy kava Tupuapou
That is thy kava Pu Fafine
The presentation of the kava again is complete.

That is thy kava Resa
I eat ten times thy excrement
Preserve thou firmly thy seating mat.

That is thy kava Taukiriti
I eat ten times thy excrement
Preserve firmly thy seating mat
Look upon thy seating mat
The kava has been made stupidly
But let it be confirmed by thee.

That is thy kava Pu Kefu
That is your kava the Bearers of the Necklet
I eat ten times your excrement
Preserve you firmly your seating mat.

This is thy kava Father!
Collect thou the gods
To watch over the kava which is being made stupidly
And let it be confirmed by thee.

That is thy kava Ruakimata
I eat ten times your excrement
The Anuta.
Preserve firmly your fruits of kin.

Evil things for the kava
Lay away at the sun which sets there
Marie!

This invocation is one of the chief formulae in the possession of
Pa Rarovi; he described it as his 'standing kava'. The privilege of
reciting it at Somosomo, particularly prior to the recital of the
Ariki Kafika, is both a token and an enhancement of his social
status as the elder next in rank to the chiefs. It is worthy of note
that in confirmation of the invocation of Pa Rarovi the Ariki
Kafika joined with the other elders in uttering the '*Kona! Kona!*'
of approval, thus putting himself in the position of an assistant
to one of his own dependants.

The general purport of this invocation will be clear from
analyses of others already given. A few expressions only need
comment. 'Cleansed son' refers to the belief that spirits of the
dead are cleansed before their entry to the spirit world, with
deities as sponsors; in this case the gods of the Brethren acted in
this capacity for the Atua i Kafika. 'The seating mat' is the elder
of Rarovi himself, on whom the gods rest when they attend the
kava. And the statement that the kava is being 'made stupidly'
involves the idea that the human performer of it may err, but
through the watchfulness of his particular tutelary deity and
immediate ancestor any mistakes can be corrected and its efficacy
assured. The appeal to 'The Anuta' to preserve their 'fruits of
kin' is to the gods of that island, since the mother of Pa Rarovi
came from there.

Following the recital of Pa Rarovi came that of the Ariki
Kafika, which was complementary to it, omitting the introduction. This morning kava, like that of the evening before, took
place outside the house site. It had to be performed before sunrise. The reason given was that in this way the Marae was not
trodden by passers-by prior to the rite, which would be offensive
to the gods and a contamination of the kava.

The main part of the ritual of Somosomo consisted of a series
of kava performances – morning, noon and evening – performed

on three successive days, on each day one of the principal participants being responsible for the food supply, the offering of which
was made at the midday celebration. The food offering was
termed the *fakaoatea* (see Canoe rites, etc.) and each day was
named after the principal food providers. Thus the first was the
'*fakaoatea Pa Rarovi*', the second the '*fakaoatea sa Kafika*' and the
third (the last full day) the '*fakaoatea sa Tavi*'. Each day, however,
the various groups brought contributions to the supplies of the
principal food provider. Moreover, whatever be the type and
quantity of food provided by the principal man on the first day,
it had also to be provided by the others on the subsequent
occasions.

The help of people of other clans might be enlisted to enable the
requisite food supplies to be obtained. An instance of this showed
how on such occasions the paramount position of the chief over-
rode ordinary family custom. The net of Pa Motuata, son of Pa
Vangatau, who had married the sister of Pa Tavi, was borrowed
by the Ariki Kafika for the 'Work' of Somosomo and used on
the lake by a son of the Ariki and a son of Pa Motuata. The result
of their labours was seven fish, which as in the normal course of
events they carried to Pa Vangatau, the head of the net-owner's
family, to 'announce' to the family net-god. The old man
scolded them for not taking the fish straight to the Ariki. He
pointed out that when a net was borrowed by a chief for any
sacred rites the catch should be taken directly to him, not brought
to the owner to handle, since the ritual and *tapu* of the chief were
paramount, no matter of what clan.

Technically the term *fakaoatea* was applied only to the bowl of
pudding carried to the Marae from which the offerings to the gods
are set out. The large basket of mixed food which accompanies it
was the specific offering to the Somosomo temple and was known
as the *tua popora*, so called because the basket was turned inside
out (*ki tua*) to hold the package. At the *fakaoatea* of Pa Rarovi
this basket was presented to the Ariki Kafika; at the *fakaoatea*
of the Ariki on the following day the compliment was returned.

The midday oven was known as 'the great oven'. From it not
only were the large baskets filled, but also the private baskets of
the elders, which were then hung up to provide the food for the
evening ritual. These were later replaced by food baskets from

their private houses from which they ate in the night if so inclined. The kava was made to the *fakaoatea* in the usual way. This time Pa Rarovi did not recite any invocation.

The remainder of the day was spent by the chief and his elders in sitting outside the canoe shed, yarning and rolling fish lines. In the evening the kava was again performed, but no ritual fish drive took place. People might arrange an excursion if they so wished, but tradition did not require it. A banana bunch, however, was again set up.

The next day was the *fakaoatea* of the Ariki Kafika, which followed the same procedure as that of Pa Rarovi. When the oven was opened the chief was invited to come and attend. As the bowl of pudding was being pounded it was 'announced' to him.

The *fakaoatea* of sa Tavi on the following day followed almost the same order of events. A particular feature of this day was the display of a bunch of areca nut, which is associated with Tavi. The areca may be 'set up' on other days also, but for Tavi it is a special obligation and privilege.

Part of this afternoon also was spent in collecting taro from all the cultivations of Te Roro to make a special *roi* for the final kava of the following morning. On this evening too the ritual fishing drive, the Sa Runga, was again put into operation. Of the songs chanted by the returning fisherfolk one was especially appropriate to the occasion. This was a dirge made to the Atua i Kafika by the former chief of the clan, Tarotu, known also as Singakitetai. It describes the descent of the deity from the heavens, his path veiled in mist, his alighting on Reani, after the fashion of gods, who come down to earth on this peak and with a bound land on their respective temples for the 'Work' undertaken there. The Atua i Kafika is in particular notice since at the time of the ceremonial season his people hear the thunder of his trailing staff in the heavens. The implication of the song is that he is desired to attend each of the spheres of interest of his worshippers – to spring to Uta, then finished there, to spring to the rites of the sacred canoe Tafurufuru in the canoe yard, then again to go out to the sea and bring in his shark after the ceremonies; and, as always, to bring fine weather. The reference to 'the ridge pole of Kafika' is to Reani, for which the former is an old poetic expression.

Translation: Ancestor! glance from side to side on your way
Your mist has veiled.
Hasten down, stand on Reani;
Clear up the crown of the land;
Make clear the ridge pole of Kafika to the skies.

We keep listening to your work.
Let there be calm,
Calm on your crown of the land.

Hasten to Uta;
Hasten down to your Tafurufuru,
Placed in the sea.

The fish from the Sa Runga were again brought in, 'announced' to the gods and then hung up in their baskets on a branch of a little tree by the lakeside.[1]

The last day of the 'Work' saw the folk awakened at dawn by one of their number for the performance of the early morning kava. Some got up at once and went down to the lake to bathe in the half-light, others, including the Ariki, lay sleepily in their bark-cloth blankets for a while, since the air was still fresh and cool to a bare skin. The women and youths went and uncovered the *roi* in the oven and carried it over for the ceremony, the women in particular being careful not to enter the Marae. The ritual took place as before, except that it was made to the *roi* instead of to the food of the 'night oven' and that an orange cloth was spread by the Ariki Kafika to his premier deity before the recital of the formula began. In a few minutes the last offerings had been cast, and the 'Work' of Somosomo was over for another year.

The men returned to the house to gather up their few belongings, and the girls and women rolled up the bedding ready to be carried home. After dispersing from Somosomo the preparations for the *nuanga*, the turmeric manufacture, began, and people went off to cut down palm stems to repair their aqueducts so as to provide an effective water supply. Attention was now concentrated on the turmeric, one of the most absorbing interests of the people at this season.

___

[1] See *Primitive Polynesian Economy*, 1939, p. 287, for a breach of this custom.

B. THE WORK OF FIORA

In point of time the ritual of Fiora actually preceded that of Somosomo, but for convenience the latter has been dealt with first. The general features of the Fiora ceremonies are similar to those already described for the other Marae – the plaiting of sacred mats, the allocation of days to certain principal 'houses' and the provision of food gifts from men who have married women of the clan. As Somosomo belongs to Kafika, so does Fiora belong to Tafua. The site of the ritual is a Marae in Namo, just above the beach, on the narrow strip of sand which divides the lake from the ocean. Now, owing to the defection of the Ariki Tafua, the seasonal rites are no longer celebrated there and the place is overgrown with bushes.

Fiora, like Somosomo, derived its sacredness from a tutelary deity, but in this case attention was concentrated on a female, not a male *atua*. Known under a variety of names, but most commonly as Nau Fiora, she is a being of unpleasant characteristics, who is believed in and feared throughout Tikopia, even by the chief and clan who have abandoned her ceremonies. Most of my information on the Fiora ritual was obtained from the Ariki Tafua in whose kava lists she plays an important part.

A reference to some of the beliefs connected with Nau Fiora will indicate the reasons for the respect in which she is held, and the importance of the 'Work' of Fiora in former days.

The origin of the ceremonies of Fiora lies in the marriage of Feke, the personified form of the octopus, who is also identified with the sun, to Faretapatapa, known as Pufine i Fiora, Nau Fiora, or Pufine Laui. In those days the sacred rites were made in Resiake, which had the primacy as between Taumako and Tafua. The Ariki Tafua said:

'As the "Work" was made first in Resiake there, and carried on, then Faretapatapa died. She caused herself to die, and indeed she was objecting that her "Work" might be carried to be performed in Matafenua (i.e. Namo). Thereupon it was lifted up: and being lifted up, thereupon she came back to life to perform the "Work". Hence the Tafua work comes first, and in the rear comes the work of sa Taumako.' This is an origin tale in which clan pride is evident; a different interpretation was given by the chief of Taumako in accounting for the absence of the presentation of *roi* at Resiake. But the desire of the goddess to attract the ritual to her own house and thereby give it prestige is a trait seen in the characters assigned to other *atua* of Tikopia.

It was said that Nau Fiora came originally from Tonga; the Ariki Tafua believed that he had confirmed the truth of this since years ago he found by comparing notes with castaways from Fiji or an adjacent group that a similar female deity was known there.

A peculiarity of Nau Fiora is that unlike other *atua* her body is white in colour. She is also very ferocious. In the evening when the sun was low she used to walk, in the nights of the trade-wind, at the time when her ceremonies were being performed, along the sand strip of Namo. Namo was not slept in on those occasions; everyone went to Te Roro to spend the night. Only in Potu i Akitunu, on the other side of the lake exit, were people left. If by chance a man did dare to stay the night in his house he took all the dirty floor-mats he could find and securely blocked the doorways, and then spreading a good new mat in the centre of the building, slept on that. The deity on her perambulations would smell only the reek of earth from within, and would pass on thinking the building untenanted. If she smelt a man she would break in, seize him, and carry him off to Fiora, there to devour him, in company with her following of spirit maidens. For, like a chieftainess, having instituted her ceremonies at Fiora, she provided herself with an attendant band, who carried out her wishes. That this was no mere ancient tale was emphasized to me by the chief. He told me of a happening in recent times, when a man, Fakaakekava, son of Pa Retiare, was seized by the goddess from the interior of the house Nukurava, and dragged off to Fiora. There he recovered from his stupor and ran, escaping from her clutches, but with cruel gashes in his back, made by her claws, which are like knives. He did not die, but slowly recovered. He was an unmarried man, which is significant, as there is always the suggestion of the motive of sexual desire in these cases, female *atua* seizing men, and male *atua* women. I cannot vouch for the injury, but only for the firm credence given it by the narrator. The incident is evidently an attempt at concrete verification of a belief.

The deity was believed to appear among men at other times also. When people were going to Namo to pluck the frangipani blossom, which was the ornamented flower of Fiora, they broke it off, and then did not turn back, or turn the head round, but proceeded straight on in the path for fear of seeing her. 'One goes and goes, goes then ahead; if one returns, there she has appeared, there one looks upon her.'

Nau Fiora among her various functions is an oven-goddess of Tafua, and again is the guardian of Rangifaerere, the heavenly abode of women who die in childbirth. The death motif seems to be strongly associated with this deity, as it occurs in several other stories connected with her.

The work of Fiora took place only once a year, in the trade-wind; and began on the day after the carpeting of Tafua, as described by the Ariki Tafua and his son Pa Rangifuri. The programme will be given briefly here, since I did not see the ceremonies, and moreover they were similar in all essential respects to those of Somosomo. The major part of the ritual took five days, on each of which the usual series of kava rites was performed. It is of interest to note that in the morning kava the list of gods and ancestors was recited downwards from the highest deity; in the afternoon kava it was recited upwards beginning with the nearest ancestor. This is a technical difference, but one of significance to a Tikopia. The formulae of Fiora were the same as those for Tafua. The presentation of roi from 'sacred children' and from men recently married to Tafua women was one of the features of the Fiora ceremony. On the first day the thatch of Fiora was pinned together, and roi was made in the evening. The food on this occasion was creamed banana; not grated into a pudding, but cooked whole. This was termed te aso o te rau, 'the day of the thatch'. The second day was te aso o a tapakau, 'the day of floor-mats'. These were plaited, and each principal person attending Fiora sat on his new mat. No one sat on the bare earth. One, two or even three mats might be plaited for one elder. The following day was that of the Tafua chief and his family, when the provision of the food of the fakaoatea was associated with them. This day was distinguished by the distribution of a special gift which was absent from the ritual of Somosomo – the fakaariki. Large baskets of food were sent out from Fiora by the Ariki Tafua to the other three chiefs, the basis of this present lying, as so often, in the sphere of the relations between clan deities. 'Shares of the gods are given to the chiefs' was the description of it by the Ariki Tafua. On the next day, the fourth, these gifts were repaid by the chiefs to Fiora. This was the day on which Pa Saukirima, the principal elder of Tafua, made the fakaoatea, and it was known as te aso sa Fusi from his lineage name. On the following day a ceremony described as *Te otaota e aoao* took place, that is, the rubbish which had accumulated during the past days was ritually gathered together (*ao*) and swept out. This was done on *te aso sa Rarupe*, the day of another lineage of importance in the Tafua clan, comprising among others the houses of Nukuofo and Rangitafuri. The head of this group was not a titled elder, but the vesting of the ritual of collecting the *otaota* in him was another indication of the way in which family pride was allowed expression in the exercise of specific traditional privileges by which for the moment the group took precedence of others of normally much greater rank. (According to Pa Rangifuri the *fakaariki* distribution was made on this day, but this statement may have been a slip. He also separated the 'Day of sa Rarupe' and the 'Sweeping out of the Rubbish', whereas according to his father they took place together. It is possible that this latter represented a curtailment of an earlier programme.)

This day was really the conclusion of the 'Work' of the Marae of Fiora, and on the following day the perfumes of Resiake were 'sunned' (see Chapter 5). As the Ariki Tafua pointed out, the Tafua goddess was thus successful in having her 'Work' performed before that of Taumako. While Taumako carried out the ceremonies of Resiake, however, Tafua proceeded with subsidiary rites of Fiora, these being connected with the temple of that name, and not with the sacred Marae. Thus on the sixth day the temple was re-carpeted, and on the seventh the *fakaoatea* of the Ariki Tafua was made for the building. For this Pa Saukirima, the principal elder, was invited to come, and after the kava had been made the food was presented to him. On the following day the situation was reversed. This was the *fakaoatea* of Pa Saukirima, who prepared the oven, carried the food to Fiora, and then in his turn invited the chief to attend and make the kava. When this was over the food was presented to the chief. This completed the final events in this place.

The ritual of Somosomo and Fiora can only be understood as part of the series of rites associated with all Tikopia temples. That of Somosomo in particular, considered in isolation, would seem to be devoid of meaning, consisting as it does essentially in spreading floor-mats on the site of a long-vanished building. Its functions would seem to lie, however, in providing yet another venue for worship of the principal gods, in giving an occasion for appeals for productivity and welfare in general, and in giving expression to some of the basic principles of the social structure such as the hierarchy of men of rank, allowing them the exercise of specific privileges by which their status is in part defined.

Postscript

In 1952 the rites of Somosomo were considerably contracted owing to shortages of food and other materials (see RM, 1963, p. 14). They also began late. I got to the house of the Ariki Fangarere by about 6.45 a.m., but after a meal of rice and fish freshly caught on the reef, and paddling across the lake, we arrived about 8 a.m. to find no one-else yet there. The Ariki Fangarere was very scornful about this, and upset at the overgrown condition of the Marae and the absence of any house shelter from sun or rain. A little later the Ariki Kafika and a few assistants arrived. The Marae was then cleared, after a formula the same in substance but slightly different in wording from that which I recorded in 1929; the process took about half an hour. Coconut fronds, which had not been got ready the night before, were then brought and three women began to plait the ritual mats. There was a threat of rain, whereupon the Ariki Kafika called on the gods:

> Clear the sky, O Gods!
> Ancient are your doings about to be performed
> Let the sky be clear.

The sun shone for a while. Then he added:

> Let your face shine to be beautiful there –

addressing the god in sun form.

This day combined the clearing of the ritual area with the noon-day rite of Kafika, that of Rarovi being omitted since Pa Rarovi had abandoned his role on converting to Christianity. The oven was prepared about midday, and the kava of the *fakaoatea* was performed in the early afternoon. (For comparative illustration of July 1929 with July 1952, see RM, plates 2 and 3.) Food for the kava and subsequent meal was provided not only from the oven but also by a basket of food sent by the Ariki Taumako, the *peni roi o Pu*, as a symbolic acknowledgment of his founding ancestor having had as mother a daughter of the Ariki Kafika (cf. p. 396). This, the only marriage celebration gift, had atop a stem of kava, as in 1929; the contents had a novel touch – a rice pudding as well as coarse taro.

After the evening kava and another meal, the Ariki Kafika drove a stick into the ground in front of his seat, set down a coarse taro leaf and leant the kava stem against the stick. 'The kava of the gods – that they may descend to the Work', he explained to me. Then he uttered another formula to clear the skies, and to provide food for the kava. The kava stem was left there until the morning kava on the morrow. The kava bowl was left lying on the ground. I asked if no one would interfere with it, since it was near the path, but was told no, with a laugh; indeed there it was next morning, half-full of rainwater. No *roi* was made, since the Ariki did not give any orders to this effect on account of the scarcity of food.

On this occasion I obtained some information about the stones in the Marae. The stone just in front of which the Ariki Kafika sat, used as a support in turmeric manufacture (p. 388 and Plate 7*b*), was a symbol of the Atua Pouri, of Porima. The stone of the Atua Fafine, the Female Deity (see Fig. 13), which was a marker for the kava bowl, was in a different position from 1929. When I asked about this, I was told that it had been taken out and moved by people of Namo – 'curse them!' – because when they used this area as a dart-match ground their darts struck it and split upon it. Of two other stones near by, one was a memorial to a Female Chief, named Setao, daughter of the Ariki Kafika Tanakiforau, who had married Pu Fenutapu; another marked the burial place of Nau Fenutapu, an Anutan woman who had died recently.

It had been hoped by Pa Fenuatara and his wife that the Somosomo rites could have been ended on the second day, because of food difficulties and the age of the Ariki Kafika (see 'A Polynesian Aristocrat', 1960, p. 29). But the two chiefs disliked this brevity, and in the end it was decided to extend the rites to a third day. The prospect of a third morning kava did not seem to disturb the young men involved, and they were very definite in assuring the Ariki Kafika that it should be exactly as he wished, that his food basket was ready for him if he wished it. On the second evening the chief decided that *roi* should be prepared after all, and the

Ariki Fangarere went off to his orchard in the vicinity to seek coarse taro for it – but it was noted that there was no coconut, a strong contrast to the situation in 1929. When after the morning kava the food was eaten there were bitter complaints from both chiefs about the famine and the improvidence of ordinary people in marrying and having large families, to the detriment of food supplies.

12

The Ritual Extraction
of Turmeric

Turmeric is a vermilion pigment extracted from the root of a
plant with large soft leaves, known generally as *Curcuma longa*,
and allied with the Canna, which it somewhat resembles in appearance. The Tikopia prepare two extracts, one edible, the other used
as a colouring material. The former is termed *tauo*, the latter *renga*,
and it is this which is primarily sought. Mixed with coconut oil
the *renga* is used for bodily decoration; mixed with water it is
used for dyeing bark-cloth; and kept in solid form in bark-cloth
wrappings, it is a highly prized object of wealth. In this last form
especially, it is known as 'property of chiefs'.[1] Application of turmeric to the body is more than simple adornment; it is a mark of
ritual significance attaching to the person or occasion. (Cases
of this have been given already in the Work of the Gods.) Part
of its meaning here lies in the belief that it is 'a perfume of the
gods', attractive to them, and a stimulus to their favourable
interest. In particular, the pigment is associated with the Atua i
Kafika. He is held to have been responsible for its original extraction, in the neighbourhood of the spring at Somosomo, though
there is no specific tale dealing with this. Bark-cloths dyed with
turmeric are especially appropriate to him, hence gifts of food
made to the Ariki Kafika by the other chiefs are normally topped
by such cloth instead of white bark-cloth. The Ariki Kafika said
to me, 'The basis of the turmeric extraction is the Atua i Kafika;
the turmeric is called his perfume, the scent of the Atua. The name
of the turmeric is the Akoako. When he lived, his desire was the

---

[1] See *We, the Tikopia*, 1936, pp. 92–4; *Primitive Polynesian Economy*, 1939,
pp. 111–12, 137–8, 276, 289–91.

turmeric; when a waistcloth is dyed red, it is his, his basis is in him; its name is the *marotafi*.'

Several factors are thus associated together: the use of turmeric for ritual; the belief that it is primarily the property of the Atua i Kafika; the *tapu* surrounding its extraction; and the craft skill demanded.

The extraction of turmeric is an annual event, in the trade-wind season, at a definite period in the Work of the Gods. The operations are complex, occupying several days, and the cycle of production is termed the *nuanga*, a term which will be retained in the following account. Since the religious aspects of the activity are intimately bound up with the technological and economic processes, these latter must be described. My material on the processes and ritual is drawn primarily from my participation in the *nuanga* of the Ariki Tafua, when at his request I observed all the rules and taboos of the work; the formulae quoted were obtained from the Ariki Tafua and the Ariki Kafika.

TURMERIC – PLANTING

The turmeric plant itself is termed *ango*. It is cultivated, and comes to maturity in about twelve months, being often planted for the next season when the roots for extraction of pigment are dug out. The planting falls outside the *nuanga* proper, and with ordinary folk is done without ritual. Small roots, or those faded at the tips by exposure to the sun, are simply set in little ledges dug out in the hillside, and covered over.

The planting of the turmeric of chiefs is a ritual affair. That of the Ariki Kafika takes precedence. On the day before the re-carpeting of the temple Mapusanga the Ariki Kafika plants a few roots in his cultivation. These are termed the *ango tapu*, or Te Akoako. Ordinarily this latter is the name of a shrub with aromatic leaves, much favoured for perfume and ornament; applied to the turmeric it indicates the 'perfume' of the Atua i Kafika. The Ariki Kafika said, 'The Akoako is made, is called the perfume of the Atua i Kafika; the turmeric of the (other) chiefs, each dedicates it only to his lesser deities.' (Actually this is not so.)

The Ariki Kafika goes alone to plant the Akoako, not because of its sacredness, but because of the trifling work involved. As he sets the tubers in the soil he says (according to his statement to me):

> Here! thy power of thy perfume, Mapusia!
> I eat ten times thy excrement.
> Thy perfume will be planted this day.
> Pour thy calms on thy crest of the land,
> Part the skies . . .

The formula may be continued at the discretion of the chief, with further appeals for fine weather, etc.

The following day the other chiefs plant their special turmeric which, however, has not the importance of that of Kafika.

ORGANIZATION OF THE 'NUANGA'

The extraction of the turmeric takes place in late July or even August.[1] One token that the time has come is the appearance of the scarlet blossoms of the *kalokalo* or *ngatae* (*Erythrina* sp.). Because of their colour this tree is designated the tree of the Atua i Kafika, and reference is made to it in the formulae of extraction; it is believed to exercise a sympathetic influence on the turmeric to produce roots of the requisite vivid hue. By this time the leaves of the turmeric plant have dried and withered. The *nuanga* season is also correlated with the movements of the Pleiades. This constellation, Matariki, appears on the eastern horizon before dawn at the opening of the trade-wind season. The Ariki Tafua said that when he saw it stand up directly over the shoulder of the mountain from his village of Matautu he knew that the turmeric was fit to dig. 'Matariki, star of the *nuanga*' is a term for it. At this time, he said, the stars of the constellation appear to oscillate in towards one another (illustrating this by moving his fingers). I was also told that another token is given by the leaves of the *ngatae*; when they begin to change colour it is time for the Work of the Trade-Wind to start, and by the time they are fully red then is the time for the *nuanga*. But though I omitted to check this, I doubt its accuracy.

The process of turmeric extraction consists essentially in grating

[1] In early August 1928 I took part in the *nuanga* of the Ariki Tafua. Since this chief no longer took part in the rest of the Work of the Gods he had more latitude in time, and on this occasion had delayed the operations to allow the incision rites for Munakina, son of the Motlav mission teacher, to take place first. In 1929, when I left on July 7th, the other chiefs were repairing their aqueducts, and I just missed the full performance. In 1952, the *nuanga* of the Ariki Kafika, which would have been normally the first of the season, but because of famine took place alone, began on July 12th and ended on July 18th. In 1966 the *nuanga* of the chiefs of Kafika and Taumako ended on July 20th.

the roots of the plant, washing and filtering the grated material, decanting the filtrate after it has settled, and baking the residual pigment in wooden cylinders in an earth oven. Incidental to this is the separation of the edible material from the pigment proper.

The organization of the *nuanga* is therefore governed to a large degree by the available water supply. There are no streams in Tikopia, and the springs which flow from the hillsides are utilized. The small flow from these debars participation of all producers as a single group, and several separate *nuanga* thus come into operation. These are headed by men of rank, the chiefs of Kafika, Tafua and Taumako each assuming responsibility for one, and having as partners a number of men of their own or of other clans. The division of producers along these lines is facilitated by the fact that each of these chiefs is acknowledged to have rights of ownership or control over an important spring. That of the Ariki Kafika is Vai Sukumarae; that of the Ariki Tafua, Vai Matautu; that of the Ariki Taumako, Vai Potu sa Taumako.[1] The Ariki Fangarere has no particular spring of his own; for this reason, it is said, he holds no separate *nuanga*, but joins with the Ariki Kafika for the purpose. His partnership with the Ariki Kafika would seem, however, to be traditional and ritual rather than technological, since some of the remaining springs are open to anyone who wishes to set up his *nuanga* there. Others, by land ownership or adjacent residence, are used primarily by specific kinship groups or villages, and in addition to the *nuanga* of the chiefs there are usually several others, headed by commoners. But whereas such commoners do not normally produce turmeric every year, the chiefs do so because of their religious obligations. (But see Epilogue.)

Another important factor in the organization is the ownership of equipment, particularly of the large troughs used in the early stages of filtration. These are costly to make, and therefore tend to be owned only by the more wealthy groups. Lack of one does not bar a man from producing turmeric, but prevents him from acting as the nucleus of a manufacturing group.

The third important factor is technical skill. As compared with the other elements of the Work of the Gods, the *nuanga* is much more of a directly practical economic activity; people of different clans mingle in the same group, and attention is concentrated on the immediate efficient production of the valued pigment rather

[1] See Map (b) in *We, the Tikopia*, 1936.

than on the maintenance of a regular sequence of traditional performances, which serve as privileges for individuals and groups. In line with this, the direction of affairs in each *nuanga* is in the hands of an expert, the *tufunga*. Though often a chief or man of rank, he assumes or is invited to take the position primarily because of his skill in the craft. It will be seen that several of the processes do really need specialist skill, and much of the success of the *nuanga* depends on the *tufunga*. The Ariki Tafua is well known as a *tufunga te renga*, and is versed in both the practical and esoteric aspects of the craft. There is no hereditary profession of turmeric expert, though a father usually hands on his knowledge to one or more of his sons.

The success of the *tufunga* is not believed to lie in his technical skill alone, but also in his command of formulae; it is through his *atua* that he secures a good yield of turmeric as a whole, and an efficient separation of *tauo* from *renga*. Ordinary commoners have a particular ancestor to whom they appeal; elders use one of the deities of their kava; chiefs have specific deities who are guardians of the water, and others who are guardians of the turmeric oven, and in addition, perhaps, a particular ancestor. In Tafua, when I was there, Tereiteata, grandfather's brother of the then Ariki Tafua and bearer of the same personal name, was the ancestor specially invoked. In addition, the *nuanga* as a whole are under the dominion of the Atua i Kafika, to whom the Ariki Kafika addresses his main appeals. He is not invoked by the other chiefs except incidentally, and not at all by commoners. The *nuanga* has thus a spiritual organization parallel to that obtaining in the case of the sacred canoes (see Chapter 3).

The basis of the *nuanga* organization is voluntary co-operation. There is no obligation upon anyone to join, nor on the other hand is a request to join normally refused. (Occasionally there may be some restriction. Thus in 1929 the Ariki Tafua requested the other chiefs to limit the number of entrants to their *nuanga* in order that the work might be soon over, and his planned *seru* take place betimes. They agreed, though his proposal was not popular.) Each *nuanga* group includes an expert, who may be the man who took the initiative in forming the group or not, and consists of a number of units. Each unit, termed *eke* or *kaueke*, is associated with a number of separate 'lots' of turmeric roots, and is the working party of the owners of the 'lots', being drawn from their kinsfolk and neighbours. All the *eke* combine as a single working group under the direction of the *tufunga*, but each 'lot' of turmeric is processed separately.

The Matautu *nuanga* of 1928 consisted of two units, representative of the 'houses' of Tafua (the chief's family) and Nukuofo; Fetauta and Nukutauriri. In the first there were the chief himself, who was also the expert for the work as a whole and the owner of the major equipment, four of his sons, two grandsons, and an 'adhering child' from Tafua in Namo; with these were Pa Nukuofo and his son, who was married to the eldest daughter of the Ariki Tafua. In the second there were Pa Fetauta and his son Rakeitino; of Kafika clan, they were related to the Ariki Tafua through his wife, as well as being members of his village. With them there was only Kavaika, eldest son of Pa Nukutauriri, of Kafika clan, but a neighbour of the chief. Ties of kinship and residence thus were the determining factors in the composition of this *nuanga*, rather than ties of clanship. And since the division into units depends largely upon the impossibility of putting the turmeric of every partner through the same stage on the same day, the relative size of each 'lot' is one factor in deciding who shall be associated in one unit. The units of the Tafua *nuanga* were small owing, it was said, to the recent death of a grandson of the chief; people had plenty of turmeric ready, but because the period of mourning had not ended they were 'ashamed' to appear. If the *nuanga* is large, then it consists of four or five units, each having three, four or five partners. But three units only are common. The number must be limited by the available equipment. 'It is arranged in proportion; we are proportioned to troughs, which are few.' Sometimes the units are spoken of as if they were individual enterprises. 'There are three *eke*; they are called three *nuanga*.'

The turmeric of each unit is begun on successive days, and the order is maintained throughout. The chief, in accordance with his rank and esoteric functions, is always leader of the first unit in his own *nuanga*. The units have titles to distinguish them. Those in Kafika, for instance, if three in number, are known as 'The Akoako', 'The Eke in the Middle', and 'The Oven-Burying'. The last is so called because after it the oven for baking the turmeric is filled in.

If there are many partners, or a large mass of material, the work of each unit is further split up, due again primarily to limitations of equipment. The initial product is termed the *Uruango*; the next the *Renga Tofua*, and the others the *Vaivai Nea*, the *Pai Nea*, the *Fakamatauo* and the *Rauwai*, in that order. These all produce *renga*, and after them comes the treatment of the *tauo*. In all cases the ritual is concentrated on the *Uruango*, the succeeding batches are regarded as of less importance, and if the turmeric of the *Uruango* turns out well, then it is thought the whole work will surely be successful. The pigment from this first batch is termed the *renga maori*, 'the true turmeric'. If the amount is large, say five or six cylinders per partner, then the expression is 'the turmeric has *aso*'. A distinction is further drawn between the first batch of a chief and those of the other partners in his unit; his is called *Te Uruango o Katea*, and theirs collectively *Te Uruango o Ama*. This description in terms of 'starboard' and 'port' brings in the concepts already discussed in the ritual of Somosomo. The true 'turmeric' (from the *Uruango*) and that of the *Renga Tofua* are the most valuable. They are usually preserved entire as cylinders, for ceremonial presentation, though occasionally they are drawn upon to dye a piece of bark-cloth to give to a chief. Hung up in their wrappings to the rafters of a house, they are treasured property, kept for years. The succeeding batches provide pigment for dyeing ordinary bark-cloth, and smearing on the body. The *Rauwai* in particular, the last batch, is the '*nuanga* of the women'. In theory its product goes to the women of the households concerned, though in practice it seems to form part of the ordinary domestic supply.

In processing, the *Uruango* of the chief goes first, and then that of the other partners in his unit; the next day the *Uruango* of the second unit is begun; the third day that of the third unit, and so on. Then comes the *Renga Tofua* of the various units in succession, and so on for the other types. But the processing once begun is continuous for each batch, so that on the second day, when the *Uruango* of the second unit is begun, that of the first unit is going through stage two. And later on all the processes are in operation together, for different batches. As a rule, the quantity of turmeric is not enough to give rise to all the divisions mentioned earlier, and the *Uruango*, the *Renga Tofua* and perhaps the *Vaivai Nea* alone are separated, with the *tauo* at the end. If any partner has a remnant of roots, not enough to justify treating it as a separate batch, it can be processed with the *Rauwai*, the 'women's turmeric', if such is being extracted.

Clearly, the organization of a *nuanga*, even a small one, is a complex affair. One of the reasons for the complex division is the wish to preserve uniformity, so that every partner gets approximately equal treatment – though a chief is allowed to have the lead. Another reason is the ritual one, of singling out a portion of each man's turmeric for special treatment in relation to the gods on whom the prosperity of the whole is believed to depend.

PRELIMINARY RITES AND WORK

Before the extraction, several preparations of a ritual and of a practical nature have to be made: the turmeric has to be dug, a water supply assured, and a shed and enclosures built.

First comes the ritual digging of the sacred turmeric. After the morning kava at Somosomo, on the fifth day of these rites, the Ariki Kafika orders one of his kinsfolk to perform this task. I did not see it done, but in 1929 was present when he sent off his son and another youth to dig up the hillock of turmeric he had planted in Maunga in the monsoon season. He said to them, 'Bruise it to be pungent to the skies; it is the perfume of the Deity.' According to him, the operator plunges his digging stick in beside the plant and levers it up. As he does so he says:

> Recite hither, Father,
> For the perfume of the Deity
> Will be turned up on this day.

And at what he judges to be the appropriate time the chief himself says:

> I eat ten times your excrement,
> My Sacred Chief.
> Your perfume will be turned up
> To be odorous to the sky.

He gave me an alternative form of words also:

> Powerful turning of your perfume, Mapusia!
> Your perfume will be cleansed in the morning.
> Let gods and men assist at it.
> Clear be the sky,
> Your perfume will be prepared.

This rite is known as 'the turning of the Akoako'. The idea is that the scent of the roots, levered up, rises to the sky, apprises the Atua i Kafika of the beginning of the work and induces him to grant good weather for it. 'The Akoako is turned to act on the sky to stand well; the *nuanga* is going to be made.'

An essential job is to assure an adequate supply of fresh water. This is helped by having the *nuanga* in the trade-wind season, when the springs are not the mere trickle they often are during the monsoon. For ordinary domestic purposes the water is made available by aqueducts of split areca palm trunks, with most of the pith removed, supported on stakes several feet above the ground. For turmeric extraction these are cleaned out and repaired, and the overhaul is incorporated into the ritual scheme. In addition a new lead to the turmeric enclosure has often to be built. On the morning of the Turning of the Akoako people go to their cultivations and get new timbers. This is known as 'the felling of the aqueduct'. The cutting of the first timber for the aqueduct of a chief's *nuanga* is prefaced by a short formula.

> Here! the aqueduct of the water.
> Fell with power the aqueduct of the water.

The appeal here is to the particular *atua* of the *nuanga*. The process of overhaul is termed 'making the waters full', that is causing a steady stream to flow. Later a libation of kava is poured and an offering of food made, with the words (by the Ariki Kafika):

> I eat ten times your excrement, My Sacred Chief.
> Your turmeric-making will be prepared,

and

> Here! Your food, Ancestor.
> Your water has been made full this day.

This is the initial kava of the *nuanga*.

Another technical operation is the erection of a shed to shelter the graters of the turmeric. It is termed the *fare kuku*, the 'grating shed', and is a flimsy erection of sago thatch, supported on poles and open on all sides. For the shed of a chief a brief formula is repeated at the pinning of the first sheet of thatch, usually done by the chief himself.

> Here! pierce with power the thatch sheet of the turmeric-
>   making.

Of more importance is the preparation of a filter-cloth, which is made or carefully supervised by the expert himself. It is made from *kaka*, the stiff porous material from the base of the coconut frond. Pieces are sewn together to form a sheet, with strips of hibiscus fibre. In olden days the sewing was done with a long whalebone needle; nowadays European pack-needles are used, even by old men, their special merit in the eyes of the expert being that the eye does not break out. The expert takes a pair of pieces of fibre at a time, and looks them over carefully for flaws. The fibre is extremely tough, and the left foot of the workman is set on the sewn material to keep it firm, while a second man often helps by turning in the edge in advance. The sewing frequently changes hands, owing to its difficulty. The completed article is a sheet about four feet square, slightly baggy in the centre owing to the tapering shape of the individual pieces and the curving seam of the join.

Another task is the collection of the raw turmeric. For several days after the Turning of the Akoako, people go and dig their turmeric, and bring it back, often at the same time as the other work is proceeding. No ritual is connected with this digging and it is done by small parties, in the same way as ordinary agricultural labour.

WASHING OF THE TURMERIC

When all the raw turmeric has been brought it is cleansed. About midday an oven is prepared, and a simple kava rite is performed; this is the *kava soronga ango*, the kava of the cleansing of the turmeric. As the sun goes down, women of the participant families in the *nuanga* come together on the grass on the beach. A large coconut leaf mat is laid down and turmeric roots piled on it. The material of each partner is kept separate, and that of a chief is always cleansed first. That of the other partners is usually done on later evenings. The women, clad in old skirts, kneel around the mat, the edge of which is lifted on to their laps; they are roughly grouped in two rows on opposite sides. Fresh water is too valuable to be used for the washing, and salt water is therefore carried up in bowls and canoe balers by children, who dash it over the pile of roots. A song is started, and to its accompaniment first one rank and then the other plunges forward with outstretched arms, hands open and together, so that their weight rolls over the heap of roots. Each side lunges and recovers alternately, keeping time to the song, rolling the turmeric backwards and forwards between them. Constantly drenched with water, the roots are thus soon freed of dirt and hair rootlets. The time taken to cleanse a batch of turmeric is less than an hour. The work is done with laughter and joking, and the women are soon thoroughly wet.

The songs during the work are usually dance chants. At Matautu in 1928, however, dirges were sung since the village was in mourning for the grandson of the chief, lost at sea some months before. The words of the song need bear no reference to the work in hand or to the *nuanga*. One of the songs at the cleansing of the turmeric of the Ariki Tafua was from a *seru*, and in praise of him.

> My great food portion from Father
> Who said to give it to me
> That I might consume the first-fruits,
>   the ripe bananas.
>
> Your kava is prepared here in the west.
> We go and shall eat from it.
>
> My Father, dwelling in Motuapi,
> Let us flock to him.[1]

Batches of turmeric after the first do not always have a song accompaniment. The women may simply give a loud grunt, for amusement, as they plunge forward. This provokes great laughter among the spectators. Petty friction also sometimes occurs. 'Why don't you rub properly instead of merely groping?' was one complaint.

The turmeric roots come up in clusters, and the parent root (*tafito*) of each cluster, covered with rootlets, is not included in the heap. These parent roots are sorted out into a basket and scraped with a small knife – in former times with a sharp shell. When the main heap is judged to have been rolled over enough the turmeric roots are put into close-woven baskets and immersed for a few minutes in the sea by boys and girls. One hand holds the basket, in water up to the breast, the other rubs the turmeric to and fro in order to remove the last remnants of dirt. At the same

---

[1] The implications of the first-fruits (*muakai*) are described in *Primitive Polynesian Economy*, 1939, pp. 213–14.

time the troughs, bowls and graters for the later stages of the work are usually washed in the sea too.

Finally the baskets are taken to the house of the chief partner to stand (or 'sleep' as it is also termed) on the *mata paito* side of the floor. There fresh water is poured over them. 'The turmeric is doused.'

REGULATIONS OF THE 'NUANGA'

The next day the *nuanga* proper begins. From this point a number of rules or taboos limit the freedom of the workers. These are distinctly onerous, involving restraint in matters of food, sleep, physical relaxation, social and sexual intercourse. Their manifest object is to secure the final product in the proper state.

It will be convenient to describe first the rules governing relations with people not engaged in the *nuanga*; second, those which refer primarily to relations between the sexes within the *nuanga*; and third, the rules relating to food.

From the evening of the day on which the turmeric is first grated a segregation of the *nuanga* workers begins. Those who have been merely helping with the grating go home, but they do not return. The partners, with their wives and any kinsfolk or neighbours they may have engaged, remain, to sleep in houses close by the scene. An intangible barrier now separates them from the rest of the village; they are 'within the *nuanga*', or 'living in the *nuanga*', and the rest are 'the crowd without' or simply 'those at the back' (*sa tua*). Limited conversation is permitted between the two groups, but they may not sit or eat together, and though the former may go outside the barrier, and do so for necessary purposes, as to get food, the latter should not come in. The question 'You are living in the *nuanga*?' and the reply 'I am living in the middle' are sufficient to keep people apart when they meet outside. Relations between them are defined by the concept of 'cold food' examined later.

Within the *nuanga* group there is also a division, on a sex basis. At night, or for rest during the day, men and women separate into two parties, the men to the house of the chief, and the women to another house vacated for them. One of the most stringent rules is this segregation of the sexes away from work. The primary basis for this is the fear lest the intrusion of sex matters affects either the turmeric or the health of the people. The anthropologist can see in this a restriction of some value for the efficient conduct of the work. But the Tikopia explain it in terms of what to us are non-rational connections.

There is a very strong prohibition on sexual intercourse during the *nuanga* (only by those 'dwelling within'). If a man should lie with his wife before it is over it is believed that the turmeric will turn out soft instead of hard, and swarms of little flies will be gathered around it, attracted by its peculiar odour. The associations here are obvious. Moreover, if the breach of taboo occurs at an early stage it is thought that it will be detected by the expert from indications in the turmeric liquid itself. 'If a man goes to a woman, we see there in the bottom of the trough the marriage-tokens that he has gone and made with the woman.' Observing what looks like a deposit of semen in the trough, the expert mentions it quietly to the others, and may make a joke at the expense of the man whose turmeric it is. 'One comes in and finds the *nuanga* laughing silently; and there! It is oneself they are laughing at, and one does not know. But the expert has related it. . . . No doings of the turmeric-making can be hidden.'

Other rules deal with positions of rest in the house. Only the floor-mats must be used to sit on; no-one, not even the chief, is allowed a stool or block of wood, and when I attended the *nuanga* I had to comply with this as with the other rules. Again, even on the mats, only certain positions are allowed. One may sit with crossed legs, or recline with the legs straight out in front, but not squat with the knees hunched up. This would spoil the turmeric. In sleeping, men must not lie on the face, but on the back; women, on the other hand, must sleep face downwards. These rules appear to be direct extensions of that debarring sexual intercourse, since that which is forbidden is more or less directly suggestive of exposure or the sexual act.

We now come to the rules about food. In the first place, the texture of foods taken is important. Semi-liquid foods and soft mushy fruits are prohibited; such are the papaya and ripe bananas. Nowadays sugar is included in the proscribed list. The Ariki Tafua was very careful to vet my proposed meals before admitting me to the *nuanga*. Dry biscuit he approved, and hot tea was allowed, but I had to promise not to take sugar with it, or eat jam. (As a matter of fact I lived almost wholly on Tikopia food during my period of seclusion there.) The reason given for these prohibitions is of the sympathetic order – lest the final pigment lose its firmness, and turn out watery.

Again, all food must be theoretically 'hot'; nothing 'cold' should be taken. The main meals during the day consisted of hot breadfruit, baked whole on the oven stones, with green or ripe coconuts, taken about mid-morning; and a hot pudding of bread-fruit, taro or green bananas eaten in the late afternoon. If the work took longer than expected this latter was sometimes cold by the time it was eaten. This was immaterial; it was 'hot food' from the ritual point of view. As such it was opposed to 'cold food'. This seems illogical. But the explanation is that these two terms have a symbolic meaning extending beyond their literal one. They apply not simply to food of different temperature, but in this context to the place of preparation. Even more figuratively, these terms are extended to the two groups of persons within and outside the *nuanga*. Persons within are 'hot', those outside are 'cold' food. The central feature of the distinction is that 'cold food' shall not come into contact with 'hot food', that those out-side shall not contaminate those within – if they do, then the turmeric will be spoiled. Hence no cooked food from outside may be brought into the *nuanga* circle, and no person from outside may enter the more sacred places where the work is being carried on.

The basis of this distinction in terms lies in the fact that nor-mally the first meal of the Tikopia day, just after sunrise, consists of cold taro or other remnants from the oven of the afternoon before. In the *nuanga* itself the same food is eaten too, at two small meals at night, and in the early morning before work begins. But in this case the meals are taken in the dark. As such they are regarded as a prolongation of the earlier 'hot food'; since a new day has not dawned on the land they have not lost their theoretical warmth. Once dawn has broken they become 'cold food' and may not be eaten. Being a thrifty folk the Tikopia do not throw the food away, but pass it on to households outside the *nuanga*. Here it is eaten, particularly by children, who thus become 'cold food' *par excellence*. As such they are warned to keep clear of anyone who is living in the *nuanga*; they themselves would not be harmed by contact, but they are contamination for him and the turmeric. (This was one of the few occasions, I noted, on which they obeyed a command to keep out of the way.)

One of the results of eating 'cold food' is said to be that a man's turmeric, when ready for decanting, 'sleeps lightly', that is, it will not settle properly. This again can be noted by the expert. A case of alleged contamination by 'cold food' came under my own observation. When the turmeric of the second unit at Matautu was 'blown' from its wooden cylinders, it was seen that the batch of Pa Fetauta had 'come down badly'; it was soft, like porridge, instead of being a hard mass. The owner at once suspected a breach of rule about 'cold food' and made inquiries. It was learned from some women that they had seen Tekarima, a member of the group of Pa Fetauta, but outside the *nuanga*, go into the house where food for the *nuanga* workers was cooking. 'He had eaten cold food, yet he came to the oven of Pa Fetauta; that's why the turmeric is bad. It is not proper!' said one of the group to me, and they talked to one another indignantly in similar terms. When taxed, Tekarima – who had heard of the mischance – denied that he had eaten 'cold food', but he was not believed, and Pa Fetauta gave him a good tongue-lashing. The view was that the guilt or innocence of the man was to be judged not by weighing statements, but by the phenomenon observed. As they put it to me, Pa Fetauta knew that Tekarima had eaten 'cold food' because the turmeric was bad. In order to test the firmness of the Tikopia belief I suggested that the reason for the failure was the presence of too much water or oil in the mixture, or too short a baking. This was not accepted for a moment. 'The turmeric was good; it was the "cold food" that acted on it.'

There are rules also for other types of behaviour. One concerns excretion. During the *nuanga* one should excrete in the sea, or at least out on the reef; one should not do so in the undergrowth. 'In the *nuanga* it is good to go and excrete in the shore waters, not to excrete inland; it will become breakable.' It is held that the turmeric will be crumbly, not firm, when turned out if this is disregarded. And when transferring it from one bowl to another it will not move smoothly, but will fall in broken lumps. Here again is an association between bodily process and natural process. Theft within the *nuanga* would seem to be rare. But a sanction against it is provided by the belief that if a man misappropriates turmeric, then his own will not settle properly.

These rules and observances are termed 'things laid down in the turmeric-making'. They are in a different category from the ritual to be described later in that firstly they are primarily of a negative, prohibitory order; and secondly, that a breach of them is believed to manifest itself directly, and not through the operation of any ancestors or gods. Moreover, the ritual tends to vary according to the precise stage of the technical operations, whereas these prohibitions run fairly evenly throughout the whole process.

We may now proceed further with the technical and ritual aspects of the activity (see Fig. 15).

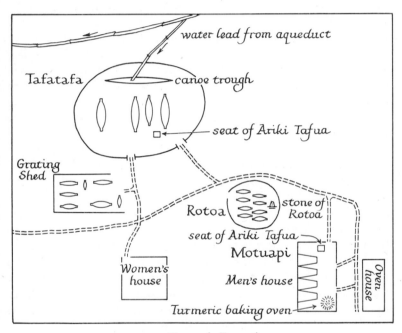

FIG. 15. Turmeric Extraction

GRATING THE TURMERIC ROOTS

The *nuanga* shows a distinct division of labour along sex lines. Though men and women dig up the roots, the building of sheds and aqueducts is done by the men, and the cleansing of the roots is the work of the women, assisted by young boys as water-carriers. Grating the roots is done by the women also, though a few men assist. The later processes of filtering are done primarily by men, though a few women may help once the most important product, that of the Ariki, has been put through. But the final stage, that of baking the turmeric, is done entirely by men. The broad principle is that the less skilled operations are allotted to the women, while those demanding more skill and technical knowledge are the domain of men; the latter also receive much greater ritual emphasis.

The roots are grated in a shed erected for the purpose. The grating implement is a stave, shaped somewhat like a slender paddle, about five feet long and four inches by half an inch at the widest part of the blade. It is made of *poumuri* or other light wood. The lower part of the stave is closely bound for about two feet with a sinnet cord, plaited and then chain-knotted to give a triangular section. It is on this, the stave cord, that the turmeric is grated. Coconut fronds are laid on the floor of the shed, wooden bowls are set out, and in each bowl is set one or more staves, with their upper ends firmly lashed to the rafters. The grating cord has been arranged in each case at kneeling height. Kneeling down, the operator takes a few roots of turmeric in the palm of the hand, and clasping it round the narrow back of the stave, rubs briskly up and down the cord. The grated material falls into the bowl. Considerable pressure is used, and the people say 'Great is the labour.' When the work is at its height the shed is full of people, and most staves are occupied by two persons. (A man and a woman may be seen grating opposite each other.) When there are not enough staves ordinary taro-graters, of wire spikes set in wood, and held horizontally, are also used. Early in the day, in the shed of the Ariki Tafua, there were five small bowls, one large bowl, and three troughs in use; sixteen staves and four taro-graters were set in them; and twenty-five women and two men were occupied in grating. An hour afterwards, at full pressure, there were twenty-eight women and five men, with one extra stave, and two boys were employed in carrying round baskets of fresh turmeric as required. The shed was full of the noise of the grating and of talk; there was much betel-chewing and smoking; and a little chewing of the turmeric itself; there was a strong smell of turmeric, and the workers were spattered with the yellow juice.

For the *nuanga* of Kafika, I was told, the first grating of the turmeric is a ritual matter. The wife of the chief, termed for this purpose 'the woman of the Akoako', sets up her stave and begins to grate; the other women watch her silently, and only when the process is well under way do they follow suit and the real work starts.

FILTERING THE GRATED TURMERIC

A few yards from the grating-shed is an area about twenty yards square, screened in by stakes, coconut and sago fronds so that the work inside cannot be seen by people who pass by. This is the *tafatafa*, the enclosure where the filtration takes place. It is floored with coconut fronds, and on one side stands a trough, collecting water from the aqueduct. The hull of a canoe, stripped of its outrigger, is often used for this purpose. Several other troughs (*nafa*) are essential to the filtration. They are from six to ten feet long, and are made specially for the extraction of turmeric and sago. For the *nuanga* of the Ariki Tafua four troughs were used. Two were his own property, one belonged to Pa Fetauta, and one was borrowed from a kinsman of the Ariki. Generically, these troughs are wooden bowls of a giant size; at succeeding stages of the work bowls of decreasing size are employed. All are of a different shape from bowls used in preparing food.

The most striking object in the *tafatafa* is the filter-stand (*kaumafuta*). (It is illustrated in plates II and IV of my *Primitive Polynesian Economy*.) To make it, three poles are set up in the form of a tripod, a circlet of coconut leaf is girt about this, and leaves of banana are bent over the circlet. A couple of leaves of the umbrella palm are added inside, with their tops pointing downwards; the corrugations in the leaves will serve as runnels for the liquid when the filtration begins. The mass of leaves is gathered in at the bottom and lashed tightly with a diamond network of strips of bark, thus forming an inverted cone. At the point of the cone a leaf of *rau tea* is set, and a pole thrust down the centre pierces the point and converts the cone into a funnel. Any extra leafage at the point is cut away, and water poured down to test for leaks. A filter-cloth of *kaka*, fibrous material from the base of the coconut frond, is added later. The completed erection stands about six feet high. I was struck by the ingenuity and speed with which an efficient piece of apparatus was made out of such simple materials. For the *nuanga* of Tafua two funnels were built; for a larger group even more may be used.

Now that the *tafatafa* was ready, a tall pole was set up at the entrance. This was 'the barrier of the women' – the sign of ritual exclusion. But though the enclosure was said to be *tapu* to women and children, I noticed that only a scolding was given to a child who strayed in before the work began. The taboo was mild compared with that, for instance, of the sacred canoes.

Meanwhile preparations were going on for feeding the graters of turmeric. During the morning the women in the grating-shed were given sugar-cane and coconuts, both green and sprouting; they ate in the shed. The men had coconuts alone, and ate in the chief's house. Other kinsfolk of the chief were cooking food in the oven house. On this day all the food provided was supplied by the chief and his kin. The custom is for the feeding of the *nuanga* group to be undertaken daily by each partner in turn, with help of supplies and labour from his kin.

The coconuts eaten by the men were called 'causing to chew betel of the turmeric', a term of depreciation. Before drinking, each partner of the group pierced the eye of a nut and poured out a libation to the ancestor or deity to whom his turmeric was dedicated. The Ariki Tafua said to me, 'They are not ashamed in the presence of the chief sitting here.' He meant that though normally ritual of this kind is left to a chief in public, it was proper on this occasion for each partner to secure any supernatural assistance he could, since the products were for the benefit of individuals.

After the brief meal came the filtration of the first batch of turmeric. The filter-cloth was drenched with water and hung over the filter-stand, supported on a pair of crossed sticks; and all troughs but one were filled with water. The empty one was set under the filter-stand, and a leaf of *rau tea* was tied at the bottom of the funnel to serve as a lead. From a large bowl of grated turmeric – known now as *pauango* – a smaller bowl was filled, and then emptied on to the filter-cloth. Water was poured on to it, and the grated mass kneaded by a pair of men. The water running down the funnel into the trough carried with it the yellow dye of the turmeric, leaving behind the waste fibres. The kneading of the *pauango* was termed *foa*. From time to time handfuls of the exhausted residue were removed, to be thrown away over the fence, and fresh material and water added. The filtering was done quickly, with little talk, and the Ariki Tafua, as expert, kept a close watch on all that was done. From time to time he was asked for advice, or proffered instruction. The impression created was one of solemnity. Each filter-stand had usually four men at work, two kneading the turmeric, one feeding it in and removing the residue, and another carrying water. Other men were busy washing bowls and troughs, shifting the filter-stand from one trough to another, and making sago-leaf thatch covers for the troughs when full.

'FISHING FOR SUCCESS'

Since the yield of turmeric depends on proper filtration and a good flow of dye at this stage, one is not surprised to find that one of the most important rites takes place at this point. At the moment when the man holding the first bowl of grated material was about to tip it into the filter-cloth he looked over to where the chief was seated, caught his eye, murmured '*Ia!*' and emptied in the bowl. The chief then began to recite under his breath a formula, known as the *Raufangota Manu* ('Fishing for Success'). Its essential theme is to secure the assistance of the spirits in getting as much turmeric pigment as possible. There are three ways by which it is thought this can be done: by facilitating proper precipitation of the filtrate; by turning some of the less valuable edible *tauo* into *renga* pigment; and by raiding alien supplies at the same time as the home supplies are protected from theft. The 'theft' here is not conceived as abstraction by human beings, but by spirits.

I received several variants of this basic formula, from the Ariki Tafua and the Ariki Kafika, differing only in a few phrases. One version will be sufficient here to show the form. It is from the Ariki Tafua.

> I eat ten times your excrement, The Chief of the Waters, E!
> Turn to your *fetau* leaf
> Stand firm your Rosy Cloud and your Rosy-Tailed Following
> Perfume of the God is this being made here.
> Be pressed down below the *tauo*
> And turned to become *renga*
> That a mark may be secured for you and your Rosy-Tailed
>   Following
> May the *renga* sleep solidly
> Be gathered together a turmeric liquid for us
> From Rotuma, from Anuta,
> Lands where the *nuanga* takes place.
> Its blood-red *kalokalo*, its blood-red *kava pi*, its blood-red
>   cordyline,

Its blood-red fish, its red fish,
Be turned to become *renga*.
Glance aside, you, to the affairs being done there,
Be scooped up hither turmeric liquid from *nuanga* being
    made there
Be gathered hither to Fiora
That a mark may be secured for you and the gods.

This formula is addressed to the Eel-God, Tuna, who is the
controller of the fresh water on the island, and hence of great
importance for the *nuanga*. He is imagined to have as attendants a
train of lesser spirits, only known by collective titles; that these
titles involve the idea of redness is in line with the colour associations given later in the appeal. The 'perfume of the God' is a
reference to the role of the Atua i Kafika, explained earlier. (This
deity, though controller of the turmeric, was said by the Ariki
Tafua to be amenable to the influence of the Eel-God, since he
was the 'cleansed son' – *tama furu* – of the latter by a rite performed in the spirit-world.) The *fetau* leaf referred to is the symbolic name given to a scrap of *kaka* fibre used later in a subsequent
filtration (in the *rotoa*). The appeal for conversion of *tauo* to *renga*
shows how the final proportions between them are believed to be
not simply a physical relation, but one governed by spirit action.
The stimulation of the gods by reference to a 'mark' refers to a
later rite of celebration of the end of the *nuanga*; it is a further
appeal to their love of prestige and recognition by men. Citation
of red plants and fish is regarded as a stimulus to the brilliance of
the colour of the turmeric; other natural objects are to be drained
of their redness to amplify that of the pigment. And the theory of
invisible abstraction of material is seen in the request that other
lands where turmeric is made may have it filched from them, and
even the *nuanga* of his fellow chiefs be raided. For this, the Ariki
Tafua relies primarily on the female deity, the Atua of Fiora, who
is believed to have long nails particularly useful for this. The
expressions also suggest the movements of a woman's hand-net,
used in a scooping manner.

Variant phrases in another formula given by the Ariki Tafua
appeal to the Eel-God to

Stand firmly in your *tafatafa*,
With eyes clear and light for the wanderers,
Looking that your mark be not snatched away.

Here the emphasis is on the protective functions of the deity; the 'wanderers' are held to be unnamed spirits of earth and woods, alert to steal turmeric; they were described somewhat indignantly as 'thieving *atua*' – with delightful inconsistency, considering other portions of the formula!

This intangible thieving of turmeric pigment is firmly believed in by the Tikopia. The Ariki Kafika said to me on this point, 'We go out in the morning and find the level in the bowl has sunk down; we look at our *renga* which has been taken away completely.' The statement, in this exaggerated form, was common to all turmeric producers. But in the Tikopia morality a distinction is drawn between stealing turmeric from foreign lands and taking it from one's fellow islanders. The Ariki Kafika denied strongly that he asked his deities to rob the other chiefs, and said that it was the Ariki Tafua alone who did so. There is a definite parallel here with the situation of the *faunga vaka* described earlier, where the personal idiosyncrasies of the Ariki Tafua have seemed to affect his formulae. The Ariki Kafika concentrates on the abstraction of turmeric from abroad. A section of the formula he gave me runs:

> Go you to fish from the direction above
> (North and East)
> That a mark may be secured for you
> (From) Samoa, and Rotuma and Anuta,
> Lands in which the *nuanga* is made.

This formula here analysed is termed *Raufangota Manu* as a whole because in essence it is an appeal for *manu*, for the efficacy or success of the operations. It is used not only as a preliminary to filtration, but also in the subsequent processes of decantation in the sacred enclosure known as the *rotoa*.

We may now return to the proceedings of the Tafua *nuanga*.

'BINDING OF THE WATER'

After reciting the formula for the initial filtration the Ariki Tafua returned to his house and made offerings to his deities and ancestors. (In olden days he would have performed the full kava ritual.) This over, he came back and performed another rite over the necessary element in the process – the water supply. This rite is termed *Te Noa o Te Vai* ('The Binding of the Water'). The

procedure, which was the same for other *nuanga*, I was told, was
to tie a bunch of leaves, symbolic of the deity in control of the
water supply, to a tree near by. In this case the tree stood in the
tafatafa enclosure, and the leaves used were of the *tafatafa a Tuna*
plant, of the cane-grass type. As its name suggests, it is a symbol
of Tuna, Eel-God and ruler of fresh water. The formula used by
the chief was given me by him as follows:

> Turn to your tie which has been set up,
> You, deity of the *nuanga*.
> Fish for success that a mark may be secured for you,
> Fish hither from the direction above,
> Lands where the turmeric pigment is made
> Be gathered together here their turmeric liquid to
>   Matautu.
> Its blood-red *kalokalo*, its blood-red cordyline, its
>   blood-red ginger,
> Its blood-red fish, its red fish.
> Turned be the liquid to turmeric,
> Raised be the turmeric to sleep thickly
> And be pressed down below the *tauo*
> Squeezed tightly be its eyes to sleep tightly.

The close resemblance of this formula to that used for the filtration is obvious, and the expression *Raufangota Manu* is even
employed in it. The point is that as the Tikopia say, 'There is only
one formula in turmeric-making, that is, the *Raufangota Manu*'.
This is true in the sense that essentially the same set of phrases is
drawn upon for all the early processes, with variation or omission
according to the particular stage reached. Here the appeal is to
the Eel-God under the title of tutelary deity of the *nuanga*, thus
linking him once more with the operations. Two other points of
interest are the introduction of a new item of colour association,
the wild ginger, one variety of which has a crimson flower; and
the sustained imagery of the turmeric 'sleeping' with tightly shut
eyes, in other words, solidly precipitated. It will be seen later how
important this is.

It is a custom in the *nuanga* of chiefs or elders to take down
certain sacred objects of the group and place them in association
with the turmeric-making. These are usually weapons of famous
ancestors which by their sacredness help to give *manu* to the operations. At Matautu a long spear, formerly the property of Pu Tafua

Lasi, namesake and familiar spirit of the present Ariki Tafua, was brought down from the house and stuck in the ground in the *tafatafa* enclosure. I was told that in other *nuanga* the *rotoa* was usually the spot selected. The object of this custom is to bring ancestors and deities still further into direct relation with the work.

A couple of hours after midday the oven was ready and men and women had a meal in their respective houses. The food was of good quality, in this case a delicacy of mashed taro with coconut oil and coconut sugar. Afterwards work was continued till darkness fell. In the late afternoon a second lot of turmeric roots was cleaned by women and girls.

The meal was termed *te osoango o te ariki*; in former days it would have been prefaced by a brief kava rite, but on this occasion libations only were poured.

POURING OFF THE WATER

The next morning the work of decanting off the water from the settled turmeric began. But first an additional enclosure, the *rotoa*, had to be built. The purpose of this was to hold the bowls of turmeric while they were being allowed to settle before the separation of *renga* from *tauo* – a process known as 'causing the turmeric to sleep'. For this work the inmates of the men's house were awakened before dawn, and after a hasty meal of last night's remnants went off to the work. The *rotoa* was quickly made. It was a circular erection of poles and rails, with a row of sago thatch at the bottom and ordinary floor-mats hung over the top, with coconut fronds laid on the ground. It was about twenty feet in diameter, with the fence about five feet high, enough to protect the work inside from prying eyes. The men then went to the *tafatafa*.

This had been closed during the night by fronds of coconut, to prevent unlawful access. The process of extraction of turmeric depends essentially upon an adequate separation first of the material in suspension in the water from the bulk of this, and second, of the lighter *renga* from the heavier *tauo*. The success of the operations of decanting depends upon the firmness of the layers of pigment, and this of course means absence of disturbance. Hence the pains to exclude all other people than the workers. Moreover, the need for a settled mass of pigment is the reason for the constant appeals for the turmeric to 'be pressed down', 'settled firmly', 'sleep tightly', etc.

When all was ready the chief, as expert, rubbed his hands well with some of the residue thrown away the day before. This seemed to be a technical rather than a ritual procedure. One of the troughs was then uncovered, and a light yellow scum which had formed on the top of the liquid was cleared off with the edge of the hand. Then a number of men gathered at one end of the trough, and the chief at the other. At his signal they lifted, pouring out the water on to the ground. The expert bent down with both hands cupped at the lip of the trough, stemming the outflow. When he saw that the deposit at the bottom was beginning to stir he called 'Leave it! Leave it!' and while he blocked the lip with his hands the assistants lowered their end. This was repeated with each trough in turn.

The deposit of turmeric was then kneaded up with the remaining water, and transferred from the troughs to medium-sized bowls, which were carried off to settle in the *rotoa*. The bowls are termed *kumete fakame tofua*. The transference was done with great care. The chief sat over the bowl with a small piece of *kaka* fibre – the '*fetau* leaf' referred to in the formula quoted. An assistant filled a coconut-shell cup with the liquid, and allowed it to dribble through the fibre into the bowl; thus a second filtration took place. The operation was termed *fakatere* ('making it run'). A little water was added to thin down the liquid when necessary, and the last dregs were removed from the trough, with a little leaf cup.

Two instances will show the care exercised by the expert. One of his sons was about to throw to one side a small cover of which a corner had dipped in the liquid; he was rebuked by his father and made to wash off the infinitesimal amount of turmeric into a bowl. Another son in carrying his end of a bowl to the *rotoa* let it dip, and a few drops splashed on the ground; this provided an indignant outburst from the old man.

When the turmeric of one *eke* had been decanted, that of the other began to be filtered.

SEPARATION OF 'RENGA' AND 'TAUO'

In the late afternoon, the chief, accompanied only by a couple of assistants, went down to the *rotoa*. This enclosure is the most sacred spot in all the *nuanga*, and all men squat down at once when they have finished any piece of work there. Talk is only in whispers, or at the most in very low tones. A prominent feature there is a low stone pillar, upright in the earth. This is the *fatu tunga nuanga*, the stone of the *nuanga* stand, marking the site of the chief's *rotoa* from one generation to another. It is not highly sacred, but has some *tapu* by being a link with ancestors, and the site of the *rotoa* when this is not in being.

Because of the sanctity of the *rotoa*, and its function as the spot where the secrets of the expert are practised to the full, it was said to be the custom of chiefs formerly not to admit commoners to the enclosure, but have members of their own family as their assistants. This rule was broken by the present Ariki Kafika, according to his own account. He said that once in Te Roro he issued an invitation to the commoners who were his partners to enter and see the operations for themselves, that they might know they were not being cheated of their turmeric. Apparently this caused a great stir. The chief said to me, 'I turned the *nuanga* upside down. I said "Come hither you, that each may look upon his property."' One result of this was that Pa Kanava, one of the commoners concerned, composed a dance song of the *mako rima* type, embodying his sensations.

> We two depart for the *nuanga*
> Chiefly brother, thou art *tapu*
> Chiefly brother proceeding with thy deity.
>
> I sit and gaze upon whom?
> I sit and gaze upon whom?
> The *renga* here will separate
> And the *tofua* will descend.
>
> I awoke with a start
> At thy *nuanga* which is made, O!
> Why not sacralize it to be sacred?

This depicts his astonishment at seeing for the first time the separation of *renga* and *tauo* (*tofua*), his praise of the chief, and the rhetorical question as to why the innovation was made.

The actual process of separation is done as before, but with even more precautions. The scum is swept off before the pouring starts, but one danger is from the light filmy suspended matter known as *toao* or *soro*. This is apt to veil the *renga*, so that if it has not set properly some of it is poured off with the water, unseen by the expert. He has to be very alert, with thumb ever-ready to check the flow immediately he sees the colour of *renga* beneath the *toao* film. It is with this critical situation in particular that the *tapu* of the *rotoa* and its silence are correlated.

Once the expert sees that the turmeric has in fact settled firmly at the bottom he orders the bowl to be tipped up and the water poured completely off. The *renga* then appears as a dark-red slime. The expert scrapes this out with his fingers into a small bowl held below; it comes away fairly cleanly, revealing beneath a yellow deposit of *tauo*. This is left untouched for the time, though a couple of cups of fresh water are run over its surface to wash down the last traces of *renga*. As each of the larger bowls is relieved of its *renga* into the smaller bowls, these are set as closely as possible round the marking stone of the *rotoa*. In this neigh-bourhood, presumably, the *manu* is strongest. They are placed carefully on little mats specially plaited from coconut frond, wedged firm with pebbles, and covered over. There are two sets of these small bowls, one containing the bulk of the *renga*, the other the small amount of pigment held in the water with which the *tauo* was washed down. The *renga* is so precious that no trace of it is wasted; this is a ritual as well as a technical precaution, since the deities would be offended at anything savouring of carelessness. The small bowls, *kumete fai renga*, are about two feet long by nine inches deep, and 25 or 30 of them are necessary for the work. Before use they are thoroughly washed out with salt water, and then with fresh, and then rubbed inside and out with the *pauango* residue.

The *rotoa* also has its ritual. Formulae of the *Raufangota Manu* type are recited, particularly with phrases to keep *renga* and *tauo* apart, and to make the yield of the former large. The Ariki Tafua told me that before beginning the separation he muttered:

> Where art thou?
> Draw hither thou
> To me who will face my *uruango*
> Thy thing will be confirmed by thee
> And thy deity there.

Then he said, 'one grasps the bowl and pours'. Another form of words he gave me as permissible to use was as follows:

> Where art thou?
> Draw hither.
> Thy thing has been little, but be it enlarged by thee.
> Be pressed down the *tauo* to sleep tightly,
> And rise only the *renga* to sleep thickly above.

These appeals are directed to an ancestor, his familiar spirit. Under the title of 'Name' (his personal name being borne by the chief), he can be addressed more fully as follows:

> Where art thou, Name, O!
> Grasp firmly the *renga* liquid
> And press down below the nose of the bowl
> And cause to run to me the *toao* to fall
> That we be not laughed at.
> Property of the folk who have come has been handed
>   over utterly to us two,
> Act so that there is a good word for thyself and us two,
> That a cry of thanks may be for thee.

This formula is reminiscent of the attitude of the Ariki Tafua in the canoe and fishing rites: an appeal to the *amour propre* of the ancestor. But it also shows the sense of responsibility of the expert for the turmeric entrusted to his charge by his partners.

According to the Ariki Tafua, when the *tauo* comes up with the *renga* this is the doing of the *atua*; but when the expert observes that the layers are solid, he knows that the deities are with him. He calls 'Lift it up', and the water is poured without fear.

The formulae used by the Ariki Kafika are of the same general type as those quoted, but he makes more play with such phrases as 'Sleep firmly your perfume . . .', in reference to the special controlling role of the Atua i Kafika.

After the *renga* had been dealt with the golden *tauo* was scraped out from the various bowls into a single bowl and kneaded up with water.

The rest of this day's work consisted of the processing of the turmeric of the second *eke* in the *tafatafa*. In this work women were brought in to help, since the taboo of the enclosure applied only while the turmeric of the chief was being handled there. But the women were given the more mechanical tasks, as the carrying of the grated turmeric and feeding the filters with water.

On the following day the *renga* of the chief was finally extracted in the *rotoa*, and the separation of *renga* and *tauo* of the second *eke* made.

BAKING THE TURMERIC

The final operation in the manufacture of the turmeric pigment is the baking. This is done by putting a thick mixture of *renga* and water, with a little coconut oil, into a wooden cylinder and cooking it for many hours in an earth oven. This oven is of a similar type to that used for preparing food, but is of less diameter and deeper, and is reserved for baking turmeric alone. The wooden cylinders, known as *taonga* (*tao* meaning to bake in an oven) or simply as *umu* (ovens) are highly valued. Each is carved from a single block of wood, nowadays with mallet and sharpened spike nail, and the interior is carefully smoothed. The exterior is frequently roughly ornamented in simple geometrical designs. The wood used is usually *fetau*, a hard timber used also for canoes, but sometimes *poumuri*, a softer wood, is employed. The range of their dimensions can be seen from the following series of measurements of six specimens (now in the collection of the Australian National University in Canberra):

Total height Inches	Interior depth Inches	Thickness of wall at mouth Inches	Interior diameter at mouth Inches
$13\frac{1}{2}$	$11\frac{1}{2}$	$\frac{9}{16}$	$4\frac{7}{8}$
$13\frac{1}{4}$	$11\frac{1}{2}$	$\frac{1}{2}$	$4\frac{3}{4}$
11	$9\frac{1}{2}$	$\frac{3}{8}$	4
$12\frac{1}{2}$	$10\frac{1}{2}$	$\frac{7}{16}$	$4\frac{3}{8}$
9	8	$\frac{3}{8}$	$3\frac{1}{2}$
$6\frac{1}{2}$	$5\frac{3}{8}$	$\frac{5}{16}$	$2\frac{5}{8}$

Greater value is attached to some cylinders than to others. Not only are the larger ones more prized, but those are deemed the best which have thin walls and a bore which is almost cylindrical, not greatly tapering. These are of course the most difficult to make. Their virtue is that they are *umu kave renga* ('ovens carrying turmeric'), or *umu kave riu* ('ovens carrying interior') – they will hold a large quantity. A cylinder with a small tapering bore is *umu kave penu* ('an oven carrying husk'). Though these *taonga* are conveniently referred to as 'cylinders' they are only approximately so; in all cases they are slightly tapered from the open end. The closed end is perforated, the hole being used to blow air through to expel the cooked turmeric, and to take a cord for hanging up the cylinder when it is not in use. The cylinders are usually kept slung together in pairs over a beam.

Large cylinders are especially appropriate for providing the turmeric of chiefs – size being here as elsewhere a correlate of rank. Such cylinders often have titles of their own, either commemorating the name of the maker, or his fancy. In Tafua, one large cylinder is known as *Fongarunga* '('Crest Above'); its fellow *Fongarenga* ('Turmeric Crest') broke and was thrown away. These larger cylinders are handed down as heirlooms, and the names of the makers are remembered from one generation to another. The decoration applied to cylinders has no ritual meaning; it is similar in style to that applied to dance-bats, betel-mortars and clubs.

On the day of turmeric-baking in Tafua the cylinders were taken down and looked over for flaws; they were then washed. The hole in the base of each was stopped with a small screw of bark-cloth, the plug. One of the larger ones was filled to the brim with water, which was emptied into a bowl, to estimate its capacity, especially with reference to the amount of dilution of the turmeric with water needed in cooking. 'The water is poured in to observe from it how great is the size of the cylinder; proportionate to the turmeric which will be brought to be mixed with water.'

Attention was then turned to the earth oven. This was at one end of the chief's house, Motuapi. The first operation was to put up a wind-shelter round it, made of poles and sheets of thatch, and for easy access some of the end thatch of the building itself was removed.

The oven is an important ritual object. It has its own tutelary deities, the most prominent being female, since the tending of ovens is largely women's work. The oven deities of Kafika are Pu Fafine, who controls the bottom of the oven; Pufine i Ravenga, under the name of Raupenapena, on one side; and Te Atua i te Uruao, under the name of Tupuasei, on the other. The two former are female deities. The principal guardian of the oven of Tafua is Pufine i Fiora. She is believed to assist the expert in a practical way by making the level of turmeric rise in the cylinder while it is baking, that is, giving a bigger yield. Of such an oven it is said *e manutia*, it is endowed with efficacy. To the oven of Tafua also come Feke, the Octopus God, husband of Pufine i Fiora, and their son Tufaretai, one of the special deities of Fusi house.

At the end of each *nuanga* the oven is filled in. It has therefore to be dug out again afresh each season. This is a ritual operation, prefaced by an appropriate formula. As the stake of the digger is driven into the soil he calls to the chief 'Here, the oven!' The chief then appeals to the oven-gods. The formula given me by the Ariki Tafua for this was:

> Turn you, Ancestress
> To your oven about to be prepared
> Excrete upon the poured-in turmeric to jump over
> To stand like the flesh of the sea-snail.

The appeal is for an increase of turmeric, the metaphor of excretion coming in again, as discussed in Chapter 10. The simile of the sea-snail was explained as due to an analogy between the opening of the turmeric cylinder and that of the snail's shell. The pigment is desired to creep up in the cylinder and overflow just as the foot of the snail spreads out from the shell.

The Ariki Kafika told me that he himself drove in the stick first, and recited:

> Pierce with efficacy your oven
> Ancestral guardians of the oven
> Tupuasei and Pu Fafine and Raupenapena.

The oven was then cleared to a depth of about three feet, the fire was started, and stones were piled over it to heat. The next operation was the preparation of the pigment. The bowls were brought from the *rotoa*, and the turmeric kneaded up with the water, more water being added if required. On the correct consistency of the liquid depends much of the success of the baking. To differences in this, in conjunction with fluctuations in the temperature of the oven, are probably due most of the failures of the finished product which the Tikopia attribute to the influence of spirits or broken taboos. Great care was used at this stage. As the chief was kneading the mass he said to the people around 'Look here first of all.' Those watching said, 'But what is going to be done? Why not yourself look after your own turmeric, act according to your own wish, to your thought!' This was largely politeness. 'It is constantly done in the *eke* as they proceed', I was told. The rest of the people did not interfere, and proffered little advice. There are three states of viscosity recognized at this stage:

Te renga e soko – it is still thick, falling in blobs. It is *suasuamatu* – thinner – but still not flowing freely. It is *tere* – of a proper thin consistency, running freely from the fingers. In this last state it is fit for the oven. A small amount of coconut oil is also needed in baking; this is poured into the cylinder first, the correct measure being that it just covers the finger-nail of the expert when he touches the bottom. According to the Ariki Kafika the expert may also repeat a formula at this point:

> Look to the valuables of your turmeric to sleep properly.

The filling of the wooden cylinder is a highly ritual affair. The Ariki Tafua wound a new bark-cloth round his waist, and kneeling, elevated the bowl of liquid in formal fashion, orienting it towards the cylinder, which was held by an assistant. In this position he recited a formula, which he gave me later, as follows:

> I eat ten times your excrement, Matapula!
> Your *uruango* is to be poured out
> Pour out with efficacy the *uruango*.

He appealed to the Atua i Kafika here, since this was one of the most critical moments of the *nuanga*. The Ariki Kafika gave me a formula, which was closely akin to a portion of the *Raufangota Manu*, its main stress being an appeal to prestige.

> Turn you to your *nuanga*
> And to your perfume, to turn out well,
> To be secured a mark for you.
> Stand firmly in your *nuanga*
> Nor lead away a rumour to other *nuanga*
> That our *nuanga* has been bad
> Lest you be laughed at here.

'It is recited only for the turmeric to be good', said the chief in comment on this formula. The formula at this stage is termed the *veronga renga*, from the action of levelling the bowl.

The turmeric liquid was then poured into the cylinder, and at the same time the Ariki Tafua said:

Tiko tiko tiko, tiko, tiko,
Solo ke pi, solo ke sa.

This was one of the very few formulae that were recited aloud. It is difficult to render the meaning of this in a form both concise and exact. It is essentially the same motif of excretion representing metaphorically productivity. *Tiko* is the ordinary word for excretion, and *solo* is an adjunct descriptive of diarrhoetic faeces. What is demanded is that the turmeric shall rise above its natural level so that the cylinder is brimful (*pi*) and the material appears (*sa*) over the edge. Another variant of the formula given me by the Ariki Kafika was:

Excrete, Ancestor, into the cylinder
To fill it that your mark may be secure.

In another variant the turmeric is required to 'jump' over the edge of the vessel. This formula is termed 'the *taurangi* of the turmeric which will appear'. While the formula of the *veronga renga* was being repeated the people present bowed their heads, and no one might look, but when they heard the *taurangi* they all looked up to see the liquid rise in the cylinder.

The liquid was stirred with a thin rod cut from the midrib of a coconut frond; this was called 'the paddle'. The expert told his assistant to stir 'pulling the liquid upwards', so that an even mixture was assured. The other cylinders were filled without ceremony. Half a dozen were baked at the one time.

The oven was prepared by spreading the glowing stones to get an even heat, and a thick lining of leaves was put in to prevent the cylinders from being burnt. As each type of leaf was put in it was announced – by implication to the invisible deities. The cylinders were then set upright in the pit and wedged firmly. As the first of them was lifted the formulae just mentioned were repeated, backed by another:

Be excreted by you, People of the Oven,
To jump over.

To protect the surface of the liquid from the oven coverings, small bars of coconut midrib were laid crosswise on top of each cylinder. Here again a formula was recited:

Here! your bar which was cut on the top of Reani,
Be it thrown to thud on the top of Tumuaki.
Here! your bar which was cut on the top of Korofau,
Be it thrown to thud on the top of Tafaronga.

A variant of this was given me by the Ariki Kafika:

Here! the bar.
Your bar was cut on the Head of the Land,
Be it glanced aside to thud on Tumuaki.

The proper names mentioned are those of hilltops on the island.[1] The Head of the Land is a metaphor for Reani, the highest peak. The demand is purely figurative – that a bar cut from a palm growing on one peak should be pushed up with such force by the rising turmeric that it will be hurled on to another peak a mile away! Moreover, it is not at all necessary that the bar should have come from the spot mentioned, and in this case they certainly did not. And all that is wanted is that the turmeric shall swell in cooking enough to fill the cylinder.

The oven was then closed with thick pads of leaves, and left for four hours or so. No formulae were directed towards the turmeric in this period, but in former days, I was told, a kava rite of the *veronga renga* was performed on the first day, when the turmeric of the chief was being baked. On subsequent occasions the 'kava' of the turmeric oven was done, with libations only. When I was there, it was made with coconut milk.

When it was judged that the pigment was baked the oven was uncovered. Mats were spread for the oven deities, and a cylinder set up on each, with food from the ordinary oven as offerings. In Motuapi one mat by the lip of the oven was for Nau Fiora and Feke, and another, by one of the posts on the south side of the house, for Tufaretai. Wrappings for the pigment were prepared from strips of bark-cloth, two for each cylinder, and carefully measured against it to leave room for tying. These are termed *kuru*.

Then came the most anxious moment of the whole *nuanga*. The turmeric was to be turned out, and it would be seen whether the operations had been successful. The method of removal was ingenious. The bark-cloth wrappings were laid on the floor, and the wooden cylinder set mouth down in the centre. The plug was

[1] See Map (a) in *We, the Tikopia*, 1936.

removed from the base of the cylinder – often by the teeth of the assistant – and handed to the expert, who tested it with his finger-tip to see if the turmeric was dry. It was so. The assistant then bent over, applied his lips to the hole and blew with all his force. When the turmeric began to move he gently raised his hands, still blowing, until he was able to lift off the cylinder, and reveal a red shining pillar of pigment. (See Plate IIB in *Social Change in Tikopia*, 1959.) This met with the admiration of all. The pigment was immediately wrapped up with extreme gentleness.

As this moment is so critical, formulae are recited to promote a safe delivery. The Ariki Tafua said that he used the following:

> Descend properly, descend
> On to your property which has been spread out.

The 'property' is the bark-cloth wrapping, spoken of in this honorific way as a kind of flattery to the turmeric. The Ariki Kafika said that he appealed to the Atua i Kafika in the following words:

> I eat ten times your excrement, Ancestor!
> Fall properly your perfume.

When the pigment proves refractory, as I saw on subsequent occasions, both practical and ritual measures are used to coax it out. The expert takes over, and strokes down the outside of the cylinder gently. This must be regarded as a sympathetic move-ment, but the Tikopia give a practical reason for not being more firm; they say if the cylinder be tapped, the pillar of turmeric inside will crack, which seems reasonable. At the same time the expert speaks:

> Come down below to be wrapped up in your property –

or some similar form of words. If the turmeric is still unrespon-sive, a little oil is poured into the plug-hole, and the cylinder allowed to stand for a few minutes. It is then stroked again, with soothing sounds of 'Down, down . . .' and blown again. This seems to be always successful. The blowing of the first cylinder after the failure of the turmeric of Pa Fetauta was a matter of great concern. The blower made all kinds of small adjustments ner-vously before beginning; as the cylinder began to move the heads of the chief and his son bent anxiously down to see if the pigment showed any signs of being too soft, and I heard the chief whisper 'Fall properly' to it. But all was well; it came out smoothly, but hard. All were elated. The chief chuckled with delight, and the blower gave a broad wink and a smile around. They told me they were glad this cylinder had turned out well since it showed that the effects of the breach of taboo by Tekarima had passed off. Moreover, it was clear that the chief was pleased because he had been successful in producing good turmeric for his partner. The blowing of the turmeric of the Akoako of the Ariki Kafika is a matter of more than domestic concern; the Ariki Kafika is a day in advance of all others, and if his pigment turns out well it is believed that this is a good augury for all the rest. People say 'There, it has fallen properly; now our *nuanga* will be well.' The Ariki Kafika himself, imbued with his responsibility, said that he recited formulae not for his turmeric alone, but that the *nuanga* of the whole land might be successful.

Sometimes, as in the case of Pa Fetauta noted, the pigment does turn out badly. This is a source of shame as well as vexation to the owner, since it implies either that he or his people have broken a taboo, or that his gods are inefficient. I was told that sometimes a man, seeing his *renga* emerge in bad condition, smashes it up in anger, and goes off to his home, to wail a dirge for his misfortune. But this must be an overstatement. When I asked if the turmeric was thrown away, the Matautu people laughed at the idea; that of Pa Fetauta was at once worked up again in a bowl and baked. In no circumstances is *renga* which is not of a good colour ever used as food, as Rivers alleges (*History of Melanesian Society*, I, 328). His statement is due to a confusion between *renga* and *tauo*.

The partners of the *nuanga* work together till the turmeric of all has been properly extracted; no one leaves when his own is through. This co-operation is expressed thus: 'We make our things, and have finished; if we have gone identically, then are we finished.'

RITES OF COMPLETION

Since the rites of the turmeric centre primarily on the various *Uruango*, the celebration of the first successful baking is known as *Fakatutu Uruango* – 'Setting Up the Uruango'. It is a kava rite performed outside the house in the early morning. Its object is a formal acknowledgment to the guardian deities. The kava bowl only is used, but the importance of the occasion is shown by the preparation of *roi* the evening before. Separate lots of this are made for men and women, that of the latter being eaten in the oven house. Another feature of importance is the offering of bark-cloth to his ancestors or deities by each partner. When the chief has laid out his cloth, each other partner follows suit, with the words, 'That is thy *maro*, Male Ancestor.' Though the Ariki Tafua did not in 1928 perform the kava, he set out his offerings, as follows:

> To: Te Atua i Kafika, an orange cloth
> Te Atua i te Vai, an orange cloth
> Pusi Uri (Atua i te Tai), a white cloth
> Te Atua i Tafua, a white cloth
> Pu Tafua Lasi (ancestor), an orange cloth
> Pu i Tai, a white cloth
> Feke, a white cloth
> Nau Fiora, a white bark-cloth square.

Some of these *maro* are set out singly, others are in bundles of two – as those of Te Atua i te Vai and Te Atua i te Tai; and Pu i Tai and his father Feke. The formulae recited are of the same general type as those already recorded. An extract from one given by the Ariki Kafika is:

> That is your kava, Guardian Deities of the *nuanga* and
> Male Ancestors.
> Your work has been well.
> Your mark has been secured.
> I eat ten times your excrement.

After this rite the rest of the work proceeds until the whole of the turmeric of each unit has been successfully baked. When this is over the concluding rite of the *nuanga* proper takes place. It is a de-sacralizing of the oven, accompanied as in the case of the canoe rites by driving off the guardian deities.

The rite of Tafua took place in the early morning, and was prefaced by a meal that for the first time since the work began was eaten in full daylight. The chief took a water bottle filled at the flume of the *tafatafa* and sprinkled the water freely over the oven.

This was the *fakatanga* rite. Calling upon the deities by name, the chief said:

> Your oven, Ancestress, is being sprinkled this morning,
> To be washed with your deities there,
> To part you from your oven . . . (and so on for the others).

This lustration was believed to render the oven and its vicinity innocuous to human beings now. The pit was then filled in, this giving the name of 'Bury Oven' to the concluding *eke* of the season, though its members do not necessarily perform this task.

The sprinkling of the oven was followed by another rite of separation, the *Fakarere Nga Atua*, the 'Causing the Gods to Fly'. No formulae were repeated, but a plain indication was given that their presence was no longer required. Buttresses of the Tahitian chestnut were beaten with staves, old canoe hulls and bowls were banged, shrieks of '*Iefu! Iefu!*' split the air. The Ariki Tafua said to me, 'The guardian deities of the *nuanga* are invited to go.' It seems an ignominious reward, but the Tikopia do not see it thus. The function of the rite was wider, also. It marked the formal conclusion of the time of *tapu*; restrictions on food, posture, social and sexual intercourse were now removed, and in actual fact as distinct from spirit theory it was really a celebration of freedom regained.

The *tauo*, which had meanwhile been lying in a bowl in the *rotoa*, now came into the proceedings again. It was put into a bag of *kaka* fibre, where it slowly dried into a yellow powder; this was drawn upon for food as required. But on the final day of the *nuanga* a special dish was prepared, in which *tauo* was the principal ingredient. This was *sua tauo*, a kind of sago pudding made by bringing a mixture of sago, coconut cream and *tauo* to the boil in a bowl, with hot stones. This pleasant yellow pudding made a kind of parting feast for the members of the *nuanga* before they left for their homes.

MARKING OF THE TURMERIC

The turmeric ritual does not end with the *nuanga*. By way of epilogue comes the imprinting of the sacred pigment in the temples of the gods. Owing to the defection of the Ariki Tafua I saw only the fragments of this ritual, and the account here is given from what I was told by him, the Ariki Kafika, and some other men, of what used to take place.

Nowadays, after the *nuanga*, the turmeric pillars are unwrapped, worked up with oil till they are of the consistency of stiff putty, then rolled up in a banana leaf and in bark-cloth. After a few months, when hard, they are re-wrapped and bound round with sinnet cord, to hang up undisturbed from the roof, perhaps for years.

In former times, a few days after the 'blowing' the turmeric 'was conveyed to Uta'. The way was led by the Akoako of Kafika, in accordance with its importance as the perfume of the presiding deity, and this gave the signal for the turmeric of the other chiefs and their elders to be taken also. Their turn came the next day. The turmeric packages were carried on long sticks, on men's shoulders, to the temples of their clan whichever it might be. There, the *renga* of the whole clan were ranged in line, before the chief, and the rite began. From the simplest point of view the rite consisted only in rubbing a succession of strokes with the turmeric-covered finger-tip on various structural portions of the building. Its significance was, however, much more than that. Each mark of the *renga* was a stroke made as an offering to an *atua* as a recognition of the part he had played in the extraction of the turmeric. And it will be remembered that various timbers of the building are regarded as sacred to specific deities, and even as embodiments of them. The marking is then a form of decoration of the god, akin to the putting of bands of turmeric on the body and arms of a spirit medium.

The procedure was for the chief to open each package in turn, rub his finger on the top of it, and then smear the appropriate post or rafter. The mark, termed *tusi* (the word being used nowadays for European writing) was about an inch in length.

The *tusi*, as so many other rites, had its definite order of precedence. On the first day the Ariki Kafika made the marks in Kafika temple; on the next the Ariki Taumako did likewise in Taumako temple. The Ariki Tafua, who came next, took three days or longer, and the Ariki Fangarere completed the ritual with a day for Nukuora.

But there was a still further order prescribed. In each case the *tusi* were not made haphazard, but in a definite sequence. Thus in Kafika temple the order was:

Pu ma (two strokes, one each for Tafaki and Karisi)
Futi o te Kere (Atua i Raropuka)
Te Ariki Tapu (Atua i Kafika)
Rakiteua (Atua i Tafua)
Sakura (Atua i Taumako)
The Kau Firifiri (chiefly ancestors, each one stroke)

Each time the chief said 'That is your mark . . .' calling the name of the deity or ancestor concerned. Then kava was performed with the *raurau kumete*, and the usual libations poured.

Events in the case of Tafua were more complex. The chief went first to Tafua temple, and made a set of markings for the benefit of his ancestors on the end of the house to the north. Then he went to the small temple known as Te Toka, or Te Fare Fiti, since its guardian deity was the Atua Fiti. A tree was cut down – a sapling of paper mulberry – and tied up horizontally at one end of the house. The chief then spread a number of bark-cloths on this beam, so that they hung down to the ground. On one side the cloth of the Atua i Tafua was hung, and that of the Eel-god; on the other that of Meteua, the Atua Fiti. The filter-cloth from the *nuanga*, a *tapu* object, was also hung up there. Then a *tusi* was made for the principal deities of the clan, one to a rafter. The order here was: Te Atua i Tafua; Tuna toto; Pusi; Te Atua Fiti; Nga Ariki (i.e. Pu ma) – the last on a single rafter. The kava was then made in the usual way.

On the following day the chief went to Tafua temple, and the marking was done on the inland side of the building. Here the order was: Te Atua i Tafua; Te Atua Lasi; Te Atua i Sao; Te Atua i Fusi; Pu Tafua Lasi. On the third day the *tusi* were made on the south side of the house, to Te Ariki Vai and Pusi toto. It will have been noted that marks had already been made for these two Eel Gods in the small temple, under other names. This was explained by the chief as due to the fact that the former were their names for the sacred adzes, while the latter were their names for the *nuanga*.

The general function of the *tusi* rite was thus in directly linking up the turmeric extraction, an external activity with primarily an economic object, to the religious system of gods, ancestors and temples which was focused upon Uta. By this means the *nuanga* was made to form an integral part of the whole season of the Work of the Gods.

Each evening the *roi* was prepared and the kava performed the next morning. On the final day a variation was made in the presentation of the kava stem. Instead of having its leaves removed, as usual, the bush had its leaves tied up, was dug up and removed entire to the temple. This is a peculiarity for which no explanation could be given by my informants. But its function probably lies simply in giving an individuality to this Tafua rite; such small differences are common in Tikopia, giving a touch of privilege to an otherwise uniform rite.

Some time after, at no fixed interval, the Ariki Tafua made his *tusi* in Motuapi in Faea. (I saw these marks when I attended his *nuanga*, and they first drew my attention to this phase of the ritual, which I had imagined to be finished.) Here the order of precedence of the deities differs somewhat from that in Uta, and some different ones are included. In Motuapi the first is the Atua i Tafua. A formula is recited asking him for general benefits:

> Here! Your mark, Rakiteua
> Turn to your mark
> Which is being marked on this morning.
> It is marked for welfare,
> That a calm may fall,
> To lay down the leaf of the wind.

Next follows a stroke to his 'Mother', whose name is unknown. 'The mark of your Mother there!' On the adjoining timber a mark is made to the Ariki Vai, and beside it one to Matapula (the Atua i Kafika), and then one to Pu Tafua Lasi. These are all at the northern end of the building. At the southern end *tusi* are then made to: Sa Tai (including Tufaretai); Tokitaitekere and Tarikotu (together); Pu Taufiti; Te Arafonu (Pu Kafika Lasi); Pu Veterei and Tangata o Namo (together); Fokimainiteni. Here several marks are made for spirits who do not figure in the direct ancestral line, but who were related to Tafua through their mothers and were men of *manu* in their lifetime.

The rite at Motuapi does not fall within the actual sequence of the Work of the Gods. The end of the *tusi* in Tafua is the signal for the Ariki Fangarere to go to Nukuora. That same evening *roi* is made for Marae, and the ground is cleared for the ritual dances there on the following day. The proceedings at Tafua often used to be a source of vexation to the other chiefs. Three days was the normal span, but no interference was possible if the Ariki Tafua extended the period. The other chiefs complained bitterly that in the time of Pukenga, the preceding chief, three or four days at the most sufficed him; but that the present chief, before he gave up the visit to Uta, delayed greatly. He would *tusi* one day, then rest for a day or two, *tusi* again, and rest again, while the other chiefs were fretting to proceed to the Dance. The other side of the matter was given by the Ariki Tafua himself. He said 'It is good for a young man to go daily to make the marks, but for an old man – he becomes sick of it. It is good if he is living in Namo and can come over by canoe, but if he is living in Faea he becomes very tired.' This illustration reinforces a general point that under-lies much of the Work of the Gods – that conformity to ritual is not an automatic affair, the easiest way of behaving; it demands a sacrifice in time and energy.

DANCE SONGS OF TURMERIC EXTRACTION

The work and ritual of turmeric extraction are now over. But the activity has repercussions on the social life of the people after-wards, which must be briefly mentioned. The yield of pigment of the different *nuanga*, the skill of experts and incidents in the *nuanga* group are topics of conversation for months afterwards. Specific-ally, they become enshrined in more permanent form by being used as themes for dance songs. I recorded nine of these songs, and there were doubtless many more that I could have secured by further inquiry. One of their most noticeable characteristics is their preoccupation with the purely technical details of the pro-cess of extraction. It seems clear that this is a correlate of the inter-est taken in the process, and the value attached to the skill of the expert. Translations of two songs will serve to illustrate this. The first, an ancient song of the *ngore* type, deals with the early stages of extraction:

Tafito: Sleep for the turmeric
        Which will be grated there.
        Plait mats
        For depositing it, O!
        Bring it hither, pour it in front of the house.

Kupu: Divide it among the turmeric-separating filters;
      Its filter-cloths have been prepared, O!
      The experts go and divide it among the bowls.

The second song was composed by Pu Torokinga, father of the present elder of that name. This refers to the preparations for baking the pigment.

Tafito: Bring it hither, and pour, pour
   Its oil first,
   First into the cylinder.
   Let the *renga* rise
   And stand up like a pudding of coconut cream.

Kupu: The expert handling the *renga* is busy, is busy;
   Are busy, are busy his hands
   With things of the land.

The phrase 'things of the land' conveys the idea of the value and interest of the product to all the people. It will be noted that in both songs reference is made to the expert, deemed to be a crucial factor in the productive process. Four out of the nine songs refer specifically to the expert by title, and three others to his functions.

One of these songs is of peculiar interest in that it refers to an archaic type of *nuanga*. This is known as the *nuanga nunu*, as distinct from the *nuanga sanasana* of today. The difference is one of technical procedure, not of ritual and organization. The exact nature of the *nuanga nunu* process is not very clear to me, since it seems to have died out about fifty years before I was in Tikopia, and no old men then living had seen it. Those of the generation immediately before them, as the mother's brother of the present Ariki Kafika, and the father of Pa Torokinga, were said to have participated in it. Its distinguishing feature appears to have been a differential decantation of *renga* and *tauo*, with the turmeric in suspension, not settled as a deposit at the bottom of the bowl. The old men said that the *pauango* was filtered with the filter-fibre not in a funnel, but held on a kind of ladder; after the filtrate had stood for a time it was transferred to smaller bowls, and the separation of *renga* and *tauo* was then made directly. The expert stirred up the *renga* with his hand, and then let it run out over his fingers, judging by its colour when it was time to stop and divert the *tauo* into another bowl. It was said that the expert needed a strong wrist, as his hand was liable to be 'gripped' by the *tauo* and held. It was said also that the *nuanga nunu* required more skill than the *nuanga sanasana*, so that while nowadays every expert, good or indifferent, gets some yield, formerly some got a yield and others got none at all. It appears in fact to have been a less efficient process than that of the present time.

The old type of *nuanga*, like the present type, was believed to have originated at Somosomo, on the initiative of the Atua i Kafika. The stone which now stands in Somosomo marks the site of the old *nuanga nunu*. Another name for this technique was *te rafu*, or *rarafu*, rendered poetically as *rorofu*.

The song mentioned commemorates an incident which befell Pu Saukirima while he was helping the expert. His hand was held in the *tauo* (as in sodden sand) and he had to call for aid.

> The *tauo* there is touched
> The trough when struck rings hither in
> turmeric-getting.

> When touched it will resound,
> When touched it will grip,
> Starting up,
> 'Some water, some water
> To (run) down quickly on to my hands.'

Postscript

Whereas in 1928 I went through the proceedings of the turmeric manufacture of the Ariki Tafua, in 1952 I was a participant in the turmeric-making of Kafika. I did not see the full kava ritual, owing to the illness of the chief, but I did get enough material to confirm my original account, as well as a few fresh details. My main informant here was Pa Fenuatara, who officiated as expert, and also took the place of his father to some degree as ritual performer.

During the rites of Somosomo the Ariki Kafika raised the question of the turmeric procedures, and was assured that the root would be dug the following day. He expressed some anxiety about the work on the grounds that there was no food for the workers. The next day he instructed one of his grandsons to go and 'turn' the turmeric in Uta, and 'announce' it (i.e. to the Atua i Kafika). The Ariki Fangarere added 'Anything that's done should be done rapidly, it's the perfume of the god indeed!'

The programme followed the same technical sequence as before, but was speeded up somewhat because of food shortage. Pa Fenuatara gave me the sequence of kava rites as follows: kava for sewing the sheets of coconut fibre; for cleansing the turmeric roots; for grating the roots; for cooking the turmeric to solidify it; and finally for despatching the gods from the scene when their work was done. But he said that whereas formerly the first two kava rites would have been performed on separate days, in this season they would be combined.

The working party of Kafika was a relatively small one owing to the food situation: grating started with only four grating staves and two bowls, and a few women at work, only about a quarter of the equivalent group in 1928 in the Tafua party.

The gods of the *nuanga*, according to Pa Fenuatara, were the Atua i Kafika, the Atua Fiti and Feke, the Atua i Faea, and to each a symbolic bark-cloth 'tie' was bound, to attach him to the turmeric manufacture. Cycas and fern fronds were used respectively for the first two deities; I observed no leaf decoration for Feke. For the Atua i Kafika the Ariki called out the formula:

> That is your tie, my Sacred Chief
> If another spirit comes, drive him away.

For the Atua i Faea he said:

> That is your tie, Feke
> May your spring of water yield turmeric
> And let the water thrive.

Meanwhile the *kaumafuta*, the filter funnel, had been constructed in traditional style and filtration proceeded normally (cf. *Primitive Polynesian Economy*, 1939, plates II and IV, with RM, 1963, Plate 4A). The troughs used by the Kafika group for this were 'Somosomo', made by Pa Fenuatara; 'Te Akaungoro' (the 'Snoring Reef'), made by his brother Pa Taramoa; and 'Fasi Onge', the chief one (*matua nafa*). The name of this trough, 'Famine District', referred to a story. Several generations ago a man Pa Ngaruefu, living in Faea, said that Ravenga was famine-struck. The chief Pu Kafika Lasi, hearing this, constructed a turmeric trough and called it by this derogatory name. Then came sa Faea and made a cream pudding with *vakiri*, a vegetable like an aerial yam. This angered Pu Kafika Lasi, who went and shot off an arrow at Mapusanga temple to express his displeasure.

After the filtration was over the trough of turmeric liquid was covered with a sheet of thatch and allowed to stand overnight. An evening kava rite was performed, with offerings to past chiefs, Pu ma on Katea and Ama, the Atua i Takarito, the Atua Pouri, Pu Fafine, Pufine i Ravenga and the Atua i Faea. The next morning the turmeric was transferred from trough to bowl, and allowed to settle ('sleep'). In the late afternoon it was decanted. This took place in the *rotoa* enclosure, with talk in whispers or low tones, and all movements quiet.

The next morning the turmeric oven was dug out at the west end of the house Teve, and thatch shelter put up to shield it from the gaze of passers-by. About eight men were present, including the Ariki Kafika. At this time he had fallen ill, and alternated between sitting up rather vacantly and lying down in a comatose state, from which he was aroused when necessary for the ritual. (At one stage, when appealed to by Pa Fenuatara he told him to get on with it himself, to which his son replied, 'Well, uncover your face then' – so that there could be symbolic communication between them.) Pa Fenuatara, as expert in charge, worked up the turmeric into a proper consistency for pouring and baking in the cylindrical wooden container. (For illustration see my 'Tikopia Woodworking Ornament', *Man*, 1960, no. 27.) The work was done with great care, and considerable anxiety was displayed. In the end the cylinder was 'blown' successfully, and there was much congratulation.

Several points of special interest arose during these operations.

The Ariki Taumako, to whom I talked at this time, told me that his main gods for the *nuanga* were: Pu ma, the Atua i Kafika, and the Atua i te Tai (the Sea Eel). The oven and the water spring were under the control of the last-named. A special basket of food was set out for him, and from this the food was never given to women and children. He pointed out that sa Kafika did not set out an offering for the Atua i te Tai. The chief's spear, bound with a decoration of red cordyline dedicated to Pu ma, was stuck in the ground in the *tafatafa* and later in the *rotoa*.

On comparing the events of this *nuanga* with the description given in the account of that in 1928, I realized that no kava rite

had taken place after the recital of the *Raufangota Manu* formula.
I tackled Pa Fenuatara about this, but he was reluctant to discuss
the matter. He said the Ariki had forgotten it – an old man, losing
his memory – and that he himself had also forgotten. All this was
very cursory. I then reverted to the subject later and again he was
rather curt. Then after a while he said suddenly 'There is a saying
"Things that the Ariki forgets, are wrong, but they are things of
the Ariki." No common man may correct him. Because if he
forgets, when another kava comes, he will remember.' In other
words, it is not for a commoner to meddle with the ritual concerns of a chief – the responsibility lies on the chief himself. (In
actual fact, ordinary people *do* jog the chief's memory on occasion.)

I also inquired of Pa Fenuatara if the Kafika *nuanga* employed
the same ritual technique of trying to steal from other chiefs as
apparently did the old Ariki Tafua (see p. 436). This made Pa
Fenuatara angry. 'It's bad', he said. 'The chiefs perform separately,
but they have one finger-marking', i.e. the symbolic acknowledgment is primarily to the Atua i Kafika. He reaffirmed that
the Ariki Kafika applies the 'Fishing' formula only to Samoa,
Rotuma and Anuta, lands in which turmeric is made. (On looking through the original account once more, I feel I may have
done some injustice to the old Ariki Tafua here!)

On the subject of licit foods for the turmeric-making Pa Fenuatara was more liberal than the old Ariki Tafua had been. He said
it was all right to go to the houses of people not engaged in the
nuanga, and eat there, provided that one was given actual hot
food. 'There is only one taboo – anything cool.' He rejected the
idea that sugar was taboo, as the old Ariki Tafua had insisted.
'Sugar is not taboo, because when you put it in, pour it into hot
water, it vanishes.' Tinned milk was also allowed, on the same
principle. (One suspected that this modern, more relaxed attitude
was perhaps linked with the growing pleasure that Tikopia took
in tea richly laced with milk and sugar.) Pumpkin was allowed, as
against papaya, which dripped water. As regards excretion, bowel
movements inland were forbidden, but urination was allowed.
When the *nuanga* took place in Te Roro, excretion was allowed in
the lake.

It was significant that after the turmeric had been successfully
'blown' Pa Fenuatara reverted again to the question of sugar. He

pointed out that he had been right about sugar being not taboo, as against Pu Tafua; no damage had been done to the turmeric! Here is an instance of a taboo not being simply blindly accepted, or rejected on arbitrary grounds. The issue is a matter of argument, and quasi-experimental putting the question to the test – with the proviso that the basic assumptions about taboos as such in a technical context are valid.

The next morning the new turmeric was taken to Uta, in company with some turmeric from a former year – since this time there was only one cylinder and this would seem inadequate. In Uta the principal members of Kafika temple were marked as described earlier (see p. 455). Later similar markings were made in the house in Tai. These markings were a formal acknowledgment to the principal gods for the success of the turmeric manufacture. They were made by elders as well as chiefs. In 1952 Pa Fatumaru, who had not made the marks that season since he had prepared no turmeric because of the famine, described the symbolic order of this procedure as follows in his temple in Uta: stone, to the Atua i Fatumaru; post, to the Atua i Kafika and Tafito; two rafters to Pu ma; a post to the Atua i Taumako; a rafter to Marapa; a rafter to Pu Lasi. After the marking, the kava was performed. In this way he acknowledged and invoked a very powerful set of deities.

In 1928 the rite of the Despatch of the Gods (*Fakarerenga Atua*) appeared to have taken place before the marking of temples, at least in Tafua. But in 1952 in Kafika it took place afterwards. The proceedings were carried out on *mata paito* of Teve, near the *rotoa*, just before 6 a.m. The Ariki Kafika, who by this time had recovered from illness, officiated, and about a dozen males of his family were present. He donned his ritual vestment and offerings of bark-cloth were laid out, with the 'ties' of cycas and fern frond laid on them. He recited a formula over the kava stem, and food portions and libations were offered to the gods in the usual form. As the kava rite concluded Pa Fenuatara, sitting quietly by, suddenly let out a wild whoop '*Iefu!*' and was followed by several other men. Then his son Pa Farikitonga (who became Ariki Kafika in 1955) fired a shot from the gun he was carrying. This noisy demonstration was, as before, the formal signalization to the gods that, their task accomplished, they could now depart from the scene.

A few details about experts, and the regularity of turmeric performance, as I was informed in 1952, are relevant in the light of the earlier situation.

A turmeric expert has high status. It is significant of the recognition of this as well as of his technical needs that a special type of stool is sometimes used by such a man, a low four-legged seat adapted to work of pouring and straining. Apart from the three-legged coconut grating stool, this was the only type of raised seat used by Tikopia. The acknowledged turmeric-making expert in Taumako was Pa Motuata, a *tufunga marama* – an 'expert clear as daylight'. He prided himself on his skill, but said that the Ariki Kafika and Pa Fenuatara were also 'good experts', also his cousin Pa Rongonafa, who made his *nuanga* at Vai Matamata. In the chiefly house of Tafua there was no expert at present; the late Ariki (Pa Rangifuri) had been such, and his brother Pa Nukunefu would have been, if he had lived. Pa Motuata was uncertain who would now act for Tafua. The Ariki Taumako himself told me that he had held ten *nuanga*, one each year since he had become chief, omitting only the year in which his father died. One year, he said, he had to do without the services of Pa Motuata (? who was ill), and he was proud of his skill in having managed thus. In explanation of his omission of one year he said that when a chief dies 'the land becomes dark' and many ordinary events are not carried out. A great exception is the turmeric manufacture of Kafika, which is never omitted. On another occasion this was confirmed by Pa Motuata, who said that because of the famine the only *nuanga* to be made in the 1952 season would be that of the Ariki Kafika. He said that the turmeric-making of the other chiefs could always be intermitted, but not that of the Ariki Kafika, because of his god. 'The Akoako is never rejected', said this Christian, in tolerant recognition of the pagan deity.

13

The Final Rites

Like the Work of the Monsoon, that of the Trade-Wind has as its climax dancing of a religious order, but the time occupied is much less. The focus of interest in the Work of the Trade-Wind is undoubtedly the extraction of turmeric, and the later rites are regarded as being really an appendage to this. The name of these succeeding rites, the *Ururenga*, literally 'Turmeric Head', bears this out. They are divided into two sets: the *Ururenga* of Marae, which is the counterpart of the *Taomatangi* of the monsoon season; and the *Ururenga Nga Vaka*, which represents the canoe rites of the monsoon season. Both are curtailed considerably from their counterparts, and no really new features are introduced, so that a very brief description of them will suffice.

The *Ururenga* of Marae begins when the 'marking' of the temple of Nukuora is over. The Marae is cleared, the little temples of Matangiaso and Rarofiroki are re-carpeted, the *epa* mat is spread, the *fare kava* set up and dismantled, and the dancing takes place. The people dance for two days only, with performance of *vetu*, and *sore* in the evening, and apportionment of areca nut, but without any women on the inland border of the sacred place. For expediency the clans pair off, Kafika and Fangarere combined on the first day, and Tafua and Taumako on the second. There is no ritual at night corresponding to the Dance of the Flaming Fire. On the following morning Marae is de-sacralized by the rite of 'clapping in the spaces between the houses' (see Chapter 9) and the people disperse.

Then comes the *Ururenga* of the Canoes, which is really a celebration of the *Fainga Vaka* type. The main question of interest at first is whether Vakamanongi shall 'fall singly' or whether the other most sacred canoes shall be also celebrated on the same day. (The only rite of the *Ururenga* which I attended, about a month after my arrival in Tikopia in 1928, was that performed by the Ariki Taumako, over his canoes Tukupasia and Te Rurua. At that time I had no conception of the huge systematic ritual structure of which this formed a part.) After the celebration of these most sacred canoes the Ariki Kafika goes to Takarito and re-carpets it, and then at intervals one or other of the remaining sacred vessels has the *Ururenga* performed for it, in the manner described. There is no fixed time for these rites; it rests at the wish of each canoe-owner and the convenience of his chief. In these intermittent canoe celebrations, then, the Work of the Gods of the trade-wind season comes to an end.

Conclusion

My account of this elaborate dual seasonal cycle of Tikopia religious rites is now finished. To use the words of the people themselves in speaking of the completion of their ritual – '*Ku fakasiki Te Raranga a Nga Atua*' ('The Plaiting of the Gods has been ornamented').

This long account is primarily an empirical record of field-observation and information imparted, with theoretical interpretation introduced when necessary only to explain. In the study of Polynesian religion so much has been reconstruction, so little the result of the actual observation of rites that a statement of the facts, in detail, has seemed to me to be the most imperative need. This citation of detail, though intricate, makes clear two important points. First, it shows that small differences in procedure are vital to the Tikopia – they give just that individuality and personal touch in each case to the relations with the unseen world which is the essence of a living cult. Secondly, it shows the fallacy of interpreting differences in a type of formula used on a certain occasion as simply deviants or corruptions of an originally 'pure' text. Failures in memory and in individual transmission do occur, but of more sociological importance is the examination of variant formulae in relation to differences in rank, social standing, individual interests and even character and personality.

In the Work of the Gods it is clear that we have a tremendous mass of detail which is not irrelevant to the main theme, but is the very stuff of religious reality to the Tikopia; it is co-ordinated, woven together into a significant pattern by a scheme of beliefs closely integrated with the particular social structure. All the ritual procedure, in its minute variants, has a self-consistency and a reality, once granted the premises of the Tikopia themselves.

The broad character of these premises has emerged in the course of this book. The most fundamental is the postulate of the existence of a set of invisible beings, ancestors and spirits who may be called deities, known by the generic term of *atua*. These beings too are co-ordinated; they have a social organization parallel to that of the Tikopia, and from our point of view are essentially an imaginative and emotional projection of this. With powers greater than those of men these beings nevertheless have human attitudes – they respond like men to the appeals of flattery, gifts, cajolery, pity; they can be shamed into action, and they can be swayed by involving their prestige. In brief, they have a moral responsibility, though this is not to be defined in terms of European notions of good and evil. They are not the personifications of chance, or of blind fate; they are bound by rules, and their essential role is to afford help to men who know and keep these rules. But they are not to be controlled by all men indiscriminately; it is necessary to have prior links with them in terms of the social structure.

A second basic premise is that the activity of these invisible beings shows itself in visible, material results. This situation is crystallized in the term *manu* (equivalent to the *mana* of other Polynesian communities). This *manu* is not the figment of anthropological theory, a vague concept of impersonal power; nor is it simply the mainspring of magic, as opposed to religion. It is an idea more concrete than the one, and more general than the other. In its broadest form it is the correlate of any belief that human efforts, unaided, are insufficient for success; that there is an unknown factor in the equation between man and nature. But it is not the principle of success in abstract form; it is the concrete manifestation of the results.

I cannot enter here into other theoretical problems raised by this material – the analysis of Tikopia formulae and their imagery; the inadequacy of commonly accepted criteria for drawing a distinction between magic and religion; or the relation between past and present which is expressed in myths, formulae and rites. But it will be clear that in this Tikopia seasonal cycle we have not only a cult of nature, but also the high point of a richly ornamented religious system which grips technology and human artefacts into an integrated scheme of belief, which provides a periodic means of expression of social differences and reaffirmation of the social structure; which idealizes the past and uses it as a tool in the processes of the present; and which while seeming to cater for the satisfaction of immediate material wants in reality exemplifies for this community a set of values far transcending their own conceptions of what they need.

Epilogue

A DECADE AFTER ABANDONMENT

The Work of the Gods as a ritual cycle was completely abandoned by 1956, when the Ariki Kafika and the Ariki Taumako finally decided to become Christian. The process by which this conversion came about and the main results will be discussed elsewhere (in *Rank and Religion in Tikopia*). In July–August 1966 I revisited Tikopia again and, in company with a Danish colleague, Dr Torben Monberg, who was very familiar with a comparable situation on Bellona,[1] studied the relics of the Work of the Gods in the light of the new religious situation.

Before analysing the situation in 1966, I outline briefly the last phases of the Work of the Gods as described to me by various participants. The Ariki Taumako had performed his sector of the Work of the Gods for many years before he decided to become a Christian. The Ariki Kafika, who only in 1955 succeeded his father (Pa Fenuatara) and grandfather (the Ariki Kafika I knew in 1929 and 1952), spent only one season in Uta, the monsoon season of the end of that year. The rites were performed as had been usual in the immediately preceding period, e.g. including the carrying of the Sacred Fire by the Ariki Kafika in substitution for Pa Rarovi (who had become a Christian earlier). The ritual in which the new Ariki Kafika participated took place during a great epidemic and the number of people attending the dance of the Taomatangi was pitifully small, perhaps a score in all. It was not long after this that the Ariki Kafika proposed to the Ariki Taumako that they should give up the traditional kava rites, go to Church, and be baptized. (The Ariki Fangarere, who had also succeeded recently, was already a Christian.)

[1] Torben Monberg: *The Religion of Bellona Island. A Study of the Place of Beliefs and Rites in the Social Life of Pre-Christian Bellona. Part I. The Concepts of Supernaturals.* (Language and Culture of Rennell and Bellona Islands, vol. II, Pt. I.) National Museum of Denmark. Copenhagen, 1966.

Having taken their decision each of the two chiefs then went to Uta, made some disposition of the ritual objects in his major temples (see later) and performed a final kava ceremony. This, the *kava fakamavae*, the 'kava of parting', was in order to announce to the gods and ancestors that their rites were now being carried out for the last time, that they should drink their kava and depart for ever, to rest in their spirit homes. This farewell kava was then performed in Tai also. 'You know that the basis of the kava in Tai is in the sacred canoes.'

The Ariki Taumako was accompanied to Church by the only two ritual elders (*pure matua*) still remaining pagan in the land at this period. From this time on, no kava rite has been performed in Tikopia, and the Work of the Gods as an integral cycle of sacerdotal performance is but a memory.

A question of distinct theoretical significance can be posed in this connection. The Work of the Gods traditionally involved an intricate combination of technological, economic and ritual procedures, linked with an elaborate set of status recognitions. Now broadly speaking, those aspects of the Work of the Gods which had been primarily of religious significance have been completely given up since 1956. The heart of the ritual, the elaborate sequence of kava ceremonies which both united and validated the sequence of technical and economic procedures, ceased to be practised, as it were, overnight. What then of the technical and economic procedures? Did they continue, shorn as it were of their supernatural trimmings, or did the discontinuance of the religious elements result in modifications or loss of the techno-economic sequences?

The answer to this question is not a completely simple one. But briefly some techno-economic procedures were hardly affected by the abandonment of ritual, and others were gravely so, though not to the point of complete cessation.

The best way to examine the situation is to consider the major sets of rites *seriatim*, as I recorded the position in 1966.

CANOES AND YAMS

In the Work of the Gods, the opening rite of the Throwing of the Firestick, the ritual release of the Freeing of the Land, and the titular commemoration of the Fono at Rarokoka had at once lost their *raison d'être*. By 1966, if not completely blotted out, they were never discussed. None of these had any technical relevance.

The 'Work' of the canoes, having technical aspects of considerable significance, while abandoned absolutely on the ritual side,
continued without check in the technical processes of canoe building and overhaul. Being denuded of all their former extra-human
referents, the ancient religious categories of *vaka tapu* and *taumauri*
were given up. All seagoing canoes are *paopao* nowadays.[1] When
thereafter what was formerly such a canoe was overhauled, this
was done at no set season. No *atua* were now associated with the
vessel. Nor was any *monotanga* carried to the chief. Here the
economic acknowledgment of suzerainty had been abandoned
together with its ritual counterpart. But in the field of social status
the traditional prescriptions continued to apply in 1966. Vessels of
large size were given personal names, and these still for the most
part perpetuated the ancestral names of the lineage and clan. 'The
names of our origin are not lost.' Such canoes were still spoken of
as '*vaka te ariki*', canoe of the chief. This was an honorific expression, the canoe being essentially the property of the man at whose
instance and cost it was built. But it carried certain implications –
as a canoe of the chief, 'no one may go and make sport of it'; it
must be handled with respect. And while the former seasonal
tribute to the chief, the *monotanga*, with its spiritual associations
with tutelary gods and ancestors, had been given up, the customary social recognition of status was retained in that any large
fish caught from the canoe, such as *para* or *varu*, were carried to a
chief; only if such fish were plentiful would they be consumed by
the canoe owner.

   With the discarding of the canoe ritual of the Work of the Gods
had also gone the ritual functions of the *mataforau*, the sacred
canoe yards. Most of these had simply been converted to secular
use. But that of the Ariki Taumako, believed earlier to be presided
over by the Taumako Eel-God of highly dangerous proclivities,
had been deserted and was now overgrown with bushes. The
area was declared by Tikopia to be no longer *tapu* as formerly, but
it is significant that it was said to have been blocked (*mono*) by the
Ariki Taumako so that no one intruded upon it. In particular it
was regarded as very important not to use it as a place of excretion.
Children told me that it was not taboo, but was forbidden to them
(*pi*) by the Ariki, that no one should excrete thereon. I myself was

   [1] Several Tikopia canoes have been made in Nukufero, where large *fetau* trees
are plentiful, and brought to the island as deck cargo on motor vessels which call.

warned of this ban by Pa Ngarumea, the chief's brother and principal executive. When I asked if the *atua* still frequented the canoe yard, the reply of one of the clan members was, 'We don't know; it's a matter for the chief; it's [part of] his dwelling-place.' It seemed evident that elements of respect, of a discretionary character, still operated in regard to things formerly dangerous as well as sacred.

The Work of the Yam had been treated similarly in that the whole ritual sequence had been abandoned with all the prescriptions of planting before dawn, silence during critical operations, etc. In 1966 there was no *ufi tapu* recognized; the yam was planted at any season, and at any time of the day. The technology and economics of yam cultivation were preserved unchanged as far as I could gather. (I did not ask about the disposition of land in the *mara ufi* – whether the plots were reserved for yam cultivation or cropped generally. But the formerly sacred *mara taro* seemed to be reserved for *taro* growing, and the yam areas would probably be reserved likewise for a time.)

DESERTED TEMPLES

The yam rites were traditionally interlineated in the timetable of the Work of the Gods with the re-carpeting and re-furbishing of the sacred temples, particularly that of Kafika. It was in this respect that the most evident change had occurred in Tikopia life.

By 1966 the temples had been completely deserted and allowed to fall into decay. Where once these impressive buildings stood, with their great posts and ridgepoles, only the merest vestiges remained. To one who remembered the many temples of Uta, the multiplicity of rites therein day by day for more than a month each season – the bustle of food preparation, the solemn moments of the kava and the handling of sacred relics, the modern sight was a melancholy one. Of all the mats that used to be laid there, only a few recent graves were tended.

Of Resiake, the great temple of Taumako dedicated to the Atua i Kafika, only a few post and the sagging ridgepole remained. The grave of the grandfather of the present chief alone was marked (see p. 213) with a coconut frond mat as formerly. There was now a stone at the head as well – the chief had it set there recently as the sign of the grave. The wife of the present chief, who died a few years ago, was buried nearby the old sacred oven house (Firth,

1939, Plates V and VI). No vestige remained of the sacred wooden symbols of gods and ancestors – including that of Tuna – which formerly were hung in the temple; all had perished.

Of the temple of Taumako the two end posts and the middle post were still standing with a much decayed ridgepole and one rafter. On the site of the former oven house a few stone seating places, a post and two formerly sacred conch shells were still visible. In some ways the temple of Kafika evoked in me the most affecting memories. The temple site was thoroughly overgrown, including the formerly impressive Tinai Ariki mound – called by analogy 'The Moana a Kafika', the Ocean of Kafika, where any mortal who set foot was believed to sink through, as in the sea, to the land of spirits. I slowly walked over this once highly sacred spot without protest from my Tikopia companions, who formerly would have reacted with horror at the sacrilege. Now they simply declared, 'It is not taboo; it is all right.' The only remnant of the huge temple that was still visible was the Post of the Samoa (p. 238), now a mere shell. The grave of the Ariki Kafika (*Social Change in Tikopia*, Plate 5) who performed the rites there for so many years lay in the centre of a mass of vegetation, marked by a simple mat and a headstone. He had been laid to rest with his head by the centre post, the symbol of his major god.

All other temples were in similar state. Fangarere was marked only by the grave of the Ariki Fangarere (*Social Change in Tikopia*, Plate 6); Porima by posts only. Of Sao only the side posts remained; its kava bowl had been taken away by the wife of the modern head of the lineage to their house on the coast. The oven house of this temple still stood, thatched and used as an orchard shelter, with the grave of my old friend Pae Sao within it, marked by a mat and a headstone. This was the only building I saw still standing in the whole of Uta, which now had for me a strange deserted appearance. People went daily there to get food, areca nut or sago palm leaf thatch, or to build a canoe, but no one now lived there for weeks or months on end, as used to be the custom.

Yet though the temple sites as such were no longer treated as sacred, and people walked over them, the recent burials meant that archaeological excavation there would have been premature, as I had guessed (Firth, 1961, p. 157 n.). When I put this question to Pa Ngarumea he looked very dubious indeed. He pointed out that the temples were still 'chiefly buildings' and were *tapu* in the sense that chiefs of old were buried there. While not ritualised, they should be respected. Another man of rank in Taumako, a sophisticate, said that while the temples were not *tapu*, people still thought they were!

Practically all the ancient furniture of the temples had disappeared. Some of the items, especially those from Fangarere, were said to have been taken away by a Bugotu Mission priest, Father Stephen Talu; others had been hidden. The Ariki Kafika was said to have been afraid to remove his sacred adzes and had buried them *in situ*; the Ariki Taumako had taken his to Tai.

Only a few conch shells and stones, formerly symbols of the gods, were left. The stone of Fatumaru, formerly very sacred, had been taken away and hidden by the Ariki Taumako who, it was reported, had said that it was not right that folk should look at it since it was something from the olden times and the growth of the land.

FROM SACRA TO HISTORICAL RELICS

One of the most interesting situations from this point of view was the position of the former sacra of the Taumako temples. Raniniu in Tai (p. 254) was the 'control centre' of the rites of the Taumako canoe yard, the kava of which validated that performed over the sacred craft. In 1966 Raniniu was the only formerly pagan temple that still stood and was not used as an ordinary dwelling. It was in poor repair and its floor had no carpeting of coconut frond mats, as formerly. But it still contained a number of the traditional symbols of the gods and historic emblems of ancestors, some formerly held in the temple and others collected there by the Ariki Taumako from Uta. The temple was declared by various people to be no longer *tapu*, and one man at least told me that ordinary people could go inside. But I observed that in fact no one went in to it and that the chief and people living around regarded the building with considerable respect.

The attitude of the Taumako chief to his once sacred objects was remarkable, in that it revealed an essential recognition of a sociological process of translation of religious symbols into historical relics of social value.

The demonstration of this was fascinating to observe. The day after our visit to Uta I was approached by Pa Ngarumea (*Social Change in Tikopia*, pp. 291–3) in my house in Ravenga, a dwelling assigned to me by the Taumako chief's family. He bore a message for me from the Ariki Taumako. 'You are different, Father [the ordinary kinship term applied to me by Tikopia of his generation], you have participated in the kava group of chiefs; your viewing of the things has already been completed. But our friend [Monberg] is otherwise. He has not seen the kava. If he wishes to see the sacred objects is it all right for him to pay – in silver? It won't be much.' To this rather astonishing proposition I asked, 'How much?' He replied, 'Four', i.e. 4s. I replied, 'I can't speak for our friend. It's up to him. But I think I know his mind. I am sure he will be glad to see the things and to pay the silver.'

Pa Ngarumea then went on to describe the situation. Some chiefs, he said, had been stupid and had given away their sacred things. But the Ariki Taumako had gathered his together in Raniniu. When formerly Father Stephen Talu, wishing to uproot all traces of paganism, had tried to obtain them the chief told him to go away – he held that this attitude was wrong and was very indignant.[1] These objects were things of olden time. Though people no longer believed in the efficacy of the powers formerly attributed to them, they were memorials of the ancestors, if only because, like the sacred shell adzes of the canoes, they represented enormous work.

I agreed with this viewpoint, holding that the chief was correct; things of the ancestors should be preserved for future generations, as Europeans do. This opinion Pa Ngarumea also enthusiastically approved, as did Pa Ngatotiu, a former ritual elder, who was present. Considering the ignorance of many visitors about the significance of such objects, however, and the offence that would be given to Tikopia if they were treated with disrespect, I stressed the importance of letting only responsible people see them. Pa Ngarumea asked me to point this out to the chief.[2] In the evening I went by invitation to talk with the chief and Pa Ngarumea, bearing Monberg's acceptance of the offer, and our discussion followed

[1] Stephen Talu later died in Honiara. I asked a Christian teacher if in Tikopia view the priest had died because he had removed the sacred objects – which would be in keeping with other modern Tikopia attitudes expressed to me. The teacher laughed and said that some Tikopia thought so.

[2] Torben Monberg has pointed out that in retrospect it seemed that he was carefully cross-examined by Pa Ngarumea on our earlier visit to Uta, on his knowledge of Bellonese gods and sacred rites. This may have been a prelude to the invitation noted.

much the same lines as before. The chief repeated his viewpoint –
that he no longer gave credence to these objects, that is, credited
them with power, but they were still very important ('weighty')
things of ancient time, things of the ancestors, and as such deserved
respect. Pa Ngarumea and the chief explained that as yet no one
who was not 'a man of the kava' had seen such things, and certainly not the Tikopia in general. But it was agreed enthusiastically
that it was good to retain such things that future generations of
Tikopia might look on them.

The upshot was that next day Monberg and I went with the
chief and Pa Ngarumea to Raniniu. There the chief had gathered
together about a score of historical relics, most of them formerly
highly sacred. They included six sacred shell adze blades, the oil
bottles from which the various sacred canoes had been anointed in
the kava, and other articles seen in 1952. Some of these objects he
had brought over from the temple in Uta. The adze blades and a
few other objects were on a shelf at the seaward end of the house,
others were hung round the beams. Of the shell adze blades, one
very fine specimen was the Principal Adze (*Matua Toki*) (p. 58).
Another, a beautiful white specimen of gouge form, was called Te
Niapu – this was probably 'the adze of the seashore', though the
chief did not say so. Both of these were termed *faingata* (p. 58), a
description applied to adzes believed to have great potency and
destructive force. (The same term was applied to a very old hafted
iron adze.) The other shell blades were described as *pipi*.

The chief led the way to the shelf and invited us to follow. He
began to describe the objects in hushed tones but as we questioned
him his voice rose to ordinary volume. It was highly significant
that he allowed us not only to see, but also to *handle* the adze
blades – which would have been inconceivable even for me, in
former days. He also allowed my colleague to photograph them,
but inquired rather anxiously as he prepared to bring them down,
if two would do! He explained how 'weighty' the adzes had been
– how the chief could call upon them at sea, for their gods to drive
away hungry sharks or allay a storm. But, he said, these things
were no longer done. His attitude was distinctly one of respect;
none of the things was handled casually and the adze blades
especially were treated very gingerly. But he said the things were
no longer *tapu*, and behaved as if they were not.

Back in my house, the reciprocation was given by my colleague, who, at first dubious as to the propriety of the transaction, gave them not the sum originally asked for but double and some tobacco in addition. Both the chief and his brother seemed very pleased, though the latter stressed that the price of seeing the objects should quite properly be high! We discussed the question of payment on future occasions and I suggested that to avoid misconceptions by Europeans the term *tauvi* (which is also used for buying) be not used since they might think that they were being invited to purchase the things and be angry to find they were expected to pay only for looking at them. *Fakapenu* (reciprocity) would be a better word, and more in accord with practice in European museums. This suggestion was very acceptable to the chief. I made out a 'museum notice' accordingly.

The theoretical significance of this incident seemed considerable, since it illustrated the process of conversion of sacra from *ritual objects* with taboo attached and symbolic *religious* value to:

i. *Secular objects* still kept in conditions of some secrecy and special care – in a 'quasi-taboo' state.

ii. *Personal memorials* or *heirlooms* of ancestors with sentimental value.

iii. *Show pieces* which people may be allowed to see for a fee.

Additional roles which such Tikopia objects fulfilled in other cases were:

iv. *Anti-sacra* – 'things of the Devil', as those destroyed by the Christian priest.

v. Alternatively *exchangeable property*, bartered or sold to visitors.

It is notable that different Tikopia behaved in different ways in this respect. In effect what we observed, at the initiative of the chief of Taumako himself, was the beginning of the process of conversion of a pagan temple of an outworn faith into a museum of historical relics – a process for which there are many analogies in the European field. As a speculation one may suggest that in a way the process of de-sacralization is the reverse of what has happened generations before. Originally, one presumes, graves and other memorials of ancestors, preserved for their social interest and sentiment as relics of dead kin, had ritual efficacy attributed to them. This is in line with Tikopia views. Now they have been stripped of their ritual significance, and once more revert, at a longer distance, to memorials of the past. This process of ritualization and de-ritualization of the past of a people may well be a characteristic feature of an agricultural community firmly rooted in the soil who in the course of time were brought into contact with an expanding social and economic universe, including a new religious faith. But it implies also a modicum of what may be termed cultural pride – a quality which the Tikopia certainly possess.

There is one aspect of the incident narrated earlier which needs further examination – the stipulation of a fee for viewing the objects. This was not, as might seem at first sight, primarily a commercial interest. The clue to the chief's attitude was given by the chief himself in our discussion. He drew the analogy between this fee and the *maro* which I had given to the chiefs when I attended the kava originally (pp. 114, 306). The analogy was not exact, for the *maro* were a tribute to gods as well as to men. But his view was essentially that these historical relics were 'weighty' and the viewing of them could not be taken casually; it had to be signalized by some 'threshold act' as one might term it.

Since the relics could still be classed as 'quasi-sacra' the viewing fee was akin to an initiation fee to participate in the 'mysteries' of a cult. It was not therefore the *amount* of the fee which was so important but that a fee was *paid*. This expressed the recognition of the value of the relics and the formalization of a relation which was regarded as of great social importance, though no longer of ritual importance.

The de-sacralization process which had taken place with the former symbols of the gods and ancestors had also taken place with their graves. No longer were any mats laid on the graves of the early ancestors and no analogous mats were offered to the gods. Only the graves of the recent dead were *fariki*, given a grave mat, and usually also a rough headstone, sometimes the symbolic seating place of a god being used for the purpose. Here too there had been a conversion of the sacred into the secular, and personal and family sentiment had replaced religious obligation.

The treatment of the sites of former temples long disappeared, even in the heyday of the pagan religion, was quite summary. The rites of Somosomo had been completely abandoned. When I visited the site the stone that marked the ancient turmeric manufacturing spot was still in position (Plate 7*b*), but the other stones had been disarranged and could no longer be identified. The glade of Somosomo was mainly overgrown, though young men had cleared out a dart match ground along the path leading from it and this had encroached upon the Somosomo itself. (The rites of Takarito in Faea had been abandoned by the old Ariki Kafika before 1952; the subsequent history of the Atua i Takarito is told elsewhere (see *Tikopia Ritual and Belief*, Ch. 13).)

THE CONDITION OF MARAE

The scene of what in many ways was the highlight of the ritual season in Uta, Marae Lasi, where the sacred dances were held, was scarcely recognizable. The ring of trees round the Marae still stood save that the umbrella palm which marked the east side (p. 288) had been cut down. But whereas the sites of the temples had been allowed to stand untouched, for the wild vegetation to take over, that of Marae had been put under manioc by Father Robert, the Tikopia priest. This was clearly a deliberate act to demonstrate to Tikopia the falsity of the concepts of the power of the ancient gods or at least their impotence. No Tikopia, even the chiefs, appeared to resent this as an intrusion. But it was said that only the priest could be successful with a crop there; ordinary people would fail. Yet the Marae was clearly regarded as no longer sacred. It was impossible to find most of the symbolic stones which had formerly stood there, though some boys and I hunted for them. The stones of the Atua i Tafua, the Atua i Taumako and the Atua i Kafika (*Pae Marae*, p. 286) were pointed out by our guide, Pa Ngarumea; they were all hidden in vegetation. Our guide also pointed out *te mono o Ruapou* – by the 'house of the Fire' – four stones said to have been set up by the Atua i Kafika near the Taurongorongo, to block the path after the Taomatangi.

Further along the path towards Te Roro was the Marae of Rarokoka, where anciently the *Fono* was held – 'the proclamation of the gods from of old', said our guide. This glade lay completely overgrown.

TURMERIC MANUFACTURE

The last of the rites of the Work of the Gods to consider are those of turmeric manufacture, the *nuanga*. Here the situation had been rather more involved. In the other cases where technology and ritual were commingled, as with canoes and yams, the ritual was abandoned but the technology continued without break. With the *nuanga* the whole process, technological as well as ritual, was given up for nearly ten years. Only in the mid-year of 1966 was turmeric manufacture resumed, and with a significant modification. For the first time, apparently, the Ariki Kafika and the Ariki Taumako combined their forces to make a joint *nuanga*. The reason given was that the amount of raw turmeric root was small. There were four partners altogether and the result was two or three cylinders apiece.

The former ritual of the *nuanga*, with the elaborate recitals of the Raufangota Manu and other formulae, had been abandoned, 'because the chiefs have as gods the One God'. Instead, prayers for the successful manufacture were said to have been recited by the chiefs in Church. The Ariki Tafua said, 'I don't know about the chiefs in Ravenga. When I and my father made turmeric, we asked in Church for the turmeric liquid to be great – the increase, that is, of anything the chiefs do.'

But despite the cessation of the positive ritual of the *nuanga*, most of the restrictive practices of the traditional *nuanga* were still in force, especially those which divided the 'people of the turmeric manufacture' (*faoa te nuanga*) from 'those at the back' (*sa tua*). Still excluded from the scene of filtration and separation were the latter, i.e. people who had not participated in the earlier grating of the root. The ideas of 'hot food' and 'cold food' (p. 429), excretion in the sea, and other taboos were still quite firmly held. I was told by the Ariki Kafika and Pa Ngarumea, both of whom participated in the recent turmeric manufacture, that if someone from 'the back' comes on to the turmeric scene the *renga* will be bad – truly bad! Also, a man of the turmeric group must excrete in the sea, not inland; the latter 'is taboo; observation of this is finished; we have observed that the results are bad'.

A problem of great interest is the ten-year gap in turmeric manufacture. I first put forward a tentative interpretation of this situation in terms of the peculiar sensitivity of turmeric technology. Results were uncertain till the very last moment, as regards quantity and quality, and consistency of the turmeric. A slight technical slip could spoil the whole process, and considerable anxiety was shown when the final moments of turning out the turmeric cylinders arrived. Rite, taboo and technology were very firmly locked together in a crisis situation.

My hypothesis then was that as far as the formerly pagan chiefs of Ravenga were concerned, the old religious associations of the turmeric – 'the perfume of the Atua i Kafika' – were probably so vivid that they intermitted its manufacture for a period. But after nearly ten years they evidently felt that the ritual was 'dead' and they could safely revive the technology. The danger of course here could be that such a considerable time-gap in production could result in a loss of technical knowledge and skill, especially through the death of technical experts, who are of prime importance in turmeric manufacture.

But this interpretation did not seem complete. It did not account for the behaviour of the Ariki Tafua, a Christian since a child, who had also intermitted production. He told me himself that he had carried out only one *nuanga*, immediately after his father's death in 1951; by 1966 he had not resumed it. My alternative hypothesis was that ecological, not ritual, reasons were probably responsible for the gap. The hurricane and drought of 1952 may have affected the sensitive turmeric plant very badly. The severe epidemic of 1955 which followed may have reduced the working population to a primary interest in food production, with the result that the supply of raw turmeric may have been so inadequate as to render manufacture not worth while.

This view was supported by various statements. Even by 1966 the amount of turmeric plant available in Tikopia still seemed fairly small. The Ariki Tafua said that he had not had enough turmeric root to make a *nuanga* with in 1966, but that he was planting some more; he would wait another year or so, plant even more, and then manufacture, probably in Te Roro. He would act as expert himself, as traditionally chiefs tend to do. I talked casually with men of Rofaea, who were also planting turmeric, and who said that they would join whatever *nuanga* happened to be available in the coming year. The *nuanga* of the Ariki Kafika and the Ariki Taumako in 1966 had been small. The Ariki Taumako in particular was busy planting *ango* and engaged in a vigorous campaign to increase the supply. In a *fono* in Ravenga instructions were given at his instance to young women to refrain from plucking turmeric leaves on the mountain, as they tended to do to make perfumed necklets.

The Ariki Kafika denied that it was because of the former religious associations of the turmeric that manufacture had ceased for a period. He said it was because people had left the turmeric plant alone and had gone to plant food instead. But he said he planted turmeric a couple of seasons before, and would have proceeded to manufacture had he not gone to the Solomons for six months. He said that now the chiefs had begun to manufacture turmeric again the process would continue.

Yet despite such views, the explanation of the gap did not yet seem completely adequate – why had a decade elapsed, since the turmeric was not such a very slow-growing plant, and why this concentration on growing food? Further inquiry revealed a very significant factor. When the Bugotu priest, Stephen Talu, was on the island he had forbidden many Tikopia customs as being harmful to Christian beliefs and morals, and labelled them 'of the Devil'. The use of turmeric had fallen under his ban. Turmeric uses included smearing on a newly married woman; on a pregnant woman; on an initiate boy; and on a person who had just completed a mourning period. In each case the function of the custom was the mark of the achievement of a new social state. To the foreign priest these were pagan customs. This ban was disliked by the Tikopia, who described their pigment, in such common use, as 'the soap of Tikopia'. But they obeyed and since they were not allowed to use the pigment, they had not manufactured it.

This position altered with the appointment in 1959 of a Tikopia priest, Robert Fakafu. Father Robert held different ideas. As he told me, he did not believe that such customs were things of the devil and told Stephen Talu so. Moreover, in due course he himself began to plant turmeric, arguing that it provided not only pigment but also food.

But all this took time to work out. The institution of turmeric manufacture, once discontinued, took time to be re-established, and several years passed before the interests of the priest, the chiefs and the people were sufficiently clearly identified to stimulate the planting of turmeric and preparations for renewed manufacture. A certain amount of 'institutional momentum' was required to maintain such complex proceedings and even more to re-institute them once they had been stopped.

So the final interpretation of the gap in turmeric production is that neither ritual nor ecological factors were ultimately responsible. Such plausible reconstructions were inaccurate. The historical accidents of personal interpretation were critical in creating first a situation of block and then one of stimulus. Reconstitution even then however was slow because different habits had been developed meanwhile.

By 1956, then, the Work of the Gods had ended, in a definitive sense. By 1966 the situation was irreversible. A series of technical processes, held together by an elaborate network of ritual links, had now been resolved into its component elements. A series of social relationships, likewise integrated by ritual, had also been dissolved. What is of interest in the Tikopia situation is that so far the dissolution of the ritual bonds and ritual values had left the technological processes relatively unimpaired, and the social relationships though modified had survived in other forms.

BIBLIOGRAPHY

COOK, JAMES, 1784. *A Voyage to the Pacific Ocean*, vol. 1, London.

CUNNISON, IAN, 1956. 'Perpetual Kinship: A Political Institution of the Luapula Peoples', *Rhodes-Livingstone Institute Journal*, vol. xx, pp. 27–48.

DURKHEIM, E., 1915. *Elementary Forms of the Religious Life*, trans. J. W. Swain, London.

FIRTH, RAYMOND, 1930. 'A Dart Match in Tikopia', *Oceania*, vol. 1, pp. 64–96.

—— 1930. 'Totemism in Polynesia', *Oceania*, vol. 1, pp. 291–321, 377–98.

—— 1936. *We, the Tikopia: A Sociological Study of Kinship in Primitive Polynesia*, London. 2nd ed. 1957.

—— 1939. *Primitive Polynesian Economy*, London. 2nd ed. 1965.

—— 1950. 'Economics and Ritual in Sago Extraction in Tikopia', *Mankind*, vol. 4, pp. 131–42, Sydney.

—— 1956. 'Ceremonies for Children and Social Frequency in Tikopia', *Oceania*, vol. 27, pp. 12–55.

—— 1959. *Social Change in Tikopia*, London.

—— 1960. 'Tikopia Woodworking Ornament', *Man*, no. 27.

—— 1960. 'The Plasticity of Myth: Cases from Tikopia', *Ethnologica N.S.*, vol. 2, pp. 181–8, Köln.

—— 1960. 'A Polynesian Aristocrat', in *The Company of Man*, ed. Joseph B. Casagrande, pp. 1–40, New York.

—— 1961. *History and Traditions of Tikopia*, Wellington, New Zealand.

—— 1964. *Essays on Social Organization and Values*, London School of Economics Monographs on Social Anthropology, no. 28, London.

—— 1966. 'Twins, Birds and Vegetables: Problems of Identification in Primitive Religious Thought', *Man*, N.S. vol. 1, pp. 1–17.

—— 1967. *Tikopia Ritual and Belief*, London.

FIRTH, RAYMOND, and SPILLIUS, JAMES, 1963. 'A Study in Ritual Modification: The Work of the Gods in Tikopia in 1929–1952', *Royal Anthropological Institute*, Occasional Paper no. 19, London.

FORDE, C. DARYLL, 1962. 'Death and Succession: An Analysis of Yakö Mortuary Ceremonial', in Gluckman, *op. cit.*, pp. 89–123.

FORTES, MEYER, 1962. 'Ritual and Office in Tribal Society', in Gluckman, *op. cit.*, pp. 53–88.

FRAZER, J. G., 1925. *The Golden Bough*, abr. ed., London.

GLUCKMAN, M. (ed.), 1962. *Essays on the Ritual of Social Relations*, Manchester.

GOODE, WILLIAM J., 1951. *Religion among the Primitives*, Glencoe, Illinois.

LEACH, E. R., 1954. *Political Systems of Highland Burma*, London.

LÉVI-STRAUSS, CL., 1962. *Le Totémisme Aujourd'hui*, Paris.

MARINER, WILLIAM, 1827. *An Account of the Natives of the Tonga Islands*, ed. J. Martin, 3rd ed., 2 vols., London.

MEAD, MARGARET, 1930. *Social Organization of Manua*, B.P. Bishop Museum Bulletin no. 76, Honolulu.

RICHARDS, AUDREY I., 1950. 'Some Types of Family Structure among the Central Bantu', in *African Systems of Kinship and Marriage*, ed. A. R. Radcliffe-Brown and D. Forde, London.

—— 1956. *Chisungu: A Girl's Initiation Ceremony among the Bemba of Northern Rhodesia*, London.

RIVERS, W. H. R., 1914. *The History of Melanesian Society*, 2 vols., Cambridge.

SMITH, W. ROBERTSON, 1907. *Religion of the Semites*, rev. ed., London.

THOMSON, BASIL, 1894. *Diversions of a Prime Minister*, Edinburgh and London.

WALEY, ARTHUR, 1949. *The Life and Times of Po Chü-i*, London.

Index

LONDON SCHOOL OF ECONOMICS
MONOGRAPHS ON SOCIAL ANTHROPOLOGY

Titles marked with an asterisk are now out of print. Those marked with a dagger have been reprinted in paperback editions and are only available in this form.